POETRY AND CRITICISM

OF

Matthew Arnold

EDITED WITH AN INTRODUCTION AND NOTES BY

A. Dwight Culler

YALE UNIVERSITY

HOUGHTON MIFFLIN COMPANY · BOSTON

The Riverside Press Cambridge

PRINTED IN THE U.S.A.

Arnold - poetry - record of his search - of ideas - intellect.

{Lit crit. / Social crit. / Lit crit.} Arnold conceived himself as a critic of all of life. Officially - an inspector of schools.

Pattern of dev.

1) Cry of revolt.

2) Aspiration for a new society

Emphasize a trust in phy. not. as a power of healing, boyhood on lake cty. (Wordsworth) - the mts.

POETRY AND CRITICISM OF

Heritage from father - imp. on shaping him. - Dr. - need to hinder the dev. of instincts to change the mind to adapt. When Arnold went to Oxford - his ironical manner - unpopularity. Public Fell in love with a Fr. - married Eng. -

Matthew Arnold

1883-85 - Came to U.S. to lecture. Preached doctrine of quiet contemplative life; died of heart attack trying to catch train.

Poems - to reflect main mvt. of mind. - thoughts of intell. who were disturbed by new subversive ideas

1. doubt - feeling for grandeur of X trad. + X. - acts as a check on his agnosticism. -

2) Subord. faith to conduct. - Faith = 9/10 morality

3) Aim high + accept the responsibility - Maintain by Trust yourself (Shks) (Sophocles)

4) Grand Chartreuse. - The self-contained soul - theme: - In memoriam.

Goethe - the ideal - need for self-sufficiency. need for estrangement from man - the sea. - poet. wanders - bewilderment. - requires a need for a fixed idea - Sophocles - possess a vision which is fixed. Substitutes for rel. -

RIVERSIDE EDITIONS

5.) Rejects illusion of Rom. - Nature, - to him world of things as opposed to moral world.

6) to obtain outward conformity - feels an impulse to flee from life. - ~~feels on in~~ Scholar gipsy.

RIVERSIDE EDITIONS

UNDER THE GENERAL EDITORSHIP OF

Gordon N. Ray

CONTENTS

POETRY

CRITICISM

Literature

Society

Religion

LETTERS

INTRODUCTION

A. Dwight Culler

I

Edith Sitwell has said that those who like Matthew Arnold "dislike poetry." Without for a moment subscribing to anything implied by this remark one may admit that people who like their poetry "pure" will not find many things in Arnold to their taste. Poetry was too closely related to life in Arnold's view for him to be interested in mere Sitwellian patterns. But beyond this one may concede that Arnold does not have more than about a dozen really fine poems. I would list them as follows: "The Strayed Reveller," "The Forsaken Merman," "Empedocles on Etna," "To Marguerite — Continued," "Tristram and Iseult," "Sohrab and Rustum," "Philomela," "The Scholar-Gipsy," "Thyrsis," "Dover Beach," and "Stanzas from the Grande Chartreuse." As will be evident from these titles, what Arnold needed in order to produce a good poem was a passionate apprehension of a theme and an image or myth in which to embody that theme. In some of his later poems, like *Balder Dead* and *Merope*, he had an image or myth but no passionate apprehension of the theme. (Indeed, he started with the myth and didn't seem to know what the theme was.) On the other hand, in many of his early poems, like "The Buried Life" or "A Summer Night," he had a theme which he felt passionately but had no adequate image or myth in which to embody it. Hence he resorted to a poetry of statement or, more properly, to a kind of rhetoric. It is this poetry especially which I am sure Miss Sitwell dislikes. I do not dislike it, for I feel that the total body of Arnold's poetry constitutes one large complex myth which, although containing an unusually large amount of *dianoia* or thought, is quite adequately rendered through character, scene, and significant action so as to establish for us a viable poetic world. I would point out that Arnold himself always approached poetry in this way. He never wrote analyses or interpretations of individual poems. In his essays on Wordsworth, Byron, Shelley, Keats, Gray, Milton, Homer, and Dante there is no discussion of either the form or the meaning of any particular work by these authors. What he is always interested in is the quality and scope of the poetic vision as a whole. This is not to be confused with biographical criticism. He is not interested in the man behind the book but in the mind in the book, in the poetic vision or spiritual life which that book embodies. It is to this vision, to the form and shape of Arnold's poetic world, that I should like to turn the reader's attention here.

Arnold's poetic world may be conceived as a history, a terrain, and a cast of characters. The history is an evolution from one world to another, the terrain the scene on which this evolution is accomplished, the characters the persons involved in the death of one world, the birth of another, and the interregnum between the two. When Arnold speaks in "Stanzas from the Grande Chartreuse" of himself as

> Wandering between two worlds, one dead,
> The other powerless to be born,

he gives the essential structure of his historic myth. The former world may be denominated by the term, so important in Arnold, of Joy. Joy is "the freshness of the early world," whether the bright, clear world of Greece, or the buoyant world of the English Renaissance, or Wordsworth's world, or the world of any individual when he was a child. The nature of the second world is hardly to be discerned in Arnold's poetry, for it barely appears there except in the new dawn of "Obermann Once More." But it too is a world of Joy — a recovered Joy — differing from the former in that it is a "Joy whose grounds are true," whereas the other had some element of a divine illusion, and differing also in that it is "Joy in widest commonalty spread," whereas the other involved a kind of aristocratic exclusiveness. Until this new Joy was recovered, however, it appeared that the poet would have to settle for a kind of makeshift Joy which he calls Calm. Calm too would be a "world" in that it possesses unity and order, but it differs from Joy in being achieved, not spontaneous, in being the painfully acquired product of culture, not the freely received gift of nature.

> 'Tis all perhaps which man acquires,
> But 'tis not what our youth desires.

Thus, considered as history, Arnold's myth assumes the form of loss, endurance, and recovery; of death, sorrow, and rebirth, which is the structure of tragedy. Had he been a poet of major forms he might have attempted tragedy, but as it is, he adopted for his more slender muse that miniature lyric equivalent, the elegy.

Since Arnold is a poet of nature, his myth characteristically evolves upon a natural landscape or terrain which we may call the "Arnold country." The central feature of this country is a river, which the poet unabashedly calls the River of Life. Characteristically it takes its rise in some hidden glen high in the forest of the far mountains, and this is the loveliest spot on its entire course. The air is cool, the grass fresh with dew and the spray from the pure mountain stream, and in its impetuous descent, sparkling among the rocks, it is unconscious of anything but the long summer evenings and the unbounded vitality with which it flows. But then comes a crisis. The gorge narrows, the rocks blacken, the current becomes turbulent and swift, and with a sudden swirl the stream plunges over the precipice into the plain below. This plain is what Arnold calls "the world," not in the sense in which we have previously used the term but rather in that of Wordsworth's sonnet:

> The world is too much with us; late and soon,
> Getting and spending, we lay waste our powers:

Hot and dusty, it is Arnold's version of T. S. Eliot's Waste Land. By night it is a "darkling plain," in whose rising mists it is impossible to distinguish friend from foe, but by day it is a burning plain, arid and sterile, frenetic in its swarming activity. The river in flowing through it loses its speed, its waters become tepid and are tainted by the offpourings from the great cities. For on the one bank of the stream there are marts of commerce, harsh with the clangor of contending voices, and on the other are tropical pleasure gardens, where the din of revelry by night is no less strident than that of commerce by day. Between these flows the river, and whether it be that it loses itself in marshes or that the city itself is a kind of labyrinth, there is a sense that the thread or clue of this stream is here lost, that it sinks underground and flows through secret, purifying channels, until at last it re-emerges beyond the burning plain and glides through open estuaries into the ocean itself.

The ocean, as one might expect, is associated by Arnold with death or with the vast continuum of nature to which all things return and from which they can be drawn up to replenish the eternal springs of the mountain. Thus it is a Calm and also a recovered Joy, a rebirth of the seasons. But sometimes it is quite a different ocean, an ocean of life, not death, a watery version of the darkling plain, over whose trackless waste man sails in perplexity and terror, isolated from human love by unplumbed, salt, estranging deeps, and feeling in the movement of the tide his fluctuating, uncertain condition. Yet not the sea but the land is the center of Arnold's country, and in the midst of the land there arises a mountain peak whence all its extent, from forest dells to ocean deeps, can be viewed. In the acrid heat of its volcanic slopes, far above the forest line, it is itself a kind of burning plain, but it is removed from the bustle of the cities, close to the stars, with their calm and their frosty solitude. It is the mountain of Manfred, the watch-tower of Teufelsdröckh, the Alpine fastness of Obermann.

Finally, Arnold's poetic world may be conceived as a group of characters appropriate to the various scenes and playing out upon them the action of the death of one world, the endurance of emptiness, and the creation of a new world in critical, creative effort. All these characters are, of course, aspects of the same character, evolving through different stages of spiritual life, and all of them are aspects of Arnold. Living in the remote forest glens where the River of Life takes its rise is one whom we may call the Youth, although actually in the poems we see him at a variety of ages. In Callicles, haunting the cool wooded slopes of Mt. Etna, and in Sohrab, whose proper terrain is a queen's secluded garden in far-off Ader-baijan, and in the Strayed Reveller, descending from his hut of rough fir-planks up at the valley's head, we see him in young manhood, but at one time he played among the children of the abbey in "Stanzas from the Grande Chartreuse" and even earlier he slept with the children of Tristram and Iseult in the remote southern wing of the castle away from the storm. Hidden as he is in secluded spots, he is as yet untroubled by problems of the modern world: he lives in nature and he possesses Joy. But he is always evoked with a feeling of nostalgia, for he is the sole inhabitant of the former world, which is now dead.

Emerging from the gorge onto the burning plain, the Youth is confronted by a life-choice which takes for Arnold the form of a dilemma. Should he subdue himself to the "world" and become a Slave, or should he revolt against the world in Byronic or Titanic defiance and become a Madman? Of the two Arnold initially prefers the Madman, for the Slave is he who leads a life of "quiet desperation" in the great cities of the plain. But ultimately it appears that the Madman is as much a slave to his own passions as the other is to the world and that his course, wandering across trackless seas or moving as an outcast through the wastes of the desert, is no more directed to a goal than is the circular movement of the Slave, within the treadmill of daily routine. The one is defeated by the finite in the world, the other by the infinite in himself.

> Is there no life, but these alone?
> Madman or slave, must man be one?

No, says Arnold, there are other alternatives, other life-choices besides these. One, the least satisfactory of all, is not to resolve the dilemma but to vacillate between one extreme and another, like Tristram, torn between his two Iseults, or like Empedocles, unable to live with men or with himself. Such a person, common among the second-generation Romantics, is a would-be Byron without the

Byronic force, a kind of Hamlet who has "the motive and the cue to passion" but in whom passion itself has petered out. Self-knowledge and the sense that it has all been done before undercut his rebellion and reduce his agony to the mere unrest of a mid-Victorian Prufrock. Using the name of Clough's hero, we may call him a Dipsychus or Divided Soul.

Finally, there is the character of the Reveller and the character of the Sage. If we were speaking in philosophic terms, we might say the Epicurean and the Stoic, but the Reveller is only an apparent Epicurean. More truly, he is one who has assumed the mask of Epicureanism in order to preserve his soul from hurt. Such a person is Mycerinus, the Egyptian king, who, finding himself in an amoral universe, retreats to the pleasure groves beyond the Nile and there gives himself up to a life of revelry. He does this only in appearance, however, for actually he is taking the measure of his own soul and finding in the knowledge of his own rectitude the reward of his virtue. "Not the less," says the poet,

> his brow was smooth,
> And his clear laugh fled ringing through the grove,

for if revelry was a mask, it was a mask very necessary in an amoral world. This, too, was the discovery of the Strayed Reveller, the youthful poet who contrived to evade the law imposed by the gods upon other poets that their vision, godlike in extent, should nevertheless differ from that of the gods in being attended with pain. They must participate in the suffering they see, but the young reveller, drinking from Circe's cup and sitting on the warm steps overlooking the valley, is able to see all day long, without pain, without labor, the bright procession of eddying forms. Even Sohrab, stout warrior that he is, seems to conceal his virility under the slight aspect of a dancing girl.

Laughter or mockery is a way of meeting the world's ills natural to youth, and that is why the Reveller (or the Strayed Reveller, as we might better call him) often emerges from the figure of Youth at the moment of his descent or disenchantment. To age it is more natural to do as Rustum does, meet the world's ills not with laughter but with fortitude and sullen pride. Recognizing that the times have passed him by, this aged and embittered warrior, who is the military version of the Sage, keeps aloof from the struggle, stubbornly enduring a fate which he cannot change. So too in the intellectual realm does Empedocles, and so too does Goethe, "physician of the iron age," in the elegy "Memorial Verses." But there is a difference among the tempers of the Sage. If he has very recently withdrawn from the conflict and is still filled with a grim, fire-eyed defiance, he may be very close to the Madman. But if he has been longer aloof and has nourished his soul in communion with the stars, he may have passed through mere endurance and icy despair to a more mellow Calm and even compassion for the human lot. He may be like Arnold's Sophocles, who "saw life steadily and saw it whole," or like his Shakespeare, who smiled enigmatically from a mountain top, "self-school'd, self-scann'd, self-honor'd, self-secure." Whatever his mood, he is always represented by the image of lofty isolation, the lonely figure brooding upon some eminence or mountain height, looking down into the tumult and misery of the plain below.

These five, then, the Slave, the Madman, the Dipsychus or Divided Soul, the Strayed Reveller, and the Sage, are the inhabitants of that burning plain or spiritual interregnum with the analysis of which Arnold's poetry is largely concerned. Who is it that inhabits the new world that is a-borning, the world foreshadowed in Arnold's poetry but brought into being by the effort of his critical prose?

Whatever his name, we know the kind of person he is likely to be. He must be one who has solved the dilemma of solitude vs. the world, of passion vs. lethargy, by giving himself to the service of others without having lost his contemplative vision. He must combine the thesis of a lost world of Joy with the antithesis of the modern waste-land into the synthesis of a recovered Joy which is a viable human faith. In this sense Arnold's father, the hero of "Rugby Chapel," would do, for he is neither the type of the Slave without purpose nor of the Madman or Sage with a selfish purpose, but of the Servant of God, who saves others along with himself. In the landscape of the poem he is not aloof on a mountain top nor yet immersed in the cities of the plain, but is engaged in leading others up the mountain, which is Sinai, not Etna or an Alp. And indeed, except in his blatant muscularity and spiritual noisiness he is one with all the *redivivus* figures who come in at the end of Arnold's elegies. An elegy is a poem in which the hero dies in order to be in some sense reborn in the final stanzas. For Arnold the elegy was a poem in which, under the guise of another person, the poet dies unto himself in order to be reborn unto another self, the "best" self of the social and religious prose. In the first Obermann poem he dies unto himself as Obermann (Madman or Sage) in order to be reborn unto himself as one of those

> Children of the Second Birth,
> Whom the world could not tame.

The phrase is significant, for it expressly connects the *redivivus* figure with the "children" of the world of Joy and yet asserts their death and subsequent rebirth as a "small, transfigured band," *in* the world but not of it. In "A Summer Night" they are one with the Christian lady and gentleman who are seen to surpass the romantic hero and heroine with whom they were at first disadvantageously compared, and in "Stanzas from Carnac" they are the fresh landscape dotted with churches which the poet's brother would have reached had he escaped the burning plains of India and the Straits (the "gorge") of Gibraltar. We may call these figures either Servants of God or Children of the Second Birth.

"The Scholar-Gipsy" and "Thyrsis," though they defy absolute categorization, are the perfect embodiment of this quiet world of a mature joy, the former a little more looking backward to the idyllic freshness of an early world, the latter, as Arnold re-explores the Cumnor country after twenty years, a little more looking forward to the recovery and persistence of the ideal in the harsh uplands dim of a too-long neglected countryside. For it is noteworthy that in these poems we have a landscape different from that of almost all the other of Arnold's major poems, a quiet English countryside with no extremes of mountain peak or burning plain but only, as its most prominent feature, a small hill with a signal elm on top. As in "Rugby Chapel," we are not on the hill but in the valley trying to reach it, and if the poet, unlike his father, never achieves his quest, he at least has the faith, unlike his Thyrsis, never to give it over. He is one with the river which flows through this country and which, if it is the River of Life, one knows not where to place it — not, certainly (though it is the "stripling" Thames), in the realm of Youth, for it is too placid, nor yet in the plain, for it is too fresh and clear. Possibly it is between the plain and the ocean, but more probably, overarched by embowering trees, it is the underground river of our "buried life," connecting Youth with Age and remaining always the same. Like the signal elm it never changes, and its tutelary god, the Scholar-Gipsy, is immortal too. As gypsy he looks backward to the world of nature and as scholar forward to the world of culture. He would be happy with Callicles in the poems and also with Joubert in the critical essays. He is waiting for the light to fall which *has* fallen in *Culture and Anarchy*, and the secret he would learn from the gypsies is the method and secret of Jesus in *Literature and Dogma*.

II

The transition from poetry to prose was made by Arnold in the decade 1853–63. The former year saw the appearance of his first piece of published prose, the Preface to *Poems* (1853), which, significantly, was a rejection of his most important poem, *Empedocles on Etna.* The latter year saw the inauguration of that remarkable series of critical essays which was to culminate in "The Function of Criticism at the Present Time," Arnold's *apologia pro vita nuova* — if one may combine two phrases and two languages — his apology for his new life as a critic. In 1857 he was elected Poetry Professor at Oxford, but to be a professor of poetry is tantamount to declaring that one is not a poet, and although the *New Poems* were published in 1867, most of those that were new were not poems, most of those that were poems were not new. From the mid-fifties on, Arnold was primarily a writer of prose.

One is naturally eager to discover the reason for this change, but it is perhaps beyond our abilities. As Lionel Trilling has said (speaking of Wordsworth), we cannot explain why a man ceases to write great poetry until we are able to explain how he once did write great poetry. And this, in the present state of our knowledge, we are unable to do. But in Arnold's case we can see that certain changes in philosophic outlook accompanied the change from poetry to prose, and we may believe that the two changes were in some way related. The philosophic change was a movement from a predominantly subjective view of the world to a predominantly objective view of the world, and it seems to have been accomplished by a deliberate process of self-discipline. Signs of it are first discerned in some of the poems and the letters to Clough, but it was not formally announced until the Preface of 1853. That document is the turning point in Arnold's critical development, for he there turns his back upon his period of *Sturm und Drang* and lays the foundations of an Olympian personality. He urges three things upon the modern poet: that he depict an action rather than give expression to his feelings, that he concentrate on the architectonics of his work rather than on details of phrasing, and that he chose his subject from ancient rather than modern times. All these counsels are obviously directed to one purpose, that of taking the artist out of himself and subjecting him to the discipline of a great external fact or form. Through this discipline he will be saved from that worst of modern maladies, the habit of writing poems which are merely "an allegory of the state of one's own mind."

It is not certain that this is bad advice. Much of the world's greatest poetry has been written upon these principles. But it was not good advice for Arnold. Why he could not evolve into serenity and remain a poet, as Tennyson did in the poems of his latest period, is unknown, but apparently he could not. The poetry he wrote upon the principles of this Preface, in *Balder Dead* and *Merope,* is the worst he ever produced. The poem which he rejected in the name of these principles, *Empedocles on Etna,* is one of the best he ever produced. *Sohrab and Rustum,* which he meant to exemplify the doctrine of the Preface, is good only because in fact it does not exemplify it, but is a rehandling of themes from *Empedocles on Etna* in a different mode. And finally, painful as it is to say it, every good poem that Arnold ever wrote is, in some degree, that object which he took such pains to repudiate, "an allegory of the state of his own mind." For with Arnold poetry derived from internal unrest and anguish, and once he achieved serenity he expressed himself in the literary medium of prose.

In issuing the critical manifesto of 1853 Arnold felt that he was challenging the dominant tendencies of his age, but we can see that this was not entirely true. His Preface and the poem which it repudiates stand pretty much in the same relation to his career as *Wilhelm Meister* and the *Sorrows of Werther* do to Goethe's. They are paralleled again by Carlyle's Everlasting Yea and Everlasting No, and by Newman's evolution from Evangelicalism to Anglicanism to the Roman Catholic Church. Wordsworth's "Immortality Ode," which records the loss of the visionary gleam and the gain of the philosophic mind, is a similar document, and if there were a more positive conclusion to Coleridge's "Dejection: an Ode," one could say that that too was autobiography of a similar kind. Even John Stuart Mill, though he started from the other side of the street and was strengthened by an access of subjectivity rather than objectivity, experienced a "mental crisis" which left him at the end pretty much where Arnold terminated in his critical prose.

The other side of the street, where Mill started from, is the Utilitarian position. This side of the street, where Arnold, Goethe, and Carlyle started from, is the Romantic position. The point on which they all converged may be called the Christian Humanist position, though it is more Christian than humanist in the case of some, more humanist than Christian in the case of others. Early nineteenth-century thought was divided among these three positions. They constitute three great ways of life, which were in dynamic tension one with another, and to understand Arnold's posture as a critic we must understand something of their interrelation.

The relation of Romanticism and Utilitarianism is a curious blend of antagonism and sympathy. The two movements are antagonistic in that Romanticism was primarily an attempt to create an interior world of meaning through the agency of the imagination, whereas Utilitarianism was primarily an attempt to manipulate the external world of physical reality through the agency of scientific method. But they were sympathetic in that they found no standard of good and evil beyond the likes and dislikes of men. They disagreed profoundly, of course, in that the one appealed to the intuition of finely touched natures and the other to a statistical computation of the pleasures and pains of the masses, but they were alike in being naturalistic and relativistic in their ethics. Christian Humanism, on the other hand, which is simply the traditional conservative ethic of the western world, disagreed with both these novel philosophies in being non-relativistic and non-naturalistic. It asserted the existence of absolute or objective values which transcended the world of nature as embodied both in physical reality and in the heart of man. It believed that the solution to the human problem lay not in accommodating reality to the likes and dislikes of the greatest number nor in freeing the heart of man from the controls of an artificial society, but in the submission of individual and society to the discipline of objective values so that they might be transformed from what they are into what they ought to be.

Viewed negatively, Arnold's criticism is directed against both the Utilitarian and the Romantic position. (By the term "Utilitarian" we wish to comprehend not merely the school properly so called but also the various associated movements of liberal reform.) Naturally, the Romantics loom larger in the literary essays and the Utilitarians in the essays on society, but both are present in that great fact with which Arnold everywhere has to deal, the French Revolution; and his principal antagonist, the Dissenting mentality, is a compound of the two. Positively, his criticism is an attempt to fashion a large objective image of human culture — of the "best that is known and thought in the world" — which shall be as a palladium to the English people; and for this purpose, though he recognizes that England has a slender continuing tradition of this culture, he goes to sources which are as remote from England as possible, to the culture of Greece and Rome as removed in time, to the continent of Europe as removed in space. He appeals, as did Newman in his quest for a similar center of authority, to the note of "apostolicity," or the judgment of history, and to the note of "catholicity," or the judgment of the whole human race. *Securus judicat orbis terrarum:* the deliberate judgment of the entire world cannot be wrong.

But the mention of Newman reminds us that it is not enough to place Arnold among the Christian humanists: one must also distinguish among the several varieties of this attitude. For it is the special character of Arnold that although his entire life as a critic was dedicated to the reform of himself and his countrymen through the establishment of absolute values, he had a saving hesitancy about these values which has made him the despair of rigorous thinkers and the admiration of more humble and flexible spirits. When Newman, for example, spoke of absolute values, he meant values that really were absolute, and he saw that they signified nothing unless they were embodied here on earth in some actual institution or center of authority. Thus in the *Apologia* he asserts, first of all, the dogmatic principle — that there is such a thing as objective truth in religious matters — and secondly, the principle of the visible church — that this truth is embodied on earth in a particular institution. The only question that remains is, which is the true church, and for Newman after 1845 it was the Church of Rome. Arnold's thought follows the pattern of Newman's up to a certain point. He clearly asserts the dogmatic principle in literature and society, and he clearly sees the incompleteness of this principle without the corollary of the visible church. But every time he approaches the problem of establishing such a church he will come right up to the point and then shy away again with the acknowledgment that such is not the way of Englishmen, such is not appropriate for this particular realm. A typical instance is "The Literary Influence of Academies." Here he speaks of the advantage which has been secured to the French nation by having in their midst a tribunal to which they can appeal in matters of literary taste and linguistic usage, and he speculates upon the beneficial effect which a similar institution might have in England. One thinks he is on the point of proposing it, when suddenly he draws back, remarks that in England special academies in special subjects might be useful but that a better solution to the general problem is for each individual to erect a personal academy within himself. That Arnold should find the solution for what Newman calls "private judgment" in private judgment itself is an enormous paradox, but it is thoroughly characteristic of Arnold's mode of proceeding. In *Culture and Anarchy* he does it again. Here, looking for a source of authority by which the anarchy of the nation may be regulated and hesitating to place it in this or that social class — hesitating, that is, to erect a visible church — he finally entrusts it to that part of our nature which he calls the "best self." Once again, in other words, the self is to be a cure for the self, for Arnold's view that there are "two selves," the best and the ordinary self, is evidently at the very heart of his humanism. The best exposition of this view is in the Preface to *Last Essays on Church and Religion,* where we are told that although the end of the individual is self-development, the means to this end lie outside of the individual, in the assimilation unto his nature of the wealth and resources of the cultural tradition. Thus, the state of being a Divided Soul, which was to the Romantic a problem or dilemma, becomes to the Christian Humanist a means of self-correction.

When we come to the subject of Arnold's religious writing, it appears as if the pattern of thought which we have just been sketching for his literary and social criticism no longer obtained, for whereas in those areas he was concerned, however hesitantly, with establishing fixed values to which the judgment of man could appeal, here he is concerned with disestablishing such values. Here he denies the dogmatic principle and would sweep away the existing visible church. The very title of his major religious work, *Literature and Dogma,* indicates that the Bible, which has been taken as a dogmatic statement of religious truth, is in his view not that at all, but is the literature of the Hebrew people. Far from denoting the objective fact of God, it denotes the subjective fact of what the Hebrew people's experience of God was. Further, its language is essentially poetic language "thrown out" to adumbrate this experience rather than scientific language set down to describe the fact. The trouble is that people have lost sight of what the Bible really is. They have allowed its metaphors to harden into creeds, its aspirations to crystallize into prophecies, its myths to petrify into history, and it has existed in this fossilized state for two thousand years. But now, with our knowledge of how these things come about, we recognize that the Bible is not "true," and the masses are on the point of rejecting it altogether. If this were to happen it would of course be a great loss to literature; but it would be much more than that. For the Hebrew people had a genius for religious experience, a genius for morality, and we can in no way better develop our religious and moral sense than by reading the Bible. Therefore, to save the Bible as a depository of subjective values which are true we must reject it as a depository of objective values which are false, and this is what Arnold wishes to do. So viewed, his criticism of religion does not really have a different tendency from his criticism of literature and society. It only appears to have because the "objective" values of the one are the "subjective" values of the other. Objective religious values are divine; objective human values are collective; subjective human values are personal. Arnold would transcend the personal but stop short of the divine. He would rest in the collective wisdom of the whole human race, in "the best that is known and thought in the world."

CHRONOLOGY

1822 Born December 24, the eldest son of Thomas and Mary Penrose Arnold at Laleham on the Thames, near Staines, where Thomas and his brother-in-law, John Buckland, kept a school. John Keble, one of the future leaders of the Oxford Movement, was MA's godfather. There were eight other children: Thomas, William Delafield, Edward Penrose, Walter; Jane (called "K"), Mary, Frances (Fanny), and Susanna.

1828 Thomas Arnold appointed Headmaster of Rugby School, a position which he held until his sudden death in 1842.

1833 The Arnolds built a home at Fox How in the English Lake District, to which they retreated in the vacations. They were friendly with the Wordsworths.

1836 After early schooling with John Buckland, MA was sent to Winchester, his father's old school, for one year, 1836–37. Summer tour of northern France with family, 1837.

1837–41 At Rugby, where, despite a certain levity displeasing to his parents, he won a prize for his poem *Alaric at Rome* (1840), was elected to an open Classical Scholarship at Balliol (1840), and won a School Exhibition at Rugby (1841).

1841 Matriculated at Balliol College, Oxford, on November 28, 1840, came into residence in autumn of 1841, after a tour of southern France and the Pyrenees with his father. His closest friends at Oxford were Arthur Hugh Clough, Theodore Walrond, A. P. Stanley, and his brother Tom, who breakfasted together on Sunday mornings, punted on the Cherwell, and rambled about the Cumnor Hills. He won the Newdigate Prize with his poem *Cromwell* (1843).

1844 Took a Second Class degree, the result of too diligent attention to fishing and French novels. Taught classics briefly at Rugby.

1845 Redeemed his failure by being elected Fellow of Oriel (March 28), as his father had thirty years before, and began his probationary year of residence in college. In September he vacationed on the Isle of Man and in Ireland with his mother and sister Jane.

1846 Made a pilgrimage to the home of George Sand, the novelist, at Nohant, France, and then on to Switzerland. Returned to France in December-February to indulge an infatuation for the French actress Élisa Rachel.

1847 Became private secretary to Lord Lansdowne, President of the Council in Lord John Russell's ministry, and so moved to London.

1848 In September of this and the next year Arnold took his holiday in Switzerland, where at the Hotel Bellevue in Thun he apparently met and fell in love with the girl called Marguerite in many of his early poems.

1849 *The Strayed Reveller, and Other Poems.*

1850 Fell in love with Frances Lucy Wightman, daughter of a judge of the Court of the Queen's Bench, but was not a welcome suitor because of his insufficient income. He apparently followed the Wightmans clandestinely to the Continent in August.

1851 Appointed Inspector of Schools by Lord Lansdowne and so was able to marry Frances Lucy ("Flu") on June 10. Honeymoon in France and Italy. For the next thirty-five years Arnold traveled widely about England and Wales inspecting elementary schools and training colleges conducted by the various dissenting sects. During the first year Flu traveled with him; thereafter she lived in London, to which MA returned on weekends. In 1868 they moved their residence to Harrow, in 1873 to Pains Hill Cottage at Cobham, Surrey. Summers were spent at Fox How or on the Continent.

1852 *Empedocles on Etna, and Other Poems.*

1853 *Poems.*

1857 Elected Professor of Poetry at Oxford, a position requiring of him three lectures annually. He held the office ten years and was the first to give his lectures in English instead of Latin.

1858 *Merope. A Tragedy.*

1859 *England and the Italian Question.* Inquiry into the state of elementary schools in France, Switzerland, and Holland, embodied in a *Report to the Education Commissioners* (1860) and *Popular Education in France* (1861).

1861 *On Translating Homer.* Death of Clough.

1865 *Essays in Criticism,* first series. Travel on the Continent on behalf of a Schools Inquiry Commission.

1867 *New Poems; On the Study of Celtic Literature.*

1868 Death of his infant son Basil (January) and of his eldest son Thomas, aged 16 (November).

1869 *Culture and Anarchy.*

1870 *St. Paul and Protestantism.*

1871 *Friendship's Garland.*

1872 Death of his son William Trevenen, aged 18.

1873 *Literature and Dogma.*

1875 *God and the Bible.*

1877 *Last Essays on Church and Religion.*

1879 *Mixed Essays.*

1882 *Irish Essays and Others.* Third educational mission to the Continent.

1883–84 Lecture tour of the United States (October-March), the lectures published as *Discourses in America* (1885).

1888 Death (April 15). *Essays in Criticism, Second Series* published posthumously.

A NOTE ON THE TEXT

The arrangement of Arnold's poems always causes difficulty to an editor. Arnold was very insistent that in matters of this kind the Greeks had the right instinct and that we shall not improve upon their categories of epic, dramatic, lyric, and so forth. Hence in the final arrangement of his poems he established five main sections: narrative poems, sonnets, lyric poems, elegiac poems, and dramatic poems, with only two lesser sections for the early and later poems when his talent was not at its height. But most readers will agree that this arrangement is not satisfactory. In the first place, in many instances the assignment of poems to section is extremely arbitrary. There are narrative poems which might just as well have been considered lyric or dramatic, and lyric poems which might just as well have been considered dramatic or narrative. Only the elegiac section really works. Further, by attempting to bring together poems which are related in form Arnold has separated poems which are related in theme, and it is surely much more important to have *Empedocles on Etna* associated with *Tristram and Iseult,* though one is a "drama" and the other a "narrative," than it is to have it associated with *Merope,* with which thematically it has nothing to do. This means that for Arnold — with whom themes come and go in the course of his spiritual development — the ideal arrangement of the poems is that of the order of their composition. Unfortunately, for the early poems this is not known, and therefore one is led to fall back on a second-best, the order of publication. But here an unexpected help arises, for in the four volumes in which most of Arnold's poems were first published he took quite as much pains about the arrangement as he did in the collected edition, and his concern at this date was usually more nearly related to the actual meaning of the poems than it was later. Thus, if we ignore the few instances of periodical publication and place the poems in the order in which they were first issued in the volumes, we will have, I believe, the best possible arrangement for an edition of selected poems.

With the prose the situation is not quite the same, for here the themes are relatively static and the development is rather in their application first to one subject and then to another. Arnold took up these subjects pretty much in successive order, first literary criticism, then social criticism, then criticism of religion, and these topics have supplied the categories by which his essays have been grouped. But there is one exception: he returned to literary criticism in his final years, and although there is some advantage in representing this "return upon himself" in the grouping of the essays, it seemed best to keep all that Arnold has to say on literature in one place, and to allow "Literature and Science" to be a transition piece into the second group. With this one exception, then, the essays are also arranged in the order of publication, the arrangement within the volumes being respected as in the poetry.

But although the order of the poems and prose is that of their original publication, the text is normally that of the last edition published in the author's lifetime. The one instance where this practice creates a difficulty is commented on in the notes.

The notes at the foot of the page are Arnold's unless otherwise indicated. The editor's notes are at the end of the volume.

The editor wishes to thank his wife and his research aide, Mr. Charles Swartz, for valuable help in preparing this edition.

A. D. C.

Poetry

The Strayed Reveller, and Other Poems

(1849)

QUIET WORK

One lesson, Nature, let me learn of thee,
One lesson which in every wind is blown,
One lesson of two duties kept at one
Though the loud world proclaim their enmity—

Of toil unsever'd from tranquillity!
Of labour, that in lasting fruit outgrows
Far noisier schemes, accomplish'd in repose,
Too great for haste, too high for rivalry!

Yes, while on earth a thousand discords ring,
Man's fitful uproar mingling with his toil,
Still do thy sleepless ministers move on,

Their glorious tasks in silence perfecting;
Still working, blaming still our vain turmoil,
Labourers that shall not fail, when man is gone.

MYCERINUS

'Not by the justice that my father spurn'd,
Not for the thousands whom my father slew,
Altars unfed and temples overturn'd,
Cold hearts and thankless tongues, where thanks are due;
Fell this dread voice from lips that cannot lie,
Stern sentence of the Powers of Destiny.

'I will unfold my sentence and my crime.
My crime — that, rapt in reverential awe,
I sate obedient, in the fiery prime
Of youth, self-govern'd, at the feet of Law;
Ennobling this dull pomp, the life of kings,
By contemplation of diviner things.

'My father loved injustice, and lived long;
Crown'd with gray hairs he died, and full of sway.
I loved the good he scorn'd, and hated wrong —
The Gods declare my recompence to-day.
I look'd for life more lasting, rule more high;
And when six years are measured, lo, I die!

'Yet surely, O my people, did I deem
Man's justice from the all-just Gods was given;
A light that from some upper fount did beam,
Some better archetype, whose seat was heaven;
A light that, shining from the blest abodes,
Did shadow somewhat of the life of Gods.

'Mere phantoms of man's self-tormenting heart,
Which on the sweets that woo it dares not feed!
Vain dreams, which quench our pleasures, then depart,
When the duped soul, self-master'd, claims its meed;
When, on the strenuous just man, Heaven bestows,
Crown of his struggling life, an unjust close!

'Seems it so light a thing, then, austere Powers,
To spurn man's common lure, life's pleasant things?
Seems there no joy in dances crown'd with flowers,
Love, free to range, and regal banquetings?
Bend ye on these, indeed, an unmoved eye,
Not Gods but ghosts, in frozen apathy?

'Or is it that some Force, too wise, too strong,
Even for yourselves to conquer or beguile,
Sweeps earth, and heaven, and men, and gods along,
Like the broad volume of the insurgent Nile?
And the great powers we serve, themselves may be
Slaves of a tyrannous necessity?

'Or in mid-heaven, perhaps, your golden cars,
Where earthly voice climbs never, wing their flight,
And in wild hunt, through mazy tracts of stars,

Sweep in the sounding stillness of the night?
Or in deaf ease, on thrones of dazzling sheen,
Drinking deep draughts of joy, ye dwell serene?

'Oh, wherefore cheat our youth, if thus it be,
Of one short joy, one lust, one pleasant dream?
Stringing vain words of powers we cannot see,
Blind divinations of a will supreme;
Lost labour! when the circumambient gloom
But hides, if Gods, Gods careless of our doom?

'The rest I give to joy. Even while I speak,
My sand runs short; and — as yon star-shot ray,
Hemm'd by two banks of cloud, peers pale and weak,
Now, as the barrier closes, dies away —
Even so do past and future intertwine,
Blotting this six years' space, which yet is mine.

'Six years — six little years — six drops of time!
Yet suns shall rise, and many moons shall wane,
And old men die, and young men pass their prime,
And languid pleasure fade and flower again,
And the dull Gods behold, ere these are flown,
Revels more deep, joy keener than their own.

'Into the silence of the groves and woods
I will go forth; though something would I say —
Something — yet what, I know not; for the Gods
The doom they pass revoke not, nor delay;
And prayers, and gifts, and tears, are fruitless all,
And the night waxes, and the shadows fall.

'Ye men of Egypt, ye have heard your king!
I go, and I return not. But the will
Of the great Gods is plain; and ye must bring
Ill deeds, ill passions, zealous to fulfil
Their pleasure, to their feet; and reap their praise,
The praise of Gods, rich boon! and length of days.'

— So spake he, half in anger, half in scorn;
And one loud cry of grief and of amaze
Broke from his sorrowing people; so he spake,
And turning, left them there; and with brief pause,
Girt with a throng of revellers, bent his way
To the cool region of the groves he loved.

There by the river-banks he wander'd on,
From palm-grove on to palm-grove, happy trees,
Their smooth tops shining sunward, and beneath
Burying their unsunn'd stems in grass and flowers;
Where in one dream the feverish time of youth
Might fade in slumber, and the feet of joy
Might wander all day long and never tire.
Here came the king, holding high feast, at morn,
Rose-crown'd; and ever, when the sun went down,
A hundred lamps beam'd in the tranquil gloom,
From tree to tree all through the twinkling grove,
Revealing all the tumult of the feast—
Flush'd guests, and golden goblets foam'd with wine;
While the deep-burnish'd foliage overhead
Splinter'd the silver arrows of the moon.
It may be that sometimes his wondering soul
From the loud joyful laughter of his lips
Might shrink half startled, like a guilty man
Who wrestles with his dream; as some pale shape
Gliding half hidden through the dusky stems,
Would thrust a hand before the lifted bowl,
Whispering: *A little space, and thou art mine!*
It may be on that joyless feast his eye
Dwelt with mere outward seeming; he, within,
Took measure of his soul, and knew its strength,
And by that silent knowledge, day by day,
Was calm'd, ennobled, comforted, sustain'd.
It may be; but not less his brow was smooth,
And his clear laugh fled ringing through the gloom,
And his mirth quail'd not at the mild reproof
Sigh'd out by winter's sad tranquillity;
Nor, pall'd with its own fulness, ebb'd and died
In the rich languor of long summer-days;
Nor wither'd when the palm-tree plumes, that roof'd
With their mild dark his grassy banquet-hall,
Bent to the cold winds of the showerless spring;
No, nor grew dark when autumn brought the clouds.
So six long years he revell'd, night and day.
And when the mirth wax'd loudest, with dull sound
Sometimes from the grove's centre echoes came,
To tell his wondering people of their king;
In the still night, across the steaming flats,
Mix'd with the murmur of the moving Nile.

TO A FRIEND

Who prop, thou ask'st, in these bad days, my mind?—
He much, the old man, who, clearest-soul'd of men,
Saw The Wide Prospect, and the Asian Fen,
And Tmolus hill, and Smyrna bay, though blind.

Much he, whose friendship I not long since won,
That halting slave, who in Nicopolis
Taught Arrian, when Vespasian's brutal son
Clear'd Rome of what most shamed him. But be his

My special thanks, whose even-balanced soul,
From first youth tested up to extreme old age,
Business could not make dull, nor passion wild;

Who saw life steadily, and saw it whole;
The mellow glory of the Attic stage,
Singer of sweet Colonus, and its child.

THE STRAYED REVELLER

THE PORTICO OF CIRCE'S PALACE. EVENING

A Youth. Circe

The Youth

FASTER, faster,
O Circe, Goddess,
Let the wild, thronging train,
The bright procession
Of eddying forms,
Sweep through my soul!

Thou standest, smiling
Down on me! thy right arm,
Lean'd up against the column there,
Props thy soft cheek;
Thy left holds, hanging loosely,
The deep cup, ivy-cinctured,
I held but now.

Is it, then, evening
So soon? I see, the night-dews,
Cluster'd in thick beads, dim
The agate brooch-stones
On thy white shoulder;
The cool night-wind, too,
Blows through the portico,
Stirs thy hair, Goddess,
Waves thy white robe!

Circe

Whence art thou, sleeper?

The Youth

When the white dawn first
Through the rough fir-planks
Of my hut, by the chestnuts,
Up at the valley-head,
Came breaking, Goddess!

I sprang up, I threw round me
My dappled fawn-skin;
Passing out, from the wet turf,
Where they lay, by the hut door,
I snatch'd up my vine-crown, my fir-staff,
All drench'd in dew —
Came swift down to join
The rout early gather'd
In the town, round the temple,
Iacchus' white fane
On yonder hill.

Quick I pass'd, following
The wood-cutters' cart-track
Down the dark valley; — I saw
On my left, through the beeches,
Thy palace, Goddess,
Smokeless, empty!
Trembling, I enter'd; beheld
The court all silent,
The lions sleeping,
On the altar this bowl.
I drank, Goddess!
And sank down here, sleeping,
On the steps of thy portico.

Circe

Foolish boy! Why tremblest thou?
Thou lovest it, then, my wine?
Wouldst more of it? See, how glows,
Through the delicate, flush'd marble,
The red, creaming liquor,
Strown with dark seeds!
Drink, then! I chide thee not,
Deny thee not my bowl.
Come, stretch forth thy hand, then — so!
Drink — drink again!

The Youth

Thanks, gracious one!
Ah, the sweet fumes again!
More soft, ah me,
More subtle-winding

Than Pan's flute-music!
Faint — faint! Ah me,
Again the sweet sleep!

Circe

Hist! Thou — within there!
Come forth, Ulysses!
Art tired with hunting?
While we range the woodland,
See what the day brings.

Ulysses

Ever new magic!
Hast thou then lured hither,
Wonderful Goddess, by thy art,
The young, languid-eyed Ampelus,
Iacchus' darling —
Or some youth beloved of Pan,
Of Pan and the Nymphs?
That he sits, bending downward
His white, delicate neck
To the ivy-wreathed marge
Of thy cup; the bright, glancing vine-leaves
That crown his hair,
Falling forward, mingling
With the dark ivy-plants —
His fawn-skin, half untied,
Smear'd with red wine-stains? Who is he,
That he sits, overweigh'd
By fumes of wine and sleep,
So late, in thy portico?
What youth, Goddess, — what guest
Of Gods or mortals?

Circe

Hist! he wakes!
I lured him not hither, Ulysses.
Nay, ask him!

The Youth

Who speaks? Ah, who comes forth
To thy side, Goddess, from within?

How shall I name him?
This spare, dark-featured,
Quick-eyed stranger?
Ah, and I see too
His sailor's bonnet,
His short coat, travel-tarnish'd,
With one arm bare! —
Art thou not he, whom fame
This long time rumours
The favour'd guest of Circe, brought by the waves?
Art thou he, stranger?
The wise Ulysses,
Laertes' son?

Ulysses

I am Ulysses.
And thou, too, sleeper?
Thy voice is sweet.
It may be thou hast follow'd
Through the islands some divine bard,
By age taught many things,
Age and the Muses;
And heard him delighting
The chiefs and people
In the banquet, and learn'd his songs,
Of Gods and Heroes,
Of war and arts,
And peopled cities,
Inland, or built
By the grey sea. — If so, then hail!
I honour and welcome thee.

The Youth

The Gods are happy.
They turn on all sides
Their shining eyes,
And see below them
The earth and men.

They see Tiresias
Sitting, staff in hand,
On the warm, grassy
Asopus bank,

His robe drawn over
His old, sightless head,
Revolving inly
The doom of Thebes.

They see the Centaurs
In the upper glens
Of Pelion, in the streams,
Where red-berried ashes fringe
The clear-brown shallow pools,
With streaming flanks, and heads
Rear'd proudly, snuffing
The mountain wind.

They see the Indian
Drifting, knife in hand,
His frail boat moor'd to
A floating isle thick-matted
With large-leaved, low-creeping melon-plants,
And the dark cucumber.
He reaps, and stows them,
Drifting — drifting; — round him,
Round his green harvest-plot,
Flow the cool lake-waves,
The mountains ring them.

They see the Scythian
On the wide stepp, unharnessing
His wheel'd house at noon.
He tethers his beast down, and makes his meal —
Mares' milk, and bread
Baked on the embers; — all around
The boundless, waving grass-plains stretch, thick-starr'd
With saffron and the yellow hollyhock
And flag-leaved iris-flowers.
Sitting in his cart
He makes his meal; before him, for long miles,
Alive with bright green lizards,
And the springing bustard-fowl,
The track, a straight black line,
Furrows the rich soil; here and there
Clusters of lonely mounds
Topp'd with rough-hewn,
Grey, rain-blear'd statues, overpeer
The sunny waste.

They see the ferry
On the broad, clay-laden
Lone Chorasmian stream; — thereon,
With snort and strain,
Two horses, strongly swimming, tow
The ferry-boat, with woven ropes
To either bow
Firm harness'd by the mane; a chief,
With shout and shaken spear,
Stands at the prow, and guides them; but astern
The cowering merchants, in long robes,
Sit pale beside their wealth
Of silk-bales and of balsam-drops,
Of gold and ivory,
Of turquoise-earth and amethyst,
Jasper and chalcedony,
And milk-barr'd onyx-stones.
The loaded boat swings groaning
In the yellow eddies;
The Gods behold them.

They see the Heroes
Sitting in the dark ship
On the foamless, long-heaving
Violet sea,
At sunset nearing
The Happy Islands.

These things, Ulysses,
The wise bards also
Behold and sing.
But oh, what labour!
O prince, what pain!

They too can see
Tiresias; — but the Gods,
Who give them vision,
Added this law:
That they should bear too
His groping blindness,
His dark foreboding,
His scorn'd white hairs;
Bear Hera's anger
Through a life lengthen'd
To seven ages.

They see the Centaurs
On Pelion; — then they feel,
They too, the maddening wine
Swell their large veins to bursting; in wild pain
They feel the biting spears
Of the grim Lapithæ, and Theseus, drive,
Drive crashing through their bones; they feel
High on a jutting rock in the red stream
Alcmena's dreadful son
Ply his bow; — such a price
The Gods exact for song:
To become what we sing.

They see the Indian
On his mountain lake; but squalls
Make their skiff reel, and worms
In the unkind spring have gnawn
Their melon-harvest to the heart. — They see
The Scythian; but long frosts
Parch them in winter-time on the bare stepp,
Till they too fade like grass; they crawl
Like shadows forth in spring.

They see the merchants
On the Oxus stream; — but care
Must visit first them too, and make them pale.
Whether, through whirling sand,
A cloud of desert robber-horse have burst
Upon their caravan; or greedy kings,
In the wall'd cities the way passes through,
Crush'd them with tolls; or fever-airs,
On some great river's marge,
Mown them down, far from home.

They see the Heroes
Near harbour; — but they share
Their lives, and former violent toil in Thebes,
Seven-gated Thebes, or Troy;
Or where the echoing oars
Of Argo first
Startled the unknown sea.

The old Silenus
Came, lolling in the sunshine,
From the dewy forest-coverts,

This way, at noon.
Sitting by me, while his Fauns
Down at the water-side
Sprinkled and smoothed
His drooping garland,
He told me these things.

But I, Ulysses,
Sitting on the warm steps,
Looking over the valley,
All day long, have seen,
Without pain, without labour,
Sometimes a wild-hair'd Mænad —
Sometimes a Faun with torches —
And sometimes, for a moment,
Passing through the dark stems
Flowing-robed, the beloved,
The desired, the divine,
Beloved Iacchus.

Ah, cool night-wind, tremulous stars!
Ah, glimmering water,
Fitful earth-murmur,
Dreaming woods!
Ah, golden-hair'd, strangely smiling Goddess,
And thou, proved, much enduring,
Wave-toss'd Wanderer!
Who can stand still?
Ye fade, ye swim, ye waver before me —
The cup again!

Faster, faster,
O Circe, Goddess,
Let the wild, thronging train,
The bright procession
Of eddying forms,
Sweep through my soul!

FRAGMENT OF AN 'ANTIGONE'

The Chorus

WELL hath he done who hath seized happiness!
For little do the all-containing hours,
    Though opulent, freely give.
    Who, weighing that life well
    Fortune presents unpray'd,
Declines her ministry, and carves his own;
    And, justice not infringed,
Makes his own welfare his unswerved-from law.

He does well too, who keeps that clue the mild
Birth-Goddess and the austere Fates first gave.
    For from the day when these
    Bring him, a weeping child,
    First to the light, and mark
A country for him, kinsfolk, and a home,
    Unguided he remains,
Till the Fates come again, this time with death.

        In little companies,
    And, our own place once left,
Ignorant where to stand, or whom to avoid,
By city and household group'd, we live; and many shocks
    Our order heaven-ordain'd
    Must every day endure:
Voyages, exiles, hates, dissensions, wars.
        Besides what waste *he* makes,
        The all-hated, order-breaking,
        Without friend, city, or home,
        Death, who dissevers all.

        Him then I praise, who dares
        To self-selected good
Prefer obedience to the primal law,
Which consecrates the ties of blood; for these, indeed,
        Are to the Gods a care;
        That touches but himself.
For every day man may be link'd and loosed
        With strangers; but the bond
        Original, deep-inwound,

Of blood, can he not bind,
Nor, if Fate binds, not bear.

But hush! Hæmon, whom Antigone,
Robbing herself of life in burying,
Against Creon's law, Polynices,
Robs of a loved bride — pale, imploring,
Waiting her passage,
Forth from the palace hitherward comes.

Hæmon

No, no, old men, Creon I curse not!
I weep, Thebans,
One than Creon crueller far!
For he, he, at least, by slaying her,
August laws doth mightily vindicate;
But thou, too-bold, headstrong, pitiless!
Ah me! — honourest more than thy lover,
O Antigone!
A dead, ignorant, thankless corpse.

The Chorus

Nor was the love untrue
Which the Dawn-Goddess bore
To that fair youth she erst,
Leaving the salt sea-beds
And coming flush'd over the stormy frith
Of loud Euripus, saw —
Saw and snatch'd, wild with love,
From the pine-dotted spurs
Of Parnes, where thy waves,
Asopus! gleam rock-hemm'd —
The Hunter of the Tanagræan Field.

But him, in his sweet prime,
By severance immature,
By Artemis' soft shafts,
She, though a Goddess born,
Saw in the rocky isle of Delos die.
Such end o'ertook that love.
For she desired to make
Immortal mortal man,

And blend his happy life,
Far from the Gods, with hers;
To him postponing an eternal law.

Hæmon

But like me, she, wroth, complaining,
Succumb'd to the envy of unkind Gods;
And, her beautiful arms unclasping,
Her fair youth unwillingly gave.

The Chorus

Nor, though enthroned too high
To fear assault of envious Gods,
His beloved Argive seer would Zeus retain
From his appointed end

In this our Thebes; but when
His flying steeds came near
To cross the steep Ismenian glen,
The broad earth open'd, and whelm'd them and him;
And through the void air sang
At large his enemy's spear.

And fain would Zeus have saved his tired son
Beholding him where the Two Pillars stand
O'er the sun-redden'd western straits,
Or at his work in that dim lower world.
Fain would he have recall'd
The fraudulent oath which bound
To a much feebler wight the heroic man.

But he preferr'd Fate to his strong desire.
Nor did there need less than the burning pile
Under the towering Trachis crags,
And the Spercheios vale, shaken with groans,
And the roused Maliac gulph,
And scared Œtæan snows,
To achieve his son's deliverance, O my child!

THE SICK KING IN BOKHARA

Hussein

O MOST just Vizier, send away
The cloth-merchants, and let them be,
Them and their dues, this day! the King
Is ill at ease, and calls for thee.

The Vizier

O merchants, tarry yet a day
Here in Bokhara! but at noon,
To-morrow, come, and ye shall pay
Each fortieth web of cloth to me,
As the law is, and go your way.

O Hussein, lead me to the King!
Thou teller of sweet tales, thine own,
Ferdousi's, and the others', lead!
How is it with my lord?

Hussein

Alone,
Ever since prayer-time, he doth wait,
O Vizier! without lying down,
In the great window of the gate,
Looking into the Registàn,
Where through the sellers' booths the slaves
Are this way bringing the dead man.—
O Vizier, here is the King's door!

The King

O Vizier, I may bury him?

The Vizier

O King, thou know'st, I have been sick
These many days, and heard no thing
(For Allah shut my ears and mind),
Not even what thou dost, O King!

Wherefore, that I may counsel thee,
Let Hussein, if thou wilt, make haste
To speak in order what hath chanced.

The King

O Vizier, be it as thou say'st!

Hussein

Three days since, at the time of prayer
A certain Moollah, with his robe
All rent, and dust upon his hair,
Watch'd my lord's coming forth, and push'd
The golden mace-bearers aside,
And fell at the King's feet, and cried:
'Justice, O King, and on myself!
On this great sinner, who did break
The law, and by the law must die!
Vengeance, O King!'

But the King spake:
'What fool is this, that hurts our ears
With folly? or what drunken slave?
My guards, what, prick him with your spears!
Prick me the fellow from the path!'
As the King said, so it was done,
And to the mosque my lord pass'd on.

But on the morrow, when the King
Went forth again, the holy book
Carried before him, as is right,
And through the square his way he took;
My man comes running, fleck'd with blood
From yesterday, and falling down
Cries out most earnestly: 'O King,
My lord, O King, do right, I pray!

'How canst thou, ere thou hear, discern
If I speak folly? but a king,
Whether a thing be great or small,
Like Allah, hears and judges all.

'Wherefore hear thou! Thou know'st, how fierce
In these last days the sun hath burn'd;

That the green water in the tanks
Is to a putrid puddle turn'd;
And the canal, which from the stream
Of Samarcand is brought this way,
Wastes, and runs thinner every day.

'Now I at nightfall had gone forth
Alone, and in a darksome place
Under some mulberry-trees I found
A little pool; and in short space,
With all the water that was there
I fill'd my pitcher, and stole home
Unseen; and having drink to spare,
I hid the can behind the door,
And went up on the roof to sleep.

'But in the night, which was with wind
And burning dust, again I creep
Down, having fever, for a drink.

'Now meanwhile had my brethren found
The water-pitcher, where it stood
Behind the door upon the ground,
And call'd my mother; and they all,
As they were thirsty, and the night
Most sultry, drain'd the pitcher there;
That they sate with it, in my sight,
Their lips still wet, when I came down.

'Now mark! I, being fever'd, sick
(Most unblest also), at that sight
Brake forth, and cursed them — dost thou hear? —
One was my mother —— Now, do right!'

But my lord mused a space, and said:
'Send him away, Sirs, and make on!
It is some madman!' the King said.
As the King bade, so was it done.

The morrow, at the self-same hour,
In the King's path, behold, the man,
Not kneeling, sternly fix'd! he stood
Right opposite, and thus began,
Frowning grim down: 'Thou wicked King,
Most deaf where thou shouldst most give ear!

What, must I howl in the next world,
Because thou wilt not listen here?

'What, wilt thou pray, and get thee grace,
And all grace shall to me be grudged?
Nay but, I swear, from this thy path
I will not stir till I be judged!'

Then they who stood about the King
Drew close together and conferr'd;
Till that the King stood forth and said:
'Before the priests thou shalt be heard.'

But when the Ulemas were met,
And the thing heard, they doubted not;
But sentenced him, as the law is,
To die by stoning on the spot.

Now the King charged us secretly:
'Stoned must he be, the law stands so.
Yet, if he seek to fly, give way;
Hinder him not, but let him go.'

So saying, the King took a stone,
And cast it softly; — but the man,
With a great joy upon his face,
Kneel'd down, and cried not, neither ran.

So they, whose lot it was, cast stones,
That they flew thick and bruised him sore.
But he praised Allah with loud voice,
And remain'd kneeling as before.

My lord had cover'd up his face;
But when one told him, 'He is dead,'
Turning him quickly to go in,
'Bring thou to me his corpse,' he said.

And truly, while I speak, O King,
I hear the bearers on the stair;
Wilt thou they straightway bring him in?
— Ho! enter ye who tarry there!

The Vizier

O King, in this I praise thee not!
Now must I call thy grief not wise.

Is he thy friend, or of thy blood,
To find such favour in thine eyes?

Nay, were he thine own mother's son,
Still, thou art king, and the law stands.
It were not meet the balance swerved,
The sword were broken in thy hands.

But being nothing, as he is,
Why for no cause make sad thy face?—
Lo, I am old! three kings, ere thee,
Have I seen reigning in this place.

But who, through all this length of time,
Could bear the burden of his years,
If he for strangers pain'd his heart
Not less than those who merit tears?

Fathers we *must* have, wife and child,
And grievous is the grief for these;
This pain alone, which *must* be borne,
Makes the head white, and bows the knees.

But other loads than this his own
One man is not well made to bear.
Besides, to each are his own friends,
To mourn with him, and show him care.

Look, this is but one single place,
Though it be great; all the earth round,
If a man bear to have it so,
Things which might vex him shall be found.

Upon the Russian frontier, where
The watchers of two armies stand
Near one another, many a man,
Seeking a prey unto his hand,

Hath snatch'd a little fair-hair'd slave;
They snatch also, towards Mervè,
The Shiah dogs, who pasture sheep,
And up from thence to Orgunjè.

And these all, labouring for a lord,
Eat not the fruit of their own hands;

Which is the heaviest of all plagues,
To that man's mind, who understands.

The kaffirs also (whom God curse!)
Vex one another, night and day;
There are the lepers, and all sick;
There are the poor, who faint alway.

All these have sorrow, and keep still,
Whilst other men make cheer, and sing.
Wilt thou have pity on all these?
No, nor on this dead dog, O King!

The King

O Vizier, thou art old, I young!
Clear in these things I cannot see.
My head is burning, and a heat
Is in my skin which angers me.

But hear ye this, ye sons of men!
They that bear rule, and are obey'd,
Unto a rule more strong than theirs
Are in their turn obedient made.

In vain therefore, with wistful eyes
Gazing up hither, the poor man,
Who loiters by the high-heap'd booths,
Below there, in the Registàn,

Says: 'Happy he, who lodges there!
With silken raiment, store of rice,
And for this drought, all kinds of fruits,
Grape-syrup, squares of colour'd ice,

'With cherries serv'd in drifts of snow.'
In vain hath a king power to build
Houses, arcades, enamell'd mosques;
And to make orchard-closes, fill'd

With curious fruit-trees brought from far;
With cisterns for the winter-rain,
And, in the desert, spacious inns
In divers places — if that pain

Is not more lighten'd, which he feels,
If his will be not satisfied;
And that it be not, from all time
The law is planted, to abide.

Thou wast a sinner, thou poor man!
Thou wast athirst; and didst not see,
That, though we take what we desire,
We must not snatch it eagerly.

And I have meat and drink at will,
And rooms of treasures, not a few.
But I am sick, nor heed I these;
And what I would, I cannot do.

Even the great honour which I have,
When I am dead, will soon grow still;
So have I neither joy, nor fame.
But what I can do, that I will.

I have a fretted brick-work tomb
Upon a hill on the right hand,
Hard by a close of apricots,
Upon the road of Samarcand;

Thither, O Vizier, will I bear
This man my pity could not save,
And, plucking up the marble flags,
There lay his body in my grave.

Bring water, nard, and linen rolls!
Wash off all blood, set smooth each limb!
Then say: 'He was not wholly vile,
Because a king shall bury him.'

SONNETS

SHAKESPEARE

Others abide our question. Thou art free.
We ask and ask — Thou smilest and art still,
Out-topping knowledge. For the loftiest hill,
Who to the stars uncrowns his majesty,

Planting his steadfast footsteps in the sea,
Making the heaven of heavens his dwelling-place,
Spares but the cloudy border of his base
To the foil'd searching of mortality;

And thou, who didst the stars and sunbeams know,
Self-school'd, self-scann'd, self-honour'd, self-secure,
Didst tread on earth unguess'd at. — Better so!

All pains the immortal spirit must endure,
All weakness which impairs, all griefs which bow,
Find their sole speech in that victorious brow.

WRITTEN IN BUTLER'S SERMONS

Affections, Instincts, Principles, and Powers,
Impulse and Reason, Freedom and Control —
So men, unravelling God's harmonious whole,
Rend in a thousand shreds this life of ours.

Vain labour! Deep and broad, where none may see,
Spring the foundations of that shadowy throne
Where man's one nature, queen-like, sits alone,
Centred in a majestic unity;

And rays her powers, like sister-islands seen
Linking their coral arms under the sea,
Or cluster'd peaks with plunging gulfs between

Spann'd by aërial arches all of gold,
Whereo'er the chariot wheels of life are roll'd
In cloudy circles to eternity.

IN HARMONY WITH NATURE

TO A PREACHER

'In harmony with Nature?' Restless fool,
Who with such heat dost preach what were to thee,
When true, the last impossibility —
To be like Nature strong, like Nature cool!

Know, man hath all which Nature hath, but more,
And in that *more* lie all his hopes of good.
Nature is cruel, man is sick of blood;
Nature is stubborn, man would fain adore;

Nature is fickle, man hath need of rest;
Nature forgives no debt, and fears no grave;
Man would be mild, and with safe conscience blest.

Man must begin, know this, where Nature ends;
Nature and man can never be fast friends.
Fool, if thou canst not pass her, rest her slave!

TO GEORGE CRUIKSHANK

ON SEEING, IN THE COUNTRY, HIS PICTURE OF 'THE BOTTLE'

Artist, whose hand, with horror wing'd, hath torn
From the rank life of towns this leaf! and flung
The prodigy of full-blown crime among
Valleys and men to middle fortune born,

Not innocent, indeed, yet not forlorn —
Say, what shall calm us when such guests intrude
Like comets on the heavenly solitude?
Shall breathless glades, cheer'd by shy Dian's horn,

Cold-bubbling springs, or caves? — Not so! The soul
Breasts her own griefs; and, urged too fiercely, says:
'Why tremble? True, the nobleness of man

May be by man effaced; man can control
To pain, to death, the bent of his own days.
Know thou the worst! So much, not more, he *can*.'

TO A REPUBLICAN FRIEND, 1848

God knows it, I am with you. If to prize
Those virtues, prized and practised by too few,
But prized, but loved, but eminent in you,
Man's fundamental life; if to despise

The barren optimistic sophistries
Of comfortable moles, whom what they do
Teaches the limit of the just and true
(And for such doing they require not eyes);

If sadness at the long heart-wasting show
Wherein earth's great ones are disquieted;
If thoughts, not idle, while before me flow

The armies of the homeless and unfed —
If these are yours, if this is what you are,
Then am I yours, and what you feel, I share.

CONTINUED

Yet, when I muse on what life is, I seem
Rather to patience prompted, than that proud
Prospect of hope which France proclaims so loud —
France, famed in all great arts, in none supreme;

Seeing this vale, this earth, whereon we dream,
Is on all sides o'ershadow'd by the high
Uno'erleap'd Mountains of Necessity,
Sparing us narrower margin than we deem.

Nor will that day dawn at a human nod,
When, bursting through the network superposed
By selfish occupation — plot and plan,

Lust, avarice, envy — liberated man,
All difference with his fellow-mortal closed,
Shall be left standing face to face with God.

RELIGIOUS ISOLATION

TO THE SAME FRIEND

CHILDREN (as such forgive them) have I known,
Ever in their own eager pastime bent
To make the incurious bystander, intent
On his own swarming thoughts, an interest own —

Too fearful or too fond to play alone.
Do thou, whom light in thine own inmost soul
(Not less thy boast) illuminates, control
Wishes unworthy of a man full-grown.

What though the holy secret, which moulds thee,
Mould not the solid earth? though never winds
Have whisper'd it to the complaining sea,

Nature's great law, and law of all men's minds? —
To its own impulse every creature stirs;
Live by thy light, and earth will live by hers!

TO A GIPSY CHILD BY THE SEA-SHORE

DOUGLAS, ISLE OF MAN

Who taught this pleading to unpractised eyes?
Who hid such import in an infant's gloom?
Who lent thee, child, this meditative guise?
Who mass'd, round that slight brow, these clouds of doom?

Lo! sails that gleam a moment and are gone;
The swinging waters, and the cluster'd pier.
Not idly Earth and Ocean labour on,
Nor idly do these sea-birds hover near.

But thou, whom superfluity of joy
Wafts not from thine own thoughts, nor longings vain,
Nor weariness, the full-fed soul's annoy —
Remaining in thy hunger and thy pain;

Thou, drugging pain by patience; half averse
From thine own mother's breast, that knows not thee;
With eyes which sought thine eyes thou didst converse,
And that soul-searching vision fell on me.

Glooms that go deep as thine I have not known:
Moods of fantastic sadness, nothing worth.
Thy sorrow and thy calmness are thine own:
Glooms that enhance and glorify this earth.

What mood wears like complexion to thy woe?
His, who in mountain glens, at noon of day,
Sits rapt, and hears the battle break below?
— Ah! thine was not the shelter, but the fray.

Some exile's, mindful how the past was glad?
Some angel's, in an alien planet born?
— No exile's dream was ever half so sad,
Not any angel's sorrow so forlorn.

Is the calm thine of stoic souls, who weigh
Life well, and find it wanting, nor deplore;
But in disdainful silence turn away,
Stand mute, self-centred, stern, and dream no more?

Or do I wait, to hear some gray-hair'd king
Unravel all his many-colour'd lore;
Whose mind hath known all arts of governing,
Mused much, loved life a little, loathed it more?

Down the pale cheek long lines of shadow slope,
Which years, and curious thought, and suffering give.
— Thou hast foreknown the vanity of hope,
Foreseen thy harvest — yet proceed'st to live.

O meek anticipant of that sure pain
Whose sureness gray-hair'd scholars hardly learn!
What wonder shall time breed, to swell thy strain?
What heavens, what earth, what sun shalt thou discern?

Ere the long night, whose stillness brooks no star,
Match that funereal aspect with her pall,
I think, thou wilt have fathom'd life too far,
Have known too much —— or else forgotten all.

The Guide of our dark steps a triple veil
Betwixt our senses and our sorrow keeps;
Hath sown with cloudless passages the tale
Of grief, and eased us with a thousand sleeps.

Ah! not the nectarous poppy lovers use,
Not daily labour's dull, Lethæan spring,
Oblivion in lost angels can infuse
Of the soil'd glory, and the trailing wing.

And though thou glean, what strenuous gleaners may,
In the throng'd fields where winning comes by strife;
And though the just sun gild, as mortals pray,
Some reaches of thy storm-vext stream of life;

Though that blank sunshine blind thee; though the cloud
That sever'd the world's march and thine, be gone;
Though ease dulls grace, and Wisdom be too proud
To halve a lodging that was all her own —

Once, ere the day decline, thou shalt discern,
Oh once, ere night, in thy success, thy chain!
Ere the long evening close, thou shalt return,
And wear this majesty of grief again.

THE FORSAKEN MERMAN

Come, dear children, let us away;
Down and away below!
Now my brothers call from the bay,
Now the great winds shoreward blow,
Now the salt tides seaward flow;
Now the wild white horses play,
Champ and chafe and toss in the spray.
Children dear, let us away!
This way, this way!

Call her once before you go —
Call once yet!
In a voice that she will know:
'Margaret! Margaret!'
Children's voices should be dear
(Call once more) to a mother's ear;
Children's voices, wild with pain —
Surely she will come again!
Call her once and come away;
This way, this way!
'Mother dear, we cannot stay!
The wild white horses foam and fret.'
Margaret! Margaret!

Come, dear children, come away down;
Call no more!
One last look at the white-wall'd town,
And the little grey church on the windy shore,
Then come down!
She will not come though you call all day;
Come away, come away!

Children dear, was it yesterday
We heard the sweet bells over the bay?
In the caverns where we lay,
Through the surf and through the swell,
The far-off sound of a silver bell?
Sand-strewn caverns, cool and deep,
Where the winds are all asleep;
Where the spent lights quiver and gleam,
Where the salt weed sways in the stream,

Where the sea-beasts, ranged all round,
Feed in the ooze of their pasture-ground;
Where the sea-snakes coil and twine,
Dry their mail and bask in the brine;
Where great whales come sailing by,
Sail and sail, with unshut eye,
Round the world for ever and aye?
When did music come this way?
Children dear, was it yesterday?

Children dear, was it yesterday
(Call yet once) that she went away?
Once she sate with you and me,
On a red gold throne in the heart of the sea,
And the youngest sate on her knee.
She comb'd its bright hair, and she tended it well,
When down swung the sound of a far-off bell.
She sigh'd, she look'd up through the clear green sea;
She said: 'I must go, for my kinsfolk pray
In the little grey church on the shore to-day.
'Twill be Easter-time in the world — ah me!
And I lose my poor soul, Merman! here with thee.'
I said: 'Go up, dear heart, through the waves;
Say thy prayer, and come back to the kind sea-caves!'
She smiled, she went up through the surf in the bay.
Children dear, was it yesterday?

Children dear, were we long alone?
'The sea grows stormy, the little ones moan;
Long prayers,' I said, 'in the world they say;
Come!' I said; and we rose through the surf in the bay.
We went up the beach, by the sandy down
Where the sea-stocks bloom, to the white-wall'd town;
Through the narrow paved streets, where all was still,
To the little grey church on the windy hill.
From the church came a murmur of folk at their prayers,
But we stood without in the cold blowing airs.
We climb'd on the graves, on the stones worn with rains,
And we gazed up the aisle through the small leaded panes.
She sate by the pillar; we saw her clear:
'Margaret, hist! come quick, we are here!
Dear heart,' I said, 'we are long alone;
The sea grows stormy, the little ones moan.'
But, ah, she gave me never a look,
For her eyes were seal'd to the holy book!

Loud prays the priest; shut stands the door.
Come away, children, call no more!
Come away, come down, call no more!

Down, down, down!
Down to the depths of the sea!
She sits at her wheel in the humming town,
Singing most joyfully.
Hark what she sings: 'O joy, O joy,
For the humming street, and the child with its toy!
For the priest, and the bell, and the holy well;
For the wheel where I spun,
And the blessed light of the sun!'
And so she sings her fill,
Singing most joyfully,
Till the spindle drops from her hand,
And the whizzing wheel stands still.
She steals to the window, and looks at the sand,
And over the sand at the sea;
And her eyes are set in a stare;
And anon there breaks a sigh,
And anon there drops a tear,
From a sorrow-clouded eye,
And a heart sorrow-laden,
A long, long sigh;
For the cold strange eyes of a little Mermaiden
And the gleam of her golden hair.

Come away, away children;
Come children, come down!
The hoarse wind blows coldly;
Lights shine in the town.
She will start from her slumber
When gusts shake the door;
She will hear the winds howling,
Will hear the waves roar.
We shall see, while above us
The waves roar and whirl,
A ceiling of amber,
A pavement of pearl.
Singing: 'Here came a mortal,
But faithless was she!
And alone dwell for ever
The kings of the sea.'

But, children, at midnight,
When soft the winds blow,
When clear falls the moonlight,
When spring-tides are low;
When sweet airs come seaward
From heaths starr'd with broom,
And high rocks throw mildly
On the blanch'd sands a gloom;
Up the still, glistening beaches,
Up the creeks we will hie,
Over banks of bright seaweed
The ebb-tide leaves dry.
We will gaze, from the sand-hills,
At the white, sleeping town;
At the church on the hill-side —
And then come back down.
Singing: 'There dwells a loved one,
But cruel is she!
She left lonely for ever
The kings of the sea.'

IN UTRUMQUE PARATUS

If, in the silent mind of One all-pure,
  At first imagined lay
The sacred world; and by procession sure
From those still deeps, in form and colour drest,
Seasons alternating, and night and day,
The long-mused thought to north, south, east, and west,
  Took then its all-seen way;

O waking on a world which thus-wise springs!
  Whether it needs thee count
Betwixt thy waking and the birth of things
Ages or hours — O waking on life's stream!
By lonely pureness to the all-pure fount
(Only by this thou canst) the colour'd dream
  Of life remount!

Thin, thin the pleasant human noises grow,
  And faint the city gleams;
Rare the lone pastoral huts — marvel not thou!
The solemn peaks but to the stars are known,

But to the stars, and the cold lunar beams;
Alone the sun arises, and alone
    Spring the great streams.

But, if the wild unfather'd mass no birth
    In divine seats hath known;
In the blank, echoing solitude if Earth,
Rocking her obscure body to and fro,
Ceases not from all time to heave and groan,
Unfruitful oft, and at her happiest throe
    Forms, what she forms, alone;

O seeming sole to awake, thy sun-bathed head
    Piercing the solemn cloud
Round thy still dreaming brother-world outspread!
O man, whom Earth, thy long-vext mother, bare
Not without joy — so radiant, so endow'd
(Such happy issue crown'd her painful care) —
    Be not too proud!

Oh when most self-exalted, most alone,
    Chief dreamer, own thy dream!
Thy brother-world stirs at thy feet unknown,
Who hath a monarch's hath no brother's part;
Yet doth thine inmost soul with yearning teem.
— Oh, what a spasm shakes the dreamer's heart!
    'I, too, but seem.'

RESIGNATION

TO FAUSTA

To die be given us, or attain!
Fierce work it were, to do again.
So pilgrims, bound for Mecca, pray'd
At burning noon; so warriors said,
Scarf'd with the cross, who watch'd the miles
Of dust which wreathed their struggling files
Down Lydian mountains; so, when snows
Round Alpine summits, eddying rose,
The Goth, bound Rome-wards; so the Hun,
Crouch'd on his saddle, while the sun
Went lurid down o'er flooded plains
Through which the groaning Danube strains
To the drear Euxine; — so pray all,
Whom labours, self-ordain'd, enthrall;
Because they to themselves propose
On this side the all-common close
A goal which, gain'd, may give repose.
So pray they; and to stand again
Where they stood once, to them were pain;
Pain to thread back and to renew
Past straits, and currents long steer'd through.

But milder natures, and more free —
Whom an unblamed serenity
Hath freed from passions, and the state
Of struggle these necessitate;
Whom schooling of the stubborn mind
Hath made, or birth hath found, resign'd —
These mourn not, that their goings pay
Obedience to the passing day.
These claim not every laughing Hour
For handmaid to their striding power;
Each in her turn, with torch uprear'd,
To await their march; and when appear'd,
Through the cold gloom, with measured race,
To usher for a destined space
(Her own sweet errands all forgone)
The too imperious traveller on.

These, Fausta, ask not this; nor thou,
Time's chafing prisoner, ask it now!

We left, just ten years since, you say,
That wayside inn we left to-day.
Our jovial host, as forth we fare,
Shouts greeting from his easy chair.
High on a bank our leader stands,
Reviews and ranks his motley bands,
Makes clear our goal to every eye —
The valley's western boundary.
A gate swings to! our tide hath flow'd
Already from the silent road.
The valley-pastures, one by one,
Are threaded, quiet in the sun;
And now beyond the rude stone bridge
Slopes gracious up the western ridge.
Its woody border, and the last
Of its dark upland farms is past —
Cool farms, with open-lying stores,
Under their burnish'd sycamores;
All past! and through the trees we glide,
Emerging on the green hill-side.
There climbing hangs, a far-seen sign,
Our wavering, many-colour'd line;
There winds, upstreaming slowly still
Over the summit of the hill.
And now, in front, behold outspread
Those upper regions we must tread!
Mild hollows, and clear heathy swells,
The cheerful silence of the fells.
Some two hours' march with serious air,
Through the deep noontide heats we fare;
The red-grouse, springing at our sound,
Skims, now and then, the shining ground;
No life, save his and ours, intrudes
Upon these breathless solitudes.
O joy! again the farms appear.
Cool shade is there, and rustic cheer;
There springs the brook will guide us down,
Bright comrade, to the noisy town.
Lingering, we follow down; we gain
The town, the highway, and the plain.
And many a mile of dusty way,
Parch'd and road-worn, we made that day;

But, Fausta, I remember well,
That as the balmy darkness fell
We bathed our hands with speechless glee,
That night, in the wide-glimmering sea.

Once more we tread this self-same road,
Fausta, which ten years since we trod;
Alone we tread it, you and I,
Ghosts of that boisterous company.
Here, where the brook shines, near its head,
In its clear, shallow, turf-fringed bed;
Here, whence the eye first sees, far down,
Capp'd with faint smoke, the noisy town;
Here sit we, and again unroll,
Though slowly, the familiar whole.
The solemn wastes of heathy hill
Sleep in the July sunshine still;
The self-same shadows now, as then,
Play through this grassy upland glen;
The loose dark stones on the green way
Lie strewn, it seems, where then they lay;
On this mild bank above the stream,
(You crush them!) the blue gentians gleam.
Still this wild brook, the rushes cool,
The sailing foam, the shining pool!
These are not changed; and we, you say,
Are scarce more changed, in truth, than they.

The gipsies, whom we met below,
They, too, have long roam'd to and fro;
They ramble, leaving, where they pass,
Their fragments on the cumber'd grass.
And often to some kindly place
Chance guides the migratory race,
Where, though long wanderings intervene,
They recognise a former scene.
The dingy tents are pitch'd; the fires
Give to the wind their wavering spires;
In dark knots crouch round the wild flame
Their children, as when first they came;
They see their shackled beasts again
Move, browsing, up the gray-wall'd lane.
Signs are not wanting, which might raise
The ghost in them of former days—
Signs are not wanting, if they would;

Suggestions to disquietude.
For them, for all, time's busy touch,
While it mends little, troubles much.
Their joints grow stiffer — but the year
Runs his old round of dubious cheer;
Chilly they grow — yet winds in March,
Still, sharp as ever, freeze and parch;
They must live still — and yet, God knows,
Crowded and keen the country grows;
It seems as if, in their decay,
The law grew stronger every day.
So might they reason, so compare,
Fausta, times past with times that are.
But no! — they rubb'd through yesterday
In their hereditary way,
And they will rub through, if they can,
To-morrow on the self-same plan,
Till death arrive to supersede,
For them, vicissitude and need.

The poet, to whose mighty heart
Heaven doth a quicker pulse impart,
Subdues that energy to scan
Not his own course, but that of man.
Though he move mountains, though his day
Be pass'd on the proud heights of sway,
Though he hath loosed a thousand chains,
Though he hath borne immortal pains,
Action and suffering though he know —
He hath not lived, if he lives so.
He sees, in some great-historied land,
A ruler of the people stand,
Sees his strong thought in fiery flood
Roll through the heaving multitude;
Exults — yet for no moment's space
Envies the all-regarded place.
Beautiful eyes meet his — and he
Bears to admire uncravingly;
They pass — he, mingled with the crowd,
Is in their far-off triumphs proud.
From some high station he looks down,
At sunset, on a populous town;
Surveys each happy group, which fleets,
Toil ended, through the shining streets,
Each with some errand of its own —

And does not say: *I am alone.*
He sees the gentle stir of birth
When morning purifies the earth;
He leans upon a gate and sees
The pastures, and the quiet trees.
Low, woody hill, with gracious bound,
Folds the still valley almost round;
The cuckoo, loud on some high lawn,
Is answer'd from the depth of dawn;
In the hedge straggling to the stream,
Pale, dew-drench'd, half-shut roses gleam;
But, where the farther side slopes down,
He sees the drowsy new-waked clown
In his white quaint-embroider'd frock
Make, whistling, tow'rd his mist-wreathed flock —
Slowly, behind his heavy tread,
The wet, flower'd grass heaves up its head.
Lean'd on his gate, he gazes — tears
Are in his eyes, and in his ears
The murmur of a thousand years.
Before him he sees life unroll,
A placid and continuous whole —
That general life, which does not cease,
Whose secret is not joy, but peace;
That life, whose dumb wish is not miss'd
If birth proceeds, if things subsist;
The life of plants, and stones, and rain,
The life he craves — if not in vain
Fate gave, what chance shall not control,
His sad lucidity of soul.

You listen — but that wandering smile,
Fausta, betrays you cold the while!
Your eyes pursue the bells of foam
Wash'd, eddying, from this bank, their home.
Those gipsies, so your thoughts I scan,
Are less, the poet more, than man.
They feel not, though they move and see;
Deeper the poet feels; but he
Breathes, when he will, immortal air,
Where Orpheus and where Homer are.
In the day's life, whose iron round
Hems us all in, he is not bound;
He leaves his kind, o'erleaps their pen,
And flees the common life of men.

He escapes thence, but we abide —
Not deep the poet sees, but wide.

The world in which we live and move
Outlasts aversion, outlasts love,
Outlasts each effort, interest, hope,
Remorse, grief, joy; — and were the scope
Of these affections wider made,
Man still would see, and see dismay'd,
Beyond his passion's widest range,
Far regions of eternal change.
Nay, and since death, which wipes out man,
Finds him with many an unsolved plan,
With much unknown, and much untried,
Wonder not dead, and thirst not dried,
Still gazing on the ever full
Eternal mundane spectacle —
This world in which we draw our breath,
In some sense, Fausta, outlasts death.

Blame thou not, therefore, him who dares
Judge vain beforehand human cares;
Whose natural insight can discern
What through experience others learn;
Who needs not love and power, to know
Love transient, power and unreal show;
Who treads at ease life's uncheer'd ways—
Him blame not, Fausta, rather praise!
Rather thyself for some aim pray
Nobler than this, to fill the day;
Rather that heart, which burns in thee,
Ask, not to amuse, but to set free;
Be passionate hopes not ill resign'd
For quiet, and a fearless mind.
And though fate grudge to thee and me
The poet's rapt security,
Yet they, believe me, who await
No gifts from chance, have conquer'd fate.
They, winning room to see and hear,
And to men's business not too near,
Through clouds of individual strife
Draw homeward to the general life.
Like leaves by suns not yet uncurl'd;
To the wise, foolish; to the world,
Weak; — yet not weak, I might reply,

Not foolish, Fausta, in His eye,
To whom each moment in its race,
Crowd as we will its neutral space,
Is but a quiet watershed
Whence, equally, the seas of life and death are fed.

Enough, we live! — and if a life,
With large results so little rife,
Though bearable, seem hardly worth
This pomp of worlds, this pain of birth;
Yet, Fausta, the mute turf we tread,
The solemn hills around us spread,
This stream which falls incessantly,
The strange-scrawl'd rocks, the lonely sky,
If I might lend their life a voice,
Seem to bear rather than rejoice.
And even could the intemperate prayer
Man iterates, while these forbear,
For movement, for an ampler sphere,
Pierce Fate's impenetrable ear;
Not milder is the general lot
Because our spirits have forgot,
In action's dizzying eddy whirl'd,
The something that infects the world.

Empedocles on Etna, and Other Poems

(1852)

EMPEDOCLES ON ETNA

A DRAMATIC POEM

PERSONS

EMPEDOCLES.
PAUSANIAS, *a Physician.*
CALLICLES, *a young Harp-player.*

The Scene of the Poem is on Mount Etna; at first in the forest region, afterwards on the summit of the mountain.

ACT I. SCENE I.

Morning. A Pass in the forest region of Etna.

CALLICLES

(*Alone, resting on a rock by the path.*)

THE mules, I think, will not be here this hour;
They feel the cool wet turf under their feet
By the stream-side, after the dusty lanes
In which they have toil'd all night from Catana,
And scarcely will they budge a yard. O Pan,
How gracious is the mountain at this hour!
A thousand times have I been here alone,
Or with the revellers from the mountain-towns,
But never on so fair a morn; — the sun
Is shining on the brilliant mountain-crests,
And on the highest pines; but farther down,
Here in the valley, is in shade; the sward
Is dark, and on the stream the mist still hangs;
One sees one's footprints crush'd in the wet grass,
One's breath curls in the air; and on these pines

That climb from the stream's edge, the long grey tufts,
Which the goats love, are jewell'd thick with dew.
Here will I stay till the slow litter comes.
I have my harp too — that is well. — Apollo!
What mortal could be sick or sorry here?
I know not in what mind Empedocles,
Whose mules I follow'd, may be coming up,
But if, as most men say, he is half mad
With exile, and with brooding on his wrongs,
Pausanias, his sage friend, who mounts with him,
Could scarce have lighted on a lovelier cure.
The mules must be below, far down. I hear
Their tinkling bells, mix'd with the song of birds,
Rise faintly to me — now it stops! — Who's here?
Pausanias! and on foot? alone?

Pausanias

And thou, then?
I left thee supping with Peisianax,
With thy head full of wine, and thy hair crown'd,
Touching thy harp as the whim came on thee,
And praised and spoil'd by master and by guests
Almost as much as the new dancing-girl.
Why hast thou follow'd us?

Callicles

The night was hot,
And the feast past its prime; so we slipp'd out,
Some of us, to the portico to breathe; —
Peisianax, thou know'st, drinks late; — and then,
As I was lifting my soil'd garland off,
I saw the mules and litter in the court,
And in the litter sate Empedocles;
Thou, too, wast with him. Straightway I sped home;
I saddled my white mule, and all night long
Through the cool lovely country follow'd you,
Pass'd you a little since as morning dawn'd,
And have this hour sate by the torrent here,
Till the slow mules should climb in sight again.
And now?

Pausanias

And now, back to the town with speed!
Crouch in the wood first, till the mules have pass'd;

They do but halt, they will be here anon.
Thou must be viewless to Empedocles;
Save mine, he must not meet a human eye.
One of his moods is on him that thou know'st;
I think, thou wouldst not vex him.

Callicles

No — and yet
I would fain stay, and help thee tend him. Once
He knew me well, and would oft notice me;
And still, I know not how, he draws me to him,
And I could watch him with his proud sad face,
His flowing locks and gold-encircled brow
And kingly gait, for ever; such a spell
In his severe looks, such a majesty
As drew of old the people after him,
In Agrigentum and Olympia,
When his star reign'd, before his banishment,
Is potent still on me in his decline.
But oh! Pausanias, he is changed of late;
There is a settled trouble in his air
Admits no momentary brightening now,
And when he comes among his friends at feasts,
'Tis as an orphan among prosperous boys.
Thou know'st of old he loved this harp of mine,
When first he sojourn'd with Peisianax;
He is now always moody, and I fear him;
But I would serve him, soothe him, if I could,
Dared one but try.

Pausanias

Thou wast a kind child ever!
He loves thee, but he must not see thee now.
Thou hast indeed a rare touch on thy harp,
He loves that in thee, too; — there was a time
(But that is pass'd), he would have paid thy strain
With music to have drawn the stars from heaven.
He hath his harp and laurel with him still,
But he has laid the use of music by,
And all which might relax his settled gloom.
Yet thou may'st try thy playing, if thou wilt —
But thou must keep unseen; follow us on,
But at a distance! in these solitudes,

In this clear mountain-air, a voice will rise,
Though from afar, distinctly; it may soothe him.
Play when we halt, and, when the evening comes
And I must leave him (for his pleasure is
To be left musing these soft nights alone
In the high unfrequented mountain-spots),
Then watch him, for he ranges swift and far,
Sometimes to Etna's top, and to the cone;
But hide thee in the rocks a great way down,
And try thy noblest strains, my Callicles,
With the sweet night to help thy harmony!
Thou wilt earn my thanks sure, and perhaps his.

Callicles

More than a day and night, Pausanias,
Of this fair summer-weather, on these hills,
Would I bestow to help Empedocles.
That needs no thanks; one is far better here
Than in the broiling city in these heats.
But tell me, how hast thou persuaded him
In this his present fierce, man-hating mood,
To bring thee out with him alone on Etna?

Pausanias

Thou hast heard all men speaking of Pantheia
The woman who at Agrigentum lay
Thirty long days in a cold trance of death,
And whom Empedocles call'd back to life.
Thou art too young to note it, but his power
Swells with the swelling evil of this time,
And holds men mute to see where it will rise.
He could stay swift diseases in old days,
Chain madmen by the music of his lyre,
Cleanse to sweet airs the breath of poisonous streams,
And in the mountain-chinks inter the winds.
This he could do of old; but now, since all
Clouds and grows daily worse in Sicily,
Since broils tear us in twain, since this new swarm
Of sophists has got empire in our schools
Where he was paramount, since he is banish'd
And lives a lonely man in triple gloom —
He grasps the very reins of life and death.
I ask'd him of Pantheia yesterday,

When we were gather'd with Peisianax,
And he made answer, I should come at night
On Etna here, and be alone with him,
And he would tell me, as his old, tried friend,
Who still was faithful, what might profit me;
That is, the secret of this miracle.

Callicles

Bah! Thou a doctor! Thou art superstitious.
Simple Pausanias, 'twas no miracle!
Pantheia, for I know her kinsmen well,
Was subject to these trances from a girl.
Empedocles would say so, did he deign;
But he still lets the people, whom he scorns,
Gape and cry *wizard* at him, if they list.
But thou, thou art no company for him!
Thou art as cross, as sour'd as himself!
Thou hast some wrong from thine own citizens,
And then thy friend is banish'd, and on that,
Straightway thou fallest to arraign the times,
As if the sky was impious not to fall.
The sophists are no enemies of his;
I hear, Gorgias, their chief, speaks nobly of him,
As of his gifted master, and once friend.
He is too scornful, too high-wrought, too bitter.
'Tis not the times, 'tis not the sophists vex him;
There is some root of suffering in himself,
Some secret and unfollow'd vein of woe,
Which makes the time look black and sad to him.
Pester him not in this his sombre mood
With questionings about an idle tale,
But lead him through the lovely mountain-paths,
And keep his mind from preying on itself,
And talk to him of things at hand and common,
Not miracles! thou art a learned man,
But credulous of fables as a girl.

Pausanias

And thou, a boy whose tongue outruns his knowledge,
And on whose lightness blame is thrown away.
Enough of this! I see the litter wind
Up by the torrent-side, under the pines.
I must rejoin Empedocles. Do thou

Crouch in the brushwood till the mules have pass'd;
Then play thy kind part well. Farewell till night!

SCENE II

Noon. A Glen on the highest skirts of the woody region of Etna.

EMPEDOCLES — PAUSANIAS

Pausanias

The noon is hot. When we have cross'd the stream,
We shall have left the woody tract, and come
Upon the open shoulder of the hill.
See how the giant spires of yellow bloom
Of the sun-loving gentian, in the heat,
Are shining on those naked slopes like flame!
Let us rest here; and now, Empedocles,
Pantheia's history!

[*A harp-note below is heard.*

Empedocles

Hark! what sound was that
Rose from below? If it were possible,
And we were not so far from human haunt,
I should have said that some one touch'd a harp.
Hark! there again!

Pausanias

'Tis the boy Callicles,
The sweetest harp-player in Catana.
He is for ever coming on these hills,
In summer, to all country-festivals,
With a gay revelling band; he breaks from them
Sometimes, and wanders far among the glens.
But heed him not, he will not mount to us;
I spoke with him this morning. Once more, therefore,
Instruct me of Pantheia's story, Master,
As I have pray'd thee.

Empedocles

That? and to what end?

Pausanias

It is enough that all men speak of it.
But I will also say, that when the Gods
Visit us as they do with sign and plague,
To know those spells of thine which stay their hand
Were to live free from terror.

Empedocles

Spells? Mistrust them!
Mind is the spell which governs earth and heaven.
Man has a mind with which to plan his safety;
Know that, and help thyself!

Pausanias

But thine own words?
'The wit and counsel of man was never clear,
Troubles confound the little wit he has.'
Mind is a light which the Gods mock us with,
To lead those false who trust it.

[*The harp sounds again.*

Empedocles

Hist! once more!
Listen, Pausanias! — Ay, 'tis Callicles;
I know these notes among a thousand. Hark!

Callicles

(*Sings unseen, from below*)

The track winds down to the clear stream,
To cross the sparkling shallows; there
The cattle love to gather, on their way
To the high mountain-pastures, and to stay,
Till the rough cow-herds drive them past,
Knee-deep in the cool ford; for 'tis the last
Of all the woody, high, well-water'd dells
On Etna; and the beam
Of noon is broken there by chestnut-boughs
Down its steep verdant sides; the air
Is freshen'd by the leaping stream, which throws
Eternal showers of spray on the moss'd roots

Of trees, and veins of turf, and long dark shoots
Of ivy-plants, and fragrant hanging bells
Of hyacinths, and on late anemonies,
That muffle its wet banks; but glade,
And stream, and sward, and chestnut-trees,
End here; Etna beyond, in the broad glare
Of the hot noon, without a shade,
Slope behind slope, up to the peak, lies bare;
The peak, round which the white clouds play.

In such a glen, on such a day,
On Pelion, on the grassy ground,
Chiron, the aged Centaur lay,
The young Achilles standing by.
The Centaur taught him to explore
The mountains; where the glens are dry
And the tired Centaurs come to rest,
And where the soaking springs abound
And the straight ashes grow for spears,
And where the hill-goats come to feed,
And the sea-eagles build their nest.
He show'd him Phthia far away,
And said: O boy, I taught this lore
To Peleus, in long distant years!
He told him of the Gods, the stars,
The tides; — and then of mortal wars,
And of the life which heroes lead
Before they reach the Elysian place
And rest in the immortal mead;
And all the wisdom of his race.

The music below ceases, and EMPEDOCLES *speaks, accompanying himself in a solemn manner on his harp.*

The out-spread world to span
A cord the Gods first slung,
And then the soul of man
There, like a mirror, hung,
And bade the winds through space impel the gusty toy.

Hither and thither spins
The wind-borne, mirroring soul,
A thousand glimpses wins,
And never sees a whole;
Looks once, and drives elsewhere, and leaves its last employ.

The Gods laugh in their sleeve
To watch man doubt and fear,
Who knows not what to believe
Since he sees nothing clear,
And dares stamp nothing false where he finds nothing sure.

Is this, Pausanias, so?
And can our souls not strive,
But with the winds must go,
And hurry where they drive?
Is fate indeed so strong, man's strength indeed so poor?

I will not judge. That man,
Howbeit, I judge as lost,
Whose mind allows a plan,
Which would degrade it most;
And he treats doubt the best who tries to see least ill.

Be not, then, fear's blind slave!
Thou art my friend; to thee,
All knowledge that I have,
All skill I wield, are free.
Ask not the latest news of the last miracle,

Ask not what days and nights
In trance Pantheia lay,
But ask how thou such sights
May'st see without dismay;
Ask what most helps when known, thou son of Anchitus!

What? hate, and awe, and shame
Fill thee to see our time;
Thou feelest thy soul's frame
Shaken and out of chime?
What? life and chance go hard with thee too, as with us;

Thy citizens, 'tis said,
Envy thee and oppress,
Thy goodness no men aid,
All strive to make it less;
Tyranny, pride, and lust, fill Sicily's abodes;

Heaven is with earth at strife,
Signs make thy soul afraid,
The dead return to life,
Rivers are dried, winds stay'd;
Scarce can one think in calm, so threatening are the Gods;

And we feel, day and night,
The burden of ourselves —
Well, then, the wiser wight
In his own bosom delves,
And asks what ails him so, and gets what cure he can.

The sophist sneers: Fool, take
Thy pleasure, right or wrong.
The pious wail: Forsake
A world these sophists throng.
Be neither saint nor sophist-led, but be a man!

These hundred doctors try
To preach thee to their school.
We have the truth! they cry;
And yet their oracle,
Trumpet it as they will, is but the same as thine.

Once read thy own breast right,
And thou hast done with fears;
Man gets no other light,
Search he a thousand years.
Sink in thyself! there ask what ails thee, at that shrine!

What makes thee struggle and rave?
Why are men ill at ease? —
'Tis that the lot they have
Fails their own will to please;
For man would make no murmuring, were his will obey'd.

And why is it, that still
Man with his lot thus fights? —
'Tis that he makes this *will*
The measure of his *rights*,
And believes Nature outraged if his will's gainsaid.

Couldst thou, Pausanias, learn
How deep a fault is this;
Couldst thou but once discern
Thou hast no *right* to bliss,
No title from the Gods to welfare and repose;

Then thou wouldst look less mazed
Whene'er of bliss debarr'd,

Nor think the Gods were crazed
When thy own lot went hard.
But we are all the same — the fools of our own woes!

For, from the first faint morn
Of life, the thirst for bliss
Deep in man's heart is born;
And, sceptic as he is,
He fails not to judge clear if this be quench'd or no.

Nor is the thirst to blame.
Man errs not that he deems
His welfare his true aim,
He errs because he dreams
The world does but exist that welfare to bestow.

We mortals are no kings
For each of whom to sway
A new-made world up-springs,
Meant merely for his play;
No, we are strangers here; the world is from of old.

In vain our pent wills fret,
And would the world subdue.
Limits we did not set
Condition all we do;
Born into life we are, and life must be our mould.

Born into life! — man grows
Forth from his parents' stem,
And blends their bloods, as those
Of theirs are blent in them;
So each new man strikes root into a far fore-time.

Born into life! — we bring
A bias with us here,
And, when here, each new thing
Affects us we come near;
To tunes we did not call our being must keep chime.

Born into life! — in vain,
Opinions, those or these,
Unalter'd to retain
The obstinate mind decrees;
Experience, like a sea, soaks all-effacing in.

Born into life! — who lists
May what is false hold dear,
And for himself make mists
Through which to see less clear;
The world is what it is, for all our dust and din.

Born into life! — 'tis we,
And not the world, are new;
Our cry for bliss, our plea,
Others have uged it too —
Our wants have all been felt, our errors made before.

No eye could be too sound
To observe a world so vast,
No patience too profound
To sort what's here amass'd;
How man may here best live no care too great to explore.

But we — as some rude guest
Would change, where'er he roam,
The manners there profess'd
To those he brings from home —
We mark not the world's course, but would have *it* take *ours*.

The world's course proves the terms
On which man wins content;
Reason the proof confirms —
We spurn it, and invent
A false course for the world, and for ourselves, false powers.

Riches we wish to get,
Yet remain spendthrifts still;
We would have health, and yet
Still use our bodies ill;
Bafflers of our own prayers, from youth to life's last scenes.

We would have inward peace,
Yet will not look within;
We would have misery cease,
Yet will not cease from sin;
We want all pleasant ends, but will use no harsh means;

We do not what we ought,
What we ought not, we do,
And lean upon the thought

That chance will bring us through;
But our own acts, for good or ill, are mightier powers.

Yet, even when man forsakes
All sin, — is just, is pure,
Abandons all which makes
His welfare insecure, —
Other existences there are, that clash with ours.

Like us, the lightning-fires
Love to have scope and play;
The stream, like us, desires
An unimpeded way;
Like us, the Libyan wind delights to roam at large.

Streams will not curb their pride
The just man not to entomb,
Nor lightnings go aside
To give his virtues room;
Nor is that wind less rough which blows a good man's barge.

Nature, with equal mind,
Sees all her sons at play;
Sees man control the wind,
The wind sweep man away;
Allows the proudly-riding and the foundering bark.

And, lastly, though of ours
No weakness spoil our lot,
Though the non-human powers
Of Nature harm us not,
The ill deeds of other men make often *our* life dark.

What were the wise man's plan? —
Through this sharp, toil-set life,
To work as best he can,
And win what's won by strife. —
But we an easier way to cheat our pains have found.

Scratch'd by a fall, with moans
As children of weak age
Lend life to the dumb stones
Whereon to vent their rage,
And bend their little fists, and rate the senseless ground;

So, loath to suffer mute,
We, peopling the void air,
Make Gods to whom to impute
The ills we ought to bear;
With God and Fate to rail at, suffering easily.

Yet grant — as sense long miss'd
Things that are now perceived,
And much may still exist
Which is not yet believed —
Grant that the world were full of Gods we cannot see;

All things the world which fill
Of but one stuff are spun,
That we who rail are still,
With what we rail at, one;
One with the o'erlabour'd Power that through the breadth and length

Of earth, and air, and sea,
In men, and plants, and stones,
Hath toil perpetually,
And travails, pants, and moans;
Fain would do all things well, but sometimes fails in strength.

And patiently exact
This universal God
Alike to any act
Proceeds at any nod,
And quietly declaims the cursings of himself.

This is not what man hates,
Yet he can curse but this.
Harsh Gods and hostile Fates
Are dreams! this only *is* —
Is everywhere; sustains the wise, the foolish elf.

Nor only, in the intent
To attach blame elsewhere,
Do we at will invent
Stern Powers who make their care
To embitter human life, malignant Deities;

But, next, we would reverse
The scheme ourselves have spun,

And what we made to curse
We now would lean upon,
And feign kind Gods who perfect what man vainly tries.

Look, the world tempts our eye,
And we would know it all!
We map the starry sky,
We mine this earthen ball,
We measure the sea-tides, we number the sea-sands;

We scrutinise the dates
Of long-past human things,
The bounds of effaced states,
The lines of deceased kings;
We search out dead men's words, and works of dead men's hands;

We shut our eyes, and muse
How our own minds are made,
What springs of thought they use,
How righten'd, how betray'd—
And spend our wit to name what most employ unnamed.

But still, as we proceed
The mass swells more and more
Of volumes yet to read,
Of secrets yet to explore.
Our hair grows grey, our eyes are dimm'd, our heat is tamed;

We rest our faculties,
And thus address the Gods:
'True science if there is,
It stays in your abodes!
Man's measures cannot mete the immeasurable All.

'You only can take in
The world's immense design.
Our desperate search was sin,
Which henceforth we resign,
Sure only that your mind sees all things which befal.'

Fools! That in man's brief term
He cannot all things view,
Affords no ground to affirm
That there are Gods who do;
Nor does being weary prove that he has where to rest.

Again. — Our youthful blood
Claims rapture as its right;
The world, a rolling flood
Of newness and delight,
Draws in the enamour'd gazer to its shining breast;

Pleasure, to our hot grasp,
Gives flowers after flowers;
With passionate warmth we clasp
Hand after hand in ours;
Now do we soon perceive how fast our youth is spent.

At once our eyes grow clear!
We see, in blank dismay,
Year posting after year,
Sense after sense decay;
Our shivering heart is mined by secret discontent;

Yet still, in spite of truth,
In spite of hopes entomb'd,
That longing of our youth
Burns ever unconsumed,
Still hungrier for delight as delights grow more rare.

We pause; we hush our heart,
And thus address the Gods:
'The world hath fail'd to impart
The joy our youth forebodes,
Fail'd to fill up the void which in our breasts we bear.

'Changeful till now, we still
Look'd on to something new;
Let us, with changeless will,
Henceforth look on to you,
To find with you the joy we in vain here require!'

Fools! That so often here
Happiness mock'd our prayer,
I think, might make us fear
A like event elsewhere;
Make us, not fly to dreams, but moderate desire.

And yet, for those who know
Themselves, who wisely take

Their way through life, and bow
To what they cannot break,
Why should I say that life need yield but *moderate* bliss?

Shall we, with temper spoil'd,
Health sapp'd by living ill,
And judgment all embroil'd
By sadness and self-will,
Shall *we* judge what for man is not true bliss or is?

Is it so small a thing
To have enjoy'd the sun,
To have lived light in the spring,
To have loved, to have thought, to have done;
To have advanced true friends, and beat down baffling foes —

That we must feign a bliss
Of doubtful future date,
And, while we dream on this,
Lose all our present state,
And relegate to worlds yet distant our repose?

Not much, I know, you prize
What pleasures may be had,
Who look on life with eyes
Estranged, like mine, and sad;
And yet the village-churl feels the truth more than you,

Who's loath to leave this life
Which to him little yields —
His hard-task'd sunburnt wife,
His often-labour'd fields,
The boors with whom he talk'd, the country-spots he knew.

But thou, because thou hear'st
Men scoff at Heaven and Fate,
Because the Gods thou fear'st
Fail to make blest thy state,
Tremblest, and wilt not dare to trust the joys there are!

I say: Fear not! Life still
Leaves human effort scope.
But, since life teems with ill,
Nurse no extravagant hope;
Because thou must not dream, thou need'st not then despair!

A long pause. At the end of it the notes of a harp below are again heard and CALLICLES *sings:—*

Far, far from here,
The Adriatic breaks in a warm bay
Among the green Illyrian hills; and there
The sunshine in the happy glens is fair,
And by the sea, and in the brakes.
The grass is cool, the sea-side air
Bouyant and fresh, the mountain flowers
More virginal and sweet than ours.
And there, they say, two bright and aged snakes,
Who once were Cadmus and Harmonia,
Bask in the glens or on the warm sea-shore,
In breathless quiet, after all their ills;
Nor do they see their country, nor the place
Where the Sphinx lived among the frowning hills,
Nor the unhappy palace of their race,
Nor Thebes, nor the Ismenus, any more.

There those two live, far in the Illyrian brakes!
They had stay'd long enough to see,
In Thebes, the billow of calamity
Over their own dear children roll'd,
Curse upon curse, pang upon pang,
For years, they sitting helpless in their home,
A grey old man and woman; yet of old
The Gods had to their marriage come,
And at the banquet all the Muses sang.

Therefore they did not end their days
In sight of blood; but were rapt, far away,
To where the west-wind plays,
And murmurs of the Adriatic come
To those untrodden mountain-lawns; and there
Placed safely in changed forms, the pair
Wholly forget their first sad life, and home,
And all that Theban woe, and stray
For ever through the glens, placid and dumb.

Empedocles

That was my harp-player again! — where is he?
Down by the stream?

Pausanias

Yes, Master, in the wood.

Empedocles

He ever loved the Theban story well!
But the day wears. Go now, Pausanias,
For I must be alone. Leave me one mule;
Take down with thee the rest to Catana.
And for young Callicles, thank him from me;
Tell him, I never fail'd to love his lyre —
But he must follow me no more to-night.

Pausanias

Thou wilt return to-morrow to the city?

Empedocles

Either to-morrow or some other day,
In the sure revolutions of the world,
Good friend, I shall revisit Catana.
I have seen many cities in my time,
Till mine eyes ache with the long spectacle,
And I shall doubtless see them all again;
Thou know'st me for a wanderer from of old.
Meanwhile, stay me not now. Farewell, Pausanias!
He departs on his way up the mountain.

Pausanias (alone)

I dare not urge him further — he must go;
But he is strangely wrought! — I will speed back
And bring Peisianax to him from the city;
His counsel could once soothe him. But, Apollo!
How his brow lighten'd as the music rose!
Callicles must wait here, and play to him;
I saw him through the chestnuts far below,
Just since, down at the stream. — Ho! Callicles!
He descends, calling.

ACT II

Evening. The Summit of Etna.

EMPEDOCLES

Alone! —
On this charr'd, blacken'd, melancholy waste,
Crown'd by the awful peak, Etna's great mouth.
Round which the sullen vapour rolls — alone!
Pausanias is far hence, and that is well,
For I must henceforth speak no more with man.
He hath his lesson too, and that debt's paid;
And the good, learned, friendly, quiet man
May bravelier front his life, and in himself
Find henceforth energy and heart. But I —
The weary man, the banish'd citizen,
Whose banishment is not his greatest ill,
Whose weariness no energy can reach,
And for whose hurt courage is not the cure —
What should I do with life and living more?

No, thou art come too late, Empedocles!
And the world hath the day, and must break thee,
Not thou the world. With men thou canst not live,
Their thoughts, their ways, their wishes, are not thine;
And being lonely thou art miserable,
For something has impair'd thy spirit's strength,
And dried its self-sufficing fount of joy.
Thou canst not live with men nor with thyself —
O sage! O sage! — Take then the one way left;
And turn thee to the elements, thy friends,
Thy well-tried friends, thy willing ministers,
And say: Ye helpers, hear Empedocles,
Who asks this final service at your hands!
Before the sophist-brood hath overlaid
The last spark of man's consciousness with words —
Ere quite the being of man, ere quite the world
Be disarray'd of their divinity —
Before the soul lose all her solemn joys,
And awe be dead, and hope impossible,
And the soul's deep eternal night come on —
Receive me, hide me, quench me, take me home!

He advances to the edge of the crater. Smoke and fire break forth with a loud noise, and CALLICLES *is heard below singing: —*

The lyre's voice is lovely everywhere;
In the court of Gods, in the city of men,
And in the lonely rock-strewn mountain-glen,
In the still mountain air.

Only to Typho it sounds hatefully;
To Typho only, the rebel o'erthrown,
Through whose heart Etna drives her roots of stone
To imbed them in the sea.

Wherefore dost thou groan so loud?
Wherefore do thy nostrils flash,
Through the dark night, suddenly,
Typho, such red jets of flame? —
Is thy tortured heart still proud?
Is thy fire-scathed arm still rash?
Still alert thy stone-crush'd frame?
Doth thy fierce soul still deplore
Thine ancient rout by the Cilician hills,
And that curst treachery on the Mount of Gore?
Do thy bloodshot eyes still weep
The fight which crown'd thine ills,
Thy last mischance on this Sicilian deep?
Hast thou sworn, in thy sad lair,
Where erst the strong sea-currents suck'd thee down,
Never to cease to writhe, and try to rest,
Letting the sea-stream wander through thy hair?
That thy groans, like thunder prest,
Begin to roll, and almost drown
The sweet notes whose lulling spell
Gods and the race of mortals love so well,
When through thy caves thou hearest music swell?

But an awful pleasure bland
Spreading o'er the Thunderer's face,
When the sound climbs near his seat,
The Olympian council sees;
As he lets his lax right hand,
Which the lightnings doth embrace,
Sink upon his mighty knees.
And the eagle, at the beck
Of the appeasing, gracious harmony,
Droops all his sheeny, brown, deep-feather'd neck,
Nestling nearer to Jove's feet;
While o'er his sovran eye

The curtains of the blue films slowly meet
And the white Olympus-peaks
Rosily brighten, and the soothed Gods smile
At one another from their golden chairs,
And no one round the charmed circle speaks.
Only the loved Hebe bears
The cup about, whose draughts beguile
Pain and care, with a dark store
Of fresh-pull'd violets wreathed and nodding o'er;
And her flushed feet glow on the marble floor.

Empedocles

He fables, yet speaks truth!
The brave, impetuous heart yields everywhere
To the subtle, contriving head;
Great qualities are trodden down,
And littleness united
Is become invincible.

These rumblings are not Typho's groans, I know!
These angry smoke-bursts
Are not the passionate breath
Of the mountain-crush'd, tortured, intractable Titan king —
But over all the world
What suffering is there not seen
Of plainness oppress'd by cunning,
As the well-counsell'd Zeus oppress'd
That self-helping son of earth!
What anguish of greatness,
Rail'd and hunted from the world,
Because its simplicity rebukes
This envious, miserable age!

I am weary of it.
— Lie there, ye ensigns
Of my unloved preëminence
In an age like this!
Among a people of children,
Who throng'd me in their cities,
Who worshipp'd me in their houses,
And ask'd, not wisdom,
But drugs to charm with,
But spells to mutter —
All the fool's-armoury of magic! — Lie there,

My golden circlet,
My purple robe!

Callicles (from below).

As the sky-brightening south-wind clears the day,
And makes the mass'd clouds roll,
The music of the lyre blows away
The clouds which wrap the soul.

Oh! that Fate had let me see
That triumph of the sweet persuasive lyre,
That famous, final victory,
When jealous Pan with Marsyas did conspire;

When, from far Parnassus' side,
Young Apollo, all the pride
Of the Phrygian flutes to tame,
To the Phrygian highlands came;
Where the long green reed-beds sway
In the rippled waters grey
Of that solitary lake
Where Mæander's springs are born;
Whence the ridged pine-wooded roots
Of Messogis westward break,
Mounting westward, high and higher.
There was held the famous strife;
There the Phrygian brought his flutes,
And Apollo brought his lyre;
And, when now the westering sun
Touch'd the hills, the strife was done,
And the attentive Muses said:
'Marsyas, thou art vanquished!'
Then Apollo's minister
Hang'd upon a branching fir
Marsyas, that unhappy Faun,
And began to whet his knife.
But the Mænads, who were there,
Left their friend, and with robes flowing
In the wind, and loose dark hair
O'er their polish'd bosoms blowing,
Each her ribbon'd tambourine
Flinging on the mountain-sod,
With a lovely frighten'd mien
Came about the youthful God.

But he turn'd his beauteous face
Haughtily another way,
From the grassy sun-warm'd place
Where in proud repose he lay,
With one arm over his head,
Watching how the whetting sped.

But aloof, on the lake-strand,
Did the young Olympus stand,
Weeping at his master's end;
For the Faun had been his friend.
For he taught him how to sing,
And he taught him flute-playing.
Many a morning had they gone
To the glimmering mountain-lakes,
And had torn up by the roots
The tall crested water-reeds
With long plumes and soft brown seeds,
And had carved them into flutes,
Sitting on a tabled stone
Where the shoreward ripple breaks.
And he taught him how to please
The red-snooded Phrygian girls,
Whom the summer evening sees
Flashing in the dance's whirls
Underneath the starlit trees
In the mountain-villages.
Therefore now Olympus stands,
At his master's piteous cries
Pressing fast with both his hands
His white garment to his eyes,
Not to see Apollo's scorn; —
Ah, poor Faun, poor Faun! ah, poor Faun!

Empedocles

And lie thou there,
My laurel bough!
Scornful Apollo's ensign, lie thou there!
Though thou hast been my shade in the world's heat —
Though I have loved thee, lived in honouring thee —
Yet lie thou there,
My laurel bough!

I am weary of thee.
I am weary of the solitude

Where he who bears thee must abide—
Of the rocks of Parnassus,
Of the gorge of Delphi,
Of the moonlit peaks, and the caves.
Thou guardest them, Apollo!
Over the grave of the slain Pytho,
Though young, intolerably severe!
Thou keepest aloof the profane,
But the solitude oppresses thy votary!
The jars of men reach him not in thy valley—
But can life reach him?
Thou fencest him from the multitude—
Who will fence him from himself?
He hears nothing but the cry of the torrents,
And the beating of his own heart.
The air is thin, the veins swell,
The temples tighten and throb there—
Air! air!

Take thy bough, set me free from my solitude;
I have been enough alone!

Where shall thy votary fly then? back to men?—
But they will gladly welcome him once more,
And help him to unbend his too tense thought,
And rid him of the presence of himself,
And keep their friendly chatter at his ear,
And haunt him, till the absence from himself,
That other torment, grow unbearable;
And he will fly to solitude again,
And he will find its air too keen for him,
And so change back; and many thousand times
Be miserably bandied to and fro
Like a sea-wave, betwixt the world and thee,
Thou young, implacable God! and only death
Can cut his oscillations short, and so
Bring him to poise. There is no other way.

And yet what days were those, Parmenides!
When we were young, when we could number friends
In all the Italian cities like ourselves,
When with elated hearts we join'd your train,
Ye Sun-born Virgins! on the road of truth.
Then we could still enjoy, then neither thought
Nor outward things were closed and dead to us;

But we received the shock of mighty thoughts
On simple minds with a pure natural joy;
And if the sacred load oppress'd our brain,
We had the power to feel the pressure eased,
The brow unbound, the thoughts flow free again,
In the delightful commerce of the world.
We had not lost our balance then, nor grown
Thought's slaves, and dead to every natural joy.
The smallest thing could give us pleasure then —
The sports of the country-people,
A flute-note from the woods,
Sunset over the sea;
Seed-time and harvest,
The reapers in the corn,
The vinedresser in his vineyard,
The village-girl at her wheel.

Fulness of life and power of feeling, ye
Are for the happy, for the souls at ease,
Who dwell on a firm basis of content!
But he, who has outlived his prosperous days —
But he, whose youth fell on a different world
From that on which his exiled age is thrown —
Whose mind was fed on other food, was train'd
By other rules than are in vogue to-day —
Whose habit of thought is fix'd, who will not change,
But, in a world he loves not, must subsist
In ceaseless opposition, be the guard
Of his own breast, fetter'd to what he guards,
That the world win no mastery over him —
Who has no friend, no fellow left, not one;
Who has no minute's breathing space allow'd
To nurse his dwindling faculty of joy —
Joy and the outward world must die to him,
As they are dead to me.

A long pause, during which EMPEDOCLES *remains motionless, plunged in thought. The night deepens. He moves forward and gazes round him, and proceeds:—*

And you, ye stars,
Who slowly begin to marshal,
As of old, in the fields of heaven,
Your distant, melancholy lines!
Have you, too, survived yourselves?
Are you, too, what I fear to become?

You, too, once lived;
You, too, moved joyfully
Among august companions,
In an older world, peopled by Gods,
In a mightier order,
The radiant, rejoicing, intelligent Sons of Heaven.
But now, ye kindle
Your lonely, cold-shining lights,
Unwilling lingerers
In the heavenly wilderness,
For a younger, ignoble world;
And renew, by necessity,
Night after night your courses,
In echoing, unnear'd silence,
Above a race you know not —
Uncaring and undelighted,
Without friend and without home;
Weary like us, though not
Weary with our weariness.

No, no, ye stars! there is no death with you,
No languor, no decay! languor and death,
They are with me, not you! ye are alive —
Ye, and the pure dark ether where ye ride
Brilliant above me! And thou, fiery world,
That sapp'st the vitals of this terrible mount
Upon whose charr'd and quaking crust I stand —
Thou, too, brimmest with life! — the sea of cloud,
That heaves its white and billowy vapours up
To moat this isle of ashes from the world,
Lives; and that other fainter sea, far down,
O'er whose lit floor a road of moonbeams leads
To Etna's Liparëan sister-fires
And the long dusky line of Italy —
That mild and luminous floor of waters lives,
With held-in joy swelling its heart; I only,
Whose spring of hope is dried, whose spirit has fail'd,
I, who have not, like these, in solitude
Maintain'd courage and force, and in myself
Nursed an immortal vigour — I alone
Am dead to life and joy, therefore I read
In all things my own deadness.

A long silence. He continues: —

Oh, that I could glow like this mountain!
Oh, that my heart bounded with the swell of the sea!

Oh, that my soul were full of light as the stars!
Oh, that it brooded over the world like the air!

But no, this heart will glow no more; thou art
A living man no more, Empedocles!
Nothing but a devouring flame of thought —
But a naked, eternally restless mind!

After a pause: —

To the elements it came from
Everything will return —
Our bodies to earth,
Our blood to water,
Heat to fire,
Breath to air.
They were well born, they will be well entomb'd —
But mind? . . .

And we might gladly share the fruitful stir
Down in our mother earth's miraculous womb;
Well would it be
With what roll'd of us in the stormy main;
We might have joy, blent with the all-bathing air,
Or with the nimble, radiant life of fire.

But mind, but thought —
If these have been the master part of us —
Where will *they* find their parent element?
What will receive *them,* who will call *them* home?
But we shall still be in them, and they in us,
And we shall be the strangers of the world,
And they will be our lords, as they are now;
And keep us prisoners of our consciousness,
And never let us clasp and feel the All
But through their forms, and modes, and stifling veils.
And we shall be unsatisfied as now;
And we shall feel the agony of thirst,
The ineffable longing for the life of life
Baffled for ever; and still thought and mind
Will hurry us with them on their homeless march,
Over the unallied unopening earth,
Over the unrecognising sea; while air
Will blow us fiercely back to sea and earth,
And fire repel us from its living waves.
And then we shall unwillingly return
Back to this meadow of calamity,

This uncongenial place, this human life;
And in our individual human state
Go through the sad probation all again,
To see if we will poise our life at last,
To see if we will now at last be true
To our own only true, deep-buried selves,
Being one with which we are one with the whole world;
Or whether we will once more fall away
Into some bondage of the flesh or mind,
Some slough of sense, or some fantastic maze
Forged by the imperious lonely thinking-power.
And each succeeding age in which we are born
Will have more peril for us than the last;
Will goad our senses with a sharper spur,
Will fret our minds to an intenser play,
Will make ourselves harder to be discern'd.
And we shall struggle awhile, gasp and rebel —
And we shall fly for refuge to past times,
Their soul of unworn youth, their breath of greatness;
And the reality will pluck us back,
Knead us in its hot hand, and change our nature
And we shall feel our powers of effort flag,
And rally them for one last fight — and fail;
And we shall sink in the impossible strife,
And be astray for ever.

Slave of sense
I have in no wise been; — but slave of thought? . . .
And who can say: I have been always free,
Lived ever in the light of my own soul? —
I cannot; I have lived in wrath and gloom,
Fierce, disputatious, ever at war with man,
Far from my own soul, far from warmth and light.
But I have not grown easy in these bonds —
But I have not denied what bonds these were.
Yea, I take myself to witness,
That I have loved no darkness,
Sophisticated no truth,
Nursed no delusion,
Allow'd no fear!

And therefore, O ye elements! I know —
Ye know it too — it hath been granted me
Not to die wholly, not to be all enslaved.
I feel it in this hour. The numbing cloud
Mounts off my soul; I feel it, I breathe free.

Is it but for a moment?
— Ah, boil up, ye vapours!
Leap and roar, thou sea of fire!
My soul glows to meet you.
Ere it flag, ere the mists
Of despondency and gloom
Rush over it again,
Receive me, save me!

[*He plunges into the crater.*

Callicles
(*from below*)

Through the black, rushing smoke-bursts,
Thick breaks the red flame;
All Etna heaves fiercely
Her forest-clothed frame.

Not here, O Apollo!
Are haunts meet for thee.
But, where Helicon breaks down
In cliff to the sea,

Where the moon-silver'd inlets
Send far their light voice
Up the still vale of Thisbe,
O speed, and rejoice!

On the sward at the cliff-top
Lie strewn the white flocks,
On the cliff-side the pigeons
Roost deep in the rocks.

In the moonlight the shepherds,
Soft lull'd by the rills,
Lie wrapt in their blankets
Asleep on the hills.

— What forms are these coming
So white through the gloom?
What garments out-glistening
The gold-flower'd broom?

What sweet-breathing presence
Out-perfumes the thyme?
What voices enrapture
The night's balmy prime? —

'Tis Apollo comes leading
His choir, the Nine.
— The leader is fairest,
But all are divine.

They are lost in the hollows!
They stream up again!
What seeks on this mountain
The glorified train? —

They bathe on this mountain,
In the spring by their road;
Then on to Olympus,
Their endless abode.

— Whose praise do they mention?
Of what is it told? —
What will be for ever;
What was from of old.

First hymn they the Father
Of all things; and then,
The rest of immortals,
The action of men.

The day in his hotness,
The strife with the palm;
The night in her silence,
The stars in their calm.

SWITZERLAND

1. MEETING

AGAIN I see my bliss at hand,
The town, the lake are here;
My Marguerite smiles upon the strand,
Unalter'd with the year.

I know that graceful figure fair,
That cheek of languid hue;
I know that soft, enkerchief'd hair,
And those sweet eyes of blue.

Again I spring to make my choice;
Again in tones of ire
I hear a God's tremendous voice:
'Be counsell'd, and retire.'

Ye guiding Powers who join and part,
What would ye have with me?
Ah, warn some more ambitious heart,
And let the peaceful be!

2. PARTING

YE storm-winds of Autumn!
Who rush by, who shake
The window, and ruffle
The gleam-lighted lake;
Who cross to the hill-side
Thin-sprinkled with farms,
Where the high woods strip sadly
Their yellowing arms —
Ye are bound for the mountains!
Ah! with you let me go
Where your cold, distant barrier,
The vast range of snow,
Through the loose clouds lifts dimly
Its white peaks in air —
How deep is their stillness!
Ah, would I were there!

But on the stairs what voice is this I hear,
Buoyant as morning, and as morning clear?
Say, has some wet bird-haunted English lawn
Lent it the music of its trees at dawn?
Or was it from some sun-fleck'd mountain-brook
That the sweet voice its upland clearness took?
Ah! it comes nearer —
Sweet notes, this way!

Hark! fast by the window
The rushing winds go,
To the ice-cumber'd gorges,
The vast seas of snow!
There the torrents drive upward
Their rock-strangled hum;
There the avalanche thunders

The hoarse torrent dumb.
— I come, O ye mountains!
Ye torrents, I come!

But who is this, by the half-open'd door,
Whose figure casts a shadow on the floor?
The sweet blue eyes — the soft, ash-colour'd hair —
The cheeks that still their gentle paleness wear —
The lovely lips, with their arch smile that tells
The unconquer'd joy in which her spirit dwells —
Ah! they bend nearer —
Sweet lips, this way!

Hark! the wind rushes past us!
Ah! with that let me go
To the clear, waning hill-side,
Unspotted by snow,
There to watch, o'er the sunk vale,
The frore mountain-wall,
Where the niched snow-bed sprays down
Its powdery fall.
There its dusky blue clusters
The aconite spreads;
There the pines slope, the cloud-strips
Hung soft in their heads.
No life but, at moments,
The mountain-bee's hum.
—I come, O ye mountains!
Ye pine-woods, I come!

Forgive me! forgive me!
Ah, Marguerite, fain
Would these arms reach to clasp thee!
But see! 'tis in vain.

In the void air, towards thee,
My stretch'd arms are cast;
But a sea rolls between us —
Our different past!

To the lips, ah! of others
Those lips have been prest,
And others, ere I was,
Were strain'd to that breast;

Far, far from each other
  Our spirits have grown;
And what heart knows another?
  Ah! who knows his own?

Blow, ye winds! lift me with you!
  I come to the wild.
Fold closely, O Nature!
  Thine arms round thy child.

To thee only God granted
  A heart ever new —
To all always open,
  To all always true.

Ah! calm me, restore me;
  And dry up my tears
On thy high mountain-platforms,
  Where morn first appears;

Where the white mists, for ever,
  Are spread and upfurl'd —
In the stir of the forces
  Whence issued the world.

3. A FAREWELL

My horse's feet beside the lake,
Where sweet the unbroken moonbeams lay,
Sent echoes through the night to wake
Each glistening strand, each heath-fringed bay.

The poplar avenue was pass'd,
And the roof'd bridge that spans the stream;
Up the steep street I hurried fast,
Led by thy taper's starlike beam.

I came! I saw thee rise! — the blood
Pour'd flushing to thy languid cheek.
Lock'd in each other's arms we stood,
In tears, with hearts too full to speak.

Days flew; — ah, soon I could discern
A trouble in thine alter'd air!

Thy hand lay languidly in mine,
Thy cheek was grave, thy speech grew rare.

I blame thee not! — this heart, I know,
To be long loved was never framed;
For something in its depths doth glow
Too strange, too restless, too untamed.

And women — things that live and move
Mined by the fever of the soul —
They seek to find in those they love
Stern strength, and promise of control.

They ask not kindness, gentle ways —
These they themselves have tried and known;
They ask a soul which never sways
With the blind gusts that shake their own.

I too have felt the load I bore
In a too strong emotion's sway;
I too have wish'd, no woman more,
This starting, feverish heart away.

I too have long'd for trenchant force,
And will like a dividing spear;
Have praised the keen, unscrupulous course,
Which knows no doubt, which feels no fear.

But in the world I learnt, what there
Thou too wilt surely one day prove,
That will, that energy, though rare,
Are yet far, far less rare than love.

Go, then! — till time and fate impress
This truth on thee, be mine no more!
They will! — for thou, I feel, not less
Than I, wast destined to this lore.

We school our manners, act our parts —
But He, who sees us through and through,
Knows that the bent of both our hearts
Was to be gentle, tranquil, true.

And though we wear out life, alas!
Distracted as a homeless wind,

In beating where we must not pass,
In seeking what we shall not find;

Yet we shall one day gain, life past,
Clear prospect o'er our being's whole;
Shall see ourselves, and learn at last
Our true affinities of soul.

We shall not then deny a course
To every thought the mass ignore;
We shall not then call hardness force,
Nor lightness wisdom any more.

Then, in the eternal Father's smile,
Our soothed, encouraged souls will dare
To seem as free from pride and guile,
As good, as generous, as they are.

Then we shall know our friends! — though much
Will have been lost — the help in strife,
The thousand sweet, still joys of such
As hand in hand face earthly life —

Though these be lost, there will be yet
A sympathy august and pure;
Ennobled by a vast regret,
And by contrition seal'd thrice sure.

And we, whose ways were unlike here,
May then more neighbouring courses ply;
May to each other be brought near,
And greet across infinity.

How sweet, unreach'd by earthly jars,
My sister! to maintain with thee
The hush among the shining stars,
The calm upon the moonlit sea!

How sweet to feel, on the boon air,
All our unquiet pulses cease!
To feel that nothing can impair
The gentleness, the thirst for peace —

The gentleness too rudely hurl'd
On this wild earth of hate and fear;
The thirst for peace a raving world
Would never let us satiate here.

4. ISOLATION. TO MARGUERITE

We were apart; yet, day by day,
I bade my heart more constant be.
I bade it keep the world away,
And grow a home for only thee;
Nor fear'd but thy love likewise grew,
Like mine, each day, more tried, more true.

The fault was grave! I might have known,
What far too soon, alas! I learn'd —
The heart can bind itself alone,
And faith may oft be unreturn'd.
Self-sway'd our feelings ebb and swell —
Thou lov'st no more; — Farewell! Farewell!

Farewell! — and thou, thou lonely heart,
Which never yet without remorse
Even for a moment didst depart
From thy remote and spheréd course
To haunt the place where passions reign —
Back to thy solitude again!

Back! with the conscious thrill of shame
Which Luna felt, that summer-night,
Flash through her pure immortal frame,
When she forsook the starry height
To hang over Endymion's sleep
Upon the pine-grown Latmian steep.

Yet she, chaste queen, had never proved
How vain a thing is mortal love,
Wandering in Heaven, far removed.
But thou hast long had place to prove
This truth — to prove, and make thine own:
'Thou hast been, shalt be, art, alone.'

Or, if not quite alone, yet they
Which touch thee are unmating things —

Ocean and clouds and night and day;
Lorn autumns and triumphant springs;
And life, and others' joy and pain,
And love, if love, of happier men.

Of happier men — for they, at least,
Have *dream'd* two human hearts might blend
In one, and were through faith released
From isolation without end
Prolong'd; nor knew, although not less
Alone than thou, their loneliness.

5. TO MARGUERITE — CONTINUED

Yes! in the sea of life enisled,
With echoing straits between us thrown,
Dotting the shoreless watery wild,
We mortal millions live *alone*.
The islands feel the enclasping flow,
And then their endless bounds they know.

But when the moon their hollows lights,
And they are swept by balms of spring,
And in their glens, on starry nights,
The nightingales divinely sing;
And lovely notes, from shore to shore,
Across the sounds and channels pour —

Oh! then a longing like despair
Is to their farthest caverns sent;
For surely once, they feel, we were
Parts of a single continent!
Now round us spreads the watery plain —
Oh might our marges meet again!

Who order'd, that their longing's fire
Should be, as soon as kindled, cool'd?
Who renders vain their deep desire? —
A God, a God their severance ruled!
And bade betwixt their shores to be
The unplumb'd, salt, estranging sea.

6. ABSENCE

In this fair stranger's eyes of grey
Thine eyes, my love! I see.
I shiver; for the passing day
Had borne me far from thee.

This is the curse of life! that not
A nobler, calmer train
Of wiser thoughts and feelings blot
Our passions from our brain;

But each day brings its petty dust
Our soon-choked souls to fill,
And we forget because we must
And not because we will.

I struggle towards the light; and ye,
Once-long'd-for storms of love!
If with the light ye cannot be,
I bear that ye remove.

I struggle towards the light — but oh,
While yet the night is chill,
Upon time's barren, stormy flow,
Stay with me, Marguerite, still!

7. THE TERRACE AT BERNE

(COMPOSED TEN YEARS AFTER THE PRECEDING)

Ten years! — and to my waking eye
Once more the roofs of Berne appear;
The rocky banks, the terrace high,
The stream! — and do I linger here?

The clouds are on the Oberland,
The Jungfrau snows look faint and far;
But bright are those green fields at hand,
And through those fields comes down the Aar,

And from the blue twin-lakes it comes,
Flows by the town, the churchyard fair;

And 'neath the garden-walk it hums,
The house! — and is my Marguerite there?

Ah, shall I see thee, while a flush
Of startled pleasure floods thy brow,
Quick through the oleanders brush,
And clap thy hands, and cry: *'Tis thou!*

Or hast thou long since wander'd back,
Daughter of France! to France, thy home;
And flitted down the flowery track
Where feet like thine too lightly come?

Doth riotous laughter now replace
Thy smile; and rouge, with stony glare,
Thy cheek's soft hue; and fluttering lace
The kerchief that enwound thy hair?

Or is it over? — art thou dead? —
Dead! — and no warning shiver ran
Across my heart, to say thy thread
Of life was cut, and closed thy span!

Could from earth's ways that figure slight
Be lost, and I not feel 'twas so?
Of that fresh voice the gay delight
Fail from earth's air, and I not know?

Or shall I find thee still, but changed,
But not the Marguerite of thy prime?
With all thy being re-arranged,
Pass'd through the crucible of time;

With spirit vanish'd, beauty waned,
And hardly yet a glance, a tone,
A gesture — anything — retain'd
Of all that was my Marguerite's own?

I will not know! For wherefore try,
To things by mortal course that live,
A shadowy durability,
For which they were not meant, to give?

Like driftwood spars, which meet and pass
Upon the boundless ocean-plain,

So on the sea of life, alas!
Man meets man — meets, and quits again.

I knew it when my life was young;
I feel it still, now youth is o'er.
— The mists are on the mountain hung,
And Marguerite I shall see no more.

HUMAN LIFE

WHAT mortal, when he saw,
Life's voyage done, his heavenly Friend,
Could ever yet dare tell him fearlessly:
'I have kept uninfringed my nature's law;
The inly-written chart thou gavest me,
To guide me, I have steer'd by to the end'?

Ah! let us make no claim,
On life's incognisable sea,
To too exact a steering of our way;
Let us not fret and fear to miss our aim,
If some fair coast have lured us to make stay,
Or some friend hail'd us to keep company.

Ay! we would each fain drive
At random, and not steer by rule.
Weakness! and worse, weakness bestow'd in vain!
Winds from our side the unsuiting consort rive,
We rush by coasts where we had lief remain;
Man cannot, though he would, live chance's fool.

No! as the foaming swath
Of torn-up water, on the main,
Falls heavily away with long-drawn roar
On either side the black deep-furrow'd path
Cut by an onward-labouring vessel's prore,
And never touches the ship-side again;

Even so we leave behind,
As, charter'd by some unknown Powers,
We stem across the sea of life by night,
The joys which were not for our use design'd; —
The friends to whom we had no natural right,
The homes that were not destined to be ours.

SELF-DECEPTION

Say, what blinds us, that we claim the glory
Of possessing powers not our share?
— Since man woke on earth, he knows his story,
But, before we woke on earth, we were.

Long, long since, undower'd yet, our spirit
Roam'd, ere birth, the treasuries of God;
Saw the gifts, the powers it might inherit,
Ask'd an outfit for its earthly road.

Then, as now, this tremulous, eager being
Strain'd and long'd and grasp'd each gift it saw;
Then, as now, a Power beyond our seeing
Staved us back, and gave our choice the law.

Ah, whose hand that day through Heaven guided
Man's new spirit, since it was not we?
Ah, who sway'd our choice, and who decided
What our gifts, and what our wants should be?

For, alas! he left us each retaining
Shreds of gifts which he refused in full.
Still these waste us with their hopeless straining,
Still the attempt to use them proves them null.

And on earth we wander, groping, reeling;
Powers stir in us, stir and disappear.
Ah! and he, who placed our master-feeling,
Fail'd to place that master-feeling clear.

We but dream we have our wish'd-for powers,
Ends we seek we never shall attain.
Ah! *some* power exists there, which is ours?
Some end is there, we indeed may gain?

YOUTH AND CALM

'Tis death! and peace, indeed, is here,
And ease from shame, and rest from fear.
There's nothing can dismarble now
The smoothness of that limpid brow.
But is a calm like this, in truth,
The crowning end of life and youth,
And when this boon rewards the dead,
Are all debts paid, has all been said?
And is the heart of youth so light,
Its step so firm, its eye so bright,
Because on its hot brow there blows
A wind of promise and repose
From the far grave, to which it goes;
Because it hath the hope to come,
One day, to harbour in the tomb?
Ah no, the bliss youth dreams is one
For daylight, for the cheerful sun,
For feeling nerves and living breath —
Youth dreams a bliss on this side death.
It dreams a rest, if not more deep,
More grateful than this marble sleep;
It hears a voice within it tell:
Calm's not life's crown, though calm is well.
'Tis all perhaps which man acquires,
But 'tis not what our youth desires.

TRISTRAM AND ISEULT

I

Tristram

Tristram

Is she not come? The messenger was sure.
Prop me upon the pillows once again —
Raise me, my page! this cannot long endure.
— Christ, what a night! how the sleet whips the pane!
What lights will those out to the northward be?

The Page

The lanterns of the fishing-boats at sea.

Tristram

Soft — who is that, stands by the dying fire?

The Page

Iseult.

Tristram

Ah! not the Iseult I desire.

* * * *

What Knight is this so weak and pale,
Though the locks are yet brown on his noble head,
Propt on pillows in his bed,
Gazing seaward for the light
Of some ship that fights the gale
On this wild December night?
Over the sick man's feet is spread
A dark green forest-dress;
A gold harp leans against the bed,
Ruddy in the fire's light.
I know him by his harp of gold,
Famous in Arthur's court of old;

I know him by his forest-dress —
The peerless hunter, harper, knight,
Tristram of Lyoness.

What Lady is this, whose silk attire
Gleams so rich in the light of the fire?
The ringlets on her shoulders lying
In their flitting lustre vying
With the clasp of burnish'd gold
Which her heavy robe doth hold.
Her looks are mild, her fingers slight
As the driven snow are white;
But her cheeks are sunk and pale.
Is it that the bleak sea-gale
Beating from the Atlantic sea
On this coast of Brittany,
Nips too keenly the sweet flower?
Is it that a deep fatigue
Hath come on her, a chilly fear,
Passing all her youthful hour
Spinning with her maidens here,
Listlessly through the window-bars
Gazing seawards many a league,
From her lonely shore-built tower,
While the knights are at the wars?
Or, perhaps, has her young heart
Felt already some deeper smart,
Of those that in secret the heart-strings rive,
Leaving her sunk and pale, though fair?
Who is this snowdrop by the sea? —
I know her by her mildness rare,
Her snow-white hands, her golden hair;
I know her by her rich silk dress,
And her fragile loveliness —
The sweetest Christian soul alive,
Iseult of Brittany.

Iseult of Britanny? — but where
Is that other Iseult fair,
That proud, first Iseult, Cornwall's queen?
She, whom Tristram's ship of yore
From Ireland to Cornwall bore,
To Tyntagel, to the side
Of King Marc, to be his bride?
She who, as they voyaged, quaff'd
With Tristram that spiced magic draught,

Which since then for ever rolls
Through their blood, and binds their souls,
Working love, but working teen? —
There were two Iseults who did sway
Each her hour of Tristram's day;
But one possess'd his waning time,
The other his resplendent prime.
Behold her here, the patient flower,
Who possess'd his darker hour!
Iseult of the Snow-White Hand
Watches pale by Tristram's bed.
She is here who had his gloom,
Where art thou who hadst his bloom?
One such kiss as those of yore
Might thy dying knight restore!
Does the love-draught work no more?
Art thou cold, or false, or dead,
Iseult of Ireland?

* * * *

Loud howls the wind, sharp patters the rain,
And the knight sinks back on his pillows again.
He is weak with fever and pain,
And his spirit is not clear.
Hark! he mutters in his sleep,
As he wanders far from here,
Changes place and time of year,
And his closéd eye doth sweep
O'er some fair unwintry sea,
Not this fierce Atlantic deep,
While he mutters brokenly: —

Tristram

The calm sea shines, loose hang the vessel's sails;
Before us are the sweet green fields of Wales,
And overhead the cloudless sky of May. —
'*Ah, would I were in those green fields at play,*
Not pent on ship-board this delicious day!
Tristram, I pray thee, of thy courtesy,
Reach me my golden phial stands by thee,
But pledge me in it first for courtesy. —'
Ha! dost thou start? are thy lips blanch'd like mine?
Child, 'tis no true draught this, 'tis poison'd wine!
Iseult! . . . .

* * * *

Ah, sweet angels, let him dream!
Keep his eyelids! let him seem
Not this fever-wasted wight
Thinn'd and paled before his time,
But the brilliant youthful knight
In the glory of his prime,
Sitting in the gilded barge,
At thy side, thou lovely charge,
Bending gaily o'er thy hand,
Iseult of Ireland!
And she too, that princess fair,
If her bloom be now less rare,
Let her have her youth again —
Let her be as she was then!
Let her have her proud dark eyes,
And her petulant quick replies —
Let her sweep her dazzling hand
With its gesture of command,
And shake back her raven hair
With the old imperious air!
As of old, so let her be,
That first Iseult, princess bright,
Chatting with her youthful knight
As he steers her o'er the sea,
Quitting at her father's will
The green isle where she was bred,
And her bower in Ireland,
For the surge-beat Cornish strand;
Where the prince whom she must wed
Dwells on loud Tyntagel's hill,
High above the sounding sea.
And that potion rare her mother
Gave her, that her future lord,
Gave her, that King Marc and she,
Might drink it on their marriage-day,
And for ever love each other —
Let her, as she sits on board,
Ah, sweet saints, unwittingly!
See it shine, and take it up,
And to Tristram laughing say:
'Sir Tristram, of thy courtesy,
Pledge me in my golden cup!'
Let them drink it — let their hands
Tremble, and their cheeks be flame,
As they feel the fatal bands

Of a love they dare not name,
With a wild delicious pain,
Twine about their hearts again!
Let the early summer be
Once more round them, and the sea
Blue, and o'er its mirror kind
Let the breath of the May-wind,
Wandering through their drooping sails,
Die on the green fields of Wales!
Let a dream like this restore
What his eye must see no more!

Tristram

Chill blows the wind, the pleasaunce-walks are drear —
Madcap, what jest was this, to meet me here?
Were feet like those made for so wild a way?
The southern winter-parlour, by my fay,
Had been the likeliest trysting-place to-day!
'Tristram! — nay, nay — thou must not take my hand! —
Tristram! — sweet love! — we are betray'd — out-plann'd.
Fly — save thyself — save me! — I dare not stay.' —
One last kiss first! — *' 'Tis vain — to horse — away!'*

* * * *

Ah! sweet saints, his dream doth move
Faster surely than it should,
From the fever in his blood!
All the spring-time of his love
Is already gone and past,
And instead thereof is seen
Its winter, which endureth still —
Tyntagel on its surge-beat hill,
The pleasaunce-walks, the weeping queen,
The flying leaves, the straining blast,
And that long, wild kiss — their last.
And this rough December-night,
And his burning fever-pain,
Mingle with his hurrying dream,
Till they rule it, till he seem
The press'd fugitive again,
The love-desperate banish'd knight
With a fire in his brain
Flying o'er the stormy main.
— Whither does he wander now?

Haply in his dreams the wind
Wafts him here, and lets him find
The lovely orphan child again
In her castle by the coast;
The youngest, fairest chatelaine,
Whom this realm of France can boast,
Our snowdrop by the Atlantic sea,
Iseult of Brittany.
And — for through the haggard air,
The stain'd arms, the matted hair
Of that stranger-knight ill-starr'd,
There gleam'd something, which recall'd
The Tristram who in better days
Was Launcelot's guest at Joyous Gard —
Welcomed here, and here install'd,
Tended of his fever here,
Haply he seems again to move
His young guardian's heart with love;
In his exiled loneliness,
In his stately, deep distress,
Without a word, without a tear.
—'Ah! 'tis well he should retrace
His tranquil life in this lone place;
His gentle bearing at the side
Of his timid youthful bride;
His long rambles by the shore
On winter-evenings, when the roar
Of the near waves came, sadly grand,
Through the dark, up the drown'd sand,
Or his endless reveries
In the woods, where the gleams play
On the grass under the trees,
Passing the long summer's day
Idle as a mossy stone
In the forest-depths alone,
The chase neglected, and his hound
Couch'd beside him on the ground.
— Ah! what trouble 's on his brow?
Hither let him wander now;
Hither, to the quiet hours
Pass'd among these heaths of ours
By the grey Atlantic sea;
Hours, if not of ecstasy,
From violent anguish surely free!

Tristram

All red with blood the whirling river flows,
The wide plain rings, the dazed air throbs with blows.
Upon us are the chivalry of Rome —
Their spears are down, their steeds are bathed in foam.
'Up, Tristram, up,' men cry, 'thou moonstruck knight!
What foul fiend rides thee? On into the fight!'
— Above the din her voice is in my ears;
I see her form glide through the crossing spears. —
Iseult! . . . .

* * * *

Ah! he wanders forth again;
We cannot keep him; now, as then,
There's a secret in his breast
Which will never let him rest.
These musing fits in the green wood
They cloud the brain, they dull the blood!
— His sword is sharp, his horse is good;
Beyond the mountains will he see
The famous towns of Italy,
And label with the blessed sign
The heathen Saxons on the Rhine.
At Arthur's side he fights once more
With the Roman Emperor.
There's many a gay knight where he goes
Will help him to forget his care;
The march, the leaguer, Heaven's blithe air,
The neighing steeds, the ringing blows —
Sick pining comes not where these are.
Ah! what boots it, that the jest
Lightens every other brow,
What, that every other breast
Dances as the trumpets blow,
If one's own heart beats not light
On the waves of the toss'd fight,
If oneself cannot get free
From the clog of misery?
Thy lovely youthful wife grows pale
Watching by the salt sea-tide
With her children at her side
For the gleam of thy white sail.
Home, Tristram, to thy halls again!
To our lonely sea complain,
To our forests tell thy pain!

Tristram

All round the forest sweeps off, black in shade,
But it is moonlight in the open glade;
And in the bottom of the glade shine clear
The forest-chapel and the fountain near.
— I think, I have a fever in my blood;
Come, let me leave the shadow of this wood,
Ride down, and bathe my hot brow in the flood.
— Mild shines the cold spring in the moon's clear light;
God! 'tis *her* face plays in the waters bright.
'Fair love,' she says, 'canst thou forget so soon,
At this soft hour, under this sweet moon?' —
Iseult! . . . .

* * * *

Ah, poor soul! if this be so,
Only death can balm thy woe.
The solitudes of the green wood
Had no medicine for thy mood;
The rushing battle clear'd thy blood
As little as did solitude.
— Ah! his eyelids slowly break
Their hot seals, and let him wake;
What new change shall we now see?
A happier? Worse it cannot be.

Tristram

Is my page here? Come, turn me to the fire!
Upon the window-panes the moon shines bright;
The wind is down — but she'll not come to-night.
Ah no! she is asleep in Cornwall now,
Far hence; her dreams are fair — smooth is her brow.
Of me she recks not, nor my vain desire.
— I have had dreams, I have had dreams, my page,
Would take a score years from a strong man's age;
And with a blood like mine, will leave, I fear,
Scant leisure for a second messenger.
— My princess, art thou there? Sweet, do not wait!
To bed, and sleep! my fever is gone by;
To-night my page shall keep me company.
Where do the children sleep? kiss them for me!
Poor child, thou art almost as pale as I;
This comes of nursing long and watching late.
To bed — good night!

* * * *

She left the gleam-lit fireplace,
She came to the bed-side;
She took his hands in hers — her tears
Down on his wasted fingers rain'd.
She raised her eyes upon his face —
Not with a look of wounded pride,
A look as if the heart complained —
Her look was like a sad embrace;
The gaze of one who can divine
A grief, and sympathise.
Sweet flower! thy children's eyes
Are not more innocent than thine.
But they sleep in shelter'd rest,
Like helpless birds in the warm nest,
On the castle's southern side;
Where feebly comes the mournful roar
Of buffeting wind and surging tide
Through many a room and corridor.
— Full on their window the moon's ray
Makes their chamber as bright as day.
It shines upon the blank white walls,
And on the snowy pillow falls,
And on two angel-heads doth play
Turn'd to each other — the eyes closed,
The lashes on the cheeks reposed.
Round each sweet brow the cap close-set
Hardly lets peep the golden hair;
Through the soft-open'd lips the air
Scarcely moves the coverlet.
One little wandering arm is thrown
At random on the counterpane,
And often the fingers close in haste
As if their baby-owner chased
The butterflies again.
This stir they have, and this alone;
But else they are so still!
—Ah, tired madcaps! you lie still;
But were you at the window now,
To look forth on the fairy sight
Of your illumined haunts by night,
To see the park-glades where you play
Far lovelier than they are by day,
To see the sparkle on the eaves,
And upon every giant-bough
Of those old oaks, whose wet red leaves
Are jewell'd with bright drops of rain —

How would your voices run again!
And far beyond the sparkling trees
Of the castle-park one sees
The bare heaths spreading, clear as day,
Moor behind moor, far, far away,
Into the heart of Brittany.
And here and there, lock'd by the land,
Long inlets of smooth glittering sea,
And many a stretch of watery sand
All shining in the white moon-beams —
But you see fairer in your dreams!

What voices are these on the clear night-air?
What lights in the court — what steps on the stair?

II

Iseult of Ireland

Tristram

Raise the light, my page! that I may see her. —
Thou art come at last, then, haughty Queen!
Long I've waited, long I've fought my fever;
Late thou comest, cruel thou hast been.

Iseult

Blame me not, poor sufferer! that I tarried;
Bound I was, I could not break the band.
Chide not with the past, but feel the present!
I am here — we meet — I hold thy hand.

Tristram

Thou art come, indeed — thou hast rejoin'd me;
Thou hast dared it — but too late to save.
Fear not now that men should tax thine honour!
I am dying: build — (thou may'st) — my grave!

Iseult

Tristram, ah, for love of Heaven, speak kindly!
What, I hear these bitter words from thee?
Sick with grief I am, and faint with travel —
Take my hand — dear Tristram, look on me!

Tristram

I forgot, thou comest from thy voyage —
Yes, the spray is on thy cloak and hair.
But thy dark eyes are not dimm'd, proud Iseult!
And thy beauty never was more fair.

Iseult

Ah, harsh flatterer! let alone my beauty!
I, like thee, have left my youth afar.
Take my hand, and touch these wasted fingers —
See my cheek and lips, how white they are!

Tristram

Thou art paler — but thy sweet charm, Iseult!
Would not fade with the dull years away.
Ah, how fair thou standest in the moonlight!
I forgive thee, Iseult! — thou wilt stay?

Iseult

Fear me not, I will be always with thee;
I will watch thee, tend thee, soothe thy pain;
Sing thee tales of true, long-parted lovers,
Join'd at evening of their days again.

Tristram

No, thou shalt not speak! I should be finding
Something alter'd in thy courtly tone.
Sit — sit by me! I will think, we've lived so
In the green wood, all our lives, alone.

Iseult

Alter'd, Tristram? Not in courts, believe me,
Love like mine is alter'd in the breast;
Courtly life is light and cannot reach it —
Ah! it lives, because so deep-suppress'd!

What, thou think'st men speak in courtly chambers
Words by which the wretched are consoled?
What, thou think'st this aching brow was cooler,
Circled, Tristram, by a band of gold?

Royal state with Marc, my deep-wrong'd husband —
 That was bliss to make my sorrows flee!
Silken courtiers whispering honied nothings —
 Those were friends to make me false to thee!

Ah, on which, if both our lots were balanced,
 Was indeed the heaviest burden thrown —
Thee, a pining exile in thy forest,
 Me, a smiling queen upon my throne?

Vain and strange debate, where both have suffer'd,
 Both have pass'd a youth consumed and sad,
Both have brought their anxious day to evening,
 And have now short space for being glad!

Join'd we are henceforth; nor will thy people,
 Nor thy younger Iseult take it ill,
That a former rival shares her office,
 When she sees her humbled, pale, and still.

I, a faded watcher by thy pillow,
 I, a statue on thy chapel-floor,
Pour'd in prayer before the Virgin-Mother,
 Rouse no anger, make no rivals more.

She will cry: 'Is this the foe I dreaded?
 This his idol? this that royal bride?
Ah, an hour of health would purge his eyesight!
 Stay, pale queen! for ever by my side.'

Hush, no words! that smile, I see, forgives me.
 I am now thy nurse, I bid thee sleep.
Close thine eyes — this flooding moonlight blinds them! —
 Nay, all's well again! thou must not weep.

Tristram

I am happy! yet I feel, there's something
 Swells my heart, and takes my breath away.
Through a mist I see thee; near — come nearer!
 Bend — bend down! — I yet have much to say.

Iseult

Heaven! his head sinks back upon the pillow —
 Tristram! Tristram! let thy heart not fail!

Call on God and on the holy angels!
  What, love, courage! — Christ! he is so pale.

Tristram

Hush, 'tis vain, I feel my end approaching!
  This is what my mother said should be,
When the fierce pains took her in the forest,
  The deep draughts of death, in bearing me.

'Son,' she said, 'thy name shall be of sorrow;
  Tristram art thou call'd for my death's sake.'
So she said, and died in the drear forest.
  Grief since then his home with me doth make.

I am dying.— Start not, nor look wildly!
  Me, thy living friend, thou canst not save.
But, since living we were ununited,
  Go not far, O Iseult! from my grave.

Close mine eyes, then seek the princess Iseult;
  Speak her fair, she is of royal blood!
Say, I will'd so, that thou stay beside me —
  She will grant it; she is kind and good.

Now to sail the seas of death I leave thee —
  One last kiss upon the living shore!

Iseult

Tristram! — Tristram! — stay — receive me with thee!
  Iseult leaves thee, Tristram! never more.

* * * *

You see them clear — the moon shines bright.
Slow, slow and softly, where she stood,
She sinks upon the ground; — her hood
Had fallen back; her arms outspread
Still hold her lover's hand; her head
Is bow'd, half-buried, on the bed.
O'er the blanch'd sheet her raven hair
Lies in disorder'd streams; and there,
Strung like white stars, the pearls still are,
And the golden bracelets, heavy and rare,
Flash on her white arms still.

The very same which yesternight
Flash'd in the silver sconces' light,
When the feast was gay and the laughter loud
In Tyntagel's palace proud.
But then they deck'd a restless ghost
With hot-flush'd cheeks and brilliant eyes,
And quivering lips on which the tide
Of courtly speech abruptly died,
And a glance which over the crowded floor,
The dancers, and the festive host,
Flew ever to the door.
That the knights eyed her in surprise,
And the dames whispered scoffingly:
'Her moods, good lack, they pass like showers!
But yesternight and she would be
As pale and still as wither'd flowers,
And now to-night she laughs and speaks
And has a colour in her cheeks;
Christ keep us from such fantasy!'—

Yes, now the longing is o'erpast,
Which, dogg'd by fear and fought by shame
Shook her weak bosom day and night,
Consumed her beauty like a flame,
And dimm'd it like the desert-blast.
And though the bed-clothes hide her face,
Yet were it lifted to the light,
The sweet expression of her brow
Would charm the gazer, till his thought
Erased the ravages of time,
Fill'd up the hollow cheek, and brought
A freshness back as of her prime—
So healing is her quiet now.
So perfectly the lines express
A tranquil, settled loveliness,
Her younger rival's purest grace.

The air of the December-night
Steals coldly around the chamber bright,
Where those lifeless lovers be;
Swinging with it, in the light
Flaps the ghostlike tapestry.
And on the arras wrought you see
A stately Huntsman, clad in green,
And round him a fresh forest-scene.
On that clear forest-knoll he stays,

With his pack round him, and delays.
He stares and stares, with troubled face,
At this huge, gleam-lit fireplace,
At that bright, iron-figured door,
And those blown rushes on the floor.
He gazes down into the room
With heated cheeks and flurried air,
And to himself he seems to say:
'*What place is this, and who are they?*
Who is that kneeling Lady fair?
And on his pillows that pale Knight
Who seems of marble on a tomb?
How comes it here, this chamber bright,
Through whose mullion'd windows clear
The castle-court all wet with rain,
The drawbridge and the moat appear,
And then the beach, and, mark'd with spray,
The sunken reefs, and far away
The unquiet bright Atlantic plain?
—What, has some glamour made me sleep,
And sent me with my dogs to sweep,
By night, with boisterous bugle-peal,
Through some old, sea-side, knightly hall,
Not in the free green wood at all?
That Knight's asleep and at her prayer
That Lady by the bed doth kneel —
Then hush, thou boisterous bugle-peal!'
— The wild boar rustles in his lair;
The fierce hounds snuff the tainted air;
But lord and hounds keep rooted there.

Cheer, cheer thy dogs into the brake,
O Hunter! and without a fear
Thy golden-tassell'd bugle blow,
And through the glades thy pastime take —
For thou wilt rouse no sleepers here!
For these thou seest are unmoved;
Cold, cold as those who lived and loved
A thousand years ago.

III

Iseult of Brittany

A YEAR had flown, and o'er the sea away,
In Cornwall, Tristram and Queen Iseult lay;

In King Marc's chapel, in Tyntagel old —
There in a ship they bore those lovers cold.

The young surviving Iseult, one bright day,
Had wander'd forth. Her children were at play
In a green circular hollow in the heath
Which borders the sea-shore — a country path
Creeps over it from the till'd fields behind.
The hollow's grassy banks are soft-inclined,
And to one standing on them, far and near
The lone unbroken view spreads bright and clear
Over the waste. This cirque of open ground
Is light and green; the heather, which all round
Creeps thickly, grows not here; but the pale grass
Is strewn with rocks, and many a shiver'd mass
Of vein'd white-gleaming quartz, and here and there
Dotted with holly-trees and juniper.
In the smooth centre of the opening stood
Three hollies side by side, and made a screen,
Warm with the winter-sun, of burnish'd green
With scarlet berries gemm'd, the fell-fare's food.
Under the glittering hollies Iseult stands,
Watching her children play; their little hands
Are busy gathering spars of quartz, and streams
Of stagshorn for their hats; anon, with screams
Of mad delight they drop their spoils, and bound
Among the holly-clumps and broken ground,
Racing full speed, and startling in their rush
The fell-fares and the speckled missel-thrush
Out of their glossy coverts; — but when now
Their cheeks were flush'd, and over each hot brow,
Under the feather'd hats of the sweet pair,
In blinding masses shower'd the golden hair —
Then Iseult call'd them to her, and the three
Cluster'd under the holly-screen, and she
Told them an old-world Breton history.

Warm in their mantles wrapt the three stood there,
Under the hollies, in the clear still air —
Mantles with those rich furs deep glistering
Which Venice ships do from swart Egypt bring.
Long they stay'd still — then, pacing at their ease,
Moved up and down under the glossy trees.
But still, as they pursued their warm dry road,
From Iseult's lips the unbroken story flow'd,

And still the children listen'd, their blue eyes
Fix'd on their mother's face in wide surprise;
Nor did their looks stray once to the sea-side,
Nor to the brown heaths round them, bright and wide,
Nor to the snow, which, though 't was all away
From the open heath, still by the hedgerows lay,
Nor to the shining sea-fowl, that with screams
Bore up from where the bright Atlantic gleams,
Swooping to landward; nor to where, quite clear,
The fell-fares settled on the thickets near.
And they would still have listen'd, till dark night
Came keen and chill down on the heather bright;
But, when the red glow on the sea grew cold,
And the grey turrets of the castle old
Look'd sternly through the frosty evening-air,
Then Iseult took by the hand those children fair,
And brought her tale to an end, and found the path,
And led them home over the darkening heath.

And is she happy? Does she see unmoved
The days in which she might have lived and loved
Slip without bringing bliss slowly away,
One after one, to-morrow like to-day?
Joy has not found her yet, nor ever will —
Is it this thought which makes her mien so still,
Her features so fatigued, her eyes, though sweet,
So sunk, so rarely lifted save to meet
Her children's? She moves slow; her voice alone
Hath yet an infantine and silver tone.
But even that comes languidly; in truth,
She seems one dying in a mask of youth.
And now she will go home, and softly lay
Her laughing children in their beds, and play
Awhile with them before they sleep; and then
She'll light her silver lamp, which fishermen
Dragging their nets through the rough waves, afar,
Along this iron coast, know like a star,
And take her broidery-frame, and there she'll sit
Hour after hour, her gold curls sweeping it;
Lifting her soft-bent head only to mind
Her children, or to listen to the wind.
And when the clock peals midnight, she will move
Her work away, and let her fingers rove
Across the shaggy brows of Tristram's hound
Who lies, guarding her feet, along the ground;

Or else she will fall musing, her blue eyes
Fixt, her slight hands clasp'd on her lap; then rise,
And at her prie-dieu kneel, until she have told
Her rosary-beads of ebony tipp'd with gold,
Then to her soft sleep — and to-morrow'll be
To-day's exact repeated effigy.

Yes, it is lonely for her in her hall.
The children, and the grey-hair'd seneschal,
Her women, and Sir Tristram's aged hound,
Are there the sole companions to be found.
But these she loves; and noisier life than this
She would find ill to bear, weak as she is.
She has her children, too, and night and day
Is with them; and the wide heaths where they play,
The hollies, and the cliff, and the sea-shore,
The sand, the sea-birds, and the distant sails,
These are to her dear as to them; the tales
With which this day the children she beguiled
She gleaned from Breton grandames, when a child,
In every hut along this sea-coast wild.
She herself loves them still, and, when they are told,
Can forget all to hear them, as of old.

Dear saints, it is not sorrow, as I hear,
Not suffering, which shuts up eye and ear
To all that has delighted them before,
And lets us be what we were once no more.
No, we may suffer deeply, yet retain
Power to be moved and soothed, for all our pain,
By what of old pleased us, and will again.
No, 'tis the gradual furnace of the world,
In whose hot air our spirits are upcurl'd
Until they crumble, or else grow like steel —
Which kills in us the bloom, the youth, the spring —
Which leaves the fierce necessity to feel,
But takes away the power — this can avail,
By drying up our joy in everything,
To make our former pleasures all seem stale.
This, or some tyrannous single thought, some fit
Of passion, which subdues our souls to it,
Till for its sake alone we live and move —
Call it ambition, or remorse, or love —
This too can change us wholly, and make seem
All which we did before, shadow and dream.

And yet, I swear, it angers me to see
How this fool passion gulls men potently;
Being, in truth, but a diseased unrest,
And an unnatural overheat at best.
How they are full of languor and distress
Not having it; which when they do possess,
They straightway are burnt up with fume and care,
And spend their lives in posting here and there
Where this plague drives them; and have little ease,
Are furious with themselves, and hard to please.
Like that bald Cæsar, the famed Roman wight,
Who wept at reading of a Grecian knight
Who made a name at younger years than he;
Or that renown'd mirror of chivalry,
Prince Alexander, Philip's peerless son,
Who carried the great war from Macedon
Into the Soudan's realm, and thundered on
To die at thirty-five in Babylon.

What tale did Iseult to the children say,
Under the hollies, that bright winter's day?

She told them of the fairy-haunted land
Away the other side of Brittany,
Beyond the heaths, edged by the lonely sea;
Of the deep forest-glades of Broce-liande,
Through whose green boughs the golden sunshine creeps,
Where Merlin by the enchanted thorn-tree sleeps.
For here he came with the fay Vivian,
One April, when the warm days first began.
He was on foot, and that false fay, his friend,
On her white palfrey; here he met his end,
In these lone sylvan glades, that April-day.
This tale of Merlin and the lovely fay
Was the one Iseult chose, and she brought clear
Before the children's fancy him and her.

Blowing between the stems, the forest-air
Had loosen'd the brown locks of Vivian's hair,
Which play'd on her flush'd cheek, and her blue eyes
Sparkled with mocking glee and exercise.
Her palfrey's flanks were mired and bathed in sweat,
For they had travell'd far and not stopp'd yet.
A brier in that tangled wilderness
Had scored her white right hand, which she allows

To rest ungloved on her green riding-dress;
The other warded off the drooping boughs.
But still she chatted on, with her blue eyes
Fix'd full on Merlin's face, her stately prize.
Her 'haviour had the morning's fresh clear grace,
The spirit of the woods was in her face.
She look'd so witching fair, that learned wight
Forgot his craft, and his best wits took flight;
And he grew fond, and eager to obey
His mistress, use her empire as she may.

They came to where the brushwood ceased, and day
Peer'd 'twixt the stems; and the ground broke away,
In a sloped sward down to a brawling brook;
And up as high as where they stood to look
On the brook's farther side was clear, but then
The underwood and trees began again.
This open glen was studded thick with thorns
Then white with blossom; and you saw the horns,
Through last year's fern, of the shy fallow-deer
Who come at noon down to the water here.
You saw the bright-eyed squirrels dart along
Under the thorns on the green sward; and strong
The blackbird whistled from the dingles near,
And the weird chipping of the woodpecker
Rang lonelily and sharp; the sky was fair,
And a fresh breath of spring stirr'd everywhere.
Merlin and Vivian stopp'd on the slope's brow,
To gaze on the light sea of leaf and bough
Which glistering plays all round them, lone and mild,
As if to itself the quiet forest smiled.
Upon the brow-top grew a thorn, and here
The grass was dry and moss'd, and you saw clear
Across the hollow; white anemonies
Starr'd the cool turf, and clumps of primroses
Ran out from the dark underwood behind.
No fairer resting-place a man could find.
'Here let us halt,' said Merlin then; and she
Nodded, and tied her palfrey to a tree.

They sate them down together, and a sleep
Fell upon Merlin, more like death, so deep.
Her finger on her lips, then Vivian rose,
And from her brown-lock'd head the wimple throws,
And takes it in her hand, and waves it over

The blossom'd thorn-tree and her sleeping lover.
Nine times she waved the fluttering wimple round,
And made a little plot of magic ground.
And in that daisied circle, as men say,
Is Merlin prisoner till the judgment-day;
But she herself whither she will can rove —
For she was passing weary of his love.

MEMORIAL VERSES

APRIL, 1850

GOETHE in Weimar sleeps, and Greece,
Long since, saw Byron's struggle cease.
But one such death remain'd to come;
The last poetic voice is dumb —
We stand to-day by Wordsworth's tomb.

When Byron's eyes were shut in death,
We bow'd our head and held our breath.
He taught us little; but our soul
Had *felt* him like the thunder's roll.
With shivering heart the strife we saw
Of passion with eternal law;
And yet with reverential awe
We watch'd the fount of fiery life
Which served for that Titanic strife.

When Goethe's death was told, we said:
Sunk, then, is Europe's sagest head.
Physician of the iron age, —
Goethe has done his pilgrimage.
He took the suffering human race,
He read each wound, each weakness clear;
And struck his finger on the place,
And said: *Thou ailest here, and here!*
He look'd on Europe's dying hour
Of fitful dream and feverish power;
His eye plunged down the weltering strife,
The turmoil of expiring life —
He said: *The end is everywhere,*
Art still has truth, take refuge there!
And he was happy, if to know
Causes of things, and far below
His feet to see the lurid flow
Of terror, and insane distress,
And headlong fate, be happiness.

And Wordsworth! — Ah, pale ghosts, rejoice!
For never has such soothing voice
Been to your shadowy world convey'd,
Since erst, at morn, some wandering shade

Heard the clear song of Orpheus come
Through Hades, and the mournful gloom.
Wordsworth has gone from us — and ye,
Ah, may ye feel his voice as we!
He too upon a wintry clime
Had fallen — on this iron time
Of doubts, disputes, distractions, fears.
He found us when the age had bound
Our souls in its benumbing round;
He spoke, and loosed our heart in tears.
He laid us as we lay at birth
On the cool flowery lap of earth,
Smiles broke from us and we had ease;
The hills were round us, and the breeze
Went o'er the sun-lit fields again;
Our foreheads felt the wind and rain.
Our youth return'd; for there was shed
On spirits that had long been dead,
Spirits dried up and closely furl'd,
The freshness of the early world.

Ah! since dark days still bring to light
Man's prudence and man's fiery might,
Time may restore us in his course
Goethe's sage mind and Byron's force;
But where will Europe's latter hour
Again find Wordsworth's healing power?
Others will teach us how to dare,
And against fear our breast to steel;
Others will strengthen us to bear —
But who, ah! who, will make us feel?
The cloud of mortal destiny,
Others will front it fearlessly —
But who, like him, will put it by?

Keep fresh the grass upon his grave
O Rotha, with thy living wave!
Sing him thy best! for few or none
Hears thy voice right, now he is gone.

SELF–DEPENDENCE

WEARY of myself, and sick of asking
What I am, and what I ought to be,

At this vessel's prow I stand, which bears me
Forwards, forwards, o'er the starlit sea.

And a look of passionate desire
O'er the sea and to the stars I send:
'Ye who from my childhood up have calm'd me,
Calm me, ah, compose me to the end!

'Ah, once more,' I cried, 'ye stars, ye waters,
On my heart your mighty charm renew;
Still, still let me, as I gaze upon you,
Feel my soul becoming vast like you!'

From the intense, clear, star-sown vault of heaven,
Over the lit sea's unquiet way,
In the rustling night-air came the answer:
'Wouldst thou *be* as these are? *Live* as they.

'Unaffrighted by the silence round them,
Undistracted by the sights they see,
These demand not that the things without them
Yield them love, amusement, sympathy.

'And with joy the stars perform their shining,
And the sea its long moon-silver'd roll;
For self-poised they live, nor pine with noting
All the fever of some differing soul.

'Bounded by themselves, and unregardful
In what state God's other works may be,
In their own tasks all their powers pouring,
These attain the mighty life you see.'

O air-born voice! long since, severely clear,
A cry like thine in mine own heart I hear:
'Resolve to be thyself; and know that he,
Who finds himself, loses his misery!'

A SUMMER NIGHT

In the deserted, moon-blanch'd street,
How lonely rings the echo of my feet!

Those windows, which I gaze at, frown,
Silent and white, unopening down,
Repellent as the world; — but see,
A break between the housetops shows
The moon! and, lost behind her, fading dim
Into the dewy dark obscurity
Down at the far horizon's rim,
Doth a whole tract of heaven disclose!

And to my mind the thought
Is on a sudden brought
Of a past night, and a far different scene.
Headlands stood out into the moonlit deep
As clearly as at noon;
The spring-tide's brimming flow
Heaved dazzlingly between;
Houses, with long white sweep,
Girdled the glistening bay;
Behind, through the soft air,
The blue haze-cradled mountains spread away,
That night was far more fair —
But the same restless pacings to and fro,
And the same vainly throbbing heart was there,
And the same bright, calm moon.

And the calm moonlight seems to say:
Hast thou then still the old unquiet breast,
Which neither deadens into rest,
Nor ever feels the fiery glow
That whirls the spirit from itself away,
But fluctuates to and fro,
Never by passion quite possess'd
And never quite benumb'd by the world's sway? —
And I, I know not if to pray
Still to be what I am, or yield and be
Like all the other men I see.

For most men in a brazen prison live,
Where, in the sun's hot eye,
With heads bent o'er their toil, they languidly
Their lives to some unmeaning taskwork give,
Dreaming of nought beyond their prison-wall.
And as, year after year,
Fresh products of their barren labour fall
From their tired hands, and rest

Never yet comes more near,
Gloom settles slowly down over their breast;
And while they try to stem
The waves of mournful thought by which they are prest,
Death in their prison reaches them,
Unfreed, having seen nothing, still unblest.

And the rest, a few,
Escape their prison and depart
On the wide ocean of life anew.
There the freed prisoner, where'er his heart
Listeth, will sail;
Nor doth he know how there prevail,
Despotic on that sea,
Trade-winds which cross it from eternity.
Awhile he holds some false way, undebarr'd
By thwarting signs, and braves
The freshening wind and blackening waves.
And then the tempest strikes him; and between
The lightning-bursts is seen
Only a driving wreck,
And the pale master on his spar-strewn deck
With anguish'd face and flying hair
Grasping the rudder hard,
Still bent to make some port he knows not where,
Still standing for some false, impossible shore.
And sterner comes the roar
Of sea and wind, and through the deepening gloom
Fainter and fainter wreck and helmsman loom,
And he too disappears, and comes no more.

Is there no life, but these alone?
Madman or slave, must man be one?

Plainness and clearness without shadow of stain!
Clearness divine!
Ye heavens, whose pure dark regions have no sign
Of languor, though so calm, and, though so great,
Are yet untroubled and unpassionate;
Who, though so noble, share in the world's toil,
And, though so task'd, keep free from dust and soil!
I will not say that your mild deeps retain
A tinge, it may be, of their silent pain
Who have long'd deeply once, and long'd in vain —
But I will rather say that you remain

A world above man's head, to let him see
How boundless might his soul's horizons be,
How vast, yet of what clear transparency!
How it were good to abide there, and breathe free;
How fair a lot to fill
Is left to each man still!

THE BURIED LIFE

LIGHT flows our war of mocking words, and yet,
Behold, with tears mine eyes are wet!
I feel a nameless sadness o'er me roll.
Yes, yes, we know that we can jest,
We know, we know that we can smile!
But there's a something in this breast,
To which thy light words bring no rest,
And thy gay smiles no anodyne.
Give me thy hand, and hush awhile,
And turn those limpid eyes on mine,
And let me read there, love! thy inmost soul.

Alas! is even love too weak
To unlock the heart, and let it speak?
Are even lovers powerless to reveal
To one another what indeed they feel?
I knew the mass of men conceal'd
Their thoughts, for fear that if reveal'd
They would by other men be met
With blank indifference, or with blame reproved;
I knew they lived and moved
Trick'd in disguises, alien to the rest
Of men, and alien to themselves — and yet
The same heart beats in every human breast!

But we, my love! — doth a like spell benumb
Our hearts, our voices? — must we too be dumb?

Ah! well for us, if even we,
Even for a moment, can get free
Our heart, and have our lips unchain'd;
For that which seals them hath been deep-ordain'd!

Fate, which foresaw
How frivolous a baby man would be —
By what distractions he would be possess'd,
How he would pour himself in every strife,
And well-nigh change his own identity —
That it might keep from his capricious play
His genuine self, and force him to obey
Even in his own despite his being's law,
Bade through the deep recesses of our breast
The unregarded river of our life
Pursue with indiscernible flow its way;
And that we should not see
The buried stream, and seem to be
Eddying at large in blind uncertainty,
Though driving on with it eternally.

But often, in the world's most crowded streets,
But often, in the din of strife,
There rises an unspeakable desire
After the knowledge of our buried life;
A thirst to spend our fire and restless force
In tracking out our true, original course;
A longing to inquire
Into the mystery of this heart which beats
So wild, so deep in us — to know
Whence our lives come and where they go.
And many a man in his own breast then delves,
But deep enough, alas! none ever mines.
And we have been on many thousand lines,
And we have shown, on each, spirit and power;
But hardly have we, for one little hour,
Been on our own line, have we been ourselves —
Hardly had skill to utter one of all
The nameless feelings that course through our breast,
But they course on for ever unexpress'd.
And long we try in vain to speak and act
Our hidden self, and what we say and do
Is eloquent, is well — but 'tis not true!
And then we will no more be rack'd
With inward striving, and demand
Of all the thousand nothings of the hour
Their stupefying power;
Ah yes, and they benumb us at our call!
Yet still, from time to time, vague and forlorn,
From the soul's subterranean depth upborne

As from an infinitely distant land,
Come airs, and floating echoes, and convey
A melancholy into all our day.

Only — but this is rare —
When a belovéd hand is laid in ours,
When, jaded with the rush and glare
Of the interminable hours,
Our eyes can in another's eyes read clear,
When our world-deafen'd ear
Is by the tones of a loved voice caress'd —
A bolt is shot back somewhere in our breast,
And a lost pulse of feeling stirs again.
The eye sinks inward, and the heart lies plain,
And what we mean, we say, and what we would, we know.
A man becomes aware of his life's flow,
And hears its winding murmur; and he sees
The meadows where it glides, the sun, the breeze.

And there arrives a lull in the hot race
Wherein he doth for ever chase
That flying and elusive shadow, rest.
An air of coolness plays upon his face,
And an unwonted calm pervades his breast.
And then he thinks he knows
The hills where his life rose,
And the sea where it goes.

STANZAS IN MEMORY OF THE AUTHOR OF 'OBERMANN'

NOVEMBER, 1849

IN front the awful Alpine track
Crawls up its rocky stair;
The autumn storm-winds drive the rack,
Close o'er it, in the air.

Behind are the abandon'd baths
Mute in their meadows lone;
The leaves are on the valley-paths,
The mists are on the Rhone —

The white mists rolling like a sea!
I hear the torrents roar.
— Yes, Obermann, all speaks of thee;
I feel thee near once more!

I turn thy leaves! I feel their breath
Once more upon me roll;
That air of languor, cold, and death,
Which brooded o'er thy soul.

Fly hence, poor wretch, whoe'er thou art,
Condemn'd to cast about,
All shipwreck in thy own weak heart,
For comfort from without!

A fever in these pages burns
Beneath the calm they feign;
A wounded human spirit turns,
Here, on its bed of pain.

Yes, though the virgin mountain-air
Fresh through these pages blows;
Though to these leaves the glaciers spare
The soul of their white snows;

Though here a mountain-murmur swells
Of many a dark-bough'd pine;
Though, as you read, you hear the bells
Of the high-pasturing kine —

Yet, through the hum of torrent lone,
And brooding mountain-bee,
There sobs I know not what ground-tone
Of human agony.

Is it for this, because the sound
Is fraught too deep with pain,
That, Obermann! the world around
So little loves thy strain?

Some secrets may the poet tell,
For the world loves new ways;
To tell too deep ones is not well —
It knows not what he says.

Yet, of the spirits who have reign'd
In this our troubled day,
I know but two, who have attain'd,
Save thee, to see their way.

By England's lakes, in grey old age,
His quiet home one keeps;
And one, the strong much-toiling sage,
In German Weimar sleeps.

But Wordsworth's eyes avert their ken
From half of human fate;
And Goethe's course few sons of men
May think to emulate.

For he pursued a lonely road,
His eyes on Nature's plan;
Neither made man too much a God,
Nor God too much a man.

Strong was he, with a spirit free
From mists, and sane, and clear;
Clearer, how much! than ours — yet we
Have a worse course to steer.

For though his manhood bore the blast
Of a tremendous time,
Yet in a tranquil world was pass'd
His tenderer youthful prime.

But we, brought forth and rear'd in hours
Of change, alarm, surprise —
What shelter to grow ripe is ours?
What leisure to grow wise?

Like children bathing on the shore,
Buried a wave beneath,
The second wave succeeds, before
We have had time to breathe.

Too fast we live, too much are tried,
Too harass'd, to attain
Wordsworth's sweet calm, or Goethe's wide
And luminous view to gain.

And then we turn, thou sadder sage,
To thee! we feel thy spell!
— The hopeless tangle of our age,
Thou too hast scann'd it well!

Immoveable thou sittest, still
As death, composed to bear!
Thy head is clear, thy feeling chill,
And icy thy despair.

Yes, as the son of Thetis said,
I hear thee saying now:
Greater by far than thou are dead;
Strive not! die also thou!

Ah! two desires toss about
The poet's feverish blood.
One drives him to the world without,
And one to solitude.

The glow, he cries, *the thrill of life,*
Where, where do these abound? —
Not in the world, not in the strife
Of men, shall they be found.

He who hath watch'd, not shared, the strife,
Knows how the day hath gone.
He only lives with the world's life,
Who hath renounced his own.

To thee we come, then! Clouds are roll'd
Where thou, O seer! art set;
Thy realm of thought is drear and cold —
The world is colder yet!

And thou hast pleasures, too, to share
With those who come to thee —
Balms floating on thy mountain-air,
And healing sights to see.

How often, where the slopes are green
On Jaman, hast thou sate
By some high chalet-door, and seen
The summer-day grow late;

And darkness steal o'er the wet grass
With the pale crocus starr'd,
And reach that glimmering sheet of glass
Beneath the piny sward,

Lake Leman's waters, far below!
And watch'd the rosy light
Fade from the distant peaks of snow;
And on the air of night

Heard accents of the eternal tongue
Through the pine branches play —
Listen'd, and felt thyself grow young!
Listen'd and wept —— Away!

Away the dreams that but deceive
And thou, sad guide, adieu!
I go, fate drives me; but I leave
Half of my life with you.

We, in some unknown Power's employ,
Move on a rigorous line;
Can neither, when we will, enjoy,
Nor, when we will, resign.

I in the world must live; but thou,
Thou melancholy shade!
Wilt not, if thou canst see me now,
Condemn me, nor upbraid.

For thou art gone away from earth,
And place with those dost claim,
The Children of the Second Birth,
Whom the world could not tame;

And with that small, transfigured band,
Whom many a different way
Conducted to their common land,
Thou learn'st to think as they.

Christian and pagan, king and slave,
Soldier and anchorite,
Distinctions we esteem so grave,
Are nothing in their sight.

They do not ask, who pined unseen,
Who was on action hurl'd,
Whose one bond is, that all have been
Unspotted by the world.

There without anger thou wilt see
Him who obeys thy spell
No more, so he but rest, like thee,
Unsoil'd! — and so, farewell.

Farewell! — Whether thou now liest near
That much-loved inland sea,
The ripples of whose blue waves cheer
Vevey and Meillerie:

And in that gracious region bland,
Where with clear-rustling wave
The scented pines of Switzerland
Stand dark round thy green grave,

Between the dusty vineyard-walls
Issuing on that green place
The early peasant still recalls
The pensive stranger's face,

And stoops to clear thy moss-grown date
Ere he plods on again; —
Or whether, by maligner fate,
Among the swarms of men,

Where between granite terraces
The blue Seine rolls her wave,
The Capital of Pleasure sees
The hardly-heard-of grave; —

Farewell! Under the sky we part,
In this stern Alpine dell.
O unstrung will! O broken heart!
A last, a last farewell!

LINES

WRITTEN IN KENSINGTON GARDENS

In this lone, open glade I lie,
Screen'd by deep boughs on either hand;
And at its end, to stay the eye,
Those black-crown'd, red-boled pine-trees stand!

Birds here make song, each bird has his,
Across the girdling city's hum.
How green under the boughs it is!
How thick the tremulous sheep-cries come!

Sometimes a child will cross the glade
To take his nurse his broken toy;
Sometimes a thrush flit overhead
Deep in her unknown day's employ.

Here at my feet what wonders pass,
What endless, active life is here!
What blowing daisies, fragrant grass!
An air-stirr'd forest, fresh and clear.

Scarce fresher is the mountain-sod
Where the tired angler lies, stretch'd out,
And, eased of basket and of rod,
Counts his day's spoil, the spotted trout.

In the huge world, which roars hard by,
Be others happy if they can!
But in my helpless cradle I
Was breathed on by the rural Pan.

I, on men's impious uproar hurl'd,
Think often, as I hear them rave,
That peace has left the upper world
And now keeps only in the grave.

Yet here is peace for ever new!
When I who watch them am away,
Still all things in this glade go through
The changes of their quiet day.

Then to their happy rest they pass!
The flowers upclose, the birds are fed,
The night comes down upon the grass,
The child sleeps warmly in his bed.

Calm soul of all things! make it mine
To feel, amid the city's jar,
That there abides a peace of thine,
Man did not make, and cannot mar.

The will to neither strive nor cry,
The power to feel with others give!
Calm, calm me more! nor let me die
Before I have begun to live.

MORALITY

We cannot kindle when we will
The fire which in the heart resides;
The spirit bloweth and is still,
In mystery our soul abides.
But tasks in hours of insight will'd
Can be through hours of gloom fulfill'd.

With aching hands and bleeding feet
We dig and heap, lay stone on stone;
We bear the burden and the heat
Of the long day, and wish 'twere done.
Not till the hours of light return,
All we have built do we discern.

Then, when the clouds are off the soul,
When thou dost bask in Nature's eye,
Ask, how *she* view'd thy self-control,
Thy struggling, task'd morality —
Nature, whose free, light, cheerful air,
Oft made thee, in thy gloom, despair.

And she, whose censure thou dost dread,
Whose eye thou wast afraid to seek,
See, on her face a glow is spread,
A strong emotion on her cheek!
'Ah, child!' she cries, 'that strife divine,
Whence was it, for it is not mine?

'There is no effort on *my* brow —
I do not strive, I do not weep;
I rush with the swift spheres and glow
In joy, and when I will, I sleep.
  Yet that severe, that earnest air,
  I saw, I felt it once — but where?

'I knew not yet the gauge of time,
Nor wore the manacles of space;
I felt it in some other clime,
I saw it in some other place.
  'Twas when the heavenly house I trod,
  And lay upon the breast of God.'

Poems

(*1853*)

SOHRAB AND RUSTUM

AN EPISODE

And the first grey of morning fill'd the east,
And the fog rose out of the Oxus stream.
But all the Tartar camp along the stream
Was hush'd, and still the men were plunged in sleep;
Sohrab alone, he slept not; all night long
He had lain wakeful, tossing on his bed;
But when the grey dawn stole into his tent,
He rose, and clad himself, and girt his sword,
And took his horseman's cloak, and left his tent,
And went abroad into the cold wet fog,
Through the dim camp to Peran-Wisa's tent.
 Through the black Tartar tents he pass'd, which stood
Clustering like bee-hives on the low flat strand
Of Oxus, where the summer-floods o'erflow
When the sun melts the snows in high Pamere;
Through the black tents he pass'd, o'er that low strand,
And to a hillock came, a little back
From the stream's brink — the spot where first a boat,
Crossing the stream in summer, scrapes the land.
The men of former times had crown'd the top
With a clay fort; but that was fall'n, and now
The Tartars built there Peran-Wisa's tent,
A dome of laths, and o'er it felts were spread.
And Sohrab came there, and went in, and stood
Upon the thick piled carpets in the tent,
And found the old man sleeping on his bed
Of rugs and felts, and near him lay his arms.
And Peran-Wisa heard him, though the step
Was dull'd; for he slept light, an old man's sleep;

And he rose quickly on one arm, and said: —
'Who art thou? for it is not yet clear dawn.
Speak! is there news, or any night alarm?'
But Sohrab came to the bedside, and said: —
'Thou know'st me, Peran-Wisa! it is I.
The sun is not yet risen, and the foe
Sleep; but I sleep not; all night long I lie
Tossing and wakeful, and I come to thee.
For so did King Afrasiab bid me seek
Thy counsel, and to heed thee as thy son,
In Samarcand, before the army march'd;
And I will tell thee what my heart desires.
Thou know'st if, since from Ader-baijan first
I came among the Tartars and bore arms,
I have still served Afrasiab well, and shown,
At my boy's years, the courage of a man.
This too thou know'st, that while I still bear on
The conquering Tartar ensigns through the world,
And beat the Persians back on every field,
I seek one man, one man, and one alone —
Rustum, my father; who I hoped should greet,
Should one day greet, upon some well-fought field,
His not unworthy, not inglorious son.
So I long hoped, but him I never find.
Come then, hear now, and grant me what I ask.
Let the two armies rest to-day; but I
Will challenge forth the bravest Persian lords
To meet me, man to man; if I prevail,
Rustum will surely hear it; if I fall —
Old man, the dead need no one, claim no kin.
Dim is the rumour of a common fight,
Where host meets host, and many names are sunk;
But of a single combat fame speaks clear.'
He spoke; and Peran-Wisa took the hand
Of the young man in his, and sigh'd, and said: —
'O Sohrab, an unquiet heart is thine!
Canst thou not rest among the Tartar chiefs,
And share the battle's common chance with us
Who love thee, but must press for ever first,
In single fight incurring single risk,
To find a father thou hast never seen?
That were far best, my son, to stay with us
Unmurmuring; in our tents, while it is war,
And when 'tis truce, then in Afrasiab's towns.
But, if this one desire indeed rules all,

To seek out Rustum — seek him not through fight!
Seek him in peace, and carry to his arms,
O Sohrab, carry an unwounded son!
But far hence seek him, for he is not here.
For now it is not as when I was young,
When Rustum was in front of every fray;
But now he keeps apart, and sits at home,
In Seistan, with Zal, his father old.
Whether that his own mighty strength at last
Feels the abhorr'd approaches of old age,
Or in some quarrel with the Persian King.
There go! — Thou wilt not? Yet my heart forebodes
Danger or death awaits thee on this field.
Fain would I know thee safe and well, though lost
To us; fain therefore send thee hence, in peace
To seek thy father, not seek single fights
In vain; — but who can keep the lion's cub
From ravening, and who govern Rustum's son?
Go, I will grant thee what thy heart desires.'
   So said he, and dropp'd Sohrab's hand, and left
His bed, and the warm rugs whereon he lay;
And o'er his chilly limbs his woollen coat
He pass'd, and tied his sandals on his feet,
And threw a white cloak round him, and he took
In his right hand a ruler's staff, no sword;
And on his head he set his sheep-skin cap,
Black, glossy, curl'd, the fleece of Kara-Kul;
And raised the curtain of his tent, and call'd
His herald to his side, and went abroad.
   The sun by this had risen, and clear'd the fog
From the broad Oxus and the glittering sands.
And from their tents the Tartar horsemen filed
Into the open plain; so Haman bade —
Haman, who next to Peran-Wisa ruled
The host, and still was in his lusty prime.
From their black tents, long files of horse, they stream'd;
As when some grey November morn the files,
In marching order spread, of long-neck'd cranes
Stream over Casbin and the southern slopes
Of Elburz, from the Aralian estuaries,
Or some frore Caspian reed-bed, southward bound
For the warm Persian sea-board — so they stream'd.
The Tartars of the Oxus, the King's guard,
First, with black sheep-skin caps and with long spears;
Large men, large steeds; who from Bokhara come

And Khiva, and ferment the milk of mares.
Next, the more temperate Toorkmuns of the south,
The Tukas, and the lances of Salore,
And those from Attruck and the Caspian sands;
Light men and on light steeds, who only drink
The acrid milk of camels, and their wells.
And then a swarm of wandering horse, who came
From far, and a more doubtful service own'd;
The Tartars of Ferghana, from the banks
Of the Jaxartes, men with scanty beards
And close-set skull-caps; and those wilder hordes
Who roam o'er Kipchak and the northern waste,
Kalmucks and unkempt Kuzzaks, tribes who stray
Nearest the Pole, and wandering Kirghizzes,
Who come on shaggy ponies from Pamere;
These all filed out from camp into the plain.
And on the other side the Persians form'd; —
First a light cloud of horse, Tartars they seem'd,
The Ilyats of Khorassan; and behind,
The royal troops of Persia, horse and foot,
Marshall'd battalions bright in burnish'd steel.
But Peran-Wisa with his herald came,
Threading the Tartar squadrons to the front,
And with his staff kept back the foremost ranks.
And when Ferood, who led the Persians, saw
That Peran-Wisa kept the Tartars back,
He took his spear, and to the front he came,
And check'd his ranks, and fix'd them where they stood.
And the old Tartar came upon the sand
Betwixt the silent hosts, and spake, and said: —
'Ferood, and ye, Persians and Tartars, hear!
Let there be truce between the hosts to-day.
But choose a champion from the Persian lords
To fight our champion Sohrab, man to man.'
As, in the country, on a morn in June,
When the dew glistens on the pearled ears,
A shiver runs through the deep corn for joy —
So, when they heard what Peran-Wisa said,
A thrill through all the Tartar squadrons ran
Of pride and hope for Sohrab, whom they loved.
But as a troop of pedlars, from Cabool,
Cross underneath the Indian Caucasus,
That vast sky-neighbouring mountain of milk snow;
Crossing so high, that, as they mount, they pass
Long flocks of travelling birds dead on the snow,

Choked by the air, and scarce can they themselves
Slake their parch'd throats with sugar'd mulberries —
In single file they move, and stop their breath,
For fear they should dislodge the o'erhanging snows —
So the pale Persians held their breath with fear.
   And to Ferood his brother chiefs came up
To counsel; Gudurz and Zoarrah came,
And Feraburz, who ruled the Persian host
Second, and was the uncle of the King;
These came and counsell'd, and then Gudurz said: —
   'Ferood, shame bids us take their challenge up,
Yet champion have we none to match this youth.
He has the wild stag's foot, the lion's heart.
But Rustum came last night; aloof he sits
And sullen, and has pitch'd his tents apart.
Him will I seek, and carry to his ear
The Tartar challenge, and this young man's name.
Haply he will forget his wrath, and fight.
Stand forth the while, and take their challenge up.'
   So spake he; and Ferood stood forth and cried: —
'Old man, be it agreed as thou hast said!
Let Sohrab arm, and we will find a man.'
   He spake: and Peran-Wisa turn'd, and strode
Back through the opening squadrons to his tent.
But through the anxious Persians Gudurz ran,
And cross'd the camp which lay behind, and reach'd,
Out on the sands beyond it, Rustum's tents.
Of scarlet cloth they were, and glittering gay,
Just pitch'd; the high pavilion in the midst
Was Rustum's, and his men lay camp'd around.
And Gudurz enter'd Rustum's tent, and found
Rustum; his morning meal was done, but still
The table stood before him, charged with food —
A side of roasted sheep, and cakes of bread,
And dark green melons; and there Rustum sate
Listless, and held a falcon on his wrist,
And play'd with it; but Gudurz came and stood
Before him; and he look'd, and saw him stand,
And with a cry sprang up and dropp'd the bird,
And greeted Gudurz with both hands, and said: —
   'Welcome! these eyes could see no better sight.
What news? but sit down first, and eat and drink.'
   But Gudurz stood in the tent-door, and said: —
'Not now! a time will come to eat and drink,
But not to-day; to-day has other needs.

The armies are drawn out, and stand at gaze;
For from the Tartars is a challenge brought
To pick a champion from the Persian lords
To fight their champion — and thou know'st his name —
Sohrab men call him, but his birth is hid.
O Rustum, like thy might is this young man's!
He has the wild stag's foot, the lion's heart;
And he is young, and Iran's chiefs are old,
Or else too weak; and all eyes turn to thee.
Come down and help us, Rustum, or we lose!'
  He spoke; but Rustum answer'd with a smile: —
'Go to! if Iran's chiefs are old, then I
Am older; if the young are weak, the King
Errs strangely; for the King, for Kai Khosroo,
Himself is young, and honours younger men,
And lets the aged moulder to their graves.
Rustum he loves no more, but loves the young —
The young may rise at Sohrab's vaunts, not I.
For what care I, though all speak Sohrab's fame?
For would that I myself had such a son,
And not that one slight helpless girl I have —
A son so famed, so brave, to send to war,
And I to tarry with the snow-hair'd Zal,
My father, whom the robber Afghans vex,
And clip his borders short, and drive his herds,
And he has none to guard his weak old age.
There would I go, and hang my armour up,
And with my great name fence that weak old man,
And spend the goodly treasures I have got,
And rest my age, and hear of Sohrab's fame,
And leave to death the hosts of thankless kings,
And with these slaughterous hands draw sword no more.'
  He spoke, and smiled; and Gudurz made reply: —
'What then, O Rustum, will men say to this,
When Sohrab dares our bravest forth, and seeks
Thee most of all, and thou, whom most he seeks,
Hidest thy face? Take heed lest men should say:
Like some old miser, Rustum hoards his fame,
And shuns to peril it with younger men.'
  And, greatly moved, then Rustum made reply: —
'O Gudurz, wherefore dost thou say such words?
Thou knowest better words than this to say.
What is one more, one less, obscure or famed,
Valiant or craven, young or old, to me?
Are not they mortal, am not I myself?

But who for men of nought would do great deeds?
Come, thou shalt see how Rustum hoards his fame!
But I will fight unknown, and in plain arms;
Let not men say of Rustum, he was match'd
In single fight with any mortal man.'
He spoke, and frown'd; and Gudurz turn'd, and ran
Back quickly through the camp in fear and joy —
Fear at his wrath, but joy that Rustum came.
But Rustum strode to his tent-door, and call'd
His followers in, and bade them bring his arms,
And clad himself in steel; the arms he chose
Were plain, and on his shield was no device,
Only his helm was rich, inlaid with gold,
And, from the fluted spine atop, a plume
Of horsehair waved, a scarlet horsehair plume.
So arm'd, he issued forth; and Ruksh, his horse,
Follow'd him like a faithful hound at heel —
Ruksh, whose renown was noised through all the earth,
The horse, whom Rustum on a foray once
Did in Bokhara by the river find
A colt beneath its dam, and drove him home,
And rear'd him; a bright bay, with lofty crest,
Dight with a saddle-cloth of broider'd green
Crusted with gold, and on the ground were work'd
All beasts of chase, all beasts which hunters know.
So follow'd, Rustum left his tents, and cross'd
The camp, and to the Persian host appear'd.
And all the Persians knew him, and with shouts
Hail'd; but the Tartars knew not who he was.
And dear as the wet diver to the eyes
Of his pale wife who waits and weeps on shore,
By sandy Bahrein, in the Persian Gulf,
Plunging all day in the blue waves, at night,
Having made up his tale of precious pearls,
Rejoins her in their hut upon the sands —
So dear to the pale Persians Rustum came.
And Rustum to the Persian front advanced,
And Sohrab arm'd in Haman's tent, and came.
And as afield the reapers cut a swath
Down through the middle of a rich man's corn,
And on each side are squares of standing corn,
And in the midst a stubble, short and bare —
So on each side were squares of men, with spears
Bristling, and in the midst, the open sand.
And Rustum came upon the sand, and cast

His eyes toward the Tartar tents, and saw
Sohrab come forth, and eyed him as he came.
As some rich woman, on a winter's morn,
Eyes through her silken curtains the poor drudge
Who with numb blacken'd fingers makes her fire —
At cock-crow, on a starlit winter's morn,
When the frost flowers the whiten'd window-panes —
And wonders how she lives, and what the thoughts
Of that poor drudge may be; so Rustum eyed
The unknown adventurous youth, who from afar
Came seeking Rustum, and defying forth
All the most valiant chiefs; long he perused
His spirited air, and wonder'd who he was.
For very young he seem'd, tenderly rear'd;
Like some young cypress, tall, and dark, and straight,
Which in a queen's secluded garden throws
Its slight dark shadow on the moonlit turf,
By midnight, to a bubbling fountain's sound —
So slender Sohrab seem'd, so softly rear'd.
And a deep pity enter'd Rustum's soul
As he beheld him coming; and he stood,
And beckon'd to him with his hand, and said: —
'O thou young man, the air of Heaven is soft,
And warm, and pleasant; but the grave is cold!
Heaven's air is better than the cold dead grave.
Behold me! I am vast, and clad in iron,
And tried; and I have stood on many a field
Of blood, and I have fought with many a foe —
Never was that field lost, or that foe saved.
O Sohrab, wherefore wilt thou rush on death?
Be govern'd! quit the Tartar host, and come
To Iran, and be as my son to me,
And fight beneath my banner till I die!
There are no youths in Iran brave as thou.'
So he spake, mildly; Sohrab heard his voice,
The mighty voice of Rustum, and he saw
His giant figure planted on the sand,
Sole, like some single tower, which a chief
Hath builded on the waste in former years
Against the robbers; and he saw that head,
Streak'd with its first grey hairs; — hope filled his soul,
And he ran forward and embraced his knees,
And clasp'd his hand within his own, and said: —
'O, by thy father's head! by thine own soul!
Art thou not Rustum? speak! art thou not he?'

But Rustum eyed askance the kneeling youth,
And turn'd away, and spake to his own soul: —
'Ah me, I muse what this young fox may mean!
False, wily, boastful, are these Tartar boys.
For if I now confess this thing he asks,
And hide it not, but say: *Rustum is here!*
He will not yield indeed, nor quit our foes,
But he will find some pretext not to fight,
And praise my fame, and proffer courteous gifts,
A belt or sword perhaps, and go his way.
And on a feast-tide, in Afrasiab's hall,
In Samarcand, he will arise and cry:
"I challenged once, when the two armies camp'd
Beside the Oxus, all the Persian lords
To cope with me in single fight; but they
Shrank, only Rustum dared; then he and I
Changed gifts, and went on equal terms away."
So will he speak, perhaps, while men applaud;
Then were the chiefs of Iran shamed through me.'
And then he turn'd, and sternly spake aloud: —
'Rise! wherefore dost thou vainly question thus
Of Rustum? I am here, whom thou hast call'd
By challenge forth; make good thy vaunt, or yield!
Is it with Rustum only thou wouldst fight?
Rash boy, men look on Rustum's face and flee!
For well I know, that did great Rustum stand
Before thy face this day, and were reveal'd,
There would be then no talk of fighting more.
But being what I am, I tell thee this —
Do thou record it in thine inmost soul:
Either thou shalt renounce thy vaunt and yield,
Or else thy bones shall strew this sand, till winds
Bleach them, or Oxus with his summer-floods,
Oxus in summer wash them all away.'
He spoke; and Sohrab answer'd on his feet: —
'Art thou so fierce? Thou wilt not fright me so!
I am no girl, to be made pale by words.
Yet this thou hast said well, did Rustum stand
Here on this field, there were no fighting then.
But Rustum is far hence, and we stand here.
Begin! thou art more vast, more dread than I,
And thou art proved, I know, and I am young —
But yet success sways with the breath of Heaven.
And though thou thinkest that thou knowest sure
Thy victory, yet thou canst not surely know.

For we are all, like swimmers in the sea,
Poised on the top of a huge wave of fate,
Which hangs uncertain to which side to fall.
And whether it will heave us up to land,
Or whether it will roll us out to sea,
Back out to sea, to the deep waves of death,
We know not, and no search will make us know;
Only the event will teach us in its hour.'
  He spoke, and Rustum answer'd not, but hurl'd
His spear; down from the shoulder, down it came,
As on some partridge in the corn a hawk,
That long has tower'd in the airy clouds,
Drops like a plummet; Sohrab saw it come,
And sprang aside, quick as a flash; the spear
Hiss'd, and went quivering down into the sand,
Which it sent flying wide; — then Sohrab threw
In turn, and full struck Rustum's shield; sharp rang,
The iron plates rang sharp, but turn'd the spear.
And Rustum seized his club, which none but he
Could wield; an unlopp'd trunk it was, and huge,
Still rough — like those which men in treeless plains
To build them boats fish from the flooded rivers,
Hyphasis or Hydaspes, when, high up
By their dark springs, the wind in winter-time
Hath made in Himalayan forests wrack,
And strewn the channels with torn boughs — so huge
The club which Rustum lifted now, and struck
One stroke; but again Sohrab sprang aside,
Lithe as the glancing snake, and the club came
Thundering to earth, and leapt from Rustum's hand.
And Rustum follow'd his own blow, and fell
To his knees, and with his fingers clutch'd the sand;
And now might Sohrab have unsheathed his sword,
And pierced the mighty Rustum while he lay
Dizzy, and on his knees, and choked with sand;
But he look'd on, and smiled, nor bared his sword,
But courteously drew back, and spoke, and said: —
  'Thou strik'st too hard! that club of thine will float
Upon the summer-floods, and not my bones.
But rise, and be not wroth! not wroth am I;
No, when I see thee, wrath forsakes my soul.
Thou say'st, thou art not Rustum; be it so!
Who art thou then, that canst so touch my soul?
Boy as I am, I have seen battles too —
Have waded foremost in their bloody waves,

And heard their hollow roar of dying men;
But never was my heart thus touch'd before.
Are they from Heaven, these softenings of the heart?
O thou old warrior, let us yield to Heaven!
Come, plant we here in earth our angry spears,
And make a truce, and sit upon this sand,
And pledge each other in red wine, like friends,
And thou shalt talk to me of Rustum's deeds.
There are enough foes in the Persian host,
Whom I may meet, and strike, and feel no pang;
Champions enough Afrasiab has, whom thou
Mayst fight; fight *them,* when they confront thy spear!
But oh, let there be peace 'twixt thee and me!'
  He ceased, but while he spake, Rustum had risen,
And stood erect, trembling with rage; his club
He left to lie, but had regain'd his spear,
Whose fiery point now in his mail'd right-hand
Blazed bright and baleful, like that autumn-star,
The baleful sign of fevers; dust had soil'd
His stately crest, and dimm'd his glittering arms.
His breast heaved, his lips foam'd, and twice his voice
Was choked with rage; at last these words broke way: —
  'Girl! nimble with thy feet, not with thy hands!
Curl'd minion, dancer, coiner of sweet words!
Fight, let me hear thy hateful voice no more!
Thou art not in Afrasiab's gardens now
With Tartar girls, with whom thou art wont to dance;
But on the Oxus-sands, and in the dance
Of battle, and with me, who make no play
Of war; I fight it out, and hand to hand.
Speak not to me of truce, and pledge, and wine!
Remember all thy valour; try thy feints
And cunning! all the pity I had is gone;
Because thou hast shamed me before both the hosts
With thy light skipping tricks, and thy girl's wiles.'
  He spoke, and Sohrab kindled at his taunts,
And he too drew his sword; at once they rush'd
Together, as two eagles on one prey
Come rushing down together from the clouds,
One from the east, one from the west; their shields
Dash'd with a clang together, and a din
Rose, such as that the sinewy woodcutters
Make often in the forest's heart at morn,
Of hewing axes, crashing trees — such blows
Rustum and Sohrab on each other hail'd.

And you would say that sun and stars took part
In that unnatural conflict; for a cloud
Grew suddenly in Heaven, and dark'd the sun
Over the fighters' heads; and a wind rose
Under their feet, and moaning swept the plain,
And in a sandy whirlwind wrapp'd the pair.
In gloom they twain were wrapp'd, and they alone;
For both the on-looking hosts on either hand
Stood in broad daylight, and the sky was pure,
And the sun sparkled on the Oxus stream.
But in the gloom they fought, with bloodshot eyes
And labouring breath; first Rustum struck the shield
Which Sohrab held stiff out; the steel-spiked spear
Rent the tough plates, but fail'd to reach the skin,
And Rustum pluck'd it back with angry groan.
Then Sohrab with his sword smote Rustum's helm,
Nor clove its steel quite through; but all the crest
He shore away, and that proud horsehair plume,
Never till now defiled, sank to the dust;
And Rustum bow'd his head; but then the gloom
Grew blacker, thunder rumbled in the air,
And lightnings rent the cloud; and Ruksh, the horse,
Who stood at hand, utter'd a dreadful cry; —
No horse's cry was that, most like the roar
Of some pain'd desert-lion, who all day
Hath trail'd the hunter's javelin in his side,
And comes at night to die upon the sand.
The two hosts heard that cry, and quaked for fear,
And Oxus curdled as it cross'd his stream.
But Sohrab heard, and quail'd not, but rush'd on,
And struck again; and again Rustum bow'd
His head; but this time all the blade, like glass,
Sprang in a thousand shivers on the helm,
And in the hand the hilt remain'd alone.
Then Rustum raised his head; his dreadful eyes
Glared, and he shook on high his menacing spear,
And shouted: *Rustum!* — Sohrab heard that shout,
And shrank amazed; back he recoil'd one step,
And scann'd with blinking eyes the advancing form;
And then he stood bewilder'd; and he dropp'd
His covering shield, and the spear pierced his side.
He reel'd, and staggering back, sank to the ground;
And then the gloom dispersed, and the wind fell,
And the bright sun broke forth, and melted all
The cloud; and the two armies saw the pair —

Saw Rustum standing, safe upon his feet,
And Sohrab, wounded, on the bloody sand.
Then, with a bitter smile, Rustum began: —
'Sohrab, thou thoughtest in thy mind to kill
A Persian lord this day, and strip his corpse,
And bear thy trophies to Afrasiab's tent.
Or else that the great Rustum would come down
Himself to fight, and that thy wiles would move
His heart to take a gift, and let thee go.
And then that all the Tartar host would praise
Thy courage or thy craft, and spread thy fame,
To glad thy father in his weak old age.
Fool, thou art slain, and by an unknown man!
Dearer to the red jackals shalt thou be
Than to thy friends, and to thy father old.'
And, with a fearless mien, Sohrab replied: —
'Unknown thou art; yet thy fierce vaunt is vain.
Thou dost not slay me, proud and boastful man!
No! Rustum slays me, and this filial heart.
For were I match'd with ten such men as thee,
And I were that which till to-day I was,
They should be lying here, I standing there.
But that belovéd name unnerved my arm —
That name, and something, I confess, in thee,
Which troubles all my heart, and made my shield
Fall; and thy spear transfix'd an unarm'd foe.
And now thou boastest, and insult'st my fate.
But hear thou this, fierce man, tremble to hear:
The mighty Rustum shall avenge my death!
My father, whom I seek through all the world,
He shall avenge my death, and punish thee!'
As when some hunter in the spring hath found
A breeding eagle sitting on her nest,
Upon the craggy isle of a hill-lake,
And pierced her with an arrow as she rose,
And follow'd her to find her where she fell
Far off; — anon her mate comes winging back
From hunting, and a great way off descries
His huddling young left sole; at that, he checks
His pinion, and with short uneasy sweeps
Circles above his eyry, with loud screams
Chiding his mate back to her nest; but she
Lies dying, with the arrow in her side,
In some far stony gorge out of his ken,
A heap of fluttering feathers — never more

Shall the lake glass her, flying over it;
Never the black and dripping precipices
Echo her stormy scream as she sails by —
As that poor bird flies home, nor knows his loss,
So Rustum knew not his own loss, but stood
Over his dying son, and knew him not.
  But, with a cold incredulous voice, he said: —
'What prate is this of fathers and revenge?
The mighty Rustum never had a son.'
  And, with a failing voice, Sohrab replied: —
'Ah yes, he had! and that lost son am I.
Surely the news will one day reach his ear,
Reach Rustum, where he sits, and tarries long,
Somewhere, I know not where, but far from here;
And pierce him like a stab, and make him leap
To arms, and cry for vengeance upon thee.
Fierce man, bethink thee, for an only son!
What will that grief, what will that vengeance be?
Oh, could I live, till I that grief had seen!
Yet him I pity not so much, but her,
My mother, who in Ader-baijan dwells
With that old king, her father, who grows grey
With age, and rules over the valiant Koords.
Her most I pity, who no more will see
Sohrab returning from the Tartar camp,
With spoils and honour, when the war is done.
But a dark rumour will be bruited up,
From tribe to tribe, until it reach her ear;
And then will that defenceless woman learn
That Sohrab will rejoice her sight no more,
But that in battle with a nameless foe,
By the far-distant Oxus, he is slain.'
  He spoke; and as he ceased, he wept aloud,
Thinking of her he left, and his own death.
He spoke; but Rustum listen'd, plunged in thought.
Nor did he yet believe it was his son
Who spoke, although he call'd back names he knew;
For he had had sure tidings that the babe,
Which was in Ader-baijan born to him,
Had been a puny girl, no boy at all —
So that sad mother sent him word, for fear
Rustum should seek the boy, to train in arms.
And so he deem'd that either Sohrab took,
By a false boast, the style of Rustum's son;
Or that men gave it him, to swell his fame.

So deem'd he; yet he listen'd, plunged in thought
And his soul set to grief, as the vast tide
Of the bright rocking Ocean sets to shore
At the full moon; tears gather'd in his eyes;
For he remember'd his own early youth,
And all its bounding rapture; as, at dawn,
The shepherd from his mountain-lodge descries
A far, bright city, smitten by the sun,
Through many rolling clouds — so Rustum saw
His youth; saw Sohrab's mother, in her bloom;
And that old king, her father, who loved well
His wandering guest, and gave him his fair child
With joy; and all the pleasant life they led,
They three, in that long-distant summer-time —
The castle, and the dewy woods, and hunt
And hound, and morn on those delightful hills
In Ader-baijan. And he saw that youth,
Of age and looks to be his own dear son,
Piteous and lovely, lying on the sand,
Like some rich hyacinth which by the scythe
Of an unskilful gardener has been cut,
Mowing the garden grass-plots near its bed,
And lies, a fragrant tower of purple bloom,
On the mown, dying grass — so Sohrab lay,
Lovely in death, upon the common sand.
And Rustum gazed on him with grief, and said: —
'O Sohrab, thou indeed art such a son
Whom Rustum, wert thou his, might well have loved.
Yet here thou errest, Sohrab, or else men
Have told thee false — thou art not Rustum's son.
For Rustum had no son; one child he had —
But one — a girl; who with her mother now
Plies some light female task, nor dreams of us —
Of us she dreams not, nor of wounds, nor war.'
But Sohrab answer'd him in wrath; for now
The anguish of the deep-fix'd spear grew fierce,
And he desired to draw forth the steel,
And let the blood flow free, and so to die —
But first he would convince his stubborn foe;
And, rising sternly on one arm, he said: —
'Man, who art thou who dost deny my words?
Truth sits upon the lips of dying men,
And falsehood, while I lived, was far from mine.
I tell thee, prick'd upon this arm I bear
That seal which Rustum to my mother gave,

That she might prick it on the babe she bore.'
He spoke; and all the blood left Rustum's cheeks,
And his knees totter'd, and he smote his hand
Against his breast, his heavy mailed hand,
That the hard iron corslet clank'd aloud;
And to his heart he press'd the other hand,
And in a hollow voice he spake, and said: —
'Sohrab, that were a proof which could not lie!
If thou show this, then art thou Rustum's son.'
Then with weak hasty fingers, Sohrab loosed
His belt, and near the shoulder bared his arm,
And show'd a sign in faint vermilion points
Prick'd; as a cunning workman, in Pekin,
Pricks with vermilion some clear porcelain vase,
An emperor's gift — at early morn he paints,
And all day long, and, when night comes, the lamp
Lights up his studious forehead and thin hands —
So delicately prick'd the sign appear'd
On Sohrab's arm, the sign of Rustum's seal.
It was that griffin, which of old rear'd Zal,
Rustum's great father, whom they left to die,
A helpless babe, among the mountain-rocks;
Him that kind creature found, and rear'd, and loved —
Then Rustum took it for his glorious sign.
And Sohrab bared that image on his arm,
And himself scann'd it long with mournful eyes,
And then he touch'd it with his hand and said: —
'How say'st thou? Is that sign the proper sign
Of Rustum's son, or of some other man's?'
He spoke; but Rustum gazed, and gazed, and stood
Speechless; and then he utter'd one sharp cry:
O boy — thy father! — and his voice choked there.
And then a dark cloud pass'd before his eyes,
And his head swam, and he sank down to earth.
But Sohrab crawl'd to where he lay, and cast
His arms about his neck, and kiss'd his lips,
And with fond faltering fingers stroked his cheeks,
Trying to call him back to life; and life
Came back to Rustum, and he oped his eyes,
And they stood wide with horror; and he seized
In both his hands the dust which lay around,
And threw it on his head, and smirch'd his hair, —
His hair, and face, and beard, and glittering arms;
And strong convulsive groanings shook his breast,
And his sobs choked him; and he clutch'd his sword,

To draw it, and for ever let life out.
But Sohrab saw his thought, and held his hands,
And with a soothing voice he spake, and said: —
'Father, forbear! for I but meet to-day
The doom which at my birth was written down
In Heaven, and thou art Heaven's unconscious hand.
Surely my heart cried out that it was thou,
When first I saw thee; and thy heart spoke too,
I know it! but fate trod those promptings down
Under its iron heel; fate, fate engaged
The strife, and hurl'd me on my father's spear.
But let us speak no more of this! I find
My father; let me feel that I have found!
Come, sit beside me on this sand, and take
My head betwixt thy hands, and kiss my cheeks,
And wash them with thy tears, and say: *My son!*
Quick! quick! for number'd are my sands of life,
And swift; for like the lightning to this field
I came, and like the wind I go away —
Sudden, and swift, and like a passing wind.
But it was writ in Heaven that this should be.'
So said he, and his voice released the heart
Of Rustum, and his tears broke forth; he cast
His arms round his son's neck, and wept aloud,
And kiss'd him. And awe fell on both the hosts,
When they saw Rustum's grief; and Ruksh, the horse,
With his head bowing to the ground and mane
Sweeping the dust, came near, and in mute woe
First to the one then to the other moved
His head, as if inquiring what their grief
Might mean; and from his dark, compassionate eyes,
The big warm tears roll'd down, and caked the sand.
But Rustum chid him with stern voice, and said: —
'Ruksh, now thou grievest; but, O Ruksh, thy feet
Should first have rotted on their nimble joints,
Or ere they brought thy master to this field!'
But Sohrab look'd upon the horse and said: —
'Is this, then, Ruksh? How often, in past days,
My mother told me of thee, thou brave steed,
My terrible father's terrible horse! and said,
That I should one day find thy lord and thee.
Come, let me lay my hand upon thy mane!
O Ruksh, thou art more fortunate than I;
For thou hast gone where I shall never go,
And snuff'd the breezes of my father's home.

And thou hast trod the sands of Seistan,
And seen the River of Helmund, and the Lake
Of Zirrah; and the aged Zal himself
Has often stroked thy neck, and given thee food,
Corn in a golden platter soak'd with wine,
And said: *O Ruksh! bear Rustum well!* — but I
Have never known my grandsire's furrow'd face,
Nor seen his lofty house in Seistan,
Nor slaked my thirst at the clear Helmund stream;
But lodged among my father's foes, and seen
Afrasiab's cities only, Samarcand,
Bokhara, and lone Khiva in the waste,
And the black Toorkmun tents; and only drunk
The desert rivers, Moorghab and Tejend,
Kohik, and where the Kalmuks feed their sheep,
The northern Sir; and this great Oxus stream,
The yellow Oxus, by whose brink I die.'
　Then, with a heavy groan, Rustum bewail'd: —
'Oh, that its waves were flowing over me!
Oh, that I saw its grains of yellow silt
Roll tumbling in the current o'er my head!'
　But, with a grave mild voice, Sohrab replied: —
'Desire not that, my father! thou must live.
For some are born to do great deeds, and live,
As some are born to be obscured, and die.
Do thou the deeds I die too young to do,
And reap a second glory in thine age;
Thou art my father, and thy gain is mine.
But come! thou seest this great host of men
Which follow me; I pray thee, slay not these!
Let me entreat for them; what have they done?
They follow'd me, my hope, my fame, my star.
Let them all cross the Oxus back in peace.
But me thou must bear hence, not send with them,
But carry me with thee to Seistan,
And place me on a bed, and mourn for me,
Thou, and the snow-hair'd Zal, and all thy friends.
And thou must lay me in that lovely earth,
And heap a stately mound above my bones,
And plant a far-seen pillar over all.
That so the passing horseman on the waste
May see my tomb a great way off, and cry:
Sohrab, the mighty Rustum's son, lies there,
Whom his great father did in ignorance kill!
And I be not forgotten in my grave.'

And, with a mournful voice, Rustum replied: —
'Fear not! as thou hast said, Sohrab, my son,
So shall it be; for I will burn my tents,
And quit the host, and bear thee hence with me,
And carry thee away to Seistan,
And place thee on a bed, and mourn for thee,
With the snow-headed Zal, and all my friends.
And I will lay thee in that lovely earth,
And heap a stately mound above thy bones,
And plant a far-seen pillar over all,
And men shall not forget thee in thy grave.
And I will spare thy host; yea, let them go!
Let them all cross the Oxus back in peace!
What should I do with slaying any more?
For would that all whom I have ever slain
Might be once more alive; my bitterest foes,
And they who were call'd champions in their time,
And through whose death I won that fame I have —
And I were nothing but a common man,
A poor, mean soldier, and without renown,
So thou mightest live too, my son, my son!
Or rather would that I, even I myself,
Might now be lying on this bloody sand,
Near death, and by an ignorant stroke of thine,
Not thou of mine! and I might die, not thou;
And I, not thou, be borne to Seistan;
And Zal might weep above my grave, not thine;
And say: *O son, I weep thee not too sore,*
For willingly, I know, thou met'st thine end!
But now in blood and battles was my youth,
And full of blood and battles is my age,
And I shall never end this life of blood.'
Then, at the point of death, Sohrab replied: —
'A life of blood indeed, thou dreadful man!
But thou shalt yet have peace; only not now,
Not yet! but thou shalt have it on that day,
When thou shalt sail in a high-masted ship,
Thou and the other peers of Kai Khosroo,
Returning home over the salt blue sea,
From laying thy dear master in his grave.'
And Rustum gazed in Sohrab's face, and said: —
'Soon be that day, my son, and deep that sea!
Till then, if fate so wills, let me endure.'
He spoke; and Sohrab smiled on him, and took
The spear, and drew it from his side, and eased

His wound's imperious anguish; but the blood
Came welling from the open gash, and life
Flow'd with the stream; — all down his cold white side
The crimson torrent ran, dim now and soil'd,
Like the soil'd tissue of white violets
Left, freshly gather'd, on their native bank,
By children whom their nurses call with haste
Indoors from the sun's eye; his head droop'd low,
His limbs grew slack; motionless, white, he lay —
White, with eyes closed; only when heavy gasps,
Deep heavy gasps quivering through all his frame,
Convulsed him back to life, he open'd them,
And fix'd them feebly on his father's face;
Till now all strength was ebb'd, and from his limbs
Unwillingly the spirit fled away,
Regretting the warm mansion which it left,
And youth, and bloom, and this delightful world.

So, on the bloody sand, Sohrab lay dead;
And the great Rustum drew his horseman's cloak
Down o'er his face, and sate by his dead son.
As those black granite pillars, once high-rear'd
By Jemshid in Persepolis, to bear
His house, now 'mid their broken flights of steps
Lie prone, enormous, down the mountain side —
So in the sand lay Rustum by his son.

And night came down over the solemn waste,
And the two gazing hosts, and that sole pair,
And darken'd all; and a cold fog, with night,
Crept from the Oxus. Soon a hum arose,
As of a great assembly loosed, and fires
Began to twinkle through the fog; for now
Both armies moved to camp, and took their meal;
The Persians took it on the open sands
Southward, the Tartars by the river marge;
And Rustum and his son were left alone.

But the majestic river floated on,
Out of the mist and hum of that low land,
Into the frosty starlight, and there moved,
Rejoicing through the hush'd Chorasmian waste,
Under the solitary moon; — he flow'd
Right for the polar star, past Orgunjè,
Brimming, and bright, and large; then sands begin
To hem his watery march, and dam his streams,
And split his currents; that for many a league
The shorn and parcell'd Oxus strains along

Through beds of sand and matted rushy isles —
Oxus, forgetting the bright speed he had
In his high mountain-cradle in Pamere,
A foil'd circuitous wanderer — till at last
The long'd-for dash of waves is heard, and wide
His luminous home of waters opens, bright
And tranquil, from whose floor the new-bathed stars
Emerge, and shine upon the Aral Sea.

PHILOMELA

Hark! ah, the nightingale —
The tawny-throated!
Hark, from that moonlit cedar what a burst!
What triumph! hark! — what pain!

O wanderer from a Grecian shore,
Still, after many years, in distant lands,
Still nourishing in thy bewilder'd brain
That wild, unquench'd, deep-sunken, old-world pain —
Say, will it never heal?
And can this fragrant lawn
With its cool trees, and night,
And the sweet, tranquil Thames,
And moonshine, and the dew,
To thy rack'd heart and brain
Afford no balm?
Dost thou to-night behold,
Here, through the moonlight on this English grass,
The unfriendly palace in the Thracian wild?
Dost thou again peruse
With hot cheeks and sear'd eyes
The too clear web, and thy dumb sister's shame?
Dost thou once more assay
Thy flight, and feel come over thee,
Poor fugitive, the feathery change
Once more, and once more seem to make resound
With love and hate, triumph and agony,
Lone Daulis, and the high Cephissian vale?
Listen, Eugenia —
How thick the bursts come crowding through the leaves!
Again — thou hearest?
Eternal passion!
Eternal pain!

THE CHURCH OF BROU

III. THE TOMB

So rest, for ever rest, O princely Pair!
In your high church, 'mid the still mountain-air,
Where horn, and hound, and vassals, never come.
Only the blessed Saints are smiling dumb,
From the rich painted windows of the nave,
On aisle, and transept, and your marble grave;
Where thou, young Prince! shalt never more arise
From the fringed mattress where thy Duchess lies,
On autumn-mornings, when the bugle sounds,
And ride across the drawbridge with thy hounds
To hunt the boar in the crisp woods till eve;
And thou, O Princess! shalt no more receive,
Thou and thy ladies, in the hall of state,
The jaded hunters with their bloody freight,
Coming benighted to the castle-gate.
So sleep, for ever sleep, O marble Pair!
Or, if ye wake, let it be then, when fair
On the carved western front a flood of light
Streams from the setting sun, and colours bright
Prophets, transfigured Saints, and Martyrs brave,
In the vast western window of the nave;
And on the pavement round the Tomb there glints
A chequer-work of glowing sapphire-tints,
And amethyst, and ruby — then unclose
Your eyelids on the stone where ye repose,
And from your broider'd pillows lift your heads,
And rise upon your cold white marble beds;
And, looking down on the warm rosy tints,
Which chequer, at your feet, the illumined flints,
Say: *What is this? we are in bliss — forgiven —*
Behold the pavement of the courts of Heaven!
Or let it be on autumn nights, when rain
Doth rustlingly above your heads complain
On the smooth leaden roof, and on the walls
Shedding her pensive light at intervals
The moon through the clere-story windows shines,
And the wind washes through the mountain-pines.
Then, gazing up 'mid the dim pillars high,
The foliaged marble forest where ye lie,
Hush, ye will say, *it is eternity!*

This is the glimmering verge of Heaven, and these
The columns of the heavenly palaces!
And, in the sweeping of the wind, your ear
The passage of the Angels' wings will hear,
And on the lichen-crusted leads above
The rustle of the eternal rain of love.

A DREAM

Was it a dream? We sail'd, I thought we sail'd,
Martin and I, down a green Alpine stream,
Border'd, each bank, with pines; the morning sun,
On the wet umbrage of their glossy tops,
On the red pinings of their forest-floor,
Drew a warm scent abroad; behind the pines
The mountain-skirts, with all their sylvan change
Of bright-leaf'd chestnuts and moss'd walnut-trees
And the frail scarlet-berried ash, began.
Swiss chalets glitter'd on the dewy slopes,
And from some swarded shelf, high up, there came
Notes of wild pastoral music — over all
Ranged, diamond-bright, the eternal wall of snow.
Upon the mossy rocks at the stream's edge,
Back'd by the pines, a plank-built cottage stood,
Bright in the sun; the climbing gourd-plant's leaves
Muffled its walls, and on the stone-strewn roof
Lay the warm golden gourds; golden, within,
Under the eaves, peer'd rows of Indian corn.
We shot beneath the cottage with the stream.
On the brown, rude-carved balcony, two forms
Came forth — Olivia's, Marguerite! and thine.
Clad were they both in white, flowers in their breast;
Straw hats bedeck'd their heads, with ribbons blue,
Which danced, and on their shoulders, fluttering, play'd.
They saw us, they conferr'd; their bosoms heaved,
And more than mortal impulse fill'd their eyes.
Their lips moved; their white arms, waved eagerly,
Flash'd once, like falling streams; we rose, we gazed.
One moment, on the rapid's top, our boat
Hung poised — and then the darting river of Life
(Such now, methought, it was), the river of Life,
Loud thundering, bore us by; swift, swift it foam'd,

Black under cliffs it raced, round headlands shone.
Soon the plank'd cottage by the sun-warm'd pines
Faded — the moss — the rocks; us burning plains,
Bristled with cities, us the sea received.

REQUIESCAT

Strew on her roses, roses,
And never a spray of yew!
In quiet she reposes;
Ah, would that I did too!

Her mirth the world required;
She bathed it in smiles of glee.
But her heart was tired, tired,
And now they let her be.

Her life was turning, turning,
In mazes of heat and sound.
But for peace her soul was yearning,
And now peace laps her round.

Her cabin'd, ample spirit,
It flutter'd and fail'd for breath.
To-night it doth inherit
The vasty hall of death.

THE SCHOLAR-GIPSY

Go, for they call you, shepherd, from the hill;
Go, shepherd, and untie the wattled cotes!
No longer leave thy wistful flock unfed,
Nor let thy bawling fellows rack their throats,
Nor the cropp'd herbage shoot another head.
But when the fields are still,
And the tired men and dogs all gone to rest,
And only the white sheep are sometimes seen
Cross and recross the strips of moon-blanch'd green,
Come, shepherd, and again begin the quest!

Here, where the reaper was at work of late —
In this high field's dark corner, where he leaves

His coat, his basket, and his earthen cruse,
And in the sun all morning binds the sheaves,
Then here, at noon, comes back his stores to use —
Here will I sit and wait,
While to my ear from uplands far away
The bleating of the folded flocks is borne,
With distant cries of reapers in the corn —
All the live murmur of a summer's day.

Screen'd is this nook o'er the high, half-reap'd field,
And here till sun-down, shepherd! will I be.
Through the thick corn the scarlet poppies peep,
And round green roots and yellowing stalks I see
Pale pink convolvulus in tendrils creep;
And air-swept lindens yield
Their scent, and rustle down their perfumed showers
Of bloom on the bent grass where I am laid,
And bower me from the August sun with shade;
And the eye travels down to Oxford's towers.

And near me on the grass lies Glanvil's book —
Come, let me read the oft-read tale again!
The story of the Oxford scholar poor,
Of pregnant parts and quick inventive brain,
Who, tired of knocking at preferment's door,
One summer-morn forsook
His friends, and went to learn the gipsy-lore,
And roam'd the world with that wild brotherhood,
And came, as most men deem'd, to little good,
But came to Oxford and his friends no more.

But once, years after, in the country-lanes,
Two scholars, whom at college erst he knew,
Met him, and of his way of life enquired;
Whereat he answer'd, that the gipsy-crew,
His mates, had arts to rule as they desired
The workings of men's brains,
And they can bind them to what thoughts they will.
'And I,' he said, 'the secret of their art,
When fully learn'd, will to the world impart;
But it needs heaven-sent moments for this skill.'

This said, he left them, and return'd no more. —
But rumours hung about the country-side,

That the lost Scholar long was seen to stray,
Seen by rare glimpses, pensive and tongue-tied,
In hat of antique shape, and cloak of grey,
The same the gipsies wore.
Shepherds had met him on the Hurst in spring;
At some lone alehouse in the Berkshire moors,
On the warm ingle-bench, the smock-frock'd boors
Had found him seated at their entering,

But, 'mid their drink and clatter, he would fly.
And I myself seem half to know thy looks,
And put the shepherds, wanderer! on thy trace;
And boys who in lone wheatfields scare the rooks
I ask if thou hast pass'd their quiet place;
Or in my boat I lie
Moor'd to the cool bank in the summer-heats,
'Mid wide grass meadows which the sunshine fills,
And watch the warm, green-muffled Cumner hills,
And wonder if thou haunt'st their shy retreats.

For most, I know, thou lov'st retired ground!
Thee at the ferry Oxford riders blithe,
Returning home on summer-nights, have met
Crossing the stripling Thames at Bab-lock-hithe,
Trailing in the cool stream thy fingers wet,
As the punt's rope chops round;
And leaning backward in a pensive dream,
And fostering in thy lap a heap of flowers
Pluck'd in shy fields and distant Wychwood bowers,
And thine eyes resting on the moonlit stream.

And then they land, and thou art seen no more! —
Maidens, who from the distant hamlets come
To dance around the Fyfield elm in May,
Oft through the darkening fields have seen thee roam,
Or cross a stile into the public way.
Oft thou hast given them store
Of flowers — the frail-leaf'd, white anemony,
Dark bluebells drench'd with dews of summer eves,
And purple orchises with spotted leaves —
But none hath words she can report of thee.

And, above Godstow Bridge, when hay-time's here
In June, and many a scythe in sunshine flames,
Men who through those wide fields of breezy grass

Where black-wing'd swallows haunt the glittering Thames,
To bathe in the abandon'd lasher pass,
Have often pass'd thee near
Sitting upon the river bank o'ergrown;
Mark'd thine outlandish garb, thy figure spare,
Thy dark vague eyes, and soft abstracted air —
But, when they came from bathing, thou wast gone!

At some lone homestead in the Cumner hills,
Where at her open door the housewife darns,
Thou hast been seen, or hanging on a gate
To watch the threshers in the mossy barns.
Children, who early range these slopes and late
For cresses from the rills,
Have known thee eying, all an April-day,
The springing pastures and the feeding kine;
And mark'd thee, when the stars come out and shine,
Through the long dewy grass move slow away.

In autumn, on the skirts of Bagley Wood —
Where most the gipsies by the turf-edged way
Pitch their smoked tents, and every bush you see
With scarlet patches tagg'd and shreds of grey,
Above the forest-ground called Thessaly —
The blackbird, picking food,
Sees thee, nor stops his meal, nor fears at all;
So often has he known thee past him stray,
Rapt, twirling in thy hand a wither'd spray,
And waiting for the spark from heaven to fall.

And once, in winter, on the causeway chill
Where home through flooded fields foot-travellers go,
Have I not pass'd thee on the wooden bridge,
Wrapt in thy cloak and battling with the snow,
Thy face tow'rd Hinksey and its wintry ridge?
And thou hast climb'd the hill,
And gain'd the white brow of the Cumner range;
Turn'd once to watch, while thick the snowflakes fall,
The line of festal light in Christ-Church hall —
Then sought thy straw in some sequester'd grange.

But what — I dream! Two hundred years are flown
Since first thy story ran through Oxford halls,
And the grave Glanvil did the tale inscribe
That thou wert wander'd from the studious walls

To learn strange arts, and join a gipsy-tribe;
And thou from earth art gone
Long since, and in some quiet churchyard laid —
Some country-nook, where o'er thy unknown grave
Tall grasses and white flowering nettles wave,
Under a dark, red-fruited yew-tree's shade.

— No, no, thou hast not felt the lapse of hours!
For what wears out the life of mortal men?
'Tis that from change to change their being rolls;
'Tis that repeated shocks, again, again,
Exhaust the energy of strongest souls
And numb the elastic powers.
Till having used our nerves with bliss and teen,
And tired upon a thousand schemes our wit,
To the just-pausing Genius we remit
Our worn-out life, and are — what we have been.

Thou hast not lived, why should'st thou perish, so?
Thou hadst *one* aim, *one* business, *one* desire;
Else wert thou long since number'd with the dead!
Else hadst thou spent, like other men, thy fire!
The generations of thy peers are fled,
And we ourselves shall go;
But thou possessest an immortal lot,
And we imagine thee exempt from age
And living as thou liv'st on Glanvil's page,
Because thou hadst — what we, alas! have not.

For early didst thou leave the world, with powers
Fresh, undiverted to the world without,
Firm to their mark, not spent on other things;
Free from the sick fatigue, the languid doubt,
Which much to have tried, in much been baffled, brings.
O life unlike to ours!
Who fluctuate idly without term or scope,
Of whom each strives, nor knows for what he strives,
And each half lives a hundred different lives;
Who wait like thee, but not, like thee, in hope.

Thou waitest for the spark from heaven! and we,
Light half-believers of our casual creeds,
Who never deeply felt, nor clearly will'd,
Whose insight never has borne fruit in deeds,
Whose vague resolves never have been fulfill'd;

For whom each year we see
Breeds new beginnings, disappointments new;
Who hesitate and falter life away,
And lose to-morrow the ground won to-day —
Ah! do not we, wanderer! await it too?

Yes, we await it! — but it still delays,
And then we suffer! and amongst us one,
Who most has suffer'd, takes dejectedly
His seat upon the intellectual throne;
And all his store of sad experience he
Lays bare of wretched days;
Tells us his misery's birth and growth and signs,
And how the dying spark of hope was fed,
And how the breast was soothed, and how the head,
And all his hourly varied anodynes.

This for our wisest! and we others pine,
And wish the long unhappy dream would end,
And waive all claim to bliss, and try to bear;
With close-lipp'd patience for our only friend,
Sad patience, too near neighbour to despair —
But none has hope like thine!
Thou through the fields and through the woods dost stray,
Roaming the country-side, a truant boy,
Nursing thy project in unclouded joy,
And every doubt long blown by time away.

O born in days when wits were fresh and clear,
And life ran gaily as the sparkling Thames;
Before this strange disease of modern life,
With its sick hurry, its divided aims,
Its heads o'ertax'd, its palsied hearts, was rife —
Fly hence, our contact fear!
Still fly, plunge deeper in the bowering wood!
Averse, as Dido did with gesture stern
From her false friend's approach in Hades turn,
Wave us away, and keep thy solitude!

Still nursing the unconquerable hope,
Still clutching the inviolable shade,
With a free, onward impulse brushing through,
By night, the silver'd branches of the glade —
Far on the forest-skirts, where none pursue.
On some mild pastoral slope

Emerge, and resting on the moonlit pales
Freshen thy flowers as in former years
With dew, or listen with enchanted ears,
From the dark dingles, to the nightingales!

But fly our paths, our feverish contact fly!
For strong the infection of our mental strife,
Which, though it gives no bliss, yet spoils for rest;
And we should win thee from thy own fair life,
Like us distracted, and like us unblest.
Soon, soon thy cheer would die,
Thy hopes grow timorous, and unfix'd thy powers,
And thy clear aims be cross and shifting made;
And then thy glad perennial youth would fade,
Fade, and grow old at last, and die like ours.

Then fly our greetings, fly our speech and smiles!
— As some grave Tyrian trader, from the sea,
Descried at sunrise an emerging prow
Lifting the cool-hair'd creepers stealthily,
The fringes of a southward-facing brow
Among the Ægæan isles;
And saw the merry Grecian coaster come,
Freighted with amber grapes, and Chian wine,
Green, bursting figs, and tunnies steep'd in brine —
And knew the intruders on his ancient home,

The young light-hearted masters of the waves —
And snatch'd his rudder, and shook out more sail;
And day and night held on indignantly
O'er the blue Midland waters with the gale,
Betwixt the Syrtes and soft Sicily,
To where the Atlantic raves
Outside the western straits; and unbent sails
There, where down cloudy cliffs, through sheets of foam,
Shy traffickers, the dark Iberians come;
And on the beach undid his corded bales.

New Poems

(1867)

THYRSIS

A MONODY, *to commemorate the author's friend,*
ARTHUR HUGH CLOUGH, *who died at Florence*, 1861

How changed is here each spot man makes or fills!
In the two Hinkseys nothing keeps the same;
The village street its haunted mansion lacks,
And from the sign is gone Sibylla's name,
And from the roofs the twisted chimney-stacks —
Are ye too changed, ye hills?
See, 'tis no foot of unfamiliar men
To-night from Oxford up your pathway strays!
Here came I often, often, in old days —
Thyrsis and I; we still had Thyrsis then.

Runs it not here, the track by Childsworth Farm,
Past the high wood, to where the elm-tree crowns
The hill behind whose ridge the sunset flames?
The signal-elm, that looks on Ilsley Downs,
The Vale, the three lone weirs, the youthful Thames? —
This winter-eve is warm,
Humid the air! leafless, yet soft as spring,
The tender purple spray on copse and briers!
And that sweet city with her dreaming spires,
She needs not June for beauty's heightening,

Lovely all times she lies, lovely to-night! —
Only, methinks, some loss of habit's power
Befalls me wandering through this upland dim.
Once pass'd I blindfold here, at any hour;
Now seldom come I, since I came with him.
That single elm-tree bright

Against the west — I miss it! is it gone?
We prized it dearly; while it stood, we said,
Our friend, the Gipsy-Scholar, was not dead;
While the tree lived, he in these fields lived on.

Too rare, too rare, grow now my visits here,
But once I knew each field, each flower, each stick;
And with the country-folk acquaintance made
By barn in threshing-time, by new-built rick.
Here, too, our shepherd-pipes we first assay'd.
Ah me! this many a year
My pipe is lost, my shepherd's holiday!
Needs must I lose them, needs with heavy heart
Into the world and wave of men depart;
But Thyrsis of his own will went away.

It irk'd him to be here, he could not rest.
He loved each simple joy the country yields,
He loved his mates; but yet he could not keep,
For that a shadow lour'd on the fields,
Here with the shepherds and the silly sheep.
Some life of men unblest
He knew, which made him droop, and fill'd his head.
He went; his piping took a troubled sound
Of storms that rage outside our happy ground;
He could not wait their passing, he is dead.

So, some tempestuous morn in early June,
When the year's primal burst of bloom is o'er,
Before the roses and the longest day —
When garden-walks and all the grassy floor
With blossoms red and white of fallen May
And chestnut-flowers are strewn —
So have I heard the cuckoo's parting cry,
From the wet field, through the vext garden-trees,
Come with the volleying rain and tossing breeze:
The bloom is gone, and with the bloom go I!

Too quick despairer, wherefore wilt thou go?
Soon will the high Midsummer pomps come on,
Soon will the musk carnations break and swell,
Soon shall we have gold-dusted snapdragon,
Sweet-William with his homely cottage-smell,
And stocks in fragrant blow;
Roses that down the alleys shine afar,

And open, jasmine-muffled lattices,
And groups under the dreaming garden-trees,
And the full moon, and the white evening-star.

He hearkens not! light comer, he is flown!
What matters it? next year he will return,
And we shall have him in the sweet spring-days,
With whitening hedges, and uncrumpling fern,
And blue-bells trembling by the forest-ways,
And scent of hay new-mown.
But Thyrsis never more we swains shall see;
See him come back, and cut a smoother reed,
And blow a strain the world at last shall heed—
For Time, not Corydon, hath conquer'd thee!

Alack, for Corydon no rival now!—
But when Sicilian shepherds lost a mate,
Some good survivor with his flute would go,
Piping a ditty sad for Bion's fate;
And cross the unpermitted ferry's flow,
And relax Pluto's brow,
And make leap up with joy the beauteous head
Of Proserpine, among whose crowned hair
Are flowers first open'd on Sicilian air,
And flute his friend, like Orpheus, from the dead.

O easy access to the hearer's grace
When Dorian shepherds sang to Proserpine!
For she herself had trod Sicilian fields,
She knew the Dorian water's gush divine,
She knew each lily white which Enna yields,
Each rose with blushing face;
She loved the Dorian pipe, the Dorian strain.
But ah, of our poor Thames she never heard!
Her foot the Cumner cowslips never stirr'd;
And we should tease her with our plaint in vain!

Well! wind-dispersed and vain the words will be,
Yet, Thyrsis, let me give my grief its hour
In the old haunt, and find our tree-topp'd hill!
Who, if not I, for questing here hath power?
I know the wood which hides the daffodil,
I know the Fyfield tree,
I know what white, what purple fritillaries
The grassy harvest of the river-fields,

Above by Ensham, down by Sandford, yields,
And what sedged brooks are Thames's tributaries;

I know these slopes; who knows them if not I? —
But many a dingle on the loved hill-side,
With thorns once studded, old, white-blossom'd trees,
Where thick the cowslips grew, and far descried
High tower'd the spikes of purple orchises,
Hath since our day put by
The coronals of that forgotten time;
Down each green bank hath gone the ploughboy's team,
And only in the hidden brookside gleam
Primroses, orphans of the flowery prime.

Where is the girl, who by the boatman's door,
Above the locks, above the boating throng,
Unmoor'd our skiff when through the Wytham flats,
Red loosestrife and blond meadow-sweet among
And darting swallows and light water-gnats,
We track'd the shy Thames shore?
Where are the mowers, who, as the tiny swell
Of our boat passing heaved the river-grass,
Stood with suspended scythe to see us pass? —
They all are gone, and thou art gone as well!

Yes, thou art gone! and round me too the night
In ever-nearing circle weaves her shade.
I see her veil draw soft across the day,
I feel her slowly chilling breath invade
The cheek grown thin, the brown hair sprent with grey;
I feel her finger light
Laid pausefully upon life's headlong train; —
The foot less prompt to meet the morning dew,
The heart less bounding at emotion new,
And hope, once crush'd, less quick to spring again.

And long the way appears, which seem'd so short
To the less practised eye of sanguine youth;
And high the mountain-tops, in cloudy air,
The mountain-tops where is the throne of Truth,
Tops in life's morning-sun so bright and bare!
Unbreachable the fort
Of the long-batter'd world uplifts its wall;
And strange and vain the earthly turmoil grows,

And near and real the charm of thy repose,
And night as welcome as a friend would fall.

But hush! the upland hath a sudden loss
Of quiet! — Look, adown the dusk hill-side,
A troop of Oxford hunters going home,
As in old days, jovial and talking, ride!
From hunting with the Berkshire hounds they come.
Quick! let me fly, and cross
Into yon farther field! — 'Tis done; and see,
Back'd by the sunset, which doth glorify
The orange and pale violet evening-sky,
Bare on its lonely ridge, the Tree! the Tree!

I take the omen! Eve lets down her veil,
The white fog creeps from bush to bush about,
The west unflushes, the high stars grow bright,
And in the scatter'd farms the lights come out.
I cannot reach the signal-tree to-night,
Yet, happy omen, hail!
Hear it from thy broad lucent Arno-vale
(For there thine earth-forgetting eyelids keep
The morningless and unawakening sleep
Under the flowery oleanders pale),

Hear it, O Thyrsis, still our tree is there! —
Ah, vain! These English fields, this upland dim,
These brambles pale with mist engarlanded,
That lone, sky-pointing tree, are not for him;
To a boon southern country he is fled,
And now in happier air,
Wandering with the great Mother's train divine
(And purer or more subtle soul than thee,
I trow, the mighty Mother doth not see)
Within a folding of the Apennine,

Thou hearest the immortal chants of old! —
Putting his sickle to the perilous grain
In the hot cornfield of the Phrygian king,
For thee the Lityerses-song again
Young Daphnis with his silver voice doth sing;
Sings his Sicilian fold,
His sheep, his hapless love, his blinded eyes —
And how a call celestial round him rang,

And heavenward from the fountain-brink he sprang,
And all the marvel of the golden skies.

There thou art gone, and me thou leavest here
Sole in these fields! yet will I not despair.
Despair I will not, while I yet descry
'Neath the mild canopy of English air
That lonely tree against the western sky.
Still, still these slopes, 'tis clear,
Our Gipsy-Scholar haunts, outliving thee!
Fields where soft sheep from cages pull the hay,
Woods with anemonies in flower till May,
Know him a wanderer still; then why not me?

A fugitive and gracious light he seeks,
Shy to illumine; and I seek it too.
This does not come with houses or with gold,
With place, with honour, and a flattering crew;
'Tis not in the world's market bought and sold —
But the smooth-slipping weeks
Drop by, and leave its seeker still untired;
Out of the heed of mortals he is gone,
He wends unfollow'd, he must house alone;
Yet on he fares, by his own heart inspired.

Thou too, O Thyrsis, on like quest wast bound;
Thou wanderedst with me for a little hour!
Men gave thee nothing; but this happy quest,
If men esteem'd thee feeble, gave thee power,
If men procured thee trouble, gave thee rest.
And this rude Cumner ground,
Its fir-topped Hurst, its farms, its quiet fields,
Here cam'st thou in thy jocund youthful time,
Here was thine height of strength, thy golden prime!
And still the haunt beloved a virtue yields.

What though the music of thy rustic flute
Kept not for long its happy, country tone;
Lost it too soon, and learnt a stormy note
Of men contention-tost, of men who groan,
Which task'd thy pipe too sore, and tired thy throat —
It fail'd, and thou wast mute!
Yet hadst thou alway visions of our light,
And long with men of care thou couldst not stay,

And soon thy foot resumed its wandering way,
Left human haunt, and on alone till night.

Too rare, too rare, grow now my visits here!
'Mid city-noise, not, as with thee of yore,
Thyrsis! in reach of sheep-bells is my home.
— Then through the great town's harsh, heart-wearying roar,
Let in thy voice a whisper often come,
To chase fatigue and fear:
Why faintest thou? I wander'd till I died.
Roam on! The light we sought is shining still.
Dost thou ask proof? Our tree yet crowns the hill,
Our Scholar travels yet the loved hill-side.

CALAIS SANDS

A THOUSAND knights have rein'd their steeds
To watch this line of sand-hills run,
Along the never-silent Strait,
To Calais glittering in the sun;

To look tow'rd Ardres' Golden Field
Across this wide aërial plain,
Which glows as if the Middle Age
Were gorgeous upon earth again.

Oh, that to share this famous scene,
I saw, upon the open sand,
Thy lovely presence at my side,
Thy shawl, thy look, thy smile, thy hand!

How exquisite thy voice would come,
My darling, on this lonely air!
How sweetly would the fresh sea-breeze
Shake loose some band of soft brown hair!

Yet now my glance but once hath roved
O'er Calais and its famous plain;
To England's cliffs my gaze is turn'd,
On the blue strait mine eyes I strain.

Thou comest! Yes! the vessel's cloud
Hangs dark upon the rolling sea.

Oh, that yon sea-bird's wings were mine,
To win one instant's glimpse of thee!

I must not spring to grasp thy hand,
To woo thy smile, to seek thine eye;
But I may stand far off, and gaze,
And watch thee pass unconscious by,

And spell thy looks, and guess thy thoughts,
Mixt with the idlers on the pier. —
Ah, might I always rest unseen,
So I might have thee always near!

To-morrow hurry through the fields
Of Flanders to the storied Rhine!
To-night those soft-fringed eyes shall close
Beneath one roof, my queen! with mine.

DOVER BEACH

THE sea is calm to-night.
The tide is full, the moon lies fair
Upon the straits; — on the French coast the light
Gleams and is gone; the cliffs of England stand,
Glimmering and vast, out in the tranquil bay.
Come to the window, sweet is the night-air!
Only, from the long line of spray
Where the sea meets the moon-blanch'd land,
Listen! you hear the grating roar
Of pebbles which the waves draw back, and fling,
At their return, up the high strand,
Begin, and cease, and then again begin,
With tremulous cadence slow, and bring
The eternal note of sadness in.

Sophocles long ago
Heard it on the Ægæan, and it brought
Into his mind the turbid ebb and flow
Of human misery; we
Find also in the sound a thought,
Hearing it by this distant northern sea.

The Sea of Faith
Was once, too, at the full, and round earth's shore
Lay like the folds of a bright girdle furl'd.
But now I only hear
Its melancholy, long, withdrawing roar,
Retreating, to the breath
Of the night-wind, down the vast edges drear
And naked shingles of the world.

Ah, love, let us be true
To one another! for the world, which seems
To lie before us like a land of dreams,
So various, so beautiful, so new,
Hath really neither joy, nor love, nor light,
Nor certitude, nor peace, nor help for pain;
And we are here as on a darkling plain
Swept with confused alarms of struggle and flight,
Where ignorant armies clash by night.

STANZAS FROM CARNAC

Far on its rocky knoll descried
Saint Michael's chapel cuts the sky.
I climb'd; — beneath me, bright and wide,
Lay the lone coast of Brittany.

Bright in the sunset, weird and still,
It lay beside the Atlantic wave,
As though the wizard Merlin's will
Yet charm'd it from his forest-grave.

Behind me on their grassy sweep,
Bearded with lichen, scrawl'd and grey,
The giant stones of Carnac sleep,
In the mild evening of the May.

No priestly stern procession now
Moves through their rows of pillars old;
No victims bleed, no Druids bow —
Sheep make the daisied aisles their fold.

From bush to bush the cuckoo flies,
The orchis red gleams everywhere;

Gold furze with broom in blossom vies,
The blue-bells perfume all the air.

And o'er the glistening, lonely land,
Rise up, all round, the Christian spires;
The church of Carnac, by the strand,
Catches the westering sun's last fires.

And there, across the watery way,
See, low above the tide at flood,
The sickle-sweep of Quiberon Bay,
Whose beach once ran with loyal blood!

And beyond that, the Atlantic wide! —
All round, no soul, no boat, no hail;
But, on the horizon's verge descried,
Hangs, touch'd with light, one snowy sail!

Ah! where is he, who should have come
Where that far sail is passing now,
Past the Loire's mouth, and by the foam
Of Finistère's unquiet brow,

Home, round into the English wave?
— He tarries where the Rock of Spain
Mediterranean waters lave;
He enters not the Atlantic main.

Oh, could he once have reach'd this air
Freshen'd by plunging tides, by showers!
Have felt this breath he loved, of fair
Cool northern fields, and grass, and flowers!

He long'd for it — press'd on. — In vain!
At the Straits fail'd that spirit brave.
The south was parent of his pain,
The south is mistress of his grave.

A SOUTHERN NIGHT

THE sandy spits, the shore-lock'd lakes,
Melt into open, moonlit sea;
The soft Mediterranean breaks
At my feet, free.

Dotting the fields of corn and vine,
  Like ghosts the huge, gnarl'd olives stand.
Behind, that lovely mountain-line!
    While, by the strand,

Cette, with its glistening houses white,
  Curves with the curving beach away
To where the lighthouse beacons bright
    Far in the bay.

Ah! such a night, so soft, so lone,
  So moonlit, saw me once of yore
Wander unquiet, and my own
    Vext heart deplore.

But now that trouble is forgot;
  Thy memory, thy pain, to-night,
My brother! and thine early lot,
    Possess me quite.

The murmur of this Midland deep
  Is heard to-night around thy grave,
There, where Gibraltar's cannon'd steep
    O'erfrowns the wave.

For there, with bodily anguish keen,
  With Indian heats at last fordone,
With public toil and private teen —
    Thou sank'st, alone.

Slow to a stop, at morning grey,
  I see the smoke-crown'd vessel come;
Slow round her paddles dies away
    The seething foam.

A boat lower'd from her side;
  Ah, gently place him on the bench!
That spirit — if all have not yet died —
    A breath might quench.

Is this the eye, the footstep fast,
  The mien of youth we used to see,
Poor, gallant boy! — for such thou wast,
    Still art, to me.

The limbs their wonted tasks refuse;
  The eyes are glazed, thou canst not speak;
And whiter than thy white burnous
    That wasted cheek!

Enough! The boat, with quiet shock,
  Unto its haven coming nigh,
Touches, and on Gibraltar's rock
    Lands thee to die.

Ah me! Gibraltar's strand is far,
  But farther yet across the brine
Thy dear wife's ashes buried are,
    Remote from thine.

For there, where morning's sacred fount
  Its golden rain on earth confers,
The snowy Himalayan Mount
    O'ershadows hers.

Strange irony of fate, alas,
  Which, for two jaded English, saves,
When from their dusty life they pass,
    Such peaceful graves!

In cities should we English lie,
  Where cries are rising ever new,
And men's incessant stream goes by —
    We who pursue

Our business with unslackening stride,
  Traverse in troops, with care-fill'd breast,
The soft Mediterranean side,
    The Nile, the East,

And see all sights from pole to pole,
  And glance, and nod, and bustle by,
And never once possess our soul
    Before we die.

Not by those hoary Indian hills,
  Not by this gracious Midland sea
Whose floor to-night sweet moonshine fills,
    Should our graves be.

Some sage, to whom the world was dead,
  And men were specks, and life a play;
Who made the roots of trees his bed,
      And once a day

With staff and gourd his way did bend
  To villages and homes of man,
For food to keep him till he end
      His mortal span

And the pure goal of being reach;
  Hoar-headed, wrinkled, clad in white,
Without companion, without speech,
      By day and night

Pondering God's mysteries untold,
  And tranquil as the glacier-snows
He by those Indian mountains old
      Might well repose.

Some grey crusading knight austere,
  Who bore Saint Louis company,
And came home hurt to death, and here
      Landed to die;

Some youthful troubadour, whose tongue
  Fill'd Europe once with his love-pain,
Who here outworn had sunk, and sung
      His dying strain;

Some girl, who here from castle-bower,
  With furtive step and cheek of flame,
'Twixt myrtle-hedges all in flower
      By moonlight came

To meet her pirate-lover's ship;
  And from the wave-kiss'd marble stair
Beckon'd him on, with quivering lip
      And floating hair;

And lived some moons in happy trance,
  Then learnt his death and pined away —
Such by these waters of romance
      'Twas meet to lay.

But you — a grave for knight or sage,
Romantic, solitary, still,
O spent ones of a work-day age!
Befits you ill.

So sang I; but the midnight breeze,
Down to the brimm'd, moon-charmed main,
Comes softly through the olive-trees,
And checks my strain.

I think of her, whose gentle tongue
All plaint in her own cause controll'd;
Of thee I think, my brother! young
In heart, high-soul'd —

That comely face, that cluster'd brow,
That cordial hand, that bearing free,
I see them still, I see them now,
Shall always see!

And what but gentleness untired,
And what but noble feeling warm,
Wherever shown, howe'er inspired,
Is grace, is charm?

What else is all these waters are,
What else is steep'd in lucid sheen,
What else is bright, what else is fair,
What else serene?

Mild o'er her grave, ye mountains, shine!
Gently by his, ye waters, glide!
To that in you which is divine
They were allied.

FRAGMENT OF CHORUS OF A 'DEJANEIRA'

O FRIVOLOUS mind of man,
Light ignorance, and hurrying, unsure thoughts!
Though man bewails you not,
How *I* bewail you!

Little in your prosperity
Do you seek counsel of the Gods.
Proud, ignorant, self-adored, you live alone.
In profound silence stern,
Among their savage gorges and cold springs,
Unvisited remain
The great oracular shrines.

Thither in your adversity
Do you betake yourselves for light,
But strangely misinterpret all you hear.
For you will not put on
New hearts with the enquirer's holy robe,
And purged, considerate minds.

And him on whom, at the end
Of toil and dolour untold,
The Gods have said that repose
At last shall descend undisturb'd —
Him you expect to behold
In an easy old age, in a happy home;
No end but this you praise.

But him, on whom, in the prime
Of life, with vigour undimm'd,
With unspent mind, and a soul
Unworn, undebased, undecay'd,
Mournfully grating, the gates
Of the city of death have for ever closed —
Him, I count *him,* well-starr'd.

GROWING OLD

What is it to grow old?
Is it to lose the glory of the form,
The lustre of the eye?
Is it for beauty to forego her wreath?
— Yes, but not this alone.

Is it to feel our strength —
Not our bloom only, but our strength — decay?
Is it to feel each limb

Grow stiffer, every function less exact,
Each nerve more loosely strung?

Yes, this, and more; but not
Ah, 'tis not what in youth we dream'd 'twould be!
'Tis not to have our life
Mellow'd and soften'd as with sunset-glow,
A golden day's decline.

'Tis not to see the world
As from a height, with rapt prophetic eyes,
And heart profoundly stirr'd;
And weep, and feel the fulness of the past,
The years that are no more.

It is to spend long days
And not once feel that we were ever young;
It is to add, immured
In the hot prison of the present, month
To month with weary pain.

It is to suffer this,
And feel but half, and feebly, what we feel.
Deep in our hidden heart
Festers the dull remembrance of a change,
But no emotion — none.

It is — last stage of all —
When we are frozen up within, and quite
The phantom of ourselves,
To hear the world applaud the hollow ghost
Which blamed the living man.

EPILOGUE TO LESSING'S LAOCOÖN

ONE morn as through Hyde Park we walk'd,
My friend and I, by chance we talk'd
Of Lessing's famed Laocoön;
And after we awhile had gone
In Lessing's track, and tried to see
What painting is, what poetry —

Diverging to another thought,
'Ah,' cries my friend, 'but who hath taught
Why music and the other arts
Oftener perform aright their parts
Than poetry? why she, than they,
Fewer fine successes can display?

'For 'tis so, surely! Even in Greece,
Where best the poet framed his piece,
Even in that Phœbus-guarded ground
Pausanias on his travels found
Good poems, if he look'd, more rare
(Though many) than good statues were —
For these, in truth, were everywhere.
Of bards full many a stroke divine
In Dante's, Petrarch's, Tasso's line,
The land of Ariosto show'd;
And yet, e'en there, the canvas glow'd
With triumphs, a yet ampler brood,
Of Raphael and his brotherhood.
And nobly perfect, in our day
Of haste, half-work, and disarray,
Profound yet touching, sweet yet strong,
Hath risen Goethe's, Wordsworth's song;
Yet even I (and none will bow
Deeper to these) must needs allow,
They yield us not, to soothe our pains,
Such multitude of heavenly strains
As from the kings of sound are blown,
Mozart, Beethoven, Mendelssohn.'

While thus my friend discoursed, we pass
Out of the path, and take the grass.
The grass had still the green of May,
And still the unblacken'd elms were gay;
The kine were resting in the shade,
The flies a summer-murmer made.
Bright was the morn and south the air;
The soft-couch'd cattle were as fair
As those which pastured by the sea,
That old-world morn, in Sicily,
When on the beach the Cyclops lay,
And Galatea from the bay
Mock'd her poor lovelorn giant's lay.
'Behold,' I said, 'the painter's sphere!

The limits of his art appear.
The passing group, the summer-morn,
The grass, the elms, that blossom'd thorn —
Those cattle couch'd, or, as they rise,
Their shining flanks, their liquid eyes —
These, or much greater things, but caught
Like these, and in one aspect brought!
In outward semblance he must give
A moment's life of things that live;
Then let him choose his moment well,
With power divine its story tell.'

Still we walk'd on, in thoughtful mood,
And now upon the bridge we stood.
Full of sweet breathings was the air,
Of sudden stirs and pauses fair.
Down o'er the stately bridge the breeze
Came rustling from the garden-trees
And on the sparkling waters play'd;
Light-plashing waves an answer made,
And mimic boats their haven near'd.
Beyond, the Abbey-towers appear'd,
By mist and chimneys unconfined,
Free to the sweep of light and wind;
While through their earth-moor'd nave below
Another breath of wind doth blow,
Sound as of wandering breeze — but sound
In laws by human artists bound.
'The world of music!' I exclaim'd: —
'This breeze that rustles by, that famed
Abbey recall it! what a sphere
Large and profound, hath genius here!
The inspired musician what a range,
What power of passion, wealth of change!
Some source of feeling he must choose
And its lock'd fount of beauty use,
And through the stream of music tell
Its else unutterable spell;
To choose it rightly is his part,
And press into its inmost heart.

'*Miserere, Domine!*
The words are utter'd, and they flee.
Deep is their penitential moan,
Mighty their pathos, but 'tis gone.

They have declared the spirit's sore
Sore load, and words can do no more.
Beethoven takes them then — those two
Poor, bounded words — and makes them new;
Infinite makes them, makes them young;
Transplants them to another tongue,
Where they can now, without constraint,
Pour all the soul of their complaint,
And roll adown a channel large
The wealth divine they have in charge.
Page after page of music turn,
And still they live and still they burn,
Eternal, passion-fraught, and free —
Miserere, Domine!'

Onward we moved, and reach'd the Ride
Where gaily flows the human tide.
Afar, in rest the cattle lay;
We heard, afar, faint music play;
But agitated, brisk, and near,
Men, with their stream of life, were here.
Some hang upon the rails, and some
On foot behind them go and come.
This through the Ride upon his steed
Goes slowly by, and this at speed.
The young, the happy, and the fair,
The old, the sad, the worn, were there;
Some vacant, and some musing went,
And some in talk and merriment.
Nods, smiles, and greetings, and farewells!
And now and then, perhaps, there swells
A sigh, a tear — but in the throng
All changes fast, and hies along.
Hies, ah, from whence, what native ground?
And to what goal, what ending, bound?
'Behold, at last the poet's sphere!
But who,' I said, 'suffices here?

'For, ah! so much he has to do;
Be painter and musician too!
The aspect of the moment show,
The feeling of the moment know!
The aspect not, I grant, express
Clear as the painter's art can dress;
The feeling not, I grant, explore

So deep as the musician's lore —
But clear as words can make revealing,
And deep as words can follow feeling.
But, ah! then comes his sorest spell
Of toil — he must life's *movement* tell!
The thread which binds it all in one,
And not its separate parts alone.
The *movement* he must tell of life,
Its pain and pleasure, rest and strife;
His eye must travel down, at full,
The long, unpausing spectacle;
With faithful unrelaxing force
Attend it from its primal source,
From change to change and year to year
Attend it of its mid career,
Attend it to the last repose
And solemn silence of its close.

'The cattle rising from the grass
His thought must follow where they pass;
The penitent with anguish bow'd
His thought must follow through the crowd.
Yes! all this eddying, motely throng
That sparkles in the sun along,
Girl, statesman, merchant, soldier bold,
Master and servant, young and old,
Grave, gay, child, parent, husband, wife,
He follows home, and lives their life.

'And many, many are the souls
Life's movement fascinates, controls;
It draws them on, they cannot save
Their feet from its alluring wave;
They cannot leave it, they must go
With its unconquerable flow.
But ah! how few, of all that try
This mighty march, do aught but die!
For ill-endow'd for such a way,
Ill-stored in strength, in wits, are they.
They faint, they stagger to and fro,
And wandering from the stream they go;
In pain, in terror, in distress,
They see, all round, a wilderness.
Sometimes a momentary gleam
They catch of the mysterious stream;

Sometimes, a second's space, their ear
The murmur of its waves doth hear.
That transient glimpse in song they say,
But not as painter can pourtray —
That transient sound in song they tell,
But not, as the musician, well.
And when at last their snatches cease,
And they are silent and at peace,
The stream of life's majestic whole
Hath ne'er been mirror'd on their soul.

'Only a few the life-stream's shore
With safe unwandering feet explore;
Untired its movement bright attend,
Follow its windings to the end.
Then from its brimming waves their eye
Drinks up delighted ecstasy,
And its deep-toned, melodious voice
For ever makes their ear rejoice.
They speak! the happiness divine
They feel, runs o'er in every line;
Its spell is round them like a shower —
It gives them pathos, gives them power.
No painter yet hath such a way,
Nor no musician made, as they,
And gather'd on immortal knolls
Such lovely flowers for cheering souls.
Beethoven, Raphael, cannot reach
The charm which Homer, Shakespeare, teach.
To these, to these, their thankful race
Gives, then, the first, the fairest place;
And brightest is their glory's sheen,
For greatest hath their labour been.'

RUGBY CHAPEL

NOVEMBER 1857

COLDLY, sadly descends
The autumn-evening. The field
Strewn with its dank yellow drifts
Of wither'd leaves, and the elms,
Fade into dimness apace,

Silent; — hardly a shout
From a few boys late at their play!
The lights come out in the street,
In the school-room windows; — but cold,
Solemn, unlighted, austere,
Through the gathering darkness, arise
The chapel-walls, in whose bound
Thou, my father! art laid.

There thou dost lie, in the gloom
Of the autumn evening. But ah!
That word, *gloom,* to my mind
Brings thee back, in the light
Of thy radiant vigour, again;
In the gloom of November we pass'd
Days not dark at thy side;
Seasons impair'd not the ray
Of thy buoyant cheerfulness clear.
Such thou wast! and I stand
In the autumn evening, and think
Of bygone autumns with thee.

Fifteen years have gone round
Since thou arosest to tread,
In the summer-morning, the road
Of death, at a call unforeseen,
Sudden. For fifteen years,
We who till then in thy shade
Rested as under the boughs
Of a mighty oak, have endured
Sunshine and rain as we might,
Bare, unshaded, alone,
Lacking the shelter of thee.

O strong soul, by what shore
Tarriest thou now? For that force,
Surely, has not been left vain!
Somewhere, surely, afar,
In the sounding labour-house vast
Of being, is practised that strength,
Zealous, beneficent, firm!

Yes, in some far-shining sphere,
Conscious or not of the past,

Still thou performest the word
Of the Spirit in whom thou dost live —
Prompt, unwearied, as here!
Still thou upraisest with zeal
The humble good from the ground,
Sternly repressest the bad!
Still, like a trumpet, dost rouse
Those who with half-open eyes
Tread the border-land dim
'Twixt vice and virtue; reviv'st,
Succourest! — this was thy work,
This was thy life upon earth.

What is the course of the life
Of mortal men on the earth? —
Most men eddy about
Here and there — eat and drink,
Chatter and love and hate,
Gather and squander, are raised
Aloft, are hurl'd in the dust,
Striving blindly, achieving
Nothing; and then they die —
Perish; — and no one asks
Who or what they have been,
More than he asks what waves,
In the moonlit solitudes mild
Of the midmost Ocean, have swell'd,
Foam'd for a moment, and gone.

And there are some, whom a thirst
Ardent, unquenchable, fires,
Not with the crowd to be spent,
Not without aim to go round
In an eddy of purposeless dust,
Effort unmeaning and vain.
Ah yes! some of us strive
Not without action to die
Fruitless, but something to snatch
From dull oblivion, nor all
Glut the devouring grave!
We, we have chosen our path —
Path to a clear-purposed goal,
Path of advance! — but it leads
A long, steep journey, through sunk
Gorges, o'er mountains in snow.
Cheerful, with friends, we set forth —

Then, on the height, comes the storm.
Thunder crashes from rock
To rock, the cataracts reply,
Lightnings dazzle our eyes.
Roaring torrents have breach'd
The track, the stream-bed descends
In the place where the wayfarer once
Planted his footstep — the spray
Boils o'er its borders! aloft
The unseen snow-beds dislodge
Their hanging ruin; alas,
Havoc is made in our train!
Friends, who set forth at our side,
Falter, are lost in the storm.
We, we only are left!
With frowning foreheads, with lips
Sternly compress'd, we strain on,
On — and at nightfall at last
Come to the end of our way,
To the lonely inn 'mid the rocks;
Where the gaunt and taciturn host
Stands on the threshold, the wind
Shaking his thin white hairs —
Holds his lantern to scan
Our storm-beat figures, and asks:
Whom in our party we bring?
Whom we have left in the snow?

Sadly we answer: We bring
Only ourselves! we lost
Sight of the rest in the storm.
Hardly ourselves we fought through,
Stripp'd, without friends, as we are.
Friends, companions, and train,
The avalanche swept from our side.

But thou would'st not *alone*
Be saved, my father! *alone*
Conquer and come to thy goal,
Leaving the rest in the wild.
We were weary, and we
Fearful, and we in our march
Fain to drop down and to die.
Still thou turnedst, and still
Beckonedst the trembler, and still
Gavest the weary thy hand.

If, in the paths of the world,
Stones might have wounded thy feet,
Toil or dejection have tried
Thy spirit, of that we saw
Nothing — to us thou wast still
Cheerful, and helpful, and firm!
Therefore to thee it was given
Many to save with thyself;
And, at the end of thy day,
O faithful shepherd! to come,
Bringing thy sheep in thy hand.

And through thee I believe
In the noble and great who are gone;
Pure souls honour'd and blest
By former ages, who else —
Such, so soulless, so poor,
Is the race of men whom I see —
Seem'd but a dream of the heart,
Seem'd but a cry of desire.
Yes! I believe that there lived
Others like thee in the past,
Not like the men of the crowd
Who all round me to-day
Bluster or cringe, and make life
Hideous, and arid, and vile;
But souls temper'd with fire,
Fervent, heroic, and good,
Helpers and friends of mankind.

Servants of God! — or sons
Shall I not call you? because
Not as servants ye knew
Your Father's innermost mind,
His, who unwillingly sees
One of his little ones lost —
Yours is the praise, if mankind
Hath not as yet in its march
Fainted, and fallen, and died!

See! In the rocks of the world
Marches the host of mankind,
A feeble, wavering line.
Where are they tending? — A God
Marshall'd them, gave them their goal.

Ah, but the way is so long!
Years they have been in the wild!
Sore thirst plagues them, the rocks,
Rising all round, overawe;
Factions divide them, their host
Threatens to break, to dissolve.
— Ah, keep, keep them combined!
Else, of the myriads who fill
That army, not one shall arrive;
Sole they shall stray; in the rocks
Stagger for ever in vain,
Die one by one in the waste.

Then, in such hour of need
Of your fainting, dispirited race,
Ye, like angels, appear,
Radiant with ardour divine!
Beacons of hope, ye appear!
Languor is not in your heart,
Weakness is not in your word,
Weariness not on your brow.
Ye alight in our van! at your voice,
Panic, despair, flee away.
Ye move through the ranks, recall
The stragglers, refresh the outworn,
Praise, re-inspire the brave!
Order, courage, return.
Eyes rekindling, and prayers,
Follow your steps as ye go.
Ye fill up the gaps in our files,
Strengthen the wavering line,
Stablish, continue our march,
On, to the bound of the waste,
On, to the City of God.

HEINE'S GRAVE

'Henri Heine' — 'tis here!
That black tombstone, the name
Carved there — no more! and the smooth,
Swarded alleys, the limes
Touch'd with yellow by hot

Summer, but under them still,
In September's bright afternoon,
Shadow, and verdure, and cool.
Trim Montmartre! the faint
Murmur of Paris outside;
Crisp everlasting-flowers,
Yellow and black, on the graves.

Half blind, palsied, in pain,
Hither to come, from the streets'
Uproar, surely not loath
Wast thou, Heine! — to lie
Quiet, to ask for closed
Shutters, and darken'd room,
And cool drinks, and an eased
Posture, and opium, no more;
Hither to come, and to sleep
Under the wings of Renown.

Ah! not little, when pain
Is most quelling, and man
Easily quell'd, and the fine
Temper of genius so soon
Thrills at each smart, is the praise,
Not to have yielded to pain!
No small boast, for a weak
Son of mankind, to the earth
Pinn'd by the thunder, to rear
His bolt-scathed front to the stars;
And, undaunted, retort
'Gainst thick-crashing, insane,
Tyrannous tempests of bale,
Arrowy lightnings of soul.

Hark! through the alley resounds
Mocking laughter! A film
Creeps o'er the sunshine; a breeze
Ruffles the warm afternoon,
Saddens my soul with its chill.
Gibing of spirits in scorn
Shakes every leaf of the grove,
Mars the benignant repose
Of this amiable home of the dead.

Bitter spirits, ye claim
Heine? — Alas, he is yours!

Only a moment I long'd
Here in the quiet to snatch
From such mates the outworn
Poet, and steep him in calm.
Only a moment! I knew
Whose he was who is here
Buried — I knew he was yours!
Ah, I knew that I saw
Here no sepulchre built
In the laurell'd rock, o'er the blue
Naples bay, for a sweet
Tender Virgil! no tomb
On Ravenna sands, in the shade
Of Ravenna pines, for a high
Austere Dante! no grave
By the Avon side, in the bright
Stratford meadows, for thee,
Shakespeare! loveliest of souls,
Peerless in radiance, in joy.

What, then, so harsh and malign,
Heine! distils from thy life?
Poisons the peace of thy grave?

I chide with thee not, that thy sharp
Upbraidings often assail'd
England, my country — for we,
Heavy and sad, for her sons,
Long since, deep in our hearts,
Echo the blame of her foes.
We, too, sigh that she flags;
We, too, say that she now —
Scarce comprehending the voice
Of her greatest, golden-mouth'd sons
Of a former age any more —
Stupidly travels her round
Of mechanic business, and lets
Slow die out of her life
Glory, and genius, and joy.

So thou arraign'st her, her foe;
So we arraign her, her sons.

Yes, we arraign her! but she,
The weary Titan, with deaf
Ears, and labour-dimm'd eyes,

Regarding neither to right
Nor left, goes passively by,
Staggering on to her goal;
Bearing on shoulders immense,
Atlanteän, the load,
Wellnigh not to be borne,
Of the too vast orb of her fate.

But was it thou — I think
Surely it was! — that bard
Unnamed, who, Goethe said,
Had every other gift, but wanted love;
Love, without which the tongue
Even of angels sounds amiss?

Charm is the glory which makes
Song of the poet divine,
Love is the fountain of charm.
How without charm wilt thou draw,
Poet! the world to thy way?
Not by the lightnings of wit —
Not by the thunder of scorn!
These to the world, too, are given;
Wit it possesses, and scorn —
Charm is the poet's alone.
Hollow and dull are the great,
And artists envious, and the mob profane.
We know all this, we know!
Cam'st thou from heaven, O child
Of light! but this to declare?
Alas, to help us forget
Such barren knowledge awhile,
God gave the poet his song!

Therefore a secret unrest
Tortured thee, brilliant and bold!
Therefore triumph itself
Tasted amiss to thy soul.
Therefore, with blood of thy foes,
Trickled in silence thine own.
Therefore the victor's heart
Broke on the field of his fame.

Ah! as of old, from the pomp
Of Italian Milan, the fair

Flower of marble of white
Southern palaces — steps
Border'd by statues, and walks
Terraced, and orange-bowers
Heavy with fragrance — the blond
German Kaiser full oft
Long'd himself back to the fields,
Rivers, and high-roof'd towns
Of his native Germany; so,
So, how often! from hot
Paris drawing-rooms, and lamps
Blazing, and brilliant crowds,
Starr'd and jewell'd, of men
Famous, of women the queens
Of dazzling converse — from fumes
Of praise, hot, heady fumes, to the poor brain
That mount, that madden — how oft
Heine's spirit outworn
Long'd itself out of the din,
Back to the tranquil, the cool
Far German home of his youth!

See! in the May-afternoon,
O'er the fresh, short turf of the Hartz,
A youth, with the foot of youth,
Heine! thou climbest again!
Up, through the tall dark firs
Warming their heads in the sun,
Chequering the grass with their shade —
Up, by the stream, with its huge
Moss-hung boulders, and thin
Musical water half-hid —
Up, o'er the rock-strewn slope,
With the sinking sun, and the air
Chill, and the shadows now
Long on the grey hill-side —
To the stone-roof'd hut at the top!

Or, yet later, in watch
On the roof of the Brocken-tower
Thou standest, gazing! — to see
The broad red sun, over field,
Forest, and city, and spire,
And mist-track'd stream of the wide,
Wide, German land, going down

In a bank of vapours — again
Standest, at nightfall, alone!

Or, next morning, with limbs
Rested by slumber, and heart
Freshen'd and light with the May,
O'er the gracious spurs coming down
Of the Lower Hartz, among oaks,
And beechen coverts, and copse
Of hazels green in whose depth
Ilse, the fairy transform'd,
In a thousand water-breaks light
Pours her petulant youth —
Climbing the rock which juts
O'er the valley, the dizzily perch'd
Rock — to its iron cross
Once more thou cling'st; to the Cross
Clingest! with smiles, with a sigh!

Goethe, too, had been there.
In the long-past winter he came
To the frozen Hartz, with his soul
Passionate, eager — his youth
All in ferment! — but he
Destined to work and to live
Left it, and thou, alas!
Only to laugh and to die.

But something prompts me: Not thus
Take leave of Heine! not thus
Speak the last word at his grave!
Not in pity, and not
With half censure — with awe
Hail, as it passes from earth
Scattering lightnings, that soul!

The Spirit of the world,
Beholding the absurdity of men —
Their vaunts, their feats — let a sardonic smile,
For one short moment, wander o'er his lips.
That smile was Heine! — for its earthly hour
The strange guest sparkled; now 'tis pass'd away.

That was Heine! and we,
Myriads who live, who have lived,
What are we all, but a mood,

A single mood, of the life
Of the Spirit in whom we exist,
Who alone is all things in one?

Spirit, who fillest us all!
Spirit, who utterest in each
New-coming son of mankind
Such of thy thoughts as thou wilt!
O thou, one of whose moods,
Bitter and strange, was the life
Of Heine — his strange, alas,
His bitter life! — may a life
Other and milder be mine!
May'st thou a mood more serene,
Happier, have utter'd in mine!
May'st thou the rapture of peace
Deep have embreathed at its core;
Made it a ray of thy thought,
Made it a beat of thy joy!

STANZAS FROM THE GRANDE CHARTREUSE

Through Alpine meadows soft-suffused
With rain, where thick the crocus blows,
Past the dark forges long disused,
The mule-track from Saint Laurent goes.
The bridge is cross'd, and slow we ride,
Through forest, up the mountain-side.

The autumnal evening darkens round,
The wind is up, and drives the rain;
While, hark! far down, with strangled sound
Doth the Dead Guier's stream complain,
Where that wet smoke, among the woods,
Over his boiling cauldron broods.

Swift rush the spectral vapours white
Past limestone scars with ragged pines,
Showing — then blotting from our sight! —
Halt — through the cloud-drift something shines!
High in the valley, wet and drear,
The huts of Courrerie appear.

Strike leftward! cries our guide; and higher
Mounts up the stony forest-way.
At last the encircling trees retire;
Look! through the showery twilight grey
What pointed roofs are these advance? —
A palace of the Kings of France?

Approach, for what we seek is here!
Alight, and sparely sup, and wait
For rest in this outbuilding near;
Then cross the sward and reach that gate.
Knock; pass the wicket! Thou art come
To the Carthusians' world-famed home.

The silent courts, where night and day
Into their stone-carved basins cold
The splashing icy fountains play —
The humid corridors behold!
Where, ghostlike in the deepening night,
Cowl'd forms brush by in gleaming white.

The chapel, where no organ's peal
Invests the stern and naked prayer —
With penitential cries they kneel
And wrestle; rising then, with bare
And white uplifted faces stand,
Passing the Host from hand to hand;

Each takes, and then his visage wan
Is buried in his cowl once more.
The cells! — the suffering Son of Man
Upon the wall — the knee-worn floor —
And where they sleep, that wooden bed,
Which shall their coffin be, when dead!

The library, where tract and tome
Not to feed priestly pride are there,
To hymn the conquering march of Rome,
Nor yet to amuse, as ours are!
They paint of souls the inner strife,
Their drops of blood, their death in life.

The garden, overgrown — yet mild,
See, fragrant herbs are flowering there!
Strong children of the Alpine wild

Whose culture is the brethren's care;
Of human tasks their only one,
And cheerful works beneath the sun.

Those halls, too, destined to contain
Each its own pilgrim-host of old,
From England, Germany, or Spain —
All are before me! I behold
The House, the Brotherhood austere!
— And what am I, that I am here?

For rigorous teachers seized my youth,
And purged its faith, and trimm'd its fire,
Show'd me the high, white star of Truth,
There bade me gaze, and there aspire.
Even now their whispers pierce the gloom:
What dost thou in this living tomb?

Forgive me, masters of the mind!
At whose behest I long ago
So much unlearnt, so much resign'd —
I come not here to be your foe!
I seek these anchorites, not in ruth,
To curse and to deny your truth;

Not as their friend, or child, I speak!
But as, on some far northern strand,
Thinking of his own Gods, a Greek
In pity and mournful awe might stand
Before some fallen Runic stone —
For both were faiths, and both are gone.

Wandering between two worlds, one dead,
The other powerless to be born,
With nowhere yet to rest my head,
Like these, on earth I wait forlorn.
Their faith, my tears, the world deride —
I come to shed them at their side.

Oh, hide me in your gloom profound,
Ye solemn seats of holy pain!
Take me, cowl'd forms, and fence me round,
Till I possess my soul again;
Till free my thoughts before me roll,
Not chafed by hourly false control!

For the world cries your faith is now
But a dead time's exploded dream;
My melancholy, sciolists say,
Is a pass'd mode, an outworn theme —
As if the world had ever had
A faith, or sciolists been sad!

Ah, if it *be* pass'd, take away,
At least, the restlessness, the pain;
Be man henceforth no more a prey
To these out-dated stings again!
The nobleness of grief is gone —
Ah, leave us not the fret alone!

But — if you cannot give us ease —
Last of the race of them who grieve
Here leave us to die out with these
Last of the people who believe!
Silent, while years engrave the brow;
Silent — the best are silent now.

Achilles ponders in his tent,
The kings of modern thought are dumb;
Silent they are, though not content,
And wait to see the future come.
They have the grief men had of yore,
But they contend and cry no more.

Our fathers water'd with their tears
This sea of time whereon we sail,
Their voices were in all men's ears
Who pass'd within their puissant hail.
Still the same ocean round us raves,
But we stand mute, and watch the waves.

For what avail'd it, all the noise
And outcry of the former men? —
Say, have their sons achieved more joys,
Say, is life lighter now than then?
The sufferers died, they left their pain —
The pangs which tortured them remain.

What helps it now, that Byron bore,
With haughty scorn which mock'd the smart,
Through Europe to the Ætolian shore

The pageant of his bleeding heart?
That thousands counted every groan,
And Europe made his woe her own?

What boots it, Shelley! that the breeze
Carried thy lovely wail away,
Musical through Italian trees
Which fringe thy soft blue Spezzian bay?
Inheritors of thy distress
Have restless hearts one throb the less?

Or are we easier, to have read,
O Obermann! the sad, stern page,
Which tells us how thou hidd'st thy head
From the fierce tempest of thine age
In the lone brakes of Fontainebleau,
Or chalets near the Alpine snow?

Ye slumber in your silent grave! —
The world, which for an idle day
Grace to your mood of sadness gave,
Long since hath flung her weeds away.
The eternal trifler breaks your spell;
But we — we learnt your lore too well!

Years hence, perhaps, may dawn an age,
More fortunate, alas! than we,
Which without hardness will be sage,
And gay without frivolity.
Sons of the world, oh, speed those years;
But, while we wait, allow our tears!

Allow them! We admire with awe
The exulting thunder of your race;
You give the universe your law,
You triumph over time and space!
Your pride of life, your tireless powers,
We laud them, but they are not ours.

We are like children rear'd in shade
Beneath some old-world abbey wall,
Forgotten in a forest-glade,
And secret from the eyes of all.
Deep, deep the greenwood round them waves,
Their abbey, and its close of graves!

But, where the road runs near the stream,
Oft through the trees they catch a glance
Of passing troops in the sun's beam —
Pennon, and plume, and flashing lance!
Forth to the world those soldiers fare,
To life, to cities, and to war!

And through the wood, another way,
Faint bugle-notes from far are borne,
Where hunters gather, staghounds bay,
Round some fair forest-lodge at morn.
Gay dames are there, in sylvan green;
Laughter and cries — those notes between!

The banners flashing through the trees
Make their blood dance and chain their eyes;
That bugle-music on the breeze
Arrests them with a charm'd surprise.
Banner by turns and bugle woo:
Ye shy recluses, follow too!

O children, what do ye reply? —
'Action and pleasure, will ye roam
Through these secluded dells to cry
And call us? — but too late ye come!
Too late for us your call ye blow,
Whose bent was taken long ago.

'Long since we pace this shadow'd nave;
We watch those yellow tapers shine,
Emblems of hope over the grave,
In the high altar's depth divine;
The organ carries to our ear
Its accents of another sphere.

'Fenced early in this cloistral round
Of reverie, of shade, of prayer,
How should we grow in other ground?
How should we flower in foreign air?
— Pass, banners, pass, and bugles, cease;
And leave our desert to its peace!'

OBERMANN ONCE MORE

Savez-vous quelque bien qui console du regret d'un monde?
OBERMANN.

GLION? —— Ah, twenty years, it cuts
All meaning from a name!
White houses prank where once were huts.
Glion, but not the same!

And yet I know not! All unchanged
The turf, the pines, the sky!
The hills in their old order ranged;
The lake, with Chillon by!

And, 'neath those chestnut-trees, where stiff
And stony mounts the way,
The crackling husk-heaps burn, as if
I left them yesterday!

Across the valley, on that slope,
The huts of Avant shine!
Its pines, under their branches, ope
Ways for the pasturing kine.

Full-foaming milk-pails, Alpine fare,
Sweet heaps of fresh-cut grass,
Invite to rest the traveller there
Before he climb the pass —

The gentian-flower'd pass, its crown
With yellow spires aflame;
Whence drops the path to Allière down,
And walls where Byron came,

By their green river, who doth change
His birth-name just below;
Orchard, and croft, and full-stored grange
Nursed by his pastoral flow.

But stop! — to fetch back thoughts that stray
Beyond this gracious bound,

The cone of Jaman, pale and grey,
See, in the blue profound!

Ah, Jaman! delicately tall
Above his sun-warm'd firs —
What thoughts to me his rocks recall,
What memories he stirs!

And who but thou must be, in truth,
Obermann! with me here?
Thou master of my wandering youth,
But left this many a year!

Yes, I forget the world's work wrought,
Its warfare waged with pain;
An eremite with thee, in thought
Once more I slip my chain,

And to thy mountain-chalet come,
And lie beside its door,
And hear the wild bee's Alpine hum,
And thy sad, tranquil lore!

Again I feel the words inspire
Their mournful calm; serene,
Yet tinged with infinite desire
For all that *might* have been —

The harmony from which man swerved
Made his life's rule once more!
The universal order served,
Earth happier than before!

— While thus I mused, night gently ran
Down over hill and wood.
Then, still and sudden, Obermann
On the grass near me stood.

Those pensive features well I knew,
On my mind, years before,
Imaged so oft! imaged so true!
— A shepherd's garb he wore,

A mountain-flower was in his hand,
A book was in his breast.

Bent on my face, with gaze which scann'd
My soul, his eyes did rest.

'And is it thou,' he cried, 'so long
Held by the world which we
Loved not, who turnest from the throng
Back to thy youth and me?

'And from thy world, with heart opprest,
Choosest thou *now* to turn? —
Ah me! we anchorites read things best,
Clearest their course discern!

'Thou fledst me when the ungenial earth,
Man's work-place, lay in gloom.
Return'st thou in her hour of birth,
Of hopes and hearts in bloom?

'Perceiv'st thou not the change of day?
  Ah! Carry back thy ken,
What, some two thousand years! Survey
The world as it was then!

'Like ours it look'd in outward air.
Its head was clear and true,
Sumptuous its clothing, rich its fare,
No pause its action knew;

'Stout was its arm, each thew and bone
Seem'd puissant and alive —
But, ah! its heart, its heart was stone,
And so it could not thrive!

'On that hard Pagan world disgust
And secret loathing fell.
Deep weariness and sated lust
Made human life a hell.

'In his cool hall, with haggard eyes,
The Roman noble lay;
He drove abroad, in furious guise,
Along the Appian way.

'He made a feast, drank fierce and fast,
And crown'd his hair with flowers —

No easier nor no quicker pass'd
The impracticable hours.

'The brooding East with awe beheld
Her impious younger world.
The Roman tempest swell'd and swell'd,
And on her head was hurl'd.

'The East bow'd low before the blast
In patient, deep disdain;
She let the legions thunder past,
And plunged in thought again.

'So well she mused, a morning broke
Across her spirit grey;
A conquering, new-born joy awoke,
And fill'd her life with day.

' "Poor world," she cried, "so deep accurst,
That runn'st from pole to pole
To seek a draught to slake thy thirst —
Go, seek it in thy soul!"

'She heard it, the victorious West,
In crown and sword array'd!
She felt the void which mined her breast,
She shiver'd and obey'd.

'She veil'd her eagles, snapp'd her sword,
And laid her sceptre down;
Her stately purple she abhorr'd,
And her imperial crown.

'She broke her flutes, she stopp'd her sports,
Her artists could not please;
She tore her books, she shut her courts,
She fled her palaces;

'Lust of the eye and pride of life
She left it all behind,
And hurried, torn with inward strife,
The wilderness to find.

'Tears wash'd the trouble from her face!
She changed into a child!

'Mid weeds and wrecks she stood — a place
Of ruin — but she smiled!

'Oh, had I lived in that great day,
How had its glory new
Fill'd earth and heaven, and caught away
My ravish'd spirit too!

'No thoughts that to the world belong
Had stood against the wave
Of love which set so deep and strong
From Christ's then open grave.

'No cloister-floor of humid stone
Had been too cold for me.
For me no Eastern desert lone
Had been too far to flee.

'No lonely life had pass'd too slow,
When I could hourly scan
Upon his Cross, with head sunk low,
That nail'd, thorn-crowned Man!

'Could see the Mother with her Child
Whose tender winning arts
Have to his little arms beguiled
So many wounded hearts!

'And centuries came and ran their course,
And unspent all that time
Still, still went forth that Child's dear force,
And still was at its prime.

'Ay, ages long endured his span
Of life — 'tis true received —
That gracious Child, that thorn-crown'd Man!
— He lived while we believed.

'While we believed, on earth he went,
And open stood his grave.
Men call'd from chamber, church, and tent;
And Christ was by to save.

'Now he is dead! Far hence he lies
In the lorn Syrian town;

And on his grave, with shining eyes,
The Syrian stars look down.

'In vain men still, with hoping new,
Regard his death-place dumb,
And say the stone is not yet to,
And wait for words to come.

'Ah, o'er that silent sacred land,
Of sun, and arid stone,
And crumbling wall, and sultry sand,
Sounds now one word alone!

'*Unduped of fancy, henceforth man*
Must labour! — must resign
His all too human creeds, and scan
Simply the way divine!

'But slow that tide of common thought,
Which bathed our life, retired;
Slow, slow the old world wore to nought,
And pulse by pulse expired.

'Its frame yet stood without a breach
When blood and warmth were fled;
And still it spake its wonted speech —
But every word was dead.

'And oh, we cried, that on this corse
Might fall a freshening storm!
Rive its dry bones, and with new force
A new-sprung world inform!

' — Down came the storm! O'er France it pass'd
In sheets of scathing fire;
All Europe felt that fiery blast,
And shook as it rush'd by her.

'Down came the storm! In ruins fell
The worn-out world we knew.
It pass'd, that elemental swell!
Again appear'd the blue;

'The sun shone in the new-wash'd sky,
And what from heaven saw he?

Blocks of the past, like icebergs high,
Float on a rolling sea!

'Upon them plies the race of man
All it before endeavour'd;
"Ye live," I cried, "ye work and plan,
And know not ye are sever'd!

' "Poor fragments of a broken world
Whereon men pitch their tent!
Why were ye too to death not hurl'd
When your world's day was spent?

' "That glow of central fire is done
Which with its fusing flame
Knit all your parts, and kept you one —
But ye, ye are the same!

' "The past, its mask of union on,
Had ceased to live and thrive.
The past, its mask of union gone,
Say, is it more alive?

' "Your creeds are dead, your rites are dead,
Your social order too!
Where tarries he, the Power who said:
See, I make all things new?

' "The millions suffer still, and grieve,
And what can helpers heal
With old-world cures men half believe
For woes they wholly feel?

' "And yet men have such need of joy!
But joy whose grounds are true;
And joy that should all hearts employ
As when the past was new.

' "Ah, not the emotion of that past,
Its common hope, were vain!
Some new such hope must dawn at last,
Or man must toss in pain.

' "But now the old is out of date,
The new is not yet born,

And who can be *alone* elate,
While the world lies forlorn?"

'Then to the wilderness I fled. —
There among Alpine snows
And pastoral huts I hid my head,
And sought and found repose.

'It was not yet the appointed hour.
Sad, patient, and resign'd,
I watch'd the crocus fade and flower,
I felt the sun and wind.

'The day I lived in was not mine,
Man gets no second day.
In dreams I saw the future shine —
But ah! I could not stay!

'Action I had not, followers, fame;
I pass'd obscure, alone.
The after-world forgets my name,
Nor do I wish it known.

'Composed to bear, I lived and died,
And knew my life was vain,
With fate I murmur not, nor chide,
At Sèvres by the Seine

'(If Paris that brief flight allow)
My humble tomb explore!
It bears: *Eternity, be thou*
My refuge! and no more.

'But thou, whom fellowship of mood
Did make from haunts of strife
Come to my mountain-solitude,
And learn my frustrate life;

'O thou, who, ere thy flying span
Was past of cheerful youth,
Didst find the solitary man
And love his cheerless truth —

'Despair not thou as I despair'd,
Nor be cold gloom thy prison!

Forward the gracious hours have fared,
And see! the sun is risen!

'He breaks the winter of the past;
A green, new earth appears.
Millions, whose life in ice lay fast,
Have thoughts, and smiles, and tears.

'What though there still need effort, strife?
Though much be still unwon?
Yet warm it mounts, the hour of life!
Death's frozen hour is done!

'The world's great order dawns in sheen,
After long darkness rude,
Divinelier imaged, clearer seen,
With happier zeal pursued.

'With hope extinct and brow composed
I mark'd the present die;
Its term of life was nearly closed,
Yet it had more than I.

'But thou, though to the world's new hour
Thou come with aspect marr'd,
Shorn of the joy, the bloom, the power
Which best befits its bard —

'Though more than half thy years be past,
And spent thy youthful prime;
Though, round thy firmer manhood cast,
Hang weeds of our sad time

'Whereof thy youth felt all the spell,
And traversed all the shade —
Though late, though dimm'd, though weak, yet tell
Hope to a world new-made!

'Help it to fill that deep desire,
The want which rack'd our brain,
Consumed our heart with thirst like fire,
Immedicable pain;

'Which to the wilderness drove out
Our life, to Alpine snow,

And palsied all our word with doubt,
And all our work with woe —

'What still of strength is left, employ
That end to help attain:
One common wave of thought and joy
Lifting mankind again!'

— The vision ended. I awoke
As out of sleep, and no
Voice moved; — only the torrent broke
The silence, far below.

Soft darkness on the turf did lie.
Solemn, o'er hut and wood,
In the yet star-sown nightly sky,
The peak of Jaman stood.

Still in my soul the voice I heard
Of Obermann! —— away
I turned; by some vague impulse stirr'd,
Along the rocks of Naye

Past Sonchaud's piny flanks I gaze
And the blanch'd summit bare
Of Malatrait, to where in haze
The Valais opens fair,

And the domed Velan, with his snows,
Behind the upcrowding hills,
Doth all the heavenly opening close
Which the Rhone's murmur fills; —

And glorious there, without a sound,
Across the glimmering lake,
High in the Valais-depth profound,
I saw the morning break.

Criticism

Literature

PREFACE TO FIRST EDITION OF *POEMS* (1853)

In two small volumes of Poems, published anonymously, one in 1849, the other in 1852, many of the Poems which compose the present volume have already appeared. The rest are now published for the first time.

I have, in the present collection, omitted the Poem from which the volume published in 1852 took its title. I have done so, not because the subject of it was a Sicilian Greek born between two and three thousand years ago, although many persons would think this a sufficient reason. Neither have I done so because I had, in my own opinion, failed in the delineation which I intended to effect. I intended to delineate the feelings of one of the last of the Greek religious philosophers, one of the family of Orpheus and Musaeus, having survived his fellows, living on into a time when the habits of Greek thought and feeling had begun fast to change, character to dwindle, the influence of the Sophists to prevail. Into the feelings of a man so situated there entered much that we are accustomed to consider as exclusively modern; how much, the fragments of Empedocles himself which remain to us are sufficient at least to indicate. What those who are familiar only with the great monuments of early Greek genius suppose to be its exclusive characteristics, have disappeared; the calm, the cheerfulness, the disinterested objectivity have disappeared: the dialogue of the mind with itself has commenced; modern problems have presented themselves; we hear already the doubts, we witness the discouragement, of Hamlet and of Faust.

The representation of such a man's feelings must be interesting, if consistently drawn. We all naturally take pleasure, says Aristotle, in any imitation or representation whatever: this is the basis of our love of Poetry: and we take pleasure in them, he adds, because all knowledge is naturally agreeable to us; not to the philosopher only, but to mankind at large. Every representation therefore which is consistently drawn may be supposed to be interesting, inasmuch as it gratifies this natural interest in knowledge of all kinds. What is *not* interesting, is that which does not add to our knowledge of any kind; that which is vaguely conceived and loosely drawn; a representation which is general, indeterminate, and faint, instead of being particular, precise, and firm.

Any accurate representation may therefore be expected to be interesting; but, if the representation be a poetical one, more than this is demanded. It is demanded, not only that it shall interest, but also that it shall inspirit and rejoice the reader: that it shall convey a charm, and infuse delight. For the Muses, as Hesiod says, were born that they might be "a forgetfulness of evils, and a truce from cares": and it is not enough that the Poet should add to the knowledge of men, it is required of him also that he should add to their happiness. "All Art," says Schiller, "is dedicated to Joy, and there is no higher and no more serious problem, than how to make men happy. The right Art is that alone, which creates the highest enjoyment."

A poetical work, therefore, is not yet justified when it has been shown to be an accurate, and therefore interesting representation; it has to be shown also that it is a representation from which men can derive enjoyment. In presence of the most tragic circumstances, represented in a work of Art, the feeling of enjoyment, as is well known, may still subsist: the representation of the most utter calamity, of the liveliest anguish, is not sufficient to destroy it: the more tragic the situation, the deeper becomes the enjoyment; and the situation is more tragic in proportion as it becomes more terrible.

What then are the situations, from the representation of which, though accurate, no poetical enjoyment can be derived? They are those in which the suffering finds no vent in action; in which a continuous state of mental distress is prolonged, unrelieved by incident, hope, or resistance; in which there is everything to be endured, nothing to be done. In such situations there is inevitably something morbid, in the description of them something monotonous. When they occur in actual life, they are painful, not tragic; the representation of them in poetry is painful also.

To this class of situations, poetically faulty as it appears to me, that of Empedocles, as I have endeavoured to represent him, belongs; and I have therefore excluded the Poem from the present collection.

And why, it may be asked, have I entered into this explanation respecting a matter so unimportant as the admission or exclusion of the Poem in question? I have done so, because I was anxious to avow that the sole reason for its exclusion was that which has been stated above; and that it has not been excluded in deference to the opinion which many critics of the present day appear to entertain against subjects chosen from distant times and countries: against the choice, in short, of any subjects but modern ones.

"The Poet," it is said,[1] and by an intelligent critic, "the Poet who would really fix the public attention must leave the exhausted past, and draw his subjects from matters of present import, and *therefore* both of interest and novelty."

Now this view I believe to be completely false. It is worth examining, inasmuch as it is a fair sample of a class of critical dicta everywhere current at the present day, having a philosophical form and air, but no real basis in fact; and which are calculated to vitiate the judgement of readers of poetry, while they exert, so far as they are adopted, a misleading influence on the practice of those who make it.

What are the eternal objects of Poetry, among all nations and at all times? They are actions; human actions; possessing an inherent interest in themselves, and which are to be communicated in an interesting manner by the art of the Poet. Vainly will the latter imagine that he has everything in his own power; that he can make an intrinsically inferior action equally delightful with a more excellent one by his treatment of it. He may indeed compel us to admire his skill, but his work will possess, within itself, an incurable defect.

The Poet, then, has in the first place to select an excellent action; and what actions are the most excellent? Those, certainly, which most powerfully appeal to the great primary human affections: to those elementary feelings which subsist permanently in the race, and which are independent of time. These feelings are permanent and the same; that which interests them is permanent and the same also. The modernness or antiquity of an action, therefore, has nothing to do with its fitness for poetical representation; this depends upon its inherent qualities. To the elementary part of our nature, to our passions, that which is great and passionate is eternally interesting; and interesting solely in proportion to its greatness and to its passion. A great human action of a thousand years ago is more interesting to it than a smaller human action of to-day, even though upon the representation of this last the most consummate skill may have been expended, and though it has the advantage of appealing by its modern language, familiar manners, and contemporary allusions, to all our transient feelings and

1 In *The Spectator* of April 2nd, 1853. The words quoted were not used with reference to poems of mine.

interests. These, however, have no right to demand of a poetical work that it shall satisfy them; their claims are to be directed elsewhere. Poetical works belong to the domain of our permanent passions: let them interest these, and the voice of all subordinate claims upon them is at once silenced.

Achilles, Prometheus, Clytemnestra, Dido — what modern poem presents personages as interesting, even to us moderns, as these personages of an "exhausted past"? We have the domestic epic dealing with the details of modern life which pass daily under our eyes; we have poems representing modern personages in contact with the problems of modern life, moral, intellectual, and social; these works have been produced by poets the most distinguished of their nation and time; yet I fearlessly assert that *Hermann and Dorothea, Childe Harold, Jocelyn, The Excursion,* leave the reader cold in comparison with the effect produced upon him by the latter books of the *Iliad,* by the *Oresteia,* or by the episode of Dido. And why is this? Simply because in the three last-named cases the action is greater, the personages nobler, the situations more intense: and this is the true basis of the interest in a poetical work, and this alone.

It may be urged, however, that past actions may be interesting in themselves, but that they are not to be adopted by the modern Poet, because it is impossible for him to have them clearly present to his own mind, and he cannot therefore feel them deeply, nor represent them forcibly. But this is not necessarily the case. The externals of a past action, indeed, he cannot know with the precision of a contemporary; but his business is with its essentials. The outward man of Oedipus or of Macbeth, the houses in which they lived, the ceremonies of their courts, he cannot accurately figure to himself; but neither do they essentially concern him. His business is with their inward man; with their feelings and behaviour in certain tragic situations, which engage their passions as men; these have in them nothing local and casual; they are as accessible to the modern Poet as to a contemporary.

The date of an action, then, signifies nothing: the action itself, its selection and construction, this is what is all-important. This the Greeks understood far more clearly than we do. The radical difference between their poetical theory and ours consists, as it appears to me, in this: that, with them, the poetical character of the action in itself, and the conduct of it, was the first consideration; with us, attention is fixed mainly on the value of the separate thoughts and images which occur in the treatment of an action. They regarded the whole; we regard the parts. With them, the action predominated over the expression of it; with us, the expression predominates over the action. Not that they failed in expression, or were inattentive to it; on the contrary, they are the highest models of expression, the unapproached masters of the *grand style.* But their expression is so excellent because it is so admirably kept in its right degree of prominence; because it is so simple and so well subordinated; because it draws its force directly from the pregnancy of the matter which it conveys. For what reason was the Greek tragic poet confined to so limited a range of subjects? Because there are so few actions which unite in themselves, in the highest degree, the conditions of excellence: and it was not thought that on any but an excellent subject could an excellent Poem be constructed. A few actions, therefore, eminently adapted for tragedy, maintained almost exclusive possession of the Greek tragic stage. Their significance appeared inexhaustible; they were as permanent problems, perpetually offered to the genius of every fresh poet. This too is the reason of what appears to us moderns a certain baldness of expression in Greek tragedy; of the trivialty with which we often reproach the remarks of the chorus, where it takes part in the dialogue: that the action itself, the situation of Orestes, or Merope, or Alcmaeon, was to stand the central point of interest, unforgotten, absorbing, principal; that no accessories were for a moment to distract the spectator's attention from this; that the tone of the parts was to be perpetually kept down, in order not to impair the grandiose effect of the whole. The terrible old mythic story on which the drama was founded stood, before he entered the theatre, traced in its bare outlines upon the spectator's mind; it stood in his memory, as a group of statuary, faintly seen, at the end of a long and dark vista: then came the Poet, embodying outlines, developing situations, not a word wasted, not a sentiment capriciously thrown in: stroke upon stroke, the drama proceeded: the light deepened upon the group; more and more it revealed itself to the rivetted gaze of the spectator: until at last, when the final words were spoken, it stood before him in broad sunlight, a model of immortal beauty.

This was what a Greek critic demanded; this was what a Greek poet endeavoured to effect. It signified nothing to what time an action belonged. We do not find that the *Persae* occupied a particularly high rank among the dramas of Aeschylus, because it represented a matter of contemporary interest: this was not what a cultivated Athenian required. He required that the permanent elements of his nature should be moved; and dramas of which the action, though taken from a long-distant mythic time, yet was calculated to accomplish this in a higher degree than that of the *Persae,* stood higher in his estimation accordingly. The Greeks felt, no doubt, with their exquisite sagacity of taste, that an action of present times was too near them, too much mixed up with what was accidental and passing, to form a sufficiently grand, detached, and self-subsistent object for a tragic poem. Such objects belonged to the domain of the comic poet, and of the lighter kinds of poetry. For the more serious kinds, for *pragmatic* poetry, to use an excellent expression of Polybius, they were more difficult and severe in the range of subjects which they permitted. Their theory and practice alike, the admirable treatise of Aristotle, and the unrivalled works of their poets, exclaim with a thousand tongues — "All depends upon the subject; choose a fitting action, penetrate yourself with the feeling of its situations; this done, everything else will follow."

But for all kinds of poetry alike there was one point on which they were rigidly exacting; the adaptability of the subject to the kind of poetry selected, and the careful construction of the poem.

How different a way of thinking from this is ours! We can hardly at the present day understand what Menander meant, when he told a man who inquired as to the progress of his comedy that he had finished it, not having yet written a single line, because he had constructed the action of it in his mind. A modern critic would have assured him that the merit of his piece depended on the brilliant things which arose under his pen as he went along. We have poems which seem to exist merely for the sake of single lines and passages; not for the sake of producing any total-impression. We have critics who seem to direct their attention merely to detached expressions, to the language about the action, not to the action itself. I verily think that the majority of them do not in their hearts believe that there is such a thing as a total-impression to be derived from a poem at all, or to be demanded from a poet; they think the term a common-place of metaphysical criticism. They will permit the Poet to select any action he pleases, and to suffer that action to go as it will, provided he gratifies them with occasional bursts of fine writing, and with a shower of isolated thoughts and images. That is, they permit him to leave their poetical sense ungratified, provided that he gratifies their rhetorical sense and their curiosity. Of his neglecting to gratify these, there is little danger. He needs rather to be warned against the danger of attempting to gratify these alone; he needs rather to be perpetually reminded to prefer his action to everything else; so to treat this, as to permit its inherent excellences to develop themselves, without interruption from the intrusion of his personal peculiarities: most fortunate, when he most entirely succeeds in effacing himself, and in enabling a noble action to subsist as it did in nature.

But the modern critic not only permits a false practice; he absolutely prescribes false aims. — "A true allegory of the state of one's own mind in a representative history," the Poet is told, "is perhaps the highest thing that one can attempt in the way of poetry." — And accordingly he attempts it. An allegory of the state of one's own mind, the highest problem of an art which imitates actions! No assuredly, it is not, it never can be so: no great poetical work has ever been produced with such an aim. *Faust* itself, in which something of the kind is attempted, wonderful passages as it contains, and in spite of the unsurpassed beauty of the scenes which relate to Margaret, *Faust* itself, judged as a whole, and judged strictly as a poetical work, is defective: its illustrious author, the greatest poet of modern times, the greatest critic of all times, would have been the first to acknowledge it; he only defended his work, indeed, by asserting it to be "something incommensurable."

The confusion of the present times is great, the multitude of voices counselling different things bewildering, the number of existing works capable of attracting a young writer's attention and of becoming his models, immense. What he wants is a hand to guide him through the confusion, a voice to prescribe to him the aim which he should keep in view, and to explain to him that the value of the literary works which offer themselves to his attention is relative to their power of helping him forward on his road towards this aim. Such a guide the English writer at the present day will nowhere find. Failing this, all that can be looked for, all indeed that can be desired, is, that his attention should be fixed on excellent models; that he may reproduce, at any rate, something of their excellence, by penetrating himself with their works and by catching their spirit, if he cannot be taught to produce what is excellent independently.

Foremost among these models for the English writer stands Shakespeare: a name the greatest perhaps of all poetical names; a name never to be mentioned without reverence. I will venture, however, to express a doubt, whether the influence of his works, excellent and fruitful for the readers of poetry, for the great majority, has been of unmixed advantage to the writers of it. Shakespeare indeed chose excellent subjects; the world could afford no better than Macbeth, or Romeo and Juliet, or Othello: he had no theory respecting the necessity of choosing subjects of present import, or the paramount interest attaching to allegories of the state of one's own mind; like all great poets, he knew well what constituted a poetical action; like them, wherever he found such an action, he took it; like them, too, he found his best in past times. But to these general characteristics of all great poets he added a special one of his own; a gift, namely, of happy, abundant, and ingenious expression, eminent and unrivalled: so eminent as irresistibly to strike the attenion first in him, and even to throw into comparative shade his other excellences as a poet. Here has been the mischief. These other excellences were his fundamental excellences *as a poet;* what distinguishes the artist from the mere amateur, says Goethe, is *Architectonicè* in the highest sense; that power of execution, which creates, forms, and constitutes: not the profoundness of single thoughts, not the richness of imagery, not the abundance of illustration. But these attractive accessories of a poetical work being more easily seized than the spirit of the whole, and these accessories being possessed by Shakespeare in an unequalled degree, a young writer having recourse to Shakespeare as his model runs great risk of being vanquished and absorbed by them, and, in consequence, of reproducing, according to the measure of his power, these, and these alone. Of this preponderating quality of Shakespeare's genius, accordingly, almost the whole of modern English poetry has, it appears to me, felt the influence. To the exclusive attention on the part of his imitators to this it is in a great degree owing, that of the majority of modern poetical works the details alone are valuable, the composition worthless. In reading them one is perpetually reminded of that terrible sentence on a modern French poet — *il dit tout ce qu'il veut, mais malheureusement il n'a rien à dire.*

Let me give an instance of what I mean. I will take it from the works of the very chief among those who seem to have been formed in the school of Shakespeare: of one whose exquisite genius and pathetic death render him for ever interesting. I will take the poem of *Isabella, or the Pot of Basil,* by Keats. I choose this rather than the *Endymion,* because the latter work (which a modern critic has classed with the *Fairy Queen!*), although undoubtedly there blows through it the breath of genius, is yet as a whole so utterly incoherent, as not strictly to merit the name of a poem at all. The poem of *Isabella,* then, is a perfect treasure-house of graceful and felicitous words and images: almost in every stanza there occurs one of those vivid and picturesque turns of expression, by which the object is made to flash upon the eye of the mind, and which thrill the reader with a sudden delight. This one short poem contains, perhaps, a greater number of happy single expressions which one could quote than all the extant tragedies of Sophocles. But the action, the story? The action in itself is an excellent one; but so feebly is it conceived by the Poet, so loosely constructed, that the effect produced by it, in and for itself, is absolutely null. Let the reader, after he has finished the poem of Keats, turn to the same story in the *Decameron:* he will then feel how pregnant and interesting the same action has become in the hands of a great artist, who above all things delineates his object; who subordinates expression to that which it is designed to express.

I have said that the imitators of Shakespeare, fixing their attention on his wonderful gift of expression, have directed their imitation to this, neglecting his other excellences. These excellences, the fundamental excellences of poetical art, Shakespeare no doubt possessed them — possessed many of them in a splendid degree; but it may perhaps be doubted whether even he himself did not sometimes give scope to his faculty of expression to the prejudice of a higher poetical duty. For we must never forget that Shakespeare is the great poet he is from his skill in discerning and firmly conceiving an excellent action, from his power of intensely feeling a situation, of intimately associating himself with a character; not from his gift of expression, which rather even leads him astray, degenerating sometimes into a fondness for curiosity of expression, into an irritability of fancy, which seems to make it impossible for him to say a thing plainly, even when the press of the action demands the very directest language, or its level character the very simplest. Mr. Hallam, than whom it is impossible to find a saner and more judicious critic, has had the courage (for at the present day it needs courage) to remark, how extremely and faultily difficult Shakespeare's language often is. It is so: you may find main scenes in some of his greatest tragedies, *King Lear* for instance, where the language is so artificial, so curiously tortured, and so difficult, that every speech has to be read two or three times before its meaning can be comprehended. This over-curiousness of expression is indeed but the excessive employment of a wonderful gift — of the power of saying a thing in a happier way than any other man; nevertheless, it is carried so far that one understands what M. Guizot meant, when he said that Shakespeare appears in his language to have tried all styles except that of simplicity. He has not the severe and scrupulous self-restraint of the ancients, partly no doubt, because he had a far less cultivated and exacting audience. He has indeed a far wider range than they had, a far richer fertility of thought; in this respect he rises above them. In his strong conception of his subject, in the genuine way in which he is penetrated with it, he resembles them, and is unlike the moderns. But in the accurate limitation of it, the conscientious rejection of superfluities, the simple and rigorous development of it from the first line of his work to the last, he falls below them, and comes nearer to the moderns. In his chief works, besides what he has of his own, he has the elementary soundness of the ancients; he has their important action and their large and broad manner: but he has not their purity of method. He is therefore a less safe model; for what he has of his own is personal, and inseparable from his own rich nature; it may be imitated and exaggerated, it cannot be learned or applied as an art. He is above all suggestive; more valuable, therefore, to young writers as men than as artists. But clearness of arrangement, rigour of development, simplicity of style

— these may to a certain extent be learned: and these may, I am convinced, be learned best from the ancients, who although infinitely less suggestive than Shakespeare, are thus, to the artist, more instructive.

What, then, it will be asked, are the ancients to be our sole models? the ancients with their comparatively narrow range of experience, and their widely different circumstances? Not, certainly, that which is narrow in the ancients, nor that in which we can no longer sympathize. An action like the action of the *Antigone* of Sophocles, which turns upon the conflict between the heroine's duty to her brother's corpse and that to the laws of her country, is no longer one in which it is possible that we should feel a deep interest. I am speaking too, it will be remembered, not of the best sources of intellectual stimulus for the general reader, but of the best models of instruction for the individual writer. This last may certainly learn of the ancients, better than anywhere else, three things which it is vitally important for him to know: — the all-importance of the choice of a subject; the necessity of accurate construction; and the subordinate character of expression. He will learn from them how unspeakably superior is the effect of the one moral impression left by a great action treated as a whole, to the effect produced by the most striking single thought or by the happiest image. As he penetrates into the spirit of the great classical works, as he becomes gradually aware of their intense significance, their noble simplicity, and their calm pathos, he will be convinced that it is this effect, unity and profoundness of moral impression, at which the ancient Poets aimed; that it is this which constitutes the grandeur of their works, and which makes them immortal. He will desire to direct his own efforts towards producing the same effect. Above all, he will deliver himself from the jargon of modern criticism, and escape the danger of producing poetical works conceived in the spirit of the passing time, and which partake of its transitoriness.

The present age makes great claims upon us: we owe it service, it will not be satisfied without our admiration. I know not how it is, but their commerce with the ancients appears to me to produce, in those who constantly practise it, a steadying and composing effect upon their judgement, not of literary works only, but of men and events in general. They are like persons who have had a very weighty and impressive experience: they are more truly than others under the empire of facts, and more independent of the language current among those with whom they live. They wish neither to applaud nor to revile their age: they wish to know what it is, what it can give them, and whether this is what they want. What they want, they know very well; they want to educe and cultivate what is best and noblest in themselves:

they know, too, that this is no easy task — χαλεπὸν, as Pittacus said, χαλεπὸν ἐσθλὸν ἔμμεναι — and they ask themselves sincerely whether their age and its literature can assist them in the attempt. If they are endeavouring to practise any art, they remember the plain and simple proceedings of the old artists, who attained their grand results by penetrating themselves with some noble and significant action, not by inflating themselves with a belief in the pre-eminent importance and greatness of their own times. They do not talk of their mission, nor of interpreting their age, nor of the coming Poet; all this, they know, is the mere delirium of vanity; their business is not to praise their age, but to afford to the men who live in it the highest pleasure which they are capable of feeling. If asked to afford this by means of subjects drawn from the age itself, they ask what special fitness the present age has for supplying them. They are told that it is an era of progress, an age commissioned to carry out the great ideas of industrial development and social amelioration. They reply that with all this they can do nothing; that the elements they need for the exercise of their art are great actions, calculated powerfully and delightfully to affect what is permanent in the human soul; that so far as the present age can supply such actions, they will gladly make use of them; but that an age wanting in moral grandeur can with difficulty supply such, and an age of spiritual discomfort with difficulty be powerfully and delightfully affected by them.

A host of voices will indignantly rejoin that the present age is inferior to the past neither in moral grandeur nor in spiritual health. He who possesses the discipline I speak of will content himself with remembering the judgements passed upon the present age, in this respect, by the two men, the one of strongest head, the other of widest culture, whom it has produced; by Goethe and by Niebuhr. It will be sufficient for him that he knows the opinions held by these two great men respecting the present age and its literature; and that he feels assured in his own mind that their aims and demands upon life were such as he would wish, at any rate, his own to be; and their judgement as to what is impeding and disabling such as he may safely follow. He will not, however, maintain a hostile attitude towards the false pretensions of his age; he will content himself with not being overwhelmed by them. He will esteem himself fortunate if he can succeed in banishing from his mind all feelings of contradiction, and irritation, and impatience; in order to delight himself with the contemplation of some noble action of a heroic time, and to enable others, through his representation of it, to delight in it also.

I am far indeed from making any claim, for myself, that I possess this discipline; or for the following Poems, that they breathe its spirit.

But I say, that in the sincere endeavour to learn and practise, amid the bewildering confusion of our times, what is sound and true in poetical art, I seemed to myself to find the only sure guidance, the only solid footing, among the ancients. They, at any rate, knew what they wanted in Art, and we do not. It is this uncertainty which is disheartening, and not hostile criticism. How often have I felt this when reading words of disparagement or of cavil: that it is the uncertainty as to what is really to be aimed at which makes our difficulty, not the dissatisfaction of the critic, who himself suffers from the same uncertainty. *Non me tua fervida terrent Dicta: Dii me terrent, et Jupiter hostis.*

Two kinds of *dilettanti,* says Goethe, there are in poetry: he who neglects the indispensable mechanical part, and thinks he has done enough if he shows spirituality and feeling; and he who seeks to arrive at poetry merely by mechanism, in which he can acquire an artisan's readiness, and is without soul and matter. And he adds, that the first does most harm to Art, and the last to himself. If we must be *dilettanti:* if it is impossible for us, under the circumstances amidst which we live, to think clearly, to feel nobly, and to delineate firmly: if we cannot attain to the mastery of the great artists — let us, at least, have so much respect for our Art as to prefer it to ourselves: let us not bewilder our successors: let us transmit to them the practice of Poetry, with its boundaries and wholesome regulative laws, under which excellent works may again, perhaps, at some future time, be produced, not yet fallen into oblivion through our neglect, not yet condemned and cancelled by the influence of their eternal enemy, Caprice.

Fox How, Ambleside,
October 1, 1853.

PREFACE TO SECOND EDITION OF *POEMS* (1854)

I HAVE allowed the Preface to the former edition of these Poems to stand almost without change, because I still believe it to be, in the main, true. I must not, however, be supposed insensible to the force of much that has been alleged against portions of it, or unaware that it contains many things incompletely stated, many things which need limitation. It leaves, too, untouched the question, how far, and in what manner, the opinions there expressed respecting the choice of subjects apply to lyric poetry; that region of the poetical field which is chiefly cultivated at present. But neither do I propose at the present time to supply these deficiencies, nor, indeed, would this be the proper place for attempting it. On one or two points alone I wish to offer, in the briefest possible way, some explanation.

An objection has been warmly urged to the classing together, as subjects equally belonging to a past time, Œdipus and Macbeth. And it is no doubt true that to Shakespeare, standing on the verge of the middle ages, the epoch of Macbeth was more familiar than that of Œdipus. But I was speaking of actions as they presented themselves to us moderns: and it will hardly be said that the European mind, in our day, has much more affinity with the times of Macbeth than with those of Œdipus. As moderns, it seems to me, we have no longer any direct affinity with the circumstances and feelings of either. As individuals, we are attracted towards this or that personage, we have a capacity for imagining him, irrespective of his times, solely according to a law of personal sympathy; and those subjects for which we feel this personal attraction most strongly, we may hope to treat successfully. Prometheus or Joan of Arc, Charlemagne or Agamemnon — one of these is not really nearer to us now than another. Each can be made present only by an act of poetic imagination: but this man's imagination has an affinity for one of them, and that man's for another.

It has been said that I wish to limit the Poet in his choice of subjects to the period of Greek and Roman antiquity: but it is not so. I only counsel him to choose for his subjects great actions, without regarding to what time they belong. Nor do I deny that the poetic faculty can and does manifest itself in treating the most trifling action, the most hopeless subject. But it is a pity that power should be wasted; and that the Poet should be compelled to impart interest and force to his subject, instead of receiving them from it, and thereby doubling his impressiveness. There is, it has been excellently said, an immortal strength in the stories of great actions: the most gifted poet, then, may well be glad to supplement with it that mortal weakness, which, in presence of the vast spectacle of life and the world, he must for ever feel to be his individual portion.

Again, with respect to the study of the classical writers of antiquity: it has been said that we should emulate rather than imitate them. I make no objection: all I say is, let us study them. They can help to cure us of what is, it seems to me, the great vice of our intellect, manifesting itself in our incredible vagaries in literature, in art, in religion, in morals; namely, that it is *fantastic,* and wants *sanity.* Sanity — that is the great virtue of the ancient literature: the want of that is the great defect of the modern, in spite of all its variety and power. It is impossible to read carefully the great ancients, without losing something of our caprice and eccentricity: and to emulate them we must at least read them.

London,
June 1, 1854.

ON TRANSLATING HOMER

. . . . *Nunquamne reponam?*

Lecture I

It has more than once been suggested to me that I should translate Homer. That is a task for which I have neither the time nor the courage; but the suggestion led me to regard yet more closely a poet whom I had already long studied, and for one or two years the works of Homer were seldom out of my hands. The study of classical literature is probably on the decline; but, whatever may be the fate of this study in general, it is certain that, as instruction spreads and the number of readers increases, attention will be more and more directed to the poetry of Homer, not indeed as part of a classical course, but as the most important poetical monument existing. Even within the last ten years two fresh translations of the *Iliad* have appeared in England: one by a man of great ability and genuine learning, Professor Newman; the other by Mr. Wright, the conscientious and painstaking translator of Dante. It may safely be asserted that neither of these works will take rank as the standard translation of Homer; that the task of rendering him will still be attempted by other translators. It may perhaps be possible to render to these some service, to save them some loss of labour, by pointing out rocks on which their predecessors have split, and the right objects on which a translator of Homer should fix his attention.

It is disputed what aim a translator should propose to himself in dealing with his original. Even this preliminary is not yet settled. On one side it is said that the translation ought to be such "that the reader should, if possible, forget that it is a translation at all, and be lulled into the illusion that he is reading an original work, — something original" (if the translation be in English), "from an English hand." The real original is in this case, it is said, "taken as a basis on which to rear a poem that shall affect our countrymen as the original may be conceived to have affected its natural hearers." On the other hand, Mr. Newman, who states the foregoing doctrine only to condemn it, declares that he "aims at precisely the opposite: to retain every peculiarity of the original, so far as he is able, *with the greater care the more foreign it may happen to be*"; so that it may "never be forgotten that he is imitating, and imitating in a different material." The translator's "first duty," says Mr. Newman, "is a historical one, to be *faith-*

ful." Probably both sides would agree that the translator's "first duty is to be faithful"; but the question at issue between them is, in what faithfulness consists.

My one object is to give practical advice to a translator; and I shall not the least concern myself with theories of translation as such. But I advise the translator not to try "to rear on the basis of the *Iliad,* a poem that shall affect our countrymen as the original may be conceived to have affected its natural hearers"; and for this simple reason, that we cannot possibly tell *how* the *Iliad* "affected its natural hearers." It is probably meant merely that he should try to affect Englishmen powerfully, as Homer affected Greeks powerfully; but this direction is not enough, and can give no real guidance. For all great poets affect their hearers powerfully, but the effect of one poet is one thing, that of another poet another thing: it is our translator's business to reproduce the effect of Homer, and the most powerful emotion of the unlearned English reader can never assure him whether he has *re*-produced this, or whether he has produced something else. So, again, he may follow Mr. Newman's directions, he may try to be "faithful," he may "retain every peculiarity of his original"; but who is to assure him, who is to assure Mr. Newman himself, that, when he has done this, he has done that for which Mr. Newman enjoins this to be done, "adhered closely to Homer's manner and habit of thought"? Evidently the translator needs some more practical directions than these. No one can tell him how Homer affected the Greeks; but there are those who can tell him how Homer affects *them.* These are scholars; who possess, at the same time with knowledge of Greek, adequate poetical taste and feeling. No translation will seem to them of much worth compared with the original; but they alone can say whether the translation produces more or less the same effect upon them as the original. They are the only competent tribunal in this matter: the Greeks are dead; the unlearned Englishman has not the data for judging; and no man can safely confide in his own single judgment of his own work. Let not the translator, then, trust to his notions of what the ancient Greeks would have thought of him; he will lose himself in the vague. Let him not trust to what the ordinary English reader thinks of him; he will be taking the blind for his guide. Let him not trust to his own judgment of his own work; he may be misled by individual caprices. Let him ask how his work affects those who both know Greek and can appreciate poetry; whether to read it gives the Provost of Eton, or Professor Thompson at Cambridge, or Professor Jowett here in Oxford, at all the same feeling which to read the original gives them. I consider that when Bentley said of Pope's translation, "It was a pretty poem, but must not be called Homer," the work, in spite of all its power and attractiveness, was judged.

Ὡς ἂν ὁ φρόνιμος ὁρίσειεν, — "as the judicious would determine," — that is a test to which every one professes himself willing to submit his works. Unhappily, in most cases, no two persons agree as to who "the judicious" are. In the present case, the ambiguity is removed: I suppose the translator at one with me as to the tribunal to which alone he should look for judgment; and he has thus obtained a practical test by which to estimate the real success of his work. How is he to proceed, in order that his work, tried by this test, may be found most successful?

First of all, there are certain negative counsels which I will give him. Homer has occupied men's minds so much, such a literature has arisen about him, that every one who approaches him should resolve strictly to limit himself to that which may directly serve the object for which he approaches him. I advise the translator to have nothing to do with the questions, whether Homer ever existed; whether the poet of the *Iliad* be one or many; whether the *Iliad* be one poem or an *Achilleis* and an *Iliad* stuck together; whether the Christian doctrine of the Atonement is shadowed forth in the Homeric mythology; whether the Goddess Latona in any way prefigures the Virgin Mary, and so on. These are questions which have been discussed with learning, with ingenuity, nay, with genius; but they have two inconveniences, — one general for all who approach them, one particular for the translator. The general inconvenience is that there really exist no data for determining them. The particular inconvenience is that their solution by the translator, even were it possible, could be of no benefit to his translation.

I advise him, again, not to trouble himself with constructing a special vocabulary for his use in translation; with excluding a certain class of English words, and with confining himself to another class, in obedience to any theory about the peculiar qualities of Homer's style. Mr. Newman says that "the entire dialect of Homer being essentially archaic, that of a translator ought to be as much Saxo-Norman as possible, and owe as little as possible to the elements thrown into our language by classical learning." Mr. Newman is unfortunate in the observance of his own theory; for I continually find in his translation words of Latin origin, which seem to me quite alien to the simplicity of Homer, — "responsive," for instance, which is a favourite word of Mr. Newman, to represent the Homeric ἀμειβόμενος:

> Great Hector of the motley helm thus spake to her *responsive*.
> But thus *responsively* to him spake god-like Alexander.

And the word "celestial," again, in the grand address of Zeus to the horses of Achilles,

> You, who are born *celestial*, from Eld and Death exempted!

seems to me in that place exactly to jar upon the feeling as too bookish. But, apart from the question of Mr. Newman's fidelity to his own theory, such a theory seems to me both dangerous for a translator and false in itself. Dangerous for a translator; because, wherever one finds such a theory announced (and one finds it pretty often), it is generally followed by an explosion of pedantry; and pedantry is of all things in the world the most un-Homeric. False in itself; because, in fact, we owe to the Latin element in our language most of that very rapidity and clear decisiveness by which it is contradistinguished from the German, and in sympathy with the languages of Greece and Rome: so that to limit an English translator of Homer to words of Saxon origin is to deprive him of one of his special advantages for translating Homer. In Voss's well-known translation of Homer, it is precisely the qualities of his German language itself, something heavy and trailing both in the structure of its sentences and in the words of which it is composed, which prevent his translation, in spite of the hexameters, in spite of the fidelity, from creating in us the impression created by the Greek. Mr. Newman's prescription, if followed, would just strip the English translator of the advantage which he has over Voss.

The frame of mind in which we approach an author influences our correctness of appreciation of him; and Homer should be approached by a translator in the simplest frame of mind possible. Modern sentiment tries to make the ancient not less than the modern world its own; but against modern sentiment in its applications to Homer the translator, if he would feel Homer truly — and unless he feels him truly, how can he render him truly? — cannot be too much on his guard. For example: the writer of an interesting article on English translations of Homer, in the last number of the *National Review*, quotes, I see, with admiration, a criticism of Mr. Ruskin on the use of the epithet φυσίζοος, "life-giving," in that beautiful passage in the third book of the *Iliad*, which follows Helen's mention of her brothers Castor and Pollux as alive, though they were in truth dead:

ὣς φάτο · τοὺς δ' ἤδη κατέχεν φυσίζοος αἶα
ἐν Λακεδαίμονι αὖθι, φίλῃ ἐν πατρίδι γαίῃ.[1]

"The poet," says Mr. Ruskin, "has to speak of the earth in sadness; but he will not let that sadness affect or change his thought of it. No; though Castor and Pollux be dead, yet the earth is our mother still, — fruitful, life-giving." This is a just specimen of that sort of application of modern sentiment to the ancients, against which a student, who wishes to feel the ancients truly, cannot too resolutely defend himself.

[1] *Iliad*, iii, 243.

It reminds one, as, alas! so much of Mr. Ruskin's writing reminds one, of those words of the most delicate of living critics: "Comme tout genre de composition a son écueil particulier, *celui du genre romanesque, c'est le faux.*" The reader may feel moved as he reads it; but it is not the less an example of "le faux" in criticism; it is false. It is not true, as to that particular passage, that Homer called the earth *φυσίζοος* because, "though he had to speak of the earth in sadness, he would not let that sadness change or affect his thought of it," but consoled himself by considering that "the earth is our mother still, — fruitful, life-giving." It is not true, as a matter of general criticism, that this kind of sentimentality, eminently modern, inspires Homer at all. "From Homer and Polygnotus I every day learn more clearly," says Goethe, "that in our life here above ground we have, properly speaking, to enact Hell:"[1] — if the student must absolutely have a keynote to the *Iliad*, let him take this of Goethe, and see what he can do with it; it will not, at any rate, like the tender pantheism of Mr. Ruskin, falsify for him the whole strain of Homer.

These are negative counsels; I come to the positive. When I say, the translator of Homer should above all be penetrated by a sense of four qualities of his author; — that he is eminently rapid; that he is eminently plain and direct, both in the evolution of his thought and in the expression of it, that is, both in his syntax and in his words; that he is eminently plain and direct in the substance of his thought, that is, in his matter and ideas; and, finally that he is eminently noble; — I probably seem to be saying what is too general to be of much service to anybody. Yet it is strictly true that, for want of duly penetrating themselves with the first-named quality of Homer, his rapidity, Cowper and Mr. Wright have failed in rendering him; that, for want of duly appreciating the second-named quality, his plainness and directness of style and diction, Pope and Mr. Sotheby have failed in rendering him; that for want of appreciating the third, his plainness and directness of ideas, Chapman has failed in rendering him; while for want of appreciating the fourth, his nobleness, Mr. Newman, who has clearly seen some of the faults of his predecessors, has yet failed more conspicuously than any of them.

Coleridge says, in his strange language, speaking of the union of the human soul with the divine essence, that this takes place

> Whene'er the mist, which stands 'twixt God and thee,
> Defecates to a pure transparency;

and so, too, it may be said of that union of the translator with his original, which alone can produce a good translation, that it takes

[1] *Briefwechsel zwischen Schiller und Goethe*, vi, 230.

place when the mist which stands between them — the mist of alien modes of thinking, speaking, and feeling on the translator's part — "defecates to a pure transparency," and disappears. But between Cowper and Homer — (Mr. Wright repeats in the main Cowper's manner, as Mr. Sotheby repeats Pope's manner, and neither Mr. Wright's translation nor Mr. Sotheby's has, I must be forgiven for saying, any proper reason for existing) — between Cowper and Homer there is interposed the mist of Cowper's elaborate Miltonic manner, entirely alien to the flowing rapidity of Homer; between Pope and Homer there is interposed the mist of Pope's literary artificial manner, entirely alien to the plain naturalness of Homer's manner; between Chapman and Homer there is interposed the mist of the fancifulness of the Elizabethan age, entirely alien to the plain directness of Homer's thought and feeling; while between Mr. Newman and Homer is interposed a cloud of more than Egyptian thickness, — namely, a manner, in Mr. Newman's version, eminently ignoble, while Homer's manner is eminently noble.

I do not despair of making all these propositions clear to a student who approaches Homer with a free mind. First, Homer is eminently rapid, and to this rapidity the elaborate movement of Miltonic blank verse is alien. The reputation of Cowper, that most interesting man and excellent poet, does not depend on his translation of Homer; and in his preface to the second edition, he himself tells us that he felt, — he had too much poetical taste not to feel, — on returning to his own version after six or seven years, "more dissatisfied with it himself than the most difficult to be pleased of all his judges." And he was dissatisfied with it for the right reason, — that "it seemed to him deficient *in the grace of ease.*" Yet he seems to have originally misconceived the manner of Homer so much, that it is no wonder he rendered him amiss. "The similitude of Milton's manner to that of Homer is such," he says, "that no person familiar with both can read either without being reminded of the other; and it is in those breaks and pauses to which the numbers of the English poet are so much indebted, both for their dignity and variety, that he chiefly copies the Grecian." It would be more true to say: "The unlikeness of Milton's manner to that of Homer is such, that no person familiar with both can read either without being struck with his difference from the other; and it is in his breaks and pauses that the English poet is most unlike the Grecian."

The inversion and pregnant conciseness of Milton or Dante are, doubtless, most impressive qualities of style; but they are the very opposites of the directness and flowingness of Homer, which he keeps alike in passages of the simplest narrative, and in those of the deepest emotion. Not only, for example, are these lines of Cowper un-Homeric:

So numerous seemed those fires the banks between
Of Xanthus, blazing, and the fleet of Greece
In prospect all of Troy;

where the position of the word "blazing" gives an entirely un-Homeric movement to this simple passage, describing the fires of the Trojan camp outside of Troy; but the following lines, in that very highly-wrought passage where the horse of Achilles answers his master's reproaches for having left Patroclus on the field of battle, are equally un-Homeric:

For not through sloth or tardiness on us
Aught chargeable, have Ilium's sons thine arms
Stript from Patroclus' shoulders; but a God
Matchless in battle, offspring of bright-haired
Latona, him contending in the van
Slew, for the glory of the chief of Troy.

Here even the first inversion, "have Ilium's sons thine arms Stript from Patroclus' shoulders," gives the reader a sense of a movement not Homeric; and the second inversion, "a God him contending in the van Slew," gives this sense ten times stronger. Instead of moving on without check, as in reading the original, the reader twice finds himself, in reading the translation, brought up and checked. Homer moves with the same simplicity and rapidity in the highly-wrought as in the simple passage.

It is in vain that Cowper insists on his fidelity: "my chief boast is that I have adhered closely to my original:" — "the matter found in me, whether the reader like it or not, is found also in Homer; and the matter not found in me, how much soever the reader may admire it, is found only in Mr. Pope." To suppose that it is *fidelity* to an original to give its matter, unless you at the same time give its manner; or, rather, to suppose that you can really give its matter at all, unless you can give its manner, is just the mistake of our pre-Raphaelite school of painters, who do not understand that the peculiar effect of nature resides in the whole and not in the parts. So the peculiar effect of a poet resides in his manner and movement, not in his words taken separately. It is well known how conscientiously literal is Cowper in his translation of Homer. It is well known how extravagantly free is Pope.

So let it be!
Portents and prodigies are lost on me:

that is Pope's rendering of the words,

Ξάνθε, τί μοι θάνατον μαντεύεαι; οὐδέ τί σε χρή·[1]

Xanthus, why prophesiest thou my death to me? thou needest not at all:

[1] *Iliad,* xix, 420.

yet, on the whole, Pope's translation of the *Iliad* is more Homeric than Cowper's, for it is more rapid.

Pope's movement, however, though rapid, is not of the same kind as Homer's; and here I come to the real objection to rhyme in a translation of Homer. It is commonly said that rhyme is to be abandoned in a translation of Homer, because "the exigences of rhyme," to quote Mr. Newman, "positively forbid faithfulness"; because "a just translation of any ancient poet in rhyme," to quote Cowper, "is impossible." This, however, is merely an accidental objection to rhyme. If this were all, it might be supposed, that if rhymes were more abundant, Homer could be adequately translated in rhyme. But this is not so; there is a deeper, a substantial objection to rhyme in a translation of Homer. It is, that rhyme inevitably tends to pair lines which in the original are independent, and thus the movement of the poem is changed. In these lines of Chapman, for instance, from Sarpedon's speech to Glaucus, in the twelfth book of the *Iliad:*

O friend, if keeping back
Would keep back age from us, and death, and that we might not wrack
In this life's human sea at all, but that deferring now
We shunned death ever, — nor would I half this vain valor show,
Nor glorify a folly so, to wish thee to advance;
But since we *must* go, though not here, and that besides the chance
Proposed now, there are infinite fates,

etc. Here the necessity of making the line,

Nor glorify a folly so, to wish thee to advance,

rhyme with the line which follows it, entirely changes and spoils the movement of the passage.

οὔτε κεν αὐτὸς ἐνὶ πρώτοισι μαχοίμην,
οὔτε κε σὲ στέλλοιμι μάχην ἐς κυδιάνειραν·[1]

Neither would I myself go forth to fight with the foremost,
Nor would I urge thee on to enter the glorious battle,

says Homer; there he stops, and begins an opposed movement:

νῦν δ'—ἔμπης γὰρ Κῆρες ἐφεστᾶσιν θανάτοιο—

But — for a thousand fates of death stand close to us always —

This line, in which Homer wishes to go away with the most marked rapidity from the line before, Chapman is forced, by the necessity of rhyming, intimately to connect with the line before.

But since we *must* go, though not here, and that besides the chance —

1 *Iliad,* xii, 324.

The moment the word *chance* strikes our ear, we are irresistibly carried back to *advance* and to the whole previous line, which, according to Homer's own feeling, we ought to have left behind us entirely, and to be moving farther and farther away from.

Rhyme certainly, by intensifying antithesis, can intensify separation, and this is precisely what Pope does; but this balanced rhetorical antithesis, though very effective, is entirely un-Homeric. And this is what I mean by saying that Pope fails to render Homer, because he does not render his plainness and directness of style and diction. Where Homer marks separation by moving away, Pope marks it by antithesis. No passage could show this better than the passage I have just quoted, on which I will pause for a moment.

Robert Wood, whose *Essay on the Genius of Homer* is mentioned by Goethe as one of the books which fell into his hands when his powers were first developing themselves, and strongly interested him, relates of this passage a striking story. He says that in 1762, at the end of the Seven Years' War, being then Under-Secretary of State, he was directed to wait upon the President of the Council, Lord Granville, a few days before he died, with the preliminary articles of the Treaty of Paris. "I found him," he continues, "so languid, that I proposed postponing my business for another time; but he insisted that I should stay, saying, it could not prolong his life to neglect his duty; and repeating the following passage out of Sarpedon's speech, he dwelled with particular emphasis on the third line, which recalled to his mind the distinguishing part he had taken in public affairs:

ὦ πέπον εἰ μὲν γὰρ πόλεμον περὶ τόνδε φυγόντε,
αἰεὶ δὴ μέλλοιμεν ἀγήρω τ' ἀθανάτω τε
ἔσσεσθ', οὔτε κεν αὐτὸς ἐνὶ πρώτοισι μαχοίμην,[1]
οὔτε κε σὲ στέλλοιμι μάχην ἐς κυδιάνειραν·
νῦν δ'—ἔμπης γὰρ Κῆρες ἐφεστᾶσιν θανάτοιο
μυρίαι, ἃς οὐκ ἔστι φυγεῖν βροτὸν οὐδ' ὑπαλύξαι—
ἴομεν.[2]

His Lordship repeated the last word several times with a calm and determinate resignation; and, after a serious pause of some minutes, he desired to hear the Treaty read, to which he listened with great attention, and recovered spirits enough to declare the approbation of a

1 These are the words on which Lord Granville "dwelled with particular emphasis."

2 ["Ah, friend, if once escaped from this battle we were for ever to be ageless and immortal, neither would I fight myself in the foremost ranks, nor would I send thee into the war that giveth men renown, but now — for assuredly ten thousand fates of death do every way beset us, and these no mortal may escape nor avoid — now let us go forward, whether we shall give glory to other men, or others to us." (Lang, Leaf, and Myers trans.) Ed. note.]

dying statesman (I use his own words) 'on the most glorious war, and most honourable peace, this nation ever saw.'"[1]

I quote this story, first, because it is interesting as exhibiting the English aristocracy at its very height of culture, lofty spirit, and greatness, towards the middle of the last century. I quote it, secondly, because it seems to me to illustrate Goethe's saying which I mentioned, that our life, in Homer's view of it, represents a conflict and a hell; and it brings out, too, what there is tonic and fortifying in this doctrine. I quote it, lastly, because it shows that the passage is just one of those in translating which Pope will be at his best, a passage of strong emotion and oratorical movement, not of simple narrative or description.

Pope translates the passage thus:

> Could all our care elude the gloomy grave
> Which claims no less the fearful than the brave,
> For lust of fame I should not vainly dare
> In fighting fields, nor urge thy soul to war:
> But since, alas! ignoble age must come,
> Disease, and death's inexorable doom;
> The life which others pay, let us bestow,
> And give to fame what we to nature owe.

Nothing could better exhibit Pope's prodigious talent, and nothing, too, could be better in its own way. But, as Bentley said, "You must not call it Homer." One feels that Homer's thought has passed through a literary and rhetorical crucible, and come out highly intellectualised; come out in a form which strongly impresses us, indeed, but which no longer impresses us in the same way as when it was uttered by Homer. The antithesis of the last two lines—

> The life which others pay, let us bestow,
> And give to fame what we to nature owe—

is excellent, and is just suited to Pope's heroic couplet; but neither the antithesis itself, nor the couplet which conveys it, is suited to the feeling or to the movement of the Homeric ἴομεν.

A literary and intellectualised language is, however, in its own way well suited to grand matters; and Pope, with a language of this kind and his own admirable talent, comes off well enough as long as he has passion, or oratory, or a great crisis to deal with. Even here, as I have been pointing out, he does not render Homer; but he and his style are in themselves strong. It is when he comes to level passages, passages of narrative or description, that he and his style are sorely tried, and

[1] Robert Wood, *Essay on the Original Genius and Writings of Homer*, London, 1775, p. vii.

prove themselves weak. A perfectly plain direct style can of course convey the simplest matter as naturally as the grandest; indeed, it must be harder for it, one would say, to convey a grand matter worthily and nobly, than to convey a common matter, as alone such a matter should be conveyed, plainly and simply. But the style of Rasselas is incomparably better fitted to describe a sage philosophising than a soldier lighting his campfire. The style of Pope is not the style of Rasselas; but it is equally a literary style, equally unfitted to describe a simple matter with the plain naturalness of Homer.

Every one knows the passage at the end of the eighth book of the *Iliad,* where the fires of the Trojan encampment are likened to the stars. It is very far from my wish to hold Pope up to ridicule, so I shall not quote the commencement of the passage, which in the original is of great and celebrated beauty, and in translating which Pope has been singularly and notoriously unfortunate. But the latter part of the passage, where Homer leaves the stars, and comes to the Trojan fires, treats of the plainest, most matter-of-fact subject possible, and deals with this, as Homer always deals with every subject, in the plainest and most straightforward style. "So many in number, between the ships and the streams of Xanthus, shone forth in front of Troy the fires kindled by the Trojans. There were kindled a thousand fires in the plain; and by each one there sat fifty men in the light of the blazing fire. And the horses, munching white barley and rye, and standing by the chariots, waited for the bright-throned Morning."[1]

In Pope's translation, this plain story becomes the following:

> So many flames before proud Ilion blaze,
> And brighten glimmering Xanthus with their rays;
> The long reflections of the distant fires
> Gleam on the walls, and tremble on the spires.
> A thousand piles the dusky horrors gild,
> And shoot a shady lustre o'er the field.
> Full fifty guards each flaming pile attend,
> Whose umbered arms, by fits, thick flashes send;
> Loud neigh the coursers o'er their heaps of corn,
> And ardent warriors wait the rising morn.

It is for passages of this sort, which, after all, form the bulk of a narrative poem, that Pope's style is so bad. In elevated passages he is powerful, as Homer is powerful, though not in the same way; but in plain narrative, where Homer is still powerful and delightful, Pope, by the inherent fault of his style, is ineffective and out of taste. Wordsworth says somewhere, that wherever Virgil seems to have

[1] *Iliad,* viii, 560.

composed "with his eye on the object," Dryden fails to render him. Homer invariably composes "with his eye on the object," whether the object be a moral or a material one: Pope composes with his eye on his style, into which he translates his object, whatever it is. That, therefore, which Homer conveys to us immediately, Pope conveys to us through a medium. He aims at turning Homer's sentiments pointedly and rhetorically; at investing Homer's description with ornament and dignity. A sentiment may be changed by being put into a pointed and oratorical form, yet may still be very effective in that form; but a description, the moment it takes its eyes off that which it is to describe, and begins to think of ornamenting itself, is worthless.

Therefore, I say, the translator of Homer should penetrate himself with a sense of the plainness and directness of Homer's style; of the simplicity with which Homer's thought is evolved and expressed. He has Pope's fate before his eyes, to show him what a divorce may be created even between the most gifted translator and Homer by an artificial evolution of thought and a literary cast of style.

Chapman's style is not artificial and literary like Pope's, nor his movement elaborate and self-retarding like the Miltonic movement of Cowper. He is plain-spoken, fresh, vigorous, and, to a certain degree, rapid; and all these are Homeric qualities. I cannot say that I think the movement of his fourteen-syllable line, which has been so much commended, Homeric; but on this point I shall have more to say by and by, when I come to speak of Mr. Newman's metrical exploits. But it is not distinctly anti-Homeric, like the movement of Milton's blank verse; and it has a rapidity of its own. Chapman's diction, too, is generally good, that is, appropriate to Homer; above all, the syntactical character of his style is appropriate. With these merits, what prevents his translation from being a satisfactory version of Homer? Is it merely the want of literal faithfulness to his original, imposed upon him, it is said, by the exigences of rhyme? Has this celebrated version, which has so many advantages, no other and deeper defect than that? Its author is a poet, and a poet, too, of the Elizabethan age; the golden age of English literature as it is called, and on the whole truly called; for, whatever be the defects of Elizabethan literature (and they are great), we have no development of our literature to compare with it for vigour and richness. This age, too, showed what it could do in translating, by producing a masterpiece, its version of the Bible.

Chapman's translation has often been praised as eminently Homeric. Keats's fine sonnet in its honour every one knows; but Keats could not read the original, and therefore could not really judge the translation. Coleridge, in praising Chapman's version, says at the same time, "It will give you small idea of Homer." But the grave authority of Mr. Hallam pronounces this translation to be "often exceedingly Homeric"; and its latest editor boldly declares that by what, with a deplorable style, he calls "his own innative Homeric genius," Chapman "has thoroughly identified himself with Homer"; and that "we pardon him even for his digressions, for they are such as we feel Homer himself would have written."

I confess that I can never read twenty lines of Chapman's version without recurring to Bentley's cry, "This is not Homer!" and that from a deeper cause than any unfaithfulness occasioned by the fetters of rhyme.

I said that there were four things which eminently distinguished Homer, and with a sense of which Homer's translator should penetrate himself as fully as possible. One of these four things was, the plainness and directness of Homer's ideas. I have just been speaking of the plainness and directness of his style; but the plainness and directness of the contents of his style, of his ideas themselves, is not less remarkable. But as eminently as Homer is plain, so eminently is the Elizabethan literature in general, and Chapman in particular, fanciful. Steeped in humours and fantasticality up to its very lips, the Elizabethan age, newly arrived at the free use of the human faculties after their long term of bondage, and delighting to exercise them freely, suffers from its own extravagance in this first exercise of them, can hardly bring itself to see an object quietly or to describe it temperately. Happily, in the translation of the Bible, the sacred character of their original inspired the translators with such respect that they did not dare to give the rein to their own fancies in dealing with it. But, in dealing with works of profane literature, in dealing with poetical works above all, which highly stimulated them, one may say that the minds of the Elizabethan translators were *too* active; that they could not forbear importing so much of their own, and this of a most peculiar and Elizabethan character, into their original, that they effaced the character of the original itself.

Take merely the opening pages to Chapman's translation, the introductory verses, and the dedications. You will find:

> An Anagram of the name of our Dread Prince
> My most gracious and sacred Mæcenas,
> Henry, Prince of Wales,
> Our Sunn, Heyr, Peace, Life, —

Henry, son of James the First, to whom the work is dedicated. Then comes an address,

> To the sacred Fountain of Princes,
> Sole Empress of Beauty and Virtue, Anne, Queen
> Of England, [etc.]

All the Middle Age, with its grotesqueness, its conceits, its irrationality, is still in these opening pages; they by themselves are sufficient to indicate to us what a gulf divides Chapman from the "clearest-souled" of poets, from Homer; almost as great a gulf as that which divides him from Voltaire. Pope has been sneered at for saying that Chapman writes "somewhat as one might imagine Homer himself to have written before he arrived at years of discretion." But the remark is excellent: Homer expresses himself like a man of adult reason, Chapman like a man whose reason has not yet cleared itself. For instance, if Homer had had to say of a poet, that he hoped his merit was now about to be fully established in the opinion of good judges, he was as incapable of saying this as Chapman says it, — "Though truth in her very nakedness sits in so deep a pit, that from Gades to Aurora, and Ganges, few eyes can sound her, I hope yet those few here will so discover and confirm [her] that, the date being out of her darkness in this morning of our poet, he shall now gird his temples with the sun," — I say, Homer was as incapable of saying this in that manner, as Voltaire himself would have been. Homer, indeed, has actually an affinity with Voltaire in the unrivalled clearness and straightforwardness of his thinking; in the way in which he keeps to one thought at a time, and puts that thought forth in its complete natural plainness, instead of being led away from it by some fancy striking him in connection with it, and being beguiled to wander off with this fancy till his original thought, in its natural reality, knows him no more. What could better show us how gifted a race was this Greek race? The same member of it has not only the power of profoundly touching that natural heart of humanity which it is Voltaire's weakness that he cannot reach, but can also address the understanding with all Voltaire's admirable simplicity and rationality.

My limits will not allow me to do more than shortly illustrate, from Chapman's version of the *Iliad,* what I mean when I speak of this vital difference between Homer and an Elizabethan poet in the quality of their thought; between the plain simplicity of the thought of the one, and the curious complexity of the thought of the other. As in Pope's case, I carefully abstain from choosing passages for the express purpose of making Chapman appear ridiculous; Chapman, like Pope, merits in himself all respect, though he too, like Pope, fails to render Homer.

In that tonic speech of Sarpedon, of which I have said so much, Homer, you may remember, has:

εἰ μὲν γὰρ πόλεμον περὶ τόνδε φυγόντε
αἰεὶ δὴ μέλλοιμεν ἀγήρω τ' ἀθανάτω τε
ἔσσεσθ', —

if indeed, but once *this* battle avoided,
We were for ever to live without growing old, and immortal.

Chapman cannot be satisfied with this, but must add a fancy to it:

if keeping back
Would keep back age from us, and death, and *that we might not wrack*
In this life's human sea at all;

and so on. Again; in another passage which I have before quoted, where Zeus says to the horses of Peleus,

τί σφῶϊ δόμεν Πηλῆϊ ἄνακτι
θνητῷ; ὑμεῖς δ' ἐστὸν ἀγήρω τ' ἀθανάτω τε·[1]

Why gave we you to royal Peleus, to a mortal? but ye are without old age, and immortal.

Chapman sophisticates this into:

Why gave we you t' a mortal king, when immortality
And *incapacity of age so dignifies your states?*

Again; in the speech of Achilles to his horses, where Achilles, according to Homer, says simply, "Take heed that ye bring your master safe back to the host of the Danaans, in some other sort than the last time, when the battle is ended," Chapman sophisticates this into:

When with blood, for this day's fast observed, revenge shall yield
Our heart satiety, bring us off.

In Hector's famous speech, again, at his parting from Andromache, Homer makes him say: "Nor does my own heart so bid me" (to keep safe behind the walls), "since I have learned to be staunch always, and to fight among the foremost of the Trojans, busy on behalf of my father's great glory, and my own."[2] In Chapman's hands this becomes:

The spirit I first did breathe
Did never teach me that; much less, since the contempt of death
Was settled in me, *and my mind knew what a worthy was,*
Whose office is to lead in fight, and give no danger pass
Without improvement. In this fire must Hector's trial shine:
Here must his country, father, friends, be in him made divine.

You see how ingeniously Homer's plain thought is *tormented,* as the French would say, here. Homer goes on: "For well I know this in my mind and in my heart, the day will be, when sacred Troy shall perish":

ἔσσεται ἦμαρ ὅτ' ἄν ποτ' ὀλώλῃ Ἴλιος ἱρή.

1 *Iliad,* xvii, 443.
2 *Iliad,* vi, 444.

Chapman makes this:

> And such a *stormy* day shall come, in mind and soul I know
> When sacred Troy *shall shed her towers, for tears of overthrow.*

I might go on for ever, but I could not give you a better illustration than this last, of what I mean by saying that the Elizabethan poet fails to render Homer because he cannot forbear to interpose a play of thought between his object and its expression. Chapman translates his object into Elizabethan, as Pope translates it into the Augustan of Queen Anne; both convey it to us through a medium. Homer, on the other hand, sees his object and conveys it to us immediately.

And yet, in spite of this perfect plainness and directness of Homer's style, in spite of this perfect plainness and directness of his ideas, he is eminently *noble;* he works as entirely in the grand style, he is as grandiose, as Phidias, or Dante, or Michael Angelo. This is what makes his translators despair. "To give relief," says Cowper, "to prosaic subjects" (such as dressing, eating, drinking, harnessing, travelling, going to bed), that is to treat such subjects nobly, in the grand style, "without seeming unreasonably tumid, is extremely difficult." It *is* difficult, but Homer has done it. Homer is precisely the incomparable poet he is, because he has done it. His translator must not be tumid, must not be artificial, must not be literary; true: but then also he must not be commonplace, must not be ignoble. I have shown you how translators of Homer fail by wanting rapidity, by wanting simplicity of style, by wanting plainness of thought: in a second lecture I will show you how a translator fails by wanting nobility.

PREFACE TO
ESSAYS IN CRITICISM

SEVERAL of the Essays which are here collected and reprinted had the good or the bad fortune to be much criticised at the time of their first appearance. I am not now going to inflict upon the reader a reply to those criticisms; for one or two explanations which are desirable, I shall elsewhere, perhaps, be able some day to find an opportunity; but, indeed, it is not in my nature, — some of my critics would rather say, not in my power, — to dispute on behalf of any opinion, even my own, very obstinately. To try and approach truth on one side after another, not to strive or cry, nor to persist in pressing forward, on any one side, with violence and self-will, — it is only thus, it seems to me, that mortals may hope to gain any vision of the mysterious Goddess, whom we shall never see except in outline, but only thus even in outline. He who will do nothing but fight impetuously towards her on his own, one, favourite, particular line, is inevitably destined to run his head into the folds of the black robe in which she is wrapped.

So it is not to reply to my critics that I write this preface, but to prevent a misunderstanding, of which certain phrases that some of them use make me apprehensive. Mr. Wright, one of the many translators of Homer, has published a Letter to the Dean of Canterbury, complaining of some remarks of mine, uttered now a long while ago, on his version of the *Iliad*. One cannot be always studying one's own works, and I was really under the impression, till I saw Mr. Wright's complaint, that I had spoken of him with all respect. The reader may judge of my astonishment, therefore, at finding, from Mr. Wright's pamphlet, that I had "declared with much solemnity that there is not any proper reason for his existing." That I never said; but, on looking back at my Lectures on translating Homer, I find that I did say, not that Mr. Wright, but that Mr. Wright's version of the *Iliad*, repeating in the main the merits and defects of Cowper's version, as Mr. Sotheby's repeated those of Pope's version, had, if I might be pardoned for saying so, no proper reason for existing. Elsewhere I expressly spoke of the merit of his version; but I confess that the phrase, qualified as I have shown, about its want of a proper reason for existing, I used. Well, the phrase had, perhaps, too much vivacity; we have all of us a right to exist, we and our works; an unpopular author should be the last person to call in question this right. So I gladly withdraw the offending phrase, and I am sorry for having used it; Mr. Wright, however, would perhaps be more indulgent to my vivacity, if he considered that we are none of us likely to be lively much longer. My vivacity is but the last sparkle of flame before we are all in the dark, the last glimpse of colour before we all go into drab, — the drab of the earnest, prosaic, practical, austerely literal future. Yes, the world will soon be the Philistines'! and then, with every voice, not of thunder, silenced, and the whole earth filled and ennobled every morning by the magnificent roaring of the young lions of the *Daily Telegraph,* we shall all yawn in one another's faces with the dismallest, the most unimpeachable gravity.

But I return to my design in writing this Preface. That design was, after apologising to Mr. Wright for my vivacity of five years ago, to beg him and others to let me bear my own burdens, without saddling the great and famous University, to which I have the honour to belong, with any portion of them. What I mean to deprecate is such phrases as, "his professorial assault," "his assertions issued *ex cathedra,*" "the sanction of his name as the representative of poetry," and so on. Proud as I am of my connection with the University of Oxford, I can truly say, that knowing how unpopular a task one is undertaking when one tries to pull out a few more stops in that powerful but at present somewhat narrow-toned organ, the modern Englishman, I have always sought to stand by myself, and to compromise others as little as possible. Besides this, my native modesty is such, that I have always been shy of assuming the honourable style of Professor, because this is a title I share with so many distinguished men, — Professor Pepper, Professor Anderson, Professor Frickel, and others, — who adorn it, I feel, much more than I do.

However, it is not merely out of modesty that I prefer to stand alone, and to concentrate on myself, as a plain citizen of the republic of letters, and not as an office-bearer in a hierarchy, the whole responsibility for all I write; it is much more out of genuine devotion to the University of Oxford, for which I feel, and always must feel, the fondest, the most reverential attachment. In an epoch of dissolution and transformation, such as that on which we are now entered, habits, ties, and associations are inevitably broken up, the action of individuals becomes more distinct, the shortcomings, errors, heats, disputes, which necessarily attend individual action, are brought into greater prominence. Who would not gladly keep clear, from all these passing clouds, an august institution which was there before they arose, and which will be there when they have blown over?

It is true, the *Saturday Review* maintains that our epoch of transformation is finished; that we have found our philosophy; that the

British nation has searched all anchorages for the spirit, and has finally anchored itself, in the fulness of perfected knowledge, on Benthamism. This idea at first made a great impression on me; not only because it is so consoling in itself, but also because it explained a phenomenon which in the summer of last year had, I confess, a good deal troubled me. At that time my avocations led me to travel almost daily on one of the Great Eastern Lines, — the Woodford Branch. Every one knows that the murderer, Müller, perpetrated his detestable act on the North London Railway, close by. The English middle class, of which I am myself a feeble unit, travel on the Woodford Branch in large numbers. Well, the demoralisation of our class, — the class which (the newspapers are constantly saying it, so I may repeat it without vanity) has done all the great things which have ever been done in England, — the demoralisation, I say, of our class, caused by the Bow tragedy, was something bewildering. Myself a transcendentalist (as the *Saturday Review* knows), I escaped the infection; and, day after day, I used to ply my agitated fellow-travellers with all the consolations which my transcendentalism would naturally suggest to me. I reminded them how Caesar refused to take precautions against assassination, because life was not worth having at the price of an ignoble solicitude for it. I reminded them what insignificant atoms we all are in the life of the world. "Suppose the worst to happen," I said, addressing a portly jeweller from Cheapside; "suppose even yourself to be the victim; *il n'y a pas d'homme nécessaire.* We should miss you for a day or two upon the Woodford Branch; but the great mundane movement would still go on, the gravel walks of your villa would still be rolled, dividends would still be paid at the Bank, omnibuses would still run, there would still be the old crush at the corner of Fenchurch Street." All was of no avail. Nothing could moderate, in the bosom of the great English middle class, their passionate, absorbing, almost bloodthirsty clinging to life. At the moment I thought this overconcern a little unworthy; but the *Saturday Review* suggests a touching explanation of it. What I took for the ignoble clinging to life of a comfortable worldling, was, perhaps, only the ardent longing of a faithful Benthamite, traversing an age still dimmed by the last mists of transcendentalism, to be spared long enough to see his religion in the full and final blaze of its triumph. This respectable man, whom I imagined to be going up to London to serve his shop, or to buy shares, or to attend an Exeter Hall meeting, or to assist at the deliberations of the Marylebone Vestry, was, perhaps, in real truth, on a pious pilgrimage, to obtain from Mr. Bentham's executors a sacred bone of his great, dissected master.

And yet, after all, I cannot but think that the *Saturday Review* has here, for once, fallen a victim to an idea, — a beautiful but deluding idea, — and that the British nation has not yet, so entirely as the reviewer seems to imagine, found the last word of its philosophy. No, we are all seekers still! seekers often make mistakes, and I wish mine to redound to my own discredit only, and not to touch Oxford. Beautiful city! so venerable, so lovely, so unravaged by the fierce intellectual life of our century, so serene!

There are our young barbarians all at play!

And yet, steeped in sentiment as she lies, spreading her gardens to the moonlight, and whispering from her towers the last enchantments of the Middle Age, who will deny that Oxford, by her ineffable charm, keeps ever calling us nearer to the true goal of all of us, to the ideal, to perfection, — to beauty, in a word, which is only truth seen from another side? — nearer, perhaps, than all the science of Tübingen. Adorable dreamer, whose heart has been so romantic! who hast given thyself so prodigally, given thyself to sides and to heroes not mine, only never to the Philistines! home of lost causes, and forsaken beliefs, and unpopular names, and impossible loyalties! what example could ever so inspire us to keep down the Philistine in ourselves, what teacher could ever so save us from that bondage to which we are all prone, that bondage which Goethe, in those incomparable lines on the death of Schiller, makes it his friend's highest praise (and nobly did Schiller deserve the praise) to have left miles out of sight behind him; — the bondage of "*was uns alle bändgit,* DAS GEMEINE!" She will forgive me, even if I have unwittingly drawn upon her a shot or two aimed at her unworthy son; for she is generous, and the cause in which I fight is, after all, hers. Apparitions of a day, what is our puny warfare against the Philistines, compared with the warfare which this queen of romance has been waging against them for centuries, and will wage after we are gone?

THE FUNCTION OF CRITICISM AT THE PRESENT TIME

MANY objections have been made to a proposition which, in some remarks of mine on translating Homer, I ventured to put forth; a proposition about criticism, and its importance at the present day. I said: "Of the literature of France and Germany, as of the intellect of Europe in general, the main effort, for now many years, has been a critical effort; the endeavour, in all branches of knowledge, theology, philosophy, history, art, science, to see the object as in itself it really is." I added, that owing to the operation in English literature of certain causes, "almost the last thing for which one would come to English literature is just that very thing which now Europe most desires, — criticism"; and that the power and value of English literature was thereby impaired. More than one rejoinder declared that the importance I here assigned to criticism was excessive, and asserted the inherent superiority of the creative effort of the human spirit over its critical effort. And the other day, having been led by a Mr. Shairp's excellent notice of Wordsworth[1] to turn again to his biography, I found, in the words of this great man, whom I, for one, must always listen to with the profoundest respect, a sentence passed on the critic's business, which seems to justify every possible disparagement of it. Wordsworth says in one of his letters:

"The writers in these publications" (the Reviews), "while they prosecute their inglorious employment, cannot be supposed to be in a state of mind very favourable for being affected by the finer influences of a thing so pure as genuine poetry."

And a trustworthy reporter of his conversation quotes a more elaborate judgment to the same effect:

"Wordsworth holds the critical power very low, infinitely lower than the inventive; and he said to-day that if the quantity of time consumed in writing critiques on the works of others were given to

[1] I cannot help thinking that a practice, common in England during the last century, and still followed in France, of printing a notice of this kind, — a notice by a competent critic, — to serve as an introduction to an eminent author's works, might be revived among us with advantage. To introduce all succeeding editions of Wordsworth, Mr. Shairp's notice might, it seems to me, excellently serve; it is written from the point of view of an admirer, nay, of a disciple, and that is right; but then the disciple must be also, as in this case he is, a critic, a man of letters, not, as too often happens, some relation or friend with no qualification for his task except affection for his author.

original composition, of whatever kind it might be, it would be much better employed; it would make a man find out sooner his own level, and it would do infinitely less mischief. A false or malicious criticism may do much injury to the minds of others; a stupid invention, either in prose or verse, is quite harmless."

It is almost too much to expect of poor human nature, that a man capable of producing some effect in one line of literature, should, for the greater good of society, voluntarily doom himself to impotence and obscurity in another. Still less is this to be expected from men addicted to the composition of the "false or malicious criticism" of which Wordsworth speaks. However, everybody would admit that a false or malicious criticism had better never have been written. Everybody, too, would be willing to admit, as a general proposition, that the critical faculty is lower than the inventive. But is it true that criticism is really, in itself, a baneful and injurious employment; is it true that all time given to writing critiques on the works of others would be much better employed if it were given to original composition, of whatever kind this may be? Is it true that Johnson had better have gone on producing more *Irenes* instead of writing his *Lives of the Poets;* is it certain that Wordsworth himself was better employed in making his Ecclesiastical Sonnets than when he made his celebrated Preface so full of criticism, and criticism of the works of others? Wordsworth was himself a great critic, and it is to be sincerely regretted that he has not left us more criticism; Goethe was one of the greatest of critics, and we may sincerely congratulate ourselves that he has left us so much criticism. Without wasting time over the exaggeration which Wordsworth's judgment on criticism clearly contains, or over an attempt to trace the causes, — not difficult, I think, to be traced, — which may have led Wordsworth to this exaggeration, a critic may with advantage seize an occasion for trying his own conscience, and for asking himself of what real service, at any given moment, the practice of criticism either is or may be made to his own mind and spirit, and to the minds and spirits of others.

The critical power is of lower rank than the creative. True; but in assenting to this proposition, one or two things are to be kept in mind. It is undeniable that the exercise of a creative power, that a free creative activity, is the highest function of man; it is proved to be so by man's finding in it his true happiness. But it is undeniable, also, that men may have the sense of exercising this free creative activity in other ways than in producing great works of literature or art; if it were not so, all but a very few men would be shut out from the true happiness of all men. They may have it in well-doing, they may have it in learning, they may have it even in criticising. This is one thing to be kept in mind. Another is, that the exercise of the creative power in the production of great works of literature or art, however high this exercise of it may rank, is not at all epochs and under all conditions possible; and that therefore labour may be vainly spent in attempting it, which might with more fruit be used in preparing for it, in rendering it possible. This creative power works with elements, with materials; what if it has not those materials, those elements, ready for its use? In that case it must surely wait till they are ready. Now, in literature, — I will limit myself to literature, for it is about literature that the question arises, — the elements with which the creative power works are ideas; the best ideas on every matter which literature touches, current at the time. At any rate we may lay it down as certain that in modern literature no manifestation of the creative power not working with these can be very important or fruitful. And I say *current* at the time, not merely accessible at the time; for creative literary genius does not principally show itself in discovering new ideas, that is rather the business of the philosopher. The grand work of literary genius is a work of synthesis and exposition, not of analysis and discovery; its gift lies in the faculty of being happily inspired by a certain intellectual and spiritual atmosphere, by a certain order of ideas, when it finds itself in them; of dealing divinely with these ideas, presenting them in the most effective and attractive combinations, — making beautiful works with them, in short. But it must have the atmosphere, it must find itself amidst the order of ideas, in order to work freely; and these it is not so easy to command. This is why great creative epochs in literature are so rare, this is why there is so much that is unsatisfactory in the productions of many men of real genius; because, for the creation of a master-work of literature two powers must concur, the power of the man and the power of the moment, and the man is not enough without the moment; the creative power has, for its happy exercise, appointed elements, and those elements are not in its own control.

Nay, they are more within the control of the critical power. It is the business of the critical power, as I said in the words already quoted, "in all branches of knowledge, theology, philosophy, history, art, science, to see the object as in itself it really is." Thus it tends, at last, to make an intellectual situation of which the creative power can profitably avail itself. It tends to establish an order of ideas, if not absolutely true, yet true by comparison with that which it displaces; to make the best ideas prevail. Presently these new ideas reach society, the touch of truth is the touch of life, and there is a stir and growth everywhere; out of this stir and growth come the creative epochs of literature.

Or, to narrow our range, and quit these considerations of the general march of genius and of society, — considerations which are apt to become too abstract and impalpable, — every one can see that a poet, for instance, ought to know life and the world before dealing with them in poetry; and life and the world being in modern times very complex things, the creation of a modern poet, to be worth much, implies a great critical effort behind it; else it must be a comparatively poor, barren, and short-lived affair. This is why Byron's poetry had so little endurance in it, and Goethe's so much; both Byron and Goethe had a great productive power, but Goethe's was nourished by a great critical effort providing the true materials for it, and Byron's was not; Goethe knew life and the world, the poet's necessary subjects, much more comprehensively and thoroughly than Byron. He knew a great deal more of them, and he knew them much more as they really are.

It has long seemed to me that the burst of creative activity in our literature, through the first quarter of this century, had about it in fact something premature; and that from this cause its productions are doomed, most of them, in spite of the sanguine hopes which accompanied and do still accompany them, to prove hardly more lasting than the productions of far less splendid epochs. And this prematureness comes from its having proceeded without having its proper data, without sufficient materials to work with. In other words, the English poetry of the first quarter of this century, with plenty of energy, plenty of creative force, did not know enough. This makes Byron so empty of matter, Shelley so incoherent, Wordsworth even, profound as he is, yet so wanting in completeness and variety. Wordsworth cared little for books, and disparaged Goethe. I admire Wordsworth, as he is, so much that I cannot wish him different; and it is vain, no doubt, to imagine such a man different from what he is, to suppose that he *could* have been different. But surely the one thing wanting to make Wordsworth an even greater poet than he is, — his thought richer, and his influence of wider application, — was that he should have read more books, among them, no doubt, those of that Goethe whom he disparaged without reading him.

But to speak of books and reading may easily lead to a misunderstanding here. It was not really books and reading that lacked to our poetry at this epoch: Shelley had plenty of reading, Coleridge had immense reading. Pindar and Sophocles, — as we all say so glibly, and often with so little discernment of the real import of what we are saying, — had not many books; Shakespeare was no deep reader. True; but in the Greece of Pindar and Sophocles, in the England of Shakespeare, the poet lived in a current of ideas in the highest degree animating and nourishing to the creative power; society was, in the fullest measure, permeated by fresh thought, intelligent and alive. And this state of things is the true basis for the creative power's exercise, in this it finds its data, its materials, truly ready for its hand; all the books and reading in the world are only valuable as they are helps to this. Even when this does not actually exist, books and reading may enable a man to construct a kind of semblance of it in his own mind, a world of knowledge and intelligence in which he may live and work. This is by no means an equivalent to the artist for the nationally diffused life and thought of the epochs of Sophocles or Shakespeare; but, besides that it may be a means of preparation for such epochs, it does really constitute, if many share in it, a quickening and sustaining atmosphere of great value. Such an atmosphere the many-sided learning and the long and widely combined critical effort of Germany formed for Goethe, when he lived and worked. There was no national glow of life and thought there as in the Athens of Pericles or the England of Elizabeth. That was the poet's weakness. But there was a sort of equivalent for it in the complete culture and unfettered thinking of a large body of Germans. That was his strength. In the England of the first quarter of this century there was neither a national glow of life and thought, such as we had in the age of Elizabeth, nor yet a culture and a force of learning and criticism such as were to be found in Germany. Therefore the creative power of poetry wanted, for success in the highest sense, materials and a basis; a thorough interpretation of the world was necessarily denied to it.

At first sight it seems strange that out of the immense stir of the French Revolution and its age should not have come a crop of works of genius equal to that which came out of the stir of the great productive time of Greece, or out of that of the Renascence, with its powerful episode the Reformation. But the truth is that the stir of the French Revolution took a character which essentially distinguished it from such movements as these. These were, in the main, disinterestedly intellectual and spiritual movements; movements in which the human spirit looked for its satisfaction in itself and in the increased play of its own activity. The French Revolution took a political, practical character. The movement, which went on in France under the old *régime,* from 1700 to 1789, was far more really akin than that of the Revolution itself to the movement of the Renascence; the France of Voltaire and Rousseau told far more powerfully upon the mind of Europe than the France of the Revolution. Goethe reproached this last expressly with having "thrown quiet culture back." Nay, and the true key to how much in our Byron, even in our Wordsworth, is this! — that they had their source in a great movement of feeling, not in a great movement of mind. The French Revolution, however, — that object of so much blind love and so much blind hatred,—found undoubtedly its motive-power in the intelligence of men, and not in their practical sense; this is what distinguishes it from the English Revolution of Charles the First's time. This is what makes it a more spiritual event than our Revolution, an event of much more powerful and world-wide interest, though practically less successful; it appeals to an order of ideas which are universal, certain, permanent. 1789 asked of a thing, Is it rational? 1642 asked of a thing, Is it legal? or, when it went furthest, Is it according to conscience? This is the English fashion, a fashion to be treated, within its own sphere, with the highest respect; for its success, within its own sphere, has been prodigious. But what is law in one place is not law in another; what is law here to-day is not law even here to-morrow; and as for conscience, what is binding on one man's conscience is not binding on another's. The old woman who threw her stool at the head of the surpliced minister in St. Giles's Church at Edinburgh obeyed an impulse to which millions of the human race may be permitted to remain strangers. But the prescriptions of reason are absolute, unchanging, of universal validity; *to count by tens is the easiest way of counting*—that is a proposition of which every one, from here to the Antipodes, feels the force; at least I should say so if we did not live in a country where it is not impossible that any morning we may find a letter in the *Times* declaring that a decimal coinage is an absurdity. That a whole nation should have been penetrated with an enthusiasm for pure reason, and with an ardent zeal for making its prescriptions triumph, is a very remarkable thing, when we consider how little of mind, or anything so worthy and quickening as mind, comes into the motives which alone, in general, impel great masses of men. In spite of the extravagant direction given to this enthusiasm, in spite of the crimes and follies in which it lost itself, the French Revolution derives from the force, truth, and universality of the ideas which it took for its law, and from the passion with which it could inspire a multitude for these ideas, a unique and still living power; it is,—it will probably long remain,—the greatest, the most animating event in history. And as no sincere passion for the things of the mind, even though it turn out in many respects an unfortunate passion, is ever quite thrown away and quite barren of good, France has reaped from hers one fruit—the natural and legitimate fruit though not precisely the grand fruit she expected: she is the country in Europe where *the people* is most alive.

But the mania for giving an immediate political and practical application to all these fine ideas of the reason was fatal. Here an Englishman is in his element: on this theme we can all go on for hours. And all we are in the habit of saying on it has undoubtedly a great deal of truth. Ideas cannot be too much prized in and for themselves, cannot be too much lived with; but to transport them abruptly into the world of politics and practice, violently to revolutionise this world to their bidding, — that is quite another thing. There is the world of ideas and there is the world of practice; the French are often for suppressing the one and the English the other; but neither is to be suppressed. A member of the House of Commons said to me the other day: "That a thing is an anomaly, I consider to be no objection to it whatever." I venture to think he was wrong; that a thing is an anomaly *is* an objection to it, but absolutely and in the sphere of ideas: it is not necessarily, under such and such circumstances, or at such and such a moment, an objection to it in the sphere of politics and practice. Joubert has said beautifully: "*C'est la force et le droit qui règlent toutes choses dans le monde; la force en attendant le droit.*" (Force and right are the governors of this world; force till right is ready.) *Force till right is ready;* and till right is ready, force, the existing order of things, is justified, is the legitimate ruler. But right is something moral, and implies inward recognition, free assent of the will; we are not ready for right, — *right,* so far as we are concerned, *is not ready,* — until we have attained this sense of seeing it and willing it. The way in which for us it may change and transform force, the existing order of things, and become, in its turn, the legitimate ruler of the world, should depend on the way in which, when our time comes, we see it and will it. Therefore for other people enamoured of their own newly discerned right, to attempt to impose it upon us as ours, and violently to substitute their right for our force, is an act of tyranny, and to be resisted. It sets at nought the second great half of our maxim, *force till right is ready.* This was the grand error of the French Revolution; and its movement of ideas, by quitting the intellectual sphere and rushing furiously into the political sphere, ran, indeed, a prodigious and memorable course, but produced no such intellectual fruit as the movement of ideas of the Renascence, and created, in opposition to itself, what I may call an *epoch of concentration.* The great force of that epoch of concentration was England; and the great voice of that epoch of concentration was Burke. It is the fashion to treat Burke's writings on the French Revolution as superannuated and conquered by the event; as the eloquent but unphilosophical tirades of bigotry and prejudice. I will not deny that they are often disfigured by the violence and passion of the moment, and that in some directions Burke's view was bounded, and his observation therefore at fault. But on the whole, and for those who can make the needful corrections, what distinguishes these writings is their profound, permanent, fruitful, philosophical truth. They contain the true philosophy of an epoch of concentration, dissipate the heavy atmosphere which its own nature is apt to engender round it, and make its resistance rational instead of mechanical.

But Burke is so great because, almost alone in England, he brings thought to bear upon politics, he saturates politics with thought. It is his accident that his ideas were at the service of an epoch of concentration, not of an epoch of expansion; it is his characteristic that he so lived by ideas, and had such a source of them welling up within him, that he could float even an epoch of concentration and English Tory politics with them. It does not hurt him that Dr. Price and the Liberals were enraged with him; it does not even hurt him that George the Third and the Tories were enchanted with him. His greatness is that he lived in a world which neither English Liberalism nor English Toryism is apt to enter; — the world of ideas, not the world of catchwords and party habits. So far is it from being really true of him that he "to party gave up what was meant for mankind," that at the very end of his fierce struggle with the French Revolution, after all his invectives against its false pretensions, hollowness, and madness, with his sincere convictions of its mischievousness, he can close a memorandum on the best means of combating it, some of the last pages he ever wrote, — the *Thoughts on French Affairs,* in December 1791, — with these striking words: —

"The evil is stated, in my opinion, as it exists. The remedy must be where power, wisdom, and information, I hope, are more united with good intentions than they can be with me. I have done with this subject, I believe, for ever. It has given me many anxious moments for the last two years. *If a great change is to be made in human affairs, the minds of men will be fitted to it; the general opinions and feelings will draw that way. Every fear, every hope will forward it; and then they who persist in opposing this mighty current in human affairs, will appear rather to resist the decrees of Providence itself, than the mere designs of men. They will not be resolute and firm, but perverse and obstinate.*"

That return of Burke upon himself has always seemed to me one of the finest things in English literature, or indeed in any literature. That is what I call living by ideas: when one side of a question has long had your earnest support, when all your feelings are engaged, when you hear all round you no language but one, when your party talks this language like a steam-engine and can imagine no other, — still to be able to think, still to be irresistibly carried, if so it be, by the current of thought to the opposite side of the question, and, like Balaam, to be unable to speak anything *but what the Lord has put in your mouth.* I know nothing more striking, and I must add that I know nothing more un-English.

For the Englishman in general is like my friend the Member of Parliament, and believes, point-blank, that for a thing to be an anomaly is absolutely no objection to it whatever. He is like the Lord Auckland of Burke's day, who, in a memorandum on the French Revolution, talks of certain "miscreants, assuming the name of philosophers, who have presumed themselves capable of establishing a new system of society." The Englishman has been called a political animal, and he values what is political and practical so much that ideas easily become objects of dislike in his eyes, and thinkers, "miscreants," because ideas and thinkers have rashly meddled with politics and practice. This would be all very well if the dislike and neglect confined themselves to ideas transported out of their own sphere, and meddling rashly with practice; but they are inevitably extended to ideas as such, and to the whole life of intelligence; practice is everything, a free play of the mind is nothing. The notion of the free play of the mind upon all subjects being a pleasure in itself, being an object of desire, being an essential provider of elements without which a nation's spirit, whatever compensations it may have for them, must, in the long run, die of inanition, hardly enters into an Englishman's thoughts. It is noticeable that the word *curiosity*, which in other languages is used in a good sense, to mean, as a high and fine quality of man's nature, just this disinterested love of a free play of the mind on all subjects, for its own sake, — it is noticeable, I say, that this word has in our language no sense of the kind, no sense but a rather bad and disparaging one. But criticism, real criticism, is essentially the exercise of this very quality. It obeys an instinct prompting it to try to know the best that is known and thought in the world, irrespectively of practice, politics, and everything of the kind; and to value knowledge and thought as they approach this best, without the intrusion of any other considerations whatever. This is an instinct for which there is, I think, little original sympathy in the practical English nature, and what there was of it has undergone a long benumbing period of blight and suppression in the epoch of concentration which followed the French Revolution.

But epochs of concentration cannot well endure for ever; epochs of expansion, in the due course of things, follow them. Such an epoch of expansion seems to be opening in this country. In the first place all danger of a hostile forcible pressure of foreign ideas upon our practice has long disappeared; like the traveller in the fable, therefore, we begin to wear our cloak a little more loosely. Then, with a long peace, the ideas of Europe steal gradually and amicably in, and mingle, though in infinitesimally small quantities at a time, with our own notions. Then, too, in spite of all that is said about the absorbing and brutalising influence of our passionate material progress, it seems to me indisputable that this progress is likely, though not certain, to lead in the end to an apparition of intellectual life; and that man, after he has made himself perfectly comfortable and has now to determine what to do with himself next, may begin to remember that he has a mind, and that the mind may be made the source of great pleasure. I grant it is mainly the privilege of faith, at present, to discern this end to our railways, our business, and our fortune-making; but we shall see if, here as elsewhere, faith is not in the end the true prophet. Our ease, our travelling, and our unbounded liberty to hold just as hard and securely as we please to the practice to which our notions have given birth, all tend to beget an inclination to deal a little more freely with these notions themselves, to canvass them a little, to penetrate a little into their real nature. Flutterings of curiosity, in the foreign sense of the word, appear amongst us, and it is in these that criticism must look to find its account. Criticism first; a time of true creative activity, perhaps, — which, as I have said, must inevitably be preceded amongst us by a time of criticism, — hereafter, when criticism has done its work.

It is of the last importance that English criticism should clearly discern what rule for its course, in order to avail itself of the field now opening to it, and to produce fruit for the future, it ought to take. The rule may be summed up in one word, — *disinterestedness.* And how is criticism to show disinterestedness? By keeping aloof from what is called "the practical view of things"; by resolutely following the law of its own nature, which is to be a free play of the mind on all subjects which it touches. By steadily refusing to lend itself to any of those ulterior, political, practical considerations about ideas, which plenty of people will be sure to attach to them, which perhaps ought often to be attached to them, which in this country at any rate are certain to be attached to them quite sufficiently, but which criticism has really nothing to do with. Its business is, as I have said, simply to know the best that is known and thought in the world, and by in its turn making this known, to create a current of true and fresh ideas. Its business is to do this with inflexible honesty, with due ability; but its business is to do no more, and to leave alone all questions of practical consequences and applications, questions which will never fail to have due prominence given to them. Else criticism, besides being really false to its own nature, merely continues in the old rut which it has hitherto followed in this country, and will certainly miss the chance now given to it. For what is at present the bane of criticism in this country? It is that practical considerations cling to it and stifle it. It subserves interests not its own. Our organs of criticism are organs of men and parties having practical ends to serve, and with them those practical ends are the first thing and the play of mind the second; so much play of mind as is compatible with the prosecution of those practical ends is all that is wanted. An organ like the *Revue des Deux Mondes,* having for its main function to understand and utter the best that is known and thought in the world, existing, it may be said, as just an organ for a free play of the mind, we have not. But we have the *Edinburgh Review,* existing as an organ of the old Whigs, and for as much play of mind as may suit its being that; we have the *Quarterly Review,* existing as an organ of the Tories, and for as much play of mind as may suit its being that; we have the *British Quarterly Review,* existing as an organ of the political Dissenters, and for as much play of mind as may suit its being that; we have the *Times,* existing as an organ of the common, satisfied, well-to-do Englishman, and for as much play of mind as may suit its being that. And so on through all the various fractions, political and religious, of our society; every fraction has, as such, its organ of criticism, but the notion of combining all fractions in the common pleasure of a free disinterested play of mind meets with no favour. Directly this play of mind wants to have more scope, and to forget the pressure of practical considerations a little, it is checked, it is made to feel the chain. We saw this the other day in the extinction, so much to be regretted, of the *Home and Foreign Review.* Perhaps in no organ of criticism in this country was there so much knowledge, so much play of mind; but these could not save it. The *Dublin Review* subordinates play of mind to the practical business of English and Irish Catholicism, and lives. It must needs be that men should act in sects and parties, that each of these sects and parties should have its organ, and should make this organ subserve the interests of its action; but it would be well, too, that there should be a criticism, not the minister of these interests, not their enemy, but absolutely and entirely independent of them. No other criticism will ever attain any real authority or make any real way towards its end, — the creating a current of true and fresh ideas.

It is because criticism has so little kept in the pure intellectual sphere, has so little detached itself from practice, has been so directly polemical and controversial, that it has so ill accomplished, in this country, its best spiritual work; which is to keep man from a self-satisfaction which is retarding and vulgarising, to lead him towards perfection, by making his mind dwell upon what is excellent in itself, and the absolute beauty and fitness of things. A polemical practical criticism makes men blind even to the ideal imperfection of their practice, makes them willingly assert its ideal perfection, in order the better to secure it against attack; and clearly this is narrowing and baneful for them. If they were reassured on the practical side, speculative considerations of ideal perfection they might be brought to entertain, and their spiritual horizon would thus gradually widen. Sir Charles Adderley says to the Warwickshire farmers:

"Talk of the improvement of breed! Why, the race we ourselves represent, the men and women, the old Anglo-Saxon race, are the best breed in the whole world. . . . The absence of a too enervating climate, too unclouded skies, and a too luxurious nature, has produced so vigorous a race of people, and has rendered us so superior to all the world."

Mr. Roebuck says to the Sheffield cutlers:

"I look around me and ask what is the state of England? Is not property safe? Is not every man able to say what he likes? Can you not walk from one end of England to the other in perfect security? I ask you whether, the world over or in past history, there is anything like it? Nothing. I pray that our unrivalled happiness may last."

Now obviously there is a peril for poor human nature in words and thoughts of such exuberant self-satisfaction, until we find ourselves safe in the streets of the Celestial City.

> *Das wenige verschwindet leicht dem Blicke*
> *Der vorwärts sieht, wie viel noch übrig bleibt—*

says Goethe; "the little that is done seems nothing when we look forward and see how much we have yet to do." Clearly this is a better line of reflection for weak humanity, so long as it remains on this earthly field of labour and trial.

But neither Sir Charles Adderley nor Mr. Roebuck is by nature inaccessible to considerations of this sort. They only lose sight of them owing to the controversial life we all lead, and the practical form which all speculation takes with us. They have in view opponents whose aim is not ideal, but practical; and in their zeal to uphold their own practice against these innovators, they go so far as even to attribute to this practice an ideal perfection. Somebody has been wanting to introduce a six-pound franchise, or to abolish church-rates, or to collect agricultural statistics by force, or to diminish local self-government. How natural, in reply to such proposals, very likely improper or ill-timed, to go a little beyond the mark and to say stoutly, "Such a race of people as we stand, so superior to all the world! The old Anglo-Saxon race, the best breed in the whole world! I pray that our unrivalled happiness may last! I ask you whether, the world over or in past history, there is anything like it?" And so long as criticism answers this dithyramb by insisting that the old Anglo-Saxon race would be still more superior to all others if it had no church-rates, or that our unrivalled happiness would last yet longer with a six-pound franchise, so long will the strain, "The best breed in the whole world!" swell louder and louder, everything ideal and refining will be lost out of sight, and both the assailed and their critics will remain in a sphere, to say the truth, perfectly unvital, a sphere in which spiritual progression is impossible. But let criticism leave church-rates and the franchise alone, and in the most candid spirit, without a single lurking thought of practical innovation, confront with our dithyramb this paragraph on which I stumbled in a newspaper immediately after reading Mr. Roebuck:

"A shocking child murder has just been committed at Nottingham. A girl named Wragg left the workhouse there on Saturday morning with her young illegitimate child. The child was soon afterwards found dead on Mapperly Hills, having been strangled. Wragg is in custody."

Nothing but that; but, in juxtaposition with the absolute eulogies of Sir Charles Adderley and Mr. Roebuck, how eloquent, how suggestive are those few lines! "Our old Anglo-Saxon breed, the best in the whole world!" — how much that is harsh and ill-favoured there is in this best! *Wragg!* If we are to talk of ideal perfection, of "the best in the whole world," has any one reflected what a touch of grossness in our race, what an original short-coming in the more delicate spiritual perceptions, is shown by the natural growth amongst us of such hideous names, — Higginbottom, Stiggins, Bugg! In Ionia and Attica they were luckier in this respect than "the best race in the world"; by the Ilissus there was no Wragg, poor thing! And "our unrivalled happiness"; — what an element of grimness, bareness, and hideousness mixes with it and blurs it; the workhouse, the dismal Mapperly Hills, — how dismal those who have seen them will remember; — the gloom, the smoke, the cold, the strangled illegitimate child! "I ask you whether, the world over or in past history, there is anything like it?" Perhaps not, one is inclined to answer; but at any rate, in that case, the world is very much to be pitied. And the final touch, — short, bleak and inhuman: *Wragg is in custody.* The sex lost in the confusion of our unrivalled happiness; or (shall I say?) the superfluous Christian name lopped off by the straightforward vigour of our old Anglo-Saxon breed! There is profit for the spirit in such contrasts as this; criticism serves the cause of perfection by establishing them. By eluding sterile conflict, by refusing to remain in the sphere where alone narrow and relative conceptions have any worth and validity, criticism may diminish its momentary importance, but only in this way has it a chance of gaining admittance for those wider and more perfect conceptions to which all its duty is really owed. Mr. Roebuck will have a poor opinion of an adversary who replies to his defiant songs of triumph only by murmuring under his breath, *Wragg is in custody;* but in no other way will these songs of triumph be induced gradually to moderate themselves, to get rid of what in them is excessive and offensive, and to fall into a softer and truer key.

It will be said that it is a very subtle and indirect action which I am thus prescribing for criticism, and that, by embracing in this manner the Indian virtue of detachment and abandoning the sphere of practical life, it condemns itself to a slow and obscure work. Slow and obscure it may be, but it is the only proper work of criticism. The mass of mankind will never have any ardent zeal for seeing things as they are; very inadequate ideas will always satisfy them. On these inadequate ideas reposes, and must repose, the general practice of the world. That is as much as saying that whoever sets himself to see small things as they are will find himself one of a very small circle; but it is only by this small circle resolutely doing its own work that adequate ideas will ever get current at all. The rush and roar of practical life will always have a dizzying and attracting effect upon the most collected spectator, and tend to draw him into its vortex; most of all will this be the case where that life is so powerful as it is in England. But it is only by remaining collected, and refusing to lend himself to the point of view of the practical man, that the critic can do the practical man any service; and it is only by the greatest sincerity in pursuing his own course, and by at last convincing even the practical man of his sincerity, that he can escape misunderstandings which perpetually threaten him.

For the practical man is not apt for fine distinctions, and yet in these distinctions truth and the highest culture greatly find their account. But it is not easy to lead a practical man, — unless you reassure him as to your practical intentions, you have no chance of leading him, — to see that a thing which he has always been used to look at from one side only, which he greatly values, and which, looked at from that side, quite deserves, perhaps, all the prizing and admiring which he bestows upon it, — that this thing, looked at from another side, may appear much less beneficent and beautiful, and yet retain all its claims to our practical allegiance. Where shall we find language innocent enough, how shall we make the spotless purity of our intentions evident enough, to enable us to say to the political Englishman that the British Constitution itself, which, seen from the practical side, looks such a magnificent organ of progress and virtue, seen from the speculative side, — with its compromises, its love of facts, its horror of theory, its studied avoidance of clear thoughts, — that, seen from this side, our august Constitution sometimes looks, — forgive me, shade of Lord Somers! — a colossal machine for the manufacture of Philistines? How is Cobbett to say this and not be misunderstood, blackened as he is with the smoke of a lifelong conflict in the field of political practice? how is Mr. Carlyle to say it and not be misunderstood, after his furious raid into this field with his *Latter-day Pamphlets*? how is Mr. Ruskin, after his pugnacious political economy? I say, the critic must keep out of the region of immediate practice in the political, social, humanitarian sphere if he wants to make a beginning for that more free speculative treatment of things, which may perhaps one day make its benefits felt even in this sphere, but in a natural and thence irresistible manner.

Do what he will, however, the critic will still remain exposed to frequent misunderstandings, and nowhere so much as in this country. For here people are particularly indisposed even to comprehend that without this free disinterested treatment of things, truth and the highest culture are out of the question. So immersed are they in practical life, so accustomed to take all their notions from this life and its processes, that they are apt to think that truth and culture themselves can be reached by the processes of this life, and that it is an impertinent singularity to think of reaching them in any other. "We are all *terræ filii*," cries their eloquent advocate; "all Philistines together. Away with the notion of proceeding by any other course than the course dear to the Philistines; let us have a social movement, let us organise and combine a party to pursue truth and new thought, let us call it *the liberal party*, and let us all stick to each other, and back each other up. Let us have no nonsense about independent criticism, and intellectual delicacy, and the few and the many. Don't let us trouble ourselves about foreign thought; we shall invent the whole thing for ourselves as we go along. If one of us speaks well, applaud him; if one of us speaks ill, applaud him too; we are all in the same movement, we are all liberals, we are all in pursuit of truth." In this way the pursuit of truth becomes really a social, practical, pleasurable affair, almost requiring a chairman, a secretary, and advertisements; with the excitement of an occasional scandal, with a little resistance to give the happy sense of difficulty overcome; but, in general, plenty of bustle and very little thought. To act is so easy, as Goethe says; to think is so hard! It is true that the critic has many temptations to go with the stream, to make one of the party movement, one of these *terræ filii*; it seems ungracious to refuse to be a *terræ filius* when so many excellent people are; but the critic's duty is to refuse, or, if resistance is vain, at least to cry with Obermann: *Périssons en résistant*.

How serious a matter it is to try and resist, I had ample opportunity of experiencing when I ventured some time ago to criticise the celebrated first volume of Bishop Colenso.[1] The echoes of the storm which was then raised I still, from time to time, hear grumbling round me. That storm arose out of a misunderstanding almost inevitable. It is a result of no little culture to attain to a clear perception that science and religion are two wholly different things. The multitude will for ever confuse them; but happily that is of no great real importance, for while the multitude imagines itself to live by its false science, it does really live by its true religion. Dr. Colenso, however, in his first volume did all he could to strengthen the confusion, and to make it dangerous. He did this with the best intentions, I freely admit, and with the most candid ignorance that this was the natural effect of what he was doing; but, says Joubert, "Ignorance, which in matters of morals extenuates the crime, is itself, in intellectual matters, a crime of the first order." I criticised Bishop Colenso's speculative confusion. Immediately there was a cry raised: "What is this? here is a liberal attacking a liberal. Do not you belong to the movement? are you not a friend of truth? Is not Bishop Colenso in pursuit of truth? then speak with proper respect of his book. Dr. Stanley is another friend of truth, and you speak with proper respect of his book; why make these invidious differences? both books are excellent, admirable, liberal; Bishop Colenso's perhaps the most so, because it is the boldest, and will have the best practical consequences for the liberal cause. Do you want to encourage to the attack of a brother liberal his, and your, and our implacable enemies, the *Church and State Review* or the *Record,* — the High Church rhinoceros and the Evangelical hyaena? Be silent, therefore; or rather speak, speak as loud as ever you can! and go into ecstasies over the eighty and odd pigeons."

But criticism cannot follow this coarse and indiscriminate method. It is unfortunately possible for a man in pursuit of truth to write a book which reposes upon a false conception. Even the practical consequences of a book are to genuine criticism no recommendation of it, if the book is, in the highest sense, blundering. I see that a lady who herself, too, is in pursuit of truth, and who writes with great ability, but a little too much, perhaps, under the influence of

1 So sincere is my dislike to all personal attack and controversy, that I abstain from reprinting, at this distance of time from the occasion which called them forth, the essays in which I criticised Dr. Colenso's book; I feel bound, however, after all that has passed, to make here a final declaration, of my sincere impenitence for having published them. Nay, I cannot forbear repeating yet once more, for his benefit and that of his readers, this sentence from my original remarks upon him. *There is truth of science and truth of religion; truth of science does not become truth of religion till it is made religious.* And I will add: Let us have all the science there is from the men of science; from the men of religion let us have religion.

the practical spirit of the English liberal movement, classes Bishop Colenso's book and M. Renan's together, in her survey of the religious state of Europe, as facts of the same order, works, both of them, of "great importance"; "great ability, power, and skill"; Bishop Colenso's, perhaps, the most powerful; at least, Miss Cobbe gives special expression to her gratitude that to Bishop Colenso "has been given the strength to grasp, and the courage to teach, truths of such deep import." In the same way, more than one popular writer has compared him to Luther. Now it is just this kind of false estimate which the critical spirit is, it seems to me, bound to resist. It is really the strongest possible proof of the low ebb at which, in England, the critical spirit is, that while the critical hit in the religious literature of Germany is Dr. Strauss's book, in that of France M. Renan's book, the book of Bishop Colenso is the critical hit in the religious literature of England. Bishop Colenso's book reposes on a total misconception of the essential elements of the religious problem, as that problem is now presented for solution. To criticism, therefore, which seeks to have the best that is known and thought on this problem, it is, however well meant, of no importance whatever. M. Renan's book attempts a new synthesis of the elements furnished to us by the Four Gospels. It attempts, in my opinion, a synthesis, perhaps premature, perhaps impossible, certainly not successful. Up to the present time, at any rate, we must acquiesce in Fleury's sentence on such recastings of the Gospel story: *Quiconque s'imagine la pouvoir mieux écrire, ne l'entend pas.* M. Renan had himself passed by anticipation a like sentence on his own work, when he said: "If a new presentation of the character of Jesus were offered to me, I would not have it; its very clearness would be, in my opinion, the best proof of its insufficiency." His friends may with perfect justice rejoin that at the sight of the Holy Land, and of the actual scene of the Gospel-story, all the current of M. Renan's thoughts may have naturally changed, and a new casting of that story irresistibly suggested itself to him; and that this is just a case for applying Cicero's maxim: Change of mind is not inconsistency — *nemo doctus unquam mutationem consilii inconstantiam dixit esse.* Nevertheless, for criticism, M. Renan's first thought must still be the truer one, as long as his new casting so fails more fully to commend itself, more fully (to use Coleridge's happy phrase about the Bible) to *find* us. Still M. Renan's attempt is, for criticism, of the most real interest and importance, since, with all its difficulty, a fresh synthesis of the New Testament *data* — not a making war on them, in Voltaire's fashion, not a leaving them out of mind, in the world's fashion, but the putting a new construction upon them, the taking them from under the old, traditional, conventional point of view and placing them under a new one, — is the very essence of the religious problem, as now presented; and only by efforts in this direction can it receive a solution.

Again, in the same spirit in which she judges Bishop Colenso, Miss Cobbe, like so many earnest liberals of our practical race, both here and in America, herself sets vigorously about a positive reconstruction of religion, about making a religion of the future out of hand, or at least setting about making it. We must not rest, she and they are always thinking and saying, in negative criticism, we must be creative and constructive; hence we have such works as her recent *Religious Duty*, and works still more considerable, perhaps, by others, which will be in every one's mind. These works often have much ability; they often spring out of sincere convictions, and a sincere wish to do good; and they sometimes, perhaps, do good. Their fault is (if I may be permitted to say so) one which they have in common with the British College of Health, in the New Road. Every one knows the British College of Health; it is that building with the lion and the statue of the Goddess Hygeia before it; at least I am sure about the lion, though I am not absolutely certain about the Goddess Hygeia. This building does credit, perhaps, to the resources of Dr. Morrison and his disciples; but it falls a good deal short of one's idea of what a British College of Health ought to be. In England, where we hate public interference and love individual enterprise, we have a whole crop of places like the British College of Health; the grand name without the grand thing. Unluckily, creditable to individual enterprise as they are, they tend to impair our taste by making us forget what more grandiose, noble, or beautiful character properly belongs to a public institution. The same may be said of the religions of the future of Miss Cobbe and others. Creditable, like the British College of Health, to the resources of their authors, they yet tend to make us forget what more grandiose, noble, or beautiful character properly belongs to religious constructions. The historic religions, with all their faults, have had this; it certainly belongs to the religious sentiment, when it truly flowers, to have this; and we impoverish our spirit if we allow a religion of the future without it. What then is the duty of criticism here? To take the practical point of view, to applaud the liberal movement and all its works, — its New Road religions of the future into the bargain, — for their general utility's sake? By no means; but to be perpetually dissatisfied with these works, while they perpetually fall short of a high and perfect ideal.

For criticism, these are elementary laws; but they never can be popular, and in this country they have been very little followed, and one meets with immense obstacles in following them. That is a reason for asserting them again and again. Criticism must maintain its independence of the practical spirit and its aims. Even with well-meant efforts of the practical spirit it must express dissatisfaction, if in the sphere of the ideal they seem impoverishing and limiting. It must not hurry on to the goal because of its practical importance. It must be patient, and know how to wait; and flexible, and know how to attach itself to things and how to withdraw from them. It must be apt to study and praise elements that for the fulness of spiritual perfection are wanted, even though they belong to a power which in the practical sphere may be maleficent. It must be apt to discern the spiritual shortcomings or illusions of powers that in the practical sphere may be beneficent. And this without any notion of favouring or injuring, in the practical sphere, one power or the other; without any notion of playing off, in this sphere, one power against the other. When one looks, for instance, at the English Divorce Court, — an institution which perhaps has its practical conveniences, but which in the ideal sphere is so hideous; an institution which neither makes divorce impossible nor makes it decent, which allows a man to get rid of his wife, or a wife of her husband, but makes them drag one another first, for the public edification, through a mire of unutterable infamy, — when one looks at this charming institution, I say, with its crowded trials, its newspaper reports, and its money compensations, this institution in which the gross unregenerate British Philistine has indeed stamped an image of himself, — one may be permitted to find the marriage theory of Catholicism refreshing and elevating. Or when Protestantism, in virtue of its supposed rational and intellectual origin, gives the law to criticism too magisterially, criticism may and must remind it that its pretensions, in this respect, are illusive and do it harm; that the Reformation was a moral rather than an intellectual event; that Luther's theory of grace no more exactly reflects the mind of the spirit than Bossuet's philosophy of history reflects it; and that there is no more antecedent probability of the Bishop of Durham's stock of ideas being agreeable to perfect reason than of Pope Pius the Ninth's. But criticism will not on that account forget the achievements of Protestantism in the practical and moral sphere; nor that, even in the intellectual sphere, Protestantism, though in a blind and stumbling manner, carried forward the Renascence, while Catholicism threw itself violently across its path.

I lately heard of a man of thought and energy contrasting the want of ardour and movement which he now found amongst young men in this country with what he remembered in his own youth, twenty years ago. "What reformers we were then!" he exclaimed; "What a zeal we had! how we canvassed every institution in Church and State, and were prepared to remodel them all on first principles!" He was inclined to regret, as a spiritual flagging, the lull which he saw. I am disposed rather to regard it as a pause in which the turn to a new mode of spiritual progress is being accomplished. Everything was long seen, by the young and ardent amongst us, in inseparable connection with politics and practical life. We have pretty well exhausted the benefits of seeing things in this connection, we have got all that can be got by so seeing them. Let us try a more disinterested mode of seeing them; let us betake ourselves more to the serener life of the mind and spirit. This life, too, may have its excesses and dangers; but they are not for us at present. Let us think of quietly enlarging our stock of true and fresh ideas, and not, as soon as we get an idea or half an idea, be running out with it into the street, and trying to make it rule there. Our ideas will, in the end, shape the world all the better for maturing a little. Perhaps in fifty years' time it will in the English House of Commons be an objection to an institution that it is an anomaly, and my friend the Member of Parliament will shudder in his grave. But let us in the meanwhile rather endeavour that in twenty years' time it may, in English literature, be an objection to a proposition that it is absurd. That will be a change so vast, that the imagination almost fails to grasp it. *Ab integro sæclorum nascitur ordo.*

If I have insisted so much on the course which criticism must take where politics and religion are concerned, it is because, where these burning matters are in question, it is most likely to go astray. I have wished, above all, to insist on the attitude which criticism should adopt towards things in general; on its right tone and temper of mind. But then comes another question as to the subject-matter which literary criticisms should most seek. Here, in general, its course is determined for it by the idea which is the law of its being; the idea of a disinterested endeavour to learn and propagate the best that is known and thought in the world, and thus to establish a current of fresh and true ideas. By the very nature of things, as England is not all the world, much of the best that is known and thought in the world cannot be of English growth, must be foreign; by the nature of things, again, it is just this that we are least likely to know, while English thought is streaming in upon us from all sides, and takes excellent care that we shall not be ignorant of its existence. The English critic of literature, therefore, must dwell much on foreign thought, and with particular heed on any part of it, which, while significant and fruitful in itself, is for any reason specially likely to escape him. Again, judging is often spoken of as the critic's one business, and so in some sense it is; but the judgment which almost insensibly forms itself in a fair and clear mind, along with fresh knowledge, is the valuable one; and thus knowledge, and ever fresh knowledge, must be the critic's great concern for himself. And it is by communicating fresh knowledge, and letting his own judgment pass along with it, — but insensibly, and in the second place, not the first, as a sort of companion and clue, not as an abstract lawgiver, — that the critic will generally do most good to his readers. Sometimes, no doubt, for the sake of establishing an author's place in literature, and his relation to a central standard (and if this is not done, how are we to get at our *best in the world?*) criticism may have to deal with a subject-matter so familiar that fresh knowledge is out of the question, and then it must be all judgment; an enunciation and detailed application of principles. Here the great safeguard is never to let oneself become abstract, always to retain an intimate and lively consciousness of the truth of what one is saying, and, the moment this fails us, to be sure that something is wrong. Still under all circumstances, this mere judgment and application of principles is, in itself, not the most satisfactory work to the critic; like mathematics, it is tautological, and cannot well give us, like fresh learning, the sense of creative activity.

But stop, some one will say; all this talk is of no practical use to us whatever; this criticism of yours is not what we have in our minds when we speak of criticism; when we speak of critics and criticism, we mean critics and criticism of the current English literature of the day; when you offer to tell criticism its function, it is to this criticism that we expect you to address yourself. I am sorry for it, for I am afraid I must disappoint these expectations. I am bound by my own definition of criticism: *a disinterested endeavour to learn and propagate the best that is known and thought in the world.* How much of current English literature comes into this "best that is known and thought in the world"? Not very much I fear; certainly less, at this moment, than of the current literature of France or Germany. Well, then, am I to alter my definition of criticism, in order to meet the requirements of a number of practising English critics, who, after all, are free in their choice of a business? That would be making criticism lend itself just to one of those alien practical considerations, which, I have said, are so fatal to it. One may say, indeed, to those who have to deal with the mass — so much better disregarded — of current English literature, that they may at all events endeavour, in dealing with this, to try it, so far as they can, by the standard of the best that is known and thought in the world; one may say, that to get anywhere near this standard, every critic should try and possess one great literature, at least, besides his own; and the more unlike his own, the better. But, after all, the criticism I am really concerned with, — the criticism which alone can much help us for the future, the criticism which, throughout Europe, is at the present day meant, when so much stress is laid on the importance of criticism and the critical spirit, — is a criticism which regards Europe as being, for intellectual and spiritual purposes, one great confederation, bound to a joint action and working to a common result; and whose members have, for their proper outfit, a knowledge of Greek, Roman, and Eastern antiquity, and of one another. Special, local, and temporary advantages being put out of account, that modern nation will in the intellectual and spiritual sphere make most progress, which most thoroughly carries out this program. And what is that but saying that we too, all of us, as individuals, the more thoroughly we carry it out, shall make the more progress?

There is so much inviting us! — what are we to take? what will nourish us in growth towards perfection? That is the question which, with the immense field of life and of literature lying before him, the critic has to answer; for himself first, and afterwards for others. In this idea of the critic's business the essays brought together in the following pages have had their origin; in this idea, widely different as are their subjects, they have, perhaps, their unity.

I conclude with what I said at the beginning: to have the sense of creative activity is the great happiness and the great proof of being alive, and it is not denied to criticism to have it; but then criticism must be sincere, simple, flexible, ardent, ever widening its knowledge. Then it may have, in no contemptible measure, a joyful sense of creative activity; a sense which a man of insight and conscience will prefer to what he might derive from a poor, starved, fragmentary, inadequate creation. And at some epochs no other creation is possible.

Still, in full measure, the sense of creative activity belongs only to genuine creation; in literature we must never forget that. But what true man of letters ever can forget it? It is no such common matter for a gifted nature to come into possession of a current of true and living ideas, and to produce amidst the inspiration of them, that we are likely to underrate it. The epochs of Æschylus and Shakespeare make us feel their pre-eminence. In an epoch like those is, no doubt, the true life of literature; there is the promised land, toward which criticism can only beckon. That promised land it will not be ours to enter, and we shall die in the wilderness: but to have desired to enter it, to have saluted it from afar, is already, perhaps, the best distinction among contemporaries; it will certainly be the best title to esteem with posterity.

THE LITERARY INFLUENCE OF ACADEMIES

It is impossible to put down a book like the history of the French Academy, by Pellisson and D'Olivet, which M. Charles Livet has lately re-edited, without being led to reflect upon the absence, in our own country, of any institution like the French Academy, upon the probable causes of this absence, and upon its results. A thousand voices will be ready to tell us that this absence is a signal mark of our national superiority; that it is in great part owing to this absence that the exhilarating words of Lord Macaulay, lately given to the world by his very clever nephew, Mr. Trevelyan, are so profoundly true: "It may safely be said that the literature now extant in the English language is of far greater value than all the literature which three hundred years ago was extant in all the languages of the world together." I daresay this is so; only, remembering Spinoza's maxim that the two great banes of humanity are self-conceit and the laziness coming from self-conceit, I think it may do us good, instead of resting in our pre-eminence with perfect security, to look a little more closely why this is so, and whether it is so without any limitations.

But first of all I must give a very few words to the outward history of the French Academy. About the year 1629, seven or eight persons in Paris, fond of literature, formed themselves into a sort of little club to meet at one another's houses and discuss literary matters. Their meetings got talked of, and Cardinal Richelieu, then minister and all-powerful, heard of them. He himself had a noble passion for letters, and for all fine culture; he was interested by what he heard of the nascent society. Himself a man in the grand style, if ever man was, he had the insight to perceive what a potent instrument of the grand style was here to his hand. It was the beginning of a great century for France, the seventeenth; men's minds were working, the French language was forming. Richelieu sent to ask the members of the new society whether they would be willing to become a body with a public character holding regular meetings. Not without a little hesitation, — for apparently they found themselves very well as they were, and these seven or eight gentlemen of a social and literary turn were not perfectly at their ease as to what the great and terrible minister could want with them, — they consented. The favours of a man like Richelieu are not easily refused, whether they are honestly meant or no; but, this favour of Richelieu's was meant quite honestly. The Parliament, however, had its doubts of this. The Parliament had none of Richelieu's enthusiasm about letters and culture; it was jealous of the apparition of a new public body in the State; above all, of a body called into existence by Richelieu. The King's letters-patent, establishing and authorising the new society, were granted early in 1635; but, by the old constitution of France, these letters-patent required the verification of the Parliament. It was two years and a half — towards the autumn of 1637 — before the Parliament would give it; and it then gave it only after pressing solicitations, and earnest assurances of the innocent intentions of the young Academy. Jocose people said that this society with its mission to purify and embellish the language, filled with terror a body of lawyers like the French Parliament, the stronghold of barbarous jargon and of chicane.

This improvement of the language was in truth the declared grand aim for the operations of the Academy. Its statutes of foundation, approved by Richelieu before the royal edict establishing it was issued, say expressly: "The Academy's principal function shall be to work with all the care and all the diligence possible at giving sure rules to our language, and rendering it pure, eloquent, and capable of treating the arts and sciences." This zeal for making a nation's great instrument of thought, — its language, — correct and worthy, is undoubtedly a sign full of promise, — a weighty earnest of future power. It is said that Richelieu had it in his mind that French should succeed Latin in its general ascendency, as Latin had succeeded Greek; if it was so, even this wish has to some extent been fulfilled. But, at any rate, the *ethical* influences of style in language, — its close relations, so often pointed out, with character, — are most important. Richelieu, a man of high culture, and, at the same time, of great character, felt them profoundly; and that he should have sought to regularise, strengthen, and perpetuate them by an institution for perfecting language, is alone a striking proof of his governing spirit and of his genius.

This was not all he had in his mind, however. The new Academy, now enlarged to a body of forty members, and meant to contain all the chief literary men of France, was to be a *literary tribunal.* The works of its members were to be brought before it previous to publication, were to be criticised by it, and finally, if it saw fit, to be published with its declared approbation. The works of other writers, not members of the Academy, might also, at the request of these writers themselves, be passed under the Academy's review. Besides this, in essays and discussions the Academy examined and judged works already published, whether by living or dead authors, and literary matters in general. The celebrated opinion on Corneille's *Cid*, delivered in 1637 by the Academy at Richelieu's urgent request, when this poem, which strongly occupied public attention, had been attacked by M. de Scudéry, shows how fully Richelieu designed his new creation to do duty as a supreme court of literature, and how early it in fact began to exercise this function. One[1] who had known Richelieu declared, after the Cardinal's death, that he had projected a yet greater institution than the Academy, a sort of grand European college of art, science, and literature, a Prytaneum, where the chief authors of all Europe should be gathered together in one central home, there to live in security, leisure, and honour; — that was a dream which will not bear to be pulled about too roughly. But the project of forming a high court of letters for France was no dream; Richelieu in great measure fulfilled it. This is what the Academy, by its idea, really is; this is what it has always tended to become; this is what it has, from time to time, really been; by being, or tending to be this, far more than even by what it has done for the language, it is of such importance in France. To give the law, the tone to literature, and that tone a high one, is its business. "Richelieu meant it," says M. Sainte-Beuve, "to be a *haut jury,*" — a jury the most choice and authoritative that could be found on all important literary matters in question before the public; to be, as it in fact became in the latter half of the eighteenth century, "a sovereign organ of opinion." "The duty of the Academy is," says M. Renan, "*maintenir la délicatesse de l'esprit français*" — to keep the fine quality of the French spirit unimpaired; it represents a kind of "*maîtrise en fait de bon ton*" — the authority of a recognised master in matters of tone and taste. "All ages," says M. Renan again, "have had their inferior literature; but the great danger of our time is that this inferior literature tends more and more to get the upper place. No one has the same advantage as the Academy for fighting against this mischief"; the Academy, which, as he says elsewhere, has even special facilities for "creating a form of intellectual culture *which shall impose itself on all around.*" M. Sainte-Beuve and M. Renan are, both of them, very keen-sighted critics; and they show it signally by seizing and putting so prominently forward this character of the French Academy.

Such an effort to set up a recognised authority, imposing on us a high standard in matters of intellect and taste, has many enemies in human nature. We all of us like to go our own way, and not to be forced out of the atmosphere of commonplace habitual to most of us; — "*was uns alle bändigt,*" says Goethe, "*das Gemeine.*" We like to be suffered to lie comfortably in the old straw of our habits, especially

1 La Mesnardière.

of our intellectual habits, even though this straw may not be very clean and fine. But if the effort to limit this freedom of our lower nature finds, as it does and must find, enemies in human nature, it finds also auxiliaries in it. Out of the four great parts, says Cicero, of the *honestum,* or good, which forms the matter on which *officium,* or human duty, finds employment, one is the fixing of a *modus* and an *ordo,* a measure and an order, to fashion and wholesomely constrain our action, in order to lift it above the level it keeps if left to itself, and to bring it nearer to perfection. Man alone of living creatures, he says, goes feeling after "*quid sit* ordo, *quid sit quod* deceat, *in factis dictisque qui* modus" — the discovery of an *order,* a law of *good taste,* a *measure* for his words and actions. Other creatures submissively follow the law of their nature; man alone has an impulse leading him to set up some other law to control the bent of his nature.

This holds good, of course, as to moral matters, as well as intellectural matters: and it is of moral matters that we are generally thinking when we affirm it. But it holds good as to intellectual matters too. Now, probably, M. Sainte-Beuve had not these words of Cicero in his mind when he made, about the French nation, the assertion I am going to quote; but, for all that, the assertion leans for support, one may say, upon the truth conveyed in those words of Cicero, and wonderfully illustrates and confirms them. "In France," says M. Sainte-Beuve, "the first consideration for us is not whether we are amused and pleased by a work of art or mind, nor is it whether we are touched by it. What we seek above all to learn is, whether *we were right* in being amused with it, and in applauding it, and in being moved by it." Those are very remarkable words, and they are, I believe, in the main quite true. A Frenchman has, to a considerable degree, what one may call a conscience in intellectual matters; he has an active belief that there is a right and a wrong in them, that he is bound to honour and obey the right, that he is disgraced by cleaving to the wrong. All the world has, or professes to have, this conscience in moral matters. The word *conscience* has become almost confined, in popular use, to the moral sphere, because this lively susceptibility of feeling is, in the moral sphere, so far more common than in the intellectual sphere; the livelier, in the moral sphere, this susceptibility is, the greater becomes a man's readiness to admit a high standard of action, an ideal authoritatively correcting his everyday moral habits; here, such willing admission of authority is due to sensitiveness of conscience. And a like deference to a standard higher than one's own habitual standard in intellectual matters, a like respectful recognition of a superior ideal, is caused, in the intellectual sphere, by sensitiveness of intelligence. Those whose intelligence is quickest, openest, most sensitive, are readiest with this deference; those whose intelligence is less delicate and sensitive are less disposed to it. Well, now we are on the road to see why the French have their Academy and we have nothing of the kind.

What are the essential characteristics of the spirit of our nation? Not, certainly, an open and clear mind, not a quick and flexible intelligence. Our greatest admirers would not claim for us that we have these in a pre-eminent degree; they might say that we had more of them than our detractors gave us credit for; but they would not assert them to be our essential characteristics. They would rather allege, as our chief spiritual characteristics, energy and honesty; and, if we are judged favourably and positively, not invidiously and negatively, our chief characteristics are no doubt, these: — energy and honesty, not an open and clear mind, not a quick and flexible intelligence. Openness of mind and flexiblity of intelligence were very signal characteristics of the Athenian people in ancient times; everybody will feel that. Openness of mind and flexibility of intelligence are remarkable characteristics of the French people in modern times; at any rate, they strikingly characterise them as compared with us; I think everybody, or almost everybody, will feel that. I will not now ask what more the Athenian or the French spirit has than this, nor what shortcomings either of them may have as a set-off against this; all I want now to point out is that they have this, and that we have it in a much lesser degree. Let me remark, however, that not only in the moral sphere, but also in the intellectual and spiritual sphere, energy and honesty are most important and fruitful qualities; that, for instance, of what we call genius energy is the most essential part. So, by assigning to a nation energy and honesty as its chief spiritual characteristics, — by refusing to it, as at all eminent characteristics, openness of mind and flexibility of intelligence, — we do not by any means, as some people might at first suppose, relegate its importance and its power of manifesting itself with effect from the intellectual to the moral sphere. We only indicate its probable special line of successful activity in the intellectual sphere, and, it is true, certain imperfections and failings to which, in this sphere, it will always be subject. Genius is mainly an affair of energy, and poetry is mainly an affair of genius; therefore a nation whose spirit is characterised by energy may well be eminent in poetry; — and we have Shakespeare. Again, the highest reach of science is, one may say, an inventive power, a faculty of divination, akin to the highest power exercised in poetry; therefore, a nation whose spirit is characterised by energy may well be eminent in science; — and we have Newton. Shakespeare and

Newton: in the intellectual sphere there can be no higher names. And what that energy, which is the life of genius, above everything demands and insists upon, is freedom; entire independence of all authority, prescription, and routine, — the fullest room to expand as it will. Therefore, a nation whose chief spiritual characteristic is energy, will not be very apt to set up, in intellectual matters, a fixed standard, an authority, like an academy. By this it certainly escapes certain real inconveniences and dangers, and it can, at the same time, as we have seen, reach undeniably splendid heights in poetry and science. On the other hand, some of the requisites of intellectual work are specially the affair of quickness of mind and flexibility of intelligence. The form, the method of evolution, the precision, the proportions, the relations of the parts to the whole, in an intellectual work, depend mainly upon them. And these are the elements of an intellectual work which are really most communicable from it, which can most be learned and adopted from it, which have, therefore, the greatest effect upon the intellectual performance of others. Even in poetry, these requisites are very important; and the poetry of a nation, not eminent for the gifts on which they depend, will, more or less, suffer by this shortcoming. In poetry, however, they are, after all, secondary, and energy is the first thing; but in prose they are of first-rate importance. In its prose literature, therefore, and in the routine of intellectual work generally, a nation with no particular gifts for these will not be so successful. These are what, as I have said, can to a certain degree be learned and appropriated, while the free activity of genius cannot. Academies consecrate and maintain them, and, therefore, a nation with an eminent turn for them naturally establishes academies. So far as routine and authority tend to embarrass energy and inventive genius, academies may be said to be obstructive to energy and inventive genius, and, to this extent, to the human spirit's general advance. But then this evil is so much compensated by the propagation, on a large scale, of the mental aptitudes and demands which an open mind and a flexible intelligence naturally engender, genius itself, in the long run, so greatly finds its account in this propagation, and bodies like the French Academy have such power for promoting it, that the general advance of the human spirit is perhaps, on the whole, rather furthered than impeded by their existence.

How much greater is our nation in poetry than prose! how much better, in general, do the productions of its spirit show in the qualities of genius than in the qualities of intelligence! One may constantly remark this in the work of individuals; how much more striking, in general, does any Englishman, — of some vigour of mind, but by no means a poet, — seem in his verse than in his prose! His verse partly suffers from his not being really a poet, partly, no doubt, from the very same defects which impair his prose, and he cannot express himself with thorough success in it. But how much more powerful a personage does he appear in it, by dint of feeling, and of originality and movement of ideas, than when he is writing prose! With a Frenchman of like stamp, it is just the reverse: set him to write poetry, he is limited, artificial, and impotent; set him to write prose, he is free, natural, and effective. The power of French literature is in its prose-writers, the power of English literature is in its poets. Nay, many of the celebrated French poets depend wholly for their fame upon the qualities of intelligence which they exhibit, — qualities which are the distinctive support of prose; many of the celebrated English prose-writers depend wholly for their fame upon the qualities of genius and imagination which they exhibit, — qualities which are the distinctive support of poetry. But, as I have said, the qualities of genius are less transferable than the qualities of intelligence; less can be immediately learned and appropriated from their product; they are less direct and stringent intellectual agencies, though they may be more beautiful and divine. Shakespeare and our great Elizabethan group were certainly more gifted writers than Corneille and his group; but what was the sequel to this great literature, this literature of genius, as we may call it, stretching from Marlowe to Milton? What did it lead up to in English literature? To our provincial and second-rate literature of the eighteenth century. What, on the other hand, was the sequel to the literature of the French "great century," to this literature of intelligence, as, by comparison with our Elizabethan literature, we may call it; what did it lead up to? To the French literature of the eighteenth century, one of the most powerful and pervasive intellectual agencies that have ever existed, — the greatest European force of the eighteenth century. In science, again, we had Newton, a genius of the very highest order, a type of genius in science, if ever there was one. On the continent, as a sort of counterpart to Newton, there was Leibnitz; a man, it seems to me (though on these matters I speak under correction), of much less creative energy of genius, much less power of divination than Newton, but rather a man of admirable intelligence, a type of intelligence in science, if ever there was one. Well, and what did they each directly lead up to in science? What was the intellectual generation that sprang from each of them? I only repeat what the men of science have themselves pointed out. The man of genius was continued by the English analysts of the eighteenth century, comparatively powerless and obscure followers of the renowned master; the man of intelligence was continued by successors like Bernouilli, Euler, Lagrange, and Laplace, the greatest names in modern mathematics.

What I want the reader to see is, that the question as to the utility of academies to the intellectual life of a nation is not settled when we say, for instance: "Oh, we have never had an academy, and yet we have, confessedly, a very great literature." It still remains to be asked: "What sort of a great literature? a literature great in the special qualities of genius, or great in the special qualities of intelligence?" If in the former, it is by no means sure that either our literature, or the general intellectual life of our nation, has got already, without academies, all that academies can give. Both the one and the other may very well be somewhat wanting in those qualities of intelligence, out of a lively sense for which a body like the French Academy, as I have said, springs, and which such a body does a great deal to spread and confirm. Our literature, in spite of the genius manifested in it, may fall short in form, method, precision, proportions, arrangement, — all of them, I have said, things where intelligence proper comes in. It may be comparatively weak in prose, that branch of literature where intelligence proper is, so to speak, all in all. In this branch it may show many grave faults to which the want of a quick flexible intelligence, and of the strict standard which such an intelligence tends to impose, makes it liable; it may be full of haphazard, crudeness, provincialism, eccentricity, violence, blundering. It may be a less stringent and effective intellectual agency, both upon our own nation and upon the world at large, than other literatures which show less genius, perhaps, but more intelligence.

The right conclusion certainly is that we should try, so far as we can, to make up our shortcomings; and that to this end, instead of always fixing our thoughts upon the points in which our literature, and our intellectual life generally, are strong, we should, from time to time, fix them upon those in which they are weak, and so learn to perceive clearly what we have to amend. What is our second great spiritual characteristic, — our honesty, — good for, if it is not good for this? But it will, — I am sure it will, — more and more, as time goes on, be found good for this.

Well, then, an institution like the French Academy, — an institution owing its existence to a national bent towards the things of the mind, towards culture, towards clearness, correctness and propriety in thinking and speaking, and, in its turn, promoting this bent, — sets standards in a number of directions, and creates, in all these directions, a force of educated opinion, checking and rebuking those who fall below these standards, or who set them at nought. Educated opinion exists here as in France; but in France the Academy serves as a sort of centre and rallying-point to it, and gives it a force which it has not got here. Why is all the *journeyman-work* of literature, as I may call it, so much worse done here than it is in France? I do not wish to hurt anyone's feelings; but surely this is so. Think of the difference between our books of reference and those of the French, between our biographical dictionaries (to take a striking instance) and theirs; think of the difference between the translations of the classics turned out for Mr. Bohn's library and those turned out for M. Nisard's collection! As a general rule, hardly any one amongst us, who knows French and German well, would use an English book of reference when he could get a French or German one; or would look at an English prose translation of an ancient author when he could get a French or German one. It is not that there do not exist in England, as in France, a number of people perfectly well able to discern what is good, in these things, from what is bad, and preferring what is good; but they are isolated, they form no powerful body of opinion, they are not strong enough to set a standard, up to which even the journeyman-work of literature must be brought, if it is to be vendible. Ignorance and charlatanism in work of this kind are always trying to pass off their wares as excellent, and to cry down criticism as the voice of an insignificant, overfastidious minority; they easily persuade the multitude that this is so when the minority is scattered about as it is here, not so easily when it is banded together as in the French Academy. So, again, with freaks in dealing with language; certainly all such freaks tend to impair the power and beauty of language; and how far more common they are with us than with the French! To take a very familiar instance. Every one has noticed the way in which the *Times* chooses to spell the word "diocese"; it always spells it "diocess"[1] deriving it, I suppose, from *Zeus* and *census*. The *Journal des Débats* might just as well write "diocess" instead of "diocèse," but imagine the *Journal des Débats* doing so! Imagine an educated Frenchman indulging himself in an orthographical antic of this sort, in face of the grave respect with which the Academy and its dictionary invest the French language! Some people will say these are little things; they are not; they are of bad example. They tend to spread the baneful notion that there is no such thing as a high correct standard in intellectual matters; that every one may as well take his own way; they are at variance with the severe discipline necessary for all real culture; they confirm us in habits of wilfulness and eccentricity, which hurt our minds, and damage our credit with serious people. The late Mr. Donaldson was certainly a man of great ability, and I,

1 The *Times* has now (1868) abandoned this spelling and adopted the ordinary one.

who am not an Orientalist, do not pretend to judge his *Jashar*: but let the reader observe the form which a foreign Orientalist's judgment of it naturally takes. M. Renan calls it a *tentative malheureuse,* a failure, in short; this it may be, or it may not be; I am no judge. But he goes on: "It is astonishing that a recent article" (in a French periodical, he means) "should have brought forward as the last word of German exegesis a work like this, composed by a doctor of the University of Cambridge, and universally condemned by German critics." You see what he means to imply: an extravagance of this sort could never have come from Germany, where there is a great force of critical opinion controlling a learned man's vagaries, and keeping him straight; it comes from the native home of intellectual eccentricity of all kinds,[1] — from England — from a doctor of the University of Cambridge: — and I daresay he would not expect much better things from a doctor of the University of Oxford. Again, after speaking of what Germany and France have done for the history of Mahomet: "America and England," M. Renan goes on, "have also occupied themselves with Mahomet." He mentions Washington Irving's *Life of Mahomet,* which does not, he says, evince much of an historical sense, a *sentiment historique fort élevé;* "but," he proceeds, "this book shows a real progress, when one thinks that in 1829 Mr. Charles Forster published two thick volumes, which enchanted the English *révérends,* to make out that Mahomet was the little horn of the he-goat that figures in the eighth chapter of Daniel, and that the Pope was the great horn. Mr. Forster founded on this ingenious parallel a whole philosophy of history, according to which the Pope represented the Western corruption of Christianity, and Mahomet the Eastern; thence the striking resemblances between Mahometanism and Popery." And in a note M. Renan adds: "This is the same Mr. Charles Forster who is the author of a mystification about the Sinaitic inscriptions, in which he declares he finds the primitive language." As much as to say: "It is an Englishman, be surprised at no extravagance." If these innuendoes had no ground, and were made in hatred and malice, they would not be worth a moment's attention; but they come from a grave Orientalist, on his own subject, and they point to a real fact; — the absence, in this country, of any force of educated literary and scientific opinion, making aberrations like those of the author of *The One Primeval Language* out of the question. Not only the author of such aberrations, often a very clever man, suffers by the want of

1 A critic declares I am wrong in saying that M. Renan's language implies this. I still think that there is a shade, a *nuance* of expression, in M. Renan's language, which does imply this; but I confess, the only person who can really settle such a question is M. Renan himself.

check, by the not being kept straight, and spends force in vain on a false road, which, under better discipline, he might have used with profit on a true one; but all his adherents, both "reverends" and others, suffer too, and the general rate of information and judgment is in this way kept low.

In a production which we have all been reading lately, a production stamped throughout with a literary quality very rare in this country, and of which I shall have a word to say presently — *urbanity;* in this production, the work of a man never to be named by any son of Oxford without sympathy, a man who alone in Oxford of his generation, alone of many generations, conveyed to us in his genius that same charm, that same ineffable sentiment which this exquisite place itself conveys, — I mean Dr. Newman, — an expression is frequently used which is more common in theological than literary language, but which seems to me fitted to be of general service; the *note* of so and so, the note of catholicity, the note of antiquity, the note of sanctity, and so on. Adopting this expressive word, I say that in the bulk of the intellectual work of a nation which has no centre, no intellectual metropolis like an academy, like M. Sainte-Beuve's "sovereign organ of opinion," like M. Renan's "recognised authority in matters of tone and taste," — there is observable a *note of provinciality.* Now to get rid of provinciality is a certain stage of culture; a stage the positive result of which we must not make of too much importance, but which is, nevertheless, indispensable; for it brings us on to the platform where alone the best and highest intellectual work can be said fairly to begin. Work done after men have reached this platform is *classical;* and that is the only work which, in the long run, can stand. All the *scoriæ* in the work of men of great genius who have not lived on this platform are due to their not having lived on it. Genius raises them to it by moments, and the portions of their work which are immortal are done at these moments; but more of it would have been immortal if they had not reached this platform at moments only, if they had had the culture which makes men live there.

The less a literature has felt the influence of a supposed centre of correct information, correct judgment, correct taste, the more we shall find in it this note of provinciality. I have shown the note of provinciality as caused by remoteness from a centre of correct information. Of course the note of provinciality from the want of a centre of correct taste is still more visible, and it is also still more common. For here great — even the greatest — powers of mind most fail a man. Great powers of mind will make him inform himself thoroughly, great powers of mind will make him think profoundly, even with ignorance and platitude all round him; but not even great powers of mind will keep his taste and style perfectly sound and sure, if he is left too much to himself, with no "sovereign organ of opinion" in these matters near him. Even men like Jeremy Taylor and Burke suffer here. Take this passage from Taylor's funeral sermon on Lady Carbery:

"So have I seen a river, deep and smooth, passing with a still foot and a sober face, and paying to the *fiscus*, the great exchequer of the sea, a tribute large and full; and hard by it a little brook, skipping and making a noise upon its unequal and neighbour bottom; and after all its talking and bragged motion, it paid to its common audit no more than the revenues of a little cloud or a contemptible vessel: so have I sometimes compared the issues of her religion to the solemnities and famed outsides of another's piety."

That passage has been much admired, and, indeed, the genius in it is undeniable. I should say, for my part, that genius, the ruling divinity of poetry, had been too busy in it, and intelligence, the ruling divinity of prose, not busy enough. But can any one, with the best models of style in his head, help feeling the note of provinciality there, the want of simplicity, the want of measure, the want of just the qualities that make prose classical? If he does not feel what I mean, let him place beside the passage of Taylor this passage from the Panegyric of St. Paul, by Taylor's contemporary, Bossuet:

"Il ira, cet ignorant dans l'art de bien dire, avec cette locution rude, avec cette phrase qui sent l'étranger, il ira en cette Grèce polie, la mère des philosophes et des orateurs; et malgré la résistance du monde, il y établira plus d'Eglises que Platon n'y a gagné de disciples par cette éloquence qu'on a crue divine."

There we have prose without the note of provinciality — classical prose, prose of the centre.

Or take Burke, our greatest English prose-writer, as I think; take expressions like this:

"Blindfold themselves, like bulls that shut their eyes when they push, they drive, by the point of their bayonets, their slaves, blindfolded, indeed, no worse than their lords, to take their fictions for currencies, and to swallow down paper pills by thirty-four millions sterling at a dose."

Or this:

"They used it" (the royal name) "as a sort of navel-string, to nourish their unnatural offspring from the bowels of royalty itself. Now that the monster can purvey for its own subsistence, it will only carry the mark about it, as a token of its having torn the womb it came from."

Or this:

"Without one natural pang, he" (Rousseau) "casts away, as a sort of offal and excrement, the spawn of his disgustful amours, and sends his children to the hospital of foundlings."

Or this:

"I confess I never liked this continual talk of resistance and revolution, or the practice of making the extreme medicine of the constitution its daily bread. It renders the habit of society dangerously valetudinary; it is taking periodical doses of mercury sublimate, and swallowing down repeated provocatives of cantharides to our love of liberty."

I say that is extravagant prose; prose too much suffered to indulge its caprices; prose at too great a distance from the centre of good taste; prose, in short, with the note of provinciality. People may reply, it is rich and imaginative; yes, that is just it, it is *Asiatic* prose, as the ancient critics would have said; prose somewhat barbarously rich and over-loaded. But the true prose is Attic prose.

Well, but Addison's prose is Attic prose. Where, then, it may be asked, is the note of provinciality in Addison? I answer, in the commonplace of his ideas.[1] This is a matter worth remarking. Addison claims to take leading rank as a moralist. To do that, you must have ideas of the first order on your subject — the best ideas, at any rate, attainable in your time — as well as be able to express them in a perfectly sound and sure style. Else you show your distance from the centre of ideas by your matter; you are provincial by your matter, though you may not be provincial by your style. It is comparatively a small matter to express oneself well, if one will be content with not expressing much, with expressing only trite ideas; the problem is to express new and profound ideas in a perfectly sound and classical style. He is the true classic, in every age, who does that. Now Addison has not, on his subject of morals, the force of ideas of the moralists of the first class — the classical moralists; he has not the best ideas attainable in or about his time, and which were, so to speak, in the air then, to be seized by the finest spirits; he is not to be compared for power, searchingness, or delicacy of thought to Pascal or La Bruyère or Vauvenargues; he is rather on a level, in this

[1] A critic says this is paradoxical, and urges that many second-rate French academicians have uttered the most commonplace ideas possible; but Addison is not a second-rate man. He is a man of the order, I will not say of Pascal, but at any rate of La Bruyère and Vauvenargues; why does he not equal them? I say because of the medium in which he finds himself, the atmosphere in which he lives and works; an atmosphere which tells unfavourably, or rather *tends* to tell unfavourably (for that is the truer way of putting it) either upon style or else upon ideas; tends to make even a man of great ability either a Mr. Carlyle or else a Lord Macaulay.

It is to be observed, however, that Lord Macaulay's style has in its turn suffered by his failure in ideas, and this cannot be said of Addison's.

respect, with a man like Marmontel; therefore, I say, he has the note of provinciality as a moralist; he is provincial by his matter, though not by his style.

To illustrate what I mean by an example. Addison, writing as a moralist on fixedness in religious faith, says:

"Those who delight in reading books of controversy do very seldom arrive at a fixed and settled habit of faith. The doubt which was laid revives again, and shows itself in new difficulties; and that generally for this reason, — because the mind, which is perpetually tossed in controversies and disputes, is apt to forget the reasons which had once set it at rest, and to be disquieted with any former perplexity when it appears in a new shape, or is started by a different hand."

It may be said, that is classical English, perfect in lucidity, measure, and propriety. I make no objection; but, in my turn, I say that the idea expressed is perfectly trite and barren, and that it is a note of provinciality in Addison, in a man whom a nation puts forward as one of its great moralists, to have no profounder and more striking idea to produce on this great subject. Compare, on the same subject, these words of a moralist really of the first order, really at the centre by his ideas, — Joubert:

"L'expérience de beaucoup d'opinions donne à l'esprit beaucoup de flexibilité et l'affermit dans celles qu'il croit les meilleures."

With what a flash of light that touches the subject! how it sets us thinking! what a genuine contribution to moral science it is!

In short, where there is no centre like an academy, if you have genius and powerful ideas, you are apt not to have the best style going; if you have precision of style and not a genius, you are apt not to have the best ideas going.

The provincial spirit, again, exaggerates the value of its ideas for want of a high standard at hand by which to try them. Or rather, for want of such a standard, it gives one idea too much prominence at the expense of others; it orders its ideas amiss; it is hurried away by fancies; it likes and dislikes too passionately, too exclusively. Its admiration weeps hysterical tears, and its disapprobation foams at the mouth. So we get the *eruptive* and the *aggressive* manner in literature; the former prevails most in our criticism, the latter in our newspapers. For, not having the lucidity of a large and centrally placed intelligence, the provincial spirit has not its graciousness; it does not persuade, it makes war; it has not urbanity, the tone of the city, of the centre, the tone which always aims at a spiritual and intellectual effect, and not excluding the use of banter, never disjoins banter itself from politeness, from felicity. But the provincial tone is more violent, and seems to aim rather at an effect upon the blood and senses than upon the spirit and intellect; it loves hard hitting rather than persuading. The newspaper, with its party spirit, its thoroughgoingness, its resolute avoidance of shades and distinctions, its short, highly charged, heavy-shotted articles, its style so unlike that style *lenis minimeque pertinax* — easy and not too violently insisting, — which the ancients so much admired, is its true literature; the provincial spirit likes in the newspaper just what makes the newspaper such bad food for it, — just what made Goethe say, when he was pressed hard about the immorality of Byron's poems, that, after all, they were not so immoral as the newspapers. The French talk of the *brutalité des journaux anglais*. What strikes them comes from the necessary inherent tendencies of newspaper-writing not being checked in England by any centre of intelligent and urbane spirit, but rather stimulated by coming in contact with a provincial spirit. Even a newspaper like the *Saturday Review*, that old friend of all of us, a newspaper expressly aiming at an immunity from the common newspaper-spirit, aiming at being a sort of organ of reason, — and, by thus aiming, it merits great gratitude and has done great good, — even the *Saturday Review*, replying to some foreign criticism on our precautions against invasion, falls into a strain of this kind:

"To do this" (to take these precautions) "seems to us eminently worthy of a great nation, and to talk of it as unworthy of a great nation, seems to us eminently worthy of a great fool."

There is what the French mean when they talk of the *brutalité des journaux anglais;* there is a style certainly as far removed from urbanity as possible, — a style with what I call the note of provinciality. And the same note may not unfrequently be observed even in the ideas of this newspaper, full as it is of thought and cleverness: certain ideas allowed to become fixed ideas, to prevail too absolutely. I will not speak of the immediate present, but, to go a little while back, it had the critic who so disliked the Emperor of the French; it had the critic who so disliked the subject of my present remarks — academies; it had the critic who was so fond of the German element in our nation, and, indeed, everywhere; who ground his teeth if one said *Charlemagne* instead of *Charles the Great*, and, in short, saw all things in Teutonism, as Malebranche saw all things in God. Certainly any one may fairly find faults in the Emperor Napoleon or in academies, and merit in the German element; but it is a note of the provincial spirit not to hold ideas of this kind a little more easily, to be so devoured by them, to suffer them to become crotchets.

In England there needs a miracle of genius like Shakespeare's to produce balance of mind, and a miracle of intellectual delicacy like

Dr. Newman's to produce urbanity of style. How prevalent all round us is the want of balance of mind and urbanity of style! How much, doubtless, it is to be found in ourselves, — in each of us! but, as human nature is constituted, every one can see it clearest in his contemporaries. There, above all, we should consider it, because they and we are exposed to the same influences; and it is in the best of one's contemporaries that it is most worth considering, because one then most feels the harm it does, when one sees what they would be without it. Think of the difference between Mr. Ruskin exercising his genius, and Mr. Ruskin exercising his intelligence; consider the truth and beauty of this:

"Go out, in the spring-time, among the meadows that slope from the shores of the Swiss lakes to the roots of their lower mountains. There, mingled with the taller gentians and the white narcissus, the grass grows deep and free; and as you follow the winding mountain paths, beneath arching boughs all veiled and dim with blossom, — paths that for ever droop and rise over the green banks and mounds sweeping down in scented undulation, steep to the blue water, studded here and there with new-mown heaps, filling all the air with fainter sweetness, — look up towards the higher hills, where the waves of everlasting green roll silently into their long inlets among the shadows of the pines. . . ."

There is what the genius, the feeling, the temperament in Mr. Ruskin, the original and incommunicable part, has to do with; and how exquisite it is! All the critic could possibly suggest, in the way of objection, would be, perhaps, that Mr. Ruskin is there trying to make prose do more than it can perfectly do; that what he is there attempting he will never, except in poetry, be able to accomplish to his own entire satisfaction: but he accomplishes so much that the critic may well hesitate to suggest even this. Place beside this charming passage another, — a passage about Shakespeare's names, where the intelligence and judgment of Mr. Ruskin, the acquired, trained, communicable part in him, are brought into play, — and see the difference:

"Of Shakespeare's names I will afterwards speak at more length; they are curiously — often barbarously — mixed out of various traditions and languages. Three of the clearest in meaning have been already noticed. Desdemona — 'δυσδαιμονία,' *miserable fortune* — is also plain enough. Othello is, I believe, 'the careful'; all the calamity of the tragedy arising from the single flaw and error in his magnificently collected strength. Ophelia, 'serviceableness,' the true, lost wife of Hamlet, is marked as having a Greek name by that of her brother, Laertes; and its signification is once exquisitely alluded to in that brother's last word of her, where her gentle preciousness is opposed to the uselessness of the churlish clergy: —'A *ministering* angel shall my sister be, when thou liest howling.' Hamlet is, I believe, connected in some way with 'homely,' the entire event of the tragedy turning on betrayal of home duty. Hermione (ἕρμα), 'pillar-like' (ἣ εἶδος ἔχε χρυσῆς Ἀφροδίτης); Titiania (τιτήνη), 'the queen'; Benedick and Beatrice, 'blessed and blessing'; Valentine and Proteus, 'enduring or strong' (*valens*), and 'changeful.' Iago and Iachimo have evidently the same root — probably the Spanish Iago, Jacob, 'the supplanter.'"

Now, really, what a piece of extravagance all that is! I will not say that the meaning of Shakespeare's names (I put aside the question as to the correctness of Mr. Ruskin's etymologies) has no effect at all, may be entirely lost sight of; but to give it that degree of prominence is to throw the reins to one's whim, to forget all moderation and proportion, to lose the balance of one's mind altogether. It is to show in one's criticism, to the highest excess, the note of provinciality.

Again, there is Mr. Palgrave, certainly endowed with a very fine critical tact: his *Golden Treasury* abundantly proves it. The plan of arrangement which he devised for that work, the mode in which he followed his plan out, nay, one might even say, merely the juxtaposition, in pursuance of it, of two such pieces as those of Wordsworth and Shelley which form the 285th and 286th in his collection, show a delicacy of feeling in these matters which is quite indisputable and very rare. And his notes are full of remarks which show it too. All the more striking, conjoined with so much justness of perception, are certain freaks and violences in Mr. Palgrave's criticism, mainly imputable, I think, to the critic's isolated position in this country, to his feeling himself too much left to take his own way, too much without any central authority representing high culture and sound judgment, by which he may be, on the one hand, confirmed as against the ignorant, on the other, held in respect when he himself is inclined to take liberties. I mean such things as this note on Milton's line,

> The great Emathian conqueror bade spare . . .

"When Thebes was destroyed, Alexander ordered the house of Pindar to be spared. *He was as incapable of appreciating the poet as Louis XIV of appreciating Racine; but even the narrow and barbarian mind of Alexander could understand the advantage of a showy act of homage to poetry.*" A note like that I call a freak or a violence; if this disparaging view of Alexander and Louis XIV, so unlike the current view, is wrong, — if the current view is, after all, the truer one of them, — the note is a freak. But, even if its disparaging view is right, the note is a violence; for abandoning the true mode of intellectual action — persuasion, the instilment of conviction, — it simply astounds and irritates the hearer by contradicting without a word of proof or preparation, his fixed and familiar notions; and this is mere violence. In either case, the fitness, the measure, the centrality, which is the soul of all good criticism, is lost, and the note of provinciality shows itself.

Thus, in the famous *Handbook*, marks of a fine power of perception are everywhere discernible, but so, too, are marks of the want of sure balance, of the check and support afforded by knowing one speaks before good and severe judges. When Mr. Palgrave dislikes a thing, he feels no pressure constraining him either to try his dislike closely or to express it moderately; he does not mince matters, he gives his dislike all its own way; both his judgment and his style would gain if he were under more restraint. "The style which has filled London with the dead monotony of Gower or Harley Streets, or the pale commonplace of Belgravia, Tyburnia, and Kensington; which has pierced Paris and Madrid with the feeble frivolities of the Rue Rivoli and the Strada de Toledo." He dislikes the architecture of the Rue Rivoli, and he puts it on a level with the architecture of Belgravia and Gower Street; he lumps them all together in one condemnation, he loses sight of the shade, the distinction which is everything here; the distinction, namely, that the architecture of the Rue Rivoli expresses show, splendour, pleasure, — unworthy things, perhaps, to express alone and for their own sakes, but it expresses them; whereas the architecture of Gower Street and Belgravia merely expresses the impotence of the architect to express anything. Then, as to style: "sculpture which stands in a contrast with Woolner hardly more shameful than diverting." . . . "passing from Davy or Faraday to the art of the mountebank or the science of the spirit-rapper." . . . "it is the old, old story with Marochetti, the frog trying to blow himself out to bull dimensions. He may puff and be puffed, but he will never do it." We all remember that shower of amenities on poor M. Marochetti. Now, here Mr. Palgrave himself enables us to form a contrast which lets us see just what the presence of an academy does for style; for he quotes a criticism by M. Gustave Planche on this very M. Marochetti. M. Gustave Planche was a critic of the very first order, a man of strong opinions, which he expressed with severity; he, too, condemns M. Marochetti's work, and Mr. Palgrave calls him as a witness to back what he has himself said; certainly Mr. Palgrave's translation will not exaggerate M. Planche's urbanity in dealing with M. Marochetti, but, even in this translation, see the difference in sobriety, in measure, between the critic writing in Paris and the critic writing in London:

"These conditions are so elementary, that I am at a perfect loss to comprehend how M. Marochetti has neglected them. There are soldiers here like the leaden playthings of the nursery: it is almost impossible to guess whether there is a body beneath the dress. We have here no question of style, not even of grammar; it is nothing beyond mere matter of the alphabet of art. To break these conditions is the same as to be ignorant of spelling."

That is really more formidable criticism than Mr. Palgrave's, and yet in how perfectly temperate a style! M. Planche's advantage is, that he feels himself to be speaking before competent judges, that there is a force of cultivated opinion for him to appeal to. Therefore, he must not be extravagant, and he need not storm; he must satisfy the reason and taste, — that is his business. Mr. Palgrave, on the other hand, feels himself to be speaking before a promiscuous multitude, with the few good judges so scattered through it as to be powerless; therefore, he has no calm confidence and no self-control; he relies on the strength of his lungs; he knows that big words impose on the mob, and that, even if he is outrageous, most of his audience are apt to be a great deal more so.[1]

Again, the first two volumes of Mr. Kinglake's *Invasion of the Crimea* were certainly among the most successful and renowned English books of our time. Their style was one of the most renowned things about them, and yet how conspicuous a fault in Mr. Kinglake's style is this overcharge of which I have been speaking! Mr. James Gordon Bennett, of the *New York Herald,* says, I believe, that the highest achievement of the human intellect is what he calls "a good editorial." This is not quite so; but, if it were so, on what a height would these two volumes by Mr. Kinglake stand! I have already spoken of the Attic and the Asiatic styles; besides these, there is the Corinthian style. That is the style for "a good editorial," and Mr. Kinglake has really reached perfection in it. It has not the warm glow, blithe movement, and soft pliancy of life, as the Attic style has; it has not the over-heavy richness and encumbered gait of the Asiatic style; it has glitter without warmth, rapidity without ease, effectiveness without charm. Its characteristic is, that it has no *soul;* all it exists for, is to get its ends, to make its points, to damage its adversaries, to be admired, to triumph. A style so bent on effect at the expense of soul, simplicity, and delicacy; a style so little studious

[1] When I wrote this I had before me the first edition of Mr. Palgrave's *Handbook.* I am bound to say that in the second edition much strong language has been expunged, and what remains, softened.

of the charm of the great models; so far from classic truth and grace, must surely be said to have the note of provinciality. Yet Mr. Kinglake's talent is a really eminent one, and so in harmony with our intellectual habits and tendencies, that, to the great bulk of English people, the faults of his style seem its merits; all the more needful that criticism should not be dazzled by them.

We must not compare a man of Mr. Kinglake's literary talent with French writers like M. de Bazancourt. We must compare him with M. Thiers. And what a superiority in style has M. Thiers from being formed in a good school, with severe traditions, wholesome restraining influences! Even in this age of Mr. James Gordon Bennett, his style has nothing Corinthian about it, its lightness and brightness make it almost Attic. It is not quite Attic, however; it has not the infallible sureness of Attic taste. Sometimes his head gets a little hot with the fumes of patriotism, and then he crosses the line, he loses perfect measure, he declaims, he raises a momentary smile. France condemned "à être l'effroi du monde *dont elle pourrait être l'amour*," — Cæsar, whose exquisite simplicity M. Thiers so much admires, would not have written like that. There is, if I may be allowed to say so, the slightest possible touch of fatuity in such language, — of that failure in good sense which comes from too warm a self-satisfaction. But compare this language with Mr. Kinglake's Marshal St. Arnaud — "dismissed from the presence" of Lord Raglan or Lord Stratford, "cowed and pressed down" under their "stern reproofs," or under "the majesty of the great Elchi's Canning brow and tight, merciless lips!" The failure in good sense and good taste there reaches far beyond what the French mean by *fatuity;* they would call it by another word, a word expressing blank defect of intelligence, a word for which we have no exact equivalent in English, — *bête.* It is the difference between a venial, momentary, good-tempered excess, in a man of the world, of an amiable and social weakness, — vanity; and a serious, settled, fierce, narrow, provincial misconception of the whole relative value of one's own things and the things of others. So baneful to the style of even the cleverest man may be the total want of checks.

In all I have said, I do not pretend that the examples given prove my rule as to the influence of academies; they only illustrate it. Examples in plenty might very likely be found to set against them; the truth of the rule depends, no doubt, on whether the balance of all the examples is in its favour or not; but actually to strike this balance is always out of the question. Here, as everywhere else, the rule, the idea, if true, commends itself to the judicious, and then the examples make it clearer still to them. This is the real use of examples, and this alone is the purpose which I have meant mine to serve. There is also another side to the whole question, — as to the limiting and prejudicial operation which academies may have; but this side of the question it rather behoves the French, not us, to study.

The reader will ask for some practical conclusion about the establishment of an Academy in this country, and perhaps I shall hardly give him the one he expects. But nations have their own modes of acting, and these modes are not easily changed; they are even consecrated, when great things have been done in them. When a literature has produced Shakespeare and Milton, when it has even produced Barrow and Burke, it cannot well abandon its traditions; it can hardly begin, at this late time of day, with an institution like the French Academy. I think academies with a limited, special, scientific scope, in the various lines of intellectual work, — academies like that of Berlin, for instance, — we with time may, and probably shall, establish. And no doubt they will do good; no doubt the presence of such influential centres of correct information will tend to raise the standard amongst us for what I have called the *journeyman-work* of literature, and to free us from the scandal of such biographical dictionaries as Chalmers's, or such translations as a recent one of Spinoza, or perhaps, such philological freaks as Mr. Forster's about the one primeval language. But an academy quite like the French Academy, a sovereign organ of the highest literary opinion, a recognised authority in matters of intellectual tone and taste, we shall hardly have, and perhaps we ought not to wish to have it. But then every one amongst us with any turn for literature will do well to remember to what shortcomings and excesses, which such an academy tends to correct, we are liable; and the more liable, of course, for not having it. He will do well constantly to try himself in respect of these, steadily to widen his culture, severely to check in himself the provincial spirit; and he will do this the better the more he keeps in mind that all mere glorification by ourselves of ourselves, or our literature, in the strain of what, at the beginning of these remarks, I quoted from Lord Macaulay, is both vulgar, and, besides being vulgar, retarding.

From MAURICE DE GUÉRIN

I will not presume to say that I now know the French language well; but at a time when I knew it even less well than at present,—some fifteen years ago,—I remember pestering those about me with this sentence, the rhythm of which had lodged itself in my head, and which, with the strangest pronunciation possible, I kept perpetually declaiming: "*Les dieux jaloux ont enfoui quelque part les témoignages de la descendance des choses; mais au bord de quel Océan ont-ils roulé la pierre qui les couvre, ô Macarée!*"

These words come from a short composition called the *Centaur*, of which the author, Georges-Maurice de Guérin, died in the year 1839, at the age of twenty-eight, without having published anything. In 1840, Madame Sand brought out the *Centaur* in the *Revue des Deux Mondes*, with a short notice of its author, and a few extracts from his letters. A year or two afterwards she reprinted these at the end of a volume of her novels; and there it was that I fell in with them. I was so much struck with the *Centaur* that I waited anxiously to hear something more of its author, and of what he had left; but it was not till the other day—twenty years after the first publication of the *Centaur* in the *Revue des Deux Mondes*, that my anxiety was satisfied. At the end of 1860 appeared two volumes with the title *Maurice de Guérin, Reliquiæ*, containing the *Centaur*, several poems of Guérin, his journals, and a number of his letters, collected and edited by a devoted friend, M. Trebutien, and preceded by a notice of Guérin by the first of living critics, M. Sainte-Beuve.

The grand power of poetry is its interpretative power; by which I mean, not a power of drawing out in black and white an explanation of the mystery of the universe, but the power of so dealing with things as to awaken in us a wonderfully full, new, and intimate sense of them, and of our relations with them. When this sense is awakened in us, as to objects without us, we feel ourselves to be in contact with the essential nature of those objects, to be no longer bewildered and oppressed by them, but to have their secret, and to be in harmony with them; and this feeling calms and satisfies us as no other can. Poetry, indeed, interprets in another way besides this; but one of its two ways of interpreting, of exercising its highest power, is by awakening this sense in us. I will not now inquire whether this sense is illusive, whether it can be proved not to be illusive, whether it does absolutely make us possess the real nature of things; all I say is, that poetry can awaken it in us, and that to awaken it is one of the highest powers of poetry. The interpretations of science do not give us this intimate sense of objects as the interpretations of poetry give it; they appeal to a limited faculty, and not to the whole man. It is not Linnæus or Cavendish or Cuvier who gives us the true sense of animals, or water, or plants, who seizes their secret for us, who makes us participate in their life; it is Shakespeare, with his

> "daffodils
> That come before the swallow dares, and take
> The winds of March with beauty;"

it is Wordsworth, with his

> "voice . . . . heard
> In spring-time from the cuckoo-bird,
> Breaking the silence of the seas
> Among the farthest Hebrides;"

it is Keats, with his

> "moving waters at their priestlike task
> Of cold ablution round Earth's human shores;"

it is Chateaubriand, with his, *"cîme indéterminée des forêts;"* it is Senancour, with his mountain birch-tree: *"Cette écorce blanche, lisse et crevassée; cette tige agreste; ces branches qui s'inclinent vers la terre; la mobilité des feuilles, et tout cet abandon, simplicité de la nature, attitude des déserts."*

Eminent manifestations of this magical power of poetry are very rare and very precious: the compositions of Guérin manifest it, I think, in singular eminence. Not his poems, strictly so called, — his verse, — so much as his prose; his poems in general take for their vehicle that favourite metre of French poetry, the Alexandrine; and, in my judgment, I confess they have thus, as compared with his prose, a great disadvantage to start with. In prose, the character of the vehicle for the composer's thoughts is not determined beforehand; every composer has to make his own vehicle; and who has ever done this more admirably than the great prose-writers of France, — Pascal, Bossuet, Fénélon, Voltaire? But in verse the composer has (with comparatively narrow liberty of modification) to accept his vehicle ready-made; it is therefore of vital importance to him that he should find at his disposal a vehicle adequate to convey the highest matters of poetry. We may even get a decisive test of the poetical power of a language and nation by ascertaining how far the principal poetical vehicle which they have employed, how far (in plainer words) the established national metre for high poetry, is adequate or inadequate. It seems to me that the established metre of this kind in France, — the Alexandrine, — is inadequate; that as a vehicle for high poetry it is greatly inferior to the hexameter or to the iambics of Greece (for example), or to the blank verse of England. Therefore the man of genius who uses it is at a disadvantage as compared with the man of genius who has for conveying his thoughts a more adequate vehicle, metrical or not. Racine is at a disadvantage as compared with Sophocles or Shakspeare, and he is likewise at a disadvantage as compared with Bossuet.

The same may be said of our own poets of the eighteenth century, a century which gave them as the main vehicle for their high poetry a metre inadequate (as much as the French Alexandrine, and nearly in the same way) for this poetry, — the ten-syllable couplet. It is worth remarking, that the English poet of the eighteenth century whose compositions wear best and give one the most entire satisfaction, — Gray, — hardly uses that couplet at all: this abstinence, however, limits Gray's productions to a few short compositions, and (exquisite as these are) he is a poetical nature repressed and without free issue. For English poetical production on a great scale, for an English poet deploying all the forces of his genius, the ten-syllable couplet was, in the eighteenth century, the established, one may almost say the inevitable, channel. Now this couplet, admirable (as Chaucer uses it) for story-telling not of the epic pitch, and often admirable for a few lines even in poetry of a very high pitch, is for continuous use in poetry of this latter kind inadequate. Pope, in his *Essay on Man*, is thus at a disadvantage compared with Lucretius in his poem on Nature: Lucretius has an adequate vehicle, Pope has not. Nay, though Pope's genius for didactic poetry was not less than that of Horace, while his satirical power was certainly greater, still one's taste receives, I cannot but think, a certain satisfaction when one reads the Epistles and Satires of Horace, which it fails to receive when one reads the Satires and Epistles of Pope. Of such avail is the superior adequacy of the vehicle used to compensate even an inferiority of genius in the user! In the same way Pope is at a disadvantage as compared with Addison. The best of Addison's composition (the "Coverley Papers" in the *Spectator*, for instance) wears better than the best of Pope's, because Addison has in his prose an intrinsically better vehicle for his genius than Pope in his couplet. But Bacon has no such advantage over Shakspeare; nor has Milton, writing prose (for no contemporary English prose-writer must be matched with Milton except Milton himself), any such advantage over Milton writing verse: indeed, the advantage here is all the other way.

It is in the prose remains of Guérin, — his journals, his letters, and the striking composition which I have already mentioned, the *Centaur*,

— that his extraordinary gift manifests itself. He has a truly interpretative faculty; the most profound and delicate sense of the life of Nature, and the most exquisite felicity in finding expressions to render that sense. To all who love poetry, Guérin deserves to be something more than a name; and I shall try, in spite of the impossibility of doing justice to such a master of expression by translations, to make English readers see for themselves how gifted an organisation his was, and how few artists have received from Nature a more magical faculty of interpreting her. . . .

In few natures, however, is there really such essential consistency as in Guérin's. He says of himself, in the very beginning of his journal: "I owe everything to poetry, for there is no other name to give to the sum total of my thoughts; I owe to it whatever I now have pure, lofty, and solid in my soul; I owe to it all my consolations in the past; I shall probably owe to it my future." Poetry, the poetical instinct, was indeed the basis of his nature; but to say so thus absolutely is not quite enough. One aspect of poetry fascinated Guérin's imagination and held it prisoner. Poetry is the interpretress of the natural world, and she is the interpretress of the moral world; it was as the interpretress of the natural world that she had Guérin for her mouthpiece. To make magically near and real the life of Nature, and man's life only so far as it is a part of that Nature, was his faculty; a faculty of naturalistic, not of moral interpretation. This faculty always has for its basis a peculiar temperament, an extraordinary delicacy of organisation and susceptibility to impressions; in exercising it the poet is in a great degree passive (Wordsworth thus speaks of a *wise passiveness*); he aspires to be a sort of human Æolian harp, catching and rendering every rustle of Nature. To assist at the evolution of the whole life of the world is his craving, and intimately to feel it all:

> . . . "the glow, the thrill of life,
> Where, where do these abound?"

is what he asks: he resists being riveted and held stationary by any single impression, but would be borne on for ever down an enchanted stream. He goes into religion and out of religion, into society and out of society, not from the motives which impel men in general, but to feel what it is all like; he is thus hardly a moral agent, and, like the passive and ineffectual Uranus of Keats's poem, he may say:

> . . . . . . "I am but a voice;
> My life is but the life of winds and tides;
> No more than winds and tides can I avail."

He hovers over the tumult of life, but does not really put his hand to it.

No one has expressed the aspirations of this temperament better than Guérin himself. In the last year of his life he writes: —

"I return, as you see, to my old brooding over the world of Nature, that line which my thoughts irresistibly take; a sort of passion which gives me enthusiasm, tears, bursts of joy, and an eternal food for musing; and yet I am neither philosopher nor naturalist, nor anything learned whatsoever. There is one word which is the God of my imagination, the tyrant, I ought rather to say, that fascinates it, lures it onward, gives it work to do without ceasing, and will finally carry it I know not where; the word *life*."

And in one place in his journal he says: —

"My imagination welcomes every dream, every impression, without attaching itself to any, and goes on for ever seeking something new."

And again in another: —

"The longer I live, and the clearer I discern between true and false in society, the more does the inclination to live, not as a savage or a misanthrope, but as a solitary man on the frontiers of society, on the outskirts of the world, gain strength and grow in me. The birds come and go and make nests around our habitations, they are fellow-citizens of our farms and hamlets with us; but they take their flight in a heaven which is boundless, but the hand of God alone gives and measures to them their daily food, but they build their nests in the heart of the thick bushes, or hang them in the height of the trees. So would I, too, live, hovering round society, and having always at my back a field of liberty vast as the sky."

In the same spirit he longed for travel. "When one is a wanderer," he writes to his sister, "one feels that one fulfils the true condition of humanity." And the last entry in his journal is, — "The stream of travel is full of delight. Oh, who will set me adrift on this Nile!"

Assuredly it is not in this temperament that the active virtues have their rise. On the contrary, this temperament, considered in itself alone, indisposes for the discharge of them. Something morbid and excessive, as manifested in Guérin, it undoubtedly has. In him, as in Keats, and as in another youth of genius, whose name, but the other day unheard of, Lord Houghton has so gracefully written in the history of English poetry, — David Gray, — the temperament, the talent itself, is deeply influenced by their mysterious malady; the temperament is *devouring;* it uses vital power too hard and too fast, paying the penalty in long hours of unutterable exhaustion and in premature death. The intensity of Guérin's depression is described to us by Guérin himself with the same incomparable touch with which he describes happier feelings; far oftener than any pleasurable sense of his gift he has "the sense profound, near, immense, of my misery, of my inward poverty." And again: "My inward misery gains upon me; I no longer dare look within." And on another day of gloom he does look within, and here is the terrible analysis:—

"Craving, unquiet, seeing only by glimpses, my spirit is stricken by all those ills which are the sure fruit of a youth doomed never to ripen into manhood. I grow old and wear myself out in the most futile mental strainings, and make no progress. My head seems dying, and when the wind blows I fancy I feel it, as if I were a tree, blowing through a number of withered branches in my top. Study is intolerable to me, or rather it is quite out of my power. Mental work brings on, not drowsiness, but an irritable and nervous disgust which drives me out, I know not where, into the streets and public places. The Spring, whose delights used to come every year stealthily and mysteriously to charm me in my retreat, crushes me this year under a weight of sudden hotness. I should be glad of any event which delivered me from the situation in which I am. If I were free I would embark for some distant country where I could begin life anew."

Such is this temperament in the frequent hours when the sense of its own weakness and isolation crushes it to the ground. Certainly it was not for Guérin's happiness, or for Keats's, as men count happiness, to be as they were. Still the very excess and predominance of their temperament has given to the fruits of their genius a unique brilliancy and flavour. I have said that poetry interprets in two ways; it interprets by expressing with magical felicity the physiognomy and movement of the outward world, and it interprets by expressing, with inspired conviction, the ideas and laws of the inward world of man's moral and spiritual nature. In other words, poetry is interpretative both by having *natural magic* in it, and by having *moral profundity*. In both ways it illuminates man; it gives him a satisfying sense of reality; it reconciles him with himself and the universe. Thus Æschylus's "δράσαντι παθεῖν" and his "ἀνήριθμον γέλασμα" are alike interpretative. Shakspeare interprets both when he says,

> "Full many a glorious morning have I seen,
> Flatter the mountain-tops with sovran eye;"

and when he says,

> "There's a divinity that shapes our ends,
> Rough-hew them as we will."

These great poets unite in themselves the faculty of both kinds of interpretation, the naturalistic and the moral. But it is observable that in the poets who unite both kinds, the latter (the moral) usually ends by making itself the master. In Shakspeare the two kinds seem wonderfully to balance one another; but even in him the balance leans; his expression tends to become too little sensuous and simple, too much intellectualised. The same thing may be yet more strongly affirmed of Lucretius and of Wordsworth. In Shelley there is not a balance of the two gifts, nor even a co-existence of them, but there is a passionate straining after them both, and this is what makes Shelley, as a man, so interesting: I will not now inquire how much Shelley achieves as a poet, but whatever he achieves, he in general fails to achieve natural magic in his expression; in Mr. Palgrave's charming *Treasury* may be seen a gallery of his failures.[1] But in Keats and Guérin, in whom the faculty of naturalistic interpretation is overpoweringly predominant, the natural magic is perfect; when they speak of the world they speak like Adam naming by divine inspiration the creatures; their expression corresponds with the thing's essential reality. Even between Keats and Guérin, however, there is a distinction to be drawn. Keats has, above all, a sense of what is pleasurable and open in the life of nature; for him she is the *Alma Parens:* his expression has, therefore, more than Guérin's, something genial, outward, and sensuous. Guérin has, above all, a sense of what there is adorable and secret in the life of Nature; for him she is the *Magna Parens;* his expression has, therefore, more than Keats's, something mystic, inward, and profound.

So he lived like a man possessed; with his eye not on his own career, not on the public, not on fame, but on the Isis whose veil he had uplifted. He published nothing: "There is more power and beauty," he writes, "in the well-kept secret of one's-self and one's thoughts, than in the display of a whole heaven that one may have inside one." "My spirit," he answers the friends who urge him to write, "is of the home-keeping order, and has no fancy for adventure; literary adventure is above all distasteful to it; for this, indeed (let me say so without the least self-sufficiency), it has a contempt. The literary career seems to me unreal, both in its own essence and in the rewards which one seeks from it, and therefore fatally marred by a secret absurdity." His acquaintances, and among them distinguished

1 Compare, for example, his "Lines Written in the Euganean Hills," with Keats's "Ode to Autumn" (*Golden Treasury*, pp. 256, 284). The latter piece *renders* Nature; the former *tries to render* her. I will not deny, however, that Shelley has natural magic in his rhythm; what I deny is, that he has it in his language. It always seems to me that the right sphere for Shelley's genius was the sphere of music, not of poetry; the medium of sounds he can master, but to master the more difficult medium of words he has neither intellectual force enough nor sanity enough.

men of letters, full of admiration for the originality and delicacy of his talent, laughed at his self-depreciation, warmly assured him of his powers. He received their assurances with a mournful incredulity, which contrasts curiously with the self-assertion of poor David Gray, whom I just now mentioned. "It seems to me intolerable," he writes, "to appear to men other than one appears to God. My worst torture at this moment is the over-estimate which generous friends form of me. We are told that at the last judgment the secret of all consciences will be laid bare to the universe; would that mine were so this day, and that every passer-by could see me as I am!" "High above my head," he says at another time, "far, far away, I seem to hear the murmur of that world of thought and feeling to which I aspire so often, but where I can never attain. I think of those of my own age who have wings strong enough to reach it, but I think of them without jealousy, and as men on earth contemplate the elect and their felicity." And, criticising his own composition, "When I begin a subject, my self-conceit" (says this exquisite artist) "imagines I am doing wonders; and when I have finished, I see nothing but a wretched made-up imitation, composed of odds and ends of colour stolen from other people's palettes, and tastelessly mixed together on mine." Such was his *passion for perfection*, his disdain for all poetical work not perfectly adequate and felicitous. The magic of expression, to which by the force of this passion he won his way, will make the name of Maurice de Guérin remembered in literature.

From HEINRICH HEINE

"I know not if I deserve that a laurel-wreath should one day be laid on my coffin. Poetry, dearly as I have loved it, has always been to me but a divine plaything. I have never attached any great value to poetical fame; and I trouble myself very little whether people praise my verses or blame them. But lay on my coffin a *sword;* for I was a brave soldier in the Liberation War of humanity."

Heine had his full share of love of fame, and cared quite as much as his brethren of the *genus irritable* whether people praised his verses or blamed them. And he was very little of a hero. Posterity will certainly decorate his tomb with the emblem of the laurel rather than with the emblem of the sword. Still, for his contemporaries, for us, for the Europe of the present century, he is significant chiefly for the reason which he himself in the words just quoted assigns. He is significant because he was, if not pre-eminently a brave, yet a brilliant, most effective soldier in the Liberation War of humanity.

To ascertain the master-current in the literature of an epoch, and to distinguish this from all minor currents, is one of the critic's highest functions; in discharging it he shows how far he possesses the most indispensable quality of his office, — justness of spirit. The living writer who has done most to make England acquainted with German authors, a man of genius, but to whom precisely this one quality of justness of spirit is perhaps wanting, — I mean Mr. Carlyle, — seems to me in the result of his labours on German literature to afford a proof how very necessary to the critic this quality is. Mr. Carlyle has spoken admirably of Goethe; but then Goethe stands before all men's eyes, the manifest centre of German literature; and from this central source many rivers flow. Which of these rivers is the main stream? which of the courses of spirit which we see active in Goethe is the course which will most influence the future, and attract and be continued by the most powerful of Goethe's successors? — that is the question. Mr. Carlyle attaches, it seems to me, far too much importance to the romantic school of Germany, — Tieck, Novalis, Jean Paul Richter, — and gives to these writers, really gifted as two, at any rate, of them are, an undue prominence. These writers, and others with aims and a general tendency the same as theirs, are not the real inheritors and continuators of Goethe's power; the current of their activity is not the main current of German literature after Goethe. Far more in Heine's works flows this main current; Heine, far more than Tieck or Jean Paul Richter, is the continuator of that which, in

Goethe's varied activity, is the most powerful and vital; on Heine, of all German authors who survived Goethe, incomparably the largest portion of Goethe's mantle fell. I do not forget that when Mr. Carlyle was dealing with German literature, Heine, though he was clearly risen above the horizon, had not shone forth with all his strength; I do not forget, too, that after ten or twenty years many things may come out plain before the critic which before were hard to be discerned by him; and assuredly no one would dream of imputing it as a fault to Mr. Carlyle that twenty years ago he mistook the central current in German literature, overlooked the rising Heine, and attached undue importance to that romantic school which Heine was to destroy; one may rather note it as a misfortune, sent perhaps as a delicate chastisement to a critic, who, — man of genius as he is, and no one recognises his genius more admirably than I do, — has, for the functions of the critic, a little too much of the self-will and eccentricity of a genuine son of Great Britain.

Heine is noteworthy, because he is the most important German successor and continuator of Goethe in Goethe's most important line of activity. And which of Goethe's lines of activity is this? — His line of activity as "a soldier in the war of liberation of humanity."

Heine himself would hardly have admitted this affiliation, though he was far too powerful-minded a man to decry, with some of the vulgar German liberals, Goethe's genius. "The wind of the Paris Revolution," he writes after the three days of 1830, "blew about the candles a little in the dark night of Germany, so that the red curtains of a German throne or two caught fire; but the old watchmen, who do the police of the German kingdoms, are already bringing out the fire engines, and will keep the candles closer snuffed for the future. Poor, fast-bound German people, lose not all heart in thy bonds! The fashionable coating of ice melts off from my heart, my soul quivers and my eyes burn, and that is a disadvantageous state of things for a writer, who should control his subject-matter and keep himself beautifully objective, as the artistic school would have us, and as Goethe has done; he has come to be eighty years old doing this, and minister, and in good condition: — poor German people! that is thy greatest man!"

But hear Goethe himself: "If I were to say what I had really been to the Germans in general, and to the young German poets in particular, I should say I had been their *liberator*."

Modern times find themselves with an immense system of institutions, established facts, accredited dogmas, customs, rules, which have come to them from times not modern. In this system their life has to be carried forward; yet they have a sense that this system is not of their own creation, that it by no means corresponds exactly with the wants of their actual life, that, for them, it is customary, not rational. The awakening of this sense is the awakening of the modern spirit. The modern spirit is now awake almost everywhere; the sense of want of correspondence between the forms of modern Europe and its spirit, between the new wine of the eighteenth and nineteenth centuries, and the old bottles of the eleventh and twelfth centuries, or even of the sixteenth and seventeenth, almost every one now perceives; it is no longer dangerous to affirm that this want of correspondence exists; people are even beginning to be shy of denying it. To remove this want of correspondence is beginning to be the settled endeavour of most persons of good sense. Dissolvents of the old European system of dominant ideas and facts we must all be, all of us who have any power of working; what we have to study is that we may not be acrid dissolvents of it.

And how did Goethe, that grand dissolvent in an age when there were fewer of them than at present, proceed in his task of dissolution, of liberation of the modern European from the old routine? He shall tell us himself. "Through me the German poets have become aware that, as man must live from within outwards, so the artist must work from within outwards, seeing that, make what contortions he will, he can only bring to light his own individuality. I can clearly mark where this influence of mine has made itself felt; there arises out of it a kind of poetry of nature, and only in this way is it possible to be original."

My voice shall never be joined to those which decry Goethe, and if it is said that the foregoing is a lame and impotent conclusion to Goethe's declaration that he had been the liberator of the Germans in general, and of the young German poets in particular, I say it is not. Goethe's profound, imperturbable naturalism is absolutely fatal to all routine thinking; he puts the standard, once for all, inside every man instead of outside him; when he is told, such a thing must be so, there is immense authority and custom in favour of its being so, it has been held to be so for a thousand years, he answers with Olympian politeness, "But *is* it so? is it so to *me?*" Nothing could be more really subversive of the foundations on which the old European order rested; and it may be remarked that no persons are so radically detached from this order, no persons so thoroughly modern, as those who have felt Goethe's influence most deeply. If it is said that Goethe professes to have in this way deeply influenced but a few persons, and those persons poets, one may answer that he could have taken no better way to secure, in the end, the ear of the world; for poetry is simply the most beautiful, impressive, and widely effective mode of saying things, and hence its importance. Nevertheless the process of liberation, as Goethe worked it, though sure, is undoubtedly slow; he came, as Heine says, to be eighty years old in thus working it, and at the end of that time the old Middle-Age machine was still creaking on, the thirty German courts and their chamberlains subsisted in all their glory; Goethe himself was a minister, and the visible triumph of the modern spirit over prescription and routine seemed as far off as ever. It was the year 1830; the German sovereigns had passed the preceding fifteen years in breaking the promises of freedom they had made to their subjects when they wanted their help in the final struggle with Napoleon. Great events were happening in France; the revolution, defeated in 1815, had arisen from its defeat, and was wresting from its adversaries the power. Heinrich Heine, a young man of genius, born at Hamburg, and with all the culture of Germany, but by race a Jew; with warm sympathies for France, whose revolution had given to his race the rights of citizenship, and whose rule had been, as is well known, popular in the Rhine provinces, where he passed his youth; with a passionate admiration for the great French Emperor, with a passionate contempt for the sovereigns who had overthrown him, for their agents, and for their policy, — Heinrich Heine was in 1830 in no humour for any such gradual process of liberation from the old order of things as that which Goethe had followed. His counsel was for open war. Taking that terrible modern weapon, the pen, in his hand, he passed the remainder of his life in one fierce battle. What was that battle? the reader will ask. It was a life and death battle with Philistinism.

Philistinism! — we have not the expression in English. Perhaps we have not the word because we have so much of the thing. At Soli, I imagine, they did not talk of solecisms; and here, at the very headquarters of Goliath, nobody talks of Philistinism. The French have adopted the term *épicier* (grocer), to designate the sort of being whom the Germans designate by the term Philistine; but the French term, — besides that it casts a slur upon a respectable class, composed of living and susceptible members, while the original Philistines are dead and buried long ago, — is really, I think, in itself much less apt and expressive than the German term. Efforts have been made to obtain in English some term equivalent to *Philister* or *épicier;* Mr. Carlyle has made several such efforts: "respectability with its thousand gigs," he says; — well, the occupant of every one of these gigs is, Mr. Carlyle means, a Philistine. However, the word *respectable* is far too valuable a word to be thus perverted from its proper meaning; if the English are ever to have a word for the thing we are speaking of, — and so prodigious are the changes which the modern spirit is introducing, that even we English shall perhaps one day come to want such a word, — I think we had much better take the term *Philistine* itself.

Philistine must have originally meant, in the mind of those who invented the nickname, a strong, dogged, unenlightened opponent of the chosen people, of the children of the light. The party of change, the would-be remodellers of the old traditional European order, the invokers of reason against custom, the representatives of the modern spirit in every sphere where it is applicable, regarded themselves, with the robust self-confidence natural to reformers as a chosen people, as children of the light. They regarded their adversaries as humdrum people, slaves to routine, enemies to light; stupid and oppressive, but at the same time very strong. This explains the love which Heine, that Paladin of the modern spirit, has for France; it explains the preference which he gives to France over Germany: "the French," he says, "are the chosen people of the new religion, its first gospels and dogmas have been drawn up in their language; Paris is the new Jerusalem, and the Rhine is the Jordan which divides the consecrated land of freedom from the land of the Philistines." He means that the French, as a people, have shown more accessibility to ideas than any other people; that prescription and routine have had less hold upon them than upon any other people; that they have shown most readiness to move and to alter at the bidding (real or supposed) of reason. This explains, too, the detestation which Heine had for the English: "I might settle in England," he says, in his exile, "if it were not that I should find there two things, coal-smoke and Englishmen; I cannot abide either." What he hated in the English was the "ächtbrittische Beschränktheit," as he calls it, — the *genuine British narrowness.* In truth, the English, profoundly as they have modified the old Middle-Age order, great as is the liberty which they have secured for themselves, have in all their changes proceeded, to use a familiar expression, by the rule of thumb; what was intolerably inconvenient to them they have suppressed, and as they have suppressed it, not because it was irrational, but because it was practically inconvenient, they have seldom in suppressing it appealed to reason, but always, if possible, to some precedent, or form, or letter, which served as a convenient instrument for their purpose, and which saved them from the necessity of recurring to general principles. They have thus become, in a certain sense, of all people the most inaccessible to ideas and the most impatient of them; inaccessible to them, because of their want of familiarity with them; and impatient of them because they have got on so well without them, that they despise those who, not having got on as well as themselves, still make a fuss for what they themselves have done so well without. But there has certainly followed from hence, in this country, somewhat of a general depression of pure intelligence: Philistia has come to be thought by us the true Land of Promise, and it is anything but that; the born lover of ideas, the born hater of commonplaces, must feel in this country, that the sky over his head is of brass and iron. The enthusiast for the idea, for reason, values reason, the idea, in and for themselves; he values them, irrespectively of the practical conveniences which their triumph may obtain for him; and the man who regards the possession of these practical conveniences as something sufficient in itself, something which compensates for the absence or surrender of the idea, of reason, is, in his eyes, a Philistine. This is why Heine so often and so mercilessly attacks the liberals; much as he hates conservatism he hates Philistinism even more, and whoever attacks conservatism itself ignobly, not as a child of light, not in the name of the idea, is a Philistine. Our Cobbett is thus for him, much as he disliked our clergy and aristocracy whom Cobbett attacked, a Philistine with six fingers on every hand and on every foot six toes, four-and-twenty in number: a Philistine, the staff of whose spear is like a weaver's beam. Thus he speaks of him: —

"While I translate Cobbett's words, the man himself comes bodily before my mind's eye, as I saw him at that uproarious dinner at the Crown and Anchor Tavern, with his scolding red face and his radical laugh, in which venomous hate mingles with a mocking exultation at his enemies' surely approaching downfall. He is a chained cur, who falls with equal fury on every one whom he does not know, often bites the best friend of the house in his calves, barks incessantly, and just because of this incessantness of his barking cannot get listened to, even when he barks at a real thief. Therefore the distinguished thieves who plunder England do not think it necessary to throw the growling Cobbett a bone to stop his mouth. This makes the dog furiously savage, and he shows all his hungry teeth. Poor old Cobbett! England's dog! I have no love for thee, for every vulgar nature my soul abhors; but thou touchest me to the inmost soul with pity, as I see how thou strainest in vain to break loose and to get at those thieves, who make off with their booty before thy very eyes, and mock at thy fruitless springs and thine impotent howling."

There is balm in Philistia as well as in Gilead. A chosen circle of children of the modern spirit, perfectly emancipated from prejudice and commonplace, regarding the ideal side of things in all its efforts for change, passionately despising half-measures and condescension to human folly and obstinacy, — with a bewildered, timid, torpid multitude behind, — conducts a country to the government of Herr von Bismarck. A nation regarding the practical side of things in its efforts for change, attacking not what is irrational, but what is pressingly inconvenient, and attacking this as one body, "moving altogether if it move at all," and treating children of light like the very harshest of stepmothers, comes to the prosperity and liberty of modern England. For all that, however, Philistia (let me say it again) is not the true promised land, as we English commonly imagine it to be; and our excessive neglect of the idea, and consequent inaptitude for it, threatens us, at a moment when the idea is beginning to exercise a real power in human society, with serious future inconvenience, and, in the meanwhile, cuts us off from the sympathy of other nations, which feel its power more than we do.

From JOUBERT

Why should we ever treat of any dead authors but the famous ones? Mainly for this reason: because, from these famous personages, home or foreign, whom we all know so well, and of whom so much has been said, the amount of stimulus which they contain for us has been in a great measure disengaged; people have formed their opinion about them, and do not readily change it. One may write of them afresh, combat received opinions about them, even interest one's readers in so doing; but the interest one's readers receive has to do, in general, rather with the treatment than with the subject; they are susceptible of a lively impression rather of the course of the discussion itself, — its turns, vivacity, and novelty, — than of the genius of the author who is the occasion of it. And yet what is really precious and inspiring, in all that we get from literature, except this sense of an immediate contact with genius itself, and the stimulus towards what is true and excellent which we derive from it? Now in literature, besides the eminent men of genius who have had their deserts in the way of fame, besides the eminent men of ability who have often had far more than their deserts in the way of fame, there are a certain number of personages who have been real men of genius, — by which I mean, that they have had a genuine gift for what is true and excellent, and are therefore capable of emitting a life-giving stimulus, — but who, for some reason or other, in most cases for very valid reasons, have remained obscure, nay, beyond a narrow circle in their own country, unknown. It is salutary from time to time to come across a genius of this kind, and to extract his honey. Often he has more of it for us, as I have already said, than greater men; for, though it is by no means true that from what is new to us there is most to be learnt, it is yet indisputably true that from what is new to us we in general learn most.

Of a genius of this kind, Joseph Joubert, I am now going to speak. His name is, I believe, almost unknown in England; and even in France, his native country, it is not famous. M. Sainte-Beuve has given of him one of his incomparable portraits; but, — besides that even M. Sainte-Beuve's writings are far less known amongst us than they deserve to be, — every country has its own point of view from which a remarkable author may most profitably be seen and studied.

Joseph Joubert was born (and his date should be remarked) in 1754, at Montignac, a little town in Périgord. His father was a doctor with small means and a large family; and Joseph, the eldest, had his own way to make in the world. He was for eight years, as pupil first, and afterwards as an assistant-master, in the public school of Toulouse, then managed by the Jesuits, who seem to have left in him a most favourable opinion, not only of their tact and address, but of their really good qualities as teachers and directors. Compelled by the weakness of his health to give up, at twenty-two, the profession of teaching, he passed two important years of his life in hard study, at home at Montignac; and came in 1778 to try his fortune in the literary world of Paris, then perhaps the most tempting field which has ever yet presented itself to a young man of letters. He knew Diderot, D'Alembert, Marmontel, Laharpe; he became intimate with one of the celebrities of the next literary generation, then, like himself, a young man, — Chateaubriand's friend, the future Grand Master of the University, Fontanes. But, even then, it began to be remarked of him, that M. Joubert, *"s'inquiétait de perfection bien plus que de gloire* — cared far more about perfecting himself than about making himself a reputation." His severity of morals may perhaps have been rendered easier to him by the delicacy of his health; but the delicacy of his health will not by itself account for his changeless preference of being to seeming, knowing to showing, studying to publishing; for what terrible public performers have some invalids been! This preference he retained all through his life, and it is by this that he is characterised. "He has chosen," Chateaubriand (adopting Epicurus's famous words) said of him, *"to hide his life."* Of a life which its owner was bent on hiding there can be but little to tell. Yet the only two public incidents of Joubert's life, slight as they are, do all concerned in them so much credit that they deserve mention. In 1790 the Constituent Assembly made the office of justice of the peace elective throughout France. The people of Montignac retained such an impression of the character of their young townsman, — one of Plutarch's men of virtue, as he had lived amongst them, simple, studious, severe, — that, though he had left them for years, they elected him in his absence without his knowing anything about it. The appointment little suited Joubert's wishes or tastes; but at such a moment he thought it wrong to decline it. He held it for two years, the legal term, discharging its duties with a firmness and integrity which were long remembered; and then, when he went out of office, his fellow-townsmen re-elected him. But Joubert thought that he had now accomplished his duty towards them, and he went back to the retirement which he loved. That seems to me a little episode of the great French Revolution worth remembering. The sage who was asked by the king, why sages were seen at the doors of kings, but not kings at the doors of sages, replied, that it was because sages knew what was good for them, and kings did not. But at Montignac the king — for in 1790 the people in France was king with a vengeance — knew what was good for him, and came to the door of the sage.

The other incident was this. When Napoleon, in 1809, reorganised the public instruction of France, founded the University, and made M. de Fontanes its Grand Master, Fontanes had to submit to the Emperor a list of persons to form the council or governing body of the new University. Third on his list, after two distinguished names, Fontanes placed the unknown name of Joubert. "This name," he said in his accompanying memorandum to the Emperor, "is not known as the two first are; and yet this is the nomination to which I attach most importance. I have known M. Joubert all my life. His character and intelligence are of the very highest order. I shall rejoice if your Majesty will accept my guarantee for him." Napoleon trusted his Grand Master, and Joubert became a councillor of the University. It is something that a man, elevated to the highest posts of State, should not forget his obscure friends; or that, if he remembers and places them, he should regard in placing them their merit rather than their obscurity. It is more, in the eyes of those whom the necessities, real or supposed, of a political system have long familiarised with such cynical disregard of fitness in the distribution of office, to see a minister and his master alike zealous, in giving away places, to give them to the best men to be found.

Between 1792 and 1809 Joubert had married. His life was passed between Villeneuve-sur-Yonne, where his wife's family lived, — a pretty little Burgundian town, by which the Lyons railroad now passes, — and Paris. Here, in a house in the Rue St.-Honoré, in a room very high up, and admitting plenty of the light which he so loved, — a room from which he saw, in his own words, "a great deal of sky and very little earth," — among the treasures of a library collected with infinite pains, taste, and skill, from which every book he thought ill of was rigidly excluded, — he never would possess either a complete Voltaire or a complete Rousseau, — the happiest hours of his life were passed. In the circle of one of those women who leave a sort of perfume in literary history, and who have the gift of inspiring successive generations of readers with an indescribable regret not to have know them, — Pauline de Montmorin, Madame de Beaumont, — he had become intimate with nearly all which at that time, in the Paris world of letters or of society, was most attractive and promising. Amongst his acquaintances one only misses the names of Madame de Staël and Benjamin Constant. Neither of them was to his taste, and with Madame de Staël he always refused to become acquainted; he thought she had more vehemence than truth, and more heat than light.

Years went on, and his friends became conspicuous authors or statesmen; but Joubert remained in the shade. His constitution was of such fragility that how he lived so long, or accomplished so much as he did, is a wonder: his soul had, for its basis of operations, hardly any body at all: both from his stomach and from his chest he seems to have had constant suffering, though he lived by rule, and was as abstemious as a Hindoo. Often, after overwork in thinking, reading, or talking, he remained for days together in a state of utter prostration, — condemned to absolute silence and inaction; too happy if the agitation of his mind would become quiet also, and let him have the repose of which he stood in so much need. With this weakness of health, these repeated suspensions of energy, he was incapable of the prolonged contention of spirit necessary for the creation of great works. But he read and thought immensely; he was an unwearied note-taker, a charming letter-writer; above all, an excellent and delightful talker. The gaiety and amenity of his natural disposition were inexhaustible; and his spirit, too, was of astonishing elasticity; he seemed to hold on to life by a single thread only, but that single thread was very tenacious. More and more, as his soul and knowledge ripened more and more, his friends pressed to his room in the Rue St.-Honoré; often he received them in bed, for he seldom rose before three o'clock in the afternoon; and at his bedroom-door, on his bad days, Madame Joubert stood sentry, trying, not always with success, to keep back the thirsty comers from the fountain which was forbidden to flow. Fontanes did nothing in the University without consulting him, and Joubert's ideas and pen were always at his friend's service.

When he was in the country, at Villeneuve, the young priests of his neighbourhood used to resort to him, in order to profit by his library and by his conversation. He, like our Coleridge, was particularly qualified to attract men of this kind and to benefit them: retaining perfect independence of mind, he was a religious philosopher. As age came on, his infirmities became more and more overwhelming; some of his friends, too, died; others became so immersed in politics, that Joubert, who hated politics, saw them seldomer than of old; but the moroseness of age and infirmity never touched him, and he never quarrelled with a friend or lost one. From these miseries he was preserved by that quality in him of which I have already spoken; a quality which is best expressed by a word, not of common use in English, — alas, we have too little in our national character of the quality which this word expresses, — his inborn, his constant amenity. He lived till the year 1824. On the 4th of May in that year he died, at the age of seventy. A day or two after his death M. de Chateaubriand inserted in the *Journal des Débats* a short notice of him, perfect for its feeling, grace, and propriety. *On ne vit dans le mémoire du monde,* he says and says truly, *que par des travaux pour le monde,* — "a man can live in the world's memory only by what he has done for the world." But Chateaubriand used the privilege which his great name gave him to assert, delicately but firmly, Joubert's real and rare merits, and to tell the world what manner of man had just left it.

Joubert's papers were accumulated in boxes and drawers. He had not meant them for publication; it was very difficult to sort them and to prepare them for it. Madame Joubert, his widow, had a scruple about giving them a publicity which her husband, she felt, would never have permitted. But, as her own end approached, the natural desire to leave of so remarkable a spirit some enduring memorial, some memorial to outlast the admiring recollection of the living who were so fast passing away, made her yield to the entreaties of his friends, and allow the printing, but for private circulation only, of a volume of his fragments. Chateaubriand edited it; it appeared in 1838, fourteen years after Joubert's death. The volume attracted the attention of those who were best fitted to appreciate it, and profoundly impressed them. M. Sainte-Beuve gave of it, in the *Revue des Deux Mondes,* the admirable notice of which I have already spoken; and so much curiosity was excited about Joubert, that the collection of his fragments, enlarged by many additions, was at last published for the benefit of the world in general. It has since been twice reprinted. The first or preliminary chapter has some fancifulness and affectation in it; the reader should begin with the second.

I have likened Joubert to Coleridge; and indeed the points of resemblance between the two men are numerous. Both of them great and celebrated talkers, Joubert attracting pilgrims to his upper chamber in the Rue St.-Honoré, as Coleridge attracted pilgrims to Mr. Gilman's at Highgate; both of them desultory and incomplete writers, — here they had an outward likeness with one another. Both of them passionately devoted to reading in a class of books, and to thinking on a class of subjects, out of the beaten line of the reading and thought of their day; both of them ardent students and critics of old literature, poetry, and the metaphysics of religion; both of them curious explorers of words, and of the latent significance hidden under the popular use of them; both of them, in a certain sense, conservative in religion and politics, by antipathy to the narrow and shallow foolishness of vulgar modern liberalism; — here they had their inward and real likeness. But that in which the essence of their likeness consisted is this, — that they both had from nature an ardent impulse for seeking the genuine truth on all matters they thought about, and a gift for finding it and recognising it when it was found. To have the impulse for seeking this truth is much rarer than most people think; to have the gift for finding it is, I need not say, very rare indeed. By this they have a spiritual relationship of the closest kind with one another, and they become, each of them, a source of stimulus and progress for all of us.

Coleridge had less delicacy and penetration than Joubert, but more richness and power; his production, though far inferior to what his nature at first seemed to promise, was abundant and varied. Yet in all his production how much is there to dissatisfy us! How many reserves must be made in praising either his poetry, or his criticism, or his philosophy! How little either of his poetry, or of his criticism, or of his philosophy, can we expect permanently to stand! But that which will stand of Coleridge is this: the stimulus of his continual effort, — not a moral effort, for he had no morals — but of his continual instinctive effort, crowned often with rich success, to get at and to lay bare the real truth of his matter in hand, whether that matter were literary, or philosophical, or political, or religious; and this in a country where at that moment such an effort was almost unknown; where the most powerful minds threw themselves upon poetry, which conveys truth, indeed, but conveys it indirectly; and where ordinary minds were so habituated to do without thinking altogether, to regard considerations of established routine and practical convenience as paramount, that any attempt to introduce within the domain of these the disturbing element of thought, they were prompt to resent as an outrage. Coleridge's great usefulness lay in his supplying in England, for many years and under critical circumstances, by the spectacle of this effort of his, a stimulus to all minds capable of profiting by it; in the generation which grew up around him. His action will still be felt as long as the need for it continues. When, with the cessation of the need, the action too has ceased, Coleridge's memory, in spite of the disesteem — nay, repugnance — which his character may and must inspire, will yet for ever remain invested with that interest and gratitude which invests the memory of founders.

M. de Rémusat, indeed, reproaches Coleridge with his *jugements saugrenus;* the criticism of a gifted truthfinder ought not to be *saugrenu,* so on this reproach we must pause for a moment. *Saugrenu* is a rather vulgar French word, but, like many other vulgar words, very expressive; used as an epithet for a judgment, it means something like *impudently absurd.* The literary judgments of one nation about another are very apt to be *saugrenus.* It is certainly true, as M. Sainte-Beuve remarks in answer to Goethe's complaint against the French that they have undervalued Du Bartas, that as to the estimate of its own authors every nation is the best judge; the *positive* estimate of them, be it understood, not, of course, the estimate of them in comparison with the authors of other nations. Therefore a foreigner's judgments about the intrinsic merit of a nation's authors will generally, when at complete variance with that nation's own, be wrong; but there is a permissible wrongness in these matters, and to that permissible wrongness there is a limit. When that limit is exceeded, the wrong judgment becomes more than wrong, it becomes *saugrenu,* or impudently absurd. For instance, the high estimate which the French have of Racine is probably in great measure deserved; or, to take a yet stronger case, even the high estimate which Joubert had of the Abbé Delille is probably in great measure deserved; but the common disparaging judgment passed on Racine by English readers is not *saugrenu,* still less is that passed by them on the Abbé Delille *saugrenu,* because the beauty of Racine, and of Delille too, so far as Delille's beauty goes, is eminently in their language, and this is a beauty which a foreigner cannot perfectly seize; — this beauty of diction, *apicibus verborum ligata,* as M. Sainte-Beuve, quoting Quintilian, says of Chateaubriand's. As to Chateaubriand himself, again, the common English judgment, which stamps him as a mere shallow rhetorician, all froth and vanity, is certainly wrong; one may even wonder that we English should judge Chateaubriand so wrongly, for his power goes far beyond beauty of diction; it is a power, as well, of passion and sentiment, and this sort of power the English can perfectly well appreciate. One production of Chateaubriand's, *René,* is akin to the most popular productions of Byron, — to the *Childe Harold* or *Manfred,* — in spirit, equal to them in power, superior to them in form. But this work, I hardly know why, is almost unread in England. And only consider this criticism of Chateaubriand's on the true pathetic! "It is a dangerous mistake, sanctioned, like so many other dangerous mistakes, by Voltaire, to suppose that the best works of imagination are those which draw most tears. One could name this or that melodrama, which no one would like to own having written, and which yet harrows the feelings far more than the *Æneid.* The true tears are those which are called forth by the *beauty* of poetry; there must be as much admiration in them as sorrow. They are the tears which come to our eyes when Priam says to Achilles, ἔτλην δ', οἷ' οὔπω . . . — 'And I have endured, — the like whereof no soul upon the earth hath yet endured, — to carry to my lips the hand of him who slew my child;' or when Joseph cries out: 'I am Joseph your brother, whom ye sold into Egypt.'" Who does not feel that the man who wrote that was no shallow rhetorician, but a born man of genius, with the true instinct of genius for what is really admirable? Nay, take these words of Chateaubriand, an old man of eighty, dying, amidst the noise and bustle of the ignoble revolution of February 1848: "Mon Dieu, mon Dieu, quand donc, quand donc serai-je délivré de tout ce monde, ce bruit; quand donc, quand donc cela finira-t-il?" Who, with any ear, does not feel that those are not the accents of a trumpery rhetorician, but of a rich and puissant nature, — the cry of the dying lion? I repeat it, Chateaubriand is most ignorantly underrated in England; and we English are capable of rating him far more correctly if we knew him better. Still Chateaubriand has such real and great faults, he falls so decidedly beneath the rank of the truly greatest authors, that the depreciatory judgment passed on him in England, though ignorant and wrong, can hardly be said to transgress the limits of permissible ignorance; it is not a *jugement saugrenu.* But when a critic denies genius to a literature which has produced Bossuet and Molière, he passes the bounds; and Coleridge's judgments on French literature and the French genius are undoubtedly, as M. de Rémusat calls them, *saugrenus.*

And yet, such is the impetuosity of our poor human nature, such its proneness to rush to a decision with imperfect knowledge, that his having delivered a *saugrenu* judgment or two in his life by no means proves a man not to have had, in comparison with his fellow-men in general, a remarkable gift for truth, or disqualifies him for being, by virtue of that gift, a source of vital stimulus for us. Joubert had far less smoke and turbid vehemence in him than Coleridge; he had also a far keener sense of what was absurd. But Joubert can write to M. Molé (the M. Molé who was afterwards Louis Philippe's well-known minister): "As to your Milton, whom the merit of the Abbé Delille" (the Abbé Delille translated *Paradise Lost*) "makes me admire, and with whom I have nevertheless still plenty of fault to find, why, I should like to know, are you scandalised that I have not enabled myself to read him? I don't understand the language in which he writes, and I don't much care to. If he is a poet one cannot put up with, even in the prose of the younger Racine, am I to blame for that? If by force you mean beauty manifesting itself with power, I maintain that the Abbé Delille has more force than Milton." That, to be sure, is a petulant outburst in a private letter; it is not, like Coleridge's, a deliberate proposition in a printed philosophical essay. But is it possible to imagine a more perfect specimen of a *saugrenu* judgment? It is even worse than Coleridge's, because it is *saugrenu* with reasons. That, however, does not prevent Joubert from having been really a man of extraordinary ardour in the search for truth, and of extraordinary fineness in the perception of it; and so was Coleridge. . . .

I do not hold up Joubert as a very astonishing and powerful genius, but rather as a delightful and edifying genius. I have not cared to exhibit him as a sayer of brilliant epigrammatic things, such things as "Notre vie est du vent tissu . . . . les dettes abrégent la vie . . . . celui qui a de l'imagination sans érudition a des ailes et n'a pas de pieds (*Our life is woven wind . . . . debts take from life . . . . the man of imagination without learning has wings and no feet*)," though for such sayings he is famous. In the first place, the French language is in itself so favourable a vehicle for such sayings, that the making them in it has the less merit; at least half the merit ought to go, not to the maker of the saying, but to the French language. In the second place, the peculiar beauty of Joubert is not there; it is not in what is exclusively intellectual, — it is in the union of *soul* with intellect, and in the delightful, satisfying result which this union produces. "Vivre, c'est penser et sentir son âme . . . . le bonheur est de sentir son âme bonne . . . toute vérité nue et crue n'a pas assez passé par l'âme . . . . les hommes ne sont justes qu'envers ceux qu'ils aiment (*The essence of life lies in thinking and being conscious of one's soul . . . . happiness is the sense of one's soul being good . . . if a truth is nude and crude, that is a proof it has not been steeped long enough in the soul, ... man cannot even be just to his neighbour, unless he loves him*);" it is much rather in sayings like these that Joubert's best and innermost nature manifests itself. He is the most prepossessing and convincing of witnesses to the good of loving light. Because he sincerely loved light, and did not prefer to it any little private darkness of his own, he found light; his eye was single, and therefore his whole body was full of light. And because he was full of light, he was also full of happiness. In spite of his infirmities, in spite of his sufferings, in spite of his obscurity, he was the happiest man alive; his life was as charming as his thoughts. For certainly it is natural that the love of light, which is already, in some measure, the possession of light, should irradiate and beatify the whole life of him who has it. There is something unnatural and shocking where, as in the case of Coleridge, it does not. Joubert pains us by no such contradiction; "the same penetration of spirit which made him such delightful company to his friends, served also to make him perfect in his own personal life, by enabling him always to perceive and do what was right;" he loved and sought light till he became so habituated to it, so accustomed to the joyful testimony of a good conscience, that, to use his own words, "he could no longer exist without this, and was obliged to live without reproach if he would live without misery."

Joubert was not famous while he lived, and he will not be famous now that he is dead. But, before we pity him for this, let us be sure what we mean, in literature, by *famous*. There are the famous men of genius in literature, — the Homers, Dantes, Shakspeares: of them we need not speak; their praise is for ever and ever. Then there are the famous men of ability in literature: their praise is in their own generation. And what makes this difference? The work of the two orders of men is at the bottom the same, — *a criticism of life*. The end and aim of all literature, if one considers it attentively, is, in truth, nothing but that. But the criticism which the men of genius pass upon human life is permanently acceptable to mankind; the criticism which the men of ability pass upon human life is transitorily acceptable. Between Shakspeare's criticism of human life and Scribe's the difference is there; — the one is permanently acceptable, the other transitorily. Whence then, I repeat, this difference? It is that the acceptableness of Shakspeare's criticism depends upon its inherent truth: the acceptableness of Scribe's upon its suiting itself, by its subject-matter, ideas, mode of treatment, to the taste of the generation that hears it. But the taste and ideas of one generation are not those of the next. This next generation in its turn arrives; — first its sharpshooters, its quick-witted, audacious light troops; then the elephantine main body. The imposing array of its predecessor it confidently assails, riddles it with bullets, passes over its body. It goes hard then with many once popular reputations, with many authorities once oracular. Only two kinds of authors are safe in the general havoc. The first kind are the great abounding fountains of truth, whose criticism of life is a source of illumination and joy to the whole human race for ever, — the Homers, the Shakspeares. These are the sacred personages, whom all civilised warfare respects. The second are those whom the out-skirmishers of the new generation, its forerunners, — quick-witted soldiers, as I have said, the select of the army — recognise, though the bulk of their comrades behind might not, as of the same family and character with the sacred personages, exercising like them an immortal function, and like them inspiring a permanent interest. They snatch them up, and set them in a place of shelter, where the on-coming multitude may not overwhelm them. These are the Jouberts. They will never, like the Shakspeares, command the homage of the multitude; but they are safe; the multitude will not trample them down. Except these two kinds, no author is safe. Let us consider, for example, Joubert's famous contemporary, Lord Jeffrey. All his vivacity and accomplishment avail him nothing; of the true critic he had in an eminent degree no quality, except one, — curiosity. Curiosity he had, but he had no gift for truth; he cannot illuminate and rejoice us; no intelligent out-skirmisher of the new generation cares about him, cares to put him in safety; at this moment we are all passing over his body. Let us consider a greater than Jeffrey, a critic whose reputation still stands firm, — will stand, many people think, for ever, — the great apostle of the Philistines, Lord Macaulay. Lord Macaulay was, as I have already said, a born rhetorician; a splendid rhetorician doubtless, and beyond that, an *English* rhetorician also, an *honest* rhetorician; still beyond the apparent rhetorical truth of things he never could penetrate; for their vital truth, for what the French call the *vraie vérité,* he had absolutely no organ; therefore his reputation, brilliant as it is, is not secure. Rhetoric so good as his excites and gives pleasure; but by pleasure alone you cannot permanently bind men's spirits to you. Truth illuminates and gives joy, and it is by the bond of joy, not of pleasure, that men's spirits are indissolubly held. As Lord Macaulay's own generation dies out, as a new generation arrives, without those ideas and tendencies of its predecessor which Lord Macaulay so deeply shared and so happily satisfied, will he give the same pleasure? and, if he ceases to give this, has he enough of light in him to make him last? Pleasure the new generation will get from its own novel ideas and tendencies; but light is another and a rarer thing, and must be treasured wherever it can be found. Will Macaulay be saved, in the sweep and pressure of time, for his light's sake, as Johnson has already been saved by two generations, Joubert by one? I think it very doubtful. But for a spirit of any delicacy and dignity, what a fate, if he could foresee it! to be an oracle for one generation, and then of little or no account for ever. How far better, to pass with scant notice through one's own generation, but to be singled out and preserved by the very iconoclasts of the next, then in their turn by those of the next, and so, like the lamp of life itself, to be handed on from one generation to another in safety! This is Joubert's lot, and it is a very enviable one. The new men of the new generations, while they let the dust deepen on a thousand Laharpes, will say of him: "He lived in the Philistine's day, in a place and time when almost every idea current in literature had the mark of Dagon upon it, and not the mark of the children of light. Nay, the children of light were as yet hardly so much as heard of: the Canaanite was then in the land. Still, there were even then a few, who, nourished on some secret tradition, or illumined, perhaps, by a divine inspiration, kept aloof from the reigning superstitions, never bowed the knee to the gods of Canaan; and one of these few was called *Joubert.*"

THE STUDY OF POETRY

"THE FUTURE of poetry is immense, because in poetry, where it is worthy of its high destinies, our race, as time goes on, will find an ever surer and surer stay. There is not a creed which is not shaken, not an accredited dogma which is not shown to be questionable, not a received tradition which does not threaten to dissolve. Our religion has materialised itself in the fact, in the supposed fact; it has attached its emotion to the fact, and now the fact is failing it. But for poetry the idea is everything; the rest is a world of illusion, of divine illusion. Poetry attaches its emotion to the idea; the idea *is* the fact. The strongest part of our religion to-day is its unconscious poetry."

Let me be permitted to quote these words of my own, as uttering the thought which should, in my opinion, go with us and govern us in all our study of poetry. In the present work it is the course of one great contributory stream to the world-river of poetry that we are invited to follow. We are here invited to trace the stream of English poetry. But whether we set ourselves, as here, to follow only one of the several streams that make the mighty river of poetry, or whether we seek to know them all, our governing thought should be the same. We should conceive of poetry worthily, and more highly than it has been the custom to conceive of it. We should conceive of it as capable of higher uses, and called to higher destinies, than those which in general men have assigned to it hitherto. More and more mankind will discover that we have to turn to poetry to interpret life for us, to console us, to sustain us. Without poetry, our science will appear incomplete; and most of what now passes with us for religion and philosophy will be replaced by poetry. Science, I say, will appear incomplete without it. For finely and truly does Wordsworth call poetry "the impassioned expression which is in the countenance of all science"; and what is a countenance without its expression? Again, Wordsworth finely and truly calls poetry "the breath and finer spirit of all knowledge": our religion, parading evidences such as those on which the popular mind relies now; our philosophy, pluming itself on its reasonings about causation and finite and infinite being; what are they but the shadows and dreams and false shows of knowledge? The day will come when we shall wonder at ourselves for having trusted to them, for having taken them seriously; and the more we perceive their hollowness, the more we shall prize "the breath and finer spirit of knowledge" offered to us by poetry.

But if we conceive thus highly of the destinies of poetry, we must also set our standard for poetry high, since poetry, to be capable of fulfilling such high destinies, must be poetry of a high order of excellence. We must accustom ourselves to a high standard and to a strict judgment. Sainte-Beuve relates that Napoleon one day said, when somebody was spoken of in his presence as a charlatan: "Charlatan as much as you please; but where is there *not* charlatanism?"—"Yes," answers Sainte-Beuve, "in politics, in the art of governing mankind, that is perhaps true. But in the order of thought, in art, the glory, the eternal honour is that charlatanism shall find no entrance; herein lies the inviolableness of that noble portion of man's being." It is admirably said, and let us hold fast to it. In poetry, which is thought and art in one, it is the glory, the eternal honour, that charlatanism shall find no entrance; that this noble sphere be kept inviolate and inviolable. Charlatanism is for confusing or obliterating the distinctions between excellent and inferior, sound and unsound or only half-sound, true and untrue or only half-true. It is charlatanism, conscious or unconscious, whenever we confuse or obliterate these. And in poetry, more than anywhere else, it is unpermissible to confuse or obliterate them. For in poetry the distinction between excellent and inferior, sound and unsound or only half-sound, true and untrue or only half-true, is of paramount importance. It is of paramount importance because of the high destinies of poetry. In poetry, as a criticism of life under the conditions fixed for such a criticism by the laws of poetic truth and poetic beauty, the spirit of our race will find, we have said, as time goes on and as other helps fail, its consolation and stay. But the consolation and stay will be of power in proportion to the power of the criticism of life. And the criticism of life will be of power in proportion as the poetry conveying it is excellent rather than inferior, sound rather than unsound or half-sound, true rather than untrue or half-true.

The best poetry is what we want; the best poetry will be found to have a power of forming, sustaining, and delighting us, as nothing else can. A clearer, deeper sense of the best in poetry, and of the strength and joy to be drawn from it, is the most precious benefit which we can gather from a poetical collection such as the present. And yet in the very nature and conduct of such a collection there is inevitably something which tends to obscure in us the consciousness of what our benefit should be, and to distract us from the pursuit of it. We should therefore steadily set it before our minds at the outset, and should compel ourselves to revert constantly to the thought of it as we proceed.

Yes; constantly in reading poetry, a sense for the best, the really excellent, and of the strength and joy to be drawn from it, should be present in our minds and should govern our estimate of what we read. But this real estimate, the only true one, is liable to be superseded, if we are not watchful, by two other kinds of estimate, the historic estimate and the personal estimate, both of which are fallacious. A poet or a poem may count to us historically, they may count to us on grounds personal to ourselves, and they may count to us really. They may count to us historically. The course of development of a nation's language, thought, and poetry, is profoundly interesting; and by regarding a poet's work as a stage in this course of development we may easily bring ourselves to make it of more importance as poetry than in itself it really is, we may come to use a language of quite exaggerated praise in criticising it; in short, to over-rate it. So arises in our poetic judgments the fallacy caused by the estimate which we may call historic. Then, again, a poet or a poem may count to us on grounds personal to ourselves. Our personal affinities, likings, and circumstances, have great power to sway our estimate of this or that poet's work, and to make us attach more importance to it as poetry than in itself it really possesses, because to us it is, or has been, of high importance. Here also we over-rate the object of our interest, and apply to it a language of praise which is quite exaggerated. And thus we get the source of a second fallacy in our poetic judgments — the fallacy caused by an estimate which we may call personal.

Both fallacies are natural. It is evident how naturally the study of the history and development of a poetry may incline a man to pause over reputations and works once conspicuous but now obscure, and to quarrel with a careless public for skipping, in obedience to mere tradition and habit, from one famous name or work in its national poetry to another, ignorant of what it misses, and of the reason for keeping what it keeps, and of the whole process of growth in its poetry. The French have become diligent students of their own early poetry, which they long neglected; the study makes many of them dissatisfied with their so-called classical poetry, the court-tragedy of the seventeenth century, a poetry which Pellisson long ago reproached with its want of the true poetic stamp, with is *politesse stérile et rampante,* but which nevertheless has reigned in France as absolutely as if it had been the perfection of classical poetry indeed. The dissatisfaction is natural; yet a lively and accomplished critic, M. Charles d'Héricault, the editor of Clément Marot, goes too far when he says that "the cloud of glory playing round a classic is a mist as dangerous to the future of a literature as it is intolerable for the purposes of history." "It hinders," he goes on, "it hinders us from seeing more than one single point, the culminating and exceptional point; the summary, fictitious and arbitrary, of a thought and of a work. It substitutes a halo for a physiognomy, it puts a statue where there was once a man, and hiding from us all trace of the labour, the attempts, the weaknesses, the failures, it claims not study but veneration; it does not show us how the thing is done, it imposes upon us a model. Above all, for the historian this creation of classic personages is inadmissible; for it withdraws the poet from his time, from his proper life, it breaks historical relationships, it blinds criticism by conventional admiration, and renders the investigation of literary origins unacceptable. It gives us a human personage no longer, but a God seated immovable amidst His perfect work, like Jupiter on Olympus; and hardly will it be possible for the young student, to whom such work is exhibited at such a distance from him, to believe that it did not issue ready made from that divine head."

All this is brilliantly and tellingly said, but we must plead for a distinction. Everything depends on the reality of a poet's classic character. If he is a dubious classic, let us sift him; if he is a false classic, let us explode him. But if he is a real classic, if his work belongs to the class of the very best (for this is the true and right meaning of the word *classic, classical*), then the great thing for us is to feel and enjoy his work as deeply as ever we can, and to appreciate the wide difference between it and all work which has not the same high character. This is what is salutary, this is what is formative; this is the great benefit to be got from the study of poetry. Everything which interferes with it, which hinders it, is injurious. True, we must read our classic with open eyes, and not with eyes blinded with superstition; we must perceive when his work comes short, when it drops out of the class of the very best, and we must rate it, in such cases, at its proper value. But the use of this negative criticism is not in itself, it is entirely in its enabling us to have a clearer sense and a deeper enjoyment of what is truly excellent. To trace the labour, the attempts, the weaknesses, the failures of a genuine classic, to acquaint oneself with his time and his life and his historical relationships, is mere literary dilettantism unless it has that clear sense and deeper enjoyment for its end. It may be said that the more we know about a classic the better we shall enjoy him; and, if we lived as long as Methuselah and had all of us heads of perfect clearness and wills of perfect steadfastness, this might be true in fact as it is plausible in theory. But the case here is much the same as the case with the Greek and Latin studies of our schoolboys. The elaborate philological groundwork which we require them to lay is in theory an admirable preparation for appreciating the Greek and Latin authors worthily. The more thoroughly we lay the groundwork, the better we shall be able, it may be said, to enjoy the authors. True, if time were not so short, and schoolboys' wits not so soon tired and their power of attention exhausted; only, as it is, the elaborate philological preparation goes on, but the authors are little known and less enjoyed. So with the investigator of "historic origins" in poetry. He ought to enjoy the true classic all the better for his investigations; he often is distracted from the enjoyment of the best, and with the less good he overbusies himself, and is prone to over-rate it in proportion to the trouble which it has cost him.

The idea of tracing historic origins and historical relationships cannot be absent from a compilation like the present. And naturally the poets to be exhibited in it will be assigned to those persons for exhibition who are known to prize them highly, rather than to those who have no special inclination towards them. Moreover the very occupation with an author, and the business of exhibiting him, disposes us to affirm and amplify his importance. In the present work, therefore, we are sure of frequent temptation to adopt the historic estimate, or the personal estimate, and to forget the real estimate; which latter, nevertheless, we must employ if we are to make poetry yield us its full benefit. So high is that benefit, the benefit of clearly feeling and of deeply enjoying the really excellent, the truly classic in poetry, that we do well, I say, to set it fixedly before our minds as our object in studying poets and poetry, and to make the desire of attaining it the one principle to which, as the *Imitation* says, whatever we may read or come to know, we always return. *Cum multa legeris et cognoveris, ad unum semper oportet redire principium.*

The historic estimate is likely in especial to affect our judgment and our language when we are dealing with ancient poets; the personal estimate when we are dealing with poets our contemporaries, or at any rate modern. The exaggerations due to the historic estimate are not in themselves, perhaps, of very much gravity. Their report hardly enters the general ear; probably they do not always impose even on the literary men who adopt them. But they lead to a dangerous abuse of language. So we hear Cædmon, amongst our own poets, compared to Milton. I have already noticed the enthusiasm of one accomplished French critic for "historic origins." Another eminent French critic, M. Vitet, comments upon that famous document of the early poetry of his nation, the *Chanson de Roland.* It is indeed a most interesting document. The *joculator* or *jongleur* Taillefer, who was with William the Conqueror's army at Hastings, marched before the Norman troops, so said the tradition, singing "of Charlemagne and of Roland and of Oliver, and of the vassals who died at Roncevaux"; and it is suggested that in the *Chanson de Roland* by one Turoldus or Théroulde, a poem preserved in a manuscript of the twelfth century in the Bodleian

Library at Oxford, we have certainly the matter, perhaps even some of the words, of the chant which Taillefer sang. The poem has vigour and freshness; it is not without pathos. But M. Vitet is not satisfied with seeing in it a document of some poetic value, and of very high historic and linguistic value; he sees in it a grand and beautiful work, a monument of epic genius. In its general design he finds the grandiose conception, in its details he finds the constant union of simplicity with greatness, which are the marks, he truly says, of the genuine epic, and distinguish it from the artificial epic of literary ages. One thinks of Homer; this is the sort of praise which is given to Homer, and justly given. Higher praise there cannot well be, and it is the praise due to epic poetry of the highest order only, and to no other. Let us try, then, the *Chanson de Roland* at its best. Roland, mortally wounded, lays himself down under a pine-tree, with his face turned towards Spain and the enemy —

> De plusurs choses à remembrer li prist,
> De tantes teres cume li bers cunquist,
> De dulce France, des humes de sun lign,
> De Carlemagne sun seignor ki l'nurrit.[1]

That is primitive work, I repeat, with an undeniable poetic quality of its own. It deserves such praise, and such praise is sufficient for it. But now turn to Homer —

> Ὣς φάτο· τοὺς δ' ἤδη κατέχεν φυσίζοος αἶα
> ἐν Λακεδαίμονι αὖθι, φίλῃ ἐν πατρίδι γαίῃ.[2]

We are here in another world, another order of poetry altogether; here is rightly due such supreme praise as that which M. Vitet gives to the *Chanson de Roland.* If our words are to have any meaning, if our judgments are to have any solidity, we must not heap that supreme praise upon poetry of an order immeasurably inferior.

Indeed there can be no more useful help for discovering what poetry belongs to the class of the truly excellent, and can therefore do us most good, than to have always in one's mind lines and expressions of the great masters, and to apply them as a touchstone to other poetry. Of course we are not to require this other poetry to resemble

[1] "Then began he to call many things to remembrance, — all the lands which his valour conquered, and pleasant France, and the men of his lineage, and Charlemagne his liege lord who nourished him." — *Chanson de Roland*, iii, 939–42.

[2] So said she; they long since in Earth's soft arms were reposing,
There, in their own dear land, their fatherland, Lacedæmon.
Iliad, iii, 243, 244 (translated by Dr. Hawtrey).

them; it may be very dissimilar. But if we have any tact we shall find them, when we have lodged them well in our minds, an infallible touchstone for detecting the presence or absence of high poetic quality, and also the degree of this quality, in all other poetry which we may place beside them. Short passages, even single lines, will serve our turn quite sufficiently. Take the two lines which I have just quoted from Homer, the poet's comment on Helen's mention of her brothers; — or take his

> Ἆ δειλώ, τί σφῶϊ δόμεν Πηλῆϊ ἄνακτι
> θνητᾷ; ὑμεῖς δ' ἐστὸν ἀγήρω τ' ἀθανάτω τε.
> ἦ ἵνα δυστήνοισι μετ' ἀνδράσιν ἄλγε' ἔχητον;[1]

the address of Zeus to the horses of Peleus; — or take finally his

> Καὶ σέ, γέρον, τὸ πρὶν μὲν ἀκούομεν ὄλβιον εἶναι·[2]

the words of Achilles to Priam, a suppliant before him. Take that incomparable line and a half of Dante, Ugolino's tremendous words —

> Io no piangeva; sì dentro impietrai.
> Piangevan elli . . .[3]

take the lovely words of Beatrice to Virgil —

> Io son fatta da Dio, sua mercè, tale,
> Che la vostra miseria non mi tange,
> Nè fiamma d'esto incendio non m'assale . . .[4]

take the simple, but perfect, single line —

> In la sua volontade è nostra pace.[5]

Take of Shakespeare a line or two of Henry the Fourth's expostulation with sleep —

> Wilt thou upon the high and giddy mast
> Seal up the ship-boy's eyes, and rock his brains
> In cradle of the rude imperious surge . . .

[1] Ah, unhappy pair, why gave we you to King Peleus, to a mortal? but ye are without old age, and immortal. Was it that with men born to misery ye might have sorrow? — *Iliad*, xvii, 443–45.

[2] "Nay, and thou too, old man, in former days wast, as we hear, happy." — *Iliad*, xxiv, 543.

[3] "I wailed not, so of stone grew I within; — *they* wailed." — *Inferno*, xxxiii, 39, 40.

[4] "Of such sort hath God, thanked be His mercy, made me, that your misery toucheth me not, neither doth the flame of this fire strike me." — *Inferno*, ii, 91–93.

[5] "In His will is our peace." — *Paradiso*, iii, 85.

and take, as well, Hamlet's dying request to Horatio —

> If thou didst ever hold me in thy heart,
> Absent thee from felicity awhile,
> And in this harsh world draw thy breath in pain
> To tell my story . . .

Take of Milton that Miltonic passage —

> Darken'd so, yet shone
> Above them all the archangel; but his face
> Deep scars of thunder had intrench'd, and care
> Sat on his faded cheek . . .

add two such lines as —

> And courage never to submit or yield
> And what is else not to be overcome . . .

and finish with the exquisite close to the loss of Proserpine, the loss

> . . . which cost Ceres all that pain
> To seek her through the world.

These few lines, if we have tact and can use them, are enough even of themselves to keep clear and sound our judgments about poetry, to save us from fallacious estimates of it, to conduct us to a real estimate.

The specimens I have quoted differ widely from one another, but they have in common this: the possession of the very highest poetical quality. If we are thoroughly penetrated by their power, we shall find that we have acquired a sense enabling us, whatever poetry may be laid before us, to feel the degree in which a high poetical quality is present or wanting there. Critics give themselves great labour to draw out what in the abstract constitutes the characters of a high quality of poetry. It is much better simply to have recourse to concrete examples; — to take specimens of poetry of the high, the very highest quality, and to say: The characters of a high quality of poetry are what is expressed *there*. They are far better recognised by being felt in the verse of the master, than by being perused in the prose of the critic. Nevertheless if we are urgently pressed to give some critical account of them, we may safely, perhaps, venture on laying down, not indeed how and why the characters arise, but where and in what they arise. They are in the matter and substance of the poetry, and they are in its manner and style. Both of these, the substance and matter on the one hand, the style and manner on the other, have a mark, an accent, of high beauty, worth, and power. But if we are asked to define this mark and accent in the abstract, our answer must be: No, for we should thereby be darkening the question, not clearing it. The mark and accent are as given by the substance and matter of that poetry, by the style and manner of that poetry, and of all other poetry which is akin to it in quality.

Only one thing we may add as to the substance and matter of poetry, guiding ourselves by Aristotle's profound observation that the superiority of poetry over history consists in its possessing a higher truth and a higher seriousness (φιλοσοφώτερον καὶ σπουδαιότερον). Let us add, therefore, to what we have said, this: that the substance and matter of the best poetry acquire their special character from possessing, in an eminent degree, truth and seriousness. We may add yet further, what is in itself evident, that to the style and manner of the best poetry their special character, their accent, is given by their diction, and, even yet more, by their movement. And though we distinguish between the two characters, the two accents, of superiority, yet they are nevertheless vitally connected one with the other. The superior character of truth and seriousness, in the matter and substance of the best poetry, is inseparable from the superiority of diction and movement marking its style and manner. The two superiorities are closely related, and are in steadfast proportion one to the other. So far as high poetic truth and seriousness are wanting to a poet's matter and substance, so far also, we may be sure, will a high poetic stamp of diction and movement be wanting to his style and manner. In proportion as this high stamp of diction and movement, again, is absent from a poet's style and manner, we shall find, also, that high poetic truth and seriousness are absent from his substance and matter.

So stated, these are but dry generalities; their whole force lies in their application. And I could wish every student of poetry to make the application of them for himself. Made by himself, the application would impress itself upon his mind far more deeply than made by me. Neither will my limits allow me to make any full application of the generalities above propounded; but in the hope of bringing out, at any rate, some significance in them, and of establishing an important principle more firmly by their means, I will, in the space which remains to me, follow rapidly from the commencement the course of our English poetry with them in my view.

Once more I return to the early poetry of France, with which our own poetry, in its origins, is indissolubly connected. In the twelfth and thirteenth centuries, that seed-time of all modern language and literature, the poetry of France had a clear predominance in Europe. Of the two divisions of that poetry, its productions in the *langue d'oil* and its productions in the *langue d'oc,* the poetry of the *langue d'oc,* of Southern France, of the troubadours, is of importance because of its effect on Italian literature; — the first literature of modern Europe to strike the true and grand note, and to bring forth, as in Dante and Petrarch it brought forth, classics. But the predominance of French poetry in Europe, during the twelfth and thirteenth centuries, is due to its poetry of the *langue d'oil,* the poetry of northern France and of the tongue which is now the French language. In the twelfth century the bloom of this romance-poetry was earlier and stronger in England, at the court of our Anglo-Norman kings, than in France itself. But it was a bloom of French poetry; and as our native poetry formed itself, it formed itself out of this. The romance-poems which took possession of the heart and imagination of Europe in the twelfth and thirteenth centuries are French; "they are," as Southey justly says, "the pride of French literature, nor have we anything which can be placed in competition with them." Themes were supplied from all quarters; but the romance-setting which was common to them all, and which gained the ear of Europe, was French. This constituted for the French poetry, literature, and language, at the height of the Middle Age, an unchallenged predominance. The Italian Brunetto Latini, the master of Dante, wrote his *Treasure* in French because, he says, "*la parleure en est plus délitable et plus commune à toutes gens.*" In the same century, the thirteenth, the French romance-writer, Christian of Troyes, formulates the claims, in chivalry and letters, of France, his native country, as follows:

Or vous ert par ce livre apris,
Que Gresse ot de chevalerie
Le premier los et de clergie;
Puis vint chevalerie à Rome,
Et de la clergie la some,
Qui ore est en France venue.
Diex doinst qu'ele i soit retenue,
Et que li lius li abelisse
Tant que de France n'isse
L'onor qui s'i est arestée!

Now by this book you will learn that first Greece had the renown for chivalry and letters; then chivalry and the primacy in letters passed to Rome, and now it is come to France. God grant it may be kept there; and that the place may please it so well, that the honour which has come to make stay in France may never depart thence!

Yet it is now all gone, this French romance-poetry, of which the weight of substance and the power of style are not unfairly represented by this extract from Christian of Troyes. Only by means of the historic estimate can we persuade ourselves now to think that any of it is of poetical importance.

But in the fourteenth century there comes an Englishman nourished on this poetry, taught his trade by this poetry, getting words, rhyme, metre from this poetry; for even of that stanza which the Italians used, and which Chaucer derived immediately from the Italians, the basis and suggestion was probably given in France. Chaucer (I have already named him) fascinated his contemporaries, but so too did Christian of Troyes and Wolfram of Eschenbach. Chaucer's power of fascination, however, is enduring; his poetical importance does not need the assistance of the historic estimate; it is real. He is a genuine source of joy and strength, which is flowing still for us and will flow always. He will be read, as time goes on, far more generally than he is read now. His language is a cause of difficulty for us; but so also, and I think in quite as great a degree, is the language of Burns. In Chaucer's case, as in that of Burns, it is a difficulty to be unhesitatingly accepted and overcome.

If we ask ourselves wherein consists the immense superiority of Chaucer's poetry over the romance-poetry — why it is that in passing from this to Chaucer we suddenly feel ourselves to be in another world, we shall find that his superiority is both in the substance of his poetry and in the style of his poetry. His superiority in substance is given by his large, free, simple, clear yet kindly view of human life, — so unlike the total want, in the romance-poets, of all intelligent command of it. Chaucer has not their helplessness; he has gained the power to survey the world from a central, a truly human point of view. We have only to call to mind the Prologue to *The Canterbury Tales*. The right comment upon it is Dryden's: "It is sufficient to say, according to the proverb, that *here is God's plenty*." And again: "He is a perpetual fountain of good sense." It is by a large, free, sound representation of things, that poetry, this high criticism of life, has truth of substance; and Chaucer's poetry has truth of substance.

Of his style and manner, if we think first of the romance-poetry and then of Chaucer's divine liquidness of diction, his divine fluidity of movement, it is difficult to speak temperately. They are irresistible, and justify all the rapture with which his successors speak of his "gold dew-drops of speech." Johnson misses the point entirely when he finds fault with Dryden for ascribing to Chaucer the first refinement of our numbers, and says that Gower also can show smooth numbers and easy rhymes. The refinement of our numbers means something far more than this. A nation may have versifiers with smooth numbers and easy rhymes, and yet may have no real poetry at all. Chaucer is the father of our splendid English poetry; he is our "well of English undefiled," because by the lovely charm of his diction, the lovely charm of his movement, he makes an epoch and founds a tradition. In Spenser, Shakespeare, Milton, Keats, we can follow the tradition of the liquid diction, the fluid movement, of Chaucer; at one time it is his liquid diction of which in these poets we feel the virtue, and at another time it is his fluid movement. And the virtue is irresistible.

Bounded as is my space, I must yet find room for an example of Chaucer's virtue, as I have given examples to show the virtue of the great classics. I feel disposed to say that a single line is enough to show the charm of Chaucer's verse; that merely one line like this—

O martyr souded[1] in virginitee!

has a virtue of manner and movement such as we shall not find in all the verse of romance-poetry;—but this is saying nothing. The virtue is such as we shall not find, perhaps, in all English poetry, outside the poets whom I have named as the special inheritors of Chaucer's tradition. A single line, however, is too little if we have not the strain of Chaucer's verse well in our memory; let us take a stanza. It is from *The Prioress's Tale,* the story of the Christian child murdered in a Jewry—

My throte is cut unto my nekke-bone
Saidè this child, and as by way of kinde
I should have deyd, yea, longè time agone;
But Jesu Christ, as ye in bookès finde,
Will that his glory last and be in minde,
And for the worship of his mother dere
Yet may I sing *O Alma* loud and clere.

Wordsworth has modernised this Tale, and to feel how delicate and evanescent is the charm of verse, we have only to read Wordsworth's first three lines of this stanza after Chaucer's—

My throat is cut unto the bone, I trow,
Said this young child, and by the law of kind
I should have died, yea, many hours ago.

The charm is departed. It is often said that the power of liquidness and fluidity in Chaucer's verse was dependent upon a free, a licentious dealing with language, such as is now impossible; upon a liberty, such as Burns too enjoyed, of making words like *neck, bird,* into a dissyllable by adding to them, and words like *cause, rhyme,* into a dissyllable by sounding the *e* mute. It is true that Chaucer's fluidity

[1] The French *soudé;* soldered, fixed fast.

is conjoined with this liberty, and is admirably served by it; but we ought not to say that it was dependent upon it. It was dependent upon his talent. Other poets with a like liberty do not attain to the fluidity of Chaucer; Burns himself does not attain to it. Poets, again, who have a talent akin to Chaucer's, such as Shakespeare or Keats, have known how to attain to his fluidity without the like liberty.

And yet Chaucer is not one of the great classics. His poetry transcends and effaces, easily and without effort, all the romance-poetry of Catholic Christendom; it transcends and effaces all the English poetry contemporary with it, it transcends and effaces all the English poetry subsequent to it down to the age of Elizabeth. Of such avail is poetic truth of substance, in its natural and necessary union with poetic truth of style. And yet, I say, Chaucer is not one of the great classics. He has not their accent. What is wanting to him is suggested by the mere mention of the name of the first great classic of Christendom, the immortal poet who died eighty years before Chaucer,—Dante. The accent of such verse as

In la sua volontade è nostra pace . . .

is altogether beyond Chaucer's reach; we praise him, but we feel that this accent is out of the question for him. It may be said that it was necessarily out of the reach of any poet in the England of that stage of growth. Possibly; but we are to adopt a real, not a historic, estimate of poetry. However we may account for its absence, something is wanting, then, to the poetry of Chaucer, which poetry must have before it can be placed in the glorious class of the best. And there is no doubt what that something is. It is the σπουδαιότης, the high and excellent seriousness, which Aristotle assigns as one of the grand virtues of poetry. The substance of Chaucer's poetry, his view of things and his criticism of life, has largeness, freedom, shrewdness, benignity; but it has not this high seriousness. Homer's criticism of life has it. Dante's has it, Shakespeare's has it. It is this chiefly which gives to our spirits what they can rest upon; and with the increasing demands of our modern ages upon poetry, this virtue of giving us what we can rest upon will be more and more highly esteemed. A voice from the slums of Paris, fifty or sixty years after Chaucer, the voice of poor Villon out of his life of riot and crime, has at its happy moments (as, for instance, in the last stanza of "La Belle Heaulmière"[1]) more of this important poetic virtue of seriousness than all

[1] The name *Heaulmière* is said to be derived from a headdress (helm) worn as a mark by courtesans. In Villon's ballad, a poor old creature of this class laments her days of youth and beauty. The last stanza of the ballad runs thus—

the productions of Chaucer. But its apparition in Villon, and in men like Villon, is fitful; the greatness of the great poets, the power of their criticism of life, is that their virtue is sustained.

To our praise, therefore, of Chaucer as a poet there must be this limitation; he lacks the high seriousness of the great classics, and therewith an important part of their virtue. Still, the main fact for us to bear in mind about Chaucer is his sterling value according to that real estimate which we firmly adopt for all poets. He has poetic truth of substance, though he has not high poetic seriousness, and corresponding to his truth of substance he has an exquisite virtue of style and manner. With him is born our real poetry.

For my present purpose I need not dwell on our Elizabethan poetry, or on the continuation and close of this poetry in Milton. We all of us profess to be agreed in the estimate of this poetry; we all of us recognise it as great poetry, our greatest, and Shakespeare and Milton as our poetical classics. The real estimate, here, has universal currency. With the next age of our poetry divergency and difficulty begin. An historic estimate of that poetry has established itself; and the question is, whether it will be found to coincide with the real estimate.

The age of Dryden, together with our whole eighteenth century which followed it, sincerely believed itself to have produced poetical classics of its own, and even to have made advance, in poetry, beyond all its predecessors Dryden regards as not seriously disputable the opinion "that the sweetness of English verse was never understood or practised by our fathers." Cowley could see nothing at all in Chaucer's poetry. Dryden heartily admired it, and, as we have seen, praised its matter admirably; but of its exquisite manner and movement all he can find to say is that "there is the rude sweetness of a Scotch tune in it, which is natural and pleasing, though not perfect." Addison, wishing to praise Chaucer's numbers, compares them with Dryden's own. And all through the eighteenth century, and down

---

Ainsi le bon temps regretons
Entre nous, pauvres vieilles sottes,
Assises bas, à croppetons,
Tout en ung tas comme pelottes;
A petit feu de chenevottes
Tost allumées, tost estainctes.
Et jadis fusmes si mignottes!
Ainsi en prend à maintz et maintes.

Thus amongst ourselves we regret the good time, poor silly old things, low-seated on our heels, all in a heap like so many balls; by a little fire of hemp-stalks, soon lighted, soon spent. And once we were such darlings! So fares it with many and many a one.

even into our own times, the stereotyped phrase of approbation for good verse found in our early poetry has been, that it even approached the verse of Dryden, Addison, Pope, and Johnson.

Are Dryden and Pope poetical classics? Is the historic estimate, which represents them as such, and which has been so long established that it cannot easily give way, the real estimate? Wordsworth and Coleridge, as is well known, denied it; but the authority of Wordsworth and Coleridge does not weigh much with the young generation, and there are many signs to show that the eighteenth century and its judgments are coming into favour again. Are the favourite poets of the eighteenth century classics?

It is impossible within my present limits to discuss the question fully. And what man of letters would not shrink from seeming to dispose dictatorially of the claims of two men who are, at any rate, such masters in letters as Dryden and Pope; two men of such admirable talent, both of them, and one of them, Dryden, a man, on all sides, of such energetic and genial power? And yet, if we are to gain the full benefit from poetry, we must have the real estimate of it. I cast about for some mode of arriving, in the present case, at such an estimate without offence. And perhaps the best way is to begin, as it is easy to begin, with cordial praise.

When we find Chapman, the Elizabethan translator of Homer, expressing himself in his preface thus: "Though truth in her very nakedness sits in so deep a pit, that from Gades to Aurora and Ganges few eyes can sound her, I hope yet those few here will so discover and confirm that, the date being out of her darkness in this morning of our poet, he shall now gird his temples with the sun," — we pronounce that such a prose is intolerable. When we find Milton writing: "And long it was not after, when I was confirmed in this opinion, that he, who would not be frustrate of his hope to write well hereafter in laudable things, ought himself to be a true poem," — we pronounce that such a prose has its own grandeur, but that it is obsolete and inconvenient. But when we find Dryden telling us: "What Virgil wrote in the vigour of his age, in plenty and at ease, I have undertaken to translate in my declining years; struggling with wants, oppressed with sickness, curbed in my genius, liable to be misconstrued in all I write," — then we exclaim that here at last we have the true English prose, a prose such as we would all gladly use if we only knew how. Yet Dryden was Milton's contemporary.

But after the Restoration the time had come when our nation felt the imperious need of a fit prose. So, too, the time had likewise come when our nation felt the imperious need of freeing itself from the absorbing preoccupation which religion in the Puritan age had exercised. It was impossible that this freedom should be brought about without some negative excess, without some neglect and impairment of the religious life of the soul; and the spiritual history of the eighteenth century shows us that the freedom was not achieved without them. Still, the freedom was achieved; the preoccupation, an undoubtedly baneful and retarding one if it had continued, was got rid of. And as with religion amongst us at that period, so it was also with letters. A fit prose was a necessity; but it was impossible that a fit prose should establish itself amongst us without some touch of frost to the imaginative life of the soul. The needful qualities for a fit prose are regularity, uniformity, precision, balance. The men of letters, whose destiny it may be to bring their nation to the attainment of a fit prose, must of necessity, whether they work in prose or in verse, give a predominating, an almost exclusive attention to the qualities of regularity, uniformity, precision, balance. But an almost exclusive attention to these qualities involves some repression and silencing of poetry.

We are to regard Dryden as the puissant and glorious founder, Pope as the splendid high priest, of our age of prose and reason, of our excellent and indispensable eighteenth century. For the purposes of their mission and destiny their poetry, like their prose, is admirable. Do you ask me whether Dryden's verse, take it almost where you will, is not good?

> A milk-white Hind, immortal and unchanged,
> Fed on the lawns and in the forest ranged.

I answer: Admirable for the purposes of the inaugurator of an age of prose and reason. Do you ask me whether Pope's verse, take it almost where you will, is not good?

> To Hounslow Heath I point, and Banstead Down;
> Thence comes your mutton, and these chicks my own.

I answer: Admirable for the purposes of the high priest of an age of prose and reason. But do you ask me whether such verse proceeds from men with an adequate poetic criticism of life, from men whose criticism of life has a high seriousness, or even, without that high seriousness, has poetic largeness, freedom, insight, benignity? Do you ask me whether the application of ideas to life in the verse of these men, often a powerful application, no doubt, is a powerful *poetic* application? Do you ask me whether the poetry of these men has either the matter or the inseparable manner of such an adequate poetic criticism; whether it has the accent of

> Absent thee from felicity awhile . . .

or of

> And what is else not to be overcome . . .

or of

> O martyr souded in virginitee!

I answer: It has not and cannot have them; it is the poetry of the builders of an age of prose and reason. Though they may write in verse, though they may in a certain sense be masters of the art of versification, Dryden and Pope are not classics of our poetry, they are classics of our prose.

Gray is our poetical classic of that literature and age; the position of Gray is singular, and demands a word of notice here. He has not the volume or the power of poets who, coming in times more favourable, have attained to an independent criticism of life. But he lived with the great poets, he lived, above all, with the Greeks, through perpetually studying and enjoying them; and he caught their poetic point of view for regarding life, caught their poetic manner. The point of view and the manner are not self-sprung in him, he caught them of others; and he had not the free and abundant use of them. But whereas Addison and Pope never had the use of them, Gray had the use of them at times. He is the scantiest and frailest of classics in our poetry, but he is a classic.

And now after Gray, we are met, as we draw towards the end of the eighteenth century, we are met by the great name of Burns. We enter now on times where the personal estimate of poets begins to be rife, and where the real estimate of them is not reached without difficulty. But in spite of the disturbing pressures of personal partiality, of national partiality, let us try to reach a real estimate of the poetry of Burns.

By his English poetry Burns in general belongs to the eighteenth century, and has little importance for us.

> Mark ruffian Violence, distain'd with crimes,
> Rousing elate in these degenerate times;
> View unsuspecting Innocence a prey,
> As guileful Fraud points out the erring way;
> While subtle Litigation's pliant tongue
> The life-blood equal sucks of Right and Wrong!

Evidently this is not the real Burns, or his name and fame would have disappeared long ago. Nor is Clarinda's love-poet, Sylvander, the real Burns either. But he tells us himself: "These English songs gravel me to death. I have not the command of the language that I have of my native tongue. In fact, I think that my ideas are more barren in English than in Scotch. I have been at 'Duncan Gray' to dress it in English, but all I can do is desperately stupid." We English turn naturally, in Burns, to the poems in our own language, because we can read them easily; but in those poems we have not the real Burns.

The real Burns is of course in his Scotch poems. Let us boldly say that of much of this poetry, a poetry dealing perpetually with Scotch drink, Scotch religion, and Scotch manners, a Scotchman's estimate is apt to be personal. A Scotchman is used to this world of Scotch drink, Scotch religion, and Scotch manners; he has a tenderness for it; he meets its poet half way. In this tender mood he reads pieces like the "Holy Fair" or "Halloween." But this world of Scotch drink, Scotch religion, and Scotch manners is against the poet, not for him, when it is not a partial countryman who reads him; for in itself it is not a beautiful world, and no one can deny that it is of advantage to a poet to deal with a beautiful world. Burns's world of Scotch drink, Scotch religion, and Scotch manners, is often a harsh, a sordid, a repulsive world; even the world of his "Cotter's Saturday Night" is not a beautiful world. No doubt a poet's criticism of life may have such truth and power that it triumphs over its world and delights us. Burns may triumph over his world, often he does triumph over his world, but let us observe how and where. Burns is the first case we have had where the bias of the personal estimate tends to mislead; let us look at him closely, he can bear it.

Many of his admirers will tell us that we have Burns, convival, genuine, delightful, here —

> Leeze me on drink! it gies us mair
>   Than either school or college;
> It kindles wit, it waukens lair,
>   It pangs us fou o' knowledge.
> Be 't whisky gill or penny wheep
>   Or ony stronger potion,
> It never fails, on drinking deep,
>   To kittle up our notion
>   By night or day.

There is a great deal of that sort of thing in Burns, and it is unsatisfactory, not because it is bacchanalian poetry, but because it has not that accent of sincerity which bacchanalian poetry, to do it justice, very often has. There is something in it of bravado, something which makes us feel that we have not the man speaking to us with his real voice; something, therefore, poetically unsound.

With still more confidence will his admirers tell us that we have the genuine Burns, the great poet, when his strain asserts the independence, equality, dignity, of men, as in the famous song "For a' that and a' that"—

A prince can mak' a belted knight,
A marquis, duke, and a' that;
But an honest man's aboon his might,
Guid faith he mauna fa' that!
For a' that, and a' that,
Their dignities, and a' that,
The pith o' sense, and pride o' worth,
Are higher rank than a' that.

Here they find his grand, genuine touches; and still more, when this puissant genius, who so often set morality at defiance, falls moralising —

The sacred lowe o' weel-placed love
Luxuriantly indulge it;
But never tempt th' illicit rove,
Tho' naething should divulge it.
I waive the quantum o' the sin,
The hazard o' concealing,
But och! it hardens a' within,
And petrifies the feeling.

Or in a higher strain —

Who made the heart, 'tis He alone
Decidedly can try us;
He knows each chord, its various tone;
Each spring, its various bias.
Then at the balance let's be mute,
We never can adjust it;
What's *done* we partly may compute,
But know not what's resisted.

Or in a better strain yet, a strain, his admirers will say, unsurpassable —

To make a happy fire-side clime
To weans and wife,
That's the true pathos and sublime
Of human life.

There is criticism of life for you, the admirers of Burns will say to us; there is the application of ideas to life! There is, undoubtedly. The doctrine of the last-quoted lines coincides almost exactly with what was the aim and end, Xenophon tells us, of all the teaching of Socrates. And the application is a powerful one; made by a man of vigorous understanding, and (need I say?) a master of language.

But for supreme poetical success more is required than the powerful application of ideas to life; it must be an application under the conditions fixed by the laws of poetic truth and poetic beauty. Those laws fix as an essential condition, in the poet's treatment of such matters as are here in question, high seriousness; — the high seriousness which comes from absolute sincerity. The accent of high seriousness, born of absolute sincerity, is what gives to such verse as

In la sua volontade è nostra pace . . .

to such criticism of life as Dante's, its power. Is this accent felt in the passages which I have been quoting from Burns? Surely not; surely, if our sense is quick, we must perceive that we have not in those passages a voice from the very inmost soul of the genuine Burns; he is not speaking to us from these depths, he is more or less preaching. And the compensation for admiring such passages less, from missing the perfect poetic accent in them, will be that we shall admire more the poetry where that accent is found.

No; Burns, like Chaucer, comes short of the high seriousness of the great classics, and the virtue of matter and manner which goes with that high seriousness is wanting to his work. At moments he touches it in a profound and passionate melancholy, as in those four immortal lines taken by Byron as a motto for *The Bride of Abydos*, but which have in them a depth of poetic quality such as resides in no verse of Byron's own —

Had we never loved sae kindly,
Had we never loved sae blindly,
Never met, or never parted,
We had ne'er been broken-hearted.

But a whole poem of that quality Burns cannot make; the rest, in the "Farewell to Nancy," is verbiage.

We arrive best at the real estimate of Burns, I think, by conceiving his work as having truth of matter and truth of manner, but not the accent or the poetic virtue of the highest masters. His genuine criticism of life, when the sheer poet in him speaks, is ironic; it is not —

Thou Power Supreme, whose mighty scheme
These woes of mine fulfil,
Here firm I rest, they must be best
Because they are Thy will!

It is far rather: "Whistle owre the lave o't!" Yet we may say of him as of Chaucer, that of life and the world, as they come before him, his view is large, free, shrewd, benignant, — truly poetic, therefore; and his manner of rendering what he sees is to match. But we must note, at the same time, his great difference from Chaucer. The freedom of Chaucer is heightened, in Burns, by a fiery, reckless energy; the benignity of Chaucer deepens, in Burns, into an overwhelming sense of the pathos of things; — of the pathos of human nature, the pathos, also, of non-human nature. Instead of the fluidity of Chaucer's manner, the manner of Burns has spring, bounding swiftness. Burns is by far the greater force, though he has perhaps less charm. The world of Chaucer is fairer, richer, more significant than that of Burns; but when the largeness and freedom of Burns get full sweep, as in *Tam o' Shanter,* or still more in that puissant and splendid production, *The Jolly Beggars,* his world may be what it will, his poetic genius triumphs over it. In the world of *The Jolly Beggars* there is more than hideousness and squalor, there is bestiality; yet the piece is a superb poetic success. It has a breadth, truth, and power which make the famous scene in Auerbach's Cellar, of Goethe's *Faust,* seem artificial and tame beside it, and which are only matched by Shakespeare and Aristophanes.

Here, where his largeness and freedom serve him so admirably, and also in those poems and songs where to shrewdness he adds infinite archness and wit, and to benignity infinite pathos, where his manner is flawless, and a perfect poetic whole is the result, — in things like the address to the mouse whose home he had ruined, in things like "Duncan Gray," "Tam Glen," "Whistle and I'll come to you my Lad," "Auld Lang Syne" (this list might be made much longer), — here we have the genuine Burns, of whom the real estimate must be high indeed. Not a classic, nor with the excellent σπουδαιότης of the great classics, nor with a verse rising to a criticism of life and a virtue like theirs; but a poet with thorough truth of substance and an answering truth of style, giving us a poetry sound to the core. We all of us have a leaning towards the pathetic, and may be inclined perhaps to prize Burns most for his touches of piercing, sometimes almost intolerable, pathos; for verse like —

> We twa hae paidl't i' the burn
> From mornin' sun till dine;
> But seas between us braid hae roar'd
> Sin auld lang syne . . .

where he is as lovely as he is sound. But perhaps it is by the perfection of soundness of his lighter and archer masterpieces that he is poetically most wholesome for us. For the votary misled by a personal estimate of Shelley, as so many of us have been, are, and will be, — of that beautiful spirit building his many-coloured haze of words and images

> Pinnacled dim in the intense inane —

no contact can be wholesomer than the contact with Burns at his archest and soundest. Side by side with the

On the brink of the night and the morning
  My coursers are wont to respire,
But the Earth has just whispered a warning
  That their flight must be swifter than fire . . .

of *Prometheus Unbound,* how salutary, how very salutary, to place this from "Tam Glen"—

My minnie does constantly deave me
  And bids me beware o' young men;
They flatter, she says, to deceive me;
  But wha can think sae o' Tam Glen?

But we enter on burning ground as we approach the poetry of times so near to us — poetry like that of Byron, Shelley, and Wordsworth — of which the estimates are so often not only personal, but personal with passion. For my purpose, it is enough to have taken the single case of Burns, the first poet we come to of whose work the estimate formed is evidently apt to be personal, and to have suggested how we may proceed, using the poetry of the great classics as a sort of touchstone, to correct this estimate, as we had previously corrected by the same means the historic estimate where we met with it. A collection like the present, with its succession of celebrated names and celebrated poems, offers a good opportunity to us for resolutely endeavoring to make our estimates of poetry real. I have sought to point out a method which will help us in making them so, and to exhibit it in use so far as to put any one who likes in a way of applying it for himself.

At any rate the end to which the method and the estimate are designed to lead, and from leading to which, if they do lead to it, they get their whole value, — the benefit of being able clearly to feel and deeply to enjoy the best, the truly classic, in poetry, — is an end, let me say it once more at parting, of supreme importance. We are often told that an era is opening in which we are to see multitudes of a common sort of readers, and masses of a common sort of literature; that such readers do not want and could not relish anything better than such literature, and that to provide it is becoming a vast and profitable industry. Even if good literature entirely lost currency with the world, it would still be abundantly worth while to continue to enjoy it by oneself. But it never will lose currency with the world, in spite of momentary appearances; it never will lose supremacy. Currency and supremacy are insured to it, not indeed by the world's deliberate and conscious choice, but by something far deeper, — by the instinct of self-preservation in humanity.

From THOMAS GRAY

To explain Gray, we must do more than allege his sterility, as we must look further than to his reclusion at Cambridge. What caused his sterility? Was it his ill-health, his hereditary gout? Certainly we will pay all respect to the powers of hereditary gout for afflicting us poor mortals. But Goethe, after pointing out that Schiller, who was so productive, was "almost constantly ill," adds the true remark that it is incredible how much the spirit can do, in these cases, to keep up the body. Pope's animation and activity through all the course of what he pathetically calls "that long disease, my life," is an example presenting itself signally, in Gray's own country and time, to confirm what Goethe here says. What gave the power to Gray's reclusion and ill-health to induce his sterility?

The reason, the indubitable reason as I cannot but think it, I have already given elsewhere. Gray, a born poet, fell upon an age of prose. He fell upon an age whose task was such as to call forth in general men's powers of understanding, wit and cleverness, rather than their deepest powers of mind and soul. As regards literary production, the task of the eighteenth century in England was not the poetic interpretation of the world, its task was to create a plain, clear, straightforward, efficient prose. Poetry obeyed the bent of mind requisite for the due fulfilment of this task of the century. It was intellectual, argumentative, ingenious; not seeing things in their truth and beauty, not interpretative. Gray, with the qualities of mind and soul of a genuine poet, was isolated in his century. Maintaining and fortifying them by lofty studies, he yet could not fully educe and enjoy them; the want of a genial atmosphere, the failure of sympathy in his contemporaries, were too great. Born in the same year with Milton, Gray would have been another man; born in the same year with Burns, he would have been another man. A man born in 1608 could profit by the larger and more poetic scope of the English spirit in the Elizabethan age; a man born in 1759 could profit by that European renewing of men's minds of which the great historical manifestation is the French Revolution. Gray's alert and brilliant young friend, Bonstetten, who would explain the void in the life of Gray by his having never loved, Bonstetten himself loved, married, and had children. Yet at the age of fifty he was bidding fair to grow old, dismal and torpid like the rest of us, when he was roused and made young again for some thirty years, says M. Sainte-Beuve, by the events of 1789. If Gray, like Burns, had been just thirty years old when the French Revolution broke out, he would have shown, probably, productiveness and animation in plenty. Coming when he did, and endowed as he was, he was a man born out of date, a man whose full spiritual flowering was impossible. The same thing is to be said of his great contemporary, Butler, the author of the *Analogy*. In the sphere of religion, which touches that of poetry, Butler was impelled by the endowment of his nature to strive for a profound and adequate conception of religious things, which was not pursued by his contemporaries, and which at that time, and in that atmosphere of mind, was not fully attainable. Hence, in Butler too, a dissatisfaction, a weariness, as in Gray; "great labour and weariness, great disappointment, pain and even vexation of mind." A sort of spiritual east wind was at that time blowing; neither Butler nor Gray could flower. They *never spoke out*.

Gray's poetry was not only stinted in quantity by reason of the age wherein he lived, it suffered somewhat in quality also. We have seen under what obligation to Dryden Gray professed himself to be — "if there was any excellence in his numbers, he had learned it wholly from that great poet." It was not for nothing that he came when Dryden had lately "embellished," as Johnson says, English poetry; had "found it brick and left it marble." It was not for nothing that he came just when "the English ear," to quote Johnson again, "had been accustomed to the mellifluence of Pope's numbers, and the diction of poetry had grown more splendid." Of the intellectualities, ingenuities, personifications, of the movement and diction of Dryden and Pope, Gray caught something, caught too much. We have little of Gray's poetry, and that little is not free from the faults of his age. Therefore it was important to go for aid, as we did, to Gray's life and letters, to see his mind and soul there, and to corroborate from thence that high estimate of his quality which his poetry indeed calls forth, but does not establish so amply and irresistibly as one could desire.

For a just criticism it does, however, clearly establish it. The difference between genuine poetry and the poetry of Dryden, Pope, and all their school, is briefly this: their poetry is conceived and composed in their wits, genuine poetry is conceived and composed in the soul. The difference between the two kinds of poetry is immense. They differ profoundly in their modes of language, they differ profoundly in their modes of evolution. The poetic language of our eighteenth century in general is the language of men composing *without their eye on the object*, as Wordsworth excellently said of Dryden; language merely recalling the object, as the common language of prose does, and then dressing it out with a certain smartness and brilliancy for the fancy and understanding. This is called "splendid diction." The evolution of the poetry of our eighteenth century is likewise intellectual; it proceeds by ratiocination, antithesis, ingenious turns and conceits. This poetry is often eloquent, and always, in the hands of such masters as Dryden and Pope, clever; but it does not take us much below the surface of things, it does not give us the emotion of seeing things in their truth and beauty. The language of genuine poetry, on the other hand, is the language of one composing with his eye on the object; its evolution is that of a thing which has been plunged in the poet's soul until it comes forth naturally and necessarily. This sort of evolution is infinitely simpler than the other, and infinitely more satisfying; the same thing is true of the genuine poetic language likewise. But they are both of them also infinitely harder of attainment; they come only from those who, as Emerson says, "live from a great depth of being."

WORDSWORTH

I REMEMBER hearing Lord Macaulay say, after Wordsworth's death, when subscriptions were being collected to found a memorial of him, that ten years earlier more money could have been raised in Cambridge alone, to do honour to Wordsworth, than was now raised all through the country. Lord Macaulay had, as we know, his own heightened and telling way of putting things, and we must always make allowance for it. But probably it is true that Wordsworth has never, either before or since, been so accepted and popular, so established in possession of the minds of all who profess to care for poetry, as he was between the years 1830 and 1840, and at Cambridge. From the very first, no doubt, he had his believers and witnesses. But I have myself heard him declare that, for he knew not how many years, his poetry had never brought him in enough to buy his shoestrings. The poetry-reading public was very slow to recognise him, and was very easily drawn away from him. Scott effaced him with this public, Byron effaced him.

The death of Byron seemed, however, to make an opening for Wordsworth. Scott, who had for some time ceased to produce poetry himself, and stood before the public as a great novelist; Scott, too genuine himself not to feel the profound genuineness of Wordsworth, and with an instinctive recognition of his firm hold on nature and of his local truth, always admired him sincerely, and praised him generously. The influence of Coleridge upon young men of ability was then powerful, and was still gathering strength; this influence told entirely in favour of Wordsworth's poetry. Cambridge was a place where Coleridge's influence had great action, and where Wordsworth's poetry, therefore, flourished especially. But even amongst the general public its sale grew large, the eminence of its author was widely recognised, and Rydal Mount became an object of pilgrimage. I remember Wordsworth relating how one of the pilgrims, a clergyman, asked him if he had ever written anything besides the *Guide to the Lakes*. Yes, he answered modestly, he had written verses. Not every pilgrim was a reader, but the vogue was established, and the stream of pilgrims came.

Mr. Tennyson's decisive appearance dates from 1842. One cannot say that he effaced Wordsworth as Scott and Byron had effaced him. The poetry of Wordsworth had been so long before the public, the suffrage of good judges was so steady and so strong in its favour, that by 1842 the verdict of posterity, one may almost say, had been already pronounced, and Wordsworth's English fame was secure. But the vogue, the ear and applause of the great body of poetry-readers, never quite thoroughly perhaps his, he gradually lost more and more, and Mr. Tennyson gained them. Mr. Tennyson drew to himself, and away from Wordsworth, the poetry-reading public, and the new generations. Even in 1850, when Wordsworth died, this diminution of popularity was visible, and occasioned the remark of Lord Macaulay which I quoted at starting.

The diminution has continued. The influence of Coleridge has waned, and Wordsworth's poetry can no longer draw succour from this ally. The poetry has not, however, wanted eulogists; and it may be said to have brought its eulogists luck, for almost every one who has praised Wordsworth's poetry has praised it well. But the public has remained cold, or, at least, undetermined. Even the abundance of Mr. Palgrave's fine and skilfully chosen specimens of Wordsworth, in the *Golden Treasury,* surprised many readers, and gave offence to not a few. To tenth-rate critics and compilers, for whom any violent shock to the public taste would be a temerity not to be risked, it is still quite permissible to speak of Wordsworth's poetry, not only with ignorance, but with impertinence. On the Continent he is almost unknown.

I cannot think, then, that Wordsworth has, up to this time, at all obtained his deserts. "Glory," said M. Renan the other day, "glory after all is the thing which has the best chance of not being altogether vanity." Wordsworth was a homely man, and himself would certainly never have thought of talking of glory as that which, after all, has the best chance of not being altogether vanity. Yet we may well allow that few things are less vain than *real* glory. Let us conceive of the whole group of civilised nations as being, for intellectual and spiritual purposes, one great confederation, bound to a joint action and working towards a common result; a confederation whose members have a due knowledge both of the past, out of which they all proceed, and of one another. This was the ideal of Goethe, and it is an ideal which will impose itself upon the thoughts of our modern societies more and more. Then to be recognised by the verdict of such a confederation as a master, or even as a seriously and eminently worthy workman, in one's own line of intellectual or spiritual activity, is indeed glory; a glory which it would be difficult to rate too highly. For what could be more beneficent, more salutary? The world is forwarded by having its attention fixed on the best things; and here is a tribunal, free from all suspicion of national and provincial partiality, putting a stamp on the best things, and recommending them for general honour and acceptance. A nation, again, is furthered by recognition of its real gifts and successes; it is encouraged to develop them further. And here is an honest verdict, telling us which of our supposed successes are really, in the judgment of the great impartial world, and not in our own private judgment only, successes, and which are not.

It is so easy to feel pride and satisfaction in one's own things, so hard to make sure that one is right in feeling it! We have a great empire. But so had Nebuchadnezzar. We extol the "unrivalled happiness" of our national civilisation. But then comes a candid friend, and remarks that our upper class is materialised, our middle class vulgarised, and our lower class brutalised. We are proud of our painting, our music. But we find that in the judgment of other people our painting is questionable, and our music non-existent. We are proud of our men of science. And here it turns out that the world is with us; we find that in the judgment of other people, too, Newton among the dead, and Mr. Darwin among the living, hold as high a place as they hold in our national opinion.

Finally, we are proud of our poets and poetry. Now poetry is nothing less than the most perfect speech of man, that in which he comes nearest to being able to utter the truth. It is no small thing, therefore, to succeed eminently in poetry. And so much is required for duly estimating success here, that about poetry it is perhaps hardest to arrive at a sure general verdict, and takes longest. Meanwhile, our own conviction of the superiority of our national poets is not decisive, is almost certain to be mingled, as we see constantly in English eulogy of Shakespeare, with much of provincial infatuation. And we know what was the opinion current amongst our neighbours the French — people of taste, acuteness, and quick literary tact — not a hundred years ago, about our great poets. The old *Biographie Universelle* notices the pretension of the English to a place for their poets among the chief poets of the world, and says that this is a pretension which to no one but an Englishman can ever seem admissible. And the scornful, disparaging things said by foreigners about Shakespeare and Milton, and about our national over-estimate of them, have been often quoted, and will be in every one's remembrance.

A great change has taken place, and Shakespeare is now generally recognised, even in France, as one of the greatest of poets. Yes, some anti-Gallican cynic will say, the French rank him with Corneille and with Victor Hugo! But let me have the pleasure of quoting a sentence about Shakespeare, which I met with by accident not long ago in the *Correspondant*, a French review which not a dozen English people, I suppose, look at. The writer is praising Shakespeare's prose. With Shakespeare, he says, "prose comes in whenever the subject, being more familiar, is unsuited to the majestic English iambic." And he goes on: "Shakespeare is the king of poetic rhythm and style, as well as the king of the realm of thought; along with his dazzling prose, Shakespeare has succeeded in giving us the most varied, the most harmonious verse which has ever sounded upon the human ear since the verse of the Greeks." M. Henry Cochin, the writer of this sentence, deserves our gratitude for it; it would not be easy to praise Shakespeare, in a single sentence, more justly. And when a foreigner and a Frenchman writes thus of Shakespeare, and when Goethe says of Milton, in whom there was so much to repel Goethe rather than to attract him, that "nothing has been ever done so entirely in the sense of the Greeks as *Samson Agonistes*," and that "Milton is in very truth a poet whom we must treat with all reverence," then we understand what constitutes a European recognition of poets and poetry as contradistinguished from a merely national recognition, and that in favour both of Milton and of Shakespeare the judgment of the high court of appeal has finally gone.

I come back to M. Renan's praise of glory, from which I started. Yes, real glory is a most serious thing, glory authenticated by the Amphictyonic Court of final appeal, definitive glory. And even for poets and poetry, long and difficult as may be the process of arriving at the right award, the right award comes at last, the definitive glory rests where it is deserved. Every establishment of such a real glory is good and wholesome for mankind at large, good and wholesome for the nation which produced the poet crowned with it. To the poet himself it can seldom do harm; for he, poor man, is in his grave, probably, long before his glory crowns him.

Wordsworth has been in his grave for some thirty years, and certainly his lovers and admirers cannot flatter themselves that this great and steady light of glory as yet shines over him. He is not fully recognised at home; he is not recognised at all abroad. Yet I firmly believe that the poetical performance of Wordsworth is, after that of Shakespeare and Milton, of which all the world now recognises the worth, undoubtedly the most considerable in our language from the Elizabethan age to the present time. Chaucer is anterior; and on other grounds, too, he cannot well be brought into the comparison. But taking the roll of our chief poetical names, besides Shakespeare and Milton, from the age of Elizabeth downwards, and going through it, — Spenser, Dryden, Pope, Gray, Goldsmith, Cowper, Burns, Coleridge, Scott, Campbell, Moore, Byron, Shelley, Keats (I mention those only who are dead), — I think it certain that Wordsworth's name deserves to stand, and will finally stand, above them all. Several of the poets named have gifts and excellences which Wordsworth has not. But taking the performance of each as a whole, I say that Wordsworth seems to me to have left a body of poetical work superior in power, in interest, in the qualities which give enduring freshness, to that which any one of the others has left.

But this is not enough to say. I think it certain, further, that if we take the chief poetical names of the Continent since the death of Molière, and, omitting Goethe, confront the remaining names with that of Wordsworth, the result is the same. Let us take Klopstock, Lessing, Schiller, Uhland, Rückert, and Heine for Germany; Filicaia, Alfieri, Manzoni, and Leopardi for Italy; Racine, Boileau, Voltaire, André Chenier, Béranger, Lamartine, Musset, M. Victor Hugo (he has been so long celebrated that although he still lives I may be permitted to name him) for France. Several of these, again, have evidently gifts and excellences to which Wordsworth can make no pretension. But in real poetical achievement it seems to me indubitable that to Wordsworth, here again, belongs the palm. It seems to me that Wordsworth has left behind him a body of poetical work which wears, and will wear, better on the whole than the performance of any one of these personages, so far more brilliant and celebrated, most of them, than the homely poet of Rydal. Wordsworth's performance in poetry is on the whole, in power, in interest, in the qualities which give enduring freshness, superior to theirs.

This is a high claim to make for Wordsworth. But if it is a just claim, if Wordsworth's place among the poets who have appeared in the last two or three centuries is after Shakespeare, Molière, Milton, Goethe, indeed, but before all the rest, then in time Wordsworth will have his due. We shall recognise him in his place, as we recognise Shakespeare and Milton; and not only we ourselves shall recognise him, but he will be recognised by Europe also. Meanwhile, those who recognise him already may do well, perhaps, to ask themselves whether there are not in the case of Wordsworth certain special obstacles which hinder or delay his due recognition by others, and whether these obstacles are not in some measure removable.

The Excursion and *The Prelude,* his poems of greatest bulk, are by no means Wordsworth's best work. His best work is in his shorter pieces, and many indeed are there of these which are of first-rate excellence. But in his seven volumes the pieces of high merit are mingled with a mass of pieces very inferior to them; so inferior to them that it seems wonderful how the same poet should have produced both. Shakespeare frequently has lines and passages in a strain quite false, and which are entirely unworthy of him. But one can imagine his smiling if one could meet him in the Elysian Fields and tell him so; smiling and replying that he knew it perfectly well himself, and what did it matter? But with Wordsworth the case is different. Work altogether inferior, work quite uninspired, flat and dull, is produced by him with evident unconsciousness of its defects, and he presents it to us with the same faith and seriousness as his best work. Now a drama or an epic fill the mind, and one does not look beyond them; but in a collection of short pieces the impression made by one piece requires to be continued and sustained by the piece following. In reading Wordsworth the impression made by one of his fine pieces is too often dulled and spoiled by a very inferior piece coming after it.

Wordsworth composed verses during a space of some sixty years; and it is no exaggeration to say that within one single decade of those years, between 1798 and 1808, almost all his really first-rate work was produced. A mass of inferior work remains, work done before and after this golden prime, imbedding the first-rate work and clogging it, obstructing our approach to it, chilling, not unfrequently, the high-wrought mood with which we leave it. To be recognised far and wide as a great poet, to be possible and receivable as a classic, Wordsworth needs to be relieved of a great deal of the poetical baggage which now encumbers him. To administer this relief is indispensable, unless he is to continue to be a poet for the few only, — a poet valued far below his real worth by the world.

There is another thing. Wordsworth classified his poems not according to any commonly received plan of arrangement, but according to a scheme of mental physiology. He has poems of the fancy, poems of the imagination, poems of sentiment and reflection, and so on. His categories are ingenious but far-fetched, and the result of his employment of them is unsatisfactory. Poems are separated one from another which possess a kinship of subject or of treatment far more vital and deep than the supposed unity of mental origin, which was Wordsworth's reason for joining them with others.

The tact of the Greeks in matters of this kind was infallible. We may rely upon it that we shall not improve upon the classification adopted by the Greeks for kinds of poetry; that their categories of epic, dramatic, lyric, and so forth, have a natural propriety, and should be adhered to. It may sometimes seem doubtful to which of two categories a poem belongs; whether this or that poem is to be called, for instance, narrative or lyric, lyric or elegiac. But there is to be found in every good poem a strain, a predominant note, which determines the poem as belonging to one of these kinds rather than the other; and here is the best proof of the value of the classification, and of the advantage of adhering to it. Wordsworth's poems will never produce their due effect until they are freed from their present artificial arrangement, and grouped more naturally.

Disengaged from the quantity of inferior work which now obscures them, the best poems of Wordsworth, I hear many people say, would indeed stand out in great beauty, but they would prove to be very few in number, scarcely more than half a dozen. I maintain, on the other hand, that what strikes me with admiration, what establishes in my opinion Wordsworth's superiority, is the great and ample body of powerful work which remains to him, even after all his inferior work has been cleared away. He gives us so much to rest upon, so much which communicates his spirit and engages ours!

This is of very great importance. If it were a comparison of single pieces, or of three or four pieces, by each poet, I do not say that Wordsworth would stand decisively above Gray, or Burns, or Coleridge, or Keats, or Manzoni, or Heine. It is in his ampler body of powerful work that I find his superiority. His good work itself, his work which counts, is not all of it, of course, of equal value. Some kinds of poetry are in themselves lower kinds than others. The ballad kind is a lower kind; the didactic kind, still more, is a lower kind. Poetry of this latter sort counts, too, sometimes, by its biographical interest partly, not by its poetical interest pure and simple; but then this can only be when the poet producing it has the power and importance of Wordsworth, a power and importance which he assuredly did not establish by such didactic poetry alone. Altogether, it is, I say, by the great body of powerful and significant work which remains to him, after every reduction and deduction has been made, that Wordsworth's superiority is proved.

To exhibit this body of Wordsworth's best work, to clear away obstructions from around it, and to let it speak for itself, is what every lover of Wordsworth should desire. Until this has been done, Wordsworth, whom we, to whom he is dear, all of us know and feel to be so great a poet, has not had a fair chance before the world. When once it has been done, he will make his way best, not by our advocacy of him, but by his own worth and power. We may safely leave him to make his way thus, we who believe that a superior worth and power in poetry finds in mankind a sense responsive to it and disposed at last to recognise it. Yet at the outset, before he has been duly known and recognised, we may do Wordsworth a service, perhaps, by indicating in what his superior power and worth will be found to consist, and in what it will not.

Long ago, in speaking of Homer, I said that the noble and profound application of ideas to life is the most essential part of poetic greatness. I said that a great poet receives his distinctive character of superiority from his application, under the conditions immutably fixed by the laws of poetic beauty and poetic truth, from his application, I say, to his subject, whatever it may be, of the ideas

On man, on nature, and on human life,

which he has acquired for himself. The line quoted is Wordsworth's own; and his superiority arises from his powerful use, in his best pieces, his powerful application to his subject, of ideas "on man, on nature, and on human life."

Voltaire, with his signal acuteness, most truly remarked that "no nation has treated in poetry moral ideas with more energy and depth than the English nation." And he adds: "There, it seems to me, is the great merit of the English poets." Voltaire does not mean, by "treating in poetry moral ideas," the composing moral and didactic poems; — that brings us but a very little way in poetry. He means just the same thing as was meant when I spoke above "of the noble and profound application of ideas to life"; and he means the application of these ideas under the conditions fixed for us by the laws of poetic beauty and poetic truth. If it is said that to call these ideas *moral* ideas is to introduce a strong and injurious limitation, I answer that it is to do nothing of the kind, because moral ideas are really so main a part of human life. The question, *how to live,* is itself a moral idea; and it is the question which most interests every man, and with which, in some way or other, he is perpetually occupied. A large sense is of course to be given to the term *moral.* Whatever bears upon the question, "how to live," comes under it.

Nor love thy life, nor hate; but, what thou liv'st,
Live well; how long or short, permit to heaven.

In those fine lines Milton utters, as every one at once perceives, a moral idea. Yes, but so too, when Keats consoles the forward-bending lover on the Grecian Urn, the lover arrested and presented in immortal relief by the sculptor's hand before he can kiss, with the line,

For ever wilt thou love, and she be fair —

he utters a moral idea. When Shakespeare says, that

We are such stuff
As dreams are made of, and our little life
Is rounded with a sleep,

he utters a moral idea.

Voltaire was right in thinking that the energetic and profound treatment of moral ideas, in this large sense, is what distinguishes the English poetry. He sincerely meant praise, not dispraise or hint of limitation; and they err who suppose that poetic limitation is a necessary consequence of the fact, the fact being granted as Voltaire states it. If what distinguishes the greatest poets is their powerful and profound application of ideas to life, which surely no good critic will deny, then to prefix to the term ideas here the term moral makes hardly any difference, because human life itself is in so preponderating a degree moral.

It is important, therefore, to hold fast to this: that poetry is at bottom a criticism of life; that the greatness of a poet lies in his powerful and beautiful application of ideas to life, — to the question: How to live. Morals are often treated in a narrow and false fashion; they are bound up with systems of thought and belief which have had their day; they are fallen into the hands of pedants and professional dealers; they grow tiresome to some of us. We find attraction, at times, even in a poetry of revolt against them; in a poetry which might take for its motto Omar Khayyam's words: "Let us make up in the tavern for the time which we have wasted in the mosque." Or we find attractions in a poetry indifferent to them; in a poetry where the contents may be what they will, but where the form is studied and exquisite. We delude ourselves in either case; and the best cure for our delusion is to let our minds rest upon that great and inexhaustible word *life,* until we learn to enter into its meaning. A poetry of revolt against moral ideas is a poetry of revolt against *life;* a poetry of indifference towards moral ideas is a poetry of indifference towards *life.*

Epictetus had a happy figure for things like the play of the senses, or literary form and finish, or argumentative ingenuity, in comparison with "the best and master thing" for us, as he called it, the concern, how to live. Some people were afraid of them, he said, or they disliked and undervalued them. Such people were wrong; they were unthankful or cowardly. But the things might also be over-prized, and treated as final when they are not. They bear to life the relation which inns bear to home. "As if a man, journeying home, and finding a nice inn on the road, and liking it, were to stay for ever at the inn! Man, thou hast forgotten thine object; thy journey was not *to* this, but *through* this. 'But this inn is taking.' And how many other inns, too, are taking, and how many fields and meadows! but as places of passage merely. You have an object, which is this: to get home, to do your duty to your family, friends, and fellow-countrymen, to attain inward freedom, serenity, happiness, contentment. Style takes your fancy, arguing takes your fancy, and you forget your home and want to make your abode with them and to stay with them, on the plea that they are taking. Who denies that they are taking? but as places of passage, as inns. And when I say this, you suppose me to be attacking the care for style, the care for argument. I am not; I attack the resting in them, the not looking to the end which is beyond them."

Now, when we come across a poet like Théophile Gautier, we have a poet who has taken up his abode at an inn, and never got farther. There may be inducements to this or that one of us, at this or that moment, to find delight in him, to cleave to him; but after all, we do not change the truth about him, — we only stay ourselves in his inn along with him. And when we come across a poet like Wordsworth, who sings

> Of truth, of grandeur, beauty, love and hope.
> And melancholy fear subdued by faith,
> Of blessed consolations in distress,
> Of moral strength and intellectual power,
> Of joy in widest commonalty spread—

then we have a poet intent on "the best and master thing," and who prosecutes his journey home. We say, for brevity's sake, that he deals with *life,* because he deals with that in which life really consists. This is what Voltaire means to praise in the English poets, — this dealing with what is really life. But always it is the mark of the greatest poets that they deal with it; and to say that the English poets are remarkable for dealing with it, is only another way of saying, what is true, that in poetry the English genius has especially shown its power.

Wordsworth deals with it, and his greatness lies in his dealing with it so powerfully. I have named a number of celebrated poets above all of whom he, in my opinion, deserves to be placed. He is to be placed above poets like Voltaire, Dryden, Pope, Lessing, Schiller, because these famous personages, with a thousand gifts and merits, never, or scarcely ever, attain the distinctive accent and utterance of the high and genuine poets —

> Quique pii vates et Phœbo digna locuti,

at all. Burns, Keats, Heine, not to speak of others in our list, have this accent; — who can doubt it? And at the same time they have treasures of humour, felicity, passion, for which in Wordsworth we shall look in vain. Where, then, is Wordsworth's superiority? It is here; he deals with more of *life* than they do; he deals with *life,* as a whole, more powerfully.

No Wordsworthian will doubt this. Nay, the fervent Wordsworthian will add, as Mr. Leslie Stephen does, that Wordsworth's poetry is precious because his philosophy is sound; that his "ethical system is as distinctive and capable of exposition as Bishop Butler's"; that his poetry is informed by ideas which "fall spontaneously into a scientific system of thought." But we must be on our guard against the Wordsworthians, if we want to secure for Wordsworth his due rank as a poet. The Wordsworthians are apt to praise him for the wrong things, and to lay far too much stress upon what they call his philosophy. His poetry is the reality, his philosophy, — so far, at least, as it may put on the form and habit of "a scientific system of thought," and the more that it puts them on, — is the illusion. Perhaps we shall one day learn to make this proposition general, and to say: Poetry is the reality, philosophy the illusion. But in Wordsworth's case, at any rate, we cannot do him justice until we dismiss his formal philosophy.

The Excursion abounds with philosophy, and therefore *The Excursion* is to the Wordsworthian what it never can be to the disinterested lover of poetry, — a satisfactory work. "Duty exists," says Wordsworth, in *The Excursion;* and then he proceeds thus —

> . . . Immutably survive,
> For our support, the measures and the forms,
> Which an abstract Intelligence supplies,
> Whose kingdom is, where time and space are not.

And the Wordsworthian is delighted, and thinks that here is a sweet union of philosophy and poetry. But the disinterested lover of poetry will feel that the lines carry us really not a step farther than the proposition which they would interpret; that they are a tissue of elevated but abstract verbiage, alien to the very nature of poetry.

Or let us come direct to the centre of Wordsworth's philosophy, as "an ethical system, as distinctive and capable of systematical exposition as Bishop Butler's" —

> . . . One adequate support
> For the calamities of mortal life
> Exists, one only; — an assured belief
> That the procession of our fate, howe'er
> Sad or disturbed, is ordered by a Being
> Of infinite benevolence and power;
> Whose everlasting purposes embrace
> All accidents, converting them to good.

That is doctrine such as we hear in church too, religious and philosophic doctrine; and the attached Wordsworthian loves passages of such doctrine, and brings them forward in proof of his poet's excellence. But however true the doctrine may be, it has, as here presented, none of the characters of *poetic* truth, the kind of truth which we require from a poet, and in which Wordsworth is really strong.

Even the "intimations" of the famous "Ode," those corner-stones of the supposed philosophic system of Wordsworth, — the idea of the high instincts and affections coming out in childhood, testifying of a divine home recently left, and fading away as our life proceeds, —

this idea, of undeniable beauty as a play of fancy, has itself not the character of poetic truth of the best kind; it has no real solidity. The instinct of delight in Nature and her beauty had no doubt extraordinary strength in Wordsworth himself as a child. But to say that universally this instinct is mighty in childhood, and tends to die away afterwards, is to say what is extremely doubtful. In many people, perhaps with the majority of educated persons, the love of nature is nearly imperceptible at ten years old, but strong and operative at thirty. In general we may say of these high instincts of early childhood, the base of the alleged systematic philosophy of Wordsworth, what Thucydides says of the early achievements of the Greek race: "It is impossible to speak with certainty of what is so remote; but from all that we can really investigate, I should say that they were no very great things."

Finally, the "scientific system of thought" in Wordsworth gives us at last such poetry as this, which the devout Wordsworthian accepts —

> O for the coming of that glorious time
> When, prizing knowledge as her noblest wealth
> And best protection, this Imperial Realm,
> While she exacts allegiance, shall admit
> An obligation, on her part, to *teach*
> Them who are born to serve her and obey;
> Binding herself by statute to secure,
> For all the children whom her soil maintains,
> The rudiments of letters, and inform
> The mind with moral and religious truth.

Wordsworth calls Voltaire dull, and surely the production of these un-Voltairian lines must have been imposed on him as a judgment! One can hear them being quoted at a Social Science Congress; one can call up the whole scene. A great room in one of our dismal provincial towns; dusty air and jaded afternoon daylight; benches full of men with bald heads and women in spectacles; an orator lifting up his face from a manuscript written within and without to declaim these lines of Wordsworth; and in the soul of any poor child of nature who may have wandered in thither, an unutterable sense of lamentation, and mourning, and woe!

"But turn we," as Wordsworth says, "from these bold, bad men," the haunters of Social Science Congresses. And let us be on our guard, too, against the exhibitors and extollers of a "scientific system of thought" in Wordsworth's poetry. The poetry will never be seen aright while they thus exhibit it. The cause of its greatness is simple, and may be told quite simply. Wordsworth's poetry is great because of the extraordinary power with which Wordsworth feels the joy offered to us in nature, the joy offered to us in the simple primary affections and duties; and because of the extraordinary power with which, in case after case, he shows us this joy, and renders it so as to make us share it.

The source of joy from which he thus draws is the truest and most unfailing source of joy accessible to man. It is also accessible universally. Wordsworth brings us word, therefore, according to his own strong and characteristic line, he brings us word

Of joy in widest commonalty spread.

Here is an immense advantage for a poet. Wordsworth tells of what all seek, and tells of it at its truest and best source, and yet a source where all may go and draw for it.

Nevertheless, we are not to suppose that everything is precious which Wordsworth, standing even at this perennial and beautiful source, may give us. Wordsworthians are apt to talk as if it must be. They will speak with the same reverence of "The Sailor's Mother," for example, as of "Lucy Gray." They do their master harm by such lack of discrimination. "Lucy Gray" is a beautiful success; "The Sailor's Mother" is a failure. To give aright what he wishes to give, to interpret and render successfully, is not always within Wordsworth's own command. It is within no poet's command; here is the part of the Muse, the inspiration, the God, the "not ourselves." In Wordsworth's case, the accident, for so it may almost be called, of inspiration, is of peculiar importance. No poet, perhaps, is so evidently filled with a new and sacred energy when the inspiration is upon him; no poet, when it fails him, is so left "weak as is a breaking wave." I remember hearing him say that Goethe's poetry was not inevitable enough." The remark is striking and true; no line in Goethe, as Goethe said himself, but its maker knew well how it came there. Wordsworth is right, Goethe's poetry is not inevitable; not inevitable enough. But Wordsworth's poetry, when he is at his best, is inevitable, as inevitable as Nature herself. It might seem that Nature not only gave him the matter for his poem, but wrote his poem for him. He has no style. He was too conversant with Milton not to catch at times his master's manner, and he has fine Miltonic lines; but he has no assured poetic style of his own, like Milton. When he seeks to have a style he falls into ponderosity and pomposity. In *The Excursion* we have his style, as an artistic product of his own creation; and although Jeffrey completely failed to recognise Wordsworth's real greatness, he was yet not wrong in saying of *The Excursion,* as a work of poetic style: "This will never do." And yet magical as is that power, which Wordsworth has not, of assured and possessed poetic style, he has something which is an equivalent for it.

Every one who has any sense for these things feels the subtle turn, the heightening, which is given to a poet's verse by his genius for style. We can feel it in the

> After life's fitful fever, he sleeps well —

of Shakespeare; in the

> . . . though fall'n on evil days,
> On evil days though fall'n, and evil tongues —

of Milton. It is the incomparable charm of Milton's power of poetic style which gives such worth to *Paradise Regained,* and makes a great poem of a work in which Milton's imagination does not soar high. Wordsworth has in constant possession, and at command, no style of this kind; but he had too poetic a nature, and had read the great poets too well, not to catch, as I have already remarked, something of it occasionally. We find it not only in his Miltonic lines; we find it in such a phrase as this, where the manner is his own, not Milton's —

> . . . the fierce confederate storm
> Of sorrow barricadoed evermore
> Within the walls of cities;

although even here, perhaps, the power of style, which is undeniable, is more properly that of eloquent prose than the subtle heightening and change wrought by genuine poetic style. It is style, again, and the elevation given by style, which chiefly makes the effectiveness of "Laodameia." Still the right sort of verse to choose from Wordsworth, if we are to seize his true and most characteristic form of expression, is a line like this from "Michael" —

> And never lifted up a single stone.

There is nothing subtle in it, no heightening, no study of poetic style, strictly so called, at all; yet it is expression of the highest and most truly expressive kind.

Wordsworth owed much to Burns, and a style of perfect plainness, relying for effect solely on the weight and force of that which with entire fidelity it utters, Burns could show him.

> The poor inhabitant below
> Was quick to learn and wise to know,
> And keenly felt the friendly glow
> And softer flame;
> But thoughtless follies laid him low
> And stain'd his name.

Every one will be conscious of a likeness here to Wordsworth; and if Wordsworth did great things with this nobly plain manner, we must remember, what indeed he himself would always have been forward to acknowledge, that Burns used it before him.

Still Wordsworth's use of it has something unique and unmatchable. Nature herself seems, I say, to take the pen out of his hand, and to write for him with her own bare, sheer, penetrating power. This arises from two causes; from the profound sincereness with which Wordsworth feels his subject, and also from the profoundly sincere and natural character of his subject itself. He can and will treat such a subject with nothing but the most plain, first-hand, almost austere naturalness. His expression may often be called bald, as, for instance, in the poem of "Resolution and Independence"; but it is bald as the bare mountain tops are bald, with a baldness which is full of grandeur.

Wherever we meet with the successful balance, in Wordsworth, of profound truth of subject with profound truth of execution, he is unique. His best poems are those which most perfectly exhibit this balance. I have a warm admiration for "Laodameia" and for the great "Ode"; but if I am to tell the very truth, I find "Laodameia" not wholly free from something artificial, and the great "Ode" not wholly free from something declamatory. If I had to pick out poems of a kind most perfectly to show Wordsworth's unique power, I should rather choose poems such as "Michael," "The Fountain," "The Highland Reaper." And poems with the peculiar and unique beauty which distinguishes these, Wordsworth produced in considerable number; besides very many other poems of which the worth, although not so rare as the worth of these, is still exceedingly high.

On the whole, then, as I said at the beginning, not only is Wordsworth eminent by reason of the goodness of his best work, but he is eminent also by reason of the great body of good work which he has left to us. With the ancients I will not compare him. In many respects the ancients are far above us, and yet there is something that we demand which they can never give. Leaving the ancients, let us come to the poets and poetry of Christendom. Dante, Shakespeare, Molière, Milton, Goethe, are altogether larger and more splendid luminaries in the poetical heaven than Wordsworth. But I know not where else, among the moderns, we are to find his superiors.

To disengage the poems which show his power, and to present them to the English-speaking public and to the world, is the object of this volume. I by no means say that it contains all which in Wordsworth's poems is interesting. Except in the case of "Margaret," a story composed separately from the rest of *The Excursion*, and which belongs to a different part of England, I have not ventured on detaching portions of poems, or on giving any piece otherwise than as Wordsworth himself gave it. But under the conditions imposed by this reserve, the volume contains, I think, everything, or nearly everything, which may best serve him with the majority of lovers of poetry, nothing which may disserve him.

I have spoken lightly of Wordsworthians; and if we are to get Wordsworth recognised by the public and by the world, we must recommend him not in the spirit of a clique, but in the spirit of disinterested lovers of poetry. But I am a Wordsworthian myself. I can read with pleasure and edification "Peter Bell," and the whole series of *Ecclesiastical Sonnets,* and the address to Mr. Wilkinson's spade, and even the "Thanksgiving Ode"; — everything of Wordsworth, I think, except "Vaudracour and Julia." It is not for nothing that one has been brought up in the veneration of a man so truly worthy of homage; that one has seen him and heard him, lived in his neighbourhood, and been familiar with his country. No Wordsworthian has a tenderer affection for this pure and sage master than I, or is less really offended by his defects. But Wordsworth is something more than the pure and sage master of a small band of devoted followers, and we ought not to rest satisfied until he is seen to be what he is. He is one of the very chief glories of English Poetry; and by nothing is England so glorious as by her poetry. Let us lay aside every weight which hinders our getting him recognised as this, and let our one study be to bring to pass, as widely as possible and as truly as possible, his own word concerning his poems: "They will co-operate with the benign tendencies in human nature and society, and will, in their degree, be efficacious in making men wiser, better, and happier."

BYRON

When at last I held in my hand the volume of poems which I had chosen from Wordsworth, and began to turn over its pages, there arose in me almost immediately the desire to see beside it, as a companion volume, a like collection of the best poetry of Byron. Alone amongst our poets of the earlier part of this century, Byron and Wordsworth not only furnish material enough for a volume of this kind, but also, as it seems to me, they both of them gain considerably by being thus exhibited. There are poems of Coleridge and of Keats equal, if not superior, to anything of Byron or Wordsworth; but a dozen pages or two will contain them, and the remaining poetry is of a quality much inferior. Scott never, I think, rises as a poet to the level of Byron and Wordsworth at all. On the other hand, he never falls below his own usual level very far; and by a volume of selections from him, therefore, his effectiveness is not increased. As to Shelley there will be more question; and indeed Mr. Stopford Brooke, whose accomplishments, eloquence, and love of poetry we must all recognise and admire, has actually given us Shelley in such a volume. But for my own part I cannot think that Shelley's poetry, except by snatches and fragments, has the value of the good work of Wordsworth and Byron; or that it is possible for even Mr. Stopford Brooke to make up a volume of selections from him which, for real substance, power, and worth, can at all take rank with a like volume from Byron or Wordsworth.

Shelley knew quite well the difference between the achievement of such a poet as Byron and his own. He praises Byron too unreservedly, but he sincerely felt, and he was right in feeling, that Byron was a greater poetical power than himself. As a man, Shelley is at a number of points immeasurably Byron's superior; he is a beautiful and enchanting spirit, whose vision, when we call it up, has far more loveliness, more charm for our soul, than the vision of Byron. But all the personal charm of Shelley cannot hinder us from at last discovering in his poetry the incurable want, in general, of a sound subject-matter, and the incurable fault, in consequence, of unsubstantiality. Those who extol him as the poet of clouds, the poet of sunsets, are only saying that he did not, in fact, lay hold upon the poet's right subject-matter; and in honest truth, with all his charm of soul and spirit, and with all his gift of musical diction and movement, he never, or hardly ever, did. Except, as I have said, for a few short things and single stanzas, his original poetry is less satisfactory than his translations, for in these the subject-matter was found for him. Nay, I doubt whether his delightful Essays and Letters, which deserve to be far more read than they are now, will not resist the wear and tear of time better, and finally come to stand higher, than his poetry.

There remain to be considered Byron and Wordsworth. That Wordsworth affords good material for a volume of selections, and that he gains by having his poetry thus presented, is an old belief of mine which led me lately to make up a volume of poems chosen out of Wordsworth, and to bring it before the public. By its kind reception of the volume, the public seems to show itself a partaker in my belief. Now Byron also supplies plenty of material for a like volume, and he too gains, I think, by being so presented. Mr. Swinburne urges, indeed, that "Byron, who rarely wrote anything either worthless or faultless, can only be judged or appreciated in the mass; the greatest of his works was his whole work taken together." It is quite true that Byron rarely wrote anything either worthless or faultless; it is quite true also that in the appreciation of Byron's power a sense of the amount and variety of his work, defective though much of his work is, enters justly into our estimate. But although there may be little in Byron's poetry which can be pronounced either worthless or faultless, there are portions of it which are far higher in worth and far more free from fault than others. And although, again, the abundance and variety of his production is undoubtedly a proof of his power, yet I question whether by reading everything which he gives us we are so likely to acquire an admiring sense even of his variety and abundance, as by reading what he gives us at his happier moments. Varied and abundant he amply proves himself even by this taken alone. Receive him absolutely without omission or compression, follow his whole outpouring stanza by stanza and line by line from the very commencement to the very end, and he is capable of being tiresome.

Byron has told us himself that *The Giaour* "is but a string of passages." He has made full confession of his own negligence. "No one," says he, "has done more through negligence to corrupt the language." This accusation brought by himself against his poems is not just; but when he goes on to say of them, that "their faults, whatever they may be, are those of negligence and not of labour," he says what is perfectly true. "*Lara,*" he declares, "I wrote while undressing after coming home from balls and masquerades, in the year of revelry, 1814. The *Bride* was written in four, *The Corsair* in ten days." He calls this "a humiliating confession, as it proves my own want of judgment in publishing, and the public's in reading, things which cannot have stamina for permanence." Again he does his poems injustice; the producer of such poems could not but publish them, the public could not but read them. Nor could Byron have produced his work in any other fashion; his poetic work could not have first grown and matured in his own mind, and then come forth as an organic whole; Byron had not enough of the artist in him for this, nor enough of self-command. He wrote, as he truly tells us, to relieve himself, and he went on writing because he found the relief become indispensable. But it was inevitable that works so produced should be, in general, "a string of passages," poured out, as he describes them, with rapidity and excitement, and with new passages constantly suggesting themselves, and added while his work was going through the press. It is evident that we have here neither deliberate scientific construction, nor yet the instinctive artistic creation of poetic wholes; and that to take passages from work produced as Byron's was is a very different thing from taking passages out of the *Oedipus* or *The Tempest,* and deprives the poetry far less of its advantage.

Nay, it gives advantage to the poetry, instead of depriving it of any. Byron, I said, has not a great artist's profound and patient skill in combining an action or in developing a character, — a skill which we must watch and follow if we are to do justice to it. But he has a wonderful power of vividly conceiving a single incident, a single situation; of throwing himself upon it, grasping it as if it were real and he saw and felt it, and of making us see and feel it too. *The Giaour* is, as he truly called it, "a string of passages," not a work moving by a deep internal law of development to a necessary end; and our total impression from it cannot but receive from this, its inherent defect, a certain dimness and indistinctness. But the incidents of the journey and death of Hassan, in that poem, are conceived and presented with a vividness not to be surpassed; and our impression from them is correspondingly clear and powerful. In *Lara,* again, there is no adequate development either of the character of the chief personage or of the action of the poem; our total impression from the work is a confused one. Yet such an incident as the disposal of the slain Ezzelin's body passes before our eyes as if we actually saw it. And in the same way as these bursts of incident, bursts of sentiment also, living and vigorous, often occur in the midst of poems which must be admitted to be but weakly conceived and loosely combined wholes. Byron cannot but be a gainer by having attention concentrated upon what is vivid, powerful, effective in his work, and withdrawn from what is not so.

Byron, I say, cannot but be a gainer by this, just as Wordsworth is a gainer by a like proceeding. I esteem Wordsworth's poetry so highly, and the world, in my opinion, has done it such scant justice, that I could not rest satisfied until I had fulfilled, on Wordsworth's behalf, a long-cherished desire; — had disengaged, to the best of my power, his good work from the inferior work joined with it, and had placed before the public the body of his good work by itself. To the poetry of Byron the world has ardently paid homage; full justice from his contemporaries, perhaps even more than justice, his torrent of poetry received. His poetry was admired, adored, "with all its imperfections on its head," — in spite of negligence, in spite of diffuseness, in spite of repetitions, in spite of whatever faults it possessed. His name is still great and brilliant. Nevertheless the hour of irresistible vogue has passed away for him; even for Byron it could not but pass away. The time has come for him, as it comes for all poets, when he must take his real and permanent place, no longer depending upon the vogue of his own day and upon the enthusiasm of his contemporaries. Whatever we may think of him, we shall not be subjugated by him as they were; for, as he cannot be for us what he was for them, we cannot admire him so hotly and indiscriminately as they. His faults of negligence, of diffuseness, of repetition, his faults of whatever kind, we shall abundantly feel and unsparingly criticise; the mere interval of time between us and him makes disillusion of this kind inevitable. But how then will Byron stand, if we relieve him too, so far as we can, of the encumbrance of his inferior and weakest work, and if we bring before us his best and strongest work in one body together? That is the question which I, who can even remember the latter years of Byron's vogue, and have myself felt the expiring wave of that mighty influence, but who certainly also regard him, and have long regarded him, without illusion, cannot but ask myself, cannot but seek to answer. The present volume is an attempt to provide adequate data for answering it.

Byron has been over-praised, no doubt. "Byron is one of our French superstitions," says M. Edmond Scherer; but where has Byron not been a superstition? He pays now the penalty of this exaggerated worship. "Alone among the English poets his contemporaries, Byron," said M. Taine, "*atteint à la cîme,* — gets to the top of the poetic mountain." But the idol that M. Taine had thus adored M. Scherer is almost for burning. "In Byron," he declares, "there is a remarkable inability ever to lift himself into the region of real poetic art, — art impersonal and disinterested, — at all. He has fecundity, eloquence, wit, but even these qualities themselves are confined within somewhat narrow limits. He has treated hardly any subject but one, — himself; now the man, in Byron, is of a nature even less sincere than the poet. This beautiful and blighted being is at bottom a coxcomb. He posed all his life long."

Our poet could not well meet with more severe and unsympathetic criticism. However, the praise often given to Byron has been so exaggerated as to provoke, perhaps, a reaction in which he is unduly disparaged. "As various in composition as Shakespeare himself, Lord Byron has embraced," says Sir Walter Scott, "every topic of human life, and sounded every string on the divine harp, from its slightest to its most powerful and heart-astounding tones." It is not surprising that some one with a cool head should retaliate, on such provocation as this, by saying: "He has treated hardly any subject but one, *himself.*" "In the very grand and tremendous drama of *Cain,*" says Scott, "Lord Byron has certainly matched Milton on his own ground." And Lord Byron has done all this, Scott adds, "while managing his pen with the careless and negligent ease of a man of quality." Alas, "managing his pen with the careless and negligent ease of a man of quality," Byron wrote in his *Cain* —

> Souls that dare look the Omnipotent tyrant in
> His everlasting face, and tell him that
> His evil is not good;

or he wrote —

> . . . And *thou* would'st go on aspiring
> To the great double Mysteries! the *two Principles!*[1]

One has only to repeat to oneself a line from *Paradise Lost* in order to feel the difference.

Sainte-Beuve, speaking of that exquisite master of language, the Italian poet Leopardi, remarks how often we see the alliance, singular though it may at first sight appear, of the poetical genius with the genius for scholarship and philology. Dante and Milton are instances which will occur to every one's mind. Byron is so negligent in his poetical style, he is often, to say the truth, so slovenly, slipshod, and infelicitous, he is so little haunted by the true artist's fine passion for the correct use and consummate management of words, that he may be described as having for this artistic gift the insensibility of the barbarian; — which is perhaps only another and a less flattering way of saying, with Scott, that he "manages his pen with the careless and negligent ease of a man of quality." Just of a piece with the rhythm of

> Dare you await the event of a few minutes'
> Deliberation?

or of

> All shall be void —
> Destroy'd!

[1] The italics are in the original.

is the diction of

> Which now is painful to these eyes,
> Which have not seen the sun to rise;

or of

> . . . there let him lay!

or of the famous passage beginning

> He who hath bent him o'er the dead;

with those trailing relatives, that crying grammatical solecism, that inextricable anacolouthon! To class the work of the author of such things with the work of the authors of such verse as

> In the dark backward and abysm of time —

or as

> Presenting Thebes, or Pelops' line,
> Or the tale of Troy divine —

is ridiculous. Shakespeare and Milton, with their secret of consummate felicity in diction and movement, are of another and an altogether higher order from Byron, nay, for that matter, from Wordsworth also; from the author of such verse as

> Sol hath dropt into his harbour —

or (if Mr. Ruskin pleases) as

> Parching summer hath no warrant —

as from the author of

> All shall be void —
> Destroy'd!

With a poetical gift and a poetical performance of the very highest order, the slovenliness and tunelessness of much of Byron's production, the pompousness and ponderousness of much of Wordsworth's are incompatible. Let us admit this to the full.

Moreover, while we are hearkening to M. Scherer, and going along with him in his fault-finding, let us admit, too, that the man in Byron is in many respects as unsatisfactory as the poet. And, putting aside all direct moral criticism of him, — with which we need not concern ourselves here, — we shall find that he is unsatisfactory in the same way. Some of Byron's most crying faults as a man, — his vulgarity, his affectation, — are really akin to the faults of commonness, of want of art, in his workmanship as a poet. The ideal nature for the poet and artist is that of the finely touched and finely gifted man, the εὐφυής of the Greeks; now, Byron's nature was in substance not that of the εὐφυής at all, but rather, as I have said, of the barbarian. The want of fine perception which made it possible for him to formulate either the comparison between himself and Rousseau, or his reason for getting Lord Delawarr excused from a "licking" at Harrow, is exactly what made possible for him also his terrible dealings in, *An ye wool; I have redde thee; Sunburn me; Oons, and it is excellent well.* It is exactly, again, what made possible for him his precious dictum that Pope is a Greek temple, and a string of other criticisms of the like force; it is exactly, in fine, what deteriorated the quality of his poetic production. If we think of a good representative of that finely touched and exquisitely gifted nature which is the ideal nature for the poet and artist, — if we think of Raphael, for instance, who truly is εὐφυής just as Byron is not, — we shall bring into clearer light the connection in Byron between the faults of the man and the faults of the poet. With Raphael's character Byron's sins of vulgarity and false criticism would have been impossible, just as with Raphael's art Byron's sins of common and bad workmanship.

Yes, all this is true, but it is not the whole truth about Byron nevertheless; very far from it. The severe criticism of M. Scherer by no means gives us the whole truth about Byron, and we have not yet got it in what has been added to that criticism here. The negative part of the true criticism of him we perhaps have; the positive part, by far the more important, we have not. Byron's admirers appeal eagerly to foreign testimonies in his favour. Some of these testimonies do not much move me; but one testimony there is among them which will always carry, with me at any rate, very great weight, — the testimony of Goethe. Goethe's sayings about Byron were uttered, it must however be remembered, at the height of Byron's vogue, when that puissant and splendid personality was exercising its full power of attraction. In Goethe's own household there was an atmosphere of glowing Byron-worship; his daughter-in-law was a passionate admirer of Byron, nay, she enjoyed and prized his poetry, as did Tieck and so many others in Germany at that time, much above the poetry of Goethe himself. Instead of being irritated and rendered jealous by this, a nature like Goethe's was inevitably led by it to heighten, not lower, the note of his praise. The Time-Spirit, or *Zeit-Geist,* he would himself have said, was working just then for Byron. This working of the *Zeit-Geist* in his favour was an advantage added to Byron's other advantages, an advantage of which he had a right to get the benefit. This is what Goethe would have thought and said to himself; and so he would have been led even to heighten somewhat his estimate of Byron, and to accentuate the emphasis of praise. Goethe speaking of Byron at that moment was not and could not be quite the same cool critic as Goethe speaking of Dante, or Molière, or Milton. This, I say, we ought to remember in reading Goethe's judgments on Byron and his poetry. Still, if we are careful to bear this in mind, and if we quote Goethe's praise correctly, — which is not always done by those who in this country quote it, — and if we add to it that great and due qualification added to it by Goethe himself, — which so far as I have seen has never yet been done by his quoters in this country at all, — then we shall have a judgment on Byron, which comes, I think, very near to the truth, and which may well command our adherence.

In his judicious and interesting *Life of Byron*, Professor Nichol quotes Goethe as saying that Byron "is undoubtedly to be regarded as the greatest genius of our century." What Goethe did really say was "the greatest *talent*," not "the greatest *genius*." The difference is important, because, while talent gives the notion of power in a man's performance, genius gives rather the notion of felicity and perfection in it; and this divine gift of consummate felicity by no means, as we have seen, belongs to Byron and to his poetry. Goethe said that Byron "must unquestionably be regarded as the greatest talent of the century."[1] He said of him moreover: "The English may think of Byron what they please, but it is certain that they can point to no poet who is his like. He is different from all the rest, and in the main greater." Here, again, Professor Nichol translates: "They can show no (living) poet who is to be compared to him"; — inserting the word *living*, I suppose, to prevent its being thought that Goethe would have ranked Byron, as a poet, above Shakespeare and Milton. But Goethe did not use, or, I think, mean to imply, any limitation such as is added by Professor Nichol. Goethe said simply, and he meant to say, "*no* poet." Only the words which follow[2] ought not, I think, to be rendered, "who is to be compared to him," that is to say, "*who is his equal as a poet.*" They mean rather, "who may properly be compared with him," "*who is his parallel.*" And when Goethe said that Byron was "in the main greater" than all the rest of the English poets, he was not so much thinking of the strict rank, as poetry, of Byron's production; he was thinking of that wonderful personality of Byron which so enters into his poetry, and which Goethe called "a personality such, for its eminence, as has never been yet, and such as is not likely to come again." He was thinking of that "daring, dash, and grandi-

1 "Der ohne Frage als das grösste Talent des Jahrhunderts anzusehen ist."
2 "Der ihm zu vergleichen wäre."

osity,"[1] of Byron, which are indeed so splendid; and which were, so Goethe maintained, of a character to do good, because "everything great is formative," and what is thus formative does us good.

The faults which went with this greatness, and which impaired Byron's poetical work, Goethe saw very well. He saw the constant state of warfare and combat, the "negative and polemical working," which makes Byron's poetry a poetry in which we can so little find rest; he saw the *Hang zum Unbegrenzten*, the straining after the unlimited, which made it impossible for Byron to produce poetic wholes such as *The Tempest* or *Lear;* he saw the *zu viel Empirie*, the promiscuous adoption of all the matter offered to the poet by life, just as it was offered, without thought or patience for the mysterious transmutation to be operated on this matter by poetic form. But in a sentence which I cannot, as I say, remember to have yet seen quoted in any English criticism of Byron, Goethe lays his finger on the cause of all these defects in Byron, and on his real source of weakness both as a man and as a poet. "The moment he reflects, he is a child," says Goethe; "*sobald er reflektiert ist er ein Kind.*"

Now if we take the two parts of Goethe's criticism of Byron, the favourable and the unfavourable, and put them together, we shall have, I think, the truth. On the one hand, a splendid and puissant personality — a personality "in eminence such as has never been yet, and is not likely to come again"; of which the like, therefore, is not to be found among the poets of our nation, by which Byron "is different from all the rest, and in the main greater." Byron is, moreover, "the greatest talent of our century." On the other hand, this splendid personality and unmatched talent, this unique Byron, "is quite too much in the dark about himself";[2] nay, "the moment he begins to reflect, he is a child." There we have, I think, Byron complete; and in estimating him and ranking him we have to strike a balance between the gain which accrues to his poetry, as compared with the productions of other poets, from his superiority, and the loss which accrues to it from his defects.

A balance of this kind has to be struck in the case of all poets except the few supreme masters in whom a profound criticism of life exhibits itself in indissoluble connection with the laws of poetic truth and beauty. I have seen it said that I allege poetry to have for its characteristic this: that it is a criticism of life; and that I make it to be thereby distinguished from prose, which is something else. So far from it, that when I first used this expression, *a criticism of life*, now

[1] "Byron's Kühnheit, Keckheit und Grandiosität, ist das nicht alles bildend? — Alles Grosse bildet, sobald wir es gewahr werden."

[2] "Gar zu dunkel über sich selbst."

many years ago, it was to literature in general that I applied it, and not to poetry in especial. "The end and aim of all literature," I said, "is, if one considers it attentively, nothing but that: *a criticism of life.*" And so it surely is; the main end and aim of all our utterance, whether in prose or in verse, is surely a criticism of life. We are not brought much on our way, I admit, towards an adequate definition of poetry as distinguished from prose by that truth; still a truth it is, and poetry can never prosper if it is forgotten. In poetry, however, the criticism of life has to be made conformably to the laws of poetic truth and poetic beauty. Truth and seriousness of substance and matter, felicity and perfection of diction and manner, as these are exhibited in the best poets, are what constitute a criticism of life made in conformity with the laws of poetic truth and poetic beauty; and it is by knowing and feeling the work of those poets, that we learn to recognise the fulfilment and non-fulfilment of such conditions.

The moment, however, that we leave the small band of the very best poets, the true classics, and deal with poets of the next rank, we shall find that perfect truth and seriousness of matter, in close alliance with perfect truth and felicity of manner, is the rule no longer. We have now to take what we can get, to forego something here, to admit compensation for it there; to strike a balance, and to see how our poets stand in respect to one another when that balance has been struck. Let us observe how this is so.

We will take three poets, among the most considerable of our century: Leopardi, Byron, Wordsworth. Giacomo Leopardi was ten years younger than Byron, and he died thirteen years after him; both of them, therefore, died young — Byron at the age of thirty-six, Leopardi at the age of thirty-nine. Both of them were of noble birth, both of them suffered from physical defect, both of them were in revolt against the established facts and beliefs of their age; but here the likeness between them ends. The stricken poet of Recanati had no country, for an Italy in his day did not exist; he had no audience, no celebrity. The volume of his poems, published in the very year of Byron's death, hardly sold, I suppose, its tens, while the volumes of Byron's poetry were selling their tens of thousands. And yet Leopardi has the very qualities which we have found wanting to Byron; he has the sense for form and style, the passion for just expression, the sure and firm touch of the true artist. Nay, more, he has a grave fulness of knowledge, an insight into the real bearings of the questions which as a sceptical poet he raises, a power of seizing the real point, a lucidity, with which the author of *Cain* has nothing to compare. I can hardly imagine Leopardi reading the

> . . . And *thou* would'st go on aspiring
> To the great double Mysteries! the *two Principles!*

or following Byron in his theological controversy with Dr. Kennedy, without having his features overspread by a calm and fine smile, and remarking of his brilliant contemporary, as Goethe did, that "the moment he begins to reflect, he is a child." But indeed whoever wishes to feel the full superiority of Leopardi over Byron in philosophic thought, and in the expression of it, has only to read one paragraph of one poem, the paragraph of *La Ginestra,* beginning

> Sovente in queste piagge,

and ending

> Non so se il riso o la pietà prevale.

In like manner, Leopardi is at many points the poetic superior of Wordsworth too. He has a far wider culture than Wordsworth, more mental lucidity, more freedom from illusions as to the real character of the established fact and of reigning conventions; above all, this Italian, with his pure and sure touch, with his fineness of perception, is far more of the artist. Such a piece of pompous dulness as

> O for the coming of that glorious time,

and all the rest of it, or such lumbering verse as Mr. Ruskin's enemy,

> Parching summer hath no warrant —

would have been as impossible to Leopardi as to Dante. Where, then, is Wordsworth's superiority? for the worth of what he has given us in poetry I hold to be greater, on the whole, than the worth of what Leopardi has given us. It is in Wordsworth's sound and profound sense

> Of joy in widest commonalty spread;

whereas Leopardi remains with his thoughts ever fixed upon the *essenza insanabile,* upon the *acerbo, indegno mistero delle cose.* It is in the power with which Wordsworth feels the resources of joy offered to us in nature, offered to us in the primary human affections and duties, and in the power with which, in his moments of inspiration, he renders this joy, and makes us, too, feel it; a force greater than himself seeming to lift him and to prompt his tongue, so that he speaks in a style far above any style of which he has the constant command, and with a truth far beyond any philosophic truth of which he has the conscious and assured possession. Neither Leopardi nor Wordsworth are of the same order with the great poets who made such verse as

> Τλητὸν γὰρ Μοῖραι θυμὸν θέσαν ἀνθρώποισιν·

or as

> In la sua volontade è nostra pace;

or as

> . . . Men must endure
> Their going hence, even as their coming hither;
> Ripeness is all.

But as compared with Leopardi, Wordsworth, though at many points less lucid, though far less a master of style, far less of an artist, gains so much by his criticism of life being, in certain matters of profound importance, healthful and true, whereas Leopardi's pessimism is not, that the value of Wordsworth's poetry, on the whole, stands higher for us than that of Leopardi's, as it stands higher for us, I think, than that of any modern poetry except Goethe's.

Byron's poetic value is also greater, on the whole, than Leopardi's; and his superiority turns in the same way upon the surpassing worth of something which he had and was, after all deduction has been made for his shortcomings. We talk of Byron's *personality,* "a personality in eminence such as has never been yet, and is not likely to come again"; and we say that by this personality Byron is "different from all the rest of English poets, and in the main greater." But can we not be a little more circumstantial, and name that in which the wonderful power of this personality consisted? We can; with the instinct of a poet Mr. Swinburne has seized upon it and named it for us. The power of Byron's personality lies in "the splendid and imperishable excellence which covers all his offences and outweighs all his defects: *the excellence of sincerity and strength.*"

Byron found our nation, after its long and victorious struggle with revolutionary France, fixed in a system of established facts and dominant ideas which revolted him. The mental bondage of the most powerful part of our nation, of its strong middle class, to a narrow and false system of this kind, is what we call British Philistinism. That bondage is unbroken to this hour, but in Byron's time it was even far more deep and dark than it is now. Byron was an aristocrat, and it is not difficult for an aristocrat to look on the prejudices and habits of the British Philistine with scepticism and disdain. Plenty of young men of his own class Byron met at Almack's or at Lady Jersey's, who regarded the established facts and reigning beliefs of the England of that day with as little reverence as he did. But these men, disbelievers in British Philistinism in private, entered English public life, the most conventional in the world, and at once they saluted with respect the habits and ideas of British Philistinism as if they were a part of the order of creation, and as if in public no sane man would think of warring against them. With Byron it was different. What he called the *cant* of the great middle part of the English nation, what we call its Philistinism, revolted him; but the cant of his own class, deferring to this Philistinism and profiting by it, while they disbelieved in it, revolted him even more. "Come what may," are his own words, "I will never flatter the million's canting in any shape." His class in general, on the other hand, shrugged their shoulders at this cant, laughed at it, pandered to it, and ruled by it. The falsehood, cynicism, insolence, misgovernment, oppression, with their consequent unfailing crop of human misery, which were produced by this state of things, roused Byron to irreconcilable revolt and battle. They made him indignant, they infuriated him; they were so strong, so defiant, so maleficent, — and yet he felt that they were doomed. "You have seen every trampler down in turn," he comforts himself with saying, "from Buonaparte to the simplest individuals." The old order, as after 1815 it stood victorious, with its ignorance and misery below, its cant, selfishness, and cynicism above, was at home and abroad equally hateful to him. "I have simplified my politics," he writes, "into an utter detestation of all existing governments." And again: "Give me a republic. The king-times are fast finishing; there will be blood shed like water and tears like mist, but the peoples will conquer in the end. I shall not live to see it, but I foresee it."

Byron himself gave the preference, he tells us, to politicians and doers, far above writers and singers. But the politics of his own day and of his own class, — even of the Liberals of his own class, — were impossible for him. Nature had not formed him for a Liberal peer, proper to move the Address in the House of Lords, to pay compliments to the energy and self-reliance of British middle-class Liberalism, and to adapt his politics to suit it. Unfitted for such politics, he threw himself upon poetry as his organ; and in poetry his topics were not Queen Mab, and the Witch of Atlas, and the Sensitive Plant — they were the upholders of the old order, George the Third and Lord Castlereagh and the Duke of Wellington and Southey, and they were the canters and tramplers of the great world, and they were his enemies and himself.

Such was Byron's personality, by which "he is different from all the rest of English poets, and in the main greater." But he posed all his life, says M. Scherer. Let us distinguish. There is the Byron who posed, there is the Byron with his affectations and silliness, the Byron whose weakness Lady Blessington, with a woman's acuteness, so admirably seized: "His great defect is flippancy and a total want of self-possession." But when this theatrical and easily criticised personage betook himself to poetry, and when he had fairly warmed to his work, then he became another man; then the theatrical personage passed away; then a higher power took possession of him and filled him; then at last came forth into light that true and puissant personality, with its direct strokes, its ever-welling force, its satire, its energy, and its agony. This is the real Byron; whoever stops at the theatrical preludings does not know him. And this real Byron may well be superior to the stricken Leopardi, he may well be declared "different from all the rest of English poets, and in the main greater," in so far as it is true of him, as M. Taine well says, that "all other souls, in comparison with his, seem inert"; in so far as it is true of him that with superb, exhaustless energy, he maintained, as Professor Nichol well says, "the struggle that keeps alive, if it does not save, the soul"; in so far, finally, as he deserves (and he does deserve) the noble praise of him which I have already quoted from Mr. Swinburne; the praise for "the splendid and imperishable excellence which covers all his offences and outweighs all his defects: *the excellence of sincerity and strength.*"

True, as a man, Byron could not manage himself, could not guide his ways aright, but was all astray. True, he has no light, cannot lead us from the past to the future; "the moment he reflects, he is a child." The way out of the false state of things which enraged him he did not see, — the slow and laborious way upward; he had not the patience, knowledge, self-discipline, virtue, requisite for seeing it. True, also, as a poet, he has no fine and exact sense for word and structure and rhythm; he has not the artist's nature and gifts. Yet a personality of Byron's force counts for so much in life, and a rhetorician of Byron's force counts for so much in literature! But it would be most unjust to label Byron, as M. Scherer is disposed to label him, as a rhetorician only. Along with his astounding power and passion he had a strong and deep sense for what is beautiful in nature, and for what is beautiful in human action and suffering. When he warms to his work, when he is inspired, Nature herself seems to take the pen from him as she took it from Wordsworth, and to write for him as she wrote for Wordsworth, though in a different fashion, with her own penetrating simplicity. Goethe has well observed of Byron, that when he is at his happiest his representation of things is as easy and real as if he were improvising. It is so; and his verse then exhibits quite another and a higher quality from the rhetorical quality, — admirable as this also in its own kind of merit is, — of such verse as

Minions of splendour shrinking from distress,

and of so much more verse of Byron's of that stamp. Nature, I say, takes the pen for him; and then, assured master of a true poetic style though he is not, any more than Wordsworth, yet as from Wordsworth at his best there will come such verse as

> Will no one tell me what she sings?

so from Byron, too, at his best, there will come such verse as

> He heard it, but he heeded not; his eyes
> Were with his heart, and that was far away.

Of verse of this high quality, Byron has much; of verse of a quality lower than this, of a quality rather rhetorical than truly poetic, yet still of extraordinary power and merit, he has still more. To separate, from the mass of poetry which Byron poured forth, all this higher portion, so superior to the mass, and still so considerable in quantity, and to present it in one body by itself, is to do a service, I believe, to Byron's reputation, and to the poetic glory of our country.

Such a service I have in the present volume attempted to perform. To Byron, after all the tributes which have been paid to him, here is yet one tribute more —

> Among thy mightier offerings here are mine!

not a tribute of boundless homage certainly, but sincere; a tribute which consists not in covering the poet with eloquent eulogy of our own, but in letting him, at his best and greatest, speak for himself. Surely the critic who does most for his author is the critic who gains readers for his author himself, not for any lucubrations on his author; — gains more readers for him, and enables those readers to read him with more admiration.

And in spite of his prodigious vogue, Byron has never yet, perhaps, had the serious admiration which he deserves. Society read him and talked about him, as it reads and talks about "Endymion" today; and with the same sort of result. It looked in Byron's glass as it looks in Lord Beaconsfield's, and sees, or fancies that it sees, its own face there; and then it goes its way, and straightway forgets what manner of man it saw. Even of his passionate admirers, how many never got beyond the theatrical Byron, from whom they caught the fashion of deranging their hair, or of knotting their neck-handkerchief, or of leaving their shirt-collar unbuttoned; how few profoundly felt his vital influence, the influence of his splendid and imperishable excellence of sincerity and strength!

His own aristocratic class, whose cynical make-believe drove him to fury; the great middle class, on whose impregnable Philistinism he shattered himself to pieces, — how little have either of these felt

Byron's vital influence! As the inevitable break-up of the old order comes, as the English middle class slowly awakens from its intellectual sleep of two centuries, as our actual present world, to which this sleep has condemned us, shows itself more clearly, — our world of an aristocracy materialised and null, a middle class purblind and hideous, a lower class crude and brutal, — we shall turn our eyes again, and to more purpose, upon this passionate and dauntless soldier of a forlorn hope, who, ignorant of the future and unconsoled by its promises, nevertheless waged against the conservation of the old impossible world so fiery battle; waged it till he fell, — waged it with such splendid and imperishable excellence of sincerity and strength.

Wordsworth's value is of another kind. Wordsworth has an insight into permanent sources of joy and consolation for mankind which Byron has not; his poetry gives us more which we may rest upon than Byron's, — more which we can rest upon now, and which men may rest upon always. I place Wordsworth's poetry, therefore, above Byron's on the whole, although in some points he was greatly Byron's inferior, and although Byron's poetry will always, probably, find more readers than Wordsworth's, and will give pleasure more easily. But these two, Wordsworth and Byron, stand, it seems to me, first and pre-eminent in actual performance, a glorious pair, among the English poets of this century. Keats had probably, indeed, a more consummate poetic gift than either of them; but he died having produced too little and being as yet too immature to rival them. I for my part can never even think of equalling with them any other of their contemporaries; — either Coleridge, poet and philosopher wrecked in a mist of opium; or Shelley, beautiful and ineffectual angel, beating in the void his luminous wings in vain. Wordsworth and Byron stand out by themselves. When the year 1900 is turned, and our nation comes to recount her poetic glories in the century which has then just ended, the first names with her will be these.

SHELLEY

NOWADAYS all things appear in print sooner or later; but I have heard from a lady who knew Mrs. Shelley a story of her which, so far as I know, has not appeared in print hitherto. Mrs. Shelley was choosing a school for her son, and asked the advice of this lady, who gave for advice — to use her own words to me — "Just the sort of banality, you know, one does come out with: Oh, send him somewhere where they will teach him to think for himself!" I have had far too long a training as a school inspector to presume to call an utterance of this kind a *banality;* however, it is not on this advice that I now wish to lay stress, but upon Mrs. Shelley's reply to it. Mrs. Shelley answered: "Teach him to think for himself? Oh, my God, teach him rather to think like other people!"

To the lips of many and many a reader of Professor Dowden's volumes a cry of this sort will surely rise, called forth by Shelley's life as there delineated. I have read those volumes with the deepest interest, but I regret their publication, and am surprised, I confess, that Shelley's family should have desired or assisted it. For my own part, at any rate, I would gladly have been left with the impression, the ineffaceable impression, made upon me by Mrs. Shelley's first edition of her husband's collected poems. Medwin and Hogg and Trelawny had done little to change the impression made by those four delightful volumes of the original edition of 1839. The text of the poems has in some places been mended since; but Shelley is not a classic, whose various readings are to be noted with earnest attention. The charm of the poems flowed in upon us from that edition and the charm of the character. Mrs. Shelley had done her work admirably; her introductions to the poems of each year, with Shelley's prefaces and passages from his letters, supplied the very picture of Shelley to be desired. Somewhat idealised by tender regret and exalted memory Mrs. Shelley's representation no doubt was. But without sharing her conviction that Shelley's character, impartially judged, "would stand in fairer and brighter light than that of any contemporary," we learned from her to know the soul of affection, of "gentle and cordial goodness," of eagerness and ardour for human happiness, which was in this rare spirit — so mere a monster unto many. Mrs. Shelley said in her general preface to her husband's poems: "I abstain from any remark on the occurrences of his private life, except inasmuch as the passions which they engendered inspired his poetry; this is not the time to relate the truth." I for my part could wish, I repeat, that that time had never come.

But come it has, and Professor Dowden has given us the *Life of Percy Bysshe Shelley* in two very thick volumes. If the work was to be done, Professor Dowden has indeed done it thoroughly. One or two things in his biography of Shelley I could wish different, even waiving the question whether it was desirable to relate in full the occurrences of Shelley's private life. Professor Dowden holds a brief for Shelley; he pleads for Shelley as an advocate pleads for his client, and this strain of pleading, united with an attitude of adoration which in Mrs. Shelley had its charm, but which Professor Dowden was not bound to adopt from her, is unserviceable to Shelley, nay, injurious to him, because it inevitably begets, in many readers of the story which Professor Dowden has to tell, impatience and revolt. Further, let me remark that the biography before us is of prodigious length, although its hero died before he was thirty years old, and that it might have been considerably shortened if it had been more plainly and simply written. I see that one of Professor Dowden's critics, while praising his style for "a certain poetic quality of fervour and picturesqueness," laments that in some important passages Professor Dowden "fritters away great opportunities for sustained and impassioned narrative." I am inclined much rather to lament that Professor Dowden has not steadily kept his poetic quality of fervour and picturesqueness more under control. Is it that the Home Rulers have so loaded the language that even an Irishman who is not one of them catches something of their full habit of style? No, it is rather, I believe, that Professor Dowden, of poetic nature himself, and dealing with a poetic nature like Shelley, is so steeped in sentiment by his subject that in almost every page of the biography the sentiment runs over. A curious note of his style, suffused with sentiment, is that it seems incapable of using the common word *child*. A great many births are mentioned in the biography, but always it is a poetic *babe* that is born, not a prosaic *child*. And so, again, André Chénier is not guillotined, but "too foully done to death." Again, Shelley after his runaway marriage with Harriet Westbrook was in Edinburgh without money and full of anxieties for the future, and complained of his hard lot in being unable to get away, in being "chained to the filth and commerce of Edinburgh." Natural enough; but why should Professor Dowden improve the occasion as follows? "The most romantic of northern cities could lay no spell upon his spirit. His eye was not fascinated by the presences of mountains and the sea, by the fantastic outlines of aërial piles seen amid the wreathing smoke of Auld Reekie, by the gloom of the Canongate illuminated with shafts of sunlight streaming from its interesting wynds and alleys; nor was his imagination kindled by storied house or palace, and the voices of old, forgotten, far-off things, which haunt their walls." If Professor Dowden, writing a book in prose, could have brought himself to eschew poetic excursions of this kind and to tell his story in a plain way, lovers of simplicity, of whom there are some still left in the world, would have been gratified, and at the same time his book would have been the shorter by scores of pages.

These reserves being made, I have little except praise for the manner in which Professor Dowden has performed his task; whether it was a task which ought to be performed at all, probably did not lie with him to decide. His ample materials are used with order and judgment; the history of Shelley's life develops itself clearly before our eyes; the documents of importance for it are given with sufficient fulness, nothing essential seems to have been kept back, although I would gladly, I confess, have seen more of Miss Clairmont's journal, whatever arrangement she may in her later life have chosen to exercise upon it. In general all documents are so fairly and fully cited, that Professor Dowden's pleadings for Shelley, though they may sometimes indispose and irritate the reader, produce no obscuring of the truth; the documents manifest it of themselves. Last but not least of Professor Dowden's merits, he has provided his book with an excellent index.

Undoubtedly this biography, with its full account of the occurrences of Shelley's private life, compels one to review one's former impression of him. Undoubtedly the brilliant and attaching rebel who in thinking for himself had of old our sympathy so passionately with him, when we come to read his full biography makes us often and often inclined to cry out: "My God! he had far better have thought like other people." There is a passage in Hogg's capitally written and most interesting account of Shelley which I wrote down when I first read it and have borne in mind ever since; so beautifully it seemed to render the true Shelley. Hogg has been speaking of the intellectual expression of Shelley's features, and he goes on: "Nor was the moral expression less beautiful than the intellectual; for there was a softness, a delicacy, a gentleness, and especially (though this will surprise many) that air of profound religious veneration that characterises the best works and chiefly the frescoes (and into these they infused their whole souls) of the great masters of Florence and of Rome." What we have of Shelley in poetry and prose suited with this charming picture of him; Mrs. Shelley's account suited with it; it was a possession which one would gladly have kept unimpaired. It still subsists, I must now add; it subsists even after one has read the present biography; it subsists, but so as by fire. It subsists with many a scar and stain; never again will it have the same pureness and beauty which it had formerly. I regret this, as I have said, and I confess I do not see what has been gained. Our ideal Shelley was the true Shelley after all; what has been gained by making us at moments doubt it? What has been gained by forcing upon us much in him which is ridiculous and odious, by compelling any fair mind, if it is to retain with a good conscience its ideal Shelley, to do that which I propose to do now? I propose to mark firmly what is ridiculous and odious in the Shelley brought to our knowledge by the new materials, and then to show that our former beautiful and lovable Shelley nevertheless survives.

Almost everybody knows the main outline of the events of Shelley's life. It will be necessary for me, however, up to the date of his second marriage, to go through them here. Percy Bysshe Shelley was born at Field Place, near Horsham, in Sussex, on the 4th of August 1792. He was of an old family of country gentlemen, and the heir to a baronetcy. He had one brother and five sisters, but the brother so much younger than himself as to be no companion for him in his boyhood at home, and after he was separated from home and England he never saw him. Shelley was brought up at Field Place with his sisters. At ten years old he was sent to a private school at Isleworth, where he read Mrs. Radcliffe's romances and was fascinated by a popular scientific lecturer. After two years of private school he went in 1804 to Eton. Here he took no part in cricket or football, refused to fag, was known as "mad Shelley" and much tormented; when tormented beyond endurance he could be dangerous. Certainly he was not happy at Eton; but he had friends, he boated, he rambled about the country. His school lessons were easy to him, and his reading extended far beyond them; he read books on chemistry, he read Pliny's *Natural History,* Godwin's *Political Justice,* Lucretius, Franklin, Condorcet. It is said he was called "atheist Shelley" at Eton, but this is not so well established as his having been called "mad Shelley." He was full, at any rate, of new and revolutionary ideas, and he declared at a later time that he was twice expelled from the school but recalled through the interference of his father.

In the spring of 1810 Shelley, now in his eighteenth year, entered University College, Oxford, as an exhibitioner. He had already written novels and poems; a poem on the Wandering Jew, in seven or eight cantos, he sent to Campbell, and was told by Campbell that there were but two good lines in it. He had solicited the correspondence of Mrs. Hemans, then Felicia Browne and unmarried; he had fallen in love with a charming cousin, Harriet Grove. In the autumn of 1810 he found a publisher for his verse; he also found a friend in a very clever and free-minded commoner of his college, Thomas Jefferson Hogg, who has admirably described the Shelley of those Oxford days, with his chemistry, his eccentric habits, his charm of look and character, his conversation, his shrill discordant voice. Shelley read incessantly. Hume's *Essays* produced a powerful impression on him; his free speculation led him to what his father, and worse still his cousin Harriet, thought "detestable principles"; his cousin and his family became estranged from him. He, on his part, became more and more incensed against the "bigotry" and "intolerance" which produced such estrangement. "Here I swear, and as I break my oaths, may Infinity, Eternity, blast me — here I swear that never will I forgive intolerance." At the beginning of 1811 he prepared and published what he called a "leaflet for letters," having for its title *The Necessity of Atheism.* He sent copies to all the bishops, to the Vice-Chancellor of Oxford, and to the heads of houses. On Lady Day he was summoned before the authorities of his College, refused to answer the question whether he had written *The Necessity of Atheism,* told the Master and Fellows that "their proceedings would become a court of inquisitors but not free men in a free country," and was expelled for contumacy. Hogg wrote a letter of remonstrance to the authorities, was in his turn summoned before them and questioned as to his share in the "leaflet," and, refusing to answer, he also was expelled.

Shelley settled with Hogg in lodgings in London. His father, excusably indignant, was not a wise man and managed his son ill. His plan of recommending Shelley to read Paley's *Natural Theology,* and of *reading it with him himself,* makes us smile. Shelley, who about this time wrote of his younger sister, then at school at Clapham, "There are some hopes of this dear little girl, she would be a divine little scion of infidelity if I could get hold of her," was not to have been cured by Paley's *Natural Theology* administered through Mr. Timothy Shelley. But by the middle of May Shelley's father had agreed to allow him two hundred pounds a year. Meanwhile in visiting his sisters at their school in Clapham, Shelley made the acquaintance of a schoolfellow of theirs, Harriet Westbrook. She was a beautiful and lively girl, with a father who had kept a tavern in Mount Street, but had now retired from business, and one sister much older than herself, who encouraged in every possible way the acquaintance of her sister of sixteen with the heir to a baronetcy and a great estate. Soon Shelley heard that Harriet met with cold looks at her school for associating with an atheist; his generosity and his ready indignation against "intolerance" were roused. In the summer Harriet wrote to him that she was persecuted not at school only but at home also, that she was lonely and miserable, and would gladly put an end to her life. Shelley went to see her; she owned her love for him, and he engaged himself to her. He told his cousin Charles Grove that his happiness had been blighted when the other Harriet, Charles's sister, cast him off; that now the only thing worth living for was self-sacrifice. Harriet's persecutors became yet more troublesome, and Shelley, at the end of August, went off with her to Edinburgh and they were married. The entry in the register is this:

> *August* 28, 1811.—Percy Bysshe Shelley, farmer, Sussex, and Miss Harriet Westbrook, St. Andrew Church Parish, daughter of Mr. John Westbrook, London.

After five weeks in Edinburgh the young farmer and his wife came southwards and took lodgings at York, under the shadow of what Shelley calls that "gigantic pile of superstition," the Minster. But his friend Hogg was in a lawyer's office in York, and Hogg's society made the Minster endurable. Mr. Timothy Shelley's happiness in his son was naturally not increased by the runaway marriage; he stopped his allowance, and Shelley determined to visit "this thoughtless man," as he calls his parent, and to "try the force of truth" upon him. Nothing could be effected; Shelley's mother, too, was now against him. He returned to York to find that in his absence his friend Hogg had been making love to Harriet, who had indignantly repulsed him. Shelley was shocked, but after a "terrible day" of explanation from Hogg, he "fully, freely pardoned him," promised to retain him still as "his friend, his bosom friend," and "hoped soon to convince him how lovely virtue was." But for the present it seemed better to separate. In November he and Harriet, with her sister Eliza, took a cottage at Keswick. Shelley was now in great straits for money; the great Sussex neighbour of the Shelley's, the Duke of Norfolk, interposed in his favour, and his father and grandfather seem to have offered him at this time an income of £2000 a year, if he would consent to entail the family estate. Shelley indignantly refused to "forswear his principles," by accepting " a proposal so insultingly hateful." But in December his father agreed, though with an ill grace, to grant him his allowance of £200 a year again, and Mr. Westbrook promised to allow a like sum to his daughter. So after four months of marriage the Shelleys began 1812 with an income of £400 a year.

Early in February they left Keswick and proceeded to Dublin, where Shelley, who had prepared an address to the Catholics, meant to "devote himself towards forwarding the great ends of virtue and happiness in Ireland." Before leaving Keswick he wrote to William

Godwin, "the regulator and former of his mind," making profession of his mental obligations to him, of his respect and veneration, and soliciting Godwin's friendship. A correspondence followed; Godwin pronounced his young disciple's plans for "disseminating the doctrines of philanthropy and freedom" in Ireland to be unwise; Shelley bowed to his mentor's decision and gave up his Irish campaign, quitting Dublin on the 4th of April 1812. He and Harriet wandered first to Nant-Gwillt in South Wales, near the upper Wye, and from thence after a month or two to Lynmouth in North Devon, where he busied himself with his poem of *Queen Mab,* and with sending to sea boxes and bottles containing a "Declaration of Rights" by him, in the hope that the winds and waves might carry his doctrines where they would do good. But his Irish servant, bearing the prophetic name of Healy, posted the "Declaration" on the walls of Barnstaple and was taken up; Shelley found himself watched and no longer able to enjoy Lynmouth in peace. He moved in September 1812 to Tremadoc, in North Wales, where he threw himself ardently into an enterprise for recovering a great stretch of drowned land from the sea. But at the beginning of October he and Harriet visited London, and Shelley grasped Godwin by the hand at last. At once an intimacy arose, but the future Mary Shelley — Godwin's daughter by his first wife, Mary Wollstonecraft — was absent on a visit in Scotland when the Shelleys arrived in London. They became acquainted, however, with the second Mrs. Godwin, on whom we have Charles Lamb's friendly comment: "A very disgusting woman, and wears green spectacles!" with the amiable Fanny, Mary Wollstonecraft's daughter by Imlay, before her marriage with Godwin; and probably also with Jane Clairmont, the second Mrs. Godwin's daughter by a first marriage, and herself afterwards the mother of Byron's Allegra. Complicated relationships, as in the Theban story! and there will be not wanting, presently, something of the Theban horrors. During this visit of six weeks to London Shelley renewed his intimacy with Hogg; in the middle of November he returned to Tremadoc. There he remained until the end of February 1813, perfectly happy with Harriet, reading widely, and working at his *Queen Mab* and at the notes to that poem. On the 26th of February an attempt was made, or so he fancied, to assassinate him, and in high nervous excitement he hurriedly left Tremadoc and repaired with Harriet to Dublin again. On this visit to Ireland he saw Killarney, but early in April he and Harriet were back again in London.

There in June 1813 their daughter Ianthe was born; at the end of July they moved to Bracknell, in Berkshire. They had for neighbours there a Mrs. Boinville and her married daughter, whom Shelley found to be fascinating women, with a culture which to his wife was altogether wanting. Cornelia Turner, Mrs. Boinville's daughter, was melancholy, required consolation, and found it, Hogg tells us, in Petrarch's poetry: "Bysshe entered at once fully into her views and caught the soft infection, breathing the tenderest and sweetest melancholy as every true poet ought." Peacock, a man of keen and cultivated mind, joined the circle at Bracknell. He and Harriet, not yet eighteen, used sometimes to laugh at the gushing sentiment and enthusiasm of the Bracknell circle; Harriet had also given offence to Shelley by getting a wet-nurse for her child; in Professor Dowden's words, "the beauty of Harriet's motherly relation to her babe was marred in Shelley's eyes by the introduction into his home of a hireling nurse to whom was delegated the mother's tenderest office." But in September Shelley wrote a sonnet to his child which expresses his deep love for the mother also, to whom in March 1814 he was remarried in London, lest the Scotch marriage should prove to have been in any point irregular. Harriet's sister Eliza, however, whom Shelley had at first treated with excessive deference, had now become hateful to him. And in the very month of the London marriage we find him writing to Hogg that he is staying with the Boinvilles, having "escaped, in the society of all that philosophy and friendship combine, from the dismaying solitude of myself." Cornelia Turner, he adds, whom he once thought cold and reserved, "is the reverse of this, as she is the reverse of everything bad; she inherits all the divinity of her mother." Then comes a stanza, beginning

> Thy dewy looks sink in my breast,
> Thy gentle words stir poison there.

It has no meaning, he says; it is only written in thought. "It is evident from this pathetic letter," says Professor Dowden, "that Shelley's happiness in his home had been fatally stricken." This is a curious way of putting the matter. To me what is evident is rather that Shelley had, to use Professor Dowden's words again — for in these things of high sentiment I gladly let him speak for me — "a too vivid sense that here (in the society of the Boinville family) were peace and joy and gentleness and love." In April come some more verses to the Boinvilles, which contain the first good stanza that Shelley wrote. In May comes a poem to Harriet, of which Professor Dowden's prose analysis is as poetic as the poem itself. "If she has something to endure (from the Boinville attachment), it is not much, and all her husband's weal hangs upon her loving endurance, for see how pale and wildered anguish has made him!" Harriet, unconvinced, seems to have gone off to Bath in resentment, from whence, however, she kept up a constant correspondence with Shelley, who was now of age, and busy in London raising money on post-obit bonds for his own wants and those of the friend and former of his mind, Godwin.

And now, indeed, it was to become true that if from the inflammable Shelley's devotion to the Boinville family poor Harriet had had "something to endure," yet this was "not much" compared with what was to follow. At Godwin's house Shelley met Mary Wollstonecraft Godwin, his future wife, then in her seventeenth year. She was a gifted person, but, as Professor Dowden says, she "had breathed during her entire life an atmosphere of free thought." On the 8th of June Hogg called at Godwin's with Shelley; Godwin was out, but "a door was partially and softly opened, a thrilling voice called 'Shelley!' a thrilling voice answered 'Mary!'" Shelley's summoner was a "very young female, fair and fair-haired, pale indeed, and with a piercing look, wearing a frock of tartan." Already they were "Shelley" and "Mary" to one another; "before the close of June they knew and felt," says Professor Dowden, "that each was to the other inexpressibly dear." The churchyard of St. Pancras, where her mother was buried, became "a place now doubly sacred to Mary, since on one eventful day Bysshe here poured forth his griefs, his hopes, his love, and she, in sign of everlasting union, placed her hand in his." In July Shelley gave her a copy of *Queen Mab,* printed but not published, and under the tender dedication to Harriet he wrote: "Count Slobendorf was about to marry a woman who, attracted solely by his fortune, proved her selfishness by deserting him in prison." Mary added an inscription on her part: "I love the author beyond all powers of expression . . . by that love we have promised to each other, although I may not be yours I can never be another's," — and a good deal more to the same effect.

Amid these excitements Shelley was for some days without writing to Harriet, who applied to Hookham the publisher to know what had happened. She was expecting her confinement; "I always fancy something dreadful has happened," she wrote, "if I do not hear from him . . . I cannot endure this dreadful state of suspense." Shelley then wrote to her, begging her to come to London; and when she arrived there, he told her the state of his feelings, and proposed separation. The shock made Harriet ill; and Shelley, says Peacock, "between his old feelings towards Harriet, and his new passion for Mary, showed in his looks, in his gestures, in his speech, the state of a mind 'suffering, like a little kingdom, the nature of an insurrection.'" Godwin grew uneasy about his daughter, and after a serious talk with her, wrote to Shelley. Under such circumstances, Professor Dowden tells us, "to youth, swift and decisive measures seem the best." In the early morning of the 28th of July 1814 "Mary Godwin stepped across her father's threshold into the summer air," she and Shelley went off together in a post-chaise to Dover, and from thence crossed to the Continent.

On the 14th of August the fugitives were at Troyes on their way to Switzerland. From Troyes Shelley addressed a letter to Harriet, of which the best description I can give is that it is precisely the letter which a man in the writer's circumstances should not have written.

> My dearest Harriet [he begins] — I write to you from this detestable town; I write to show that I do not forget you; I write to urge you to come to Switzerland, where you will at last find one firm and constant friend to whom your interests will be always dear — by whom your feelings will never wilfully be injured. From none can you expect this but me — all else are either unfeeling or selfish, or have beloved friends of their own.

Then follows a description of his journey with Mary from Paris "through a fertile country, neither interesting from the character of its inhabitants nor the beauty of the scenery, with a mule to carry our baggage, as Mary, who has not been sufficiently well to walk, fears the fatigue of walking." Like St. Paul to Timothy, he ends with commissions:

> I wish you to bring with you the two deeds which Tahourdin has to prepare for you, as also a copy of the settlement. Do not part with any of your money. But what shall be done about the books? You can consult on the spot. With love to my sweet little Ianthe, ever most affectionately yours, S.
>
> I write in great haste; we depart directly.

Professor Dowden's flow of sentiment is here so agitating, that I relieve myself by resorting to a drier world. Certainly my comment on this letter shall not be his, that it "assures Harriet that her interests were still dear to Shelley, though now their lives had moved apart." But neither will I call the letter an odious letter, a hideous letter. I prefer to call it, applying an untranslatable French word, a *bête* letter. And it is *bête* from what is the signal, the disastrous want and weakness of Shelley, with all his fine intellectual gifts — his utter deficiency in humour.

Harriet did not accept Shelley's invitation to join him and Mary in Switzerland. Money difficulties drove the travellers back to England in September. Godwin would not see Shelley, but he sorely needed, continually demanded, and eagerly accepted, pecuniary help from his erring "spiritual son." Between Godwin's wants and his own, Shelley was hard pressed. He got from Harriet, who still believed that he would return to her, twenty pounds which remained in her hands. In November she was confined; a son and heir was born to Shelley.

He went to see Harriet, but "the interview left husband and wife each embittered against the other." Friends were severe; "when Mrs. Boinville wrote, her letter seemed cold and even sarcastic," says Professor Dowden. "Solitude," he continues, "unharassed by debts and duns, with Mary's companionship, the society of a few friends, and the delights of study and authorship, would have made these winter months to Shelley months of unusual happiness and calm." But, alas! creditors were pestering, and even Harriet gave trouble. In January 1815 Mary had to write in her journal this entry: "Harriet sends her creditors here; nasty woman. Now we must change our lodgings."

One day about this time Shelley asked Peacock, "Do you think Wordsworth could have written such poetry if he ever had dealings with money-lenders?" Not only had Shelley dealings with money-lenders, he now had dealings with bailiffs also. But still he continued to read largely. In January 1815 his grandfather, Sir Bysshe Shelley, died. Shelley went down into Sussex; his father would not suffer him to enter the house, but he sat outside the door and read *Comus,* while the reading of his grandfather's will went on inside. In February was born Mary's first child, a girl, who lived but a few days. All the spring Shelley was ill and harassed, but by June it was settled that he should have an allowance from his father of £1000 a year, and that his debts (including £1200 promised by him to Godwin) should be paid. He on his part paid Harriet's debts and allowed her £200 a year. In August he took a house on the borders of Windsor Park, and made a boating excursion up the Thames as far as Lechlade, an excursion which produced his first entire poem of value, the beautiful *Stanzas in Lechlade Churchyard.* They were followed, later in the autumn, by *Alastor.* Henceforth, from this winter of 1815 until he was drowned between Leghorn and Spezzia in July 1822, Shelley's literary history is sufficiently given in the delightful introductions prefixed by Mrs. Shelley to the poems of each year. Much of the history of his life is there given also; but with some of those "occurrences of his private life" on which Mrs. Shelley forbore to touch, and which are now made known to us in Professor Dowden's book, we have still to deal.

Mary's first son, William, was born in January 1816, and in February we find Shelley declaring himself "strongly urged, by the perpetual experience of neglect or enmity from almost every one but those who are supported by my resources, to desert my native country, hiding myself and Mary from the contempt which we so unjustly endure." Early in May he left England with Mary and Miss Clairmont; they met Lord Byron at Geneva and passed the summer by the Lake of Geneva in his company. Miss Clairmont had already in London, without the knowledge of the Shelleys, made Byron's acquaintance and become his mistress. Shelley determined, in the course of the summer, to go back to England, and, after all, "to make that most excellent of nations my perpetual resting-place." In September he and his ladies returned; Miss Clairmont was then expecting her confinement. Of her being Byron's mistress the Shelleys were now aware; but "the moral indignation," says Professor Dowden, "which Byron's act might justly arouse, seems to have been felt by neither Shelley nor Mary." If Byron and Clair Clairmont, as she was now called, loved and were happy, all was well.

The eldest daughter of the Godwin household, the amiable Fanny, was unhappy at home and in deep dejection of spirits. Godwin was, as usual, in terrible straits for money. The Shelleys and Miss Clairmont settled themselves at Bath; early in October Fanny Godwin passed through Bath without their knowing it, travelled on to Swansea, took a bedroom at the hotel there, and was found in the morning dead, with a bottle of laudanum on the table beside her and these words in her handwriting:

> I have long determined that the best thing I could do was to put an end to the existence of a being whose birth was unfortunate,[1] and whose life has only been a series of pain to those persons who have hurt their health in endeavouring to promote her welfare. Perhaps to hear of my death will give you pain, but you will soon have the blessing of forgetting that such a creature ever existed as . . .

There is no signature.

A sterner tragedy followed. On the 9th of November 1816 Harriet Shelley left the house in Brompton where she was then living, and did not return. On the 10th of December her body was found in the Serpentine; she had drowned herself. In one respect Professor Dowden resembles Providence: his ways are inscrutable. His comment on Harriet's death is: "There is no doubt she wandered from the ways of upright living." But, he adds: "That no act of Shelley's, during the two years which immediately preceded her death, tended to cause the rash act which brought her life to its close, seems certain." Shelley had been living with Mary all the time; only that!

On the 30th of December 1816 Mary Godwin and Shelley were married. I shall pursue "the occurrences of Shelley's private life" no further. For the five years and a half which remain, Professor Dowden's book adds to our knowledge of Shelley's life much that is interesting; but what was chiefly important we knew already. The new and grave matter which we did not know, or knew in the vaguest way only,

[1] She was Mary Wollstonecraft's natural daughter by Imlay.

but which Shelley's family and Professor Dowden have now thought it well to give us in full, ends with Shelley's second marriage.

I regret, I say once more, that it has been given. It is a sore trial for our love of Shelley. What a set! what a world! is the exclamation that breaks from us as we come to an end of this history of "the occurrences of Shelley's private life." I used the French word *bête* for a letter of Shelley's; for the world in which we find him I can only use another French word, *sale.* Godwin's house of sordid horror, and Godwin preaching and holding the hat, and the green-spectacled Mrs. Godwin, and Hogg the faithful friend, and Hunt the Horace of this precious world, and, to go up higher, Sir Timothy Shelley, a great country gentleman, feeling himself safe while "the exalted mind of the Duke of Norfolk [the drinking Duke] protects me with the world," and Lord Byron with his deep grain of coarseness and commonness, his affectation, his brutal selfishness — what a set! The history carries us to Oxford, and I think of the clerical and respectable Oxford of those old times, the Oxford of Copleston and the Kebles and Hawkins, and a hundred more, with the relief Keble declares himself to experience from Izaak Walton,

> When, wearied with the tale thy times disclose,
> The eye first finds thee out in thy secure repose.

I am not only thinking of morals and the house of Godwin, I am thinking also of tone, bearing, dignity. I appeal to Cardinal Newman, if perchance he does me the honour to read these words, is it possible to imagine Copleston or Hawkins declaring himself safe "while the exalted mind of the Duke of Norfolk protects me with the world"?

Mrs. Shelley, after her marriage and during Shelley's closing years, becomes attractive; up to her marriage her letters and journal do not please. Her ability is manifest, but she is not attractive. In the world discovered to us by Professor Dowden as surrounding Shelley up to 1817, the most pleasing figure is poor Fanny Godwin; after Fanny Godwin, the most pleasing figure is Harriet Shelley herself.

Professor Dowden's treatment of Harriet is not worthy — so much he must allow me in all kindness, but also in all seriousness, to say — of either his taste or his judgment. His pleading for Shelley is constant, and he does more harm than good to Shelley by it. But here his championship of Shelley makes him very unjust to a cruelly used and unhappy girl. For several pages he balances the question whether or not Harriet was unfaithful to Shelley before he left her for Mary, and he leaves the question unsettled. As usual Professor Dowden (and it is his signal merit) supplies the evidence decisive against himself. Thornton Hunt, not well disposed to Harriet, Hogg, Peacock, Trelawny, Hookham, and a member of Godwin's own family, are all clear in their evidence that up to her parting from Shelley Harriet was perfectly innocent. But that precious witness, Godwin, wrote in 1817 that "she had proved herself unfaithful to her husband before their separation. . . . Peace be to her shade!" Why, Godwin was the father of Harriet's successor. But Mary believed the same thing. She was Harriet's successor. But Shelley believed it too. He had it from Godwin. But he was convinced of it earlier. The evidence for this is, that, in writing to Southey in 1820, Shelley declares that "the single passage of a life, otherwise not only spotless but spent in an impassioned pursuit of virtue, which looks like a blot," bears that appearance "merely because I regulated my domestic arrangements without deferring to the notions of the vulgar, although I might have done so quite as conveniently had I descended to their base thoughts." From this Professor Dowden concludes that Shelley believed he could have got a divorce from Harriet had he so wished. The conclusion is not clear. But even were the evidence perfectly clear that Shelley believed Harriet unfaithful when he parted from her, we should have to take into account Mrs. Shelley's most true sentence in her introduction to *Alastor:* "In all Shelley did, he, at the time of doing it, believed himself justified to his own conscience."

Shelley's asserting a thing vehemently does not prove more than that he chose to believe it and did believe it. His extreme and violent changes of opinion about people show this sufficiently. Eliza Westbrook is at one time "a diamond not so large" as her sister Harriet but "more highly polished"; and then: "I certainly hate her with all my heart and soul. I sometimes feel faint with the fatigue of checking the overflowings of my unbounded abhorrence for this miserable wretch." The antipathy, Hogg tells us, was as unreasonable as the former excess of deference. To his friend Miss Hitchener he says: "Never shall that intercourse cease, which has been the day-dawn of my existence, the sun which has shed warmth on the cold drear length of the anticipated prospect of life." A little later, and she has become "the Brown Demon, a woman of desperate views and dreadful passions, but of cool and undeviating revenge." Even Professor Dowden admits that this is absurd; that the real Miss Hitchener was not seen by Shelley, either when he adored or when he detested.

Shelley's power of persuading himself was equal to any occasion; but would not his conscientiousness and high feeling have prevented his exerting this power at poor Harriet's expense? To abandon her as he did, must he not have known her to be false? Professor Dowden insists always on Shelley's "conscientiousness." Shelley himself speaks of his "impassioned pursuit of virtue." Leigh Hunt compared his life to that of "Plato himself, or, still more, a Pythagorean," and added that he "never met a being who came nearer, perhaps so near, to the height of humanity," to being an "angel of charity." In many respects Shelley really resembled both a Pythagorean and an angel of charity. He loved high thoughts, he cared nothing for sumptuous lodging, fare, and raiment, he was poignantly afflicted at the sight of misery, he would have given away his last farthing, would have suffered in his own person, to relieve it. But in one important point he was like neither a Pythagorean nor an angel: he was extremely inflammable. Professor Dowden leaves no doubt on the matter. After reading his book, one feels sickened forever on the subject of irregular relations; God forbid that I should go into the scandals about Shelley's "Neapolitan charge," about Shelley and Emilia Viviani, about Shelley and Miss Clairmont, and the rest of it! I will say only that it is visible enough that when the passion of love was aroused in Shelley (and it was aroused easily) one could not be sure of him, his friends could not trust him. We have seen him with the Boinville family. With Emilia Viviani he is the same. If he is left much alone with Miss Clairmont, he evidently makes Mary uneasy; nay, he makes Professor Dowden himself uneasy. And I conclude that an entirely human inflammability, joined to an inhuman want of humour and a superhuman power of self-deception, are the causes which chiefly explain Shelley's abandonment of Harriet in the first place, and then his behavior to her and his defence of himself afterwards.

His misconduct to Harriet, his want of humour, his self-deception, are fully brought before us for the first time by Professor Dowden's book. Good morals and good criticism alike forbid that when all this is laid bare to us we should deny, or hide, or extenuate it. Nevertheless I go back after all to what I said at the beginning; still our ideal Shelley, the angelic Shelley, subsists. Unhappily the data for this Shelley we had and knew long ago, while the data for the unattractive Shelley are fresh; and what is fresh is likely to fix our attention more than what is familiar. But Professor Dowden's volumes, which give so much, which give too much, also afford data for picturing anew the Shelley who delights, as well as for picturing for the first time a Shelley who, to speak plainly, disgusts; and with what may renew and restore our impression of the delightful Shelley I shall end.

The winter at Marlow, and the ophthalmia caught among the cottages of the poor, we knew, but we have from Professor Dowden more details of this winter and of Shelley's work among the poor; we have above all, for the first time I believe, a line of verse of Shelley's own which sums up truly and perfectly this most attractive side of him —

> I am the friend of the unfriended poor.

But that in Shelley on which I would especially dwell is that in him which contrasts most with the ignobleness of the world in which we have seen him living, and with the pernicious nonsense which we have found him talking. The Shelley of "marvellous gentleness," of feminine refinement with gracious and considerate manners, "a perfect gentleman, entirely without arrogance or aggressive egotism," completely devoid of the proverbial and ferocious vanity of authors and poets, always disposed to make little of his own work and to prefer that of others, of reverent enthusiasm for the great and wise, of high and tender seriousness, of heroic generosity, and of a delicacy in rendering services which was equal to his generosity — the Shelley who was all this is the Shelley with whom I wish to end. He may talk nonsense about tyrants and priests, but what a high and noble ring in such a sentence as the following, written by a young man who is refusing £2000 a year rather than consent to entail a great property!

> That I should entail £120,000 of command over labour, of power to remit this, to employ it for benevolent purposes, on one whom I know not — who might, instead of being the benefactor of mankind, be its bane, or use this for the worst purposes, which the real delegates of my chance-given property might convert into a most useful instrument of benevolence! No! this you will not suspect me of.

And again:

> I desire money because I think I know the use of it. It commands labour, it gives leisure; and to give leisure to those who will employ it in the forwarding of truth is the noblest present an individual can make to the whole.

If there is extravagance here, it is extravagance of a beautiful and rare sort, like Shelley's "underhand ways" also, which differed singularly, the cynic Hogg tells us, from the underhand ways of other people; "the latter were concealed because they were mean, selfish, sordid; Shelley's secrets, on the contrary (kindnesses done by stealth), were hidden through modesty, delicacy, generosity, refinement of soul."

His forbearance to Godwin, to Godwin lecturing and renouncing him and at the same time holding out, as I have said, his hat to him for alms, is wonderful; but the dignity with which he at last, in a letter perfect for propriety of tone, reads a lesson to his ignoble father-in-law, is in the best possible style:

> Perhaps it is well that you should be informed that I consider your last letter to be written in a style of haughtiness and encroachment which neither awes nor imposes on me; but I have no desire to transgress the limits which you place to our intercourse, nor in any future instance will I make any remarks but such as arise from the strict question in discussion.

And again:

> My astonishment, and, I will confess, when I have been treated with most harshness and cruelty by you, my indignation, has been extreme, that, knowing as you do my nature, any considerations should have prevailed on you to have been thus harsh and cruel. I lamented also over my ruined hopes of all that your genius once taught me to expect from your virtue, when I found that for yourself, your family, and your creditors, you would submit to that communication with me which you once rejected and abhorred, and which no pity for my poverty or sufferings, assumed willingly for you, could avail to extort.

Moreover, though Shelley has no humour, he can show as quick and sharp a tact as the most practised man of the world. He has been with Byron and the Countess Guiccioli, and he writes of the latter:

> La Guiccioli is a very pretty, sentimental, innocent Italian, who has sacrificed an immense future for the sake of Lord Byron, and who, if I know anything of my friend, of her, and of human nature, will hereafter have plenty of opportunity to repent her rashness.

Tact also, and something better than tact, he shows in his dealings, in order to befriend Leigh Hunt, with Lord Byron. He writes to Hunt:

> Particular circumstances, or rather, I should say, particular dispositions in Lord Byron's character, render the close and exclusive intimacy with him, in which I find myself, intolerable to me; thus much, my best friend, I will confess and confide to you. No feelings of my own shall injure or interfere with what is now nearest to them — your interest; and I will take care to preserve the little influence I may have over this Proteus, in whom such strange extremes are reconciled, until we meet.

And so we have come back again, at last, to our original Shelley — to the Shelley of the lovely and well-known picture, to the Shelley with "flushed, feminine, artless face," the Shelley "blushing like a girl," of Trelawny. Professor Dowden gives us some further attempts at portraiture. One by a Miss Rose, of Shelley at Marlow:

> He was the most interesting figure I ever saw; his eyes like a deer's, bright but rather wild; his white throat unfettered; his slender but to me almost faultless shape; his brown long coat with curling lambs' wool collar and cuffs — in fact, his whole appearance — are as fresh in my recollection as an occurrence of yesterday.

Feminine enthusiasm may be deemed suspicious, but a Captain Kennedy must surely be able to keep his head. Captain Kennedy was quartered at Horsham in 1813, and saw Shelley when he was on a stolen visit, in his father's absence, at Field Place:

> He received me with frankness and kindliness, as if he had known me from childhood, and at once won my heart. I fancy I see him now as he sate by the window, and hear his voice, the tones of which impressed me with his sincerity and simplicity. His resemblance to his sister Elizabeth was as striking as if they had been twins. His eyes were most expressive; his complexion beautifully fair, his features exquisitely fine; his hair was dark, and no peculiar attention to its arrangement was manifest. In person he was slender and gentlemanlike, but inclined to stoop; his gait was decidedly not military. The general appearance indicated great delicacy of constitution. One would at once pronounce of him that he was different from other men. There was an earnestness in his manner and such perfect gentleness of breeding and freedom from everything artificial as charmed every one. I never met a man who so immediately won upon me.

Mrs. Gisborne's son, who knew Shelley well at Leghorn, declared Captain Kennedy's description of him to be "the best and most truthful I have ever seen."

To all this we have to add the charm of the man's writings — of Shelley's poetry. It is his poetry, above everything else, which for many people establishes that he is an angel. Of his poetry I have not space now to speak. But let no one suppose that a want of humour and a self-delusion such as Shelley's have no effect upon a man's poetry. The man Shelley, in very truth, is not entirely sane, and Shelley's poetry is not entirely sane either. The Shelley of actual life is a vision of beauty and radiance, indeed, but availing nothing, effecting nothing. And in poetry, no less than in life, he is "a beautiful *and ineffectual* angel, beating in the void his luminous wings in vain."

LITERATURE AND SCIENCE

PRACTICAL people talk with a smile of Plato and of his absolute ideas; and it is impossible to deny that Plato's ideas do often seem unpractical and impracticable, and especially when one views them in connection with the life of a great work-a-day world like the United States. The necessary staple of the life of such a world Plato regards with disdain; handicraft and trade and the working professions he regards with disdain; but what becomes of the life of an industrial modern community if you take handicraft and trade and the working professions out of it? The base mechanic arts and handicrafts, says Plato, bring about a natural weakness in the principle of excellence in a man, so that he cannot govern the ignoble growths in him, but nurses them, and cannot understand fostering any other. Those who exercise such arts and trades, as they have their bodies, he says, marred by their vulgar businesses, so they have their souls, too, bowed and broken by them. And if one of these uncomely people has a mind to seek self-culture and philosophy, Plato compares him to a bald little tinker, who has scraped together money, and has got his release from service, and has had a bath, and bought a new coat, and is rigged out like a bridegroom about to marry the daughter of his master who has fallen into poor and helpless estate.

Nor do the working professions fare any better than trade at the hands of Plato. He draws for us an inimitable picture of the working lawyer, and of his life of bondage; he shows how this bondage from his youth up has stunted and warped him, and made him small and crooked of soul, encompassing him with difficulties which he is not man enough to rely on justice and truth as means to encounter, but has recourse, for help out of them, to falsehood and wrong. And so, says Plato, this poor creature is bent and broken, and grows up from boy to man without a particle of soundness in him, although exceedingly smart and clever in his own esteem.

One cannot refuse to admire the artist who draws these pictures. But we say to ourselves that his ideas show the influence of a primitive and obsolete order of things, when the warrior caste and the priestly caste were alone in honour, and the humble work of the world was done by slaves. We have now changed all that; the modern majesty consists in work, as Emerson declares; and in work, we may add, principally of such plain and dusty kind as the work of cultivators of the ground, handicraftsmen, men of trade and business, men of the working professions. Above all is this true in a great industrious community such as that of the United States.

Now education, many people go on to say, is still mainly governed by the ideas of men like Plato, who lived when the warrior caste and the priestly or philosophical class were alone in honour, and the really useful part of the community were slaves. It is an education fitted for persons of leisure in such a community. This education passed from Greece and Rome to the feudal communities of Europe, where also the warrior caste and the priestly caste were alone held in honour, and where the really useful and working part of the community, though not nominally slaves as in the pagan world, were practically not much better off than slaves, and not more seriously regarded. And how absurd it is, people end by saying, to inflict this education upon an industrious modern community, where very few indeed are persons of leisure, and the mass to be considered has not leisure, but is bound, for its own great good, and for the great good of the world at large, to plain labour and to industrial pursuits, and the education in question tends necessarily to make men dissatisfied with these pursuits and unfitted for them!

That is what is said. So far I must defend Plato, as to plead that his view of education and studies is in the general, as it seems to me, sound enough, and fitted for all sorts and conditions of men, whatever their pursuits may be. "An intelligent man," says Plato, "will prize those studies which result in his soul getting soberness, righteousness, and wisdom, and will less value the others." I cannot consider *that* a bad description of the aim of education, and of the motives which should govern us in the choice of studies, whether we are preparing ourselves for a hereditary seat in the English House of Lords or for the pork trade in Chicago.

Still I admit that Plato's world was not ours, that his scorn of trade and handicraft is fantastic, that he had no conception of a great industrial community such as that of the United States, and that such a community must and will shape its education to suit its own needs. If the usual education handed down to it from the past does not suit it, it will certainly before long drop this and try another. The usual education in the past has been mainly literary. The question is whether the studies which were long supposed to be the best for all of us are practically the best now; whether others are not better. The tyranny of the past, many think, weighs on us injuriously in the predominance given to letters in education. The question is raised whether, to meet the needs of our modern life, the predominance ought not now to pass from letters to science; and naturally the question is nowhere raised with more energy than here in the United States. The design of abasing what is called "mere literary instruction and education," and of exalting what is called "sound, extensive, and practical scientific knowledge," is, in this intensely modern world of the United States, even more perhaps than in Europe, a very popular design, and makes great and rapid progress.

I am going to ask whether the present movement for ousting letters from their old predominance in education, and for transferring the predominance in education to the natural sciences, whether this brisk and flourishing movement ought to prevail, and whether it is likely that in the end it really will prevail. An objection may be raised which I will anticipate. My own studies have been almost wholly in letters, and my visits to the field of the natural sciences have been very slight and inadequate, although those sciences have always strongly moved my curiosity. A man of letters, it will perhaps be said, is not competent to discuss the comparative merits of letters and natural science as means of education. To this objection I reply, first of all, that his incompetence, if he attempts the discussion but is really incompetent for it, will be abundantly visible; nobody will be taken in; he will have plenty of sharp observers and critics to save mankind from that danger. But the line I am going to follow is, as you will soon discover, so extremely simple, that perhaps it may be followed without failure even by one who for a more ambitious line of discussion would be quite incompetent.

Some of you may possibly remember a phrase of mine which has been the object of a good deal of comment; an observation to the effect that in our culture, the aim being *to know ourselves and the world*, we have, as the means to this end, *to know the best which has been thought and said in the world*. A man of science, who is also an excellent writer and the very prince of debaters, Professor Huxley, in a discourse at the opening of Sir Josiah Mason's college at Birmingham, laying hold of this phrase, expanded it by quoting some more words of mine, which are these: "The civilised world is to be regarded as now being, for intellectual and spiritual purposes, one great confederation, bound to a joint action and working to a common result; and whose members have for their proper outfit a knowledge of Greek, Roman, and Eastern antiquity, and of one another. Special local and temporary advantages being put out of account, that modern nation will in the intellectual and spiritual sphere make most progress, which most thoroughly carries out this programme."

Now on my phrase, thus enlarged, Professor Huxley remarks that when I speak of the above-mentioned knowledge as enabling us to know ourselves and the world, I assert *literature* to contain the materials which suffice for thus making us know ourselves and the world.

But it is not by any means clear, says he, that after having learnt all which ancient and modern literatures have to tell us, we have laid a sufficiently broad and deep foundation for that criticism of life, that knowledge of ourselves and the world, which constitutes culture. On the contrary, Professor Huxley declares that he finds himself "wholly unable to admit that either nations or individuals will really advance, if their outfit draws nothing from the stores of physical science. An army without weapons of precision, and with no particular base of operations, might more hopefully enter upon a campaign on the Rhine, than a man, devoid of a knowledge of what physical science has done in the last century, upon a criticism of life."

This shows how needful it is for those who are to discuss any matter together, to have a common understanding as to the sense of the terms they employ, — how needful, and how difficult. What Professor Huxley says, implies just the reproach which is so often brought against the study of *belles lettres*, as they are called: that the study is an elegant one, but slight and ineffectual; a smattering of Greek and Latin and other ornamental things, of little use for any one whose object is to get at truth, and to be a practical man. So, too, M. Renan talks of the "superficial humanism" of a school-course which treats us as if we were all going to be poets, writers, preachers, orators, and he opposes this humanism to positive science, or the critical search after truth. And there is always a tendency in those who are remonstrating against the predominance of letters in education, to understand by letters *belles lettres*, and by *belles lettres* a superficial humanism, the opposite of science or true knowledge.

But when we talk of knowing Greek and Roman antiquity, for instance, which is the knowledge people have called the humanities, I for my part mean a knowledge which is something more than a superficial humanism, mainly decorative. "I call all teaching *scientific*," says Wolf, the critic of Homer, "which is systematically laid out and followed up to its original sources. For example: a knowledge of classical antiquity is scientific when the remains of classical antiquity are correctly studied in the original languages." There can be no doubt that Wolf is perfectly right; that all learning is scientific which is systematically laid out and followed up to its original sources, and that a genuine humanism is scientific.

When I speak of knowing Greek and Roman antiquity, therefore, as a help to knowing ourselves and the world, I mean more than a knowledge of so much vocabulary, so much grammar, so many portions of authors in the Greek and Latin languages. I mean knowing the Greeks and Romans, and their life and genius, and what they were and did in the world; what we get from them, and what is its value.

That, at least, is the ideal; and when we talk of endeavouring to know Greek and Roman antiquity, as a help to knowing ourselves and the world, we mean endeavouring so to know them as to satisfy this ideal, however much we may still fall short of it.

The same also as to knowing our own and other modern nations, with the like aim of getting to understand ourselves and the world. To know the best that has been thought and said by the modern nations, is to know, says Professor Huxley, "only what modern *literatures* have to tell us; it is the criticism of life contained in modern literature." And yet "the distinctive character of our times," he urges, "lies in the vast and constantly increasing part which is played by natural knowledge." And how, therefore, can a man, devoid of knowledge of what physical science has done in the last century enter hopefully upon a criticism of modern life?

Let us, I say, be agreed about the meaning of the terms we are using. I talk of knowing the best which has been thought and uttered in the world; Professor Huxley says this means knowing *literature.* Literature is a large word; it may mean everything written with letters or printed in a book. Euclid's *Elements* and Newton's *Principia* are thus literature. All knowledge that reaches us through books is literature. But by literature Professor Huxley means *belles lettres.* He means to make me say, that knowing the best which has been thought and said by the modern nations is knowing their *belles lettres* and no more. And this is no sufficient equipment, he argues, for a criticism of modern life. But as I do not mean, by knowing ancient Rome, knowing merely more or less of Latin *belles lettres,* and taking no account of Rome's military, and political, and legal, and administrative work in the world; and as, by knowing ancient Greece, I understand knowing her as the giver of Greek art, and the guide to a free and right use of reason and to scientific method, and the founder of our mathematics and physics and astronomy and biology, — I understand knowing her as all this, and not merely knowing certain Greek poems, and histories, and treatises, and speeches, — so as to the knowledge of modern nations also. By knowing modern nations, I mean not merely knowing their *belles lettres,* but knowing also what has been done by such men as Copernicus, Galileo, Newton, Darwin. "Our ancestors learned," says Professor Huxley, "that the earth is the centre of the visible universe, and that man is the cynosure of things terrestrial; and more especially was it inculcated that the course of nature had no fixed order, but that it could be, and constantly was, altered." But for us now, continues Professor Huxley, "the notions of the beginning and the end of the world entertained by our forefathers are no longer credible. It is very certain that the earth is not the chief body in the material universe, and that the world is not subordinated to man's use. It is even more certain that nature is the expression of a definite order, with which nothing interferes." "And yet," he cries, "the purely classical education advocated by the representatives of the humanists in our day gives no inkling of all this!"

In due place and time I will just touch upon that vexed question of classical education; but at present the question is as to what is meant by knowing the best which modern nations have thought and said. It is not knowing their *belles lettres* merely which is meant. To know Italian *belles lettres* is not to know Italy, and to know English *belles lettres* is not to know England. Into knowing Italy and England there comes a great deal more, Galileo and Newton, amongst it. The reproach of being a superficial humanism, a tincture of *belles lettres,* may attach rightly enough to some other disciplines; but to the particular discipline recommended when I proposed knowing the best that has been thought and said in the world, it does not apply. In that best I certainly include what in modern times has been thought and said by the great observers and knowers of nature.

There is, therefore, really no question between Professor Huxley and me as to whether knowing the great results of the modern scientific study of nature is not required as a part of our culture, as well as knowing the products of literature and art. But to follow the processes by which those results are reached, ought, say the friends of physical science, to be made the staple of education for the bulk of mankind. And here there does arise a question between those whom Professor Huxley calls with playful sarcasm "the Levites of culture," and those whom the poor humanist is sometimes apt to regard as its Nebuchadnezzars.

The great results of the scientific investigation of nature we are agreed upon knowing, but how much of our study are we bound to give to the processes by which those results are reached? The results have their visible bearing on human life. But all the processes, too, all the items of fact, by which those results are reached and established, are interesting. All knowledge is interesting to a wise man, and the knowledge of nature is interesting to all men. It is very interesting to know, that, from the albuminous white of the egg, the chick in the egg gets the materials for its flesh, bones, blood, and feathers; while, from the fatty yolk of the egg, it gets the heat and energy which enable it at length to break its shell and begin the world. It is less interesting, perhaps, but still it is interesting, to know that when a taper burns, the wax is converted into carbonic acid and water. Moreover, it is quite true that the habit of dealing with facts, which is given by the study of nature, is, as the friends of physical science praise it for being, an excellent discipline. The appeal, in the study of nature, is constantly to observation and experiment; not only is it said that the thing is so, but we can be made to see that it is so. Not only does a man tell us that when a taper burns the wax is converted into carbonic acid and water, as a man may tell us, if he likes, that Charon is punting his ferry-boat on the river Styx, or that Victor Hugo is a sublime poet, or Mr. Gladstone the most admirable of statesmen; but we are made to see that the conversion into carbonic acid and water does actually happen. This reality of natural knowledge it is, which makes the friends of physical science contrast it, as a knowledge of things, with the humanist's knowledge, which is, say they, a knowledge of words. And hence Professor Huxley is moved to lay it down that, "for the purpose of attaining real culture, an exclusively scientific education is at least as effectual as an exclusively literary education." And a certain President of the Section for Mechanical Science in the British Association is, in Scripture phrase, "very bold," and declares that if a man, in his mental training, "has substituted literature and history for natural science, he has chosen the less useful alternative." But whether we go these lengths or not, we must all admit that in natural science the habit gained of dealing with facts is a most valuable discipline, and that every one should have some experience of it.

More than this, however, is demanded by the reformers. It is proposed to make the training in natural science the main part of education, for the great majority of mankind at any rate. And here, I confess, I part company with the friends of physical science, with whom up to this point I have been agreeing. In differing from them, however, I wish to proceed with the utmost caution and diffidence. The smallness of my own acquaintance with the disciplines of natural science is ever before my mind, and I am fearful of doing these disciplines an injustice. The ability and pugnacity of the partisans of natural science make them formidable persons to contradict. The tone of tentative inquiry, which befits a being of dim faculties and bounded knowledge, is the tone I would wish to take and not to depart from. At present it seems to me, that those who are for giving to natural knowledge, as they call it, the chief place in the education of the majority of mankind, leave one important thing out of their account: the constitution of human nature. But I put this forward on the strength of some facts not at all recondite, very far from it; facts capable of being stated in the simplest possible fashion, and to which, if I so state them, the man of science will, I am sure, be willing to allow their due weight.

Deny the facts altogether, I think, he hardly can. He can hardly deny, that when we set ourselves to enumerate the powers which go to the building up of human life, and say that they are the power of conduct, the power of intellect and knowledge, the power of beauty, and the power of social life and manners, — he can hardly deny that this scheme, though drawn in rough and plain lines enough, and not pretending to scientific exactness, does yet give a fairly true representation of the matter. Human nature is built up by these powers; we have the need for them all. When we have rightly met and adjusted the claims of them all, we shall then be in a fair way for getting soberness and righteousness, with wisdom. This is evident enough, and the friends of physical science would admit it.

But perhaps they may not have sufficiently observed another thing: namely, that the several powers just mentioned are not isolated, but there is, in the generality of mankind, a perpetual tendency to relate them one to another in divers ways. With one such way of relating them I am particularly concerned now. Following our instinct for intellect and knowledge, we acquire pieces of knowledge; and presently, in the generality of men, there arises the desire to relate these pieces of knowledge to our sense for conduct, to our sense for beauty, — and there is weariness and dissatisfaction if the desire is baulked. Now in this desire lies, I think, the strength of that hold which letters have upon us.

All knowledge is, as I said just now, interesting; and even items of knowledge which from the nature of the case cannot well be related, but must stand isolated in our thoughts, have their interest. Even lists of exceptions have their interest. If we are studying Greek accents, it is interesting to know that *pais* and *pas,* and some other monosyllables of the same form of declension, do not take the circumflex upon the last syllable of the genitive plural, but vary, in this respect, from the common rule. If we are studying physiology, it is interesting to know that the pulmonary artery carries dark blood and the pulmonary vein carries bright blood, departing in this respect from the common rule for the division of labour between the veins and the arteries. But every one knows how we seek naturally to combine the pieces of our knowledge together, to bring them under general rules, to relate them to principles; and how unsatisfactory and tiresome it would be to go on for ever learning lists of exceptions, or accumulating items of fact which must stand isolated.

Well, that same need of relating our knowledge, which operates here within the sphere of our knowledge itself, we shall find operating, also, outside that sphere. We experience, as we go on learning and knowing, — the vast majority of us experience, — the need of relating what we have learnt and known to the sense which we have in us for conduct, to the sense which we have in us for beauty.

A certain Greek prophetess of Mantineia in Arcadia, Diotima by name, once explained to the philosopher Socrates that love, and impulse, and bent of all kinds, is, in fact, nothing else but the desire in men that good should for ever be present to them. This desire for good, Diotima assured Socrates, is our fundamental desire, of which fundamental desire every impulse in us is only some one particular form. And therefore this fundamental desire it is, I suppose, — this desire in men that good should be for ever present to them, — which acts in us when we feel the impulse for relating our knowledge to our sense for conduct and to our sense for beauty. At any rate, with men in general the instinct exists. Such is human nature. And the instinct, it will be admitted, is innocent, and human nature is preserved by our following the lead of its innocent instincts. Therefore, in seeking to gratify this instinct in question, we are following the instinct of self-preservation in humanity.

But, no doubt, some kinds of knowledge cannot be made to directly serve the instinct in question, cannot be directly related to the sense for beauty, to the sense for conduct. These are instrument-knowledges; they lead on to other knowledges, which can. A man who passes his life in instrument-knowledges is a specialist. They may be invaluable as instruments to something beyond, for those who have the gift thus to employ them; and they may be disciplines in themselves wherein it is useful for every one to have some schooling. But it is inconceivable that the generality of men should pass all their mental life with Greek accents or with formal logic. My friend Professor Sylvester, who is one of the first mathematicians in the world, holds transcendental doctrines as to the virtue of mathematics, but those doctrines are not for common men. In the very Senate House and heart of our English Cambridge I once ventured, though not without an apology for my profaneness, to hazard the opinion that for the majority of mankind a little of mathematics, even, goes a long way. Of course this is quite consistent with their being of immense importance as an instrument to something else; but it is the few who have the aptitude for thus using them, not the bulk of mankind.

The natural sciences do not, however, stand on the same footing with these instrument-knowledges. Experience shows us that the generality of men will find more interest in learning that, when a taper burns, the wax is converted into carbonic acid and water, or in learning the explanation of the phenomenon of dew, or in learning how the circulation of the blood is carried on, than they find in learning that the genitive plural of *pais* and *pas* does not take the circumflex on the termination. And one piece of natural knowledge is added to another, and others are added to that, and at last we come to propositions so interesting as Mr. Darwin's famous proposition that "our ancestor was a hairy quadruped furnished with a tail and pointed ears, probably arboreal in his habits." Or we come to propositions of such reach and magnitude as those which Professor Huxley delivers, when he says that the notions of our forefathers about the beginning and the end of the world were all wrong, and that nature is the expression of a definite order with which nothing interferes.

Interesting, indeed, these results of science are, important they are, and we should all of us be acquainted with them. But what I now wish you to mark is, that we are still, when they are propounded to us and we receive them, we are still in the sphere of intellect and knowledge. And for the generality of men there will be found, I say, to arise, when they have duly taken in the proposition that their ancestor was "a hairy quadruped furnished with a tail and pointed ears, probably arboreal in his habits," there will be found to arise an invincible desire to relate this proposition to the sense in us for conduct, and to the sense in us for beauty. But this the men of science will not do for us, and will hardly even profess to do. They will give us other pieces of knowledge, other facts, about other animals and their ancestors, or about plants, or about stones, or about stars; and they may finally bring us to those great "general conceptions of the universe, which are forced upon us all," says Professor Huxley, "by the progress of physical science." But still it will be *knowledge* only which they give us; knowledge not put for us into relation with our sense for conduct, our sense for beauty, and touched with emotion by being so put; not thus put for us, and therefore, to the majority of mankind, after a certain while, unsatisfying, wearying.

Not to the born naturalist, I admit. But what do we mean by a born naturalist? We mean a man in whom the zeal for observing nature is so uncommonly strong and eminent, that it marks him off from the bulk of mankind. Such a man will pass his life happily in collecting natural knowledge and reasoning upon it, and will ask for nothing, or hardly anything, more. I have heard it said that the sagacious and admirable naturalist whom we lost not very long ago, Mr. Darwin, once owned to a friend that for his part he did not experience the necessity for two things which most men find so necessary to them, — religion and poetry; science and the domestic affections, he thought, were enough. To a born naturalist, I can well understand that this should seem so. So absorbing is his occupation with nature, so strong his love for his occupation, that he goes on acquiring natural knowledge and reasoning upon it, and has little time or inclination for thinking about getting it related to the desire in man for conduct, the desire in man for beauty. He relates it to them for himself as he goes along, so far as he feels the need; and he draws from the domestic affections all the additional solace necessary. But then Darwins are extremely rare. Another great and admirable master of natural knowledge, Faraday, was a Sandemanian. That is to say, he related his knowledge to his instinct for conduct and to his instinct for beauty, by the aid of that respectable Scottish sectary, Robert Sandeman. And so strong, in general, is the demand of religion and poetry to have their share in a man, to associate themselves with his knowing, and to relieve and rejoice it, that, probably, for one man amongst us with the disposition to do as Darwin did in this respect, there are at least fifty with the disposition to do as Faraday.

Education lays hold upon us, in fact, by satisfying this demand. Professor Huxley holds up to scorn mediæval education, with its neglect of the knowledge of nature, its poverty even of literary studies, its formal logic devoted to "showing how and why that which the Church said was true must be true." But the great mediæval Universities were not brought into being, we may be sure, by the zeal for giving a jejune and contemptible education. Kings have been their nursing fathers, and queens have been their nursing mothers, but not for this. The mediæval Universities came into being, because the supposed knowledge, delivered by Scripture and the Church, so deeply engaged men's hearts, by so simply, easily, and powerfully relating itself to their desire for conduct, their desire for beauty. All other knowledge was dominated by this supposed knowledge and was subordinated to it, because of the surpassing strength of the hold which it gained upon the affections of men, by allying itself profoundly with their sense for conduct, their sense for beauty.

But now, says Professor Huxley, conceptions of the universe fatal to the notions held by our forefathers have been forced upon us by physical science. Grant to him that they are thus fatal, that the new conceptions must and will soon become current everywhere, and that every one will finally perceive them to be fatal to the beliefs of our forefathers. The need of humane letters, as they are truly called, because they serve the paramount desire in men that good should be for ever present to them, — the need of humane letters, to establish a relation between the new conceptions, and our instinct for beauty, our instinct for conduct, is only the more visible. The Middle Age could do without humane letters, as it could do without the study of nature, because its supposed knowledge was made to engage its emotions so powerfully. Grant that the supposed knowledge disappears, its power of being made to engage the emotions will of course disappear along with it, — but the emotions themselves, and their claim to be engaged and satisfied, will remain. Now if we find by experience that humane letters have an undeniable power of engaging the emotions, the importance of humane letters in a man's training becomes not less, but greater, in proportion to the success of modern science in extirpating what it calls "mediæval thinking."

Have humane letters, then, have poetry and eloquence, the power here attributed to them of engaging the emotions, and do they exercise it? And if they have it and exercise it, *how* do they exercise it, so as to exert an influence upon man's sense for conduct, his sense for beauty? Finally, even if they both can and do exert an influence upon the senses in question, how are they to relate to them the results, — the modern results, — of natural science? All these questions may be asked. First, have poetry and eloquence the power of calling out the emotions? The appeal is to experience. Experience shows that for the vast majority of men, for mankind in general, they have the power. Next, do they exercise it? They do. But then, *how* do they exercise it so as to affect man's sense for conduct, his sense for beauty? And this is perhaps a case for applying the Preacher's words: "Though a man labour to seek it out, yet he shall not find it; yea, farther, though a wise man think to know it, yet shall he not be able to find it."[1] Why should it be one thing, in its effect upon the emotions, to say, "Patience is a virtue," and quite another thing, in its effect upon the emotions, to say with Homer,

τλητὸν γὰρ Μοῖραι θυμὸν θέσαν ἀνθρώποισιν—[2]

"for an enduring heart have the destinies appointed to the children of men"? Why should it be one thing, in its effect upon the emotions, to say with the philosopher Spinoza, *Felicitas in eo consistit quod homo suum esse conservare potest* — "Man's happiness consists in his being able to preserve his own essence," and quite another thing, in its effect upon the emotions, to say with the Gospel, "What is a man advantaged, if he gain the whole world, and lose himself, forfeit himself?" How does this difference of effect arise? I cannot tell, and I am not much concerned to know; the important thing is that it does arise, and that we can profit by it. But how, finally, are poetry and eloquence to exercise the power of relating the modern results of natural science to man's instinct for conduct, his instinct for beauty? And here again I answer that I do not know *how* they will exercise it, but that they can and will exercise it I am sure. I do not mean that modern philosophical poets and modern philosophical moralists are to come and relate for us, in express terms, the results of modern scientific research to our instinct for conduct, our instinct for beauty. But I mean that we shall find, as a matter of experience, if we know

1 *Ecclesiastes,* viii, 17.
2 *Iliad,* xxiv, 49.

the best that has been thought and uttered in the world, we shall find that the art and poetry and eloquence of men who lived, perhaps, long ago, who had the most limited natural knowledge, who had the most erroneous conceptions about many important matters, we shall find that this art, and poetry, and eloquence, have in fact not only the power of refreshing and delighting us, they have also the power, — such is the strength and worth, in essentials, of their authors' criticism of life, — they have a fortifying, and elevating, and quickening, and suggestive power, capable of wonderfully helping us to relate the results of modern science to our need for conduct, our need for beauty. Homer's conceptions of the physical universe were, I imagine, grotesque; but really, under the shock of hearing from modern science that "the world is not subordinated to man's use, and that man is not the cynosure of things terrestrial," I could, for my own part, desire no better comfort than Homer's line which I quoted just now,

τλητὸν γὰρ Μοῖραι θυμὸν θέσαν ἀνθρώποισιν—

"for an enduring heart have the destinies appointed to the children of men!"

And the more that men's minds are cleared, the more that the results of science are frankly accepted, the more that poetry and eloquence come to be received and studied as what in truth they really are, — the criticism of life by gifted men, alive and active with extraordinary power at an unusual number of points; — so much the more will the value of humane letters, and of art also, which is an utterance having a like kind of power with theirs, be felt and acknowledged, and their place in education be secured.

Let us therefore, all of us, avoid indeed as much as possible any invidious comparison between the merits of humane letters, as means of education, and the merits of the natural sciences. But when some President of a Section for Mechanical Science insists on making the comparison, and tells us that "he who in his training has substituted literature and history for natural science has chosen the less useful alternative," let us make answer to him that the student of humane letters only, will, at least, know also the great general conceptions brought in by modern physical science; for science, as Professor Huxley says, forces them upon us all. But the student of the natural sciences only, will, by our very hypothesis, know nothing of humane letters; not to mention that in setting himself to be perpetually accumulating natural knowledge, he sets himself to do what only specialists have in general the gift for doing genially. And so he will probably be unsatisfied, or at any rate incomplete, and even more incomplete than the student of humane letters only.

I once mentioned in a school-report, how a young man in one of our English training colleges having to paraphrase the passage in *Macbeth* beginning,

> Can'st thou not minister to a mind diseased?

turned this line into, "Can you not wait upon the lunatic?" And I remarked what a curious state of things it would be, if every pupil of our national schools knew, let us say, that the moon is two thousand one hundred and sixty miles in diameter, and thought at the same time that a good paraphrase for

> Can'st thou not minister to a mind diseased?

was, "Can you not wait upon the lunatic?" If one is driven to choose, I think I would rather have a young person ignorant about the moon's diameter, but aware that "Can you not wait upon the lunatic?" is bad, than a young person whose education had been such as to manage things the other way.

Or to go higher than the pupils of our national schools. I have in my mind's eye a member of our British Parliament who comes to travel here in America, who afterwards relates his travels, and who shows a really masterly knowledge of the geology of this great country and of its mining capabilities, but who ends by gravely suggesting that the United States should borrow a prince from our Royal Family, and should make him their king, and should create a House of Lords of great landed proprietors after the pattern of ours; and then America, he thinks, would have her future happily and perfectly secured. Surely, in this case, the President of the Section for Mechanical Science would himself hardly say that our member of Parliament, by concentrating himself upon geology and mineralogy, and so on, and not attending to literature and history, had "chosen the more useful alternative."

If then there is to be separation and option between humane letters on the one hand, and the natural sciences on the other, the great majority of mankind, all who have not exceptional and overpowering aptitudes for the study of nature, would do well, I cannot but think, to choose to be educated in humane letters rather than in the natural sciences. Letters will call out their being at more points, will make them live more.

I said that before I ended I would just touch on the question of classical education, and I will keep my word. Even if literature is to retain a large place in our education, yet Latin and Greek, say the friends of progress, will certainly have to go. Greek is the grand offender in the eyes of these gentlemen. The attackers of the established course of study think that against Greek, at any rate, they have irresistible arguments. Literature may perhaps be needed in education, they say; but why on earth should it be Greek literature? Why not French or German? Nay, "has not an Englishman models in his own literature of every kind of excellence?" As before, it is not on any weak pleadings of my own that I rely for convincing the gainsayers; it is on the constitution of human nature itself, and on the instinct of self-preservation in humanity. The instinct for beauty is set in human nature, as surely as the instinct for knowledge is set there, or the instinct for conduct. If the instinct for beauty is served by Greek literature and art as it is served by no other literature and art, we may trust to the instinct of self-preservation in humanity for keeping Greek as part of our culture. We may trust to it for even making the study of Greek more prevalent than it is now. Greek will come, I hope, some day to be studied more rationally than at present; but it will be increasingly studied as men increasingly feel the need in them for beauty, and how powerfully Greek art and Greek literature can serve this need. Women will again study Greek, as Lady Jane Grey did; I believe that in that chain of forts, with which the fair host of the Amazons are now engirdling our English universities, I find that here in America, in colleges like Smith College in Massachusetts, and Vassar College in the State of New York, and in the happy families of the mixed universities out West, they are studying it already.

Defuit una mihi symmetria prisca, — "The antique symmetry was the one thing wanting to me," said Leonardo da Vinci; and he was an Italian. I will not presume to speak for the Americans, but I am sure that, in the Englishman, the want of this admirable symmetry of the Greeks is a thousand times more great and crying than in any Italian. The results of the want show themselves most glaringly, perhaps, in our architecture, but they show themselves, also, in all our art. *Fit details strictly combined, in view of a large general result nobly conceived;* that is just the beautiful *symmetria prisca* of the Greeks, and it is just where we English fail, where all our art fails. Striking ideas we have, and well-executed details we have; but that high symmetry which, with satisfying and delightful effect, combines them, we seldom or never have. The glorious beauty of the Acropolis at Athens did not come from single fine things stuck about on that hill, a statue here, a gateway there; — no, it arose from all things being perfectly combined for a supreme total effect. What must not an Englishman feel about our deficiencies in this respect, as the sense for beauty, whereof this symmetry is an essential element, awakens and strengthens within him! what will not one day be his respect and desire for Greece and its *symmetria prisca,* when the scales drop from his eyes as he walks the London streets, and he sees such a lesson in meanness as the Strand, for instance, in its true deformity! But here we are coming to our friend Mr. Ruskin's province, and I will not intrude upon it, for he is its very sufficient guardian.

And so we at last find, it seems, we find flowing in favour of the humanities the natural and necessary stream of things, which seemed against them when we started. The "hairy quadruped furnished with a tail and pointed ears, probably arboreal in his habits," this good fellow carried hidden in his nature, apparently, something destined to develop into a necessity for humane letters. Nay, more; we seem finally to be even led to the further conclusion that our hairy ancestor carried in his nature, also, a necessity for Greek.

And therefore, to say the truth, I cannot really think that humane letters are in much actual danger of being thrust out from their leading place in education, in spite of the array of authorities against them at this moment. So long as human nature is what it is, their attractions will remain irresistible. As with Greek, so with letters generally: they will some day come, we may hope, to be studied more rationally, but they will not lose their place. What will happen will rather be that there will be crowded into education other matters besides, far too many; there will be, perhaps, a period of unsettlement and confusion and false tendency; but letters will not in the end lose their leading place. If they lose it for a time, they will get it back again. We shall be brought back to them by our wants and aspirations. And a poor humanist may possess his soul in patience, neither strive nor cry, admit the energy and brilliancy of the partisans of physical science, and their present favour with the public, to be far greater than his own, and still have a happy faith that the nature of things works silently on behalf of the studies which he loves, and that, while we shall all have to acquaint ourselves with the great results reached by modern science, and to give ourselves as much training in its disciplines as we can conveniently carry, yet the majority of men will always require humane letters; and so much the more, as they have the more and the greater results of science to relate to the need in man for conduct, and to the need in him for beauty.

Society

FRIENDSHIP'S GARLAND:

Being the Conversations, Letters, and Opinions of the late Arminius, Baron von Thunder-Ten-Tronckh

Letter VI

I become intrusted with the Views of Arminius on Compulsory Education

Grub Street, April 20, 1867.

Sir, —

It is a long while since you have heard anything of Arminius and me, though I do hope you have sometimes given a thought to us both. The truth is we have been in the country. You may imagine how horribly disagreeable Arminius made himself during the famous snow in London at the beginning of this year. About the state of the streets he was bad enough, but about the poor frozen-out working men who went singing without let or hindrance before our houses, he quite made my blood creep. "The dirge of a society *qui s'en va*," he used to call their pathetic songs. It is true I had always an answer for him — "Thank God, we are not Hausmannised yet!" and if that was not enough, and he wanted the philosophy of the thing, why I turned to a sort of constitutional commonplace book, or true Englishman's *vade mecum*, which I have been these many years forming for my own use by potting extracts from the *Times* and which I hope one day to give to the world, and I read him this golden aphorism: "Administrative, military, and clerical tyranny are unknown in this country, because the educated class discharges all the corresponding functions through committees of its own body." "Well, then," Arminius would answer, "show me your administrative committee for ridding us of these cursed frozen-out impostors." "My dear Arminius," was my quiet reply, "voluntary organisations are not to be dealt with in this peremptory manner. The administrative committee you ask for will develop itself in good time; its future members are probably now at nurse. In England we like our improvements to *grow,* not to be manufactured."

However the mental strain, day after day, of this line of high constitutional argument was so wearing, that I gladly acceded to a proposal made by Arminius in one of his fits of grumbling to go with him for a little while into the country. So into the country we went, and there, under his able guidance, I have been assiduously pursuing the study of German philosophy. As a rule, I attend to nothing else just now; but when we were taking one of our walks abroad the other morning, an incident happened which led us to discuss the subject of compulsory education, and, as this subject is beginning to awaken deep interest in the public mind, I think you may be glad to have an account of the incident, and of the valuable remarks on compulsory education which were drawn from Arminius by it.

We were going out the other morning on one of our walks, as I said, when we saw a crowd before the inn of the country town where we have been staying. It was the magistrates' day for sitting, and I was glad of an opportunity to show off our local self-government to a bureaucracy-ridden Prussian like Arminius. So I stopped in the crowd, and there we saw an old fellow in a smock-frock, with a white head, a low forehead, a red nose, and a foxy expression of countenance, being taken along to the justice-room. Seeing among the bystanders a contributor to the *Daily Telegraph,*[1] whom I formerly knew well enough, — for he had the drawing-room floor underneath me in Grub Street, but the magnificent circulation of that journal has long since carried him, like the course of empire, westward, — I asked him if he could tell me what the prisoner was charged with. I found it was a hardened old poacher, called Diggs, — Zephaniah Diggs, — and that he was had up for snaring a hare, — probably his ten-thousandth. The worst of the story, to my mind, was that the old rogue had a heap of young children by a second wife whom he had married late in life, and that not one of these children would he send to school, but persisted in letting them all run wild, and grow up in utter barbarism.

I hastened to tell Arminius that it was a poaching case; and I added that it was not always, perhaps, in poaching cases that our local self-government appeared to the best advantage. "In the present case,

1 Do you recognise yourself, Leo? Is it presumptuous in me, upon giving this volume to the world, to bid you too, my friend, say with the poet: *Non omnis moriar?* — Ed. [i.e., Arnold, the supposed "editor" of these letters].

however, there is," said I, "no danger; for a representative of the *Daily Telegraph* is down here, to be on the look-out for justices' justice, and to prevent oppression." Immediately afterwards I was sorry I had said this, for there are unfortunately several things which operate on Arminius like scarlet on a bull, making him vicious the moment he comes across them; and the *Daily Telegraph* is one of these things. He declares it foments our worst faults; and he is fond of applying to it Dryden's dictum on Elkanah Settle, that its style is boisterous and its prose incorrigibly lewd. Though I do certainly think its prose a little full-bodied, yet I cannot bear to hear Arminius apply such a term to it as "incorrigibly lewd;" and I always remonstrate with him. "No, Arminius," I always say, "I hope not *incorrigibly;* I should be sorry to think that of a publication which is forming the imagination and taste of millions of Englishmen." "Pleasant news," was Arminius's answer, the last time I urged this to him, "pleasant news; the next batch of you, then, will be even more charming than the present!"

I trouble you with all this, Sir, to account for the acerbity of tone in some of Arminius's subsequent conversation; an acerbity he too often manifests, and which tends, as I tell him, to detract from the influence which his talents and acquirements would otherwise give him. On the present occasion he took no direct notice of my mention of the *Daily Telegraph*, but seemed quite taken up with scrutinising old Diggs. "Such a peasant as that wretched old creature," he said at last, "is peculiar, my dear friend, to your country. Only look at that countenance! Centuries of feudalism have effaced in it every gleam of humane life." . . . "Centuries of fiddlesticks!" interrupted I (for I assure you, Sir, I can stand up to Arminius well enough on a proper occasion). "My dear Arminius, how can you allow yourself to talk such rubbish? Gleam of humane life, indeed! do but look at the twinkle in the old rogue's eye. He has plenty of life and wits about him, has old Diggs, I can assure you; you just try and come round him about a pot of beer!" "The mere cunning of an animal!" retorted Arminius. "For my part," pursued I, "it is his children I think most about; I am told not one of them has ever seen the inside of a school. Do you know, Arminius, I begin to think, and many people in this country begin to think, that the time has almost come for taking a leaf out of your Prussian book, and applying, in the education of children of this class, what the great Kant calls the categorical imperative. The gap between them and our educated and intelligent classes is really too frightful." "Your educated and intelligent classes!" sneered Arminius, in his very most offensive manner; "where are they? I should like to see them."

I was not going to stand and hear our aristocracy and middle-class set down in this way; so, treating Arminius's ebullition of spite as beneath my notice, I pushed my way through the crowd to the inn-door. I asked the policeman there what magistrates were on the bench to-day. "Viscount Lumpington," says the man, "Reverend Esau Hittall, and Bottles Esquire." "Good heavens!" I exclaimed, turning round to Arminius, who had followed me, and forgetting, in my excitement, my just cause of offence with him, — "Good heavens, Arminius, if Bottles hasn't got himself made a county magistrate! *Sic itur ad astra.*" "Yes," says Arminius, with a smile, "one of your educated and intelligent classes, I suppose. And I dare say the other two are to match. Your magistrates are a sort of judges, I know; just the people who are drawn from the educated and intelligent classes. Now, what's sauce for the goose is sauce for the gander; if you put a pressure on one class to make it train itself properly, you must put a pressure on others to the same end. That is what we do in Prussia, if you are going to take a leaf out of our book. I want to hear what steps you take to put this pressure on people above old Diggs there, and then I will talk to you about putting it on old Diggs. Take his judges who are going to try him to-day; how about them? What training have you made them give themselves, and what are their qualifications?"

I luckily happen to know Lord Lumpington and Hittall pretty well, having been at college with them in former days, when I little thought the Philistines would have brought my grey hairs to a garret in Grub Street; and I have made the acquaintance of Mr. Bottles since, and know all about him. So I was able to satisfy Arminius's curiosity, and I had great pleasure in making him remark, as I did so, the rich diversity of our English life, the healthy natural play of our free institutions, and the happy blending of classes and characters which this promotes. "The three magistrates in that inn," said I, "are not three Government functionaries all cut out of one block; they embody our whole national life; — the land, religion, commerce, are all represented by them. Lord Lumpington is a peer of old family and great estate; Esau Hittall is a clergyman; Mr. Bottles is one of our self-made middle-class men. Their politics are not all of one colour, and that colour the Government's. Lumpington is a Constitutional Whig; Hittall is a benighted old Tory. As for Mr. Bottles, he is a Radical of the purest water; quite one of the Manchester school. He was one of the earliest free-traders; he has always gone as straight as an arrow about Reform; he is an ardent voluntary in every possible line, opposed the Ten Hours' Bill, was one of the leaders of the Dissenting opposition out of Parliament which smashed up the education clauses of Sir James Graham's Factory Act; and he paid the whole expenses of a most important church-rate contest out of his own pocket. And, finally, he looks forward to marrying his deceased wife's sister. Table, as my friend Mr. Grant Duff says, the whole Liberal creed, and in not a single point of it will you find Bottles tripping!"

"That is all very well as to their politics," said Arminius, "but I want to hear about their education and intelligence." "There, too, I can satisfy you," I answered. "Lumpington was at Eton. Hittall was on the foundation at Charterhouse, placed there by his uncle, a distinguished prelate, who was one of the trustees. You know we English have no notion of your bureaucratic tyranny of treating the appointments to these great foundations as public patronage, and vesting them in a responsible minister; we vest them in independent magnates, who relieve the State of all work and responsibility, and never take a shilling of salary for their trouble. Hittall was the last of six nephews nominated to the Charterhouse by his uncle, this good prelate, who had thoroughly learnt the divine lesson that charity begins at home." "But I want to know what his nephew learnt," interrupted Arminius, "and what Lord Lumpington learnt at Eton." "They followed," said I, "the grand, old, fortifying, classical curriculum." Did they know anything when they left?" asked Arminius. "I have seen some longs and shorts of Hittall's," said I, "about the Calydonian Boar, which were not bad. But you surely don't need me to tell you, Arminius, that it is rather in training and bracing the mind for future acquisition, — a course of mental gymnastics we call it, — than in teaching any set thing, that the classical curriculum is so valuable." "Were the minds of Lord Lumpington and Mr. Hittall much braced by their mental gymnastics?" inquired Arminius. "Well," I answered, "during their three years at Oxford they were so much occupied with Bullingdon and hunting that there was no great opportunity to judge. But for my part I have always thought that their both getting their degree at last with flying colours, after three weeks of a famous coach for fast men, four nights without going to bed, and an incredible consumption of wet towels, strong cigars, and brandy-and-water, was one of the most astonishing feats of mental gymnastics I ever heard of."

"That will do for the land and the Church," said Arminius. "And now let us hear about commerce." "You mean how was Bottles educated?" answered I. "Here we get into another line altogether, but a very good line in its way, too. Mr. Bottles was brought up at the Lycurgus House Academy, Peckham. You are not to suppose from the name of Lycurgus that any Latin and Greek was taught in the establishment; the name only indicates the moral discipline, and the strenuous earnest character, imparted there. As to the instruction, the thoughtful educator who was principal of the Lycurgus House Academy, — Archimedes Silverpump, Ph.D., you must have heard of him in Germany? — had modern views. 'We must be men of our age,' he used to say. 'Useful knowledge, living languages, and the forming of the mind through observation and experiment, these are the fundamental articles of my educational creed.' Or, as I have heard his pupil Bottles put it in his expansive moments after dinner (Bottles used to ask me to dinner till that affair of yours with him in the Reigate train): 'Original man, Silverpump! fine mind! fine system! None of your antiquated rubbish — all practical work — latest discoveries in science — mind constantly kept excited — lots of interesting experiments — lights of all colours — fizz! fizz! bang! bang! That's what I call forming a man.' "

"And pray," cried Arminius, impatiently, "what sort of man do you suppose this infernal quack really formed in your precious friend Mr. Bottles?" "Well," I replied, "I hardly know how to answer that question. Bottles has certainly made an immense fortune; but as to Silverpump's effect on his mind, whether it was from any fault in the Lycurgus House system, whether it was that with a sturdy self-reliance thoroughly English, Bottles, ever since he quitted Silverpump, left his mind wholly to itself, his daily newspaper, and the Particular Baptist minister under whom he sate, or from whatever cause it was, certainly his mind, *quâ* mind——" "You need not go on," interrupted Arminius, with a magnificent wave of his hand, "I know what that man's mind, *quâ* mind, is, well enough."

But, Sir, the midnight oil is beginning to run very low; I hope, therefore, you will permit me to postpone the rest of Arminius's discourse till to-morrow. And meanwhile, Sir, I am, with all respect,

Your humble servant,

MATTHEW ARNOLD.

To

The EDITOR *of the* PALL MALL GAZETTE.

Letter VII

More about Compulsory Education

Grub Street, April 21, 1867.

SIR, —

I take up the thread of the interesting and important discussion on compulsory education between Arminius and me where I left it last night.

"But," continued Arminius, "you were talking of compulsory education, and your common people's want of it. Now, my dear friend, I want you to understand what this principle of compulsory education really means. It means that to ensure, as far as you can, every man's being fit for his business in life, you put education as a bar, or condition, between him and what he aims at. The principle is just as good for one class as another, and it is only by applying it impartially that you save its application from being insolent and invidious. Our Prussian peasant stands our compelling him to instruct himself before he may go about his calling, because he sees we believe in instruction, and compel our own class, too, in a way to make it really feel the pressure, to instruct itself before it may go about its calling. Now, you propose to make old Diggs's boys instruct themselves before they may go bird-scaring or sheep-tending. I want to know what you do to make those three worthies in that justice-room instruct themselves before they may go acting as magistrates and judges." "Do?" said I; "why, just look what they have done all of themselves. Lumpington and Hittall have had a public-school and university education; Bottles has had Dr. Silverpump's, and the practical training of business. What on earth would you have us make them do more?" "Qualify themselves for administrative or judicial functions, if they exercise them," said Arminius. "That is what really answers, in their case, to the compulsion you propose to apply to Diggs's boys. Sending Lord Lumpington and Mr. Hittall to school is nothing; the natural course of things takes them there. Don't suppose that, by doing this, you are applying the principle of compulsory education fairly, and as you apply it to Diggs's boys. You are not interposing, for the rich, education as a bar or condition between them and that which they aim at. But interpose it, as we do, between the rich and things they aim at, and I will say something to you. I should like to know what has made Lord Lumpington a magistrate?" "Made Lord Lumpington a magistrate?" said I; "why, the Lumpington estate, to be sure." "And the Reverend Esau Hittall?" continued Arminius. "Why, the Lumpington living, of course," said I. "And that man Bottles?" he went on. "His English energy and self-reliance," I answered very stiffly, for Arminius's incessant carping began to put me in a huff; "those same incomparable and truly British qualities which have just triumphed over every obstacle and given us the Atlantic telegraph! — and let me tell you, Von T., in my opinion it will be a long time before the 'Geist' of any pedant of a Prussian professor gives us anything half so valuable as that." "Pshaw!" replied Arminius, contemptuously; "that great rope, with a Philistine at each end of it talking inutilities!

"But in my country," he went on, "we should have begun to put a pressure on these future magistrates at school. Before we allowed Lord Lumpington and Mr. Hittall to go to the university at all, we should have examined them, and we should not have trusted the keepers of that absurd cockpit you took me down to see, to examine them as they chose, and send them jogging comfortably off to the university on their lame longs and shorts. No; there would have been some Mr. Grote as School Board Commissary, pitching into them questions about history, and some Mr. Lowe, as Crown Patronage Commissary, pitching into them questions about English literature; and these young men would have been kept from the university, as Diggs's boys are kept from their bird-scaring, till they had instructed themselves. Then, if, after three years of their university, they wanted to be magistrates, another pressure!—a great Civil Service examination before a board of experts, an examination in English law, Roman law, English history, history of jurisprudence——" "A most abominable liberty to take with Lumpington and Hittall!" exclaimed I. "Then your compulsory education is a most abominable liberty to take with Diggs's boys," retorted Arminius. "But good gracious! my dear Arminius," expostulated I, "do you really mean to maintain that a man can't put old Diggs in quod for snaring a hare without all this elaborate apparatus of Roman law and history of jurisprudence?" "And do you really mean to maintain," returned Arminius, "that a man can't go bird-scaring or sheep-tending without all this elaborate apparatus of a compulsory school?" "Oh, but," I answered, "to live at all, even at the lowest stage of human life, a man needs instruction." "Well," returned Arminius, "and to administer at all, even at the lowest stage of public administration, a man needs instruction." "We have never found it so," said I.

Arminius shrugged his shoulders and was silent. By this time the proceedings in the justice-room were drawn to an end, the majesty of the law had been vindicated against old Diggs, and the magistrates were coming out. I never saw a finer spectacle than my friend Arminius presented, as he stood by to gaze on the august trio as they passed. His pilot-coat was tightly buttoned round his stout form, his light blue eye shone, his sanguine cheeks were ruddier than ever with the cold morning and the excitement of discourse, his fell of tow was blown about by the March wind, and volumes of tobacco-smoke issued from his lips. So in old days stood, I imagine, his great namesake by the banks of the Lippe, glaring on the Roman legions before their destruction.

Lord Lumpington was the first who came out. His lordship good-naturedly recognised me with a nod, and then eyeing Arminius with surprise and curiosity: "Whom on earth have you got there?" he whispered. "A very distinguished young Prussian *savant*," replied I; and then dropping my voice, in my most impressive undertones I added: "And a young man of very good family, besides, my Lord." Lord Lumpington looked at Arminius again; smiled, shook his head, and then, turning away, and half aloud: "Can't compliment you on your friend," says he.

As for that centaur Hittall, who thinks of nothing on earth but field-sports, and in the performance of his sacred duties never warms up except when he lights on some passage about hunting or fowling, he always, whenever he meets me, remembers that in my unregenerate days, before Arminius inoculated me with a passion for intellect, I was rather fond of shooting, and not quite such a successful shot as Hittall himself. So, the moment he catches sight of me: "How d'ye do, old fellow?" he blurts out; "well, been shooting any straighter this year than you used to, eh?"

I turned from him in pity, and then I noticed Arminius, who had unluckily heard Lord Lumpington's unfavourable comment on him, absolutely purple with rage and blowing like a turkey-cock. "Never mind, Arminius," said I soothingly; "run after Lumpington, and ask him the square root of thirty-six." But now it was my turn to be a little annoyed, for at the same instant Mr. Bottles stepped into his brougham, which was waiting for him, and observing Arminius, his old enemy of the Reigate train, he took no notice whatever of me who stood there, with my hat in my hand, practising all the airs and graces I have learnt on the Continent; but, with that want of amenity I so often have to deplore in my countrymen, he pulled up the glass on our side with a grunt and a jerk, and drove off like the wind, leaving Arminius in a very bad temper indeed, and me, I confess, a good deal shocked and mortified.

However, both Arminius and I got over it, and have now returned to London, where I hope we shall before long have another good talk about educational matters. Whatever Arminius may say, I am still for going straight, with all our heart and soul, at compulsory education for the lower orders. Why, good heavens! Sir, with our present squeezable Ministry, we are evidently drifting fast to household suffrage, pure and simple; and I observe, moreover a Jacobinical spirit growing up in some quarters which gives me more alarm than even household suffrage. My elevated position in Grub Street, Sir, where I sit commercing with the stars, commands a view of a certain spacious and secluded back yard; and in that back yard, Sir, I tell you confidentially that I saw the other day with my own eyes that powerful young publicist, Mr. Frederic Harrison, in full evening costume, furbishing up a guillotine. These things are very serious; and I say, if the masses are to have power, let them be instructed, and don't swamp with ignorance and unreason the education and intelligence which now bear rule amongst us. For my part, when I think of Lumpington's estate, family, and connections, when I think of Hittall's shooting, and of the energy and self-reliance of Bottles, and when I see the unexampled pitch of splendour and security to which these have conducted us, I am bent, I own, on trying to make the new elements of our political system worthy of the old; and I say kindly, but firmly, to the compound householder in the French poet's beautiful words,[1] slightly altered: "Be great, O working class, for the middle and upper class are great!"

I am, Sir,
Your humble servant,
MATTHEW ARNOLD.

To
The EDITOR *of the* PALL MALL GAZETTE.

[1] "Et tâchez d'être grand, car le peuple grandit."

CULTURE AND ANARCHY

Introduction

In one of his speeches a short time ago, that fine speaker and famous Liberal, Mr. Bright, took occasion to have a fling at the friends and preachers of culture. "People who talk about what they call *culture!*" said he, contemptuously; "by which they mean a smattering of the two dead languages of Greek and Latin." And he went on to remark, in a strain with which modern speakers and writers have made us very familiar, how poor a thing this culture is, how little good it can do to the world, and how absurd it is for its possessors to set much store by it. And the other day a younger Liberal than Mr. Bright, one of a school whose mission it is to bring into order and system that body of truth with which the earlier Liberals merely fumbled, a member of the University of Oxford, and a very clever writer, Mr. Frederic Harrison, developed, in the systematic and stringent manner of his school, the thesis which Mr. Bright had propounded in only general terms. "Perhaps the very silliest cant of the day," said Mr. Frederic Harrison, "is the cant about culture. Culture is a desirable quality in a critic of new books, and sits well on a possessor of *belles lettres;* but as applied to politics, it means simply a turn for small fault-finding, love of selfish ease, and indecision in action. The man of culture is in politics one of the poorest mortals alive. For simple pedantry and want of good sense no man is his equal. No assumption is too unreal, no end is too unpractical for him. But the active exercise of politics requires common sense, sympathy, trust, resolution, and enthusiasm, qualities which your man of culture has carefully rooted up, lest they damage the delicacy of his critical olfactories. Perhaps they are the only class of responsible beings in the community who cannot with safety be entrusted with power."

Now for my part I do not wish to see men of culture asking to be entrusted with power; and, indeed, I have freely said, that in my opinion the speech most proper, at present, for a man of culture to make to a body of his fellow-countrymen who get him into a committee-room, is Socrates's: *Know thyself!* and this is not a speech to be made by men wanting to be entrusted with power. For this very indifference to direct political action I have been taken to task by the *Daily Telegraph,* coupled, by a strange perversity of fate, with just that very one of the Hebrew prophets whose style I admire the least, and called "an elegant Jeremiah." It is because I say (to use the words which the *Daily Telegraph* puts in my mouth): — "You mustn't make a fuss because you have no vote, — that is vulgarity; you mustn't hold big meetings to agitate for reform bills and to repeal corn laws, — that is the very height of vulgarity," — it is for this reason that I am called sometimes an elegant Jeremiah, sometimes a spurious Jeremiah, a Jeremiah about the reality of whose mission the writer in the *Daily Telegraph* has his doubts. It is evident, therefore, that I have so taken my line as not to be exposed to the whole brunt of Mr. Frederic Harrison's censure. Still, I have often spoken in praise of culture, I have striven to make all my works and ways serve the interests of culture. I take culture to be something a great deal more than what Mr. Frederic Harrison and others call it: "a desirable quality in a critic of new books." Nay, even though to a certain extent I am disposed to agree with Mr. Frederic Harrison, that men of culture are just the class of responsible beings in this community of ours who cannot properly, at present, be entrusted with power, I am not sure that I do not think this the fault of our community rather than of the men of culture. In short, although, like Mr. Bright and Mr. Frederic Harrison, and the editor of the *Daily Telegraph*, and a large body of valued friends of mine, I am a Liberal, yet I am a Liberal tempered by experience, reflection, and renouncement, and I am, above all, a believer in culture. Therefore I propose now to try and inquire, in the simple unsystematic way which best suits both my taste and my powers, what culture really is, what good it can do, what is our own special need of it; and I shall seek to find some plain grounds on which a faith in culture, — both my own faith in it and the faith of others, — may rest securely.

I. *Sweetness and Light*

The disparagers of culture make its motive curiosity; sometimes, indeed, they make its motive mere exclusiveness and vanity. The culture which is supposed to plume itself on a smattering of Greek and Latin is a culture which is begotten by nothing so intellectual as curiosity; it is valued either out of sheer vanity and ignorance or else as an engine of social and class distinction, separating its holder, like a badge or title, from other people who have not got it. No serious man would call this *culture*, or attach any value to it, as culture, at all. To find the real ground for the very different estimate which serious people will set upon culture, we must find some motive for culture in the terms of which may lie a real ambiguity; and such a motive the word *curiosity* gives us.

I have before now pointed out that we English do not, like the foreigners, use this word in a good sense as well as in a bad sense. With us the word is always used in a somewhat disapproving sense. A liberal and intelligent eagerness about the things of the mind may be meant by a foreigner when he speaks of curiosity, but with us the word always conveys a certain notion of frivolous and unedifying activity. In the *Quarterly Review*, some little time ago, was an estimate of the celebrated French critic, M. Sainte-Beuve, and a very inadequate estimate it in my judgment was. And its inadequacy consisted chiefly in this: that in our English way it left out of sight the double sense really involved in the word *curiosity*, thinking enough was said to stamp M. Sainte-Beuve with blame if it was said that he was impelled in his operations as a critic by curiosity, and omitting either to perceive that M. Sainte-Beuve himself, and many other people with him, would consider that this was praiseworthy and not blameworthy, or to point out why it ought really to be accounted worthy of blame and not of praise. For as there is a curiosity about intellectual matters which is futile, and merely a disease, so there is certainly a curiosity, — a desire after the things of the mind simply for their own sakes and for the pleasure of seeing them as they are, — which is, in an intelligent being, natural and laudable. Nay, and the very desire to see things as they are implies a balance and regulation of mind which is not often attained without fruitful effort, and which is the very opposite of the blind and diseased impulse of mind which is what we mean to blame when we blame curiosity. Montesquieu says: "The first motive which ought to impel us to study is the desire to augment the excellence of our nature, and to render an intelligent being yet more intelligent." This is the true ground to assign for the genuine scientific passion, however manifested, and for culture, viewed simply as a fruit of this passion; and it is a worthy ground, even though we let the term *curiosity* stand to describe it.

But there is of culture another view, in which not solely the scientific passion, the sheer desire to see things as they are, natural and proper in an intelligent being, appears as the ground of it. There is a view in which all the love of our neighbour, the impulses towards action, help, and beneficence, the desire for removing human error, clearing human confusion, and diminishing human misery, the noble aspiration to leave the world better and happier than we found it, — motives eminently such as are called social, — come in as part of the grounds of culture, and the main and pre-eminent part. Culture is then properly described not as having its origin in curiosity, but as having its origin in the love of perfection; it is *a study of perfection*. It moves by the force, not merely or primarily of the scientific passion for pure knowledge, but also of the moral and social passion for doing good. As, in the first view of it, we took for its worthy motto Montesquieu's words: "To render an intelligent being yet more intelligent!" so, in the second view of it, there is no better motto which it can have than these words of Bishop Wilson: "To make reason and the will of God prevail!"

Only, whereas the passion for doing good is apt to be overhasty in determining what reason and the will of God say, because its turn is for acting rather than thinking and it wants to be beginning to act; and whereas it is apt to take its own conceptions, which proceed from its own state of development and share in all the imperfections and immaturities of this, for a basis of action; what distinguishes culture is, that it is possessed by the scientific passion as well as by the passion of doing good; that it demands worthy notions of reason and the will of God, and does not readily suffer its own crude conceptions to substitute themselves for them. And knowing that no action or institution can be salutary and stable which is not based on reason and the will of God, it is not so bent on acting and instituting, even with the great aim of diminishing human error and misery ever before its thoughts, but that it can remember that acting and instituting are of little use, unless we know how and what we ought to act and to institute.

This culture is more interesting and more far-reaching than that other, which is founded solely on the scientific passion for knowing. But it needs times of faith and ardour, times when the intellectual horizon is opening and widening all round us, to flourish in. And is not the close and bounded intellectual horizon within which we have long lived and moved now lifting up, and are not new lights finding free passage to shine in upon us? For a long time there was no passage for them to make their way in upon us, and then it was of no use to think of adapting the world's action to them. Where was the hope of making reason and the will of God prevail among people who had a routine which they had christened reason and the will of God, in which they were inextricably bound, and beyond which they had no power of looking? But now the iron force of adhesion to the old routine, — social, political, religious, — has wonderfully yielded; the iron force of exclusion of all which is new has wonderfully yielded. The danger now is, not that people should obstinately refuse to allow anything but their old routine to pass for reason and the will of God, but either that they should allow some novelty or other to pass for these too easily, or else that they should underrate the importance of them altogether, and think it enough to follow action for its own sake, without troubling themselves to make reason and the will of God prevail therein. Now, then, is the moment for culture to be of service, culture which believes in making reason and the will of God prevail, believes in perfection, is the study and pursuit of perfection, and is no longer debarred, by a rigid invincible exclusion of whatever is new, from getting acceptance for its ideas, simply because they are new.

The moment this view of culture is seized, the moment it is regarded not solely as the endeavour to see things as they are, to draw towards a knowledge of the universal order which seems to be intended and aimed at in the world, and which it is a man's happiness to go along with or his misery to go counter to, — to learn, in short, the will of God, — the moment, I say, culture is considered not merely as the endeavour to *see* and *learn* this, but as the endeavour, also, to make it *prevail,* the moral, social, and beneficent character of culture becomes manifest. The mere endeavour to see and learn the truth for our own personal satisfaction is indeed a commencement for making it prevail, a preparing the way for this, which always serves this, and is wrongly, therefore, stamped with blame absolutely in itself and not only in its caricature and degeneration. But perhaps it has got stamped with blame, and disparaged with the dubious title of curiosity, because in comparison with this wider endeavour of such great and plain utility it looks selfish, petty, and unprofitable.

And religion, the greatest and most important of the efforts by which the human race has manifested its impulse to perfect itself, — religion, that voice of the deepest human experience, — does not only enjoin and sanction the aim which is the great aim of culture, the aim of setting ourselves to ascertain what perfection is and to make it prevail; but also, in determining generally in what human perfection consists, religion comes to a conclusion identical with that which culture, — culture seeking the determination of this question through *all* the voices of human experience which have been heard upon it, of art, science, poetry, philosophy, history, as well as of religion, in order to give a greater fulness and certainty to its solution, — likewise reaches. Religion says: *The kingdom of God is within you;* and culture, in like manner, places human perfection in an *internal* condition, in the growth and predominance of our humanity proper, as distinguished from our animality. It places it in the ever-increasing efficacy and in the general harmonious expansion of those gifts of thought and feeling, which make the peculiar dignity, wealth, and happiness of human nature. As I have said on a former occasion: "It is in making endless additions to itself, in the endless expansion of its powers, in endless growth in wisdom and beauty, that the spirit of the human race finds its ideal. To reach this ideal, culture is an indispensable aid, and that is the true value of culture." Not a having and a resting, but a growing and a becoming, is the character of perfection as culture conceives it; and here, too, it coincides with religion.

And because men are all members of one great whole, and the sympathy which is in human nature will not allow one member to be indifferent to the rest or to have a perfect welfare independent of the rest, the expansion of our humanity, to suit the idea of perfection which culture forms, must be a *general* expansion. Perfection, as culture conceives it, is not possible while the individual remains isolated. The individual is required, under pain of being stunted and enfeebled in his own development if he disobeys, to carry others along with him in his march towards perfection, to be continually doing all he can to enlarge and increase the volume of the human stream sweeping thitherward. And here, once more, culture lays on us the same obligation as religion, which says, as Bishop Wilson has admirably put it, that "to promote the kingdom of God is to increase and hasten one's own happiness."

But, finally, perfection, — as culture from a thorough disinterested study of human nature and human experience learns to conceive it, — is a harmonious expansion of *all* the powers, which make the beauty and worth of human nature, and is not consistent with the over-development of any one power at the expense of the rest. Here culture goes beyond religion, as religion is generally conceived by us.

If culture, then, is a study of perfection, and of harmonious perfection, general perfection, and perfection which consists in becoming something rather than in having something, in an inward condition of the mind and spirit, not in an outward set of circumstances, — it is clear that culture, instead of being the frivolous and useless thing which Mr. Bright, and Mr. Frederic Harrison, and many other Liberals are apt to call it, has a very important function to fulfil for mankind. And this function is particularly important in our modern world, of which the whole civilisation is, to a much greater degree than the civilisation of Greece and Rome, mechanical and external, and tends constantly to become more so. But above all in our own country has culture a weighty part to perform, because here that mechanical character, which civilisation tends to take everywhere, is shown in the most eminent degree. Indeed nearly all the characters of perfection, as culture teaches us to fix them, meet in this country with some powerful tendency which thwarts them and sets them at defiance. The idea of perfection as an *inward* condition of the mind and spirit is at variance with the mechanical and material civilisation in esteem with us, and nowhere, as I have said, so much in esteem as with us. The idea of perfection as a *general* expansion of the human family is at variance with our strong individualism, our hatred of all limits to the unrestrained swing of the individual's personality, our maxim of "every man for himself." Above all, the idea of perfection as a *harmonious* expansion of human nature is at variance with our want of flexibility, with our inaptitude for seeing more than one side of a thing, with our intense energetic absorption in the particular pursuit we happen to be following. So culture has a rough task to achieve in this country. Its preachers have, and are likely long to have, a hard time of it, and they will much oftener be regarded, for a great while to come, as elegant or spurious Jeremiahs than as friends and benefactors. That, however, will not prevent their doing in the end good service if they persevere. And, meanwhile, the mode of action they have to pursue, and the sort of habits they must fight against, ought to be made quite clear for every one to see, who may be willing to look at the matter attentively and dispassionately.

Faith in machinery is, I said, our besetting danger; often in machinery most absurdly disproportioned to the end which this machinery, if it is to do any good at all, is to serve; but always in machinery, as if it had a value in and for itself. What is freedom but machinery? what is population but machinery? what is coal but machinery? what are railroads but machinery? what is wealth but machinery? what are, even, religious organisations but machinery? Now almost every voice in England is accustomed to speak of these things as if they were precious ends in themselves, and therefore had some of the characters of perfection indisputably joined to them. I have before now noticed Mr. Roebuck's stock argument for proving the greatness and happiness of England as she is, and for quite stopping the mouths of all gainsayers. Mr. Roebuck is never weary of reiterating this argument of his, so I do not know why I should be weary of noticing it. "May not every man in England say what he likes?" — Mr. Roebuck perpetually asks; and that, he thinks, is quite sufficient, and when every man may say what he likes, our aspirations ought to be satisfied. But the aspirations of culture, which is the study of perfection, are not satisfied, unless what men say, when they may say what they like, is worth saying, — has good in it, and more good than bad. In the same way the *Times*, replying to some foreign strictures on the dress, looks, and behaviour of the English abroad, urges that the English ideal is that every one should be free to do and to look just as he likes. But culture indefatigably tries, not to make what each raw person may like the rule by which he fashions himself; but to draw ever nearer to a sense of what is indeed beautiful, graceful, and becoming, and to get the raw person to like that.

And in the same way with respect to railroads and coal. Every one must have observed the strange language current during the late discussions as to the possible failures of our supplies of coal. Our coal, thousands of people were saying, is the real basis of our national greatness; if our coal runs short, there is an end of the greatness of England. But what *is* greatness? — culture makes us ask. Greatness is a spiritual condition worthy to excite love, interest, and admiration; and the outward proof of possessing greatness is that we excite love, interest, and admiration. If England were swallowed up by the sea to-morrow, which of the two, a hundred years hence, would most excite the love, interest, and admiration of mankind, — would most, therefore, show the evidences of having possessed greatness, — the England of the last twenty years, or the England of Elizabeth, of a time of splendid spiritual effort, but when our coal, and our industrial operations depending on coal, were very little developed? Well, then, what an unsound habit of mind it must be which makes us talk of things like coal or iron as constituting the greatness of England, and how salutary a friend is culture, bent on seeing things as they are, and thus dissipating delusions of this kind and fixing standards of perfection that are real!

Wealth, again, that end to which our prodigious works for material advantage are directed, — the commonest of commonplaces tells us how men are always apt to regard wealth as a precious end in itself; and certainly they have never been so apt thus to regard it as they are in England at the present time. Never did people believe anything more firmly than nine Englishmen out of ten at the present day believe that our greatness and welfare are proved by our being so very rich. Now, the use of culture is that it helps us, by means of its spiritual standard of perfection, to regard wealth as but machinery, and not only to say as a matter of words that we regard wealth as but machinery, but really to perceive and feel that it is so. If it were not for this purging effect wrought upon our minds by culture, the whole world, the future as well as the present, would inevitably belong to the Philistines. The people who believe most that our greatness and welfare are proved by our being very rich, and who most give their lives and thoughts to becoming rich, are just the very people whom we call Philistines. Culture says: "Consider these people, then, their way of life, their habits, their manners, the very tones of their voice; look at them attentively; observe the literature they read, the things which give them pleasure, the words which come forth out of their mouths, the thoughts which make the furniture of their minds; would any amount of wealth be worth having with the condition that one was to become just like these people by having it?" And thus culture begets a dissatisfaction which is of the highest possible value in stemming the common tide of men's thoughts in a wealthy and industrial community, and which saves the future, as one may hope, from being vulgarised, even if it cannot save the present.

Population, again, and bodily health and vigour, are things which are nowhere treated in such an unintelligent, misleading, exaggerated way as in England. Both are really machinery; yet how many people all around us do we see rest in them and fail to look beyond them! Why, one has heard people, fresh from reading certain articles of the *Times* on the Registrar-General's returns of marriages and births in this country, who would talk of our large English families in quite a solemn strain, as if they had something in itself beautiful, elevating, and meritorious in them; as if the British Philistine would have only to present himself before the Great Judge with his twelve children, in order to be received among the sheep as a matter of right!

But bodily health and vigour, it may be said, are not to be classed with wealth and population as mere machinery; they have a more real and essential value. True; but only as they are more intimately connected with a perfect spiritual condition than wealth or population are. The moment we disjoin them from the idea of a perfect spiritual condition, and pursue them, as we do pursue them, for their own sake and as ends in themselves, our worship of them becomes as mere worship of machinery, as our worship of wealth or population, and as unintelligent and vulgarising a worship as that is. Every one with anything like an adequate idea of human perfection has distinctly marked this subordination to higher and spiritual ends of the cultivation of bodily vigour and activity. "Bodily exercise profiteth little; but godliness is profitable unto all things," says the author of the Epistle to Timothy. And the utilitarian Franklin says just as explicitly: — "Eat and drink such an exact quantity as suits the constitution of thy body, *in reference to the services of the mind.*" But the point of view of culture, keeping the mark of human perfection simply and broadly in view, and not assigning to this perfection, as religion or utilitarianism assigns to it, a special and limited character, this point of view, I say, of culture is best given by these words of Epictetus: — "It is a sign of ἀφυΐα," says he, — that is, of a nature not finely tempered, — "to give yourselves up to things which relate to the body; to make, for instance, a great fuss about exercise, a great fuss about eating, a great fuss about drinking, a great fuss about walking, a great fuss about riding. All these things ought to be done merely by the way: the formation of the spirit and character must be our real concern." This is admirable; and, indeed, the Greek word εὐφυΐα, a finely tempered nature, gives exactly the notion of perfection as culture brings us to conceive it: a harmonious perfection, a perfection in which the characters of beauty and intelligence are both present, which unites "the two noblest of things," — as Swift, who of one of the two, at any rate, had himself all too little, most happily calls them in his *Battle of the Books,* — "the two noblest of things, *sweetness and light.*" The εὐφυής is the man who tends towards sweetness and light; the ἀφυής, on the other hand, is our Philistine. The immense spiritual significance of the Greeks is due to their having been inspired with this central and happy idea of the essential character of human perfection; and Mr. Bright's misconception of culture, as a smattering of Greek and Latin, comes itself, after all, from this wonderful significance of the Greeks having affected the very machinery of our education, and is in itself a kind of homage to it.

In thus making sweetness and light to be characters of perfection, culture is of like spirit with poetry, follows one law with poetry. Far more than on our freedom, our population, and our industrialism, many amongst us rely upon our religious organisations to save us. I have called religion a yet more important manifestation of human nature than poetry, because it has worked on a broader scale for perfection, and with greater masses of men. But the idea of beauty and of a human nature perfect on all its sides, which is the dominant idea of poetry, is a true and invaluable idea, though it has not yet had the success that the idea of conquering the obvious faults of our animality, and of a human nature perfect on the moral side, — which is the dominant idea of religion, — has been enabled to have; and it is destined, adding to itself the religious idea of a devout energy, to transform and govern the other.

The best art and poetry of the Greeks, in which religion and poetry are one, in which the idea of beauty and of a human nature perfect on all sides adds to itself a religious and devout energy, and works in the strength of that, is on this account of such surpassing interest and instructiveness for us, though it was, — as, having regard to the human race in general, and, indeed, having regard to the Greeks themselves, we must own, — a premature attempt, an attempt which for success needed the moral and religious fibre in humanity to be more braced and developed than it had yet been. But Greece did not err in having the idea of beauty, harmony, and complete human perfection, so present and paramount. It is impossible to have this idea too present and paramount; only, the moral fibre must be braced too. And we, because we have braced the moral fibre, are not on that account in the right way, if at the same time the idea of beauty, harmony, and complete human perfection, is wanting or misapprehended amongst us; and evidently it *is* wanting or misapprehended at present. And when we rely as we do on our religious organisations, which in themselves do not and cannot give us this idea, and think we have done enough if we make them spread and prevail, then, I say, we fall into our common fault of overvaluing machinery.

Nothing is more common than for people to confound the inward peace and satisfaction which follows the subduing of the obvious faults of our animality with what I may call absolute inward peace and satisfaction, — the peace and satisfaction which are reached as we draw near to complete spiritual perfection, and not merely to moral perfection, or rather to relative moral perfection. No people in the world have done more and struggled more to attain this relative moral perfection than our English race has. For no people in the world has the command to *resist the devil, to overcome the wicked one,* in the nearest and most obvious sense of those words, had such a pressing force and reality. And we have had our reward, not only in the great worldly prosperity which our obedience to this command has brought us, but also, and far more, in great inward peace and satisfaction. But to me few things are more pathetic than to see people, on the strength of the inward peace and satisfaction which their rudimentary efforts towards perfection have brought them, employ, concerning their incomplete perfection and the religious organisations within which they have found it, language which properly applies only to complete perfection, and is a far-off echo of the human soul's prophecy of it. Religion itself, I need hardly say, supplies them in abundance with this grand language. And very freely do they use it; yet it is really the severest possible criticism of such an incomplete perfection as alone we have yet reached through our religious organisations.

The impulse of the English race towards moral development and self-conquest has nowhere so powerfully manifested itself as in Puritanism. Nowhere has Puritanism found so adequate an expression as in the religious organisation of the Independents. The modern Independents have a newspaper, the *Noncomformist,* written with great sincerity and ability. The motto, the standard, the profession of faith which this organ of theirs carries aloft, is: "The Dissidence of Dissent and the Protestantism of the Protestant religion." There is sweetness light, and an ideal of complete harmonious human perfection! One need not go to culture and poetry to find language to judge it. Religion, with its instinct for perfection, supplies language to judge it, language, too, which is in our mouths every day. "Finally, be of one mind, united in feeling," says St. Peter. There is an ideal which judges the Puritan ideal: "The Dissidence of Dissent and the Protestantism of the Protestant religion!" And religious organisations like this are what people believe in, rest in, would give their lives for!

Such, I say, is the wonderful virtue of even the beginnings of perfection, of having conquered even the plain faults of our animality, that the religious organisation which has helped us to do it can seem to us something precious, salutary, and to be propagated, even when it wears such a brand of imperfection on its forehead as this. And men have got such a habit of giving to the language of religion a special application, of making it a mere jargon, that for the condemnation which religion itself passes on the shortcomings of their religious organisations they have no ear; they are sure to cheat themselves and to explain this condemnation away. They can only be reached by the criticism which culture, like poetry, speaking a language not to be sophisticated, and resolutely testing these organisations by the ideal of a human perfection complete on all sides, applies to them.

But men of culture and poetry, it will be said, are again and again failing, and failing conspicuously, in the necessary first stage to a harmonious perfection, in the subduing of the great obvious faults of our animality, which it is the glory of these religious organisations to have helped us to subdue. True, they do often so fail. They have often been without the virtues as well as the faults of the Puritan; it has been one of their dangers that they so felt the Puritan's faults that they too much neglected the practice of his virtues. I will not, however, exculpate them at the Puritan's expense. They have often failed in morality, and morality is indispensable. And they have been punished for their failure, as the Puritan has been rewarded for his performance. They have been punished wherein they erred; but their ideal of beauty, of sweetness and light, and a human nature complete on all its sides, remains the true ideal of perfection still; just as the Puritan's ideal of perfection remains narrow and inadequate, although for what he did well he has been richly rewarded. Notwithstanding the mighty results of the Pilgrim Fathers' voyage, they and their standard of perfection are rightly judged when we figure to ourselves Shakespeare or Virgil, — souls in whom sweetness and light, and all that in human nature is most humane, were eminent, — accompanying them on their voyage, and think what intolerable company Shakespeare and Virgil would have found them! In the same way let us judge the religious organisations which we see all around us. Do not let us deny the good and the happiness which they have accomplished; but do not let us fail to see clearly that their idea of human perfection is narrow and inadequate, and that the Dissidence of Dissent and the Protestantism of the Protestant religion will never bring humanity to its true goal. As I said with regard to wealth: Let us look at the life of those who live in and for it, — so I say with regard to the religious organisations. Look at the life imaged in such a newspaper as the *Nonconformist,* — a life of jealousy of the Establishment, disputes, tea-meetings, openings of chapels, sermons; and then think of it as an ideal of a human life completing itself on all sides, and aspiring with all its organs after sweetness, light, and perfection!

Another newspaper, representing, like the *Nonconformist,* one of the religious organisations of this country, was a short time ago giving an account of the crowd at Epsom on the Derby day, and of all the vice and hideousness which was to be seen in that crowd; and then the writer turned suddenly round upon Professor Huxley, and asked him how he proposed to cure all this vice and hideousness without religion. I confess I felt disposed to ask the asker this question: and how do you propose to cure it with such a religion as yours? How is the ideal of a life so unlovely, so unattractive, so incomplete, so narrow, so far removed from a true and satisfying ideal of human perfection, as is the life of your religious organisation as you yourself reflect it, to conquer and transform all this vice and hideousness? Indeed, the strongest plea for the study of perfection as pursued by culture, the clearest proof of the actual inadequacy of the idea of perfection held by the religious organisations, — expressing, as I have said, the most widespread effort which the human race has yet made after perfection, — is to be found in the state of our life and society with these in possession of it, and having been in possession of it I know not how many hundred years. We are all of us included in some religious organisation or other; we all call ourselves, in the sublime and aspiring language of religion which I have before noticed, *children of God.* Children of God; — it is an immense pretension! — and how are we to justify it? By the works which we do, and the words which we speak. And the work which we collective children of God do, our grand centre of life, our *city* which we have builded for us to dwell in, is London! London, with its unutterable external hideousness, and with its internal canker of *publice egestas, privatim opulentia,* — to use the words which Sallust puts into Cato's mouth about Rome, — unequalled in the world! The word, again, which we children of God speak, the voice which most hits our collective thought, the newspaper with the largest circulation in England, nay, with the largest circulation in the whole world, is the *Daily Telegraph!* I say that when our religious organisations, — which I admit to express the most considerable effort after perfection that our race has yet made, — land us in no better result than this, it is high time to examine carefully their idea of perfection, to see whether it does not leave out of account sides and forces of human nature which we might turn to great use; whether it would not be more operative if it were more complete. And I say that the English reliance on our religious organisations and on their ideas of human perfection just as they stand, is like our reliance on freedom, on muscular Christianity, on population, on coal, on wealth, — mere belief in machinery, and unfruitful; and that it is wholesomely counteracted by culture, bent on seeing things as they are, and on drawing the human race onwards to a more complete, a harmonious perfection.

Culture, however, shows its single-minded love of perfection, its desire simply to make reason and the will of God prevail, its freedom from fanaticism, by its attitude towards all this machinery, even while it insists that it *is* machinery. Fanatics, seeing the mischief men do themselves by their blind belief in some machinery or other, — whether it is wealth and industrialism, or whether it is the cultivation of bodily strength and activity, or whether it is a political organisation, — or whether it is a religious organisation, — oppose with might and main the tendency to this or that political and religious organisation, or to games and athletic exercises, or to wealth and industrialism, and try violently to stop it. But the flexibility which sweetness and light give, and which is one of the rewards of culture pursued in good faith, enables a man to see that a tendency may be necessary, and even, as a preparation for something in the future, salutary, and yet that the generations or individuals who obey this tendency are sacrificed to it, that they fall short of the hope of perfection by following it; and that its mischiefs are to be criticised, lest it should take too firm a hold and last after it has served its purpose.

Mr. Gladstone well pointed out, in a speech at Paris, — and others have pointed out the same thing, — how necessary is the present great movement towards wealth and industrialism, in order to lay broad foundations of material well-being for the society of the future. The worst of these justifications is, that they are generally addressed to the very people engaged, body and soul, in the movement in question; at all events, that they are always seized with the greatest avidity by these people, and taken by them as quite justifying their life; and that thus they tend to harden them in their sins. Now, culture admits the necessity of the movement towards fortune-making and exaggerated industrialism, readily allows that the future may derive benefit from it; but insists, at the same time, that the passing generations of industrialists, — forming, for the most part, the stout main body of Philistinism, — are sacrificed to it. In the same way, the result of all the games and sports which occupy the passing generation of boys and young men may be the establishment of a better and sounder physical type for the future to work with. Culture does not set itself against the games and sports; it congratulates the future, and hopes it will make a good use of its improved physical basis; but it points out that our passing generation of boys and young men is, meantime, sacrificed. Puritanism was perhaps necessary to develop the moral fibre of the English race, Nonconformity to break the yoke of ecclesiastical domination over men's minds and to prepare the way for freedom of thought in the distant future; still, culture points out that the harmonious perfection of generations of Puritans and Nonconformists have been in consequence, sacrificed. Freedom of speech may be necessary for the society of the future, but the young lions of the *Daily Telegraph* in the meanwhile are sacrificed. A voice for every man in his country's government may be necessary for the society of the future, but meanwhile Mr. Beales and Mr. Bradlaugh are sacrificed.

Oxford, the Oxford of the past, has many faults; and she has heavily paid for them in defeat, in isolaton, in want of hold upon the modern world. Yet we in Oxford, brought up amidst the beauty and sweetness of that beautiful place, have not failed to seize one truth, — the truth that beauty and sweetness are essential characters of a complete human perfection. When I insist on this, I am all in the faith and tradition of Oxford. I say boldly that this our sentiment for beauty and sweetness, our sentiment against hideousness and rawness, has been at the bottom of our attachment to so many beaten causes, of our opposition to so many triumphant movements. And the sentiment is true, and has never been wholly defeated, and has shown its power even in its defeat. We have not won our political battles, we have not carried our main points, we have not stopped our adversaries' advance, we have not marched victoriously with the modern world; but we have told silently upon the mind of the country, we have prepared currents of feeling which sap our adversaries' position when it seems gained, we have kept up our own communications with the future. Look at the course of the great movement which shook Oxford to its centre some thirty years ago! It was directed, as any one who reads Dr. Newman's *Apology* may see, against what in one word may be called "Liberalism." Liberalism prevailed; it was the appointed force to do the work of the hour; it was necessary, it was inevitable that it should prevail. The Oxford movement was broken, it failed; our wrecks are scattered on every shore:

> Quæ regio in terris nostri non plena laboris?

But what was it, this liberalism, as Dr. Newman saw it, and as it really broke the Oxford movement? It was the great middle-class liberalism, which had for the cardinal points of its belief the Reform Bill of 1832, and local self-government, in politics; in the social sphere, free-trade, unrestricted competition, and the making of large industrial fortunes; in the religious sphere, the Dissidence of Dissent and the

Protestantism of the Protestant religion. I do not say that other and more intelligent forces than this were not opposed to the Oxford movement: but this was the force which really beat it; this was the force which Dr. Newman felt himself fighting with; this was the force which till only the other day seemed to be the paramount force in this country, and to be in possession of the future; this was the force whose achievements fill Mr. Lowe with such inexpressible admiration, and whose rule he was so horror-struck to see threatened. And where is this great force of Philistinism now? It is thrust into the second rank, it is become a power of yesterday, it has lost the future. A new power has suddenly appeared, a power which it is impossible yet to judge fully, but which is certainly a wholly different force from middle-class liberalism; different in its cardinal points of belief, different in its tendencies in every sphere. It loves and admires neither the legislation of middle-class Parliaments, nor the local self-government of middle-class vestries, nor the unrestricted competition of middle-class industrialists, nor the dissidence of middle-class Dissent and the Protestantism of middle-class Protestant religion. I am not now praising this new force, or saying that its own ideals are better; all I say is, that they are wholly different. And who will estimate how much the currents of feeling created by Dr. Newman's movements, the keen desire for beauty and sweetness which it nourished, the deep aversion it manifested to the hardness and vulgarity of middle-class liberalism, the strong light it turned on the hideous and grotesque illusions of middle-class Protestantism, — who will estimate how much all these contributed to swell the tide of secret dissatisfaction which has mined the ground under self-confident liberalism of the last thirty years, and has prepared the way for its sudden collapse and supersession? It is in this manner that the sentiment of Oxford for beauty and sweetness conquers, and in this manner long may it continue to conquer!

In this manner it works to the same end as culture, and there is plenty of work for it yet to do. I have said that the new and more democratic force which is now superseding our old middle-class liberalism cannot yet be rightly judged. It has its main tendencies still to form. We hear promises of its giving us administrative reform, law reform, reform of education, and I know not what; but those promises come rather from its advocates, wishing to make a good plea for it and to justify it for superseding middle-class liberalism, than from clear tendencies which it has itself yet developed. But meanwhile it has plenty of well-intentioned friends against whom culture may with advantage continue to uphold steadily its ideal of human perfection; that this is *an inward spiritual activity, having for its characters increased sweetness, increased light, increased life, increased sym-*

pathy. Mr. Bright, who has a foot in both worlds, the world of middle-class liberalism and the world of democracy, but who brings most of his ideas from the world of middle-class liberalism in which he was bred, always inclines to inculcate that faith in machinery to which, as we have seen, Englishmen are so prone, and which has been the bane of middle-class liberalism. He complains with a sorrowful indignation of people who "appear to have no proper estimate of the value of the franchise"; he leads his disciples to believe, — what the Englishman is always too ready to believe, — that the having a vote, like the having a large family, or a large business, or large muscles, has in itself some edifying and perfecting effect upon human nature. Or else he cries out to the democracy, — "the men," as he calls them, "upon whose shoulders the greatness of England rests," — he cries out to them: "See what you have done! I look over this country and see the cities you have built, the railroads you have made, the manufactures you have produced, the cargoes which freight the ships of the greatest mercantile navy the world has ever seen! I see that you have converted by your labours what was once a wilderness, these islands, into a fruitful garden; I know that you have created this wealth, and are a nation whose name is a word of power throughout all the world." Why, this is just the very style of laudation with which Mr. Roebuck or Mr. Lowe debauches the minds of the middle classes, and makes such Philistines of them. It is the same fashion of teaching a man to value himself not on what he *is,* not on his progress in sweetness and light, but on the number of the railroads he has constructed, or the bigness of the tabernacle he has built. Only the middle classes are told they have done it all with their energy, self-reliance, and capital, and the democracy are told they have done it all with their hands and sinews. But teaching the democracy to put its trust in achievements of this kind is merely training them to be Philistines to take the place of the Philistines whom they are superseding; and they too, like the middle class, will be encouraged to sit down at the banquet of the future without having on a wedding garment, and nothing excellent can then come from them. Those who know their besetting faults, those who have watched them and listened to them, or those who will read the instructive account recently given of them by one of themselves, the *Journeyman Engineer,* will agree that the idea which culture sets before us of perfection, — an increased spiritual activity, having for its characters increased sweetness, increased light, increased life, increased sympathy, — is an idea which the new democracy needs far more than the idea of the blessedness of the franchise, or the wonderfulness of its own industrial performances.

Other well-meaning friends of this new power are for leading it, not in the old ruts of middle-class Philistinism, but in ways which are naturally alluring to the feet of democracy, though in this country they are novel and untried ways. I may call them the ways of Jacobinism. Violent indignation with the past, abstract systems of renovation applied wholesale, a new doctrine drawn up in black and white for elaborating down to the very smallest details a rational society for the future, — these are the ways of Jacobinism. Mr. Frederic Harrison and other disciples of Comte, — one of them, Mr. Congreve, is an old friend of mine, and I am glad to have an opportunity of publicly expressing my respect for his talents and character, — are among the friends of democracy who are for leading it in paths of this kind. Mr. Frederic Harrison is very hostile to culture, and from a natural enough motive; for culture is the eternal opponent of the two things which are the signal marks of Jacobinism, — its fierceness, and its addiction to an abstract system. Culture is always assigning to system-makers and systems a smaller share in the bent of human destiny than their friends like. A current in people's minds sets towards new ideas; people are dissatisfied with their old narrow stock of Philistine ideas, Anglo-Saxon ideas, or any other; and some man, some Bentham or Comte, who has the real merit of having early and strongly felt and helped the new current, but who brings plenty of narrowness and mistakes of his own into his feeling and help of it, is credited with being the author of the whole current, the fit person to be entrusted with its regulation and to guide the human race.

The excellent German historian of the mythology of Rome, Preller, relating the introduction at Rome under the Tarquins of the worship of Apollo, the god of light, healing, and reconciliation, will have us observe that it was not so much the Tarquins who brought to Rome the new worship of Apollo, as a current in the mind of the Roman people which set powerfully at that time towards a new worship of this kind, and away from the old run of Latin and Sabine religious ideas. In a similar way, culture directs our attention to the natural current there is in human affairs, and to its continual working, and will not let us rivet our faith upon any one man and his doings. It makes us see not only his good side, but also how much in him was of necessity limited and transient; nay, it even feels a pleasure, a sense of an increased freedom and of an ampler future, in so doing.

I remember, when I was under the influence of a mind to which I feel the greatest obligations, the mind of a man who was the very incarnation of sanity and clear sense, a man the most considerable, it seems to me, whom America has yet produced, — Benjamin Franklin, — I remember the relief with which, after long feeling the sway of Franklin's imperturbable common-sense, I came upon a project of his for a new version of the Book of Job, to replace the old version, the style of which, says Franklin, has become obsolete, and thence less agreeable. "I give," he continues, "a few verses, which may serve as a sample of the kind of version I would recommend." We all recollect the famous verse in our translation: "Then Satan answered the Lord and said: 'Doth Job fear God for nought?'" Franklin makes this: "Does your Majesty imagine that Job's good conduct is the effect of mere personal attachment and affection?" I well remember how, when first read that, I drew a deep breath of relief, and said to myself: "After all, there is a stretch of humanity beyond Franklin's victorious good sense!" So, after hearing Bentham cried loudly up as the renovator of modern society, and Bentham's mind and ideas proposed as the rulers of our future, I open the *Deontology*. There I read: "While Xenophon was writing his history and Euclid teaching geometry, Socrates and Plato were talking nonsense under pretence of talking wisdom and morality. This morality of theirs consisted in words; this wisdom of theirs was the denial of matters known to every man's experience." From the moment of reading that, I am delivered from the bondage of Bentham! the fanaticism of his adherents can touch me no longer. I feel the inadequacy of his mind and ideas for supplying the rule of human society, for perfection.

Culture tends always thus to deal with the men of a system, of disciples, of a school; with men like Comte, or the late Mr. Buckle, or Mr. Mill. However much it may find to admire in these personages, or in some of them, it nevertheless remembers the text: "Be not ye called Rabbi!" and it soon passes on from any Rabbi. But Jacobinism loves a Rabbi; it does not want to pass on from its Rabbi in pursuit of a future and still unreached perfection; it wants its Rabbi and his ideas to stand for perfection, that they may with the more authority recast the world; and for Jacobinism, therefore, culture, — eternally passing onwards and seeking, — is an impertinence and an offence. But culture, just because it resists this tendency of Jacobinism to impose on us a man with limitations and errors of his own along with the true ideas of which he is the organ, really does the world and Jacobinism itself a service.

So, too, Jacobinism, in its fierce hatred of the past and of those whom it makes liable for the sins of the past, cannot away with the inexhaustible indulgence proper to culture, the consideration of circumstances, the severe judgment of actions joined to the merciful judgment of persons. "The man of culture is in politics," cries Mr. Frederic Harrison, "one of the poorest mortals alive!" Mr. Frederic Harrison wants to be doing business, and he complains that the man of culture stops him with a "turn for small fault-finding, love of selfish ease, and indecision in action." Of what use is culture, he asks, except for "a critic of new books or a professor of *belles lettres?*" Why, it is of use because, in presence of the fierce exasperation which breathes, or rather, I may say, hisses through the whole production in which Mr. Frederic Harrison asks that question, it reminds us that the perfection of human nature is sweetness and light. It is of use because, like religion, — that other effort after perfection, — it testifies that, where bitter envying and strife are, there is confusion and every evil work.

The pursuit of perfection, then, is the pursuit of sweetness and light. He who works for sweetness and light, works to make reason and the will of God prevail. He who works for machinery, he who works for hatred, works only for confusion. Culture looks beyond machinery, culture hates hatred; culture has one great passion, the passion for sweetness and light. It has one even yet greater! — the passion for making them *prevail.* It is not satisfied till we *all* come to a perfect man; it knows that the sweetness and light of the few must be imperfect until the raw and unkindled masses of humanity are touched with sweetness and light. If I have not shrunk from saying that we must work for sweetness and light, so neither have I shrunk from saying that we must have a broad basis, must have sweetness and light for as many as possible. Again and again I have insisted how those are the happy moments of humanity, how those are the marking epochs of a people's life, how those are the flowering times for literature and art and all the creative power of genius, when there is a *national* glow of life and thought, when the whole of society is in the fullest measure permeated by thought, sensible to beauty, intelligent and alive. Only it must be *real* thought and *real* beauty; *real* sweetness and *real* light. Plenty of people will try to give the masses, as they call them, an intellectual food prepared and adapted in the way they think proper for the actual condition of the masses. The ordinary popular literature is an example of this way of working on the masses. Plenty of people will try to indoctrinate the masses with the set of ideas and judgments constituting the creed of their own profession or party. Our religious and political organisations give an example of this way of working on the masses. I condemn neither way; but culture works differently. It does not try to teach down to the level of inferior classes; it does not try to win them for this or that sect of its own, with ready-made judgments and watchwords. It seeks to do away with classes; to make the best that has been thought and known in the world current everywhere; to make all men live in an atmosphere of sweetness and light, where they may use ideas, as it uses them itself, freely, — nourished, and not bound by them.

This is the *social idea;* and the men of culture are the true apostles of equality. The great men of culture are those who have had a passion for diffusing, for making prevail, for carrying from one end of society to the other, the best knowledge, the best ideas of their time; who have laboured to divest knowledge of all that was harsh, uncouth, difficult, abstract, professional, exclusive; to humanise it, to make it efficient outside the clique of the cultivated and learned, yet still remaining the *best* knowledge and thought of the time, and a true source, therefore, of sweetness and light. Such a man was Abelard in the Middle Ages, in spite of all his imperfections; and thence the boundless emotion and enthusiasm which Abelard excited. Such were Lessing and Herder in Germany, at the end of the last century; and their services to Germany were in this way inestimably precious. Generations will pass, and literary monuments will accumulate, and works far more perfect than the works of Lessing and Herder will be produced in Germany; and yet the names of these two men will fill a German with a reverence and enthusiasm such as the names of the most gifted masters will hardly awaken. And why? Because they *humanised* knowledge; because they broadened the basis of life and intelligence; because they worked powerfully to diffuse sweetness and light, to make reason and the will of God prevail. With Saint Augustine they said: "Let us not leave thee alone to make in the secret of thy knowledge, as thou didst before the creation of the firmament, the division of light from darkness; let the children of thy spirit, placed in their firmament, make their light shine upon the earth, mark the division of night and day, and announce the revolution of the times; for the old order is passed, and the new arises; the night is spent, the day is come forth; and thou shalt crown the year with thy blessing, when thou shalt send forth labourers into thy harvest sown by other hands than theirs; when thou shalt send forth new labourers to new seed-times, whereof the harvest shall be not yet."

II. *Doing as One Likes*

I have been trying to show that culture is, or ought to be, the study and pursuit of perfection; and that of perfection as pursued by culture, beauty and intelligence, or, in other words, sweetness and light, are the main characters. But hitherto I have been insisting chiefly on beauty, or sweetness, as a character of perfection. To complete rightly my design, it evidently remains to speak also of intelligence, or light, as a character of perfection.

First, however, I ought perhaps to notice that, both here and on the other side of the Atlantic, all sorts of objections are raised against the "religion of culture," as the objectors mockingly call it, which I am supposed to be promulgating. It is said to be a religion proposing parmaceti, or some scented salve or other, as a cure for human miseries; a religion breathing a spirit of cultivated inaction, making its believer refuse to lend a hand at uprooting the definite evils on all sides of us, and filling him with antipathy against the reforms and reformers which try to extirpate them. In general, it is summed up as being not practical, or, — as some critics familiarly put it, — all moonshine. That Alcibiades, the editor of the *Morning Star,* taunts me, as its promulgator, with living out of the world and knowing nothing of life and men. That great austere toiler, the editor of the *Daily Telegraph,* upbraids me, — but kindly, and more in sorrow than in anger, — for trifling with æsthetics and poetical fancies, while he himself, in that arsenal of his in Fleet Street, is bearing the burden and heat of the day. An intelligent American newspaper, the *Nation,* says that it is very easy to sit in one's study and find fault with the course of modern society, but the thing is to propose practical improvements for it. While, finally, Mr. Frederic Harrison, in a very good-tempered and witty satire, which makes me quite understand his having apparently achieved such a conquest of my young Prussian friend, Arminius, at last gets moved to an almost stern moral impatience, to behold, as he says, "Death, sin, cruelty stalk among us, filling their maws with innocence and youth," and me, in the midst of the general tribulation, handing out my pouncet-box.

It is impossible that all these remonstrances and reproofs should not affect me, and I shall try my very best, in completing my design and in speaking of light as one of the characters of perfection, and of culture as giving us light, to profit by the objections I have heard and read, and to drive at practice as much as I can, by showing the communications and passages into practical life from the doctrine which I am inculcating.

It is said that a man with my theories of sweetness and light is full of antipathy against the rougher or coarser movements going on around him, that he will not lend a hand to the humble operation of uprooting evil by their means, and that therefore the believers in action grow impatient with him. But what if rough and coarse action, ill-calculated action, action with insufficient light, is, and has for a long time been, our bane? What if our urgent want now is, not to act at any price, but rather to lay in a stock of light for our difficulties? In that case, to refuse to lend a hand to the rougher and coarser movements going on round us, to make the primary need, both for oneself and others, to consist in enlightening ourselves and qualifying ourselves to act less at random, is surely the best and in real truth the most practical line our endeavours can take. So that if I can show what my opponents call rough or coarse action, but what I would rather call random and ill-regulated action, — action with insufficient light, action pursued because we like to be doing something and doing it as we please, and do not like the trouble of thinking and the severe constraint of any kind of rule, — if I can show this to be, at the present moment, a practical mischief and dangerous to us, then I have found a practical use for light in correcting this state of things, and have only to exemplify how, in cases which fall under everybody's observation, it may deal with it.

When I began to speak of culture, I insisted on our bondage to machinery, on our proneness to value machinery as an end in itself, without looking beyond it to the end for which alone, in truth, it is valuable. Freedom, I said, was one of those things which we thus worshipped in itself, without enough regarding the ends for which freedom is to be desired. In our common notions and talk about freedom, we eminently show our idolatry of machinery. Our prevalent notion is, — and I quoted a number of instances to prove it, — that it is a most happy and important thing for a man merely to be able to do as he likes. On what he is to do when he is thus free to do as he likes, we do not lay so much stress. Our familiar praise of the British Constitution under which we live, is that it is a system of checks, — a system which stops and paralyses any power in interfering with the free action of individuals. To this effect Mr. Bright, who loves to walk in the old ways of the Constitution, said forcibly in one of his great speeches, what many other people are every day saying less forcibly, that the central idea of English life and politics is *the assertion of personal liberty*. Evidently this is so; but evidently, also, as feudalism, which with its ideas and habits of subordination was for many centuries silently behind the British Constitution, dies out, and we are left with nothing but our system of checks, and our notion of its being the great right and happiness of an Englishman to do as far as possible what he likes, we are in danger of drifting towards anarchy. We have not the notion, so familiar on the Continent and to antiquity, of *the State,* — the nation in its collective and corporate character, entrusted with stringent powers for the general advantage, and controlling individual wills in the name of an interest wider than that of individuals. We say, what is very true, that this notion is often made instrumental to tyranny; we say that a State is in reality made up of the individuals who compose it, and that every individual is the best judge of his own interests. Our leading class is an aristocracy, and no aristocracy likes the notion of a State-authority greater than itself, with a stringent administrative machinery superseding the decorative inutilities of lord-lieutenancy, deputy-lieutenancy, and the *posse comitatus,* which are all in its own hands. Our middle class, the great representative of trade and Dissent, with its maxims of every man for himself in business, every man for himself in religion, dreads a powerful administration which might somehow interfere with it; and besides, it has its own decorative inutilities of vestrymanship and guardianship, which are to this class what lord-lieutenancy and the county magistracy are to the aristocratic class, and a stringent administration might either take these functions out of its hands, or prevent its exercising them in its own comfortable, independent manner, as at present.

Then as to our working class. This class, pressed constantly by the hard daily compulsion of material wants, is naturally the very centre and stronghold of our national idea, that it is man's ideal right and felicity to do as he likes. I think I have somewhere related how M. Michelet said to me of the people of France, that it was "a nation of barbarians civilised by the conscription." He meant that through their military service the idea of public duty and of discipline was brought to the mind of these masses, in other respects so raw and uncultivated. Our masses are quite as raw and uncultivated as the French; and so far from their having the idea of public duty and of discipline, superior to the individual's self-will, brought to their mind by a universal obligation of military service, such as that of the conscription, — so far from their having this, the very idea of a conscription is so at variance with our English notion of the prime right and blessedness of doing as one likes, that I remember the manager of the Clay Cross works in Derbyshire told me during the Crimean war, when our want of soldiers was much felt and some people were talking of a conscription, that sooner than submit to a conscription the population of that district would flee to the mines, and lead a sort of Robin Hood life under ground.

For a long time, as I have said, the strong feudal habits of subordination and deference continued to tell upon the working class. The modern spirit has now almost entirely dissolved those habits, and the anarchical tendency of our worship of freedom in and for itself, of our superstitious faith, as I say, in machinery, is becoming very manifest. More and more, because of this our blind faith in machinery, because of our want of light to enable us to look beyond machinery to the end for which machinery is valuable, this and that man, and this and that body of men, all over the country, are beginning to assert and put in practice an Englishman's right to do what he likes; his right to march where he likes, meet where he likes, enter where he likes, hoot as he likes, threaten as he likes, smash as he likes. All this, I say, tends to anarchy; and though a number of excellent people, and particularly my friends of the Liberal or progressive party, as they call themselves, are kind enough to reassure us by saying that these are trifles, that a few transient outbreaks of rowdyism signify nothing, that our system of liberty is one which itself cures all the evils which it works, that the educated and intelligent classes stand in overwhelming strength and majestic repose, ready, like our military force in riots, to act at a moment's notice, — yet one finds that one's Liberal friends generally say this because they have such faith in themselves and their nostrums, when they shall return, as the public welfare requires, to place and power. But this faith of theirs one cannot exactly share, when one has so long had them and their nostrums at work, and sees that they have not prevented our coming to our present embarrassed condition. And one finds, also, that the outbreaks of rowdyism tend to become less and less of trifles, to become more frequent rather than less frequent; and that meanwhile our educated and intelligent classes remain in their majestic repose, and somehow or other, whatever happens, their overwhelming strength, like our military force in riots, never does act.

How, indeed, *should* their overwhelming strength act, when the man who gives an inflammatory lecture, or breaks down the park railings, or invades a Secretary of State's office, is only following an Englishman's impulse to do as he likes; and our own conscience tells us that we ourselves have always regarded this impulse as something primary and sacred? Mr. Murphy lectures at Birmingham, and showers on the Catholic population of that town "words," says the Home Secretary, "only fit to be addressed to thieves or murderers." What then? Mr. Murphy has his own reasons of several kinds. He suspects the Roman Catholic Church of designs upon Mrs. Murphy; and he says if mayors and magistrates do not care for their wives and daughters, he does. But, above all, he is doing as he likes; or, in worthier language, asserting his personal liberty. "I will carry out my lectures if they walk over my body as a dead corpse; and I say to the Mayor of Birmingham that he is my servant while I am in Birmingham, and as my servant he must do his duty and protect me." Touching and beautiful words, which find a sympathetic chord in every British bosom! The moment it is plainly put before us that a man is asserting his personal liberty, we are half disarmed; because we are believers in freedom, and not in some dream of a right reason to which the assertion of our freedom is to be subordinated. Accordingly, the Secretary of State had to say that although the lecturer's language was "only fit to be addressed to thieves or murderers," yet, "I do not think he is to be deprived, I do not think that anything I have said could justify the inference that he is to be deprived, of the right of protection in a place built by him for the purpose of these lectures; because the language was not language which afforded grounds for a criminal prosecution." No, nor to be silenced by Mayor, or Home Secretary, or any administrative authority on earth, simply on their notion of what is discreet and reasonable! This is in perfect consonance with our public opinion, and with our national love for the assertion of personal liberty.

In quite another department of affairs, an experienced and distinguished Chancery Judge relates an incident which is just to the same effect as this of Mr. Murphy. A testator bequeathed £300 a year, to be for ever applied as a pension to some person who had been unsuccessful in literature, and whose duty should be to support and diffuse, by his writings, the testator's own views, as enforced in the testator's publications. The views were not worth a straw, and the bequest was appealed against in the Court of Chancery on the ground of its absurdity; but, being only absurd, it was upheld, and the so-called charity was established. Having, I say, at the bottom of our English hearts a very strong belief in freedom, and a very weak belief in right reason, we are soon silenced when a man pleads the prime right to do as he likes, because this is the prime right for ourselves too; and even if we attempt now and then to mumble something about reason, yet we have ourselves thought so little about this and so much about liberty, that we are in conscience forced, when our brother Philistine with whom we are meddling turns boldly round upon us and asks: *Have you any light?* — to shake our heads ruefully, and to let him go his own way after all.

There are many things to be said on behalf of this exclusive attention of ours to liberty, and of the relaxed habits of government which it has engendered. It is very easy to mistake or to exaggerate the sort of anarchy from which we are in danger through them. We are not in danger from Fenianism, fierce and turbulent as it may show itself; for against this our conscience is free enough to let us act resolutely and put forth our overwhelming strength the moment there is any real need for it. In the first place, it never was any part of our creed that the great right and blessedness of an Irishman, or, indeed, of anybody on earth except an Englishman, is to do as he likes; and we can have no scruple at all about abridging, if necessary, a non-Englishman's assertion of personal liberty. The British Constitution, its checks, and its prime virtues, are for Englishmen. We may extend them to others out of love and kindness; but we find no real divine law written on our hearts constraining us so to extend them. And then the difference between an Irish Fenian and an English rough is so immense, and the case, in dealing with the Fenian, so much more clear! He is so evidently desperate and dangerous, a man of a conquered race, a Papist, with centuries of ill-usage to inflame him against us, with an alien religion established in his country by us at his expense, with no admiration of our institutions, no love of our virtues, no talents for our business, no turn for our comfort! Show him our symbolical Truss Manufactory on the finest site in Europe, and tell him that British industrialism and individualism can bring a man to that, and he remains cold! Evidently, if we deal tenderly with a sentimentalist like this, it is out of pure philanthropy.

But with the Hyde Park rioter how different! He is our own flesh and blood; he is a Protestant; he is framed by nature to do as we do, hate what we hate, love what we love; he is capable of feeling the symbolical force of the Truss Manufactory; the question of questions, for him, is a wages question. That beautiful sentence Sir Daniel Gooch quoted to the Swindon workmen, and which I treasure as Mrs. Gooch's Golden Rule, or the Divine Injunction "Be ye Perfect" done into British, — the sentence Sir Daniel Gooch's mother repeated to him every morning when he was a boy going to work: — *"Ever remember, my dear Dan, that you should look forward to being some day manager of that concern!"* — this truthful maxim is perfectly fitted to shine forth in the heart of the Hyde Park rough also, and to be his guiding-star through life. He has no visionary schemes of revolution and transformation, though of course he would like his class to rule, as the aristocratic class like their class to rule, and the middle class theirs. But meanwhile our social machine is a little out of order; there are a good many people in our paradisiacal centres of industrialism and individualism taking the bread out of one another's mouths. The rough has not yet quite found his groove and settled down to his work, and so he is just asserting his personal liberty a little, going where he likes, assembling where he likes, bawling as he likes, hustling as he likes. Just as the rest of us, — as the country squires in the aristocratic class, as the political dissenters in the middle class, — he has no idea of a *State,* of the nation in its collective and corporate character controlling, as government, the free swing of this or that one of its members in the name of the higher reason of all of them, his own as well as that of others. He sees the rich, the aristocratic class, in occupation of the executive government, and so if he is stopped from making Hyde Park a bear-garden or the streets impassable, he says he is being butchered by the aristocracy.

His apparition is somewhat embarrassing, because too many cooks spoil the broth; because, while the aristocratic and middle classes have long been doing as they like with great vigour, he has been too undeveloped and submissive hitherto to join in the game; and now, when he does come, he comes in immense numbers, and is rather raw and rough. But he does not break many laws, or not many at one time; and, as our laws were made for very different circumstances from our present (but always with an eye to Englishmen doing as they like), and as the clear letter of the law must be against our Englishman who does as he likes and not only the spirit of the law and public policy, and as Government must neither have any discretionary power nor act resolutely on its own interpretation of the law if any one disputes it, it is evident our laws give our playful giant, in doing as he likes, considerable advantage. Besides, even if he can be clearly proved to commit an illegality in doing as he likes, there is always the resource of not putting the law in force, or of abolishing it. So he has his way, and if he has his way he is soon satisfied for the time. However, he falls into the habit of taking it oftener and oftener, and at last begins to create by his operations a confusion of which mischievous people can take advantage, and which, at any rate, by troubling the common course of business throughout the country, tends to cause distress, and so to increase the sort of anarchy and social disintegration which had previously commenced. And thus that profound sense of settled order and security, without which a society like ours cannot live and grow at all, sometimes seems to be beginning to threaten us with taking its departure.

Now, if culture, which simply means trying to perfect oneself, and one's mind as part of oneself, brings us light, and if light shows us that there is nothing so very blessed in merely doing as one likes, that the worship of the mere freedom to do as one likes is worship of machinery, that the really blessed thing is to like what right reason ordains, and to follow her authority, then we have got a practical benefit out of culture. We have got a much wanted principle, a principle of authority, to counteract the tendency to anarchy which seems to be threatening us.

But how to organise this authority, or to what hands to entrust the wielding of it? How to get your *State*, summing up the right reason of the community, and giving effect to it, as circumstances may require, with vigour? And here I think I see my enemies waiting for me with a hungry joy in their eyes. But I shall elude them.

The *State*, the power most representing the right reason of the nation, and most worthy, therefore, of ruling, — of exercising, when circumstances require it, authority over us all, — is for Mr. Carlyle the aristocracy. For Mr. Lowe, it is the middle class with its incomparable Parliament. For the Reform League, it is the working class, the class with "the brightest powers of sympathy and readiest powers of action." Now culture, with its disinterested pursuit of perfection, culture, simply trying to see things as they are in order to seize on the best and to make it prevail, is surely well fitted to help us to judge rightly, by all the aids of observing, reading, and thinking, the qualifications and titles to our confidence of these three candidates for authority, and can thus render us a practical service of no mean value.

So when Mr. Carlyle, a man of genius to whom we have all at one time or other been indebted for refreshment and stimulus, says we should give rule to the aristocracy, mainly because of its dignity and politeness, surely culture is useful in reminding us, that in our idea of perfection the characters of beauty and intelligence are both of them present, and sweetness and light, the two noblest of things, are united. Allowing, therefore, with Mr. Carlyle, the aristocratic class to possess sweetness, culture insists on the necessity of light also, and shows us that aristocracies, being by the very nature of things inaccessible to ideas, unapt to see how the world is going, must be somewhat wanting in light, and must therefore be, at a moment when light is our great requisite, inadequate to our needs. Aristocracies, those children of the established fact, are for epochs of concentration. In epochs of expansion, epochs such as that in which we now live, epochs when always the warning voice is again heard: *Now is the judgment of this world,*—in such epochs aristocracies with their natural clinging to the established fact, their want of sense for the flux of things, for the inevitable transitoriness of all human institutions, are bewildered and helpless. Their serenity, their high spirit, their power of haughty resistance,—the great qualities of an aristocracy, and the secret of its distinguished manners and dignity,—these very qualities, in an epoch of expansion, turn against their possessors. Again and again I have said how the refinement of an aristocracy may be precious and educative to a raw nation as a kind of shadow of true refinement; how its serenity and dignified freedom from petty cares may serve as a useful foil to set off the vulgarity and hideousness of that type of life which a hard middle class tends to establish, and to help people to see this vulgarity and hideousness in their true colours. But the true grace and serenity is that of which Greece and Greek art suggest the admirable ideals of perfection,—a serenity which comes from having made order among ideas and harmonised them; whereas the serenity of aristocracies, at least the peculiar serenity of aristocracies of Teutonic origin, appears to come from their never having had any ideas to trouble them. And so, in a time of expansion like the present, a time for ideas, one gets perhaps, in regarding an aristocracy, even more than the idea of serenity, the idea of futility and sterility.

One has often wondered whether upon the whole earth there is anything so unintelligent, so unapt to perceive how the world is really going, as an ordinary young Englishman of our upper class. Ideas he has not, and neither has he that seriousness of our middle class which is, as I have often said, the great strength of this class, and may become its salvation. Why, a man may hear a young Dives of the aristocratic class, when the whim takes him to sing the praises of wealth and material comfort, sing them with a cynicism from which the conscience of the veriest Philistine of our industrial middle class would recoil in affright. And when, with the natural sympathy of aristocracies for firm dealing with the multitude, and his uneasiness at our feeble dealing with it at home, an unvarnished young Englishman of our aristocratic class applauds the absolute rulers on the Continent, he in general manages completely to miss the grounds of reason and intelligence which alone can give any colour of justification, any possibility of existence, to those rulers, and applauds them on grounds which it would make their own hair stand on end to listen to.

And all this time we are in an epoch of expansion; and the essence of an epoch of expansion is a movement of ideas, and the one salvation of an epoch of expansion is a harmony of ideas. The very principle of the authority which we are seeking as a defence against anarchy is right reason, ideas, light. The more, therefore, an aristocracy calls to its aid its innate forces, — its impenetrability, its high spirit, its power of haughty resistance, — to deal with an epoch of expansion, the graver is the danger, the greater the certainty of explosion, the surer the aristocracy's defeat; for it is trying to do violence to nature instead of working along with it. The best powers shown by the best men of an aristocracy at such an epoch are, it will be observed, non-aristocratical powers, powers of industry, powers of intelligence; and these powers thus exhibited, tend really not to strengthen the aristocracy, but to take their owners out of it, to expose them to the dissolving agencies of thought and change, to make them men of the modern spirit and of the future. If, as sometimes happens, they add to their non-aristocratical qualities of labour and thought, a strong dose of aristocratical qualities also, — of pride, defiance, turn for resistance, — this truly aristocratical side of them, so far from adding any strength to them, really neutralises their force and makes them impracticable and ineffective.

Knowing myself to be indeed sadly to seek, as one of my many critics says, in "a philosophy with coherent, interdependent, subordinate, and derivative principles," I continually have recourse to a plain man's expedient of trying to make what few simple notions I have, clearer and more intelligible to myself by means of example and illustration. And having been brought up at Oxford in the bad old times, when we were stuffed with Greek and Aristotle, and thought nothing of preparing ourselves by the study of modern languages,— as after Mr. Lowe's great speech at Edinburgh we shall do,—to fight the battle of life with the waiters in foreign hotels, my head is still full of a lumber of phrases we learnt at Oxford from Aristotle, about virtue being in a mean, and about excess and defect, and so on. Once when I had had the advantage of listening to the Reform debates in the House of Commons, having heard a number of interesting speakers, and among them a well-known lord and a well-known baronet, I remember it struck me, applying Aristotle's machinery of the mean to my ideas about our aristocracy, that the lord was exactly the perfection, or happy mean, or virtue, of aristocracy, and the baronet the excess. And I fancied that by observing these two we might see both the inadequacy of aristocracy to supply the principle of authority needful for our present wants, and the danger of its trying to supply it when it was not really competent for the business. On the one hand, in the brilliant lord, showing plenty of high spirit, but remarkable, far above and beyond his gift of high spirit, for the fine tempering of his high spirit, for ease, serenity, politeness,—the great virtues, as Mr. Carlyle says, of aristocracy,—in this beautiful and virtuous mean, there seemed evidently some insufficiency of light; while, on the other hand, the worthy baronet, in whom the high spirit of aristocracy, its impenetrability, defiant courage, and pride of resistance, were developed even in excess, was manifestly capable, if he had his way given him, of causing us greater danger, and, indeed, of throwing the whole commonwealth into confusion. Then I reverted to that old fundamental notion of mine about the grand merit of our race being really our honesty. And the very helplessness of our aristocratic or governing class in dealing with our perturbed social condition, their jealousy of entrusting too much power to the State as it now actually exists—that is to themselves —gave me a sort of pride and satisfaction; because I saw they were, as a whole, too honest to try and manage a business for which they did not feel themselves capable.

Surely, now, it is no inconsiderable boon which culture confers upon us, if in embarrassed times like the present it enables us to look at the ins and the outs of things in this way, without hatred and without partiality, and with a disposition to see the good in everybody all round. And I try to follow just the same course with our middle class as with our aristocracy. Mr. Lowe talks to us of this strong middle part of the nation, of the unrivalled deeds of our Liberal middle-class Parliament, of the noble, the heroic work it has performed in the last thirty years; and I begin to ask myself if we shall not, then, find in our middle class the principle of authority we want, and if we had not better take administration as well as legislation away from the weak extreme which now administers for us, and commit both to the strong middle part. I observe, too, that the heroes of middle-class liberalism, such as we have hitherto known it, speak with a kind of prophetic anticipation of the great destiny which awaits them, and as if the future was clearly theirs. The advanced party, the progressive party, the party in alliance with the future, are the names they like to give themselves. "The principles which will obtain recognition in the future," says Mr. Miall, a personage of deserved eminence among the political Dissenters, as they are called, who have been the backbone of middle-class liberalism, — "the principles which will obtain recognition in the future are the principles for which I have long and zealously laboured. I qualified myself for joining in the work of harvest by doing to the best of my ability the duties of seedtime." These duties, if one is to gather them from the works of the great Liberal party in the last thirty years, are, as I have elsewhere summed them up, the advocacy of free trade, of Parliamentary reform, of abolition of church-rates, of voluntaryism in religion and education, of non-interference of the State between employers and employed, and of marriage with one's deceased wife's sister.

Now I know, when I object that all this is machinery, the great Liberal middle class has by this time grown cunning enough to answer that it always meant more by these things than meets the eye; that it has had that within which passes show, and that we are soon going to see, in a Free Church and all manner of good things, what it was. But I have learned from Bishop Wilson (if Mr. Frederic Harrison will forgive my again quoting that poor old hierophant of a decayed superstition): "If we would really know our heart let us impartially view our actions"; and I cannot help thinking that if our Liberals had had so much sweetness and light in their inner minds as they allege, more of it must have come out in their sayings and doings.

An American friend of the English Liberals says, indeed, that their Dissidence of Dissent has been a mere instrument of the political Dissenters for making reason and the will of God prevail (and no doubt he would say the same of marriage with one's deceased wife's sister); and that the abolition of a State Church is merely the Dissenter's means to this end, just as culture is mine. Another American defender of theirs says just the same of their industrialism and free trade; indeed, this gentleman, taking the bull by the horns, proposes that we should for the future call industrialism culture, and the industrialists the men of culture, and then of course there can be no longer any misapprehension about their true character; and besides the pleasure of being wealthy and comfortable, they will have authentic recognition as vessels of sweetness and light.

All this is undoubtedly specious; but I must remark that the culture of which I talked was an endeavour to come at reason and the will of God by means of reading, observing, and thinking; and that whoever calls anything else culture, may, indeed, call it so if he likes, but then he talks of something quite different from what I talked of. And, again, as culture's way of working for reason and the will of God is by directly trying to know more about them, while the Dissidence of Dissent is evidently in itself no effort of this kind, nor is its Free Church, in fact, a church with worthier conceptions of God and the ordering of the world than the State Church professes, but with mainly the same conceptions of these as the State Church has, only that every man is to comport himself as he likes in professing them, — this being so, I cannot at once accept the Nonconformity any more than the industrialism and the other great works of our Liberal middle class as proof positive that this class is in possession of light, and that here is the true seat of authority for which we are in search; but I must try a little further, and seek for other indications which may enable me to make up my mind.

Why should we not do with the middle class as we have done with the aristocratic class, — find in it some representative men who may stand for the virtuous mean of this class, for the perfection of its present qualities and mode of being, and also for the excess of them. Such men must clearly not be men of genius like Mr. Bright; for, as I have formerly said, so far as a man has genius he tends to take himself out of the category of class altogether, and to become simply a man. Some more ordinary man would be more to the purpose, — would sum up better in himself, without disturbing influences, the general liberal force of the middle class, the force by which it has done its great works of free trade, Parliamentary reform, voluntaryism, and so on, and the spirit in which it has done them. Now it happens that a typical middle-class man, the member for one of our chief industrial cities, has given us a famous sentence which bears directly on the resolution of our present question: whether there is light enough in our middle class to make it the proper seat of the authority we wish to establish. When there was a talk some little while ago about the state of middle-class education, our friend, as the representative of that class, spoke some memorable words: — "There had been a cry that middle-class education ought to receive more attention. He confessed himself very much surprised by the clamour that was raised. He did not think that class need excite the sympathy either of the legislature or the public." Now this satisfaction of our middle-class member of Parliament with the mental state of the middle class was truly representative, and makes good his claim to stand as the beautiful and virtuous mean of that class. But it is obviously at variance with our definition of culture, or the pursuit of light and perfection, which made light and perfection consist, not in resting and being, but in growing and becoming, in a perpetual advance in beauty and wisdom. So the middle class is by its essence, as one may say, by its incomparable self-satisfaction decisively expressed through its beautiful and virtuous mean, self-excluded from wielding an authority of which light is to be the very soul.

Clear as this is, it will be made clearer still if we take some representative man as the excess of the middle class, and remember that the middle class, in general, is to be conceived as a body swaying between the qualities of its mean and of its excess, and on the whole, of course, as human nature is constituted, inclining rather towards the excess than the mean. Of its excess no better representative can possibly be imagined than a Dissenting minister from Walsall, who came before the public in connection with the proceedings at Birmingham of Mr. Murphy, already mentioned. Speaking in the midst of an irritated population of Catholics, this Walsall gentleman exclaimed: "I say, then, away with the Mass! It is from the bottomless pit; and in the bottomless pit shall all liars have their part, in the lake that burneth with fire and brimstone." And again: "When all the praties were black in Ireland, why didn't the priests say the hocus-pocus over them, and make them all good again?" He shared, too, Mr. Murphy's fears of some invasion of his domestic happiness: "What I wish to say to you as Protestant husbands is, *Take care of your wives!*" And finally, in the true vein of an Englishman doing as he likes, a vein of which I have at some length pointed out the present dangers, he recommended for imitation the example of some churchwardens at Dublin, among whom, said he, "there was a Luther and also a Melanchthon," who had made very short work with some ritualist or other, hauled him down from his pulpit, and kicked him out of church. Now it is manifest, as I said in the case of our aristocratical baronet, that if we let this excess of the sturdy English middle class, this conscientious Protestant Dissenter, so strong, so self-reliant, so fully persuaded in his own mind, have his way, he would be capable, with his want of light, — or, to use the language of the religious world, with his zeal without knowledge, — of stirring up strife which neither he nor any one else could easily compose.

And then comes in, as it did also with the aristocracy, the honesty of our race, and by the voice of another middle-class man, Alderman of the City of London and Colonel of the City of London Militia, proclaims that it has twinges of conscience, and that it will not attempt to cope with our social disorders, and to deal with a business which it feels to be too high for it. Every one remembers how this virtuous Alderman-Colonel, or Colonel-Alderman, led his militia through the London streets; how the bystanders gathered to see him pass; how the London roughs, asserting an Englishman's best and most blissful right of doing what he likes, robbed and beat the bystanders; and how the blameless warrior-magistrate refused to let his troops interfere. "The crowd," he touchingly said afterwards, "was mostly composed of fine healthy strong men, bent on mischief; if he had allowed his soldiers to interfere they might have been overpowered, their rifles taken from them and used against them by the mob; a riot, in fact, might have ensued, and been attended with bloodshed, compared with which the assaults and loss of property that actually occurred would have been as nothing." Honest and affecting testimony of the English middle class to its own inadequacy for the authoritative part one's admiration would sometimes incline one to assign to it! "Who are we," they say by the voice of their Alderman-Colonel, "that we should not be overpowered if we attempt to cope with social anarchy, our rifles taken from us and used against us by the mob, and we, perhaps, robbed and beaten ourselves? Or what light have we, beyond a free-born Englishman's impulse to do as he likes, which could justify us in preventing, at the cost of bloodshed, other free-born Englishmen from doing as they like, and robbing and beating us as much as they please?"

This distrust of themselves as an adequate centre of authority does not mark the working class, as was shown by their readiness the other day in Hyde Park to take upon themselves all the functions of government. But this comes from the working class being, as I have often said, still an embryo, of which no one can yet quite foresee the final development; and from its not having the same experience and self-knowledge as the aristocratic and middle classes. Honesty it no doubt has, just like the other classes of Englishmen, but honesty in an inchoate and untrained state; and meanwhile its powers of action, which are, as Mr. Frederic Harrison says, exceedingly ready, easily run away with it. That it cannot at present have a sufficiency of light which comes by culture, — that is, by reading, observing, and thinking, — is clear from the very nature of its condition; and, indeed, we saw that Mr. Frederic Harrison, in seeking to make a free stage for its bright powers of sympathy and ready powers of action, had to begin by throwing overboard culture, and flouting it as only fit for a professor of *belles-lettres*. Still, to make it perfectly manifest that no more in the working class than in the aristocratic and middle classes can one find an adequate centre of authority, — that is, as culture teaches us to conceive our required authority, of light, — let us again follow, with this class, the method we have followed with the aristocratic and middle classes, and try to bring before our minds representative men, who may figure to us its virtue and its excess.

We must not take, of course, men like the chiefs of the Hyde Park demonstration, Colonel Dickson or Mr. Beales; because Colonel Dickson, by his martial profession and dashing exterior, seems to belong properly, like Julius Cæsar and Mirabeau and other great popular leaders, to the aristocratic class, and to be carried into the popular ranks only by his ambition or his genius; while Mr. Beales belongs to our solid middle class, and, perhaps, if he had not been a great popular leader, would have been a Philistine. But Mr. Odger, whose speeches we have all read, and of whom his friends relate, besides, much that is favourable, may very well stand for the beautiful and virtuous mean of our present working class; and I think everybody will admit that in Mr. Odger there is manifestly, with all his good points, some insufficiency of light. The excess of the working class, in its present state of development, is perhaps best shown in Mr. Bradlaugh, the iconoclast, who seems to be almost for baptizing us all in blood and fire into his new social dispensation, and to whose reflections, now that I have once been set going on Bishop Wilson's track, I cannot forbear commending this maxim of the good old man: "Intemperance in talk makes a dreadful havoc in the heart." Mr. Bradlaugh, like our types of excess in the aristocratic and middle classes, is evidently capable, if he had his head given him, of running us all into great dangers and confusion. I conclude, therefore, — what indeed, few of those who do me the honour to read this disquisition are likely to dispute, — that we can as little find in the working class as in the aristocratic or in the middle class our much-wanted source of authority, as culture suggests it to us.

Well, then, what if we tried to rise above the idea of class to the idea of the whole community, *the State,* and to find our centre of light and authority there? Every one of us has the idea of country, as a sentiment; hardly any one of us has the idea of *the State,* as a working power. And why? Because we habitually live in our ordinary selves, which do not carry us beyond the ideas and wishes of the class to which we happen to belong. And we are all afraid of giving to the State too much power, because we only conceive of the State as something equivalent to the class in occupation of the executive government, and are afraid of that class abusing power to its own purposes. If we strengthen the State with the aristocratic class in occupation of the executive government, we imagine we are delivering ourselves up captive to the ideas and wishes of our fierce aristocratical baronet; if with the middle class in occupation of the executive government, to those of our truculent middle-class Dissenting minister; if with the working class, to those of its notorious tribune, Mr. Bradlaugh. And with much justice; owing to the exaggerated notion which we English, as I have said, entertain of the right and blessedness of the mere doing as one likes, of the affirming oneself, and oneself just as it is. People of the aristocratic class want to affirm their ordinary selves, their likings and dislikings; people of the middle class the same, people of the working class the same. By our every day selves, however, we are separate, personal, at war; we are only safe from one another's tyranny when no one has any power; and this safety, in its turn, cannot save us from anarchy. And when, therefore, anarchy presents itself as a danger to us, we know not where to turn.

But by our *best self* we are united, impersonal, at harmony. We are in no peril from giving authority to this, because it is the truest friend we all of us can have; and when anarchy is a danger to us, to this authority we may turn with sure trust. Well, and this is the very self which culture, or the study of perfection, seeks to develop in us; at the expense of our old untransformed self, taking pleasure only in doing what it likes or is used to do, and exposing us to the risk of clashing with every one else who is doing the same! So that our poor culture, which is flouted as so unpractical, leads us to the very ideas capable of meeting the great want of our present embarrassed times! We want an authority, and we find nothing but jealous classes, checks, and a deadlock; culture suggests the idea of *the State*. We find no basis for a firm State-power in our ordinary selves; culture suggests one to us in our *best self*.

It cannot but acutely try a tender conscience to be accused, in a practical country like ours, of keeping aloof from the work and hope of a multitude of earnest-hearted men, and of merely toying with poetry and æsthetics. So it is with no little sense of relief that I find myself thus in the position of one who makes a contribution in aid of the practical necessities of our times. The great thing, it will be observed, is to find our *best* self, and to seek to affirm nothing but that; not, — as we English with our over-value for merely being free and busy have been so accustomed to do, — resting satisfied with a self which comes uppermost long before our best self, and affirming that with blind energy. In short, — to go back yet once more to Bishop Wilson, — of these two excellent rules of Bishop Wilson's for a man's guidance: "Firstly, never go against the best light you have; secondly, take care that your light be not darkness," we English have followed with praiseworthy zeal the first rule, but we have not given so much heed to the second. We have gone manfully according to the best light we have; but we have not taken enough care that this should be really the best light possible for us, that it should not be darkness. And, our honesty being very great, conscience has whispered to us that the light we were following, our ordinary self, was, indeed, perhaps, only an inferior self, only darkness; and that it would not do to impose this seriously on all the world.

But our best self inspires faith, and is capable of affording a serious principle of authority. For example. We are on our way to what the late Duke of Wellington, with his strong sagacity, foresaw and admirably described as "a revolution by due course of law." This is undoubtedly, — if we are still to live and grow, and this famous nation is not to stagnate and dwindle away on the one hand, or, on the other, to perish miserably in mere anarchy and confusion, — what we are on the way to. Great changes there must be, for a revolution cannot accomplish itself without great changes; yet order there must be, for without order a revolution cannot accomplish itself by due course of law. So whatever brings risk of tumult and disorder, multitudinous processions in the streets of our crowded towns, multitudinous meetings in their public places and parks, — demonstrations perfectly unnecessary in the present course of our affairs, — our best self, or right reason, plainly enjoins us to set our faces against. It enjoins us to encourage and uphold the occupants of the executive power, whoever they may be, in firmly prohibiting them. But it does this clearly and resolutely, and is thus a real principle of authority, because it does it with a free conscience; because in thus provisionally strengthening the executive power, it knows that it is not doing this merely to enable our aristocratical baronet to affirm himself as against our working-men's tribune, or our middle-class Dissenter to affirm himself as against both. It knows that it is establishing *the State*, or organ of our collective best self, of our national right reason. And it has the testimony of conscience that it is stablishing the State on behalf of whatever great changes are needed, just as much as on behalf of order; stablishing it to deal just as stringently, when the time comes, with our baronet's aristocratical prejudices, or with the fanaticism of our middle-class Dissenter, as it deals with Mr. Bradlaugh's street-processions.

III. *Barbarians, Philistines, Populace*

From a man without a philosophy no one can expect philosophical completeness. Therefore I may observe without shame, that in trying to get a distinct notion of our aristocratic, our middle, and our working class, with a view of testing the claims of each of these classes to become a centre of authority, I have omitted, I find, to complete the old-fashioned analysis which I had the fancy of applying, and have not shown in these classes, as well as the virtuous mean and the excess, the defect also. I do not know that the omission very much matters. Still, as clearness is the one merit which a plain, unsystematic writer, without a philosophy, can hope to have, and as our notion of the three great English classes may perhaps be made clearer if we see their distinctive qualities in the defect, as well as in the excess and in the mean, let us try, before proceeding further, to remedy this omission.

It is manifest, if the perfect and virtuous mean of that fine spirit which is the distinctive quality of aristocracies, is to be found in a high, chivalrous style, and its excess in a fierce turn for resistance, that its defect must lie in a spirit not bold and high enough, and in an excessive and pusillanimous unaptness for resistance. If, again, the perfect and virtuous mean of that force by which our middle class has done its great works, and of that self-reliance with which it contemplates itself and them, is to be seen in the performances and speeches of our commercial member of Parliament, and the excess of that force and of that self-reliance in the performances and speeches of our fanatical Dissenting minister, then it is manifest that their defect must lie in a helpless inaptitude for the great works of the middle class, and in a poor and despicable lack of its self-satisfaction.

To be chosen to exemplify the happy mean of a good quality, or set of good qualities, is evidently a praise to a man; nay, to be chosen to exemplify even their excess, is a kind of praise. Therefore I could have no hesitation in taking actual personages to exemplify, respectively, the mean and the excess of aristocratic and middle-class qualities. But perhaps there might be a want of urbanity in singling out this or that personage as the representative of defect. Therefore I shall leave the defect of aristocracy unillustrated by any representative man. But with oneself one may always, without impropriety, deal quite freely; and, indeed, this sort of plain-dealing with oneself has in it, as all the moralists tell us, something very wholesome. So I will venture to humbly offer myself as an illustration of defect in those forces and qualities which make our middle class what it is. The too well-founded reproaches of my opponents declare how little I have lent a hand to the great works of the middle class; for it is evidently these works, and my slackness at them, which are meant, when I am said to "refuse to lend a hand to the humble operation of uprooting certain definite evils" (such as church-rates and others), and that therefore "the believers in action grow impatient" with me. The line, again, of a still unsatisfied seeker which I have followed, the idea of self-transformation, of growing towards some measure of sweetness and light not yet reached, is evidently at clean variance with the perfect self-satisfaction current in my class, the middle class, and may serve to indicate in me, therefore, the extreme defect of this feeling. But these confessions, though salutary, are bitter and unpleasant.

To pass, then, to the working class. The defect of this class would be the falling short in what Mr. Frederic Harrison calls those "bright powers of sympathy and ready powers of action," of which we saw in Mr. Odger the virtuous mean, and in Mr. Bradlaugh the excess. The working class is so fast growing and rising at the present time, that instances of this defect cannot well be now very common. Perhaps Canning's "Needy Knife-Grinder" (who is dead, and therefore cannot be pained at my taking him for an illustration) may serve to give us the notion of defect in the essential quality of a working class; or I might even cite (since, though he is alive in the flesh, he is dead to all heed of criticism) my poor old poaching friend, Zephaniah Diggs, who, between his hare-snaring and his gin-drinking, has got his powers of sympathy quite dulled and his powers of action in any great movement of his class hopelessly impaired. But examples of this defect belong, as I have said, to a bygone age rather than to the present.

The same desire for clearness, which has led me thus to extend a little my first analysis of the three great classes of English society, prompts me also to improve my nomenclature for them a little, with a view to making it thereby more manageable. It is awkward and tiresome to be always saying the aristocratic class, the middle class, the working class. For the middle class, for that great body which, as we know, "has done all the great things that have been done in all departments," and which is to be conceived as moving between its two cardinal points of our commercial member of Parliament and our fanatical Protestant Dissenter, — for this class we have a designation which now has become pretty well known, and which we may as well still keep for them, the designation of Philistines. What this term means I have so often explained that I need not repeat it here. For the aristocratic class, conceived mainly as a body moving between the two cardinal points of our chivalrous lord and our defiant baronet, we have as yet got no special designation. Almost all my attention has naturally been concentrated on my own class, the middle class, with which I am in closest sympathy, and which has been, besides, the great power of our day, and has had its praises sung by all speakers and newspapers.

Still the aristocratic class is so important in itself, and the weighty functions which Mr. Carlyle proposes at the present critical time to commit to it, must add so much to its importance, that it seems neglectful, and a strong instance of that want of coherent philosophic method for which Mr. Frederic Harrison blames me, to leave the aristocratic class so much without notice and denomination. It may be thought that the characteristic which I have occasionally mentioned as proper to aristocracies, — their natural inaccessibility, as children of the established fact, to ideas, — points to our extending to this class also the designation of Philistines; the Philistine being, as is well known, the enemy of the children of light or servants of the idea. Nevertheless, there seems to be an inconvenience in thus giving one and the same designation to two very different classes; and besides, if we look into the thing closely, we shall find that the term Philistine conveys a sense which makes it more peculiarly appropriate to our middle class than to our aristocratic. For *Philistine* gives the notion of something particularly stiff-necked and perverse in the resistance to light and its children; and therein it specially suits our middle class, who not only do not pursue sweetness and light, but who even prefer to them that sort of machinery of business, chapels, tea-meetings, and the addresses from Mr. Murphy, which makes up the dismal and illiberal life on which I have so often touched. But the aristocratic class has actually, as we have seen, in its well-known politeness, a kind of image or shadow of sweetness; and as for light, if it does not pursue light, it is not that it perversely cherishes some dismal and illiberal existance in preference to light, but it is lured off from following light by those mighty and eternal seducers of our race which weave for this class their most irresistible charms, — by worldly splendour, security, power, and pleasure. These seducers are exterior goods, but in a way they are goods; and he who is hindered by them from caring for light and ideas, is not so much doing what is perverse as what is too natural.

Keeping this in view, I have in my own mind often indulged myself with the fancy of employing, in order to designate our aristocratic class, the name of *The Barbarians*. The Barbarians, to whom we all owe so much, and who reinvigorated and renewed our worn-out Europe, had, as is well known, eminent merits; and in this country, where we are for the most part sprung from the Barbarians, we have never had the prejudice against them which prevails among the races of Latin origin. The Barbarians brought with them that staunch individualism, as the modern phrase is, and that passion for doing as one likes, for the assertion of personal liberty, which appears to Mr. Bright the central idea of English life, and of which we have, at any rate, a very rich supply. The stronghold and natural seat of this passion was in the nobles of whom our aristocratic class are the inheritors; and this class, accordingly, have signally manifested it, and have done much by their example to recommend it to the body of the nation, who already, indeed, had it in their blood. The Barbarians, again, had the passion for field-sports; and they have handed it on to our aristocratic class, who of this passion too, as of the passion for asserting one's personal liberty, are the great natural stronghold. The care of the Barbarians for the body, and for all manly exercises; the vigour, good looks, and fine complexion which they acquired and perpetuated in their families by these means,—all this may be observed still in our aristocratic class. The chivalry of the Barbarians, with its characteristics of high spirit, choice manners, and distinguished bearing,—what is this but the attractive commencement of the politeness of our aristocratic class? In some Barbarian noble, no doubt, one would have admired, if one could have been then alive to see it, the rudiments of our politest peer. Only, all this culture (to call it by that name) of the Barbarians was an exterior culture mainly. It consisted principally in outward gifts and graces, in looks, manners, accomplishments, prowess. The chief inward gifts which had part in it were the most exterior, so to speak, of inward gifts, those which come nearest to outward ones; they were courage, a high spirit, self-confidence. Far within, and unawakened, lay a whole range of powers of thought and feeling, to which these interesting productions of nature had, from the circumstances of their life, no access. Making allowances for the difference of the times, surely we can observe precisely the same thing now in our aristocratic class. In general its culture is exterior chiefly; all the exterior graces and accomplishments, and the more external of the inward virtues, seem to be principally its portion. It now, of course, cannot but be often in contact with those studies by which, from the world of thought and feeling, true culture teaches us to fetch sweetness and light; but its hold upon these very studies appears remarkably external, and unable to exert any deep power upon its spirit. Therefore the one insufficiency which we noted in the perfect mean of this class was an insufficiency of light. And owing to the same causes, does not a subtle criticism lead us to make, even on the good looks and politeness of our aristocratic class, and of even the most fascinating half of that class, the feminine half, the one qualifying remark, that in these charming gifts there should perhaps be, for ideal perfection, a shade more *soul*?

I often, therefore, when I want to distinguish clearly the aristocratic class from the Philistines proper, or middle class, name the former, in my own mind, *the Barbarians.* And when I go through the country, and see this and that beautiful and imposing seat of theirs crowning the landscape, "There," I say to myself, "is a great fortified post of the Barbarians."

It is obvious that that part of the working class which, working diligently by the light of Mrs. Gooch's Golden Rule, looks forward to the happy day when it will sit on thrones with commercial members of Parliament and other middle-class potentates, to survey, as Mr. Bright beautifully says, "the cities it has built, the railroads it has made, the manufactures it has produced, the cargoes which freight the ships of the greatest mercantile navy the world has ever seen," — it is obvious, I say, that this part of the working class is, or is in a fair way to be, one in spirit with the industrial middle class. It is notorious that our middle-class Liberals have long looked forward to this consummation, when the working class shall join forces with them, aid them heartily to carry forward their great works, go in a body to their tea-meetings, and, in short, enable them to bring about their millennium. That part of the working class, therefore, which does really seem to lend itself to these great aims, may, with propriety, be numbered by us among the Philistines. That part of it, again, which so much occupies the attention of philanthropists at present, — the part which gives all its energies to organising itself, through trades' unions and other means, so as to constitute, first, a great working-class power independent of the middle and aristocratic classes, and then, by dint of numbers, give the law to them and itself reign absolutely, — this lively and promising part must also, according to our definition, go with the Philistines; because it is its class and its class instinct which it seeks to affirm — its ordinary self, not its best self; and it is a machinery, an industrial machinery, and power and pre-eminence and other external goods, which fill its thoughts, and not an inward perfection. It is wholly occupied, according to Plato's subtle expression, with the things of itself and not its real self, with the things of the State and not the real State. But that vast portion, lastly, of the working class which, raw and half-developed, has long lain half-hidden amidst its poverty and squalor, and is now issuing from its hiding-place to assert an Englishman's heaven-born privilege of doing as he likes, and is beginning to perplex us by marching where it likes, meeting where it likes, bawling what it likes, breaking what it likes, — to this vast residuum we may with great propriety give the name of *Populace.*

Thus we have got three distinct terms, *Barbarians, Philistines, Populace,* to denote roughly the three great classes into which our society is divided; and though this humble attempt at a scientific nomenclature falls, no doubt, very far short in precision of what might be required from a writer equipped with a complete and coherent philosophy, yet, from a notoriously unsystematic and unpretending writer, it will, I trust, be accepted as sufficient.

But in using this new, and, I hope, convenient division of English society, two things are to be borne in mind. The first is, that since, under all our class divisions, there is a common basis of human nature, therefore, in every one of us, whether we be properly Barbarians, Philistines, or Populace, there exists, sometimes only in germ and potentially, sometimes more or less developed, the same tendencies and passions which have made our fellow-citizens of other classes what they are. This consideration is very important, because it has great influence in begetting that spirit of indulgence which is a necessary part of sweetness, and which, indeed, when our culture is complete, is, as I have said, inexhaustible. Thus, an English Barbarian who examines himself will, in general, find himself to be not so entirely a Barbarian but that he has in him, also, something of the Philistine, and even something of the Populace as well. And the same with Englishmen of the two other classes.

This is an experience which we may all verify every day. For instance, I myself (I again take myself as a sort of *corpus vile* to serve for illustration in a matter where serving for illustration may not by every one be thought agreeable), I myself am properly a Philistine, — Mr. Swinburne would add, the son of a Philistine. And although, through circumstances which will perhaps one day be known if ever the affecting history of my conversion comes to be written, I have, for the most part, broken with the ideas and the tea-meetings of my own class, yet I have not, on that account, been brought much the nearer to the ideas and works of the Barbarians or of the Populace. Nevertheless, I never take a gun or a fishing-rod in my hands without feeling that I have in the ground of my nature the self-same seeds which, fostered by circumstances, do so much to make the Barbarian; and that, with the Barbarian's advantages, I might have rivalled him. Place me in one of his great fortified posts, with these seeds of a love for field-sports sown in my nature, with all the means of developing them, with all pleasures at my command, with most whom I met deferring to me, every one I met smiling on me, and with every appearance of permanence and security before me and behind me, — then I too might have grown, I feel, into a very passable child of the established fact, of commendable spirit and politeness, and, at the same time, a little inaccessible to ideas and light; not, of course, with either the eminent fine spirit of our type of aristocratic perfection, or the eminent turn for resistance of our type of aristocratic excess, but according to the measure of the common run of mankind, something between the two. And as to the Populace, who, whether he be Barbarian or Philistine, can look at them without sympathy, when he remembers how often, — every time that we snatch up a vehement opinion in ignorance and passion, every time that we long to crush an adversary by sheer violence, every time that we are envious, every time that we are brutal, every time that we adore mere power or success, every time that we add our voice to swell a blind clamour against some unpopular personage, every time that we trample savagely on the fallen, — he has found in his own boson the eternal spirit of the Populace, and that there needs only a little help from circumstances to make it triumph in him untamably.

The second thing to be borne in mind I have indicated several times already. It is this. All of us, so far as we are Barbarians, Philistines, or Populace, imagine happiness to consist in doing what one's ordinary self likes. What one's ordinary self likes differs according to the class to which one belongs, and has its severer and its lighter side; always, however, remaining machinery, and nothing more. The graver self of the Barbarian likes honours and consideration; his more relaxed self, field-sports and pleasure. The graver self of one kind of Philistine likes fanaticism, business, and money-making; his more relaxed self, comfort and tea-meetings. Of another kind of Philistine, the graver self likes rattening; the relaxed self, deputations, or hearing Mr. Odger speak. The sterner self of the Populace likes bawling, hustling, and smashing; the lighter self, beer. But in each class there are born a certain number of natures with a curiosity about their best self, with a bent for seeing things as they are, for disentangling themselves from machinery, for simply concerning themselves with reason and the will of God, and doing their best to make these prevail; — for the pursuit, in a word, of perfection. To certain manifestations of this love for perfection mankind have accustomed themselves to give the name of genius; implying, by this name, something original and heaven-bestowed in the passion. But the passion is to be found far beyond those manifestations of it to which the world usually gives the name of genius, and in which there is, for the most part, a *talent* of some kind or other, a special and striking faculty of execution, informed by the heaven-bestowed ardour, or genius. It is to be found in many manifestations besides these, and may best be called, as we have called it, the love and pursuit of perfection; culture being the true nurse of the pursuing love, and sweetness and light the true character of the pursued perfection. Natures with this bent emerge in all classes, — among the Barbarians, among the Philistines, among the Populace. And this bent always tends to take them out of their class, and to make their distinguishing characteristic not their Barbarianism or their Philistinism, but their *humanity*. They have, in general, a rough time of it in their lives; but they are sown more abundantly than one might think, they appear where and when one least expects it, they set up a fire which enfilades, so to speak, the class with which they are ranked; and, in general, by the extrication of their best self as the self to develop, and by the simplicity of the ends fixed by them as paramount, they hinder the unchecked predominance of that class-life which is the affirmation of our ordinary self, and seasonably disconcert mankind in their worship of machinery.

Therefore, when we speak of ourselves as divided into Barbarians, Philistines, and Populace, we must be understood always to imply that within each of these classes there are a certain number of *aliens*, if we may so call them, — persons who are mainly led, not by their class spirit, but by a general *humane* spirit, by the love of human perfection; and that this number is capable of being diminished or augmented. I mean, the number of those who will succeed in developing this happy instinct will be greater or smaller, in proportion both to the force of the original instinct within them, and to the hindrance or encouragement which it meets with from without. In almost all who have it, it is mixed with some infusion of the spirit of an ordinary self, some quantity of class-instinct, and even, as has been shown, of more than one class-instinct at the same time; so that, in general, the extrication of the best self, the predominance of the *humane* instinct, will very much depend upon its meeting, or not, with what is fitted to help and elicit it. At a moment, therefore, when it is agreed that we want a source of authority, and when it seems probable that the right source is our best self, it becomes of vast importance to see whether or not the things around us are, in general, such as to help and elicit our best self, and if they are not, to see why they are not, and the most promising way of mending them.

Now, it is clear that the very absence of any powerful authority amongst us, and the prevalent doctrine of the duty and happiness of doing as one likes, and asserting our personal liberty, must tend to prevent the erection of any very strict standard of excellence, the belief in any very paramount authority of right reason, the recognition of our best self as anything very recondite and hard to come at. It may be, as I have said, a proof of our honesty that we do not attempt to give to our ordinary self, as we have it in action, predominant authority, and to impose its rule upon other people. But it is evident also, that it is not easy, with our style of proceeding, to get beyond the notion of an ordinary self at all, or to get the paramount authority of a commanding best self, or right reason, recognised. The learned Martinus Scriblerus well says: — "the taste of the bathos is implanted by nature itself in the soul of man; till, perverted by custom or example, he is taught, or rather compelled, to relish the sublime." But with us everything seems directed to prevent any such perversion of us by custom or example as might compel us to relish the sublime; by all means we are encouraged to keep our natural taste for the bathos unimpaired.

I have formerly pointed out how in literature the absence of any authoritative centre, like an Academy, tends to do this. Each section of the public has its own literary organ, and the mass of the public is without any suspicion that the value of these organs is relative to their being nearer a certain ideal centre of correct information, taste, and intelligence, or farther away from it. I have said that within certain limits, which any one who is likely to read this will have no difficulty in drawing for himself, my old adversary, the *Saturday Review,* may, on matters of literature and taste, be fairly enough regarded, relatively to the mass of newspapers which treat these matters, as a kind of organ of reason. But I remember once conversing with a company of Nonconformist admirers of some lecturer who had let off a great firework, which the *Saturday Review* said was all noise and false lights, and feeling my way as tenderly as I could about the effect of this unfavourable judgment upon those with whom I was conversing. "Oh," said one who was their spokesman, with the most tranquil air of conviction, "it is true the *Saturday Review* abuses the lecture, but the *British Banner*" (I am not quite sure it was the *British Banner*, but it was some newspaper of that stamp) "says that the *Saturday Review* is quite wrong." The speaker had evidently no notion that there was a scale of value for judgments on these topics, and that the judgments of the *Saturday Review* ranked high on this scale, and those of the *British Banner* low; the taste of the bathos implanted by nature in the literary judgments of man had never, in my friend's case, encountered any let or hindrance.

Just the same in religion as in literature. We have most of us little idea of a high standard to choose our guides by, of a great and profound spirit which is an authority while inferior spirits are none. It is enough to give importance to things that this or that person says them decisively, and has a large following of some strong kind when he says them. This habit of ours is very well shown in that able and interesting work of Mr. Hepworth Dixon's, which we were all reading lately, *The Mormons, by One of Themselves*. Here, again, I am not quite sure that my memory serves me as to the exact title, but I mean the well-known book in which Mr. Hepworth Dixon described the Mormons, and other similar religious bodies in America, with so much detail and such warm sympathy. In this work it seems enough for Mr. Dixon that this or that doctrine has its Rabbi, who talks big to him, has a staunch body of disciples, and, above all, has plenty of rifles. That there are any further stricter tests to be applied to a doctrine, before it is pronounced important, never seems to occur to him. "It is easy to say," he writes of the Mormons, "that these saints are dupes and fanatics, to laugh at Joe Smith and his church, but what then? *The great facts remain*. Young and his people are at Utah; a church of 200,000 souls; an army of 20,000 rifles." But if the followers of a doctrine are really dupes, or worse, and its promulgators are really fanatics, or worse, it gives the doctrine no seriousness or authority the more that there should be found 200,000 souls, — 200,000 of the innumerable multitude with a natural taste for the bathos, — to hold it, and 20,000 rifles to defend it. And again, of another religious organisation in America: "A fair and open field is not to be refused when hosts so mighty throw down wager of battle on behalf of what they hold to be true, however strange their faith may seem." A fair and open field is not to be refused to any speaker; but this solemn way of heralding him is quite out of place, unless he has, for the best reason and spirit of man, some significance. "Well, but," says Mr. Hepworth Dixon, "a theory which has been accepted by men like Judge Edmonds, Dr. Hare, Elder Frederick, and Professor Bush!" And again: "Such are, in brief, the bases of what Newman Weeks, Sarah Horton, Deborah Butler, and the associated brethren, proclaimed in Rolt's Hall as the new covenant!" If he was summing up an account of the doctrine of Plato, or of St. Paul, and of its followers, Mr. Hepworth Dixon could not be more earnestly reverential. But the question is, Have personages like Judge Edmonds, and Newman Weeks, and Elderess Polly, and Elderess Antoinette, and the rest of Mr. Hepworth Dixon's heroes and heroines, anything of the weight and significance for the best reason and spirit of man that Plato and St. Paul have? Evidently they, at present, have not; and a very small taste of them and their doctrines ought to have convinced Mr. Hepworth Dixon that they never could have. "But," says he, "the magnetic power which Shakerism is exercising on American thought would of itself compel us," — and so on. Now, so far as real thought is concerned, — thought which affects the best reason and spirit of man, the scientific or the imaginative thought of the world, the only thought which deserves speaking of in this solemn way, — America has up to the present time been hardly more than a province of England, and even now would not herself claim to be more than abreast of England; and of this only real human thought, English thought itself is not just now, as we must all admit, the most significant factor. Neither, then, can American thought be; and the magnetic power which Shakerism exercises on American thought is about as important, for the best reason and spirit of man, as the magnetic power which Mr. Murphy exercises on Birmingham Protestantism. And as we shall never get rid of our natural taste for the bathos in religion, — never get access to a best self and right reason which may stand as a serious authority, — by treating Mr. Murphy as his own disciples treat him, seriously, and as if he was as much an authority as any one else; so we shall never get rid of it while our able and popular writers treat their Joe Smiths and Deborah Butlers, with their so many thousand souls and so many thousand rifles, in the like exaggerated and misleading manner, and so do their best to confirm us in a bad mental habit to which we are already too prone.

If our habits make it hard for us to come at the idea of a high best self, of a paramount authority, in literature or religion, how much more do they make this hard in the sphere of politics! In other countries the governors, not depending so immediately on the favour of the governed, have everything to urge them, if they know anything of right reason (and it is at least supposed that governors should know more of this than the mass of the governed), to set it authoritatively before the community. But our whole scheme of government being representative, every one of our governors has all possible temptation, instead of setting up before the governed who elect him, and on whose favour he depends, a high standard of right reason, to accommodate himself as much as possible to their natural taste for the bathos; and even if he tries to go counter to it, to proceed in this with so much flattering and coaxing, that they shall not suspect their ignorance and prejudices to be anything very unlike right reason, or their natural taste for the bathos to differ much from a relish for the sublime. Every one is thus in every possible way encouraged to trust in his own heart; but, "he that trusteth in his own heart," says the Wise Man, "is a fool"; and at any rate this, which Bishop Wilson says, is undeniably true: "The number of those who need to be awakened is far greater than that of those who need comfort."

But in our political system everybody is comforted. Our guides and governors who have to be elected by the influence of the Barbarians, and who depend on their favour, sing the praises of the Barbarians, and say all the smooth things that can be said of them.

With Mr. Tennyson, they celebrate "the great broad-shouldered genial Englishman," with his "sense of duty," his "reverence for the laws," and his "patient force," who saves us from the "revolts, republics, revolutions, most no graver than a schoolboy's barring out," which upset other and less broad-shouldered nations. Our guides who are chosen by the Philistines and who have to look to their favour, tell the Philistines how "all the world knows that the great middle class of this country supplies the mind, the will, and the power requisite for all the great and good things that have to be done," and congratulate them on their "earnest good sense, which penetrates through sophisms, ignores commonplaces, and gives to conventional illusions their true value." Our guides who look to the favour of the Populace, tell them that "theirs are the brightest powers of sympathy, and the readiest powers of action."

Harsh things are said too, no doubt, against all the great classes of the community; but these things so evidently come from a hostile class, and are so manifestly dictated by the passions and prepossessions of a hostile class, and not by right reason, that they make no serious impression on those at whom they are launched, but slide easily off their minds. For instance, when the Reform League orators inveigh against our cruel and bloated aristocracy, these invectives so evidently show the passions and point of view of the Populace, that they do not sink into the minds of those at whom they are addressed, or awaken any thought or self-examination in them. Again, when our aristocratical baronet describes the Philistines and the Populace as influenced with a kind of hideous mania for emasculating the aristocracy, that reproach so clearly comes from the wrath and excited imagination of the Barbarians, that it does not much set the Philistines and the Populace thinking. Or when Mr. Lowe calls the Populace drunken and venal, he so evidently calls them this in an agony of apprehension for his Philistine or middle-class Parliament, which has done so many great and heroic works, and is now threatened with mixture and debasement, that the Populace do not lay his words seriously to heart.

So the voice which makes a permanent impression on each of our classes is the voice of its friends, and this is from the nature of things, as I have said, a comforting voice. The Barbarians remain in the belief that the great broad-shouldered genial Englishman may be well satisfied with himself; the Philistines remain in the belief that the great middle class of this country, with its earnest common-sense penetrating through sophisms and ignoring commonplaces, may be well satisfied with itself; the Populace, that the working man with his bright powers of sympathy and ready powers of action, may be well satisfied with himself. What hope, at this rate, of extinguishing the taste of the bathos implanted by nature itself in the soul of man, or of inculcating the belief that excellence dwells among high and steep rocks, and can only be reached by those who sweat blood to reach her?

But it will be said, perhaps, that candidates for political influence and leadership, who thus caress the self-love of those whose suffrages they desire, know quite well that they are not saying the sheer truth as reason sees it, but that they are using a sort of conventional language, or what we call clap-trap, which is essential to the working of representative institutions. And therefore, I suppose, we ought rather to say with Figaro: *Qui est-ce qu'on trompe ici?* Now, I admit that often, but not always, when our governors say smooth things to the self-love of the class whose political support they want, they know very well that they are overstepping, by a long stride, the bounds of truth and soberness; and while they talk, they in a manner, no doubt, put their tongue in their cheek. Not always; because, when a Barbarian appeals to his own class to make him their representative and give him political power, he, when he pleases their self-love by extolling broad-shouldered genial Englishmen with their sense of duty, reverence for the laws, and patient force, pleases his own self-love and extols himself, and is, therefore, himself ensnared by his own smooth words. And so, too, when a Philistine wants to be sent to Parliament by his brother Philistines, and extols the earnest good sense which characterises Manchester and supplies the mind, the will, and the power, as the *Daily News* eloquently says, requisite for all the great and good things that have to be done, he intoxicates and deludes himself as well as his brother Philistines who hear him.

But it is true that a Barbarian often wants the political support of the Philistines; and he unquestionably, when he flatters the self-love of Philistinism, and extols, in the approved fashion, its energy, enterprise, and self-reliance, knows that he is talking clap-trap, and so to say, puts his tongue in his cheek. On all matters where Nonconformity and its catchwords are concerned, this insincerity of Barbarians needing Nonconformist support, and, therefore, flattering the self-love of Nonconformity and repeating its catchwords without the least real belief in them, is very noticeable. When the Nonconformists, in a transport of blind zeal, threw out Sir James Graham's useful Education Clauses in 1843, one-half of their Parliamentary advocates, no doubt, who cried aloud against "trampling on the religious liberty of the Dissenters by taking the money of Dissenters to teach the tenets of the Church of England," put their tongue in their cheek while they so cried out. And perhaps there is even a sort of motion of Mr. Frederic Harrison's tongue towards his cheek when he talks of "the shriek of superstition," and tells the working class that "theirs are the brightest powers of sympathy and the readiest powers of action." But the point on which I would insist is, that this involuntary tribute to truth and soberness on the part of certain of our governors and guides never reaches at all the mass of us governed, to serve as a lesson to us, to abate our self-love, and to awaken in us a suspicion that our favourite prejudices may be, to a higher reason, all nonsense. Whatever by-play goes on among the more intelligent of our leaders, we do not see it; and we are left to believe that, not only in our own eyes, but in the eyes of our representative and ruling men, there is nothing more admirable than our ordinary self, whatever our ordinary self happens to be, Barbarian, Philistine, or Populace.

Thus everything in our political life tends to hide from us that there is anything wiser than our ordinary selves, and to prevent our getting the notion of a paramount right reason. Royalty itself, in its idea the expression of the collective nation, and a sort of constituted witness to its best mind, we try to turn into a kind of grand advertising van, meant to give publicity and credit to the inventions, sound or unsound, of the ordinary self of individuals.

I remember, when I was in North Germany, having this very strongly brought to my mind in the matter of schools and their institution. In Prussia, the best schools are Crown patronage schools, as they are called; schools which have been established and endowed (and new ones are to this day being established and endowed) by the Sovereign himself out of his own revenues, to be under the direct control and management of him or of those representing him, and to serve as types of what schools should be. The Sovereign, as his position raises him above many prejudices and littlenesses, and as he can always have at his disposal the best advice, has evident advantages over private founders in well planning and directing a school; while at the same time his great means and his great influence secure, to a well-planned school of his, credit and authority. This is what, in North Germany, the governors do in the matter of education for the governed; and one may say that they thus give the governed a lesson, and draw out in them the idea of a right reason higher than the suggestions of an ordinary man's ordinary self.

But in England how different is the part which in this matter our governors are accustomed to play! The Licensed Victuallers or the Commercial Travellers propose to make a school for their children; and I suppose, in the matter of schools, one may call the Licensed Victuallers or the Commercial Travellers ordinary men, with their natural taste for the bathos still strong; and a Sovereign with the advice of men like Wilhelm von Humboldt or Schleiermacher may, in this matter, be a better judge, and nearer to right reason. And it will be allowed, probably, that right reason would suggest that, to have a sheer school of Licensed Victuallers' children, or a sheer school of Commercial Travellers' children, and to bring them all up, not only at home but at school too, in a kind of odour of licensed victualism or of bagmanism, is not a wise training to give to these children. And in Germany, I have said, the action of the national guides or governors is to suggest and provide a better. But, in England, the action of the national guides or governors is, for a Royal Prince or a great Minister to go down to the opening of the Licensed Victuallers' or of the Commercial Travellers' school, to take the chair, to extol the energy and self-reliance of the Licensed Victuallers or the Commercial Travellers, to be all of their way of thinking, to predict full success to their schools, and never so much as to hint to them that they are probably doing a very foolish thing, and that the right way to go to work with their children's education is quite different. And it is the same in almost every department of affairs. While, on the Continent, the idea prevails that it is the business of the heads and representatives of the nation, by virtue of their superior means, power, and information, to set an example and to provide suggestions of right reason, among us the idea is that the business of the heads and representatives of the nation is to do nothing of the kind, but to applaud the natural taste for the bathos showing itself vigorously in any part of the community, and to encourage its works.

Now I do not say that the political system of foreign countries has not inconveniences which may outweigh the inconveniences of our own political system; nor am I the least proposing to get rid of our own political system and to adopt theirs. But a sound centre of authority being what, in this disquisition, we have been led to seek, and right reason, or our best self, appearing alone to offer such a sound centre of authority, it is necessary to take note of the chief impediments which hinder, in this country, the extrication or recognition of this right reason as a paramount authority, with a view to afterwards trying in what way they can best be removed.

This being borne in mind, I proceed to remark how not only do we get no suggestions of right reason, and no rebukes of our ordinary self, from our governors, but a kind of philosophical theory is widely spread among us to the effect that there is no such thing at all as a best self and a right reason having claim to paramount authority, or, at any rate, no such thing ascertainable and capable of being made use of; and that there is nothing but an infinite number of ideas and works of our ordinary selves, and suggestions of our natural taste for the bathos, pretty nearly equal in value, which are doomed either to an irreconcilable conflict, or else to a perpetual give and take; and that wisdom consists in choosing the give and take rather than the conflict, and in sticking to our choice with patience and good humour.

And, on the other hand, we have another philosophical theory rife among us, to the effect that without the labour of perverting ourselves by custom or example to relish right reason, but by continuing all of us to follow freely our natural taste for the bathos, we shall, by the mercy of Providence, and by a kind of natural tendency of things, come in due time to relish and follow right reason.

The great promoters of these philosophical theories are our newspapers, which, no less than our parliamentary representatives, may be said to act the part of guides and governors to us; and these favourite doctrines of theirs I call, — or should call, if the doctrines were not preached by authorities I so much respect, — the first, a peculiarly British form of Atheism, the second, a peculiarly British form of Quietism. The first-named melancholy doctrine is preached in the *Times* with great clearness and force of style; indeed, it is well known, from the example of the poet Lucretius and others, what great masters of style the atheistic doctrine has always counted among its promulgators. "It is of no use," says the *Times,* "for us to attempt to force upon our neighbours our several likings and dislikings. We must take things as they are. Everybody has his own little vision of religious or civil perfection. Under the evident impossibility of satisfying everybody, we agree to take our stand on equal laws and on a system as open and liberal as is possible. The result is that everybody has more liberty of action and of speaking here than anywhere else in the Old World." We come again here upon Mr. Roebuck's celebrated definition of happiness, on which I have so often commented: "I look around me and ask what is the state of England? Is not every man able to say what he likes? I ask you whether the world over, or in past history, there is anything like it? Nothing. I pray that our unrivalled happiness may last." This is the old story of our system of checks and every Englishman doing as he likes, which we have already seen to have been convenient enough so long as there were only the Barbarians and the Philistines to do what they liked, but to be getting inconvenient, and productive of anarchy, now that the Populace wants to do what it likes too.

But for all that, I will not at once dismiss this famous doctrine, but will first quote another passage from the *Times*, applying the doctrine to a matter of which we have just been speaking, — education. "The difficulty here" (in providing a national system of education), says the *Times*, "does not reside in any removable arrangements. It is inherent and native in the actual and inveterate state of things in this country. All these powers and personages, all these conflicting influences and varieties of character, exist, and have long existed among us; they are fighting it out, and will long continue to fight it out, without coming to that happy consummation when some one element of the British character is to destroy or to absorb all the rest." There it is! the various promptings of the natural taste for the bathos in this man and that amongst us are fighting it out; and the day will never come (and, indeed, why should we wish it to come?) when one man's particular sort of taste for the bathos shall tyrannise over another man's; nor when right reason (if that may be called an element of the British character) shall absorb and rule them all. "The whole system of this country, like the constitution we boast to inherit, and are glad to uphold, is made up of established facts, prescriptive authorities, existing usages, powers that be, persons in possession, and communities or classes that have won dominion for themselves, and will hold it against all comers." Every force in the world, evidently, except the one reconciling force, right reason! Barbarian here, Philistine there, Mr. Bradlaugh and Populace striking in! — pull devil, pull baker! Really, presented with the mastery of style of our leading journal, the sad picture, as one gazes upon it, assumes the iron and inexorable solemnity of tragic Destiny.

After this, the milder doctrine of our other philosophical teacher, the *Daily News,* has, at first, something very attractive and assuaging. The *Daily News* begins, indeed, in appearance, to weave the iron web of necessity round us like the *Times.* "The alternative is between a man's doing what he likes and his doing what some one else, probably not one whit wiser than himself, likes." This points to the tacit compact, mentioned in my last paper, between the Barbarians and the Philistines, and into which it is hoped that the Populace will one day enter; the compact, so creditable to English honesty, that since each class has only the ideas and aims of its ordinary self to give effect to, none of them shall, if it exercise power, treat its ordinary self too seriously, or attempt to impose it on others; but shall let these others, — the fanatical Protestant, for instance, in his Papist-baiting, and the popular tribune in his Hyde Park anarchy-mongering, — have their fling. But then the *Daily News* suddenly lights up the gloom of necessitarianism with bright beams of hope. "No doubt," it says, "the common reason of society ought to check the aberrations of individual eccentricity." This common reason of society looks very like our best self or right reason, to which we want to give authority, by making the action of the *State,* or nation in its collective character, the expression of it. But of this project of ours, the *Daily News,* with its subtle dialectics, makes havoc. "Make the State the organ of the common reason?" — it says. "You make it the organ of something or other, but how can you be certain that reason will be the quality which will be embodied in it?" You cannot be certain of it, undoubtedly, if you never try to bring the thing about; but the question is, the action of the State being the action of the collective nation, and the action of the collective nation carrying naturally great publicity, weight, and force of example with it, whether we should not try to put into the action of the State as much as possible of right reason or our best self, which may, in this manner, come back to us with new force and authority; may have visibility, form, and influence; and help to confirm us, in the many moments when we are tempted to be our ordinary selves merely, in resisting our natural taste of the bathos rather than in giving way to it?

But no! says our teacher: "It is better there should be an infinite variety of experiments in human action; the common reason of society will in the main check the aberrations of individual eccentricity well enough, if left to its natural operation." This is what I call the specially British form of Quietism, or a devout, but excessive reliance on an over-ruling Providence. Providence, as the moralists are careful to tell us, generally works in human affairs by human means; so, when we want to make right reason act on individual inclination, our best self on our ordinary self, we seek to give it more power of doing so by giving it public recognition and authority, and embodying it, so far as we can, in the State. It seems too much to ask of Providence, that while we, on our part, leave our congenital taste for the bathos to its natural operation and its infinite variety of experiments, Providence should mysteriously guide it into the true track, and compel it to relish the sublime. At any rate, great men and great institutions have hitherto seemed necessary for producing any considerable effect of this kind. No doubt we have an infinite variety of experiments and an ever-multiplying multitude of explorers. Even in these few chapters I have enumerated many: the *British Banner*, Judge Edmonds, Newman Weeks, Deborah Butler, Elderess Polly, Brother Noyes, Mr. Murphy, the Licensed Victuallers, the Commercial Travellers, and I know not how many more; and the members of the noble army are swelling every day. But what a depth of Quietism, or rather, what an overbold call on the direct interposition of Providence, to believe that these interesting explorers will discover the true track, or at any rate, "will do so in the main well enough" (whatever that may mean) if left to their natural operation; that is, by going on as they are! Philosophers say, indeed, that we learn virtue by performing acts of virtue; but to say that we shall learn virtue by performing any acts to which our natural taste for the bathos carries us, that the fanatical Protestant comes at his best self by Papist-baiting, or Newman Weeks and Deborah Butler at right reason by following their noses, this certainly does appear over-sanguine.

It is true, what we want is to make right reason act on individual reason, the reason of individuals; all our search for authority has that for its end and aim. The *Daily News* says, I observe, that all my argument for authority "has a non-intellectual root"; and from what I know of my own mind and its poverty I think this so probable, that I should be inclined easily to admit it, if it were not that, in the first place, nothing of this kind, perhaps, should be admitted without examination; and, in the second, a way of accounting for the charge being made, in this particular instance, without good grounds, appears to present itself. What seems to me to account here, perhaps, for the charge, is the want of flexibility of our race, on which I have so often remarked. I mean, it being admitted that the conformity of the individual reason of the fanatical Protestant or the popular rioter with right reason is our true object, and not the mere restraining them, by the strong arm of the State, from Papist-baiting, or railing-breaking, — admitting this, we English have so little flexibility that we cannot readily perceive that the State's restraining them from these indulgences may yet fix clearly in their minds that, to the collective nation, these indulgences appear irrational and unallowable, may make them pause and reflect, and may contribute to bringing, with time, their individual reason into harmony with right reason. But in no country, owing to the want of intellectual flexibility above mentioned, is the leaning which is our natural one, and, therefore, needs no recommending to us, so sedulously recommended, and the leaning which is not our natural one, and, therefore, does not need dispraising to us, so sedulously dispraised, as in ours. To rely on the individual being, with us, the natural leaning, we will hear of nothing but the good of relying on the individual; to act through the collective nation on the individual being not our natural leaning, we will hear nothing in recommendation of it. But the wise know that we often need to hear most of that to which we are least inclined, and even to learn to employ, in certain circumstances, that which is capable, if employed amiss, of being a danger to us.

Elsewhere this is certainly better understood than here. In a recent number of the *Westminister Review,* an able writer, but with precisely our national want of flexibility of which I have been speaking, has unearthed, I see, for our present needs, an English translation, published some years ago, of Wilhelm von Humboldt's book, *The Sphere and Duties of Government.* Humboldt's object in this book is to show that the operation of government ought to be severely limited to what directly and immediately relates to the security of person and property. Wilhelm von Humboldt, one of the most beautiful souls that have ever existed, used to say that one's business in life was first to perfect one's self by all the means in one's power, and secondly, to try and create in the world around one an aristocracy, the most numerous that one possibly could, of talents and characters. He saw, of course, that, in the end, everything comes to this, — that the individual must act for himself, and must be perfect in himself; and he lived in a country, Germany, where people were disposed to act too little for themselves, and to rely too much on the Government. But even thus, such was his flexibility, so little was he in bondage to a mere abstract maxim, that he saw very well that for his purpose itself, of enabling the individual to stand perfect on his own foundations and to do without the State, the action of the State would for long, long years be necessary. And soon after he wrote his book on *The Sphere and Duties of Government,* Wilhelm von Humboldt became Minister of Education in Prussia; and from his ministry all the great reforms which give the control of Prussian education to the State, — the transference of the management of public schools from their old boards of trustees to the State, the obligatory State-examination for schoolmasters, and the foundation of the great State-University of Berlin, — take their origin. This his English reviewer says not a word of. But, writing for a people whose dangers lie, as we have seen, on the side of their unchecked and unguided individual action, whose dangers none of them lie on the side of an over-reliance on the State, he quotes just so much of Wilhelm von Humboldt's example as can flatter them in their propensities, and do them no good; and just what might make them think, and be of use to them, he leaves on one side. This precisely recalls the manner, it will be observed, in which we have seen that our royal and noble personages proceed with the Licensed Victuallers.

In France the action of the State on individuals is yet more preponderant than in Germany; and the need which friends of human perfection feel for what may enable the individual to stand perfect on his own foundations is all the stronger. But what says one of the staunchest of these friends, M. Renan, on State action; and even State action in that very sphere where in France it is most excessive, the sphere of education? Here are his words: — "A Liberal believes in liberty, and liberty signifies the non-intervention of the State. *But such an ideal is still a long way off from us, and the very means to remove it to an indefinite distance would be precisely the State's withdrawing its action too soon.*" And this, he adds, is even truer of education than of any other department of public affairs.

We see, then, how indispensable to that human perfection which we seek is, in the opinion of good judges, some public recognition and establishment of our best self, or right reason. We see how our habits and practice oppose themselves to such a recognition, and the many inconveniences which we therefore suffer. But now let us try to go a little deeper, and to find, beneath our actual habits and practice, the very ground and cause out of which they spring.

IV. *Hebraism and Hellenism*

This fundamental ground is our preference of doing to thinking. Now this preference is a main element in our nature, and as we study it we find ourselves opening up a number of large questions on every side.

Let me go back for a moment to Bishop Wilson, who says: "First, never go against the best light you have; secondly, take care that your light be not darkness." We show, as a nation, laudable energy and persistence in walking according to the best light we have, but are not quite careful enough, perhaps, to see that our light be not darkness. This is only another version of the old story that energy is our strong point and favourable characteristic, rather than intelligence. But we may give to this idea a more general form still, in which it will have a yet larger range of application. We may regard this energy driving at practice, this paramount sense of the obligation of duty, self-control, and work, this earnestness in going manfully with the best light we have, as one force. And we may regard the intelligence driving at those ideas which are, after all, the basis of right practice, the ardent sense for all the new and changing combinations of them which man's development brings with it, the indomitable impulse to know and adjust them perfectly, as another force. And these two forces we may regard as in some sense rivals, — rivals not by the necessity of their own nature, but as exhibited in man and his history, — and rivals dividing the empire of the world between them. And to give these forces names from the two races of men who have supplied the most signal and splendid manifestations of them, we may call them respectively the forces of Hebraism and Hellenism. Hebraism and Hellenism, — between these two points of influence moves our world. At one time it feels more powerfully the attraction of one of them, at another time of the other; and it ought to be, though it never is, evenly and happily balanced between them.

The final aim of both Hellenism and Hebraism, as of all great spiritual disciplines, is no doubt the same: man's perfection or salvation. The very language which they both of them use in schooling us to reach this aim is often identical. Even when their language indicates by variation, — sometimes a broad variation, often a but slight and subtle variation, — the different courses of thought which are uppermost in each discipline, even then the unity of the final end and aim is still apparent. To employ the actual words of that discipline with which we ourselves are all of us most familiar, and the words of which, therefore, come most home to us, that final end and aim is "that we might be partakers of the divine nature." These are the words of a Hebrew apostle, but of Hellenism and Hebraism alike this is, I say, the aim. When the two are confronted, as they very often are confronted, it is nearly always with what I may call a rhetorical purpose; the speaker's whole design is to exalt and enthrone one of the two, and he uses the other only as a foil and to enable him the better to give effect to his purpose. Obviously, with us, it is usually Hellenism which is thus reduced to minister to the triumph of Hebraism. There is a sermon on Greece and the Greek spirit by a man never to be mentioned without interest and respect, Frederick Robertson, in which this rhetorical use of Greece and the Greek spirit, and the inadequate exhibition of them necessarily consequent upon this, is almost ludicrous, and would be censurable if it were not to be explained by the exigencies of a sermon. On the other hand, Heinrich Heine, and other writers of his sort, give us the spectacle of the tables completely turned, and of Hebraism brought in just as a foil and contrast to Hellenism, and to make the superiority of Hellenism more manifest. In both these cases there is injustice and misrepresentation. The aim and end of both Hebraism and Hellenism is, as I have said, one and the same, and this aim and end is august and admirable.

Still, they pursue this aim by very different courses. The uppermost idea with Hellenism is to see things as they really are; the uppermost idea with Hebraism is conduct and obedience. Nothing can do away with this ineffaceable difference. The Greek quarrel with the body and its desires is, that they hinder right thinking; the Hebrew quarrel with them is, that they hinder right acting. "He that keepeth the law, happy is he"; "Blessed is the man that feareth the Eternal, that delighteth greatly in his commandments"; — that is the Hebrew notion of felicity; and, pursued with passion and tenacity, this notion would not let the Hebrew rest till, as is well known, he had at last got out of the law a network of prescriptions to enwrap his whole life, to govern every moment of it, every impulse, every action. The Greek notion of felicity, on the other hand, is perfectly conveyed in these words of a great French moralist: *"C'est le bonheur des hommes,"* — when? when they abhor that which is evil? — no; when they exercise themselves in the law of the Lord day and night?

— no; when they die daily? — no; when they walk about the New Jerusalem with palms in their hands? — no; but when they think aright, when their thought hits: *"quand ils pensent juste."* At the bottom of both the Greek and the Hebrew notion is the desire, native in man, for reason and the will of God, the feeling after the universal order, — in a word, the love of God. But, while Hebraism seizes upon certain plain, capital intimations of the universal order, and rivets itself, one may say, with unequalled grandeur of earnestness and intensity on the study and observance of them, the bent of Hellenism is to follow, with flexible activity, the whole play of the universal order, to be apprehensive of missing any part of it, of sacrificing one part to another, to slip away from resting in this or that intimation of it, however capital. An unclouded clearness of mind, an unimpeded play of thought, is what this bent drives at. The governing idea of Hellenism is *spontaneity of consciousness;* that of Hebraism, *strictness of conscience.*

Christianity changed nothing in this essential bent of Hebraism to set doing above knowing. Self-conquest, self-devotion, the following not our own individual will, but the will of God, *obedience,* is the fundamental idea of this form, also, of the discipline to which we have attached the general name of Hebraism. Only, as the old law and the network of prescriptions with which it enveloped human life were evidently a motive-power not driving and searching enough to produce the result aimed at, — patient continuance in well-doing, self-conquest, — Christianity substituted for them boundless devotion to that inspiring and affecting pattern of self-conquest offered by Jesus Christ; and by the new motive-power, of which the essence was this, though the love and admiration of Christian churches have for centuries been employed in varying, amplifying, and adorning the plain description of it, Christianity, as St. Paul truly says, "establishes the law," and in the strength of the ampler power which she has thus supplied to fulfil it, has accomplished the miracles, which we all see, of her history.

So long as we do not forget that both Hellenism and Hebraism are profound and admirable manifestations of man's life, tendencies, and powers, and that both of them aim at a like final result, we can hardly insist too strongly on the divergence of line and of operation with which they proceed. It is a divergence so great that it most truly, as the prophet Zechariah says, "has raised up thy sons, O Zion, against thy sons, O Greece!" The difference whether it is by doing or by knowing that we set most store, and the practical consequences which follow from this difference, leave their mark on all the history of our race and of its development. Language may be abundantly quoted from both Hellenism and Hebraism to make it seem that one follows the same current as the other towards the same goal. They are, truly, borne towards the same goal; but the currents which bear them are infinitely different. It is true, Solomon will praise knowing: "Understanding is a well-spring of life unto him that hath it." And in the New Testament, again, Jesus Christ is a "light," and "truth makes us free." It is true, Aristotle will undervalue knowing: "In what concerns virtue," says he, "three things are necessary — knowledge, deliberate will, and perseverance; but, whereas the two last are all-important, the first is a matter of little importance." It is true that with the same impatience with which St. James enjoins a man to be not a forgetful hearer, but a *doer of the work*, Epictetus exhorts us to *do* what we have demonstrated to ourselves we ought to do; or he taunts us with futility, for being armed at all points to prove that lying is wrong, yet all the time continuing to lie. It is true, Plato, in words which are almost the words of the New Testament or the Imitation, calls life a learning to die. But underneath the superficial agreement the fundamental divergence still subsists. The understanding of Solomon is "the walking in the way of the commandments"; this is "the way of peace," and it is of this that blessedness comes. In the New Testament, the truth which gives us the peace of God and makes us free, is the love of Christ constraining us to crucify, as he did, and with a like purpose of moral regeneration, the flesh with its affections and lusts, and thus establishing, as we have seen, the law. The moral virtues, on the other hand, are with Aristotle but the porch and access to the intellectual, and with these last is blessedness. That partaking of the divine life, which both Hellenism and Hebraism, as we have said, fix as their crowning aim, Plato expressly denies to the man of practical virtue merely, of self-conquest with any other motive than that of perfect intellectual vision. He reserves it for the lover of pure knowledge, of seeing things as they really are, — the φιλομαθής.

Both Hellenism and Hebraism arise out of the wants of human nature, and address themselves to satisfying those wants. But their methods are so different, they lay stress on such different points, and call into being by their respective disciplines such different activities, that the face which human nature presents when it passes from the hands of one of them to those of the other, is no longer the same. To get rid of one's ignorance, to see things as they are, and by seeing them as they are to see them in their beauty, is the simple and attractive ideal which Hellenism holds out before human nature; and from the simplicity and charm of this ideal, Hellenism, and human life in the hands of Hellenism, is invested with a kind of aërial ease, clearness, and radiancy; they are full of what we call sweetness and light. Difficulties are kept out of view, and the beauty and rationalness of the ideal have all our thoughts. "The best man is he who most tries to perfect himself, and the happiest man is he who most feels that he *is* perfecting himself," — this account of the matter by Socrates, the true Socrates of the *Memorabilia,* has something so simple, spontaneous, and unsophisticated about it, that it seems to fill us with clearness and hope when we hear it. But there is a saying which I have heard attributed to Mr. Carlyle about Socrates, — a very happy saying, whether it is really Mr. Carlyle's or not, — which excellently marks the essential point in which Hebraism differs from Hellenism. "Socrates," this saying goes, "is terribly *at ease in Zion.*" Hebraism, — and here is the source of its wonderful strength, — has always been severely preoccupied with an awful sense of the impossibility of being at ease in Zion; of the difficulties which oppose themselves to man's pursuit or attainment of that perfection of which Socrates talks so hopefully, and, as from this point of view one might almost say, so glibly. It is all very well to talk of getting rid of one's ignorance, of seeing things in their reality, seeing them in their beauty; but how is this to be done when there is something which thwarts and spoils all our efforts?

This something is *sin;* and the space which sin fills in Hebraism, as compared with Hellenism, is indeed prodigious. This obstacle to perfection fills the whole scene, and perfection appears remote and rising away from earth, in the background. Under the name of sin, the difficulties of knowing oneself and conquering oneself which impede man's passage to perfection, become, for Hebraism, a positive, active entity hostile to man, a mysterious power which I heard Dr. Pusey the other day, in one of his impressive sermons, compare to a hideous hunchback seated on our shoulders, and which it is the main business of our lives to hate and oppose. The discipline of the Old Testament may be summed up as a discipline teaching us to abhor and flee from sin; the discipline of the New Testament, as a discipline teaching us to die to it. As Hellenism speaks of thinking clearly, seeing things in their essence and beauty, as a grand and precious feat for man to achieve, so Hebraism speaks of becoming conscious of sin, of awakening to a sense of sin, as a feat of this kind. It is obvious to what wide divergence these differing tendencies, actively followed, must lead. As one passes and repasses from Hellenism to Hebraism, from Plato to St. Paul, one feels inclined to rub one's eyes and ask oneself whether man is indeed a gentle and simple being, showing the traces of a noble and divine nature; or an unhappy chained captive, labouring with groanings that cannot be uttered to free himself from the body of this death.

Apparently it was the Hellenic conception of human nature which was unsound, for the world could not live by it. Absolutely to call it unsound, however, is to fall into the common error of its Hebraising enemies; but it was unsound at that particular moment of man's development, it was premature. The indispensable basis of conduct and self-control, the platform upon which alone the perfection aimed at by Greece can come into bloom, was not to be reached by our race so easily; centuries of probation and discipline were needed to bring us to it. Therefore the bright promise of Hellenism faded, and Hebraism ruled the world. Then was seen that astonishing spectacle, so well marked by the often-quoted words of the prophet Zechariah, when men of all languages and nations took hold of the skirt of him that was a Jew, saying: — "*We will go with you, for we have heard that God is with you.*" And the Hebraism which thus received and ruled a world all gone out of the way and altogether become unprofitable, was, and could not but be, the later, the more spiritual, the more attractive development of Hebraism. It was Christianity; that is to say, Hebraism aiming at self-conquest and rescue from the thrall of vile affections, not by obedience to the letter of a law, but by conformity to the image of a self-sacrificing example. To a world stricken with moral enervation Christianity offered its spectacle of an inspired self-sacrifice; to men who refused themselves nothing, it showed one who refused himself everything; — "*my Saviour banished joy!*" says George Herbert. When the *alma Venus*, the life-giving and joy-giving power of nature, so fondly cherished by the Pagan world, could not save her followers from self-dissatisfaction and ennui, the severe words of the apostle came bracingly and refreshingly: "Let no man deceive you with vain words, for because of these things cometh the wrath of God upon the children of disobedience." Through age after age and generation after generation, our race, or all that part of our race which was most living and progressive, was *baptized into a death;* and endeavoured, by suffering in the flesh, to cease from sin. Of this endeavour, the animating labours and afflictions of early Christianity, the touching asceticism of mediæval Christianity, are the great historical manifestations. Literary monuments of it, each in its own way incomparable, remain in the Epistles of St. Paul, in St. Augustine's *Confessions*, and in the two original and simplest books of the *Imitation*.[1]

Of two disciplines laying their main stress, the one, on clear intelligence, the other, on firm obedience; the one, on comprehensively knowing the grounds of one's duty, the other, on diligently practising it; the one, on taking all possible care (to use Bishop Wilson's words

1 The two first books.

again) that the light we have be not darkness, the other, that according to the best light we have we diligently walk, — the priority naturally belongs to that discipline which braces all man's moral powers, and founds for him an indispensable basis of character. And, therefore, it is justly said of the Jewish people, who were charged with setting powerfully forth that side of the divine order to which the words *conscience* and *self-conquest* point, that they were "entrusted with the oracles of God"; as it is justly said of Christianity, which followed Judaism and which set forth this side with a much deeper effectiveness and a much wider influence, that the wisdom of the old Pagan world was foolishness compared to it. No words of devotion and admiration can be too strong to render thanks to these beneficent forces which have so borne forward humanity in its appointed work of coming to the knowledge and possession of itself; above all, in those great moments when their action was the wholesomest and the most necessary.

But the evolution of these forces, separately and in themselves, is not the whole evolution of humanity, — their single history is not the whole history of man; whereas their admirers are always apt to make it stand for the whole history. Hebraism and Hellenism are, neither of them, the *law* of human development, as their admirers are prone to make them; they are, each of them, *contributions* to human development, — august contributions, invaluable contributions; and each showing itself to us more august, more invaluable, more preponderant over the other, according to the moment in which we take them, and the relation in which we stand to them. The nations of our modern world, children of that immense and salutary movement which broke up the Pagan world, inevitably stand to Hellenism in a relation which dwarfs it, and to Hebraism in a relation which magnifies it. They are inevitably prone to take Hebraism as the law of human development, and not as simply a contribution to it, however precious. And yet the lesson must perforce be learned, that the human spirit is wider than the most priceless of the forces which bear it onward, and that to the whole development of man Hebraism itself is, like Hellenism, but a contribution.

Perhaps we may help ourselves to see this clearer by an illustration drawn from the treatment of a single great idea which has profoundly engaged the human spirit, and has given it eminent opportunities for showing its nobleness and energy. It surely must be perceived that the idea of immortality, as this idea rises in its generality before the human spirit, is something grander, truer, and more satisfying, than it is in the particular forms by which St. Paul, in the famous fifteenth chapter of the Epistle to the Corinthians, and Plato, in the *Phædo*, endeavour to develop and establish it. Surely we cannot but feel, that the argumentation with which the Hebrew apostle goes about to expound this great idea is, after all, confused and inconclusive; and that the reasoning, drawn from analogies of likeness and equality, which is employed upon it by the Greek philosopher, is over-subtle and sterile. Above and beyond the inadequate solutions which Hebraism and Hellenism here attempt, extends the immense and august problem itself, and the human spirit which gave birth to it. And this single illustration may suggest to us how the same thing happens in other cases also.

But meanwhile, by alternations of Hebraism and Hellenism, of a man's intellectual and moral impulses, of the effort to see things as they really are, and the effort to win peace by self-conquest, the human spirit proceeds; and each of these two forces has its appointed hours of culmination and seasons of rule. As the great movement of Christianity was a triumph of Hebraism and man's moral impulses, so the great movement which goes by the name of the Renascence[1] was an uprising and re-instatement of man's intellectual impulses and of Hellenism. We in England, the devoted children of Protestantism, chiefly know the Renascence by its subordinate and secondary side of the Reformation. The Reformation has been often called a Hebraising revival, a return to the ardour and sincereness of primitive Christianity. No one, however, can study the development of Protestantism and of Protestant churches without feeling that into the Reformation too, — Hebraising child of the Renascence and offspring of its fervour, rather than its intelligence, as it undoubtedly was, — the subtle Hellenic leaven of the Renascence found its way, and that the exact respective parts, in the Reformation, of Hebraism and of Hellenism, are not easy to separate. But what we may with truth say is, that all which Protestantism was to itself clearly conscious of, all which it succeeded in clearly setting forth in words, had the characters of Hebraism rather than of Hellenism. The Reformation was strong, in that it was an earnest return to the Bible and to doing from the heart the will of God as there written. It was weak, in that it never consciously grasped or applied the central idea of the Renascence, — the Hellenic idea of pursuing, in all lines of activity, the law and science, to use Plato's words, of things as they really are. Whatever direct superiority, therefore, Protestantism had over Catholicism was a moral superiority, a superiority arising out of its greater sincerity and earnestness, — at the moment of its apparition at any

[1] I have ventured to give to the foreign word *Renaissance*, — destined to become of more common use amongst us as the movement which it denotes comes, as it will come, increasingly to interest us,—an English form.

rate, — in dealing with the heart and conscience. Its pretensions to an intellectual superiority are in general quite illusory. For Hellenism, for the thinking side in man as distinguished from the acting side, the attitude of mind of Protestantism towards the Bible in no respect differs from the attitude of mind of Catholicism towards the Church. The mental habit of him who imagines that Balaam's ass spoke, in no respect differs from the mental habit of him who imagines that a Madonna of wood or stone winked; and the one, who says that God's Church makes him believe what he believes, and the other, who says that God's Word makes him believe what he believes, are for the philosopher perfectly alike in not really and truly knowing, when they say *God's Church* and *God's Word*, what it is they say, or whereof they affirm.

In the sixteenth century, therefore, Hellenism re-entered the world, and again stood in presence of Hebraism, — a Hebraism renewed and purged. Now, it has not been enough observed, how, in the seventeenth century, a fate befell Hellenism in some respects analogous to that which befell it at the commencement of our era. The Renascence, that great re-awakening of Hellenism, that irresistible return of humanity to nature and to seeing things as they are, which in art, in literature, and in physics, produced such splendid fruits, had, like the anterior Hellenism of the Pagan world, a side of moral weakness and of relaxation or insensibility of the moral fibre, which in Italy showed itself with the most startling plainness, but which in France, England, and other countries was very apparent too. Again this loss of spiritual balance, this exclusive preponderance given to man's perceiving and knowing side, this unnatural defect of his feeling and acting side, provoked a reaction. Let us trace that reaction where it most nearly concerns us.

Science has now made visible to everybody the great and pregnant elements of difference which lie in race, and in how signal a manner they make the genius and history of an Indo-European people vary from those of a Semitic people. Hellenism is of Indo-European growth, Hebraism is of Semitic growth; and we English, a nation of Indo-European stock, seem to belong naturally to the movement of Hellenism. But nothing more strongly marks the essential unity of man, than the affinities we can perceive, in this point or that, between members of one family of peoples and members of another. And no affinity of this kind is more strongly marked than that likeness in the strength and prominence of the moral fibre, which, notwithstanding immense elements of difference, knits in some special sort the genius and history of us English, and our American descendants across the Atlantic, to the genius and history of the Hebrew people. Puritanism, which has been so great a power in the English nation, and in the strongest part of the English nation, was originally the reaction in the seventeenth century of the conscience and moral sense of our race, against the moral indifference and lax rule of conduct which in the sixteenth century came in with the Renascence. It was a reaction of Hebraism against Hellenism; and it powerfully manifested itself, as was natural, in a people with much of what we call a Hebraising turn, with a signal affinity for the bent which was the master-bent of Hebrew life. Eminently Indo-European by its *humour*, by the power it shows, through this gift, of imaginatively acknowledging the multiform aspects of the problem of life, and of thus getting itself unfixed from its own over-certainty, of smiling at its own over-tenacity, our race has yet (and a great part of its strength lies here), in matters of practical life and moral conduct, a strong share of the assuredness, the tenacity, the intensity of the Hebrews. This turn manifested itself in Puritanism, and has had a great part in shaping our history for the last two hundred years. Undoubtedly it checked and changed amongst us that movement of the Renascence which we see producing in the reign of Elizabeth such wonderful fruits. Undoubtedly it stopped the prominent rule and direct development of that order of ideas which we call by the name of Hellenism, and gave the first rank to a different order of ideas. Apparently, too, as we said of the former defeat of Hellenism, if Hellenism was defeated, this shows that Hellenism was imperfect, and that its ascendency at that moment would not have been for the world's good.

Yet there is a very important difference between the defeat inflicted on Hellenism by Christianity eighteen hundred years ago, and the check given to the Renascence by Puritanism. The greatness of the difference is well measured by the difference in force, beauty, significance, and usefulness, between primitive Christianity and Protestantism. Eighteen hundred years ago it was altogether the hour of Hebraism. Primitive Christianity was legitimately and truly the ascendant force in the world at that time, and the way of mankind's progress lay through its full development. Another hour in man's development began in the fifteenth century, and the main road of his progress then lay for a time through Hellenism. Puritanism was no longer the central current of the world's progress, it was a side stream crossing the central current and checking it. The cross and the check may have been necessary and salutary, but that does not do away with the essential difference between the main stream of man's advance and a cross or side stream. For more than two hundred years the main stream of man's advance has moved towards knowing himself and the world, seeing things as they are, spontaneity of consciousness; the main impulse of a great part, and that the strongest part, of our nation has been towards strictness of conscience. They have made the secondary the principal at the wrong moment, and the principal they have at the wrong moment treated as secondary. This contravention of the natural order has produced, as such contravention always must produce, a certain confusion and false movement, of which we are now beginning to feel, in almost every direction, the inconvenience. In all directions our habitual courses of action seem to be losing efficaciousness, credit, and control, both with others and even with ourselves. Everywhere we see the beginnings of confusion, and we want a clue to some sound order and authority. This we can only get by going back upon the actual instincts and forces which rule our life, seeing them as they really are, connecting them with other instincts and forces, and enlarging our whole view and rule of life.

EQUALITY

THERE IS a maxim which we all know, which occurs in our copy-books, which occurs in that solemn and beautiful formulary against which the Nonconformist genius is just now so angrily chafing, — the Burial Service. The maxim is this: "Evil communications corrupt good manners." It is taken from a chapter of the First Epistle to the Corinthians; but originally it is a line of poetry, of Greek poetry. *Quid Athenis et Hierosolymis?* asks a Father; what have Athens and Jerusalem to do with one another? Well, at any rate, the Jerusalemite Paul, exhorting his converts, enforces what he is saying by a verse of Athenian comedy, — a verse, probably, from the great master of that comedy, a man unsurpassed for fine and just observation of human life, Menander. *Φθείρουσιν ἤθη χρήσθ' ὁμιλίαι κακαί* — "Evil communications corrupt good manners."

In that collection of single, sententious lines, printed at the end of Menander's fragments, where we now find the maxim quoted by St. Paul, there is another striking maxim, not alien certainly to the language of the Christian religion, but which has not passed into our copy-books: "Choose equality and flee greed." The same profound observer, who laid down the maxim so universally accepted by us that it has become commonplace, the maxim that evil communications corrupt good manners, laid down also, as a no less sure result of the accurate study of human life, this other maxim as well: "Choose equality and flee greed" — *Ἰσότητα δ' αἱροῦ καὶ πλεονεξίαν φύγε.*

Pleonexia, or greed, the wishing and trying for the bigger share, we know under the name of covetousness. We understand by covetousness something different from what *pleonexia* really means: we understand by it the longing for other people's goods: and covetousness, so understood, it is a commonplace of morals and of religion with us that we should shun. As to the duty of pursuing equality, there is no such consent amongst us. Indeed, the consent is the other way, the consent is against equality. Equality before the law we all take as a matter of course; that is not the equality which we mean when we talk of equality. When we talk of equality, we understand social equality; and for equality in this Frenchified sense of the term almost everybody in England has a hard word. About four years ago Lord Beaconsfield held it up to reprobation in a speech to the students at Glasgow; — a speech so interesting, that being asked soon afterwards to hold a discourse at Glasgow, I said that if one spoke there at all at that time it would be impossible to speak on any other subject but equality. However, it is a great way to Glasgow, and I never yet have been able to go and speak there.

But the testimonies against equality have been steadily accumulating from the date of Lord Beaconsfield's Glasgow speech down to the present hour. Sir Erskine May winds up his new and important *History of Democracy* by saying: "France has aimed at social equality. The fearful troubles through which she has passed have checked her prosperity, demoralised her society, and arrested the intellectual growth of her people." Mr. Froude, again, who is more his own master than I am, has been able to go to Edinburgh and to speak there upon equality. Mr. Froude told his hearers that equality splits a nation into a "multitude of disconnected units," that "the masses require leaders whom they can trust," and that "the natural leaders in a healthy country are the gentry." And only just before the *History of Democracy* came out, we had that exciting passage of arms between Mr. Lowe and Mr. Gladstone, where equality, poor thing, received blows from them both. Mr. Lowe declared that "no concession should be made to the cry for equality, unless it appears that the State is menaced with more danger by its refusal than by its admission. No such case exists now or ever has existed in this country." And Mr. Gladstone replied that equality was so utterly unattractive to the people of this country, inequality was so dear to their hearts, that to talk of concessions being made to the cry for equality was absurd. "There is no broad political idea," says Mr. Gladstone quite truly, "which has entered less into the formation of the political system of this country than the love of equality." And he adds: "It is not the love of equality which has carried into every corner of the country the distinct undeniable popular preference, wherever other things are equal, for a man who is a lord over a man who is not. The love of freedom itself is hardly stronger in England than the love of aristocracy." Mr. Gladstone goes on to quote a saying of Sir William Molesworth, that with our people the love of aristocracy "is a religion." And he concludes in his copious and eloquent way: "Call this love of inequality by what name you please, — the complement of the love of freedom, or its negative pole, or the shadow which the love of freedom casts, or the reverberation of its voice in the halls of the constitution, — it is an active, living, and life-giving power, which forms an inseparable essential element in our political habits of mind, and asserts itself at every step in the processes of our system."

And yet, on the other side, we have a consummate critic of life like Menander, delivering, as if there were no doubt at all about the matter, the maxim: "Choose equality!" An Englishman with any curiosity must surely be inclined to ask himself how such a maxim can ever have got established, and taken rank along with "Evil communications corrupt good manners." Moreover, we see that among the French, who have suffered so grievously, as we hear, from choosing equality, the most gifted spirits continue to believe passionately in it nevertheless. "The human ideal, as well as the social ideal, is," says George Sand, "to achieve equality." She calls equality "the goal of man and the law of the future." She asserts that France is the most civilised of nations, and that its pre-eminence in civilisation it owes to equality.

But Menander lived a long while ago, and George Sand was an enthusiast. Perhaps their differing from us about equality need not trouble us much. France, too, counts for but one nation, as England counts for one also. Equality may be a religion with the people of France, as inequality, we are told, is a religion with the people of England. But what do other nations seem to think about the matter?

Now, my discourse to-night is most certainly not meant to be a disquisition on law, and on the rules of bequest. But it is evident that in the societies of Europe, with a constitution of property such as that which the feudal Middle Age left them with, — a constitution of property full of inequality, — the state of the law of bequest shows us how far each society wishes the inequality to continue. The families in possession of great estates will not break them up if they can help it. Such owners will do all they can, by entail and settlement to prevent their successors from breaking them up. They will preserve inequality. Freedom of bequest, then, the power of making entails and settlements, is sure, in an old European country like ours, to maintain inequality. And with us, who have the religion of inequality, the power of entailing and settling, and of willing property as one likes, exists, as is well known, in singular fulness, — greater fulness than in any country of the Continent. The proposal of a measure such as the Real Estates Intestacy Bill is, in a country like ours, perfectly puerile. A European country like ours, wishing not to preserve inequality but to abate it, can only do so by interfering with the freedom of bequest. This is what Turgot, the wisest of French statesmen, pronounced before the Revolution to be necessary, and what was done in France at the great Revolution. The *Code Napoléon*, the actual law of France, forbids entails altogether, and leaves a man free to dispose of but one-fourth of his property, of whatever kind, if he have three children or more, of one-third if he have two children, of one-half if he have but one child. Only in the rare case, therefore, of a man's having but one child, can that child take the whole of his father's property. If there are two children, two-thirds of the property must be equally divided between them; if there are more than two, three-fourths. In this way has France, desiring equality, sought to bring equality about.

Now the interesting point for us is, I say, to know how far other European communities, left in the same situation with us and with France, having immense inequalities of class and property created for them by the Middle Age, have dealt with these inequalities by means of the law of bequest. Do they leave bequest free, as we do? then, like us, they are for inequality. Do they interfere with the freedom of bequest, as France does? then, like France, they are for equality. And we shall be most interested, surely, by what the most civilised European communities do in this matter, — communities such as those of Germany, Italy, Belgium, Holland, Switzerland. And among those communities we are most concerned, I think, with such as, in the conditions of freedom and of self-government which they demand for their life, are most like ourselves. Germany, for instance, we shall less regard, because the conditions which the Germans seem to accept for their life are so unlike what we demand for ours; there is so much personal government there, so much *junkerism*, militarism, officialism; the community is so much more trained to submission than we could bear, so much more used to be, as the popular phrase is, sat upon. Countries where the community has more a will of its own, or can more show it, are the most important for our present purpose, — such countries as Belgium, Holland, Italy, Switzerland. Well, Belgium adopts purely and simply, as to bequest and inheritance, the provisions of the *Code Napoléon*. Holland adopts them purely and simply. Italy has adopted them substantially. Switzerland is a republic, where the general feeling against inequality is strong, and where it might seem less necessary, therefore, to guard against inequality by interfering with the power of bequest. Each Swiss canton has its own law of bequest. In Geneva, Vaud, and Zurich, — perhaps the three most distinguished cantons, — the law is identical with that of France. In Berne, one-third is the fixed proportion which a man is free to dispose of by will; the rest of his property must go among his children equally. In all the other cantons there are regulations of a like kind. Germany, I was saying, will interest us less than these freer countries. In Germany, — though there is not the English freedom of bequest, but the rule of the Roman law prevails, the rule obliging the parent to assign a certain portion to each child, — in Germany entails and settlements in favour of an eldest son are generally permitted. But there is a remarkable exception. The Rhine countries, which in the early part of this century were under French rule, and which then received the *Code Napoléon*, these countries refused to part with it when they were restored to Germany; and to this day Rhenish Prussia, Rhenish Hesse, and Baden, have the French law of bequest, forbidding entails, and dividing property in the way we have seen.

The United States of America have the English liberty of bequest. But the United States are, like Switzerland, a republic, with the republican sentiment for equality. Theirs is, besides, a new society; it did not inherit the system of classes and of property which feudalism established in Europe. The class by which the United States were settled was not a class with feudal habits and ideas. It is notorious that to acquire great landed estates and to entail them upon an eldest son, is neither the practice nor the desire of any class in America. I remember hearing it said to an American in England: "But, after all, you have the same freedom of bequest and inheritance as we have, and if a man to-morrow chose in your country to entail a great landed estate rigorously, what could you do?" The American answered: "Set aside the will on the ground of insanity."

You see we are in a manner taking the votes for and against equality. We ought not to leave out our own colonies. In general they are, of course, like the United States of America, new societies. They have the English liberty of bequest. But they have no feudal past, and were not settled by a class with feudal habits and ideas. Nevertheless it happens that there have arisen, in Australia, exceedingly large estates, and that the proprietors seek to keep them together. And what have we seen happen lately? An Act has been passed which in effect inflicts a fine upon every proprietor who holds a landed estate of more than a certain value. The measure has been severely blamed in England; to Mr. Lowe such a "concession to the cry for equality" appears, as we might expect, pregnant with warnings. At present I neither praise it nor blame it; I simply count it as one of the votes for equality. And is it not a singular thing, I ask you, that while we have the religion of inequality, and can hardly bear to hear equality spoken of, there should be, among the nations of Europe which have politically most in common with us, and in the United States of America, and in our own colonies, this diseased appetite, as we must think it, for equality? Perhaps Lord Beaconsfield may not have turned your minds to this subject as he turned mine, and what Menander or George Sand happens to have said may not interest you much; yet surely, when you think of it, when you see what a practical revolt against inequality there is amongst so many people not so very unlike to ourselves, you must feel some curiosity to sift the matter a little further, and may be not ill-disposed to follow me while I try to do so.

I have received a letter from Clerkenwell, in which the writer reproaches me for lecturing about equality at this which he calls "the most aristocratic and exclusive place out." I am here because your secretary invited me. But I am glad to treat the subject of equality before such an audience as this. Some of you may remember that I have roughly divided our English society into Barbarians, Philistines, Populace, each of them with their prepossessions, and loving to hear what gratifies them. But I remarked at the same time, that scattered throughout all these classes were a certain number of generous and humane souls, lovers of man's perfection, detached from the prepossessions of the class to which they might naturally belong, and desirous that he who speaks to them should, as Plato says, not try to please his fellow-servants, but his true and legitimate master — the heavenly Gods. I feel sure that among the members and frequenters of an institution like this, such humane souls are apt to congregate in numbers. Even from the reproach which my Clerkenwell friend brings against you of being too aristocratic, I derive some comfort. Only I give to the term *aristocratic* a rather wide extension. An accomplished American, much known and much esteemed in this country, the late Mr. Charles Sumner, says that what particularly struck him in England was the large class of gentlemen as distinct from the nobility, and the abundance amongst them of serious knowledge, high accomplishment, and refined taste, — taste fastidious perhaps, says Mr. Sumner, to excess, but erring on virtue's side. And he goes on: "I do not know that there is much difference between the manners and social observances of the highest classes of England and those of the corresponding classes of France and Germany; but in the rank immediately below the highest, — as among the professions, or military men, or literary men, — there you will find that the Englishmen have the advantage. They are better educated and better bred, more careful in their personal habits and in social conventions, more refined." Mr. Sumner's remark is just and important; this large class of gentlemen in the professions, the services, literature, politics, — and a good contingent is now added from business also, — this large class, not of the nobility, but with the accomplishments and taste of an upper class, is something peculiar to England. Of this class I may probably assume that my present audience is in large measure composed. It is aristocratic in this sense, that it has the tastes of a cultivated class, a certain high standard of civilisation. Well, it is in its effects upon *civilisation* that equality interests me. And I speak to an audience with a high standard of civilisation. If I say that certain things in certain classes do not come up to a high standard of civilisation, I need not prove how and why they do not; you will feel instinctively whether they do or no. If they do not, I need not prove that this is a bad thing, that a high standard of civilisation is desirable; you will instinctively feel that it is. Instead of calling this "the most aristocratic and exclusive place out," I conceive of it as a *civilised* place; and in speaking about civilisation half one's labour is saved when one speaks about it among those who are civilised.

Politics are forbidden here; but equality is not a question of English politics. The abstract right to equality may, indeed, be a question of speculative politics. French equality appeals to this abstract natural right as its support. It goes back to a state of nature where all were equal, and supposes that "the poor consented," as Rousseau says, "to the existence of rich people," reserving always a natural right to return to the state of nature. It supposes that a child has a natural right to his equal share in his father's goods. The principle of abstract right, says Mr. Lowe, has never been admitted in England, and is false. I so entirely agree with him, that I run no risk of offending by discussing equality upon the basis of this principle. So far as I can sound human consciousness, I cannot, as I have often said, perceive that man is really conscious of any abstract natural rights at all. The natural right to have work found for one to do, the natural right to have food found for one to eat — rights sometimes so confidently and so indignantly asserted — seem to me quite baseless. It cannot be too often repeated: peasants and workmen have no natural rights, not one. Only we ought instantly to add, that kings and nobles have none either. If it is the sound English doctrine that all rights are created by law and are based on expediency, and are alterable as the public advantage may require, certainly that orthodox doctrine is mine. Property is created and maintained by law. It would disappear in that state of private war and scramble which legal society supersedes. Legal society creates, for the common good, the right of property; and for the common good that right is by legal society limitable. That property should exist, and that it should be held with a sense of security and with a power of disposal, may be taken, by us here at any rate, as a settled matter of expediency. With these conditions a good deal of inequality is inevitable. But that the power of disposal should be practically *unlimited,* that the inequality should be *enormous,* or that the degree of inequality admitted at one time should be admitted *always,* — this is by no means so certain. The right of bequest was in early times, as Sir Henry Maine and Mr. Mill have pointed out, seldom recognised. In later times it has been limited in many countries in the way that we have seen; even in England itself it is not formally quite unlimited. The question is one of expediency. It is assumed, I grant, with great unanimity amongst us, that our signal inequality of classes and property is expedient for our civilisation and welfare. But this assumption, of which the distinguished personages who adopt it seem so sure that they think it needless to produce grounds for it, is just what we have to examine.

Now, there is a sentence of Sir Erskine May, whom I have already quoted, which will bring us straight to the very point that I wish to raise. Sir Erskine May, after saying, as you have heard, that France has pursued social equality, and has come to fearful troubles, demoralisation, and intellectual stoppage by doing so, continues thus: "Yet is she high, if not the first, in the scale of civilised nations." Why, here is a curious thing, surely! A nation pursues social equality, supposed to be an utterly false and baneful ideal; it arrives, as might have been expected, at fearful misery and deterioration by doing so; and yet, at the same time, it is high, if not the first, in the scale of civilised nations. What do we mean by *civilised*? Sir Erskine May does not seem to have asked himself the question, so we will try to answer it for ourselves. Civilisation is the humanisation of man in society. To be humanised is to comply with the true law of our human nature: *servare modum, finemque tenere, Naturamque sequi,* says Lucan; "to keep our measure, and to hold fast our end, and to follow Nature." To be humanised is to make progress towards this, our true and full humanity. And to be civilised is to make progress towards this in civil society; in that civil society "without which," says Burke, "man could not by any possibility arrive at the perfection of which his nature is capable, nor even make a remote and faint approach to it." To be the most civilised of nations, therefore, is to be the nation which comes nearest to human perfection, in the state which that perfection essentially demands. And a nation which has been brought by the pursuit of social equality to moral deterioration, intellectual stoppage, and fearful troubles, is perhaps the nation which has come nearest to human perfection in that state which such perfection essentially demands! Michelet himself, who would deny the demoralisation and the stoppage, and call the fearful troubles a sublime expiation for the sins of the whole world, could hardly say more for France than this. Certainly Sir Erskine May never intended to say so much. But into what a difficulty has he somehow run himself, and what a good action would it be to extricate him from it! Let us see whether the performance of that good action may not also be a way of clearing our minds as to the uses of equality.

When we talk of man's advance towards his full humanity, we think of an advance, not along one line only, but several. Certain races and nations, as we know, are on certain lines pre-eminent and representative. The Hebrew nation was pre-eminent on one great line. "What nation," it was justly asked by their lawgiver, "hath statutes and judgments so righteous as the law which I set before you this day? Keep therefore and do them; for this is your wisdom and your understanding in the sight of the nations which shall hear all these statutes and say: Surely this great nation is a wise and understanding people!"

The Hellenic race was pre-eminent on other lines. Isocrates could say of Athens: "Our city has left the rest of the world so far behind in philosophy and eloquence, that those educated by Athens have become the teachers of the rest of mankind; and so well has she done her part, that the name of Greeks seems no longer to stand for a race but to stand for intelligence itself, and they who share in our culture are called Greeks even before those who are merely of our own blood." The power of intellect and science, the power of beauty, the power of social life and manners, — these are what Greece so felt, and fixed, and may stand for. They are great elements in our humanisation. The power of conduct is another great element; and this was so felt and fixed by Israel that we can never with justice refuse to permit Israel, in spite of all his shortcomings, to stand for it.

So you see that in being humanised we have to move along several lines, and that on certain lines certain nations find their strength and take a lead. We may elucidate the thing yet further. Nations now existing may be said to feel or to have felt the power of this or that element in our humanisation so signally that they are characterised by it. No one who knows this country would deny that it is characterised, in a remarkable degree, by a sense of the power of conduct. Our feeling for religion is one part of this; our industry is another. What foreigners so much remark in us, — our public spirit, our love, amidst all our liberty, for public order and for stability, — are parts of it too. Then the power of beauty was so felt by the Italians that their art revived, as we know, the almost lost idea of beauty, and the serious and successful pursuit of it. Cardinal Antonelli, speaking to me about the education of the common people in Rome, said that they were illiterate indeed, but whoever mingled with them at any public show, and heard them pass judgment on the beauty or ugliness of what came before them, — "*è brutto,*" "*è bello,*" — would find that their judgment agreed admirably, in general, with just what the most cultivated people would say. Even at the present time, then, the Italians are pre-eminent in feeling the power of beauty. The power of knowledge, in the same way, is eminently an influence with the Germans. This by no means implies, as is sometimes supposed, a high and fine general culture. What it implies is a strong sense of the necessity of knowing *scientifically,* as the expression is, the things which have to be known by us; of knowing them systematically, by the regular and right process, and in the only real way. And this sense the Germans especially have. Finally, there is the power of social life and manners. And even the Athenians themselves, perhaps, have hardly felt this power so much as the French.

Voltaire, in a famous passage where he extols the age of Louis the

Fourteenth and ranks it with the chief epochs in the civilisation of our race, has to specify the gift bestowed on us by the age of Louis the Fourteenth, as the age of Pericles, for instance, bestowed on us its art and literature, and the Italian Renascence its revival of art and literature. And Voltaire shows all his acuteness in fixing on the gift to name. It is not the sort of gift which we expect to see named. The great gift of the age of Louis the Fourteenth to the world, says Voltaire, was this: *l'esprit de société,* the spirit of society, the social spirit. And another French writer, looking for the good points in the old French nobility, remarks that this at any rate is to be said in their favour: they established a high and charming ideal of social intercourse and manners, for a nation formed to profit by such an ideal, and which has profited by it ever since. And in America, perhaps, we see the disadvantages of having social equality before there has been any such high standard of social life and manners formed.

We are not disposed in England, most of us, to attach all this importance to social intercourse and manners. Yet Burke says: "There ought to be a system of manners in every nation which a well-formed mind would be disposed to relish." And the power of social life and manners is truly, as we have seen, one of the great elements in our humanisation. Unless we have cultivated it, we are incomplete. The impulse for cultivating it is not, indeed, a moral impulse. It is by no means identical with the moral impulse to help our neighbour and to do him good. Yet in many ways it works to a like end. It brings men together, makes them feel the need of one another, be considerate of one another, understand one another. But, above all things, it is a promoter of equality. It is by the humanity of their manners that men are made equal. "A man thinks to show himself my equal," says Goethe, "by being *grob,* — that is to say, coarse and rude; he does not show himself my equal, he shows himself *grob.*" But a community having humane manners is a community of equals, and in such a community great social inequalities have really no meaning, while they are at the same time a menace and an embarrassment to perfect ease of social intercourse. A community with the spirit of society is eminently, therefore, a community with the spirit of equality. A nation with a genius for society, like the French or the Athenians, is irresistibly drawn towards equality. From the first moment when the French people, with its congenital sense for the power of social intercourse and manners, came into existence, it was on the road to equality. When it had once got a high standard of social manners abundantly established, and at the same time the natural, material necessity for the feudal inequality of classes and property pressed upon it no longer, the French people introduced equality and made the French Revolution. It was not the spirit of philanthropy which mainly impelled the French to that Revolution, neither was it the spirit of envy, neither was it the love of abstract ideas, though all these did something towards it; but what did most was the spirit of society.

The well-being of the many comes out more and more distinctly, in proportion as time goes on, as the object we must pursue. An individual or a class, concentrating their efforts upon their own well-being exclusively, do but beget troubles both for others and for themselves also. No individual life can be truly prosperous, passed, as Obermann says, in the midst of men who suffer; *passée au milieu des générations qui souffrent.* To the noble soul, it cannot be happy; to the ignoble, it cannot be secure. Socialistic and communistic schemes have generally, however, a fatal defect; they are content with too low and material a standard of well-being. That instinct of perfection, which is the master-power in humanity, always rebels at this, and frustrates the work. Many are to be made partakers of well-being, true; but the ideal of well-being is not to be, on that account, lowered and coarsened. M. de Laveleye, the political economist, who is a Belgian and a Protestant, and whose testimony therefore we may the more readily take about France, says that France, being the country of Europe where the soil is more divided than anywhere except in Switzerland and Norway, is at the same time the country where material well-being is most widely spread, where wealth has of late years increased most, and where population is least outrunning the limits which, for the comfort and progress of the working classes themselves, seem necessary. This may go for a good deal. It supplies an answer to what Sir Erskine May says about the bad effects of equality upon French prosperity. But I will quote to you from Mr. Hamerton what goes, I think, for yet more. Mr. Hamerton is an excellent observer and reporter, and has lived for many years in France. He says of the French peasantry that they are exceedingly ignorant. So they are. But he adds: "They are at the same time full of intelligence; their manners are excellent, they have delicate perceptions, they have tact, they have a certain refinement which a brutalised peasantry could not possibly have. If you talk to one of them at his own home, or in his field, he will enter into conversation with you quite easily, and sustain his part in a perfectly becoming way, with a pleasant combination of dignity and quiet humour. The interval between him and a Kentish labourer is enormous."

This is indeed worth your attention. Of course all mankind are, as Mr. Gladstone says, of our own flesh and blood. But you know how often it happens in England that a cultivated person, a person of the sort that Mr. Charles Sumner describes, talking to one of the lower class, or even of the middle class, feels, and cannot but feel, that there is somehow a wall of partition between himself and the other, that they seem to belong to two different worlds. Thoughts, feelings, perceptions, susceptibilities, language, manners, — everything is different. Whereas, with a French peasant, the most cultivated man may find himself in sympathy, may feel that he is talking to an equal. This is an experience which has been made a thousand times, and which may be made again any day. And it may be carried beyond the range of mere conversation, it may be extended to things like pleasures, recreations, eating and drinking, and so on. In general the pleasures, recreations, eating and drinking of English people, when once you get below that class which Mr. Charles Sumner calls the class of gentlemen, are to one of that class unpalatable and impossible. In France there is not this incompatibility. Whether he mix with high or low, the gentleman feels himself in a world not alien or repulsive, but a world where people make the same sort of demands upon life, in things of this sort, which he himself does. In all these respects France is the country where the people, as distinguished from a wealthy refined class, most lives what we call a humane life, the life of civilised man.

Of course, fastidious persons can and do pick holes in it. There is just now, in France, a *noblesse* newly revived, full of pretension, full of airs and graces and disdains; but its sphere is narrow, and out of its own sphere no one cares very much for it. There is a general equality in a humane kind of life. This is the secret of the passionate attachment with which France inspires all Frenchmen, in spite of her fearful troubles, her checked prosperity, her disconnected units, and the rest of it. There is so much of the goodness and agreeableness of life there, and for so many. It is the secret of her having been able to attach so ardently to her the German and Protestant people of Alsace, while we have been so little able to attach the Celtic and Catholic people of Ireland. France brings the Alsatians into a social system so full of the goodness and agreeableness of life; we offer to the Irish no such attraction. It is the secret, finally, of the prevalence which we have remarked in other continental countries of a legislation tending, like that of France, to social equality. The social system which equality creates in France is, in the eyes of others, such a giver of the goodness and agreeableness of life, that they seek to get the goodness by getting the equality.

Yet France has had her fearful troubles, as Sir Erskine May justly says. She suffers too, he adds, from demoralisation and intellectual stoppage. Let us admit, if he likes, this to be true also. His error is that he attributes all this to equality. Equality, as we have seen, has brought France to a really admirable and enviable pitch of humanisation in one important line. And this, the work of equality, is so much a good in Sir Erskine May's eyes, that he has mistaken it for the whole of which it is a part, frankly identifies it with civilisation, and is inclined to pronounce France the most civilised of nations.

But we have seen how much goes to full humanisation, to true civilisation, besides the power of social life and manners. There is the power of conduct, the power of intellect and knowledge, the power of beauty. The power of conduct is the greatest of all. And without in the least wishing to preach, I must observe, as a mere matter of natural fact and experience, that for the power of conduct France has never had anything like the same sense which she has had for the power of social life and manners. Michelet, himself a Frenchman, gives us the reason why the Reformation did not succeed in France. It did not succeed, he says, because *la France ne voulait pas de réforme morale* — moral reform France would not have; and the Reformation was above all a moral movement. The sense in France for the power of conduct has not greatly deepened, I think, since. The sense for the power of intellect and knowledge has not been adequate either. The sense for beauty has not been adequate. Intelligence and beauty have been, in general, but so far reached, as they can be and are reached by men who, of the elements of perfect humanisation, lay thorough hold upon one only, — the power of social intercourse and manners. I speak of France in general; she has had, and she has, individuals who stand out and who form exceptions. Well then, if a nation laying no sufficient hold upon the powers of beauty and knowledge, and a most failing and feeble hold upon the power of conduct, comes to demoralisation and intellectual stoppage and fearful troubles, we need not be inordinately surprised. What we should rather marvel at is the healing and bountiful operation of Nature, whereby the laying firm hold on one real element in our humanisation has had for France results so beneficient.

And thus, when Sir Erskine May gets bewildered between France's equality and fearful troubles on the one hand, and the civilisation of France on the other, let us suggest to him that perhaps he is bewildered by his data because he combines them ill. France has not exemplary disaster and ruin as the fruits of equality, and at the same time, and independently of this, an exemplary civilisation. She has a large measure of happiness and success as the fruits of equality, and she has a very large measure of dangers and troubles as the fruits of something else.

We have more to do, however, than to help Sir Erskine May out of his scrape about France. We have to see whether the considerations which we have been employing may not be of use to us about England.

We shall not have much difficulty in admitting whatever good is to be said of ourselves, and we will try not to be unfair by excluding all that is not so favourable. Indeed, our less favourable side is the one which we should be the most anxious to note, in order that we may mend it. But we will begin with the good. Our people has energy and honesty as its good characteristics. We have a strong sense for the chief power in the life and progress of man, — the power of conduct. So far we speak of the English people as a whole. Then we have a rich, refined, and splendid aristocracy. And we have, according to Mr. Charles Sumner's acute and true remark, a class of gentlemen, not of the nobility, but well-bred, cultivated, and refined, larger than is to be found in any other country. For these last we have Mr. Sumner's testimony. As to the splendour of our aristocracy, all the world is agreed. Then we have a middle class and a lower class; and they, after all, are the immense bulk of the nation.

Let us see how the civilisation of these classes appears to a Frenchman, who has witnessed, in his own country, the considerable humanisation of these classes by equality. To such an observer our middle class divides itself into a serious portion and a gay or rowdy portion; both are a marvel to him. With the gay or rowdy portion we need not much concern ourselves; we shall figure it to our minds sufficiently if we conceive it as the source of that war-song produced in these recent days of excitement:

> We don't want to fight, but by jingo, if we do,
> We've got the ships, we've got the men, and we've got
> the money too.

We may also partly judge its standard of life, and the needs of its nature, by the modern English theatre, perhaps the most contemptible in Europe. But the real strength of the English middle class is in its serious portion. And of this a Frenchman, who was here some little time ago as the correspondent, I think, of the *Siècle* newspaper, and whose letters were afterwards published in a volume, writes as follows. He had been attending some of the Moody and Sankey meetings, and he says: "To understand the success of Messrs. Moody and Sankey, one must be familiar with English manners, one must know the mind-deadening influence of a narrow Biblism, one must have experienced the sense of acute ennui, which the aspect and the frequentation of this great division of English society produce in others, the want of elasticity and the chronic ennui which characterise this class itself, petrified in a narrow Protestantism and in a perpetual reading of the Bible."

You know the French; — a little more Biblism, one may take leave to say, would do them no harm. But an audience like this, — and here, as I said, is the advantage of an audience like this, — will have no difficulty in admitting the amount of truth which there is in the Frenchman's picture. It is the picture of a class which, driven by its sense for the power of conduct, in the beginning of the seventeenth century entered, — as I have more than once said, and as I may more than once have occasion in future to say, — *entered the prison of Puritanism, and had the key turned upon its spirit there for two hundred years.* They did not know, good and earnest people as they were, that to the building up of human life there belong all those other powers also, — the power of intellect and knowledge, the power of beauty, the power of social life and manners. And something, by what they became, they gained, and the whole nation with them; they deepened and fixed for this nation the sense of conduct. But they created a type of life and manners, of which they themselves indeed are slow to recognise the faults, but which is fatally condemned by its hideousness, its immense ennui, and against which the instinct of self-preservation in humanity rebels.

Partisans fight against facts in vain. Mr. Goldwin Smith, a writer of eloquence and power, although too prone to acerbity, is a partisan of the Puritans, and of the Noncomformists who are the special inheritors of the Puritan tradition. He angrily resents the imputation upon that Puritan type of life, by which the life of our serious middle class has been formed, that it was doomed to hideousness, to immense ennui. He protests that it had beauty, amenity, accomplishment. Let us go to facts. Charles the First, who, with all his faults, had the just idea that art and letters are great civilisers, made, as you know, a famous collection of pictures, — our first National Gallery. It was, I suppose, the best collection at that time north of the Alps. It contained nine Raphaels, eleven Correggios, twenty-eight Titians. What became of that collection? The journals of the House of Commons will tell you. There you may see the Puritan Parliament disposing of this Whitehall or York House collection as follows: "Ordered, that all such pictures and statues there as are without any superstition, shall be forthwith sold. . . . Ordered, that all such pictures there as have the representation of the Second Person in Trinity upon them, shall be forthwith burnt. Ordered, that all such pictures there as have the representation of the Virgin Mary upon them, shall be forthwith burnt." There we have the weak side of our parliamentary government and our serious middle class. We are incapable of sending Mr.

Gladstone to be tried at the Old Bailey because he proclaims his antipathy to Lord Beaconsfield. A majority in our House of Commons is incapable of hailing, with frantic laughter and applause, a string of indecent jests against Christianity and its Founder. But we are not, or were not, incapable of producing a Parliament which burns or sells the masterpieces of Italian art. And one may surely say of such a Puritan Parliament, and of those who determine its line for it, that they had not the spirit of beauty.

What shall we say of amenity? Milton was born a humanist, but the Puritan temper, as we know, mastered him. There is nothing more unlovely and unamiable than Milton the Puritan disputant. Some one answers his *Doctrine and Discipline of Divorce*. "I mean not," rejoins Milton, "to dispute philosophy with this pork, who never read any." However, he does reply to him, and throughout the reply Milton's great joke is, that his adversary, who was anonymous, is a serving-man. "Finally, he winds up his text with much doubt and trepidation; for it may be his trenchers were not scraped, and that which never yet afforded corn of favour to his noddle, — the salt-cellar, — was not rubbed; and therefore, in this haste, easily granting that his answers fall foul upon each other, and praying you would not think he writes as a prophet, but as a man, he runs to the black jack, fills his flagon, spreads the table, and serves up dinner." There you have the same spirit of urbanity and amenity, as much of it, and as little, as generally informs the religious controversies of our Puritan middle class to this day.

But Mr. Goldwin Smith insists, and picks out his own exemplar of the Puritan type of life and manners; and even here let us follow him. He picks out the most favourable specimen he can find, — Colonel Hutchinson, whose well-known memoirs, written by his widow, we have all read with interest. "Lucy Hutchinson," says Mr. Goldwin Smith, "is painting what she thought a perfect Puritan would be; and her picture presents to us not a coarse, crop-eared, and snuffling fanatic, but a highly accomplished, refined, gallant, and most amiable, though religious and seriously minded, gentleman." Let us, I say, in this example of Mr. Goldwin Smith's own choosing, lay our finger upon the points where this type deflects from the truly humane ideal.

Mrs. Hutchinson relates a story which gives us a good notion of what the amiable and accomplished social intercourse, even of a picked Puritan family, was. Her husband was governor of Nottingham. He had occasion, she says, "to go and break up a private meeting in the cannoneer's chamber"; and in the cannoneer's chamber "were found some notes concerning pædobaptism, which, being brought into the governor's lodgings, his wife having perused them and compared them with the Scriptures, found not what to say against the truths they asserted concerning the misapplication of that ordinance to infants." Soon afterwards she expects her confinement, and communicates the cannoneer's doubts about pædobaptism to her husband. The fatal cannoneer makes a breach in him too. "Then he bought and read all the eminent treatises on both sides, which at that time came thick from the presses, and still was cleared in the error of the pædobaptists." Finally, Mrs. Hutchinson is confined. Then the governor "invited all the ministers to dinner, and propounded his doubt and the ground thereof to them. None of them could defend their practice with any satisfactory reason, but the tradition of the Church from the primitive times, and their main buckler of federal holiness, which Tombs and Denne had excellently overthrown. He and his wife then, professing themselves unsatisfied, desired their opinions." With the opinions I will not trouble you, but hasten to the result: "Whereupon that infant was not baptized."

No doubt to a large division of English society at this very day, that sort of dinner and discussion, and, indeed, the whole manner of life and conversation here suggested by Mrs. Hutchinson's narrative, will seem both natural and amiable, and such as to meet the needs of man as a religious and social creature. You know the conversation which reigns in thousands of middle-class families at this hour, about nunneries, teetotalism, the confessional, eternal punishment, ritualism, disestablishment. It goes wherever the class goes which is moulded on the Puritan type of life. In the long winter evenings of Toronto Mr. Goldwin Smith has had, probably, abundant experience of it. What is its enemy? The instinct of self-preservation in humanity. Men make crude types and try to impose them, but to no purpose. *"L'homme s'agite, Dieu le mène,"* says Bossuet. "There are many devices in a man's heart; nevertheless the counsel of the Eternal, that shall stand." Those who offer us the Puritan type of life offer us a religion not true, the claims of intellect and knowledge not satisfied, the claim of beauty not satisfied, the claim of manners not satisfied. In its strong sense for conduct that life touches truth; but its other imperfections hinder it from employing even this sense aright. The type mastered our nation for a time. Then came the reaction. The nation said: "This type, at any rate, is amiss; we are not going to be all like *that!*" The type retired into our middle class, and fortified itself there. It seeks to endure, to emerge, to deny its own imperfections, to impose itself again; — impossible! If we continue to live, we must outgrow it. The very class in which it is rooted, our middle class, will have to acknowledge the type's inadequacy, will have to acknowledge the hideousness, the immense ennui of the life which this type has created, will have to transform itself thoroughly. It will have to admit the large part of truth which there is in the criticisms of our Frenchman, whom we have too long forgotten.

After our middle class he turns his attention to our lower class. And of the lower and larger portion of this, the portion not bordering on the middle class and sharing its faults, he says: "I consider this multitude to be absolutely devoid, not only of political principles, but even of the most simple notions of good and evil. Certainly it does not appeal, this mob, to the principles of '89, which you English make game of; it does not insist on the rights of man; what it wants is beer, gin, and *fun*." [1]

That is a description of what Mr. Bright would call the residuum, only our author seems to think the residuum a very large body. And its condition strikes him with amazement and horror. And surely well it may. Let us recall Mr. Hamerton's account of the most illiterate class in France; what an amount of civilisation they have notwithstanding! And this is always to be understood, in hearing or reading a Frenchman's praise of England. He envies our liberty, our public spirit, our trade, our stability. But there is always a reserve in his mind. He never means for a moment that he would like to change with us. Life seems to him so much better a thing in France for so many more people, that, in spite of the fearful troubles of France, it is best to be a Frenchman. A Frenchman might agree with Mr. Cobden, that life is good in England for those people who have at least £5000 a year. But the civilisation of that immense majority who have not £5000 a year, or £500, or even £100, — of our middle and lower class, — seems to him too deplorable.

And now what has this condition of our middle and lower class to tell us about equality? How is it, must we not ask, how is it that, being without fearful troubles, having so many achievements to show and so much success, having as a nation a deep sense for conduct, having signal energy and honesty, having a splendid aristocracy, having an exceptionally large class of gentlemen, we are yet so little civilised? How is it that our middle and lower classes, in spite of the individuals among them who are raised by happy gifts of nature to a more humane life, in spite of the seriousness of the middle class, in spite of the honesty and power of true work, the *virtus verusque labor,* which are to be found in abundance throughout the lower, do yet present, as a whole, the characters which we have seen?

And really it seems as if the current of our discourse carried us of itself to but one conclusion. It seems as if we could not avoid concluding, that just as France owes her fearful troubles to other things

[1] So in the original.

and her civilisedness to equality, so we owe our immunity from fearful troubles to other things, and our uncivilisedness to inequality. "Knowledge is easy," says the wise man, "to him that understandeth"; easy, he means, to him who will use his mind simply and rationally, and not to make him think he can know what he cannot, or to maintain, *per fas et nefas*, a false thesis with which he fancies his interests to be bound up. And to him who will use his mind as the wise man recommends, surely it is easy to see that our shortcomings in civilisation are due to our inequality; or in other words, that the great inequality of classes and property, which came to us from the Middle Age and which we maintain because we have the religion of inequality, that this constitution of things, I say, has the natural and necessary effect, under present circumstances, of materialising our upper class, vulgarising our middle class, and brutalising our lower class. And this is to fail in civilisation.

For only just look how the facts combine themselves. I have said little as yet about our aristocratic class, except that it is splendid. Yet these, "our often very unhappy brethren," as Burke calls them, are by no means matter for nothing but ecstasy. Our charity ought certainly, Burke says, to "extend a due and anxious sensation of pity to the distresses of the miserable great." Burke's extremely strong language about their miseries and defects I will not quote. For my part, I am always disposed to marvel that human beings, in a position so false, should be so good as these are. Their reason for existing was to serve as a number of centres in a world disintegrated after the ruin of the Roman Empire, and slowly re-constituting itself. Numerous centres of material force were needed, and these a feudal aristocracy supplied. Their large and hereditary estates served this public end. The owners had a positive function, for which their estates were essential. In our modern world the function is gone; and the great estates, with an infinitely multiplied power of ministering to mere pleasure and indulgence, remain. The energy and honesty of our race does not leave itself without witness in this class, and nowhere are there more conspicuous examples of individuals raised by happy gifts of nature far above their fellows and their circumstances. For distinction of all kinds this class has an esteem. Everything which succeeds they tend to welcome, to win over, to put on their side; genius may generally make, if it will, not bad terms for itself with them. But the total result of the class, its effect on society at large and on national progress, are what we must regard. And on the whole, with no necessary function to fulfil, never conversant with life as it really is, tempted, flattered, and spoiled from childhood to old age, our aristocratic class is inevitably materialised, and the more so the more the development of industry and ingenuity augments the means of luxury. Every one can see how bad is the action of such an aristocracy upon the class of newly enriched people, whose great danger is a materialistic ideal, just because it is the ideal they can easiest comprehend. Nor is the mischief of this action now compensated by signal services of a public kind. Turn even to that sphere which aristocracies think specially their own, and where they have under other circumstances been really effective, — the sphere of politics. When there is need, as now, for any large forecast of the course of human affairs, for an acquaintance with the ideas which in the end sway mankind, and for an estimate of their power, aristocracies are out of their element, and materialised aristocracies most of all. In the immense spiritual movement of our day, the English aristocracy, as I have elsewhere said, always reminds me of Pilate confronting the phenomenon of Christianity. Nor can a materialised class have any serious and fruitful sense for the power of beauty. They may imagine themselves to be in pursuit of beauty; but how often, alas, does the pursuit come to little more than dabbling a little in what they are pleased to call art, and making a great deal of what they are pleased to call love!

Let us return to their merits. For the power of manners an aristocratic class, whether materialised or not, will always, from its circumstances, have a strong sense. And although for this power of social life and manners, so important to civilisation, our English race has no special natural turn, in our aristocracy this power emerges and marks them. When the day of general humanisation comes, they will have fixed the standard of manners. The English simplicity, too, makes the best of the English aristocracy more frank and natural than the best of the like class anywhere else, and even the worst of them it makes free from the incredible fatuities and absurdities of the worst. Then the sense of conduct they share with their countrymen at large. In no class has it such trials to undergo; in none is it more often and more grievously overborne. But really the right comment on this is the comment of Pepys upon the evil courses of Charles the Second and the Duke of York and the court of that day: "At all which I am sorry; but it is the effect of idleness, and having nothing else to employ their great spirits upon."

Heaven forbid that I should speak in dispraise of that unique and most English class which Mr. Charles Sumner extols — the large class of gentlemen, not of the landed class or of the nobility, but cultivated and refined. They are a seemly product of the energy and of the power to rise in our race. Without, in general, rank and splendour and wealth and luxury to polish them, they have made their own the high standard of life and manners of an aristocratic and refined class. Not having all the dissipations and distractions of this class, they are much more seriously alive to the power of intellect and knowledge, to the power of beauty. The sense of conduct, too, meets with fewer trials in this class. To some extent, however, their contiguousness to the aristocratic class has now the effect of materialising them, as it does the class of newly enriched people. The most palpable action is on the young amongst them, and on their standard of life and enjoyment. But in general, for this whose class, established facts, the materialism which they see regnant, too much block their mental horizon, and limit the possibilities of things to them. They are deficient in openness and flexibility of mind, in free play of ideas, in faith and ardour. Civilised they are, but they are not much of a civilising force; they are somehow bounded and ineffective.

So on the middle class they produce singularly little effect. What the middle class sees is that splendid piece of materialism, the aristocratic class, with a wealth and luxury utterly out of their reach, with a standard of social life and manners, the offspring of that wealth and luxury, seeming utterly out of their reach also. And thus they are thrown back upon themselves — upon a defective type of religion, a narrow range of intellect and knowledge, a stunted sense of beauty, a low standard of manners. And the lower class see before them the aristocratic class, and its civilisation, such as it is, even infinitely more out of *their* reach than out of that of the middle class; while the life of the middle class, with its unlovely types of religion, thought, beauty, and manners, has naturally, in general, no great attractions for them either. And so they too are thrown back upon themselves; upon their beer, their gin, and their *fun*. Now, then, you will understand what I meant by saying that our inequality materialises our upper class, vulgarises our middle class, brutalises our lower.

And the greater the inequality the more marked is its bad action upon the middle and lower classes. In Scotland the landed aristocracy fills the scene, as is well known, still more than in England; the other classes are more squeezed back and effaced. And the social civilisation of the lower middle class and of the poorest class, in Scotland, is an example of the consequences. Compared with the same class even in England, the Scottish lower middle class is most visibly, to vary Mr. Charles Summer's phrase, *less* well-bred, *less* careful in personal habits and in social conventions, *less* refined. Let any one who doubts it go, after issuing from the aristocratic solitudes which possess Loch Lomond, let him go and observe the shopkeepers and the middle class in Dumbarton, and Greenock, and Gourock, and the places along the mouth of the Clyde. And for the poorest class, who that has seen it can ever forget the hardly human horror, the abjection and uncivilisedness of Glasgow?

What a strange religion, then, is our religion of inequality! Romance often helps a religion to hold its ground, and romance is good in its way; but ours is not even a romantic religion. No doubt our aristocracy is an object of very strong public interest. The *Times* itself bestows a leading article by way of epithalamium on the Duke of Norfolk's marriage. And those journals of a new type, full of talent, and which interest me particularly because they seem as if they were written by the young lion of our youth, — the young lion grown mellow and, as the French say, *viveur,* arrived at his full and ripe knowledge of the world, and minded to enjoy the smooth evening of his days, — those journals, in the main a sort of social gazette of the aristocracy, are apparently not read by that class only which they most concern, but are read with great avidity by other classes also. And the common people too have undoubtedly, as Mr. Gladstone says, a wonderful preference for a lord. Yet our aristocracy, from the action upon it of the Wars of the Roses, the Tudors, and the political necessities of George the Third, is for the imagination a singularly modern and uninteresting one. Its splendour of station, its wealth, show, and luxury, is then what the other classes really admire in it; and this is not an elevating admiration. Such an admiration will never lift us out of our vulgarity and brutality, if we chance to be vulgar and brutal to start with; it will rather feed them and be fed by them. So that when Mr. Gladstone invites us to call our love of inequality "the complement of the love of freedom or its negative pole, or the shadow which the love of freedom casts, or the reverberation of its voice in the halls of the constitution," we must surely answer that all this mystical eloquence is not in the least necessary to explain so simple a matter; that our love of inequality is really the vulgarity in us, and the brutality, admiring and worshipping the splendid materiality.

Our present social organisation, however, will and must endure until our middle class is provided with some better ideal of life than it has now. Our present organisation has been an appointed stage in our growth; it has been of good use, and has enabled us to do great things. But the use is at an end, and the stage is over. Ask yourselves if you do not sometimes feel in yourselves a sense, that in spite of the strenuous efforts for good of so many excellent persons amongst us, we begin somehow to flounder and to beat the air; that we seem to be finding ourselves stopped on this line of advance and on that, and to be threatened with a sort of standstill. It is that we are trying to live on with a social organisation of which the day is over. Certainly equality will never of itself alone give us a perfect civilisation. But, with such inequality as ours, a perfect civilisation is impossible.

To that conclusion, facts, and the stream itself of this discourse, do seem, I think, to carry us irresistibly. We arrive at it because they so choose, not because we so choose. Our tendencies are all the other way. We are all of us politicians, and in one of two camps, the Liberal or the Conservative. Liberals tend to accept the middle class as it is, and to praise the nonconformists; while Conservatives tend to accept the upper class as it is, and to praise the aristocracy. And yet here we are at the conclusion, that whereas one of the great obstacles to our civilisation is, as I have often said, British nonconformity, another main obstacle to our civilisation is British aristocracy! And this while we are yet forced to recognise excellent special qualities as well as the general English energy and honesty, and a number of emergent humane individuals, in both noncomformists and aristocracy. Clearly such a conclusion can be none of our own seeking.

Then again, to remedy our inequality, there must be a change in the law of bequest, as there has been in France; and the faults and inconveniences of the present French law of bequest are obvious. It tends to over-divide property; it is unequal in operation, and can be eluded by people limiting their families; it makes the children, however ill they may behave, independent of the parent. To be sure, Mr. Mill and others have shown that a law of bequest fixing the maximum, whether of land or money, which any one individual may take by bequest or inheritance, but in other respects leaving the testator quite free, has none of the inconveniences of the French law, and is in every way preferable. But evidently these are not questions of practical politics. Just imagine Lord Hartington going down to Glasgow, and meeting his Scotch Liberals there, and saying to them: "You are ill at ease, and you are calling for change, and very justly. But the cause of your being ill at ease is not what you suppose. The cause of your being ill at ease is the profound imperfectness of your social civilisation. Your social civilisation is indeed such as I forbear to characterise. But the remedy is not disestablishment. The remedy is social equality. Let me direct your attention to a reform in the law of bequest and entail." One can hardly speak of such a thing without laughing. No, the matter is at present one for the thoughts of those who think. It is a thing to be turned over in the minds of those who, on the one hand, have the spirit of scientific inquirers, bent on seeing things as they really are; and, on the other hand, the spirit of friends of the humane life, lovers of perfection. To your thoughts I commit it. And perhaps, the more you think of it, the more you will be persuaded that Menander showed his wisdom quite as much when he said *Choose equality,* as when he assured us that *Evil communications corrupt good manners.*

Religion

PREFACE TO
LAST ESSAYS ON CHURCH AND RELIGION

Qu'on fonde la foi profonde!

THE PRESENT volume closes the series of my attempts to deal directly with questions concerning religion and the Church. Indirectly such questions must often, in all serious literary work, present themselves; but in this volume I make them my direct object for the last time. Assuredly it was not for my own pleasure that I entered upon them at first, and it is with anything but reluctance that I now part from them. Neither can I be ignorant what offence my handling of them has given to many whose goodwill I value, and with what relief they will learn that the handling is now to cease. Personal considerations, however, ought not in a matter like this to bear sway; and they have not, in fact, determined me to bring to an end the work which I had been pursuing. But the thing which I proposed to myself to do has, so far as my powers enabled me to do it, been done. What I wished to say has been said. And in returning to devote to literature, more strictly so-called, what remains to me of life and strength and leisure, I am returning, after all, to a field where work of the most important kind has now to be done, though indirectly, for religion. I am persuaded that the transformation of religion, which is essential for its perpetuance, can be accomplished only by carrying the qualities of flexibility, perceptiveness, and judgment, which are the best fruits of letters, to whole classes of the community which now know next to nothing of them, and by procuring the application of those qualities to matters where they are never applied now.

A survey of the forms and tendencies which religion exhibits at the present day in England has been made lately by a man of genius, energy, and sympathy — Mr. Gladstone. Mr. Gladstone seems disposed to fix as the test of value, for those several forms, their greater or lesser adaptedness to the mind of masses of our people. It may be admitted that religion ought to be capable of reaching the mind of masses of men. It may be admitted that a religion not plain and simple, a religion of abstractions and intellectual refinements, cannot influence masses of men. But it is an error to imagine that the mind of our masses, or even the mind of our religious world, is something which may remain just as it now is, and that religion will have to adapt itself to that mind just as it now is. At least as much change is required, and will have to take place, in that mind as in religion. Gross of perception and materialising that mind is, at present, still disposed to be. Yet at the same time it is undeniable that the old anthropomorphic and miraculous religion, suited in many respects to such a mind, no longer reaches and rules it as it once did. A check and disturbance to religion thence arises. But let us impute the disturbance to the right cause. It is not to be imputed merely to the inadequacy of the old materialising religion, and to be remedied by giving to this religion a form still materialising, but more acceptable. It is to be imputed, in at least an equal degree, to the grossness of perception and materialising habits of the popular mind, which unfit it for any religion not lending itself, like the old popular religion, to those habits; while yet, from other causes, that old religion cannot maintain its sway. And it is to be remedied by a gradual transformation of the popular mind, by slowly curing it of its grossness of perception and of its materialising habits, not by keeping religion materialistic that it may correspond to them.

The conditions of the religious question are, in truth, profoundly misapprehended in this country. In England and in America religion has retained so much hold upon the affections of the community, that the partisans of poplar religion are easily led to entertain illusions; to fancy that the difficulties of their case are much less than they are, that they can make terms which they cannot make, and save things which they cannot save. A good medicine for such illusions would be the perusal of the criticisms which *Literature and Dogma* has encountered on the Continent. Here in England that book passes, in general, for a book revolutionary and anti-religious. In foreign critics of the liberal school it provokes a feeling of mingled astonishment and impatience; impatience, that religion should be set on new grounds when they had hoped that religion, the old ground having in the judgment of all rational persons given way, was going to ruin as fast as could fairly be expected; astonishment, that any man of liberal tendencies should not agree with them.

Particularly striking, in this respect, were the remarks upon *Literature and Dogma* of M. Challemel-Lacour, in France, and of

Professor de Gubernatis, in Italy. Professor de Gubernatis is perhaps the most accomplished man in Italy; he is certainly one of the most intelligent. M. Challemel-Lacour is, or was, one of the best, gravest, most deeply interesting and instructive, of French writers. His admirable series of articles on Wilhelm von Humboldt, which I read a good many years ago in the *Revue des Deux Mondes,* still live as fresh in my memory as if I had read them yesterday. M. Challemel-Lacour has become an ardent politician. It is well known how politics, in France, govern men's treatment of the religious question. Some little temper and heat are excusable, undoubtedly, when religion raises in a man's mind simply the image of the clerical party and of his sworn political foes. Perhaps a man's view of religion, however, must necessarily in this case be somewhat warped. Professor de Gubernatis is not a politician; he is an independent friend of progress, of high studies, and of intelligence. His remarks on *Literature and Dogma,* therefore, and on the attempt made in that book to give a new life to religion by giving a new sense to words of the Bible, have even a greater significance than M. Challemel-Lacour's. For Italy and for Italians, says Professor de Gubernatis, such an attempt has and can have no interest whatever. "In Italy the Bible is just this: — for priests, a sacred text; for infidels, a book full of obscurities and contradictions; for the learned, an historical document to be used with great caution; for lovers of literature, a collection of very fine specimens of Oriental poetic eloquence. But it never has been, and never will be, a fruitful inspirer of men's daily life." "And how wonderful," Professor de Gubernatis adds, "that any one should wish to make it so, and should raise intellectual and literary discussions having this for their object!" "It is strange that the human genius should take pleasure in combating in such narrow lists, with such treacherous ground under one's feet, with such a cloudy sky over one's head; — and all this in the name of freedom of discussion!" "What would the author of *Literature and Dogma* say," concludes Professor de Gubernatis, "if Plato had based his republic upon a text of Hesiod; — *se Platone avesse fondata la sua Repubblica sopra un testo d'Esiodo?*" That is to say, the Bible has no more solidity and value, as a basis for human life, than the *Theogony*.

Here we have, undoubtedly, the genuine opinion of Continental liberalism concerning the religion of the Bible and its future. It is stated with unusual frankness and clearness, but it is the genuine opinion. It is not an opinion which at present prevails at all widely either in this country or in America. But when we consider the immense change which, in other matters where tradition and convention were the obstacles to change, has befallen the thought of this country since the Continent was opened at the end of the great war, we cannot doubt that in religion, too, the mere barriers of tradition and convention will finally give way, that a common European level of thought will establish itself, and will spread to America also. Of course there will be backwaters, more or less strong, of superstition and obscurantism; but I speak of the probable development of opinion in those classes which are to be called progressive and liberal. Such classes are undoubtedly the multiplying and prevailing body both here and in America. And I say that, if we judge the future from the past, these classes, in any matter where it is tradition and convention that at present isolates them from the common liberal opinion of Europe, will, with time, be drawn almost inevitably into that opinion.

The partisans of traditional religion in this country do not know, I think, how decisively the whole force of progressive and liberal opinion on the Continent has pronounced against the Christian religion. They do not know how surely the whole force of progressive and liberal opinion in this country tends to follow, so far as traditional religion is concerned, the opinion of the Continent. They dream of patching up things unmendable, of retaining what can never be retained, of stopping change at a point where it can never be stopped. The undoubted tendency of liberal opinion is to reject the whole anthropomorphic and miraculous religion of tradition, as unsound and untenable. On the Continent such opinion has rejected it already. One cannot blame the rejection. "Things are what they are," and the religion of tradition, Catholic or Protestant, *is* unsound and untenable. A greater force of tradition in favour of religion is all which now prevents the liberal opinion in this country from following Continental opinion. That force is not of a nature to be permanent, and it will not, in fact, hold out long. But a very grave question is behind.

Rejecting, henceforth, all concern with the obsolete religion of tradition, the liberalism of the Continent rejects also, and on the like grounds, all concern with the Bible and Christianity. To claim for the Bible the direction, in any way, of modern life, is, we hear, as if Plato had sought to found his ideal republic "upon a text of Hesiod." The real question is whether this conclusion, too, of modern liberalism is to be admitted, like the conclusion that traditionary religion is unsound and obsolete. And it does not find many gainsayers. Obscurantists are glad to see the question placed on this footing: that the cause of traditionary religion, and the cause of Christianity in general, must stand or fall together. For they see but very little way into the future; and in the immediate present this way of putting the question tells, as they clearly perceive, in their favour. In the immediate present many will be tempted to cling to the traditionary religion with their eyes shut, rather than accept the extinction of Christianity. Other friends of religion are busy with fantastic projects, which can never come to anything, but which prevent their seeing the real character of the situation. So the thesis of modern liberals on the Continent, that Christianity in general stands on the same footing as traditionary religion and must share its fate, meets with little direct discussion or opposition. And liberal opinion everywhere will at last grow accustomed to finding that thesis put forward as certain, will become familiarised with it, will suppose that no one disputes it. This in itself will tend to withhold men from any serious return upon their own minds in the matter. Meanwhile the day will most certainly arrive, when the great body of liberal opinion in this country will adhere to the first half of the doctrine of Continental liberals; — will admit that traditionary religion is utterly untenable. And the danger is, that from the habits of their minds, and from seeing the thing treated as certain, and from hearing nothing urged against it, our liberals may admit as indisputable the second half of the doctrine too: that Christianity, also, is untenable.

And therefore is it so all-important to insist on what I call the *natural truth* of Christianity, and to bring this out all we can. Liberal opinion tends, as we have seen, to treat traditional religion and Christianity as identical; if one is unsound, so is the other. Especially, however, does liberal opinion show this tendency among the Latin nations, on whom Protestantism did not lay hold; and it shows it most among those Latin nations of whom Protestantism laid hold least, such as Italy and Spain. For Protestantism was undoubtedly, whatever may have been its faults and miscarriages, an assertion of the natural truth of Christianity for the mind and conscience of men. The question is, whether Christianity has this natural truth or not. It is a question of fact. In the end the victory belongs to facts, and he who contradicts them finds that he runs his head against a wall. Our traditional religion turns out not to have, in fact, natural truth, the only truth which can stand. The miracles of our traditional religion, like other miracles, did not happen; its metaphysical proofs of God are mere words. Has or has not Christianity, in fact, the same want of natural truth as our traditional religion? It is a question of immense importance. Of questions about religion, it may be said to be at the present time, for a serious man, the only important one.

Now, whoever seeks to show the natural truth of a thing which professes to be for general use, ought to try to be as simple as possible. He ought not to allow himself to have any recourse either to intellectual refinements or to sentimental rhetoric. And therefore it is well to start, in bringing out the truth of Christianity, with a plain proposition such as everybody, one would think, must admit: the proposition that conduct is a very important matter. I have called conduct three-fourths of life. M. Challemel-Lacour quarrels greatly with the proposition. Certainly people in general do not behave as if they were convinced that conduct is three-fourths of life. Butler well says that even religious people are always for placing the stress of their religion anywhere other than on virtue; — virtue being simply the good direction of conduct. We know, too, that the Italians at the Renascence changed the very meaning of the word virtue altogether, and made their *virtù* mean a love of the fine arts and of intellectual culture. And we see the fruits of the new definition in the Italy of the seventeenth and eighteenth centuries. We will not, then, there being all this opposition, offer to settle the exact proportion of life which conduct may be said to be. But that conduct is, at any rate, a very considerable part of life, will generally be admitted.

It will generally be admitted, too, that all experience as to conduct brings us at last to the fact of two selves, or instincts, or forces, — name them how we will, and however we may suppose them to have arisen, — contending for the mastery in man: one, a movement of first impulse and more involuntary, leading us to gratify any inclination that may solicit us, and called generally a movement of man's ordinary or passing self, of sense, appetite, desire; the other, a movement of reflection and more voluntary, leading us to submit inclination to some rule, and called generally a movement of man's higher or enduring self, of reason, spirit, will. The thing is described in different words by different nations and men relating their experience of it, but as to the thing itself they all, or all the most serious and important among them, agree. This, I think, will be admitted. Nor will it be denied that they all come to the conclusion that for a man to obey the higher self, or reason, or whatever it is to be called, is happiness and life for him; to obey the lower is death and misery. It will be allowed, again, that whatever men's minds are to fasten and rest upon, whatever is to hold their attention and to rule their practice, naturally embodies itself for them in certain examples, precepts, and sayings, to which they perpetually recur. Without a frame or body of this kind, a set of thoughts cannot abide with men and sustain them. "If ye abide in me," says Jesus, "ye shall know the truth, and the truth shall make you free;" — not if you keep skipping about all over the world for various renderings of it. "It behoves us to know," says Epictetus, "that a principle can hardly establish itself with a man, unless he every day utters the same things, hears the same things, and applies them withal to his life." And naturally the body of examples and precepts, which men should use for this purpose, ought to be those which most impressively represent the principle, or the set of thoughts, commending itself to their minds for respect and attention. And the more the precepts are used, the more will men's sentiments cluster around them, and the more dear and solemn will they be.

Now to apply this to Christianity. It is evident that to what they called *righteousness,* — a name which covers all that we mean by conduct, — the Jewish nation attached pre-eminent, unique importance. This impassioned testimony of theirs to the weight of a thing admittedly of very considerable importance, has its own value of a special kind. But it is well known how imperfectly and amiss the Jewish nation conceived righteousness. And finally, when their misconceived righteousness failed them in actual life more and more, they took refuge in imaginings about the future, and filled themselves with hopes of a *kingdom of God,* a *resurrection,* a *judgment,* an *eternal life,* bringing in and establishing for ever this misconceived righteousness of theirs. As God's agent in this work of restoring the kingdom to Israel they promised to themselves an Anointed and Chosen One, *Christ the son of God.*[1]

Jesus Christ found, when he came among his countrymen, all these phrases and ideas ruling their minds. Conduct or righteousness, a matter admittedly of very considerable importance, and which the Jews thought of paramount importance, they had come entirely to misconceive, and had created an immense poetry of hopes and imaginings in favour of their misconception. What did Jesus do? From his countrymen's errors about righteousness he reverted to the solid, authentic, universal fact of experience about it: the fact of the higher and lower self in man, inheritors the one of them of happiness, the other of misery. He possessed himself of it, he made it the centre of his teaching. He made it so in the well-known formula, his *secret:* "He that will save his life shall lose it; he that do lose his life shall save it." And by his admirable figure of the *two lives* of man, the real life and the seeming life, he connected this profound fact of experience with that attractive poetry of hopes and imaginings which possessed the minds of his countrymen. Eternal life? Yes, the life in the higher and undying self of man. Judgment? Yes, the trying, in conscience, of the claims and instigations of the two lives, and the decision between them. Resurrection? Yes, the rising from bondage and transience with the lower life to victory and permanence with

[1] John xx. 31.

the higher. The kingdom of God? Yes, the reign amongst mankind of the higher life. The Christ the son of God? Yes, the bringer-in and founder of this reign of the higher life, this true kingdom of God.

But we can go farther. Observers say, with much appearance of truth, that all our passions may be run up into two elementary instincts: the reproductive instinct and the instinct of self-preservation. It is evident to what these instincts will in themselves carry the man who follows the lower self of sense, and appetite, and first impulse. It is evident, also, that they are directly controlled by two forces which Christianity, following that law of the higher life which St. Paul names indifferently the *law of God,* the *law of our mind,* the *line of thought of the spirit*[1] — has set up as its two grand virtues: kindness and pureness, charity and chastity. If any virtues could stand for the whole of Christianity, these might. Let us have them from the mouth of Jesus Christ himself. "He that loveth his life shall lose it; a new commandment give I unto you that ye love *one another.*" There is charity. "Blest are the pure in heart, for they shall see God." There is purity.

We go here simply on experience, having to establish the *natural truth* of Christianity. That the "new commandment" of charity is enjoined by the Bible, gives it therefore, we shall suppose, no force at all, unless it turns out to be enjoined also by experience. And it is enjoined by experience if experience shows that it is necessary to human happiness, — that men cannot get on without it. Now really if there is a lesson which in our day has come to force itself upon everybody, in all quarters and by all channels, it is the lesson of the *solidarity,* as it is called by modern philosophers, of men. If there was ever a notion tempting to common human nature, it was the notion that the rule of "every man for himself" was the rule of happiness. But at last it turns out as a matter of experience, and so plainly that it is coming to be even generally admitted, — it turns out that the only real happiness is in a kind of impersonal higher life, where the happiness of others counts with a man as essential to his own. He that loves his life does really turn out to lose it, and the new commandment proves its own truth by experience.

And the other great Christian virtue, pureness? Here the case is somewhat different. One hears doubts raised, nowadays, as to the natural truth of this virtue. While science has adopted, as a truth confirmed by experience, the Christian idea of charity, long supposed to conflict with experience, and has decked it out with the grand title of *human solidarity,* one may hear many doubts thrown, in the name of science and reason, on the truth and validity of the

[1] φοόνημα τοῦ πνεύματος.

Christian idea of pureness. As a mere *commandment* this virtue cannot have the authority which it once had, for the notion of *commandments* in this sense is giving way. And on its natural truth, when the thing comes to be tested by experience, doubts are thrown. Well, experience must decide. It is a question of fact. "There is no honest woman who is not sick of her trade," says La Rochefoucauld. "I pass for having enjoyed life," said Ninon in old age, "but if any one had told me beforehand what my life was going to be I would have hanged myself." Who is right? On which side is *natural truth*? It will be admitted that there can hardly be a more vital question for human society. And those who doubt on which side is natural truth, and who raise the question, will have to learn by experience. But finely touched souls have a presentiment of a thing's natural truth even though it be questioned, and long before the palpable proof by experience convinces all the world. They have it quite independently of their attitude toward traditional religion. "May the idea of *pureness,* extending itself to the very morsel which I take into my mouth, grow ever clearer in me and clearer!"[1] So prayed Goethe. And all such well-inspired souls will perceive the profound natural truth of the idea of pureness, and will be sure therefore, that the more boldly it is challenged, the more sharply and signally will experience mark its truth. So that of the two great Christian virtues, charity and chastity, kindness and pureness, the one has at this moment the most signal testimony from experience to its intrinsic truth and weight, and the other is expecting it.

All this may enable us to understand how admirably fitted are Jesus Christ and his precepts to serve as mankind's standing reminder as to conduct, — to serve as men's religion. Jesus Christ and his precepts are found to hit the moral experience of mankind, to hit it in the critical points, to hit it lastingly; and, when doubts are thrown upon their really hitting it, then to come out stronger than ever. And we know how Jesus Christ and his precepts won their way from the very first, and soon became the religion of all that part of the world which most counted, and are now the religion of all that part of the world which most counts. This they certainly in great part owed, even from the first, to that instinctive sense of their natural fitness for such a service, of their natural truth and weight, which amidst all misapprehensions of them they inspired.

Moreover, we must always keep in sight one specially important element in the power exercised by Jesus Christ and his precepts. And that is, the impression left by Jesus of what we call *sweet reason* in

1 "Möge die Idee des *Reinen,* die sich auf den Bissen erstreckt den ich in den Mund nehme, immer lichter in mir werden!"

the highest degree; of consummate justness in what he said, perfect balance, unerring felicity. For this impression has been a great element of progress. It made half the charm of the religion of Jesus in the first instance, and it makes it still. But it also serves in an admirable way against the misapprehensions with which men received, as we have said, and could not but receive, the natural truth he gave them, and which they made up along with that truth into their religion. For it is felt that anything exaggerated, distorted, false, cannot be from Jesus; that it must be human perversion of him. There is always an appeal open, and a return possible, to the acknowledged sweet reason of Jesus, to his "grace and truth." And thus Christians, instead of sticking for ever because of their religion to errors which they themselves have put into their religion, find in their religion itself a ground for breaking with them. For example: medieval charity and medieval chastity are manifestly misgrowths, however natural, — misgrowths unworkable and dangerous, — of the ideas of kindness and pureness. Then they cannot have come from Jesus; they cannot be what Jesus meant. Such is the inevitable inference; and Christianity here touches a spring for self-correction and self-readjustment which is of the highest value.

And, finally, the figure and sayings of Jesus, embodying and representing men's moral experience to them, serving them as a perpetual reminder of it, by a fixed form of words and observances holding their attention to it, and thus attaching them, have attracted to themselves, by the very force of time, and use, and association, a mass of additional attachment, and a host of sentiments the most tender and profound.

This, then, is what we mean by saying that Christianity has natural truth. By this truth things must stand, not by people's wishes and asseverations about them. *Omnium Deus est, cujus, velimus aut nolimus, omnes sumus,* says Tertullian. "The God of all of us is the God that we all belong to whether we will or no." The Eternal that makes for righteousness is such a God; and he is the God of Christianity. Jesus explains what this God would have of us; and the strength of Jesus is that he explains it right. The natural experimental truth of his explanations is their one claim upon us; but this is claim enough. Does the thing, being admittedly most important, turn out to be as he says? If it does, then we "belong to him whether we will or no."

A recent German writer, wishing to exhalt Schopenhauer at the expense of Jesus, says that both Jesus and Schopenhauer taught the true doctrine of self-renouncement, but that Schopenhauer faced the pessimism which is that doctrine's natural accompaniment, whereas Jesus sought to escape from it by the dream of a paradise to come. This critic credits Jesus, as usual, with the very misconceptions against which he strove. It was the effort of Jesus to place the bliss, the eternal life of popular religion, not where popular religion placed it, in a fantastic paradise to come, but in the joy of self-renouncement. This was the "eternal life" of Jesus; this was his "joy;" — the joy which he desired that his disciples, too, might have full and complete, might have "fulfilled in themselves." His depth, his truth, his rightness, come out in this very point; that he saw that self-renouncement *is* joy, and that human life, in which it takes place, is therefore a blessing and a benefit. And just exactly here is his superiority to Schopenhauer. Jesus hits the plain natural truth that human life is a blessing and a benefit, while Schopenhauer misses it. "It is evident, even *a priori,* that the world is doomed to evil, and that it is the domain of irrationality. In abstinence from the further propagation of mankind is salvation. This would gradually bring about the extinction of our species, and, with our extinction, that of the universe, since the universe requires for its existence the co-operation of human thought." The fault of this sort of thing is, that it is plainly, somehow or other, a paradox, and that human thought (I say it with due deference to the many persons for whom Schopenhauer is just now in fashion) instinctively feels it to be absurd. The *fact* is with Jesus. "The Eternal is king, the earth may be *glad* thereof." Human life is a blessing and a benefit, and constantly improvable, because in self-renouncement is a fount of joy, "springing up unto everlasting life." Not only, "It is more *right* to give than to receive," more rational, more necessary; but, "It is more *blessed* to give than to receive."

The *fact*, I say, the real *fact*, is what it imports us to reach. A writer of remarkable knowledge, judgment, and impartiality, M. Maurice Vernes, of the *Revue Scientifique*, objects to the contrast of an earlier intuition of Israel, *Righteousness tendeth to life, the righteous is an everlasting foundation*, with a later "Aberglaube," such as we find in the Book of Daniel, and such as Jesus had to deal with. He objects to the contrast of the doctrine of Jesus with the metaphysics of the Church. M. Maurice Vernes is one of those, of whom there are so many, who have a philosophical system of history, — a history ruled by the law of progress, of evolution. Between the eighth century before our era and the second, the law of evolution must have been at work. Progress must have gone on. Therefore the Messianic ideas of the Book of Daniel must be a higher stage than the ideas of the great prophets and wise men of the eighth and ninth centuries. Again. The importation of metaphysics into Christianity means the arrival of Greek thought, Western thought, — the enrichment of the early Christian thought with new elements. This is evolution, development. And therefore, apparently, the Athanasian Creed must be a higher stage than the Sermon on the Mount.

Let us salute with respect that imposing generality, the law of evolution. But let us remember that, in each particular case which comes before us, what concerns us is, surely, the *fact* as to that particular case. And surely, as a matter of fact, the ideas of the great prophets and wise men of the eighth or ninth century before Christ are profounder and more true than the ideas of the eschatologist of the Book of Daniel. As a matter of fact, again, the ideas of Jesus in the Sermon on the Mount are surely profounder and more true than the ideas of the theologian of the Athanasian Creed. Ins and outs of this kind may settle their business with the general law of evolution as they can; but our business is with the fact. And the fact, surely, is here as we have stated it.

M. Vernes further objects to our picking and choosing among the records of Jesus, and pronouncing that whatever suits us shall be held to come from Jesus, and whatever does not suit us from his reporters. But here, again, it is a question of fact; — a question, which of two things is, in fact, more likely? It is, in fact, more likely that Jesus, being what we can see from certain of the data about him that he was, should have been in many points misunderstood and misrepresented by his followers; or that, being what by those data he was, he should also have been at the same time the thaumaturgical personage that his followers imagined? The more reasonable Jesus is likewise, surely, the more real one.

I believe, then, that the real God, the real Jesus, will continue to command allegiance, because we do, in fact, "belong to them." I believe that Christianity will survive because of its natural truth. Those who fancied that they had done with it, those who had thrown it aside because what was presented to them under its name was so unreceivable, will have to return to it again, and to learn it better. The Latin nations, — even the southern Latin nations, — will have to acquaint themselves with that fundamental document of Christianity, the Bible, and to discover wherein it differs from "a text of Hesiod." Neither will the old forms of Christian worship be extinguished by the growth of a truer conception of their essential contents. Those forms, thrown out at dimly-grasped truth, approximative and provisional representations of it, and which are now surrounded with such an atmosphere of tender and profound sentiment, will not disappear. They will survive as poetry. Above all, among the Catholic nations will this be the case. And, indeed, one must wonder at the fatuity of the Roman Catholic Church, that she should not herself see what a future there is for her here. Will there never arise among Catholics some great soul, to perceive that the eternity and universality, which is vainly claimed for Catholic dogma and the ultramontane system, might really be possible for Catholic worship? But to rule over the moment and the credulous has more attraction than to work for the future and the sane.

Christianity, however, will find the ways for its own future. What is certain is that it will not disappear. Whatever progress may be made in science, art, and literary culture, — however much higher, more general, and more effective than at present the value for them may become, — Christianity will be still there as what these rest against and imply; as the indispensable background, the *three-fourths of life*. It is true, while the remaining fourth is ill-cared for, the three-fourths themselves must also suffer with it. But this does but bring us to the old and true Socratic thesis of the interdependence of virtue and knowledge. And we cannot, then, do better than conclude with some excellent words of Mr. Jowett, doing homage, in the preface introducing his translation of Plato's Protagoras, to that famous thesis. "This is an aspect of the truth which was lost almost as soon as it was found; and yet has to be recovered by every one for himself who would pass the limits of proverbial and popular philosophy. The moral and intellectual are always dividing, yet they must be reunited, and in the highest conception of them are inseparable."

Letters

TO ARTHUR HUGH CLOUGH[1]

[London]
[shortly after December 6, 1847]

My dear Clough

I sent you a beastly vile note the other day: but I was all rasped by influenza and a thousand other bodily discomforts. Upon this came all the exacerbation produced by your apostrophes to duty: and put me quite wrong: so that I did not at all do justice to the great precision and force you have attained in those inward ways. I do think however that rare as individuality is you have to be on your guard against it — you particularly: — tho: indeed I do not really know that I think so. Shakspeare says that if imagination would apprehend some joy it comprehends some bringer of that joy: and this latter operation which makes palatable the bitterest or most arbitrary original apprehension you seem to me to despise. Yet to *solve* the Universe as you try to do is as irritating as Tennyson's dawdling with its painted shell is fatiguing to me to witness: and yet I own that to *re-construct* the Universe is not a satisfactory attempt either — I keep saying, Shakspeare, Shakspeare, you are as obscure as life is: yet this unsatisfactoriness goes against the poetic office in general: for this must I think certainly be its end. But have I been inside you, or Shakspeare? Never. Therefore heed me not, but come to what you can. Still my first note was cynical and beastly-vile. To compensate it, I have got you the Paris diamond edition of Beranger, like mine. Tell me when you are coming up hither. I think it possible Tom may have trotted into Arthur's Bosom in some of the late storms; which would have been a pity as he meant to enjoy himself in New Zealand. It is like your noble abstemiousness not to have shown him the Calf Poem: he would have worshipped like the children of Israel. Farewell.

yours most truly
M. Arnold

TO ARTHUR HUGH CLOUGH

[London, about February 24, 1848]

A growing sense of the deficiency of the *beautiful* in your poems, and of this alone being properly *poetical* as distinguished from rhetor-

[1] The letters to Clough are reprinted with the kind permission of Professor H. L. Lowry, from his edition of *The Letters of Matthew Arnold to Arthur Hugh Clough* (London and New York: Oxford University Press, 1932).

ical, devotional or metaphysical, made me speak as I did. But your line is a line: and you have most of the promising English verse-writers with you now: Festus for instance. Still, problem as the production of the beautiful remains still to me, I will die protesting against the world that the other is false and JARRING.

No — I doubt your being an artist: but have you read Novalis? He certainly is not one either: but in the way of direct communication, insight, and report, his tendency has often reminded me of yours, though tenderer and less systematic than you. And there are the sciences: in which I think the passion for truth, not special curiosities about birds and beasts, makes the great professor. —

— Later news than any of the papers have, is, that the National Guard have declared against a Republic, and were on the brink of a collision with the people when the express came away.

— I trust in God that feudal industrial class as the French call it, you worship, will be clean trodden under. Have you seen Michelet's characterisation (superb) of your brothers — "La dure inintelligence des Anglo-Americains." — Tell Edward I shall be ready to take flight with him the very moment the French land, and have engaged a Hansom to convey us both from the possible scene of carnage.

— yours

M. A.

TO ARTHUR HUGH CLOUGH

Baths of Leuk. Sept[ber] 29, 1848.

My dear Clough

A woodfire is burning in the grate and I have been forced to drink champagne to guard against the cold and the café noir is about to arrive, to enable me to write a little. For I am all alone in this vast hotel: and the weather having been furious rain for the last few days, has tonight turned itself towards frost. Tomorrow I repass the Gemmi and get to Thun: linger one day at the Hotel Bellevue for the sake of the blue eyes of one of its inmates: and then proceed by slow stages down the Rhine to Cologne, thence to Amiens and Boulogne and England.

The day before yesterday I passed the Simplon — and yesterday I repassed it. The day before yesterday I lay at Domo d'Ossola and yesterday morning the old man within me and the guide were strong for proceeding to the Lago Maggiore: but no, I said, first impressions must not be trifled with: I have but 3 days and they, according to the public voice will be days of rain: coupons court à notre voyage — revenons en Suisse — So I ordered a char yesterday morning to remount the Simplon. It rained still . . . here and there was something unblurred by rain. Précisons: I have noticed in Italy — the chestnuts: the vines: the courtliness and kingliness of buildings and people as opposed to this land of a republican peasantry: and one or two things more: but d — n description. My guide assures me he saw one or two "superbes filles" in Domo d'Ossola (nothing improper): but I rose late and disheartened by the furious rain, and saw nothing but what I saw from the carriage. So Italy remains for a second entry. From Isella to Simplon the road is glory to God. In these rains maps and guides have suffered more or less: but your Keller very little: I travel with a live guide as well as Murray: an expensive luxury: but if he is a good Xtian and a family man like mine, a true comfort. I gave him today a foulard for his daughter who is learning French at Neufchatel to qualify her first for the place of fille de chambre in a hotel and afterwards for that of soubrette in a private family. I love gossip and the small-wood of humanity generally among these raw mammoth-belched half-delightful objects the Swiss Alps. The lime stone is terribly gingerbready: the pines terribly larchy: and above all the grand views being ungifted with self-controul almost invariably desinunt in piscem. And the curse of the dirty water — the real pain it occasions to one who looks upon water as the Mediator between the inanimate and man is not to be described. — I have seen clean water in parts of the lake of Geneva (w[hi]ch whole locality is spoiled by the omnipresence there of that furiously flaring bethiefed rushlight, the vulgar Byron): in the Aar at the exit of the Lac de Thoune: and in the little stream's beginnings on the Italian side of the Simplon. I have however done very little, having been baffled in two main wishes — the Tschingel Glacier and the Monte Moro, by the weather. My golies, how jealous you would have been of the first: "we fools accounted his calves meagre, and his legs to be without honor." All I have done however is to ascend the Faulhorn — 8300 above the sea, my duck.

This people, the Swiss, are on the whole what they should be; so I am satisfied. — L'homme sage ne cherche point le sentiment parmi les habitans des montagnes: ils ont quelque chose de mieux — le bonheur. That is but indifferent French though. For their extortion, it is all right I think — as the wise man pumpeth the fool, who is made for to be pumped.

I have with me only Béranger and Epictetus: the latter tho: familiar to me, yet being Greek, when tired I am, is not much read by me: of the former I am getting tired. Horace whom he resembles had to write only for a circle of highly cultivated desillusionés roués, in a sceptical age: we have the sceptical age, but a far different and wider audience: voilà pourquoi, with all his genius, there is something "fade" about Beranger's Epicureanism. Perhaps you don't see the pourquoi, but I think my love does and the paper draws to an end. In the reste, I am glad to be tired of an author: one link in the immense series of cognoscenda et indagenda despatched. More particularly is this my feeling with regard to (I hate the word) women. We know beforehand all they can teach us: yet we are obliged to learn it directly from them. Why here is a marvellous thing. The following is curious —

"Say this of her:
The day was, thou wert not: the day will be,
Thou wilt be most unlovely: shall I chuse
Thy little moment life of loveliness
Betwixt blank nothing and abhorred decay
To glue my fruitless gaze on, and to pine,
Sooner than those twin reaches of great time,
When thou are either nought, and so not loved,
Or somewhat, but that most unloveable,
That preface and post-scribe thee?" —

Farewell, my love, to meet I hope at Oxford: not alas in Heaven: tho: thus much I cannot but think: that our spirits retain their conquests: that from the height they succeed in raising themselves to, they can never fall. Tho: this uti possedetes principle may be compatible with entire loss of individuality and of the power to recognize one another. Therefore, my well-known love, accept my heartiest greeting and farewell, while it is called today.

Yours,
M. Arnold.

TO ARTHUR HUGH CLOUGH

London. Monday. [after September 1848–49]

My dearest Clough

What a brute you were to tell me to read Keats' Letters. However it is over now: and reflexion resumes her power over agitation.

What harm he has done in English Poetry. As Browning is a man with a moderate gift passionately desiring movement and fulness, and obtaining but a confused multitudinousness, so Keats with a very high gift, is yet also consumed by this desire: and cannot produce the truly living and moving, as his conscience keeps telling him. They will not be patient neither understand that they must begin with an Idea of the world in order not to be prevailed over by the world's multitudinousness: or if they cannot get that, at least with isolated ideas: and all other things shall (perhaps) be added unto them.

— I recommend you to follow up these letters with the Laocoön of Lessing: it is not quite satisfactory, and a little mare's nesty — but very searching.

— I have had that desire of fulness without respect of the means, which may become almost maniacal: but nature had placed a bar thereto not only in the conscience (as with all men) but in a great numbness in that direction. But what perplexity Keats Tennyson et id genus omne must occasion to young writers of the ὁπλίτης sort: yes and those d——d Elizabethan poets generally. Those who cannot read G[ree]k sh[ou]ld read nothing but Milton and parts of Wordsworth: the state should see to it: for the failures of the σταθμοί may leave them good citizens enough, as Trench: but the others go to the dogs failing or succeeding.

So much for this inspired "cheeper" as they are saying on the moon.

My own good man farewell.

M. A.

TO ARTHUR HUGH CLOUGH

Thun. Sunday. Sept[ber] 23 [1849]

My dear Clough

I wrote to you from this place last year. It is long since I have communicated with you and I often think of you among the untoward generation with whom I live and of whom all I read testifies. With me it is curious at present: I am getting to feel more independent and unaffectible as to all intellectual and poetical performance the impatience at being faussé in which drove me some time since so strongly into myself, and more snuffing after a moral atmosphere to respire in than ever before in my life. Marvel not that I say unto you, ye must be born again. While I will not much talk of these things, yet the considering of them has led me constantly to you the only living one almost that I know of of

The children of the second birth
Whom the world could not tame —

for my dear Tom has not sufficient besonnenheit for it to be any *rest* to think of him any more than it is a *rest* to think of mystics and such cattle — not that Tom is in any sense cattle or even a mystic but he has not a "still, considerate mind."

What I must tell you is that I have never yet succeeded in any one great occasion in consciously mastering myself: I can go thro: the imaginary process of mastering myself and see the whole affair as it would then stand, but at the critical point I am too apt to hoist up the mainsail to the wind and let her drive. However as I get more awake to this it will I hope mend for I find that with me a clear almost palpable intuition (damn the logical senses of the word) is necessary before I get into prayer: unlike many people who set to work at their duty self-denial etc. like furies in the dark hoping to be gradually illuminated as they persist in this course. Who also perhaps may be sheep but not of my fold, whose one natural craving is not for profound thoughts, mighty spiritual workings etc. etc. but a distinct seeing of my way as far as my own nature is concerned: which I believe to be the reason why the mathematics were ever foolishness to me.

— I am here in a curious and not altogether comfortable state: however tomorrow I carry my aching head to the mountains and to my cousin the Blümlis Alp.

Fast, fast by my window
The rushing winds go
Towards the ice-cumber'd gorges,
The vast fields of snow.
There the torrents drive upward
Their rock strangled hum,
And the avalanche thunders
The hoarse torrent dumb.
I come, O ye mountains —
Ye torrents, I come.

Yes, I come, but in three or four days I shall be back here, and then I must try how soon I can ferociously turn towards England.

My dearest Clough these are damned times — everything is against one — the height to which knowledge is come, the spread of luxury, our physical enervation, the absence of great *natures*, the unavoidable contact with millions of small ones, newspapers, cities, light profligate friends, moral desperadoes like Carlyle, our own selves, and the sickening consciousness of our difficulties: but for God's sake let us neither be fanatics nor yet chaff blown by the wind but let us be ὡς ο φρονιμος διαρισειεν and not as any one else διαρισειεν. When

I come to town I tell you beforehand I will have a real effort at managing myself as to newspapers and the talk of the day. Why the devil do I read about L[d]. Grey's sending convicts to the Cape and excite myself thereby, when I can thereby produce no possible good. But public opinion consists in a multitude of such excitements. Thou fool — that which is morally worthless remains so, and undesired by Heaven, whatever results flow from it. And which of the units which has felt the excitement caused by reading of Lord Grey's conduct has been made one iota a better man thereby, or can honestly call his excitement a *moral* feeling.

You will not I know forget me. You cannot answer this letter for I know not how I come home.

Yours faithfully,

M. A.

TO HIS WIFE

Oldham Road Lancasterian School,
Manchester, October 15, 1851.

I think I shall get interested in the schools after a little time; their effects on the children are so immense, and their future effects in civilising the next generation of the lower classes, who, as things are going, will have most of the political power of the country in their hands, may be so important. It is really a fine sight in Manchester to see the anxiety felt about them, and the time and money the heads of their cotton-manufacturing population are willing to give to them. In arithmetic, geography, and history the excellence of the schools I have seen is quite wonderful, and almost all the children have an equal amount of information; it is not confined, as in schools of the richer classes, to the one or two cleverest boys. We shall certainly have a good deal of moving about; but we both like that well enough, and we can always look forward to retiring to Italy on £200 a year. I intend seriously to see what I can do in such a case in the literary way that might increase our income. But for the next three or four years I think we shall both like it well enough.

TO ARTHUR HUGH CLOUGH

Edgbaston. February 12th, 1853

My dear Clough

I received your letter ten days since — just as I was leaving London — but I have since that time had too much to do to attempt answering it, or indeed to attempt any thing else that needed any thing of "recueillement." I do not like to put off writing any longer, but to say the truth I do not feel in the vein to write even now, nor do I feel certain that I can write as I should wish. I am past thirty, and three parts iced over — and my pen, it seems to me is even stiffer and more cramped than my feeling.

But I will write historically, as I can write naturally in no other way. I did not really think you had been hurt at anything I did or left undone while we were together in town: that is, I did not think any impression of hurt you might have had for a moment, had lasted. I remember your being annoyed once or twice, and that I was vexed with myself: but at that time I was absorbed in my speculations and plans and agitations respecting Fanny Lucy, and was as egoistic and anti-social as possible. People in the condition in which I then was always are. I thought I had said this and explained one or two pieces of apparent carelessness in this way: and that you had quite understood it. So entirely indeed am I convinced that being in love generally unfits a man for the society of his friends, that I remember often smiling to myself at my own selfishness in half compelling you several times to meet me in the last few months before you left England, and thinking that it was only I who could make such unreasonable demands or find pleasure in meeting and being with a person, for the mere sake of meeting and being with them, without regarding whether they would be absent and preoccupied or not. I never, while we were both in London, had any feeling towards you but one of attachment and affection: if I did not enter into much explanation when you expressed annoyance, it was really because I thought the mention of my circumstances accounted for all and more than all that had annoyed you. I remember Walrond telling me you were vexed one day that on a return to town after a longish absence I let him stop in Gordon Square without me: I was then expecting to find a letter — or something of that sort — it all seems trivial now, but it was enough at the time to be the cause of heedlessness selfishness and heartlessness — in all directions but one — without number. It ought not to have been so perhaps — but it was so — and I quite thought you had understood that it was so.

There was one time indeed — shortly after you had published the Bothie — that I felt a strong disposition to intellectual seclusion, and to the barring out all influences that I felt troubled without advancing me: but I soon found that it was needless to secure myself against a danger from which my own weakness even more than my strength — my coldness and want of intellectual robustness — sufficiently exempted me — and besides your company and mode of being always had a charm and a salutary effect for me, and I could not have foregone these on a mere theory of intellectual dietetics.

In short, my dear Clough, I cannot say more than that I really have clung to you in spirit more than to any other man — and have never been seriously estranged from you at any time — for the estrangement I have just spoken of was merely a contemplated one and it never took place: I remember saying something about it to you at the time — and your answer, which struck me for the genuineness and faith it exhibited as compared with my own — not want of faith exactly — but invincible languor of spirit, and fickleness and insincerity even in the gravest matters. All this is dreary work — and I cannot go on with it now: but tomorrow night I will try again — for I have one or two things more to say. Good-night now. —

Sunday, 6 P.M.

I will not look at what I wrote last night — one endeavours to write deliberately out what is in one's mind, without any veils of flippancy levity metaphor or demi-mot, and one succeeds only in putting upon the paper a string of dreary dead sentences that correspond to nothing in one's inmost heart or mind, and only represent themselves. It was your own fault partly for forcing me to it. I will not go on with it: only remember, *pray* remember that I am and always shall be, whatever I do or say, powerfully attracted towards you, and vitally connected with you: this I am sure of: the period of my development (God forgive me the d——d expression!) coincides with that of my friendship with you so exactly that I am for ever linked with you by intellectual bonds — the strongest of all: more than you are with me: for your development was really over before you knew me, and you had properly speaking come to your *assiette* for life. You ask me in what I think or have thought you going wrong: in this: that you would never take your assiette as something determined final and unchangeable for you and proceed to work away on the basis of that: but were always poking and patching and cobbling at the assiette itself — could never finally, as it seemed — "resolve to be thyself" — but were looking for this and that experience, and doubting whether you ought not to adopt this or that mode of being of persons qui ne vous valaient pas because it might possibly be nearer the truth than your own: you had no reason for thinking it *was*, but it *might* be — and so you would try to adapt yourself to it. You have I am convinced lost infinite time in this way: it is what I call your morbid conscientiousness — you are the most conscientious man I ever knew: but on some lines morbidly so, and it spoils your action.

There — but now we will have done with this: we are each very near to the other — write and tell me that you feel this: as to my behaviour in London I have told you the simple truth: it is I fear too simple than that (excuse the idiom) you with your raffinements should believe and appreciate it.

There is a power of truth in your letter and in what you say about America and this country: yes — *congestion of the brain* is what we suffer from — I always feel it and say it — and cry for air like my own Empedocles. But this letter shall be what it is. I have a number of things I want to talk to you about — they shall wait till I have heard again from you. Pardon me, but we *will* exchange intellectual aperçus — we shall both be the better for it. Only let us pray all the time — God keep us both from aridity! *Arid* — that is what the times are. — Write soon and tell me you are well — I was sure you were not well. God bless you. Flu sends her kindest remembrances.
ever yours

M. A.

We called the other day at Combe Hurst but found vacuas sedes et inania arcana. But we shall meet in town. What does Emerson say to my poems — or is he gone crazy as Miss Martineau says. But this is probably one of her d——d lies. Once more fare*well*, in every sense.

TO HIS SISTER JANE[1]

London, Saturday. 1853(?)

My dearest K,

The parcel shall be carried to Miss Cottman when it arrives.

Fret not yourself to make my poems square in all their parts, but like what you can my darling. The true reason why parts suit you while others do not is that my poems are fragments — i.e. that I am fragments, while you are a whole; the whole effect of my poems is quite vague and indeterminate — this is their weakness; a person

[1] By permission of the Yale University Press.

therefore who endeavoured to make them accord would only lose his labor; and a person who has any inward completeness can at best only like parts of them; in fact such a person stands firmly and knows what he is about while the poems stagger weakly & are at their wits end. I shall do better some day I hope — meanwhile change nothing, resign nothing that you have in deference to me or my oracles; & do not plague yourself to find a consistent meaning for these last, which in fact they do not possess through my weakness.

There — I would not be so frank as that with everyone.

I am a wicked wicked beast about the Spectator; you shall have last week's — it has been lying on my sopha all this week; but I have been putting a bookcase up & changing servants. I must try & get up at 5 in the morning.

I quite agree about Rome, only there is a certain excuse for the French in their not bad intentions at first. When once beaten, one does not like to give in before trying to set oneself right.

Yours,
M. A.

I cannot after all find last week's Spectator.

TO HIS SISTER JANE

Martigny, August 6, 1858

My dearest K. —

Here is a pouring wet day, to give me an opportunity of paying my long-standing debt to you. I have never thanked you for sending me Kingsley's remarks on my poems, which you rightly judged I should like to hear. They reached me when I was worried with an accumulation of all sorts of business, and I kept putting off and putting off writing to thank you for them; at last, when I had fairly made up my mind to write, I heard you were gone to Holland. What on earth did you do there?

Kingsley's remarks were very *handsome*, especially coming from a brother in the craft. I should like to send you a letter which I had from Froude about *Merope*, just at the same time that your record of Kingsley's criticisms reached me. If I can find it when I return to England I will send it to you. It was to beg me to discontinue the *Merope* line, but entered into very interesting developments, as the French say, in doing so. Indeed, if the opinion of the general public about my poems were the same as that of the leading literary men, I should make more money by them than I do. But, more than this, I should gain the stimulus necessary to enable me to produce my best — all that I have in me, whatever that may be, — to produce which is no light matter with an existence so hampered as mine is. People do not understand what a temptation there is, if you cannot bear anything not *very good,* to transfer your operations to a region where form is everything. Perfection of a certain kind may there be attained, or at least approached, without knocking yourself to pieces, but to attain or approach perfection in the region of thought and feeling, and to unite this with perfection of form, demands not merely an effort and a labour, but an actual tearing of oneself to pieces, which one does not readily consent to (although one is sometimes forced to it) unless one can devote one's whole life to poetry. Wordsworth could give his whole life to it, Shelley and Byron both could, and were besides driven by their demon to do so. Tennyson, a far inferior natural power to either of the three, can; but of the moderns Goethe is the only one, I think, of those who have had an *existence assujettie,* who has thrown himself with a great result into poetry. And even he felt what I say, for he could, no doubt, have done more, *poetically,* had he been freer; but it is not so light a matter, when you have other grave claims on your powers, to submit voluntarily to the exhaustion of the best poetical production in a time like this. Goethe speaks somewhere of the endless matters on which he had employed himself, and says that with the labour he had given to them he might have produced half a dozen more good tragedies; but to produce these, he says, I must have been *sehr zerrissen.* It is only in the best poetical epochs (such as the Elizabethan) that you can descend into yourself and produce the best of your thought and feeling naturally, and without an overwhelming and in some degree morbid effort; for then all the people around you are more or less doing the same thing. It is natural, it is the bent of the time to do it; its being the bent of the time, indeed, is what makes the time a *poetical* one. But enough of this.

It is nearly a fortnight since Walrond and I started, and in ten days I hope to be at home again. They will have kept you more or less informed from Fox How, I daresay, of our travelling proceedings. We have hitherto done just what we intended: Geneva, Bex and the Diablerets, Zermatt, and the Grand St. Bernard. The fates are against us to-day for the first time, for at this moment we ought to be on the Col de Balme, and we are here kept to the house by good heavy Westmorland rain. It will be curious if I again miss Chamouni, which I have missed so often; but we are resolutely staying over the day here, not to miss it if the weather will give us a chance. If it rains to-morrow, however, we shall go on to Geneva. I am glad to have been here again, and Walrond has admirable qualities for a travelling companion; but I have found two things: one, that I am not sure but I have begun to feel with papa about the time lost of mere mountain and lake hunting (though every one should see the Alps once to know what they are), and to desire to bestow my travelling solely on eventful countries and cities; the other that I miss Flu as a travelling companion more than I could have believed possible, and will certainly never travel again for *mere pleasure* without her. . . .

Your ever affectionate
M.A.

TO HIS MOTHER

Aston Clinton Park, Tring,
January 28, 1864.

My dearest Mother

It will take at least this sheet added to the one I wrote the other night to make my proper weekly letter. I have so often refused to come here, alleging my inspecting duties, that I thought this time I would come, and I am glad I have. I inspected yesterday in Bethnal Green, got home to a late luncheon, and a little before five left home again in a hansom for Euston Square. When I got to Tring I found the court outside the station full of carriages bound for Aston Clinton and no means of getting a fly; but Count d'Apponyi, the Austrian Ambassador, took me with him. We got here just after the Bishop, at half-past seven, just in time to dress, and a little after eight we dined. The house was quite full last night. Count d'Apponyi, the Bishop of Oxford, the Disraelis, Sir Edward and Lady Filmer, Lord John Hay, the young Lord Huntly, the young Nathaniel Rothschild, Mr. Dawson Damer, Mr. Raikes Currie, Mr. John Abel Smith, Archdeacon Bickersteth, and one or two other clergy were the party at dinner, almost all of them staying in the house. I took Constance Rothschild in to dinner, and was placed between her and Mrs. Disraeli; on Mrs. Disraeli's other side was the Bishop of Oxford. I thought the Bishop a little subdued and guarded, though he talked incessantly. Mrs. Disraeli is not much to my taste, though she is a clever woman, and told me some amusing stories. Dizzy sat opposite, looking moody, black, and silent, but his head and face, when you see him near and for some time, are very striking. After the ladies went he was called over by the Bishop to take Mrs. Disraeli's vacant place.

After a little talk to the Bishop he turned to me and asked me very politely if this was my first visit to Buckinghamshire, how I liked the country, etc.; then he said he thought he had seen me somewhere, and I said Lord Houghton had introduced me to him eight or nine years ago at a literary dinner among a crowd of other people. "Ah yes, I remember," he said, and then he went on: "At that time I had a great respect for the name you bore, but you yourself were little known. Now you are well known. You have made a reputation, but you will go further yet. You have a great future before you, and you deserve it." I bowed profoundly, and said something about his having given up literature. "Yes," he said, "one does not settle these things for oneself, and politics and literature both are very attractive; still, in the one one's work lasts, and in the other it doesn't." He went on to say that he had given up literature because he was not one of those people who can do two things at once, but that he admired most the men like Cicero, who could. Then we talked of Cicero, Bolingbroke, and Burke. Later in the evening, in the drawing-room, we talked again. I mentioned William Forster's name, telling him my connexion with him, and he spoke most highly of him and of his prospects, saying, just as I always say, how his culture and ideas distinguished him from the mob of Radicals. He spoke strongly of the harm he and Stansfeld and such men suffered in letting themselves be "appropriated," as he called it, by Palmerston, with whom they really had not the least agreement. Of Bright's powers as a speaker he spoke very highly, but thought his cultivation defective and his powers of mind not much; for Cobden's powers of mind he professed the highest admiration. "He was born a Statesman," he said, "and his reasoning is always like a Statesman's, and striking." He ended by asking if I lived in London, and begging me to come and see him. I daresay this will not go beyond my leaving a card, but at all events what I have already seen of him is very interesting. I daresay the chief of what he said about me myself was said in consequence of Lady de Rothschild, for whom he has a great admiration, having told him she had a high opinion of me; but it is only from politicians who have themselves felt the spell of literature that one gets these charming speeches. Imagine Palmerston or Lord Granville making them; or again, Lowe or Cardwell. The Disraelis went this morning. Of the Bishop and his sermon I must tell you in my next. I had hardly any talk with him. He too is now gone, but there is a large party tonight again; early tomorrow morning I return to London. My love to Fan.

Your ever affectionate

M. A.

TO HIS SISTER JANE

January 4, 1868.

My dearest K.

Poor little Basil died this afternoon, a few minutes before one o'clock. I sat up with him till four this morning, looking over my papers, that Flu and Mrs. Tuffin might get some sleep, and at the end of every second paper I went to him, stroked his poor twitching hand and kissed his soft warm cheek, and though he never slept he seemed easy, and hardly moaned at all. This morning, about six, after I had gone to bed, he became more restless; about eleven he had another convulsion; from that time he sank. Flu, Mrs. Tuffin, and I were all round him as his breathing gradually ceased, then the spasm of death passed over his face; after that the eyes closed, all the features relaxed, and now as he lies with his hands folded, and a white camellia Georgina Wightman brought him lying on his breast, he is the sweetest and most beautiful sight possible.

And so this loss comes to me just after my forty-fifth birthday, with so much other "suffering in the flesh," — the departure of youth, cares of many kinds, an almost painful anxiety about public matters, — to remind me that *the time past of our life may suffice us!* — words which have haunted me for the last year or two, and that we "should no longer live the rest of our time in the flesh to the lusts of men, but to the will of God." However different the interpretation we put on much of the facts and history of Christianity, we may unite in the bond of this call, which is true for all of us, and for me, above all, how full of meaning and warning.

Ever, my dearest K., your most affectionate

M. A.

TO HIS MOTHER

Harrow, June 5, 1869

My dearest Mother —

At Fox How to-day it must be quite heavenly, and how I wish I was there! I have had a hard week, and indeed my work will not leave me a single free day till the end of July. But from the 1st of August I shall be free and ready for Fox How whenever you like. The summer holidays here are a strict six weeks, and end quite early in September. . . .

My book [*Poems,* two volumes, 1869] was out yesterday. This new edition is really a very pretty book, but you had better not buy it, because I am going to give it Fan, and shall bring it with me to Fox How, and the order of arrangement in this edition is not quite the final one I shall adopt. On this final order I could not decide till I saw this collected edition. The next edition will have the final order, and then the book will be stereotyped. That edition I shall then have bound, and give you. I expect the present edition will be sold out in about a year. Macmillan tells me the booksellers are subscribing very well for it. My poems represent the main movement of mind of the last quarter of a century, and thus they will probably have their day as people become conscious to themselves of what that movement of mind is, and interested in the literary productions which reflect it. It might be fairly urged that I have less poetical sentiment than Tennyson, and less intellectual vigour and abundance than Browning; yet, because I have perhaps more of a fusion of the two than either of them, and have more regularly applied that fusion to the main line of modern development, I am likely enough to have my turn, as they have had theirs. . . . Your ever affectionate

M. A.

BIBLIOGRAPHY

Editions

Complete Prose Works, ed. R. H. Super. Ann Arbor: University of Michigan Press, 1960– Vol. I–

Note-Books, ed. H. F. Lowry, K. Young, and W. H. Dunn. Oxford University Press, 1952.

Poetical Works, ed. C. B. Tinker and H. F. Lowry. Oxford University Press, 1950.

Works. Edition de Luxe. London, 1903–04. 15 vols. Vol. XV contains the revised and expanded *Bibliography of Matthew Arnold* by T. B. Smart.

Letters

Letters, 1848–1888, ed. G. W. E. Russell. London, 1895. 2 vols.

Letters to Arthur Hugh Clough, ed. H. F. Lowry. Oxford University Press, 1932.

Unpublished Letters, ed. A. Whitridge. New Haven: Yale University Press, 1923.

Books

Baum, Paull F. *Ten Studies in the Poetry of Matthew Arnold.* Durham: Duke University Press, 1958.

Bonnerot, Louis. *Matthew Arnold, poète: Essai de biographie psychologique.* Paris: Didier, 1947.

Chambers, Sir E. K. *Matthew Arnold: a Study.* Oxford, 1947.

Connell, W. F. *The Educational Thought and Influence of Matthew Arnold.* London, 1950.

Faverty, Frederic E. *Matthew Arnold the Ethnologist.* Evanston, 1951.

Garrod, H. W. *Poetry and the Criticism of Life.* Oxford, 1931.

Jamison, William A. *Arnold and the Romantics.* Copenhagen, 1958.

Johnson, E. D. H. *The Alien Vision of Victorian Poetry.* Princeton, 1952.

Robbins, William. *The Ethical Idealism of Matthew Arnold.* Toronto, 1959.

Sells, Iris Esther. *Matthew Arnold and France: the Poet.* Cambridge, 1935.

Stanley, Carleton. *Matthew Arnold.* Toronto, 1938.

Tinker, C. B., and H. F. Lowry. *The Poetry of Matthew Arnold: a Commentary.* Oxford University Press, 1940.

Trilling, Lionel. *Matthew Arnold.* New York, 1949.

Articles and Essays

Dewey, John. "Arnold and Browning," *Characters and Events* (New York, 1929), I, 3–17.

Eliot, T. S. "Arnold and Pater," *Selected Essays* (New York, 1932).

———. "Matthew Arnold," *The Use of Poetry and the Use of Criticism* (Cambridge, Mass., 1933).

Garrod, H. W. "Matthew Arnold's 1853 Preface," *RES*, XVII (July, 1941), 310–21.

Harris, Alan. "Matthew Arnold, the 'Unknown Years,'" *Nineteenth Century,* CXIII (April, 1933), 498–509.

Holloway, John. "Matthew Arnold and the Modern Dilemma," *Essays in Criticism,* I (1951), 1–16.

Hutton, R. H. "The Poetry of Matthew Arnold," *Essays in Literary Criticism* (London, 1888).

———. "The Two Great Oxford Thinkers: Cardinal Newman and Matthew Arnold," *Essays on Some of the Modern Guides of English Thought in Matters of Faith* (London, 1887).

Tillotson, Kathleen. "Matthew Arnold and Carlyle," *Proceedings of the British Academy,* XLII (1956), 133–53.

———. "Yes: in the Sea of Life," *RES*, III, n.s. (October, 1952), 346–64.

Tinker, C. B. "Arnold's Poetic Plans," *Yale Review,* XXII (1933), 782–93.

The indispensable works in the above list are those by Bonnerot, Tinker and Lowry, and Trilling, and the *Letters to Clough.* Books and articles dealing with particular poems and essays of Arnold are listed in the notes.

The following abbreviations have been used in the bibliography and notes:

Commentary	C. B. Tinker and H. F. Lowry, *The Poetry of Matthew Arnold: A Commentary* (1940), also referred to as "Tinker and Lowry."
JEGP	*Journal of English and Germanic Philology*
Letters	*Letters of Matthew Arnold,* ed. Russell (1895), 2 vols.
MLN	*Modern Language Notes*
MLR	*Modern Language Review*
MP	*Modern Philology*
N & Q	*Notes and Queries*
PMLA	*Publications of the Modern Language Association*
RES	*Review of English Studies*
TLS	*Times Literary Supplement*

The editor acknowledges a particular debt to the *Commentary* of Professors Tinker and Lowry.

NOTES TO THE POETRY

Quiet Work *Page 3*

Originally the introductory poem to Arnold's first volume, this sonnet was later transferred to the page facing the opening page of the volume and printed, without title, in italics, as a kind of motto to the entire book. It retained this position in the final arrangement of Arnold's poems. Originally called simply "Sonnet," it received the title "Quiet Work" in 1869. The original version, reprinted in the *Commentary,* differs considerably from that of the later editions. The influence of Epictetus, Plotinus, Goethe, Senancour, and Wordsworth has been suggested. Fraser Neiman, "Plotinus and Arnold's 'Quiet Work,'" *MLN,* LXV (1950), 52–55.

Mycerinus *Page 3*

Arnold's note cites the original story from Herodotus as follows:

> After Cephren, Mycerinus, son of Cheops, reigned over Egypt. He abhorred his father's courses, and judged his subjects more justly than any of their kings had done. — To him there came an oracle from the city of Buto, to the effect that he was to live but six years longer, and to die in the seventh year from that time.

The rest of the account in Herodotus, not quoted by Arnold, is as follows:

> The king deemed this unjust, and sent back to the oracle a message of reproach, blaming the god: why must he die so soon who was pious, whereas his father and his uncle had lived long, who shut up the temples, and regarded not the gods, and destroyed men? But a second utterance from the place of divination declared to him that his good deeds were the very cause of shortening his life; for he had done what was contrary to fate; Egypt should have been afflicted for an hundred and fifty years, whereof the two kings before him had been aware, but not Mycerinus. Hearing this, he knew that his doom was fixed. Therefore he caused many lamps to be made, and would light these at nightfall and drink and make merry; by day or night he never ceased from reveling, roaming to the marsh country and the groves and wherever he heard of the likeliest places of pleasure. Thus he planned, that by turning night into day he might make his six years into twelve and so prove the oracle false. (Bk. II, 133)

As Douglas Bush observes, the original tale is "an anecdote of oriental ingenuity in cheating death rather than the statement of a moral problem." (*Mythology and the Romantic Tradition,* 1937, p. 248n.) With

Arnold, however, it becomes a moral problem, namely, that of the stance a young man should assume on finding himself in an amoral world.

103–6 Cf. Herodotus, II, 78 (speaking of the customs of the Egyptians): "At rich men's banquets, after dinner a man carries round an image of a corpse in a coffin, painted and carved in exact imitation, a cubit or two cubits long. This he shows to each of the company, saying, 'Drink and make merry, but look on this; for such shalt thou be when thou art dead.' Such is the custom at their drinking-bouts."

To a Friend *Page 7*

Wyndham Slade, a close friend of Arnold's, conjectured that Patrick Cumin, a Balliol man who later entered the law, was the friend addressed. But it is more likely to have been Arthur Hugh Clough, to whom Arnold, in a letter written in August or September, 1848, quoted lines 6–8 of the sonnet. The phrase "these bad days" of course suggests the revolutionary movements of 1848, but it may also recall a passage in Thomas Carlyle's *Past and Present* (1843), a work with which Arnold and Clough were perfectly familiar, where Hero-worship is represented as "the port and happy haven, towards which, through all these stormtost seas, French Revolutions, Chartisms, Manchester Insurrections, that make the heart sick in these bad days, the Supreme Powers are driving us." (Bk. I, chap. vi) If so, Arnold is announcing Homer, Epictetus, and Sophocles as his "heroes." (K. Tillotson, "Matthew Arnold and Carlyle," *Proceed. of the British Academy,* XLII, 1956, p. 143) Probably, too, there is something of Emerson's "Compensation" in the idea of a disability overcome by each of the three.

3 (Arnold's note) "The name Europe (Εὐρώπη, *the wide prospect*) probably describes the appearance of the European coast to the Greeks on the coast of Asia Minor opposite. The name Asia, again, comes, it has been thought, from the muddy fens of the rivers of Asia Minor, such as the Cayster or Mæander, which struck the imagination of the Greeks living near them."

6 Epictetus (c. 50–120 A.D.), born a slave and lamed early in life, had become a recognized leader of the Stoic school of philosophy in Rome by the time the emperor Domitian ("Vespasian's brutal son") banished all such persons from the city. He then settled in Nicopolis, in Epirus, Greece, where he lived with great simplicity. He is the author of eight books of *Discourses,* from which his pupil Arrian compiled a manual or *Encheiridion,* which, wrote Arnold in the letter to Clough cited above, "I have been reading with equal surprise and profit lately. . . ." "Lately," of course, confirms line 5 of the sonnet.

9 In the same letter Arnold speaks of Sophocles, the Greek tragic dramatist, as differing from Herodotus in that the latter "sought over all the world's surface for that interest [which the former] found within man."

The Strayed Reveller *Page 8*

This poem, the title poem in Arnold's first volume of verse, is concerned with three antagonist theories of poetry: the romantic theory, voiced especially by Keats and Hazlitt, that the poet must project himself into his subject, suffer with the suffering he depicts, and so experience some loss of life in the creation of a work of art; the classical theory, associated with Goethe and the Greeks, that the poet's vision is detached, serene, perfectly objective; and a third theory, that for those not strong enough to achieve Olympian objectivity something like its serenity is possible through a draught from Circe's bowl. In other words, the poem deals with the conflict between art and life, the sacrifice of life which the creation of art normally entails and how this sacrifice may be evaded; and with the conflict between two kinds of art, subjective and objective. It is Arnold's first statement of his poetic creed and a kind of explanation of himself to his family and friends. For throughout his school and college days Arnold had adopted the pose of the dandy, affecting an elegance in dress and assuming a certain airy manner and light bantering tone which were misunderstood by people who expected something else in a son of Dr. Arnold. They thought he was not serious, and Arnold is here telling them, "I am serious. Don't be misled by the pose. I am a reveller, but a strayed reveller — one belonging more truly to the court of Circe than the temple of Bacchus." Poems related in theme are "Mycerinus," "Shakespeare," "The Sick King in Bokhara," and "Resignation" — also Tennyson's "The Lady of Shalott."

38 Iacchus, a little-known Greek god invoked in the Eleusinian mysteries. But Arnold evidently equates him, as was commonly done in antiquity, with Bacchus (Dionysus), a vegetation deity and god of wine. He was usually represented as a youth of effeminate aspect and luxuriant hair, reposing with grapes or a wine-cup in his hand or holding the *thyrsis,* a rod encircled with vines or ivy. He was often accompanied by a rout of votaries, Satyrs, Sileni, Maenads, Bassarids, dancing about him, tearing animals to pieces, intoxicated or possessed.

78 Ampelus: a satyr beloved of Bacchus; the name means "vine."

135–42 See also lines 212–22. Tiresias, the Theban, having for a time been transformed into a woman, was asked by Zeus and Hera to resolve their dispute as to which sex derives more pleasure from the act of love. When Tiresias supported the opinion of Zeus (that women are more favored), Hera struck him blind, but Zeus rewarded him with the inner vision of the seer and lengthened his life to seven generations. In the war of the Seven against Thebes and at the time of Oedipus he saw the truth about the city which others could not see.

143–50 See also lines 222–32. The Centaurs were beings, half man and half horse, who lived on the wooded slopes of Mt. Pelion in Thessaly. Invited by the Lapithae, their neighbors, to the wedding-feast of their king, the Centaurs attempted to carry off the bride, Hippodamia, and a battle resulted in which they were defeated and driven from their haunts. The Centaur shot by Alcmena's son (line 231), Heracles, was Nessus, who, after carrying Heracles' wife across a river, offered violence to her.

151–61, 181–200 For the source of these passages in Captain Sir Alexander Burnes's *Travels into Bokhara* (1834) see Tinker and Lowry.

232–34 Cf. Emerson, "History," *Essays* (1841), p. 14: "A painter told me that nobody could draw a tree without in some sort becoming a tree. . . ."

261 Silenus was an elderly drunken satyr sometimes described as the tutor of Dionysus and so associated with music and wisdom.

Fragment of an "Antigone" *Page 16*

This "Fragment" probably does not represent any intention on Arnold's part to retell *in toto* the story of Sophocles' *Antigone*. It is a self-contained exploration of the moral problem of the play and is related in theme to "The Sick King in Bokhara." It may be to this poem that Arnold referred when he wrote to Clough in March, 1849: "But my Antigone supports me, and in some degree subjugates destiny." Or he may be referring simply to Sophocles.

In Sophocles' tragedy Creon, king of Thebes, has forbidden on pain of death the burial of the corpse of his enemy Polyneices, but Polyneices' sister, Antigone, placing the law of the gods above that of the king, defies him. She is condemned to death, and Haemon, Creon's son and the betrothed of Antigone, pleads for her life in vain.

54–64 The myth of Aurora's snatching up Orion to be her lover (*Odyssey,* V, 121) is associated with Thebes by the place-names Euripus, a strait by the coast of Boeotia; Parnes, a mountain; and Asopus, a river flowing into the Euripus.

64 (Arnold's note) "Orion, the Wild Huntsman of Greek legend, and in this capacity appearing in both earth and sky." Tanagra is a town in Boeotia.

80–103 The Chorus offers two instances where Zeus himself was subject to primal law: (1) that of the seer Amphiaraus, one of the Seven against Thebes: just as an enemy spear was descending upon him the earth opened and swallowed him and his charioteer; (2) that of Zeus's son Heracles, whose tenth labor was to steal the oxen of Geryones on the island of Erytheia (so called, says Arnold's note to line 92, "from the redness of the West under which the Greeks saw it."). Zeus's "fradulent oath" (line 95) provided that the person born on the day Heracles was expected should hold sway over the Peralidae, but Hera, as goddess of childbirth, cunningly delayed his birth and advanced that of Eurystheus, so that Heracles throughout his life was bound to the latter. Thus, the only means of his deliverance was the fated one of his being caught up into heaven from the funeral pyre built for him by Apollo in Trachis, Thessaly, by Mt. Œta and the Maliac gulf.

The Sick King in Bokhara *Page 19*

Bokhara is a city and a kingdom in western Asia between the mountains of Pamere and the Aral Sea. It is drained by the river Oxus. In 1831 it was penetrated by Captain Sir Alexander Burnes, whose narrative, *Travels into Bokhara* (1833), supplied Arnold with the central episode of his poem:

> I have already mentioned the rigour of the Mohammedan law, which is enforced in Bokhara. A few additional instances will further illustrate it. About twelve years since, a person who had violated the law proceeded to the palace, and, in the presence of the King, stated his crime, and demanded justice according to the Koran. The singularity of an individual appearing as his own accuser induced the King to direct him to be driven away. The man appeared the following day with the same tale, and was again turned out. He repaired a third time to the palace, repeated his sins, and upbraided the King for his remissness in declining to dispense justice, which, as a believer of Mahommed, he intreated, that it might lead to his punishment in this world instead of the next. The Ulema, or congress of divines, was assembled: death was the punishment; and the man himself, who was a Moollah, was prepared for this decision. He was condemned to be stoned till dead. He turned his face to Mecca, and, drawing his garment over his head, repeated the kuluma, ("There is but one God, and Mahommed is his prophet!") and met his fate. The King was present, and threw the first stone: but he had instructed his officers to permit the deluded man to escape if he made the attempt. When dead the King wept over his corpse, ordered it to be washed and buried, and proceeded in person to the grave, over which he read the funeral service. It is said that he was much affected; and to this day verses commemorate the death of this unfortunate man, whom we must either pronounce a bigot or a madman. An incident similar to the above happened within this very year. A son who had cursed his mother appeared as a suppliant for justice, and his own accuser. The mother solicited his pardon and forgiveness; the son demanded punishment: the Ulema directed his death, and he was executed as a criminal in the streets of Bokhara. (I, 307–8)

For a discussion of Arnold's use of his source see Tinker and Lowry; F. L. Jouard, "The Source of Matthew Arnold's Poem, *The Sick King in Bokhara*," *JEGP*, VI (1906), 92–98; and J. E. MacNeill, *TLS*, April 11, 1936; January 15, 1938. In interpreting the poem the best guide is the analogy of the sick king in T. S. Eliot's *Waste Land* and especially the comment in Arnold's own "Fragment of an 'Antigone,'" "The Strayed Reveller" (lines 207–34), and the fifth stanza of "Thyrsis." Indeed, Clough is as good a candidate as any for the original of the Sick King, for his sentimental humanitarianism seemed to Arnold to lead into a denial of absolute values which was quite wrong and especially dangerous to the poet-king.

12 **Ferdousi:** Persian epic poet (10th cent.), whose work contains the story of Sohrab and Rustum.

17 **Registàn:** the bazaar of Bokhara.

31 **Moolah:** among Mohammedans, one learned in theology and sacred law.

167 **Shiah dogs:** a sect of Mohammedans considered by those of Bokhara not to be true believers.

173 **kaffirs:** infidels of the Hindu Koosh.

Shakespeare *Page 26*

According to Mrs. Humphry Ward, who was Arnold's niece, this sonnet was written out in a letter addressed to the poet's sister, Jane. (*A Writer's Recollections,* 1918, p. 39) There is a manuscript of it in the British Museum dated August 1, 1844. The poem has proved difficult to the critics, whose efforts to interpret it may be traced in *N & Q,* CLXXXII (January–June, 1942), 221, 276, 348; CLXXXIII (July–December, 1942), 52, 264; *Explicator,* IV (1946), 57; V (1946), 24; VI (1947), 4; F. R. Leavis, *Education and the University* (1943), pp. 73–76; and Baum, *Ten Studies.* The main fact which needs to be known is that in the early 1830's and 1840's there was a great deal of research done on Shakespeare's life, by J. P. Collier, Edmund Malone, and others, which produced singularly small results — so small that the stage was all set for attributing Shakespeare's works to Bacon, as was done for the first time in 1857. Arnold's sonnet probably was occasioned by his reading a work like Charles Knight's *Life of Shakespeare* (1843), which offers as its motto a remark by the Shakespearean scholar George Steevens: "All that is known with any degree of certainty concerning Shakspere is — that he was born at Stratford-upon-Avon — married and had children there — went to London, where he commenced actor, and wrote poems and plays — returned to Stratford, made his will, died, and was buried." Opposite this motto is an engraved title page which presents, with gleaming baldness, five different representations of Shakespeare's "victorious brow" (line 14) — the Stratford bust, the Droeshout portrait, and three others. Or Arnold may have read Barry Cornwall's Memoir of Shakespeare in the 1843 edition of his *Works:* "Of the personal history of Shakspere — the greatest genius, beyond doubt or cavil, that ever the world produced — little now can with certainty be shewn. . . . What he did, or thought, or suffered, in his own individual person [cf. lines 12–13], is now mere matter for ingenious conjecture. We are sure that his mind was vast, liberal, compassionate, generous; — that he saw human nature on every side, detecting it in its many masks and changes; — that he penetrated into the innermost mysteries of man; that

'From this bank and shoal of time'

his intellect soared upward, and held commerce with the stars [line 9]; with our dim 'Hereafter;' and with worlds and agencies beyond our own;

and knowing all this, our curiosity as to the possessor of faculties so varied and wonderful, and our consequent disappointment on being baffled at every point of inquiry [line 8], becomes proportionably greater." (p. i) Joined to this paucity of biographical materials is the fact that Shakespeare did not obtrude himself into his works. Unlike Byron and Wordsworth, he was the sort of artist (admired by Keats and Hazlitt) who projected himself into the world rather than assimilating the world unto himself. These considerations are probably more germane to the sonnet than Arnold's remark to Clough three years later, "I keep saying, Shakspeare, Shakspeare, you are as obscure as life is: . . . Have I ever been inside you [Clough], or Shakspeare? Never." (*Letters to Clough*, p. 63)

3 The mountain image is a commonplace as applied to Shakespeare, being especially associated with the conception of him as an Olympian artist developed by Goethe, Carlyle, and Emerson.

5 Cf. William Cowper's hymn, which presents God as enigmatic:

> God moves in a mysterious way
> His wonders to perform;
> He plants his footsteps in the sea,
> And rides upon the storm.

Written in Butler's Sermons *Page 26*

Bishop Joseph Butler (1692–1752), best known for his *Analogy of Religion* (1736), a defence of Christianity against the deists, had ten years previously published a book of *Fifteen Sermons,* which in Arnold's day was used as a textbook at Oxford. Arnold's tutor in the subject was Archibald Campbell Tait, who in 1842 succeeded Arnold's father as headmaster of Rugby and later became Archbishop of Canterbury. The poem may have been written, then, as early as 1841–42 or in 1844, when Arnold would have been reviewing Butler for his final examination. His attitude toward the book may be gathered from a lecture, "Bishop Butler and the Zeit-Geist," which he delivered in 1876 in Tait's native city of Edinburgh. Speaking of "the reverent devotion formerly, at any rate, paid at Oxford to text-books in philosophy," he says, "Your text-book was right; there were no mistakes *there.* If there was anything obscure, anything hard to be comprehended, it was your ignorance which was in fault, your failure of comprehension. Just such was our mode of dealing with Butler's *Sermons* and Aristotle's *Ethics.*" (*Last Essays,* 1877, pp. 62–3) Going on to analyze Butler's philosophy of mind, Arnold declares that his view that all human instincts work together for good under the guidance of conscience simply does not stand the test of experience. What experience does show us is that "out of the simple primary instinct, which we may call the instinct or effort *to live,* grew our affections; and out of the experience of those affections, in their result upon the instinctive effort to live, grew reflexion, practical reason, conscience." (p. 114) "But into this vast, dimly lighted, primordial region of the natural genesis of man's affections and principles, Butler never enters." (p. 113)

In Harmony with Nature *Page 27*

The identity of the preacher who occasioned this poem is unknown. Its original title was "To an Independent Preacher, who preached that we should be 'In Harmony with Nature.'" As Arnold later said, "What pitfalls lie in that word Nature!" Cf. "Morality."

To George Cruikshank *Page 27*

George Cruikshank (1792–1878), artist and caricaturist, published in 1847, in support of the cause of total abstinence, a series of eight plates entitled *The Bottle.* Which one of these Arnold saw (they were available individually) is uncertain. Tinker and Lowry suggest the eighth, where "The bottle has done its work," the children being reduced to vice and the father a hopeless maniac; Müller-Schwefe considers No. VII more likely, in which "The Husband, in a state of furious drunkenness, kills his wife with the instrument of all their misery," namely, the Bottle.

2–3 Cf. *Hamlet,* I.ii.136; v.76; III.iii.81–82, and Hamlet's discourse on drunkenness, I.iv.8 ff.

11–14 The thought of these lines is emphasized by a new title supplied in the edition of 1869, and only there: "Human Limits."

To a Republican Friend, 1848 *Page 28*

The friend is Arthur Hugh Clough, who because of his enthusiasm for the revolutionary movements of 1848 was, in his own words, accounted at Oxford "the wildest and most écervelé republican going" — so much so that on March 7, 1848, Arnold jokingly addressed a letter to him as "Citizen Clough, Oriel Lyceum, Oxford." Since when, wrote Clough, "I . . . bear that title par excellence." (*Correspondence of Arthur Hugh Clough,* I, 216) In May, Clough went over to Paris to observe the march of events at first hand, and in October he took the not unrelated step of resigning his Oriel Fellowship. The question as to what might be accomplished of lasting significance by direct social action, especially on the part of two Oxford poets, was one which increasingly divided Arnold and his republican friend (*Letters to Clough,* p. 68); yet on the basic issue they agreed "like two lambs in a world of wolves.' (Mrs. Humphry Ward, *A Writer's Recollections,* 1918, p. 47)

Religious Isolation *Page 29*

Originally entitled "To the Same" (i.e., Clough), but not, as Tinker and Lowry assert, part of the sequence formed by "To a Republican Friend" and "Continued."

To a Gipsy Child by the Sea-Shore *Page 30*

This poem was presumably written in the period July 9 to August 19, 1845, when Arnold was vacationing on the Isle of Man with his mother and sister Jane. Mary Arnold found it "surely more poetical than true" (Mrs. Humphry Ward, *A Writer's Recollections,* 1918, p. 45), but Tom, the poet's brother, has recounted the occasion of it as follows: "Matthew and a companion were one afternoon on the pier, watching the passengers landing from the Liverpool steamer. There was a crowd, and just in front of them stood a poor woman: she might have been a gipsy, or might not; she was looking down at the steamer, and the child in her arms was looking backwards over her shoulder. Its pitiful wan face and dark sad eyes rested on Matthew for some time, without change of expression; what thoughts they inspired in him he has told in the poem." (*Manchester Guardian,* May 18, 1888, p. 8.) In 1869 Arnold revised the opening stanzas (reprinted in Tinker and Lowry, p. 53), but the revision was unsuccessful, and the poem was later restored to its original form. For other uses of the gipsy, see "Resignation," 108 ff., and, of course, "The Scholar-Gipsy."

The Forsaken Merman *Page 32*

The ultimate source of this poem is a Danish ballad, "The Deceived Merman." It is not known where Arnold encountered it or in what particular form, but two prose versions that he could have known are cited by Tinker and Lowry. The first is from Hans Christian Andersen's *The True Story of My Life,* trans. Mary Howitt (1847), the other from George Borrow's review of a book of Danish folktales in the *Universal Review,* II (1825), 563–64. The chief change Arnold has made — if these versions reflect the story as he knew it — is in shifting the sympathy from the wife to the merman. For example, Borrow's version of the tale concludes: "He [the merman] came once more, the third time, and cried, 'Grethe! Grethe! will you come quick? your children are crying for you.' But when she did not come, he began to weep bitterly, and went back to the bottom of the sea. But Grethe ever after stayed with her parents, and let the merman himself take care of his ugly little children, and his weeping and lamentation have been often heard from the bottom of the deep."

The poem has been associated both with the Marguerite episode and with a visit of the Arnold family in 1845 to the Isle of Man, where mermaid legends abound and the scenery is said to resemble that of the poem. See P. Fitzgerald, "Matthew Arnold's Summer Holiday," *English,* VI (1946), 77–81; E. Hoch, "Matthew Arnold's 'Forsaken Merman,'" *Neuphilologische Monatsschrift,* V (1934), 157–75; H. Wright, "The Source of Matthew Arnold's 'Forsaken Merman,'" *MLR,* XIII (1918), 90–94.

In Utrumque Paratus *Page 35*

The title, from *Aeneid* II, 61, means "prepared for either (eventuality, alternative)." The poem was not reprinted until 1869 (apparently at Swinburne's request), when the following lines replaced the final stanza:

> Thy native world stirs at thy feet unknown,
> Yet there thy secret lies!
> Out of this stuff, these forces, thou art grown,
> And proud self-severance from them were disease.
> O scan thy native world with pious eyes!
> High as thy life be risen, 'tis from these;
> And these, too, rise.

In the next edition (1877) Arnold restored the original ending. The poem has been variously interpreted by Tinker and Lowry; Trilling, pp. 90–91; and W. S. Johnson, *Explicator,* X (1952), 46.

Resignation *Page 37*

Arnold's note to line 41 is as follows: "Those who have been long familiar with the English Lake-Country will find no difficulty in recalling, from the description in the text, the roadside inn at Wythburn on the descent from Dunmail Raise towards Keswick; its sedentary landlord of thirty years ago, and the passage over the Wythburn Fells to Watendlath." The "thirty years ago" was dating from 1877; in the edition of 1869 it read "twenty years ago." In other words, the date of the walk with "Fausta," Arnold's elder sister Jane (called "K"), was 1847–49, and the previous walk "just ten years since" (line 40), with which it is compared, was 1837–39. This seems to be confirmed by a letter of Thomas Arnold, Jr., to his mother on August 7, 1849; "Does Fausta mean K., and is the walk 'ten years ago' alluded to in 'Resignation' that which we took over Wythburn Fells to Keswick with Captain Hamilton [a friend of Wordsworth]? Or was no particular walk intended?" (Tinker and Lowry, pp. 63–64) The earlier dates 1833 and 1843 accepted by Tinker and Lowry on the evidence of a memorial stone now marking the spot are shown by E. K. Chambers to be improbable (pp. 41–43). The route taken can be traced on a detailed map of the Lake Country: walking north from Rydal and Grasmere, the party left the main road at Wythburn (line 41), crossed the ridge and fells, descending along side the Watendlath brook (line 76) to Derwentwater and Keswick, the "noisy town." If they actually bathed their hands in the sea (line 85), they must have gone on to Workington or Maryport some twenty miles further, but doubtless Derwentwater is meant. The theme of retracing a journey is also employed in "Thyrsis," "Obermann Once More," and, in a negative way, in "The Terrace at Berne." "Tintern Abbey," of course, affords a precedent.

The thought of the poem is best apprehended by distinguishing clearly among the ways of life represented by (1) the various daemonic types in lines 1–21, (2) the gipsies, (3) the poet, and (4) the ordinary man who nevertheless draws homeward to "the general life." An important passage from Goethe's *Wilhelm Meister* bearing on Arnold's conception of the poet both here and in "The Strayed Reveller" is quoted in Tinker and Lowry, pp. 65–66. See also Baum, *Ten Studies.*

Empedocles on Etna *Page 44*

Empedocles on Etna, Arnold's most considerable poem, was composed between 1849 and 1852. In notes for poems to be composed in the former year Arnold has listed, "Empedocles — refusal of limitation by the religious sentiment." In the summer of that same year J. Campbell Shairp, an Oxford friend, wrote to Clough: "I saw the said Hero — Matt — the day I left London. . . . He was working at an "Empedocles" — which seemed to be not much about the man who leapt in the crater — but his name & outward circumstances are used for the drapery of his own thoughts." (*Commentary,* p. 287) In later years Arnold denied that "I merely use Empedocles and Obermann as mouthpieces through which to vent my own opinions. . . . Empedocles was composed fifteen years ago [1852], when I had been much studying the remains of the early Greek religious philosophers, as they are called; he greatly impressed me, and I desired to gather up and draw out as a whole the hints which his remains offered. Traces of an impatience with the language and assumptions of the popular theology of the day may very likely be visible in my work, and I have now, and no doubt had still more then, a sympathy with the figure Empedocles presents to the imagination; but neither then nor now would my creed, if I wished or were able to draw it out in black and white, be by any means identical with that contained in the preachment of Empedocles." (*Commentary,* pp. 287–88) It is true that Arnold studied the remains of the fifth-century Sicilian philosopher in Simon Karsten's *Philosophorum Graecorum veterum* (*praesertim qui ante Platonem floruerunt*) *operum reliquiae* (1830) and derived from Karsten's introduction to the fragments of Empedocles most of the facts for his opening scene, but it is also true that his figure owes less to the original than it does to ancient Stoicism and the modern Romantic hero. The influence of Lucretius, Epictetus, and Marcus Aurelius has been noted, and also that of "Obermann," Carlyle's Teufelsdröckh, Byron's Manfred, Hamlet, and Faust. *Empedocles* is, indeed, Arnold's *Werther,* and the best comment on it is Arnold's own letter to Clough, September 23, 1849: "These are damned times — everything is against one — the height to which knowledge is come, the spread of luxury, our physical enervation, the absence of great *natures,* the unavoidable contact with millions of small ones, newspapers, cities, light profligate friends, moral desperadoes like Carlyle, — our own selves, and the sickening consciousness of our difficulties." (*Letters to Clough,* p. 111)

Empedocles on Etna was first published in the volume of 1852. It was excluded by Arnold from *Poems* (1853) for the reasons assigned in the Preface to that volume and was not revived until the publication of *New*

Poems (1867), when Arnold announced that he reprinted it "at the request of a man of genius, whom it had the honor and the good fortune to interest, — Mr. Robert Browning." It has been suggested that Browning's "Cleon" (1855) is a kind of refutation of *Empedocles* (A. W. Crawford, "Browning's 'Cleon,'" *JEGP,* XXVI, 1927, p. 485 ff.; W. C. DeVane, *A Browning Handbook,* 1955, p. 264), and comparisons with Browning's *Paracelsus* (1835) have also been made (L. Bonnerot, ed., *Empédocle sur l'Etna,* 1947, pp. 86–88).

The most comprehensive study of the poem is L. Bonnerot's Introduction to his *Empédocle sur l'Etna* (Paris, [1947]), pp. 13–91; see also W. E. Houghton, "Arnold's 'Empedocles on Etna,'" *Victorian Studies,* I (1958), 311–36; *Commentary,* pp. 286–303, where Arnold's notes on Empedocles and a preliminary prose sketch of the poem are reprinted; D. Bush, *Mythology and the Romantic Tradition* (1937), pp. 253–58; and for a translation of the fragments of Empedocles, John Burnet, *Early Greek Philosophy* (1930), pp. 197–250.

Persons: Pausanias, Peisianax (I,i,31), and Pantheia (I,i,108) are historical figures appearing in the life of Empedocles by Diogenes Laertius. Callicles is Arnold's invention and seems to have no relation to the Callicles in Plato's *Gorgias.* The name is from the Greek *kallos,* beauty.

Act I, scene ii:

4–5 Cf. "Obermann Once More," 21–22 and note.

36 Callicles' lyrics were the only portions of the drama reprinted between 1852 and 1867. They were grouped under the title "The Harp-player on Etna," and this particular lyric was called "The Last Glen."

57–76 The Centaurs were creatures, half-man and half-horse, who lived on the slopes of Mt. Pelion in Thessaly. (Cf. "The Strayed Reveller," 143–50, 222–32 and note.) Chiron, who was wise, just, and learned in music and medicine, educated some of the most famous of the Greek heroes, including Achilles, son of Peleus. He had previously saved the life of Peleus, king of Phthia, when he was abandoned on Mt. Pelion by Acastus. Arnold's classical sources were probably Pindar, *Nem.* iii, 43 ff.; *Pyth.* vi, 19 ff. (Bush)

77 ff. For the sources of Empedocles' discourse in Parmenides, Lucretius, Epictetus, Marcus Aurelius, "Obermann," and Carlyle, see Bonnerot's edition, cited above, and *Commentary.* The main divisions of the discourse are as follows: 77–146, introductory discussion of the human situation; 147–266, analysis of the problem of evil; 267–386, man's relation to the gods; 387–426, concluding advice.

152–61 The following sentence was written by Arnold on the back of a sheet of notes on Empedocles' career: "Man has an impulse for happiness: he sees something of it, hears traditions of much of it: he thinks therefore he *ought* to have it: what is true is, he *may* have it if he *can.*" (*Commentary,* p. 290n.) Arnold is here reflecting Carlyle's view in *Sartor Resartus,* II, ix.

397–411 Arnold's notes suggest that these three stanzas were originally written for a projected drama on Lucretius. (*Commentary,* pp. 293–94)

427 Cadmus, the founder of Thebes, was a culture hero who civilized the Bœotians, taught them the founding of metal and the use of letters. He married Harmonia, daughter of Ares and Aphrodite. Having accidentally killed a serpent sacred to the gods, he and his line suffered many woes until at last he cried out, "If a serpent be so dear to the Gods, would that I too were one," whereupon he and Harmonia were transformed into serpents and lived happily in the brakes of Illyria. Bush cites as sources: Pindar, *Pyth.* iii, 88 ff.; Euripides, *Bacchae;* Apollodorus, III, 4; Hyginus, *Fab.,* VI; Ovid, *Metamorphoses,* IV, 563 ff.

Act II:

7–10 In the letter quoted above in which Arnold denied that Empedocles' philosophy was his own, he went on: "No critic appears to remark that if Empedocles throws himself into Etna his creed can hardly be meant to be one to live by. If the creed of Empedocles were, as exhibited in my poem, a satisfying one, he ought to have lived after delivering himself of it, not died." (*Commentary,* p. 288) But these lines make it clear that Empedocles' creed is one to live by for some people, though not for himself.

18–23 Cf. "Stanzas in Memory of the Author of 'Obermann,'" 93 ff.; "A Summer Night," 37–75; *Tristram and Iseult,* III, 112 ff.

37–88 Typho, one of the giants who warred on the Olympian gods, was pinned by Jove under Mt. Etna, whence he spews lava and fire. Classical sources of the myth are: Hesiod, *Theogony,* 820 ff.; Pindar, *Pyth.* i, 15 ff.; Aeschylus, *Prometheus Bound,* 351 ff.; Ovid, *Metamorphoses,* V, 321 ff. (Bush)

54 (Arnold's note) "Mount Hæmus, so called, said the legend, from Typho's blood spilt on it in his last battle with Zeus, when the giant's strength failed, owing to the Destinies having a short time before given treacherously to him, for his refreshment, perishable fruits. See Apollodorus, *Bibliotheca,* book i, chap. vi."

109–20 Note that here, after Empedocles has seen himself in Typho, and the Sophists in the Olympians, he renounces the symbols of his necromancy, which connect him with the "world"; whereas in lines 191–219, after he has seen himself in Apollo, he renounces the symbols of his intellectual and poetic supremacy, which enforced solitude upon him.

112–17 Cf. Matthew 12:38–39: "Then certain of the scribes and of the Pharisees answered, saying, Master, we would see a sign from thee. But he answered and said unto them, An evil and adulterous generation seeketh after a sign; and there shall be no sign given to it. . . ."

125–90 Marsyas, a satyr, became so proficient on the flute that he challenged Apollo to a contest, it being agreed that the victor should treat the vanquished as he wished. The victory was adjudged to Apollo by the Muses, whereupon he had Marsyas tied to a tree and cut up, or flayed, by a Scythian. The tears of Marsyas' friends formed a river carrying his name, which flowed into the Maeander (136) in Phrygia, Asia Minor. Olympus (168) was a poet of Mysia, in Asia Minor, and the pupil of Marsyas. Pan (127) had previously had a musical contest with Apollo which he had lost in the judgment of all except Midas, who was given ass's ears for his stupidity. The classical sources are: Hyginus, *Fab.* CLXV; Ovid, *Metamorphoses,* VI, 393 ff. (Bush)

235–57 With Empedocles' relation to Parmenides compare that of Olympus to Marsyas (171–84). The Wordsworthian note of lines 242–43 suggests extending the parallel to Arnold and Wordsworth.

276–300 Printed separately in 1855 as "The Philosopher and the Stars."

320–22 Cf. Coleridge's "Dejection: an Ode," iii-v.

423 Helicon, a mountain in Bœotia sacred to the Muses.

Switzerland *Page 74*

"Switzerland" is the core of a group of love poems centering about a figure called "Marguerite." During his lifetime Arnold always insisted, according to his daughter, that Marguerite was imaginary. "What else," says Professor Chambers, "can a paterfamilias say when his children question him as to the object of his early love poems?" That Marguerite was a real person, however, was essentially proved by the publication in 1932 of Arnold's letters to Clough. On September 29, 1848, the poet wrote to his friend from the Baths of Leuk, Switzerland: "Tomorrow I repass the Gemmi and get to Thun: linger one day at the Hôtel Bellevue for the sake of the blue eyes of one of its inmates: and then proceed by slow stages down the Rhine to . . . England." Apparently Arnold was vacationing at Thun, an old Swiss town near Berne where the river Aar flows into lake Thun and then on past Interlaken into Lake Brienz. The Hotel Bellevue et du Parc is on a steep street running from the Castle, which dominates the town, down to a covered bridge leading across a portion of the lake to an island. Visible to the south are the Bernese Alps, particularly the Blümlis Alp. Arnold had evidently walked across this range via the Gemmi Pass to the Rhone valley and then taken the Simplon Pass to Domo d'Ossola and Italy. There, ignoring his guide's account of the "superbes filles" in Domo d'Ossola, he had retraced his steps as far as the Baths of Leuk, near the Rhone, and was intending to return to Thun. In the following year (1849) he visited Thun again, and presumably again saw Marguerite. It should be emphasized, however, that unless we take the poems for fact, we know absolutely nothing about Marguerite or her relation with Arnold except what is contained in the single sentence quoted above. Nevtheless the poems do have the stamp upon them of an actual experience, and this experience was certainly a major crisis in Arnold's life. The best interpretation of it is to be found in the letters to Clough, but there are also secondary studies in Bonnerot, pp. 57–98; Tinker and Lowry, pp. 153–57; Chambers, pp. 46–54; and Baum, pp. 58–84.

Most of the poems in the "Switzerland" group were published in 1852, but they were not distinguished as a series until 1853, and the number, order, and titles of the poems were not finally settled until 1877 (for details see Tinker and Lowry, pp. 151–53 and Baum, pp. 79–84). There is disagreement among scholars as to how many of Arnold's other poems reflect the Marguerite episode. Some would say as many as eighteen, others only four or five. Among the poems included in this volume the following may plausibly be associated with Marguerite: "The Church of Brou. III. The Tomb," "A Dream," "Human Life," "Tristram and Iseult," "The Forsaken Merman," "A Summer Night," "The Buried Life," and "Stanzas in Memory of the Author of 'Obermann.'"

1. Meeting *Page 74*

Originally entitled "The Lake," this poem was from 1853 to 1869 the second poem of the series, following "To my Friends, who ridiculed a tender leave-taking." Arnold himself connected the two poems by a note, and thus, if they are autobiographical in character, the former presumably represents his leave-taking from Marguerite in September, 1848, fearful that they would never meet again, and "The Meeting" recounts their reunion in 1849.

2. Parting *Page 75*

From 1853 to 1857 this was the fourth poem of the series, following "A Dream." See Arnold's letter to Clough, September 23, [1849], where lines 25–34 of this poem are quoted.

3. A Farewell *Page 77*

Not included in the "Switzerland" series until 1854, and then as the fifth in order.

4. Isolation. To Marguerite *Page 80*

This poem did not appear in the volume *Empedocles on Etna* (1852). It was first published (as the sixth in the "Switzerland" series) in 1857 with the title "To Marguerite." The present title was adopted in 1869.

5. To Marguerite — Continued *Page 81*

Originally entitled "To Marguerite, In Returning a Volume of the Letters of Ortis," this poem suffered two changes of title to distinguish it from the preceding lyric: "Isolation" in 1857 and the present title in 1869. The *Letters of Jacopo von Ortis,* a romantic novel modelled upon Goethe's *Sorrows of Werther,* is by the Italian patriot, Ugo Foscolo (1778–1827). Arnold probably read it in the French translation by Alexandre Dumas. The hero, Ortis, is isolated from his beloved by her prior engagement and by her father's low prudential outlook. For this and related poems see Kathleen Tillotson, "Yes: in the Sea of Life," *RES,* III, n.s., (1952), 346–64.

6. Absence *Page 82*

The "fair stranger" has been associated by Tinker and Lowry (p. 170) with Lucy Wightman, whom Arnold courted in the summer of 1850 and married in June, 1851. There is no evidence to support this suggestion, however, except the fact that in several other poems where Miss Wightman is referred to her eyes are called "grey." But the whole point of this poem, that the poet's passion for Marguerite has been blotted out not by anything important but by the "petty dust" of daily life, would seem to demand that the stranger be a person indifferent to the poet.

7. The Terrace at Berne *Page 82*

This poem was not in the volume *Empedocles on Etna* (1852) but was first published in *New Poems* (1867). It is included here to complete the "Switzerland" series in its final form.

In the spring and summer of 1859 Arnold toured the Continent with his wife on business for the Education Office. They arrived at Berne, Switzerland, on Wednesday, June 29, and spent all day Thursday there. ("Bathed. Weather clearing. Drove in the evening.") Thun was twenty miles and ten years away, but they did not visit it. On the following day they took a train in the opposite direction, to Yverdon and Geneva.

19–24 The commentators have been very severe upon Arnold for this reflection upon Marguerite's virtue. Stopford Brooke says that if Arnold had really loved the girl he "would have spared her that conjecture," and E. K. Chambers delivers the severe rebuke, "I do not think that this stanza was worthy of Matthew Arnold."

Youth and Calm *Page 86*

This poem is first found, without title and dated December 28, 1851, in the album of Rotha Quillinan, Wordsworth's granddaughter and a friend of the Arnold family. It was first published in October, 1852, as the second paragraph of a poem entitled "Lines written by a Death-bed." Then, in *New Poems* (1867) the first paragraph was dropped and the title "Youth and Calm" was adopted for the remainder. Two years later the omitted first paragraph was inserted into *Tristram and Iseult* as lines II, 131–46, where they form part of the description of Iseult of Ireland in death. The interpretation put upon these facts by Tinker and Lowry is that "Lines written by a Death-bed" was originally an independent poem, that the first part was suppressed to avoid comparison with the more successful "Requiescat" (both referring to the same death), and that it was later inserted into *Tristram and Iseult* so as not to sacrifice the lines altogether. This view is certainly wrong. Close scrutiny of *Tristram and Iseult,* II, 131–46, and the surrounding context, will show that the lines originally belonged there, as, it may be, so also did the second paragraph now called "Youth and

Calm." It is more likely, however, that the second paragraph, which is in a different rhyme scheme from the first, was written as an independent poem on the occasion of the death of Edward Quillinan, Rotha's father, in 1851, for Arnold's acknowledged elegy on this subject, "Stanzas in Memory of Edward Quillinan," appears in Rotha's album with the date December 27, 1851. Since "Stanzas" presents Quillinan as having achieved in death a calm one would not wish to change, the present poem, which begins in Rotha's album with line 5, "— Yet ah, is Calm alone, in truth," may be considered as a kind of reply. Why Arnold removed the description of the dying Iseult from *Tristram* to add to this poem or why he incorporated this into *Tristram* and then removed both before publication is uncertain. But the suppression of the first paragraph of "Lines written by a Death-bed" in 1867 was certainly made with a view to its restoration in *Tristram* when that poem was next reprinted in 1869. For without the passage one could not be sure that Tristram and Iseult were dead.

Tristram and Iseult

Page 87

It must be remembered that Arnold's is the first modern treatment of the Tristram story, preceding Wagner's by thirteen years and Tennyson's in "The Last Tournament" by nineteen years. Thus, the fact that he gives it a different interpretation from that with which we are familiar need not be considered a defect. In his own day no version of the story was familiar. Indeed, he soon discovered that readers had great difficulty in following his narrative, and therefore, in the second edition, at the suggestion of his friend J. A. Froude, he prefaced the poem with the following condensation of a passage from John Dunlop's *History of Fiction* (1814):

> In the court of his uncle King Marc, the king of Cornwall, who at this time resided at the castle of Tyntagel, Tristram became expert in all knightly exercises. — The king of Ireland, at Tristram's solicitations, promised to bestow his daughter Iseult in marriage on King Marc. The mother of Iseult gave to her daughter's confidante a philtre, or love-potion, to be administered on the night of her nuptials. Of this beverage Tristram and Iseult, on their voyage to Cornwall, unfortunately partook. Its influence, during the remainder of their lives, regulated the affections and destiny of the lovers. —
>
> After the arrival of Tristram and Iseult in Cornwall, and the nuptials of the latter with King Marc, a great part of the romance is occupied with their contrivances to procure secret interviews. — Tristram, being forced to leave Cornwall, on account of the displeasure of his uncle, repaired to Brittany, where lived Iseult with the White Hands. — He married her — more out of gratitude than love. — Afterwards he proceeded to the dominions of Arthur, which became the theatre of unnumbered exploits.
>
> Tristram, subsequent to these events, returned to Brittany, and to his long-neglected wife. There, being wounded and sick, he was soon reduced to the lowest ebb. In this situation, he despatched a confidant to the queen of Cornwall, to try if he could induce her to follow him to Brittany, etc.

Dunlop, however, was not Arnold's source. Writing to Clough on May 1, 1853, he said, "My version of Tristram and Iseult comes from an article in the Revue de Paris, on Fauriel, I think." To Herbert Hill, a friend and former tutor, he explained on November 5, 1852: "I read the story of Tristram and Iseult some years ago at Thun [Switzerland] in an article in a French Review on the romance literature: I had never met with it before, and it fastened upon me: when I got back to England I looked at the Morte d'Arthur and took what I could, but the poem was in the main formed, and I could not well disturb it. If I had read the story first in the Morte d'Arthur I should have managed it differently. I am by no means satisfied with Tristram in the second part myself." The article in the French Review has been identified as "Les poèmes gallois et les romans de la Table-Ronde" by Théodore de la Villemarqué in the *Revue de Paris,* ser. 3, XXXIV (1841), 266–82 and 335–48. The most important passage, a prose summary of the legend, is quoted by Tinker and Lowry, pp. 109–110.

The reason why this story "fastened" upon Arnold is doubtless to be found in the symbolic figure of Tristram, the man of sorrows, whose sick-bed is the sick-bed of modern Europe, and in his relation to the two poles of passion and calm represented by the two Iseults. The fact that the poem was begun during Arnold's acquaintance with Marguerite in Switzerland (see headnote to the "Switzerland" series) but was not published until after his marriage to Lucy Wightman in England has led critics to identify Arnold with his own protagonist. Certainly the poem has thematic relations with *Empedocles on Etna,* "Stanzas in Memory of the Author of 'Obermann,'" "A Summer Night," and "Philomela."

Part I

1 she: Iseult of Ireland, who had been summoned by the dying Tristram to his bed-side in Britanny. The detail that the ship bearing her reply would have white sails if she were coming and black if she were not was absent from Arnold's primary source, La Villemarqué. Writing to Swinburne on July 26, 1882, shortly before reading the younger poet's *Tristram of Lyonesse,* he said, "I suppose you have taken the *sails* as the issue of your story; a beautiful way of ending, which I should perhaps have used, had I known of it, but I did not." (Gosse, "Matthew Arnold and Swinburne," *TLS,* August 12, 1920, p. 517) Presumably Arnold means that he did not know of it when he began writing, for the detail is in Dunlop.

325–73 The description of the sleeping children is the first of the three "end symbols" whose relation to the main theme of the poem the reader will want to work out for himself. The other two symbols are the huntsman on the arras (II, 147–93) and the story of Merlin and Vivian (III, 151–224).

Part II

131–46 These lines, though probably written originally for this scene, were not originally published here but first appeared as the opening paragraph of a short poem entitled "Lines written by a Death-bed" (1852). They were detached from that poem, the title of which was then altered to "Youth and Calm," in 1867 and were first inserted in their present position in *Tristram and Iseult* in 1869. It is barely possible that the rest of the poem was also once intended for *Tristram and Iseult* (following l. 146); if so, it would provide a key to the interpretation of the two Iseults. See the headnote to "Youth and Calm."

164 ff. Cf. "The Church of Brou. III. The Tomb."

Part III

78–81 Cf. Wordsworth's "Michael," 139.

112–50 These lines, which are set apart from the rest of Part III by a certain quaintness of manner, were omitted from the second and third editions but restored in the fourth (1857). Cf. "A Summer Night," 37–75; *Empedocles on Etna,* II, 18–23; the Preface of 1853; and Coleridge's "Dejection: an Ode."

151 ff. Arnold wrote to Herbert Hill on November 5, 1852, "The story of Merlin, of which I am particularly fond, was brought in on purpose to relieve the poem which would else I thought have ended too sadly; but perhaps the new element introduced is too much." (*Commentary,* p. 124) The kind of "relief" intended is perhaps suggested by the following quotation from the German poet Heinrich Heine, which is cited in Arnold's essay on Heine: "My body is so shrunk that there is hardly anything of me left but my voice, and my bed makes me think of the melodious grave of the enchanter Merlin, which is in the forest of Broceliand in Brittany, under high oaks whose tops shine like green flames to heaven. Ah, I envy thee those trees, brother Merlin, and their fresh waving; for over my mattress-grave here in Paris no green leaves rustle; and early and late I hear nothing but the rattle of carriages, hammering, scolding, and the jingle of the piano." Arnold was reading Heine in 1848.

As to source, Arnold wrote Clough that "the story of Merlin is imported from the Morte d'Arthur." Since the story does not actually occur in that work, scholars have suggested as Arnold's source two articles in the same *Revue de Paris* which supplied the Tristram story: La Villemarqué, "Visite au Tombeau de Merlin," ser. 2, XLI (1837), 45–62, and Louandre, "L'enchanteur Merlin," ser. 3, XVI (1840), 109–122. But it is more likely that Arnold was referring to Robert Southey's introduction to the 1817 edition of the *Morte d'Arthur,* which retells the Merlin and Vivian story at length. In all versions Merlin is a great bard and magician who is so infatuated with Vivian, one of the damosels of the Lake, that he pursues her even to his own destruction. On one particular day Vivian, having been made jealous, asks him how she may immure a man without tower or wall or iron, and Merlin, though knowing very well her mischievous intent, tells her and falls asleep in her lap. She invokes the enchantment, never guessing that it will work, and Merlin is imprisoned forever. Vivian is truly sorry and for a time lingers near the spot, but this does not help the old magician who was so foolish as to be immured by his own devices.

Memorial Verses *Page 108*

This poem, first published in *Fraser's Magazine* in June, 1850, was written at the request of Edward Quillinan, Wordsworth's son-in-law and a neighbor of the Arnold family at Fox How in the English Lake District. Wordsworth died on April 23, and Arnold's verses were apparently written almost immediately, for a MS. at Yale is dated "April 27th 1850." Though Arnold speaks ironically in a letter to Clough of having "dirged W.W. *in the grand style,*" the poem was not merely a command performance. For Arnold's attitude toward Wordsworth see the headnote to the essay "Wordsworth."

6 ff. For a similar contrast, but with Obermann replacing Byron, see "Stanzas in Memory of the Author of 'Obermann,'" 47 ff.

29–33 Virgil, *Georgics,* II, 490–92.

Self-Dependence *Page 109*

From 1854 to 1881 the final stanza was set off from the rest of the poem.

31 See Arnold's letter to Clough, February 12, 1853, where this line is quoted.

A Summer Night *Page 110*

Neither of the two scenes (lines 1–10, 11–25) has been identified. One of them, probably the second, is alluded to in "A Southern Night." With the dilemma of lines 37–75, cf. *Tristram and Iseult,* III, 112–33; *Empedocles on Etna,* II, 18–23; "Stanzas in Memory of the Author of 'Obermann,'" 93–96.

62 ff. Arnold wrote to Clough from Thun, September 23, [1849]: "What I must tell you is that I have never yet succeeded in any one great occasion in consciously mastering myself: I can go thro: the imaginary process of mastering myself and see the whole affair as it would then stand, but at the critical point I am too apt to hoist up the mainsail to the wind and let her drive."

78ff. Cf. "Quiet Work."

The Buried Life *Page 113*

Presumably the lady is Marguerite, who elsewhere is described as "arch" and "mocking" ("A Memory-Picture" and "Parting"). Arnold's problem is illuminated by his letter to Clough written from Thun, September 23, [1849]: "I feel that with me a clear almost palpable intuition (damn the logical senses of the word) is necessary before I get into prayer. . . . [My] one natural craving is not for profound thoughts, mighty spiritual workings etc. etc. but a distinct seeing of my way as far as my own nature is concerned. . . ."

Stanzas in Memory of the Author of 'Obermann' *Page 115*

"Senancour, the author of Obermann," wrote Arnold in 1867, "was a French writer of the beginning of this century, too melancholy and too much without a direct aim to be popular, but who, from his gravity, sincerity, and feeling for nature, produced on me when I happened, at 25, to fall in with his works, an extraordinary impression. My separation of myself, finally, from him and his influence, is related in a poem in my Second Series [i.e., this poem]. . . ." (*Commentary,* p. 271)

Arnold's note to this poem is as follows:

> The author of *Obermann,* Étienne Pivert de Senancour, has little celebrity in France, his own country; and out of France he is almost unknown. But the profound inwardness, the austere sincerity, of his principal work, *Obermann,* the delicate feeling for nature which it exhibits, and the melancholy eloquence of many passages of it, have attracted and charmed some of the most remarkable spirits of this century, such as George Sand and Sainte-Beuve, and will probably always find a certain number of spirits whom they touch and interest.
>
> Senancour was born in 1770. He was educated for the priesthood, and passed some time in the seminary of St. Sulpice; broke away from the Seminary and from France itself, and passed some years in Switzerland, where he married; returned to France in middle life, and followed thenceforward the career of a man of letters, but with hardly any fame or success. He died an old man in 1846, desiring that on his grave might be placed these words only: *Éternité, deviens mon asile!*
>
> The influence of Rousseau, and certain affinities with more famous and fortunate authors of his own day, — Chateaubriand and Madame de Staël, — are everywhere visible in Senancour. But though, like these eminent personages, he may be called a sentimental writer, and though *Obermann,* a collection of letters from Switzerland treating almost entirely of nature and of the human soul, may be called a work of sentiment, Senancour has a gravity and severity which distinguish him from all other writers of the sentimental school. The world is with him in his solitude far less than it is with them; of all writers he is the most perfectly isolated and the least attitudinising. His chief work, too, has a value and power of its own, apart from these merits of its author. The stir of all the main forces, by which modern life is and has been impelled, lives in the letters of *Obermann;* the dissolving agencies of the eighteenth century, the fiery storm of the French Revolution, the first faint promise and dawn of that new world which our own time is but now more fully bringing to light, — all these are to be felt, almost to be touched, there. To me, indeed, it will always seem that the impressiveness of this production can hardly be rated too high.
>
> Besides *Obermann* there is one other of Senancour's works which, for those spirits who feel his attraction, is very interesting; its title is, *Libres Méditations d'un Solitaire Inconnu.*

See Arnold's essay "Senancour," *Essays in Criticism, Third Series;* Iris E. Sells, *Matthew Arnold and France* (1934).

5 (Arnold's note) "The Baths of Leuk. This poem was conceived, and partly composed, in the valley going down from the foot of the Gemmi Pass towards the Rhone." Arnold had travelled the same route the previous September (1848).

45–80 Cf. "Memorial Verses."

93–96 Cf. *Empedocles on Etna,* II, 18–23; "A Summer Night, 37–75.

114 The Dent de Jaman is a peak on the shores of Lake Leman (Geneva). Although Arnold had written the year before that the "whole locality is spoiled by the omnipresence there of that furiously flaring bethiefed rushlight, the vulgar Byron," he inevitably saw the region partly through Byron's eyes.

143 Arnold wrote to Clough from Thun, September 23 [1849]: "Marvel not that I say unto you, ye must be born again. While I will not much talk of these things, yet the considering of them has led me constantly to you as the only living one almost that I know of of

> The children of the second birth
> Whom the world could not tame —"

161–80 Sainte-Beuve wrote Arnold in 1854: "You are perhaps unaware that the author, M. de Senancour, died several years ago at Sèvres near Paris, whither he had been taken. There were only two persons present at his funeral, and engraved upon his tomb were the words which he had requested: *Éternité, deviens mon asyle.*" (*Unpublished Letters,* p. 68)

Lines Written in Kensington Gardens *Page 121*

A pencilled draft of this poem with several variants is printed in the *Commentary.*

Morality *Page 122*

See "In Harmony with Nature."

Sohrab and Rustum *Page 124*

"Sohrab and Rustum" opens the volume of 1853 immediately after the Preface in which Arnold announced his new literary creed. Undoubtedly he considered the poem to be an exemplification of that creed; and, looking forward to his lectures *On Translating Homer,* one may say that he also considered it a sample of how to render the Homeric style into English. He was, indeed, very pleased with the poem, thinking it "by far the best thing I have yet done. . . . I have had the greatest pleasure in composing it — a rare thing with me, and, as I think, a good test of the pleasure what you write is likely to afford to others; but then the story is a very noble and excellent one." (*Letters,* I, 30)

The story, one of many versions of the myth of a combat between a father and a son who are unknown to one another, is drawn from a tenth-century Persian epic, the *Shah Nameh,* or *Book of Kings,* by Firdausi. Arnold had a long-standing interest in the literature and thought of the East, but in this instance he did not go to Firdausi's own work, just recently translated into French by Jules Mohl, but depended upon secondary accounts in Sir

John Malcolm's *History of Persia* and especially upon a review of Mohl's translation by the French critic Sainte-Beuve. He also derived details for "orientalizing" his similes from Captain Sir Alexander Burnes's *Travels into Bokhara* (1833). For a fuller account of Arnold's sources see Tinker and Lowry, pp. 75–85, and the works cited there. Part of Arnold's own note on the subject, first published in 1854 in response to a charge of plagiarism made by John Duke Coleridge in the *Christian Remembrancer,* is given below.

> The story of Sohrab and Rustum is told in Sir John Malcolm's *History of Persia,* as follows: —
>
> "The young Sohrab was the fruit of one of Rustum's early amours. He had left his mother, and sought fame under the banners of Afrasiab, whose armies he commanded, and soon obtained a renown beyond that of all contemporary heroes but his father. He had carried death and dismay into the ranks of the Persians, and had terrified the boldest warriors of that country, before Rustum encountered him, which at last that hero resolved to do, under a feigned name. They met three times. The first time they parted by mutual consent, though Sohrab had the advantage; the second, the youth obtained a victory, but granted life to his unknown father; the third was fatal to Sohrab, who, when writhing in the pangs of death, warned his conqueror to shun the vengeance that is inspired by parental woes, and bade him dread the rage of the mighty Rustum, who must soon learn that he had slain his son Sohrab. These words, we are told, were as death to the aged hero; and when he recovered from a trance, he called in despair for proofs of what Sohrab had said. The afflicted and dying youth tore open his mail, and showed his father a seal which his mother had placed on his arm when she discovered to him the secret of his birth, and bade him seek his father. The sight of his own signet rendered Rustum quite frantic; he cursed himself, attempting to put an end to his existence, and was only prevented by the efforts of his expiring son. After Sohrab's death, he burnt his tents and all his goods, and carried the corpse to Seistan, where it was interred; the army of Turan was, agreeably to the last request of Sohrab, permitted to cross the Oxus unmolested. To reconcile us to the improbability of this tale, we are informed that Rustum could have no idea his son was in existence. The mother of Sohrab had written to him her child was a daughter, fearing to lose her darling infant if she revealed the truth; and Rustum, as before stated, fought under a feigned name, an usage not uncommon in the chivalrous combats of those days."
>
> M. Sainte-Beuve, also, that most delightful of critics, in a notice of an edition of Ferdousi's great poem by M. Mohl now in course of publication at Paris, containing the original text and a prose translation, gives an analysis of this episode, with extracts from M. Mohl's translation . . . , commencing from the point where Rustum leaves Tehmineh, the future mother of Sohrab, before the birth of her child; having given her an onyx with instructions to let the child wear it in her hair, if a girl, and on his arm, if a boy. Of M. Mohl's book itself I have not been able to obtain sight. . . .
>
> A writer in the *Christian Remembrancer* (of the general tenour of

whose remarks I have, assuredly, no right to complain) having made the discovery of this notice by M. Sainte-Beuve, has pointed out the passages in which I have made use of the extracts from M. Mohl's translation which it contains; has observed, apparently with blame, that I "have not thought fit to offer a single syllable of acknowledgment to an author to whom I have been manifestly very largely indebted"; has complained of being "under some embarrassment from not being sure how much of the treatment is Mr. Arnold's own"; and, finally, has suggested that "the whole work of M. Mohl may have been used throughout, and the study of antiquity carried so far as simply to reproduce an ancient poem as well as an ancient subject."

It would have been more charitable, perhaps, had the reviewer, before making this goodnatured suggestion, ascertained, by reference to M. Mohl's work, how far it was confirmed by the fact.

The reader, however, is now in possession of the whole of the sources from which I have drawn the story of *Sohrab and Rustum,* and can determine, if he pleases, the exact amount of my obligation to M. Mohl. But I hope that it will not in future be supposed, if I am silent as to the sources from which a poem has been derived, that I am trying to conceal obligations, or to claim an absolute originality for all parts of it. When any man endeavours to *"remanier et réinventer à sa manière"* a great story, which, as M. Sainte-Beuve says of that of *Sohrab and Rustum,* has *"couru le monde,"* it may be considered quite certain that he has not drawn all the details of his work out of his own head. The reader is not, I think, concerned to ask, from what sources these have been drawn; but only how the whole work, as it stands, affects him. Real plagiarism, such as the borrowing without acknowledgement of passages from other English poets — real dishonesty, such as the endeavouring to pass off the mere translation of a poem as an original work — are always certain enough to be discovered.

I must not be led on, from defending the morality of my imitation, to defend at length its aesthetics; but I cannot forbear adding, that it would be a most unfortunate scruple which should restrain an author, treating matter of history or tradition, from placing, where he can, in the mouths of his personages the very words of the old chronicle, or romance, or poem (when the poem embodies, as that of Ferdousi, the tradition of a people); and which should lead him to substitute for these any *"eigene* [sic] *grossen Erfindungen."* For my part, I only regret that I could not meet with a translation from Ferdousi's poem of the whole of the episode of *Sohrab and Rustum:* with a prose translation, that is: for in a verse translation no original work is any longer recognizable. I should certainly have made all the use I could of it. The use of the tradition, above everything else, gives to a work that *naïveté,* that flavour of reality and truth, which is the very life of poetry.

156 corn: grain (the English sense).

160 ff. Cf. Burnes, *Travels in Bokhara,* II, 247–48: "This great peak [Hindoo Koosh] is visible from Cabool, and entirely enveloped in milk-white snow. . . . Its altitude must be considerable, for the travellers complain of the difficulty of breathing, and carry sugar and mulberries with them, to ease their respiration; and the strongest of men suffer from giddiness and vomiting. Thousands of birds are also found dead on the snow, for it is believed that they are unable to fly from the violence of the winds; but it is more probable that they are prevented by the rarity of the atmosphere: . . . The greatest silence is preserved in crossing Hindoo Koosh; and no one speaks loud, or fires a gun, lest the reverberation cause a fall of snow: such, at least, is the reason assigned; nor does it appear to be destitute of foundation." Cf. "Rugby Chapel," 99–100.

634 Hyacinthus, a Greek youth beloved of Apollo and unwittingly killed by him at a game of quoits. From his blood sprang a flower marked with the Greek letters AI, meaning "alas."

875 For Arnold's source in the description of the course of the Oxus see Tinker and Lowry, p. 80. For other uses of the river symbol see "Mycerinus," "A Dream," "The Buried Life," "The Scholar-Gipsy," and "Memorial Verses."

Philomela *Page 144*

In the Latin version of this Greek myth Philomela was married to Tereus, king of Thrace. The latter became enamoured of Philomela's sister, Procne, and having seduced or outraged her, cut out her tongue that she might not reveal his crime. But Procne managed to depict her misfortunes in a tapestry, whereupon Philomela in revenge killed her own son, Itylus, and served up his flesh to her husband. Tereus drew his sword to slay the sisters but was changed into a hoopoe, Procne being simultaneously changed into a swallow and Philomela into a nightingale. In the Greek version the roles of the sisters are reversed. For an analysis of the theme of this poem in Arnold's work, see R. A. Donovan, "Philomela," *Victorian Newsletter* (1957), 1–6.

The Church of Brou. III. The Tomb *Page 145*

"The Tomb" is Part III of a narrative poem entitled "The Church of Brou." Part I ("The Castle") tells, in ballad stanza, of the Duchess Marguerite, whose husband, the Duke of Savoy, was killed on a boar hunt a few months after their marriage. The Duchess thereupon determined to complete an unfinished church begun many years before in the Savoy mountains and to rear there a tomb with her own and the Duke's figure sculptured upon it. As soon as the work was completed, she died. Part II ("The Church") tells how the lonely church is visited by worshippers from the surrounding country, who wonder at the beauty of the tomb. But Part III is the real *raison d'être* of the poem and its only successful portion. In 1877 Arnold published Part III by itself under the title "A Tomb among the Mountains," partly, perhaps because he recognized the inferiority of the narrative sections but more particularly because he had been sharply criticized for having gotten his facts all wrong and wished to dissociate the poem from the actual church and the historical duchess. For material on this question and on Arnold's source, Edgar Quinet's essay, "Des Arts de la Renaissance et de l'Église de Brou" (1839), see Tinker and Lowry. The poem has been associated with the Marguerite group, especially with "Tristram and Iseult," Part II.

A Dream *Page 146*

From 1853 to 1857 this was the third poem in the "Switzerland" series. (See headnote to that group.) It is clearly one of the Marguerite poems, but nothing is known about the originals, if any, of Olivia and Martin. The scenery, as Tinker and Lowry note, is that of Thun and the Aar valley.

Requiescat *Page 147*

The title is from the phrase *requiescat in pace,* may he (or she) rest in peace. It is unknown whether the poem refers to an actual person.

The Scholar-Gipsy *Page 147*

The source of "The Scholar-Gipsy" is a passage in Joseph Glanvill's *The Vanity of Dogmatizing* (1661), a work attacking the scholastic philosophy:

> There was very lately a Lad in the *University of Oxford,* who being of very pregnant and ready parts, and yet wanting the encouragement of preferment; was by his poverty forc'd to leave his studies there, and to cast himself upon the wide world for a livelyhood. Now, his necessities growing dayly on him, and wanting the help of friends to relieve him; he was at last forced to joyn himself to a company of *Vagabond Gypsies,* whom occasionally he met with, and to follow their Trade for a maintenance. Among these extravagant people, by the insinuating subtilty of his carriage, he quickly got so much of their love, and esteem; as that they discover'd to him their *Mystery:* in the practice of which, by the pregnancy of his wit and parts he soon grew so good a proficient, as to be able to out-do his Instructours. After he had been a pretty while well exercis'd in the Trade; there chanc'd to ride by a couple of *Scholars* who had formerly bin of his acquaintance. The *Scholars* had quickly spyed out their old friend, among the *Gypsies;* and their amazement to see him among such society, had well-nigh discover'd him: but by a sign he prevented their owning him before that Crew: and taking one of them aside privately, desired him with his friend to go to an *Inn,* not far distant thence, promising there to come to them. They accordingly went thither, and he follows: after their first salutations, his friends enquire how he came to lead so odd a life as that was, and to joyn himself to such a *cheating beggerly* company. The Scholar-Gypsy having given them an account of the necessity, which drove him to that kind of life; told them, that the people he went with were not such *Impostours* as they were taken for,

> but that they had a *traditional* kind of *learning* among them, and could do wonders by the power of *Imagination*, and that himself had learnt much of their Art, and improved it further then themselves could. And to evince the truth of what he told them, he said, he'd remove into another room, leaving them to discourse together; and upon his return tell them the sum of what they had talked of: which accordingly he perform'd, giving them a full account of what had pass'd between them in his absence. The *Scholars* being amaz'd at so unexpected a discovery, earnestly desir'd him to unriddle the *mystery*. In which he gave them satisfaction, by telling them, that what he did was by the power of *Imagination*, his Phancy *binding* theirs; and that himself had dictated to them the discourse, they held together, while he was from them: That there were warrantable wayes of heightening the *Imagination* to that pitch, as to bind anothers; and that when he had compass'd the whole *secret*, some parts of which he said he was yet ignorant of, he intended to leave their company, and give the world an account of what he had learned.

As Arnold purchased a copy of Glanvill in 1844 and in his pocket almanac listed it first among books to be read "From October 1845 to ——," it is likely that the experiences which lie behind the poem date principally from 1845–46, when he was a probationer fellow of Oriel. That was the time when he, his brother Tom, Clough, and Theodore Walrond used to breakfast in each other's rooms on Sunday mornings and then ramble in the Cumnor hills two or three miles to the south and west. The poem is in part a monument to those free and happy days. Even then, if we may believe "Thyrsis" (lines 26–30), they saw in the Scholar-Gipsy a symbol of a spiritual ideal, at once an emantion of their beloved landscape and its tutelary genius. This being so, it is unwise to place too much emphasis on the early titles of the poems — "the first mesmerist" in a list of poems to be composed in 1849, and "the wandering Mesmerist" in a later list (? 1851) — as indicating that Arnold once intended to treat the magical element seriously. (C. B. Tinker, "Arnold's Poetic Plans," *Yale Review,* XXII, 1933, 791–93; Curgenven, below.) True, there was much interest in mesmerism in the 1840's: Harriet Martineau, a friend of the Arnolds, was ostensibly cured by this means in 1844 and published an account of the matter in five articles in *The Athenaeum.* And Mrs. Arnold, the mother of the poet, was "almost a convert." But gipsies were even more in the air, chiefly through George Borrow's books: *The Zincali, or an Account of the Gypsies in Spain* (1841), *The Bible in Spain* (1843), and *Lavengro* (1851). The subtitle of the last is "The Scholar — The Gypsy — The Priest," and its hero is an wandering "philologist" who lives among the gipsies. Of course, Arnold had already used the gipsies in "To a Gipsy Child by the Sea-Shore" and "Resignation."

The literary tradition to which "The Scholar-Gipsy" belongs is that of the pastoral elegy and the odes of Keats, especially "To Autumn" and, for theme, the "Ode on a Grecian Urn" and "Ode to a Nightingale."

The best critical treatments are: Brooks and Warren, *Understanding Poetry;* G. Wilson Knight, "*The Scholar Gipsy:* an Interpretation," *RES*, n.s., VI

(1955), 53–62; J. P. Curgenven, "*The Scholar Gipsy:* A Study of the Growth, Meaning, and Integration of a Poem," *Litera* (Istanbul), II (1955), 41–58; III (1956), 1–13; A. E. Dyson, "The Last Enchantments," *RES*, n.s., VIII (1957), 257–65. There are notes by the following in *Explicator:* R. M. Gay, II (1944), 28; C. K. Hyder, IX (1950), 23; L. Perrine, XV (1957), 33; G. Montague, XVIII (1959), 15.

1 The "shepherd" is undoubtedly Clough, who in quitting Oxford in 1848 out of a dissatisfaction with the state of English society, seemed to Arnold to be indulging in a morbid and sentimental restlessness. He urges him, after "the fields are still" (6), i.e., after the revolutionary movements of 1848 are over, to return and begin again the quest for the Scholar-Gipsy. The stanza would also apply to Thomas Arnold, Jr., the poet's brother, who on November 24, 1847, sailed for New Zealand under somewhat similar circumstances. Beyond these, of course, the shepherd is anyone who abandons the quest for the ideal in favor of direct social action.

57–130 For the topography of the poem see Sir Francis Wylie, "The Scholar-Gipsy Country," in *Commentary*, pp. 351–73.

182–86 In a reading of his poems in Boston on November 24, 1883, "Mr. Arnold said he had Goethe in mind when he wrote [these lines]. . . . They were written just after Mr. Arnold had read Goethe's *Dichtung und Wahrheit*, and while he still felt the impression of its sadness." (*Worcester* [Mass.] *Spy*, November 29, 1883, quoted by Chilson H. Leonard, *MLN*, XLVI, 1931, 119) Some scholars have been dissatisfied with this identification and have suggested Tennyson or Leopardi. (*Commentary;* J. C. Maxwell, "One who most has suffered," *RES*, n.s., VI, 1955, 182–83)

208–9 *Aeneid,* VI, 450–76.

231–50 The relevance of this "end-symbol" has been defended by E. K. Brown, "The Scholar-Gipsy; an Interpretation," *Revue anglo-américaine*, XII (1935), 219–25; and by Knight and Curgenven in the articles cited above.

Thyrsis *Page 154*

When Arthur Hugh Clough, the poet, died in Florence on November 13, 1861, Arnold wrote that he could not, as requested, write about him in a newspaper or a review, "but I shall some day in some way or other relieve myself of what I think about him." (*Letters,* I, 176–77) Within the month he delivered at Oxford the public tribute contained in his "Last Words on Translating Homer," but the more personal statement required a process of time. In January, 1862, thanking Mrs. Clough for some of her husband's verses, he said, "I shall take them with me to Oxford, where I shall go alone after Easter; — and there, among the Cumner hills where we have so often rambled, I shall be able to think him over as I could wish." (*Letters to Clough,* p. 160) Presumably it was on this visit that Arnold retraced the walks which he and Clough had taken almost twenty years before and in that retracing found the structure of his poem. Composition, however, did not come easily. In 1863 "Clough & the Cumner hill-side" was on a list of works to be composed, and in April, 1866, we learn that the elegy had been "forming itself" in the poet's mind for the past two years. It was published in *Macmillan's Magazine* in April, 1866.

The reason for this delay is doubtless to be found in the peculiar nature of Arnold's relation with Clough. As Dr. Arnold's prize pupil, preceding his friend through Rugby, Balliol, and Oriel, Clough was a kind of intellectual older brother to Arnold and profoundly influenced his development. But his tendency to plumb all religious and social questions to their depths, even to his own bewilderment, represented to Arnold a spiritual danger latent in himself. He tried to fend off this danger by fending off Clough, and it must be confessed that he sometimes used his friend as a whipping-boy for his own errors. When Clough renounced his Oriel fellowship in 1848, no longer able to stomach the Thirty-Nine Articles of the Anglican Church, and went over to Paris and Rome to witness the revolutionary movements of that year, it must have seemed to Arnold that this was a far more glamorous gesture than his own decision to abandon Marguerite, subdue his restlessness, get married, and become a School Inspector. Yet now, in the 1860's, Clough was dead with very little accomplished and Arnold was just emerging into fame. Could it be that he was right after all? The signal elm, the symbol of the shy, unglamorous ideal of the Scholar-Gipsy, was standing still and Clough had been wrong to abandon it so soon. No wonder that "Thyrsis" is rather critical of its protagonist — that it comes to bury Caesar not to praise him — and that the usual elegiac structure of the death and rebirth of the hero is replaced by that of the loss and recovery of the elm. Arnold admitted, in respect to the pastoral form, that "there is much in Clough (the whole *prophet* side, in fact) which one cannot deal with in this way, and one has the feeling, if one reads the poem as a memorial poem, that not enough is said about Clough in it; I feel this so much that I do not send the poem to Mrs. Clough. Still Clough *had* this idyllic side, too; to deal with this suited my desire to deal with that Cumner country: anyway, only so could I treat the matter this time." (*Letters,* I, 380)

"The diction of the poem," Arnold wrote to his mother, "was modelled on that of Theocritus, whom I have been much reading during the two years this poem has been forming itself, and . . . I meant the diction to be so artless as to be almost heedless. . . . It is probably too *quiet* a poem for the general taste, but I think it will stand wear." (*Letters,* I, 378)

J. P. Curgenven, "Thyrsis," *Litera* (Istanbul), IV (1957), 27–39; V (1958), 7–16 (to be concluded); W. S. Knickerbocker, *Explicator,* VIII (1950), 51; Sir Francis Wylie, "The Scholar-Gipsy Country," *Commentary,* pp. 351–73.

10 Thyrsis is the shepherd-poet of Theocritus' first idyll, where he sings a lament for Daphnis (cf. line 185), and of Virgil's seventh eclogue, where the singing-match between Thyrsis and Corydon is recounted (cf. lines 80 ff.).

19ff. Cf. Arnold's lovely apostrophe to Oxford at the end of the Preface to *Essays in Criticism,* written contemporaneously with this poem.

38–39 Cf. "Stanzas in Memory of the Author of 'Obermann,'" 131–40.

82–97 "The Hellenic focus of the poem is . . . Sicily, home of the Doric Greek of Theocritus and Bion, the haunt thence . . . of the pastoral muse, and the place whence Proserpine was abducted by Pluto. . . . The fancy that Sicilian poets might recover their lost friends from the shades by piping a ditty to Proserpine is directly inspired by Moschus' lament for Bion." (Curgenven)

167 Clough was buried in the Protestant cemetery in Florence.

185 (Arnold's note) "Daphnis, the ideal Sicilian shepherd of Greek pastoral poetry, was said to have followed into Phrygia his mistress Piplea, who had been carried off by robbers, and to have found her in the power of the king of Phrygia, Lityerses. Lityerses used to make strangers try a contest with him in reaping corn, and to put them to death if he overcame them. Hercules arrived in time to save Daphnis, took upon himself the reaping-contest with Lityerses, overcame him, and slew him. The Lityerses-song connected with this tradition was, like the Linus-song, one of the early plaintive strains of Greek popular poetry, and used to be sung by corn-reapers. Other traditions represented Daphnis as beloved by a nymph who exacted from him an oath to love no one else. He fell in love with a princess, and was struck blind by the jealous nymph. Mercury, who was his father, raised him to Heaven, and made a fountain spring up in the place from which he ascended. At this fountain the Sicilians offered yearly sacrifices.—See Servius, *Comment. in Virgil. Bucol.*, v. 20, and viii. 68."

Calais Sands *Page 160*

This poem was addressed to Frances Lucy Wightman, daughter of a judge of the Court of Queen's Bench, whom Arnold began to court in 1850. A manuscript draft of the poem bears the heading, "By the seaside near Calais, August, 1850." Family tradition says that Miss Wightman's father, not sure that Arnold could support a wife, had forbidden any further meeting of the two, but that Arnold secretly placed himself in their way on their trip to the Continent that summer. "Matt comes to Switzerland in a month. . . ," wrote Clough on July 23. "He is deep in flirtation with Miss Wightman, daughter of the Judge. It is thought it will come to something, for he has actually been to Church to meet her." Come to something it did: on April 14, 1851, Arnold was assured an adequate income by his appointment as Inspector of Schools, and the wedding took place on June 10.

Dover Beach *Page 161*

Very little is known certainly about the date or occasion of "Dover Beach." Although it was first published in 1867, it was probably written much earlier, perhaps in June, 1851, when Arnold passed through Dover on his wedding journey to the Continent. A pencilled draft of the first twenty-eight lines of the poem occurs on the back of a sheet of notes on the career of Empedocles which Arnold presumably made about 1850. The draft ends with line 28 followed by the words "Ah love &c.," as though the last nine lines of the poem already existed and were to be understood as following upon this introduction. (C. B. Tinker and H. F. Lowry, "Arnold's 'Dover Beach,'" *TLS,* October 10, 1935, p. 631; and *Commentary*) The fact that the image of the night-battle (lines 35–37) occurs in Clough's poem *The Bothie of Tober-na-vuolich* (IX, 48–54), which Arnold read in November, 1848, and rather disliked, has led one critic to interpret "Dover Beach" as a reaction against the optimism of that poem. (P. Turner, "*Dover Beach* and *The Bothie of Tober-na-vuolich,*" *English Studies,* XXVIII, 1947, pp. 173–78; B. Trawick, "The Sea of Faith and the Battle by Night in *Dover Beach,*" *PMLA,* LXV, 1950, pp. 1282–83.) Another has seen Clough's "Say not the struggle naught availeth" as being a reply to "Dover Beach." (D. A. Robertson, "'Dover Beach' and 'Say not the struggle naught availeth,'" *PMLA,* LXVI, 1951, pp. 919–20; reply by P. F. Baum, "Clough and Matthew Arnold," *MLN,* LXVII, 1952, pp. 546–47.) Both views are possible but presuppose a rather early date, around 1848–49; and if this were the case the poem would have to be associated with Marguerite rather than Mrs. Arnold.

There is good criticism as well as amusement in Theodore Morrison's classic "Dover Beach Revisited: a New Fable for Critics," *Harper's Magazine,* CLXXX (1940), 235–44; see also M. Krieger, "'Dover Beach' and the Tragic Sense of Eternal Recurrence," *Univ. of Kansas City Review,* XXIII (1956), 73–79; and comment by the following in *Explicator:* J. P. Kirby, I (1943), 42; F. A. Pottle, II (1944), 45; F. L. Gwynn, VIII (1950), 46; N. C. Stageberg, IX (1951), 34; R. Delasanta, XVIII (1959), 7; G. Montague, XVIII (1959), 15. Archibald MacLeish's poem, "'Dover Beach'—A Note to that Poem," is suggestive.

15–18 Cf. Sophocles, *Antigone,* 583 ff.; *Trachiniae,* 112 ff.; and *Oedipus at Colonus,* 1239 ff., quoted in the *Commentary* from *N & Q,* CLXXIV (1938), 57–58.

21–28 Cf. Sainte-Beuve, *Portraits littéraires* (Paris, 1864; 1st ed., 1851), III, 540: "Mon âme est pareille à ces plages où l'on dit que Saint Louis s'est embarqué; la mer et la foi se sont depuis longtemps, hélas, retirées, et c'est tout si parfois, à travers les sables, sous l'aride chaleur ou le froid mistral, je trouve un instant à m'asseoir à l'ombre d'un rare tamarin." (C. C. Clark, "A Possible Source of Matthew Arnold's 'Dover Beach,'" *MLN,* XVII, 1902, pp. 484–85)

28 shingles: beaches strewn with coarse gravel.

35–37 Whether or not the image of the night-battle alludes to Clough's poem, it is ultimately derived from Thucydides' famous account of the battle of Epipolae (VII, 43–44) between the Athenians and the Syracusans. In that battle, fought on a moonlit plain at the top of a cliff, the adversaries "saw one another [in Thomas Arnold's rendering] as men naturally would by moonlight; that is, to see before them the form of the object but to mistrust their knowing who was friend and who was foe." Arnold and Clough would have studied Thucydides in the fifth and sixth forms at Rugby, for the *History* was a favorite text with Dr. Arnold, who published a three-volume edition in 1830–35. There is some evidence that the night-battle was a common symbol among Rugby and Oxford men for the spiritual conflict of the age. Cf. Newman's sermon (published 1843) on "Faith and Reason, contrasted as Habits of Mind," which concludes: "Controversy, at least in this age, does not lie between the hosts of heaven, Michael and his Angels on the one side, and the powers of evil on the other; but it is a sort of night battle, where each fights for himself, and friend and foe stand together." (Cited by J. W. Cameron, "The Night Battle: Newman and Empiricism," *Victorian Studies,* IV, 1960, p. 99)

Stanzas from Carnac *Page 162*

Arnold's note to line 33 of the poem reads: "The author's brother, William Delafield Arnold, Director of Public Instruction in the Punjab, and author of *Oakfield, or Fellowship in the East,* died at Gibraltar on his way home from India, April the 9th, 1859." Arnold received the news while he was in Paris making a tour of French schools. On May 6, the date which the poem bears in the original edition, he was at Auray on the west coast of Britanny. "I left the diligence at Auray. . . ," he wrote to his wife, "and immediately ordered a conveyance for Carnac, about ten miles off on the sea-shore. The great Druidical monument is there, and I stopped at Auray on purpose to see it. It is a very wild country — broom and furze, broom and furze everywhere — and a few patches of pine forest. The sea runs into the land everywhere, and beautiful church towers rise on all sides of you, for this is a land of churches. The stones of Carnac are very singular, but the chapel of St. Michel, on a hill between the stones and the village of Carnac, I liked better still; the view over the stones and the strange country of Morbihan (the little sea), on the spur of Carnac by the sea, and beyond the bay and peninsula of Quiberon, where the emigrants landed, and beyond that the Atlantic. All this at between six and seven on a perfectly still, cloudless evening in May, with the sea like glass, and the solitude all round entire. I got back to Auray at eight." (*Letters,* I, 95)

28 Lazare Hoche, French general under the Revolution, inflicted a crushing blow on the Royalist cause by defeating and capturing Sombreuil's expedition at Quiberon in July, 1795.

A Southern Night *Page 163*

See the headnote to "Stanzas from Carnac." On learning of his brother's death Arnold wrote his mother from Paris as follows: "How strange it seems that he should have overlived his first terrible illness when his wife was alive to nurse him and he had but one child to suffer by his loss, to die now alone, with only a chance acquaintance to attend him, and leaving those four poor little orphans, to whom no tenderness can ever quite replace a father and a mother! And then that he should have overlived the misery of his poor wife's death to struggle through a year's loneliness, and then to die too. Poor Fanny! she at Dhurmsala, and he by the Rock of Gibraltar."

(*Letters,* I, 92) The poem was first published in *Victoria Regia* (1861), a miscellany edited by Adelaide Ann Procter and published by Emily Faithful at the Victoria Press for the Employment of Women. Tennyson, Thackeray, and other well-known authors contributed.

9 Cette is on the Gulf of Lions in southern France.

14 (Arnold's note) "See the poem, *A Summer Night.*" Presumably the night referred to is not that which provides the setting of "A Summer Night" but the night alluded to in lines 11–25.

Fragment of Chorus of a "Dejaneira" *Page 167*

A "Dejaneira" would presumably be a tragedy modelled on Sophocles' *Trachiniae,* in which Dejaneira, the wife of Heracles, attempts to win back the love of her husband by smearing his robe with a love-charm. Too late she discovers that the charm is in fact a deadly poison.

Growing Old *Page 168*

It has been suggested that this poem is a reply to Browning's "Rabbi Ben Ezra" (1864), as that poem apparently was to Fitzgerald's "Rubáiyát of Omar Khayyám." (W. C. DeVane, *A Browning Handbook,* 1955, p. 295) But poems on growing old are generally written by young men, and it seems to have been just as Arnold was turning thirty, in the early 1850's, that he felt "three parts iced over." Toward the end of 1851 he wrote to Clough, "We are growing old, and advancing towards the deviceless darkness," and again the next year, "What a difference there is between reading in poetry and morals of the loss of youth, and experiencing it!" Cf. "Youth and Calm."

Epilogue to Lessing's Laocoön *Page 169*

The *Laocoön* (1764) by Gotthold Ephraim Lessing uses the celebrated group of statuary representing Laocoön and his sons in the coils of a serpent, and Virgil's description of the incident, as the basis for analyzing the differences between poetry and the plastic arts. Arnold read the work in the autumn of 1848 and recommended it to Clough with the caution, "it is not quite satisfactory, and a little mare's nesty — but very searching." (*Letters to Clough,* p. 97)

16 Pausanias (2nd cent., A.D.), the author of a *Description of Hellas,* was especially interested in statues, paintings, and tombs.

44–48 Theocritus tells the story (*Id.* xi) of Galatea, a Nereid beloved by the Cyclops Polyphemus, who ignored him in favor of a youth called Acis.

107 *The Ride:* an avenue along the southern border of Hyde Park where it was fashionable to ride; pedestrians walked or lounged just beyond the railings which surrounded the Park.

Rugby Chapel *Page 174*

Dr. Thomas Arnold, the poet's father and headmaster of Rugby School, died in the prime of life in 1842. He was not the portentous figure he is represented as being in Lytton Strachey's *Eminent Victorians,* but was a great liberal educator, a historian of modern views, and a Broad Church divine. Nevertheless, his children, though they loved him, were a little in awe of him, and Matthew's youthful levity was undoubtedly put on partly for the Doctor's benefit. By the 1850's, however, as Arnold turned from poetry to literary and social criticism, he realized that he was more and more approximating his father's position and in a sense continuing his father's work. This it was, undoubtedly, that made possible the belated writing of the elegy. But the immediate occasion was apparently Arnold's reading, in November, 1857, of Thomas Hughes' novel, *Tom Brown's School Days,* which contains a final solemn scene representing the Doctor's funeral in Rugby Chapel. Then in January, 1858, the novel was reviewed in the *Edinburgh Review* by Fitzjames Stephen, and "it was [his] thesis . . . ," wrote Arnold, "of Papa's being a narrow bustling fanatic, which moved me first to the poem." The poem was not published until 1867 and probably not completed much before that date (see note to line 162).

98–100 Cf. "Sohrab and Rustum," 168.

124–27 Arnold wrote to his mother in 1855: "He [Dr. Arnold] was not only a good man saving his soul by righteousness, but . . . he carried so many others with him in his hand, and saved them, if they would let him, along with himself." (*Letters,* I, 42)

162–65 The source of these lines is evidently J. H. Newman, *Apologia pro Vita Sua* (1864), pp. 79–80: "Mr. Keble used to quote the words of the Psalm: 'I will guide thee with mine *eye.* Be ye not like to horse and mule, which have no understanding; whose mouths must be held with bit and bridle, lest they fall upon thee.' This is the very difference, he used to say, between slaves, and friends or children. Friends do not ask for literal commands; but, from their knowledge of the speaker, they understand his half-words, and from love of him they anticipate his wishes. . . . The view thus suggested by Mr. Keble, is brought forward in one of the earliest of the 'Tracts for the Times.' In No. 8 I say, 'The Gospel is a Law of Liberty. We are treated as sons, not as servants; not subjected to a code of formal commandments, but addressed as those who love God, and wish to please Him.' " Arnold notes in "The Literary Influence of Academies" (published August, 1864) that he had "lately" been reading the *Apologia.*

Heine's Grave *Page 179*

See the headnote to Arnold's essay "Heinrich Heine." Arnold's visit to Heine's grave in the Montmartre Cemetery in Paris was apparently made on September 14, 1858, but the poem was not completed until the spring of 1863. The sources are chiefly Heine's *Reisebilder* and an article by Saint-René Taillandier, "Poètes contemporains de l'Allemagne," *Revue des deux mondes* (April 1, 1852). J. B. Orrick has pointed out that Arnold's assumption (lines 98–100) that Heine is "that bard/Unnamed, who, Goethe said, / Had every other gift, but wanted love," is incorrect. The reference is to the *Conversations with Eckermann*, where the bard is unnamed, but later editions identify him as Platen.

Stanzas from the Grande Chartreuse *Page 185*

Arnold visited the monastery of the Grande Chartreuse, in the French Alps, on Sunday, September 7, 1851, while on his wedding journey. He may have begun the poem immediately, for "the Chartreuse" is in a list of three poems to be written or completed in the year 1852, but it was not published until April, 1855, in *Fraser's Magazine*. There is some evidence that a poem with this general theme had been in Arnold's mind for several years. Lines 139–44, for example, seem to represent the note, in a list of subjects from 1849, "Shelley — Spezzia — ah an eternal grief. The Alexandrian pessimism;" and it may be that another poem from this list, "To Meta — the cloister & the life liveable," was abandoned in favor of the "Stanzas." In any case, the poem reflects Arnold's attitude towards the so-called Oxford or Tractarian Movement (1833–45), which, attempting to revitalize the Church of England, carried so many of Arnold's contemporaries over to the Church of Rome. The question of line 65, "And what am I, that I am here?" is asked with a certain grim irony, for Arnold was well aware that a young Oxford man visiting a continental monastery in 1851 might be suspected of an intention to convert. Thus, he "reassures" his imaginary interlocutor with the statement that "rigorous teachers" (such as his father and the other anti-Tractarians) had seized his youth and so rationalized his faith that he had very little left to convert with. This pretty well represents Arnold's attitude toward the Anglo-Catholic movement: as an undergraduate he had listened to the Sunday afternoon sermons of the great Tractarian leader, John Henry Newman, and was deeply moved. Newman, he said later, was one of the "four people, in especial, from whom I am conscious of having learnt — a very different thing from merely receiving a strong impression." But when Newman went over to Rome he adopted, in Arnold's view, a solution which, "frankly speaking, is impossible."

1–24 After the French Revolution the monastery of the Grande Chartreuse became a favorite spot for English travellers to visit. Wordsworth, Hazlitt, and Ruskin have all left records of their impressions; Dr. Arnold went there when Matthew was a child.

31–48 Arnold is characteristically inaccurate in his description of the monastic life. (*Commentary*, pp. 249–51)

80–84 Cf. "Dover Beach," 15–20; "Stanzas from Carnac," 9–16.

115–16 These lines have never been satisfactorily explained, but probably the three lines 114–16 are parallel statements of the same idea — that the intellectual leaders of the modern world (cf. "The Scholar-Gipsy," 182–84) have adopted a stoical silence like that of Teufelsdröckh when he was between the two worlds of the "Everlasting Nay" and the "Everlasting Yea." (Carlyle, *Sartor Resartus,* II, viii) Goethe and Carlyle might be meant, but Chambers' suggestion of Newman is certainly wrong (*Commentary,* p. 249n.) Newman would not have been called "Achilles" in 1851–52 when he was in process of being sued for libel by a defrocked priest named Achilli.

146 See note to "Stanzas in Memory of the Author of 'Obermann.'"

164 The *Times* newspaper was nicknamed "The Thunderer" in allusion to the style of writing of Edward Sterling (1773–1847), a member of its staff.

169 Cf. the children in "Tristram and Iseult," I, 325–71; III; "Stanzas in Memory of the Author of 'Obermann,'" 73–76, 143. The *Commentary* notes the influence of Chateaubriand's *Génie du Christianisme.*

Obermann Once More *Page 191*

See note to "Stanzas in Memory of the Author of 'Obermann.'" In the early 1850's Arnold had felt himself "between two worlds, one dead, the other powerless to be born." But by 1865, through the effort of his critical writings, the second world — a world of social, religious, and literary order — had gradually been brought into being. Thus, when he revisited the Obermann country around Lake Geneva in 1865 and turned again to the book which had influenced him so profoundly, he was led to embody his new religious position in a new poem, regenerating in a transfigured form the Obermann whom he had dismissed in the "Stanzas" of seventeen years before. The best comment on the poem is Arnold's own religious writings, e.g. the Preface to *Last Essays on Church and Religion.*

1 (Arnold's note) "Probably all who know the Vevey end of the Lake of Geneva, will recollect Glion, the mountain-village above the castle of Chillon. Glion now has hotels, *pensions,* and villas; but twenty years ago it was hardly more than the huts of Avant opposite to it, — huts through which goes that beautiful path over the Col de Jaman, followed by so many foot-travelers on their way from Vevey to the Simmenthal and Thun."

22 (Arnold's note) "The blossoms of the *Gentiana lutea.*" See *Empedocles on Etna,* I, ii, 4–5.

24 (Arnold's note) "Montbovon. See Byron's Journal in his *Works,* vol. iii, p. 258. The river Saane becomes the Sarine below Montbovon."

66 Tinker and Lowry suggest (p. 266) that the "book" is the *Manuel de Pseusophanes,* attributed to Aristippus, which Obermann reprints; but it may, of course, simply be his own book.

232 Revelation, 21:5.

NOTES TO THE CRITICISM

Preface to First Edition of *Poems* — Page 203

In the preface to the 1853 edition of *Poems,* Arnold's first piece of criticism and one of his best, he is formulating the poetical creed which he will adhere to for the rest of his life. It is evident that he is doing this in opposition to a dominant literary tendency of the day, and Professor H. W. Garrod ("Matthew Arnold's 1853 Preface," *RES,* XVII, 1941, pp. 310–21) has shown that this is the tradition not only of Shakespeare and Keats, whom Arnold mentions, but also of Alexander Smith, the "spasmodic" poet whose *Poems* were published earlier in the year and attracted considerably more, and more favorable, attention than Arnold's. Clough, for example, reviewed the two works together in the *North American Review* (July, 1853) and gave the preference to Smith. But Arnold was also speaking against Keats, whose *Life, Letters and Literary Remains,* edited by Monckton Milnes, he had read four or five years earlier, and against Tennyson and Browning. Needless to say, he was also speaking against his own earlier self, which he was rapidly outgrowing. The principal positive influence on the Preface is that of Aristotle's *Poetics.*

The "intelligent critic" quoted by Arnold who demands that the poet choose subjects of "present import" was Robert Stephen Rintoul, editor of the *Spectator;* and the "modern critic" who declares that "a true allegory of the state of one's own mind" is the highest thing one can attempt in poetry is an anonymous reviewer (apparently J. M. Ludlow, a Christian socialist) in the *North British Review* for August, 1853. Garrod points out that if Arnold had read the review more carefully he would have noted that the authority for this statement was not Ludlow but Goethe!

For studies of the Preface, see Garrod, cited above; J. D. Jump, "Matthew Arnold and the *Spectator,*" *RES,* XXV (1949), 61–64; Alba H. Warren, Jr., *English Poetic Theory, 1825–1865* (1950), chap. IX.

Preface to Second Edition of *Poems* — Page 215

One of the principal causes of the misunderstanding of Arnold's Preface of 1853 was his failure to state that by "poetry" he meant epic and dramatic poetry, not lyric. He was also attacked in the *Spectator* (December 3, 1853) for considering Macbeth and Œdipus to be equally legendary for the purposes of the poet, and by his friends J. A. Froude and J. D. Coleridge for apparently limiting the poet to subjects from classical antiquity (*Westminster Review,* January, 1854; *Christian Remembrancer,* April, 1854).

On Translating Homer *Page 217*

As Professor of Poetry at Oxford from 1857 to 1867 Arnold was expected to deliver three public lectures annually, the topic which he had chosen for himself being "The Modern Element in Literature." But in the autumn of 1860 he decided to interrupt this course with some remarks "On Translating Homer." At first he intended only a single lecture, but the subject extended itself into three, delivered on November 3 and December 8, 1860, and on January 26, 1861. When Arnold's views were resented by the translator with whom he was principally concerned, F. W. Newman, who published a reply, *Homeric Translation in Theory and Practice,* Arnold added a fourth lecture, "On Translating Homer: Last Words," which he delivered on November 30, 1861.

The subject attracted Arnold because Homer was for him the very symbol of that world-wide literary culture which the English people needed to assimilate as the antidote to their narrowness and provinciality. Clearly the first step toward such assimilation was translation, by which Arnold meant not the transformation of Homer into the likeness of a middle-class Englishman but the true carrying over of his qualities of mind and style into a different medium so that the middle-class Englishman might himself be transformed into the likeness of Homer. But it so happened that in 1856 there appeared a translation into English by one who was the very antithesis of European culture (and the symbol of English provinciality), Francis W. Newman, the brother of the great Tractarian leader, John Henry Newman. Francis Newman had taken a brilliant degree at Oxford but then, diverging from his brother's High Church views, had married a member of a small dissenting sect, the Plymouth Brethren, and had embarked on a fantastic missionary expedition to Syria. Returning disillusioned, he became a Unitarian, then a freethinker; and at the same time he was made Professor of Latin at University College, London. He combined astonishing erudition in languages (he knew French, Italian, Spanish, Latin, Greek, Hebrew, Sanskrit, Danish, Berber, Libyan, Arabic, Abyssinian, Gothic, Chaldean, Syriac, and Numidian) with equally astonishing inability to put this erudition to any sensible use. (He translated *Hiawatha* into Latin and *Robinson Crusoe* into Latin and Arabic.) His dress was fantastic: in winter his cloak was a rug with a hole in the center for his head and his trousers were trimmed with six inches of leather against the wet. His translation of Homer was of a piece with his dress and his life, an expression of that "muscular classicality" which delighted in rudeness, violence, and all things odd and uncouth. Of course, modern scholarship has revealed that if Newman's "Non-conformist" Homer was created in his own image, so too in some degree was Arnold's bland Oxonian Homer. But it is clear that the conflict between the two men was not simply over the pedantics of translation but was a conflict between two conceptions of culture.

F. W. Newman's reply to Arnold has been reprinted in the Everyman and Oxford editions of Arnold's essays. The edition of Arnold's lectures by W. H. D. Rouse (1905) contains a valuable introduction, and there are useful remarks on Arnold's theory of translation in William Frost, *Dryden and the Art of Translation* (Yale Studies in English, No. 128). See also T. S. Omond, "Arnold and Homer," *Essays and Studies by Members of the English Association,* III (1912), 71–91; N. Annan, in *New Statesman,* XXVII (1944), 191.

Preface to *Essays in Criticism* — *Page 233*

Although Arnold had shown his power as a critic in the preface to *Poems* (1853) and the lectures *On Translating Homer,* he first came before the world as England's leading litterateur with the publication of *Essays in Criticism,* first series (1865). Most of the nine essays had been lectures delivered at Oxford and then published in periodicals, but they made their full impact when gathered together in a volume. With the preface which Arnold wrote to introduce them he was rather tickled, for it was full of "vivacities." "The Preface will make you laugh," he wrote to his mother; but it may be that he was mistaken, for a few days later he was writing to Lady de Rothschild: "I had read the Preface to a brother and sister of mine, and they received it in such solemn silence that I began to tremble; then —— [presumably either his mother or his wife] is always thrown into a nervous tremor by my writing anything which she thinks likely to draw down attacks on me; so altogether I needed the refreshment of your sympathy." (*Letters,* I, 286, 288) When the book appeared, Arnold was generally pleased by the results: "The best justification of the Preface is the altered tone of the *Saturday* [*Review*]." (I, 290) But within a month he was eager to talk to Lady de Rothschild "about some of the notices of my *Essays.* I think if I republish the book I shall leave out some of the preface and notes, as being too much of mere temporary matter. . . ." (I, 294) This he did in the second edition (1869), the text of which is reprinted here. A reprint of the preface in its original form may be found in Fraser Neiman's *Essays, Letters, and Reviews by Matthew Arnold* (Cambridge, Mass., 1960), 92–101.

The Function of Criticism at the Present Time — *Page 237*

"The Function of Criticism at the Present Time" was originally a lecture delivered by Arnold on October 29, 1864, in his capacity as Professor of Poetry at the University of Oxford. It was then published in the *National Review* in November, 1864, and republished the following year as the opening essay in *Essays in Criticism,* first series. In this position it seems to lay down a general program for criticism which the later essays on individual figures — Maurice and Eugénie de Guérin, Heine, Joubert, Spinoza, and so on — carry out. But we must remember that it was originally written and published after those essays, not before. In other words, its function in Arnold's life may have been not so much to lay down a program for the nation as to explain why the author had been writing criticism for the past ten years instead of poetry. The handling of the quotation from Wordsworth at the beginning of the essay seems to suggest this view. Cf. T. S. Eliot, "The Function of Criticism"; F. W. Bateson, "The Function of Criticism at the Present Time," *Essays in Criticism,* III (1953), 1–27.

The Literary Influence of Academies *Page 259*

"The Literary Influence of Academies" was originally a lecture delivered by Arnold on June 4, 1864, in his capacity as Professor of Poetry at the University of Oxford. It was then published in the *Cornhill Magazine* in April, 1864, and republished the following year as the second essay in *Essays in Criticism,* first series. Thus, the remarks made about "The Function of Criticism at the Present Time" in the preceding note apply in a lesser degree to this essay. It was published second in the collected series but was originally written second from last, and it occupies a position midway between the general theoretical essay and the specialized practical ones: it applies the theory to the general problem of an institution. For a discussion of the academy as Arnold's "Visible Church" of literature, see the Introduction, section ii.

from Maurice de Guérin *Page 280*

This essay was probably the lecture on "A Modern French Poet" which Arnold delivered at Oxford as Professor of Poetry on November 15, 1862. It was published in *Fraser's Magazine* in January, 1863, and republished in *Essays in Criticism,* first series. It is thoroughly characteristic of this series, which is more concerned with widening the horizons of the English people by supplying them with fresh ideas and information than it is with helping them evaluate material already familiar to them. That will be the task of *Essays in Criticism,* second series. Hence Arnold chooses by preference little known figures from foreign lands, selecting those who may not be important in themselves but who represent some idea or ideal. For this reason we have omitted from this and three other essays the large portions of merely factual material which they contain and have concentrated on Arnold's own contribution, the idea which he distilled from this material.

from Heinrich Heine *Page 288*

Arnold first read Heinrich Heine (1797–1856), the German poet and man of letters, in 1848 and was at once fascinated and disgusted by him. "He has a good deal of power, though more trick. . . . The Byronism of a German, of a man trying to be gloomy, cynical, impassioned, *moqueur,* etc., all *à la fois,* with their honest bonhommistic language and total want of experience of the kind that Lord Byron, an English peer with access everywhere, possessed, is the most ridiculous thing in the world." (*Letters,* I, 11) Nevertheless, Heine took hold of him as a symbol of the modern spirit, of one who, finding himself on the sick-bed of modern Europe, rose above his suffering through derision and scorn. That this was not the best way Arnold knew, and he expressed this judgment in his elegy, "Heine's Grave," written in 1862–63. But when he came to treat the same subject in prose in one of his Oxford lectures, he felt that the English people could do with a little of the Heinesque spirit. Writing to his mother immediately after the lecture, which was delivered on June 13, 1863, he commented on the "schoolboy instruction" at Oxford which resulted in a slight attendance at professorial lectures. "I have almost always a very fair attendance; to be sure, it is chiefly composed of ladies, but the above [stricture] is so far true that I am obliged always to think, in composing my lectures, of the public who will read me, not of the dead bones who will hear me, or my spirit would fail. Tell Edward that there was, nevertheless, one thing which even a wooden Oxford audience gave way to — Heine's wit. I gave them about two pages of specimens of it, and they positively laughed aloud. I have had two applications for the lecture from magazines, but I shall print it, if I can, in the *Cornhill*, because it both pays best and has much the largest circle of readers." (*Letters*, I, 226) The lecture appeared in the August issue of *Cornhill Magazine* and later in *Essays in Criticism*, first series.

See: Elsie M. Butler, "Heine in England and Matthew Arnold," *German Life and Letters* (April, 1956), 157–65; Sol Liptzin, "Heine, the Continuator of Goethe: a Mid-Victorian Legend," *JEGP*, XLIII (1944), 317–25, and "The English Reception of Heine," *Victorian Newsletter* (Spring, 1957), 14–16.

from Joubert — *Page 295*

Coleridge is the only one of the English Romantic poets whom Arnold never made the subject of a separate essay. It may be said that the piece on Joubert supplies the place, for when it was first delivered as a lecture at Oxford on November 28, 1863, it was entitled "A French Coleridge," and that phrase too supplied the subtitle on its periodical publication in the *National Review*, January, 1864. When it appeared in *Essays in Criticism*, however, it was called "Joubert," and that is right, for the parallel with Coleridge is a little odd and illustrates the imperfect sympathy which Arnold had for one too magical and too metaphysical for his comprehension. The omitted portions of the essay consist almost entirely of lengthy extracts from Joubert's writings.

The Study of Poetry — *Page 306*

"The Study of Poetry" was composed by Arnold as a General Introduction to an anthology, *The English Poets* (4 vols., 1880), edited by Thomas Humphry Ward, the husband of Arnold's niece. Arnold also contributed separate introductions to the selections by Gray and Keats. Eight years later the Introduction was reprinted as the opening essay in *Essays in Criticism, Second Series*, a volume planned by Arnold but not published until after his death. "The Study of Poetry" bears the same relation to the second series of critical essays as "The Function of Criticism at the Present Time" did to the first, that of formulating the nature of the criticism therein practiced, and a comparison of the two essays perfectly indicates the difference between the two volumes. In the former Arnold was mainly concerned with information, in the latter with evaluation. Hence in the former he dealt with little-known figures from other literatures, here with well-known English authors who need to be reassessed. The means of arriving at a reassessment, especially the "touchstone" method, may not seem attractive to the modern reader, but one should examine Arnold's Notebooks and see upon what depth of meditative experience the "touchstone" method is based before he dismisses it completely. The quotation with which the essay opens is a revision of a passage from Arnold's introduction to volume one of a work called *The Hundred Greatest Men* (1879).

from Thomas Gray *Page 328*

The essay on Gray was originally written as an introduction to the selections from that poet included in T. H. Ward's *The English Poets* (1880) (see preceding note). It was later reprinted in *Essays in Criticism, Second Series*. The first part of the essay, omitted here, is largely biographical and is concerned with posing the question, which is answered in the present selection, as to why Gray "never spoke out" — i.e., why his poetic production was so scanty. Arnold's answer is particularly interesting not only for the light it sheds on his view of eighteenth-century literature but also because, under cover of an essay on Gray, he seems to be inquiring into the causes of his own poetic sterility.

Wordsworth *Page 331*

The essay on Wordsworth, Arnold's finest on an individual figure, was written as an introduction to a selection of Wordsworth's poems made by Arnold for the Golden Treasury series (1879). It largely determined the view of Wordsworth for many decades. On this subject Arnold was profoundly qualified to speak, for he had meditated lovingly upon the poetry of Wordsworth since childhood and was, more than any other Victorian poet, the continuator of the Wordsworthian tradition in his age. Ever since his father, who was also a "lover of the hills," built a summer home at Fox How near the Wordsworth's home at Rydal Mount, there was a constant friendly intercourse between the two families, and Arnold grew up accustomed not only to see the great bard and hear him recite his poems but also to roam the hills and lakes which were their theme. In 1848, damning "Keats, Tennyson, et id genus omne," he declared, "Those who cannot read Greek should read nothing but Milton and parts of Wordsworth: the state should see to it." (*Clough Letters*, p. 97) Of course, as the younger poet grew into his own ways he found himself turning critical of his master, partly because in Wordsworth's more didactic poems he used "poetry as a channel for thinking aloud, instead of making anything" (*Unpublished Poems,* p. 17) and partly because in his simple nature philosophy he averted his eyes from "half of human fate," which Arnold in a more complex world could not do. But the death of Wordsworth was, for Arnold, nothing less than the death of poetry in the modern world ("Memorial Verses"), and in 1872 he listed Wordsworth as one of the "four people, in especial, from whom I am conscious of having learnt — a very different thing from merely receiving a strong impression — learnt habits, methods, ruling ideas, which are constantly with me." (*Unpublished Letters,* pp. 65–66) William A. Jamison, *Arnold and the Romantics* (Copenhagen, 1958).

Byron *Page 347*

Next to Wordsworth, Byron is the English poet who entered most deeply into Arnold's consciousness. His two youthful poems, *Alaric at Rome* and *Cromwell,* are pure Byronic posing of the "Childe Harold" variety, and although in later years he began to react against the vulgarity and shallowness of his idol, he never ceased to regard him as a great Titanic force of admirable power. It is significant, as Lionel Trilling notes, that Arnold never criticizes Byron for his sexual lapses, as he does Keats and Shelley. Apparently he considered that these were not morbid and enervating, as theirs were, and also that they were part of a protest against a social order. Byron was like Heine, a soldier in the warfare of the liberation of humanity, and it apparently did not detract from his stature as an artist that he conducted this warfare partly through the medium of his personal life.

The essay on Byron was written as the introduction to a selection of Byron's poems made by Arnold for the Golden Treasury series, but it was also published in *Macmillan's Magazine* (March, 1881) and in *Essays in Criticism, Second Series.* William A. Jamison, *Arnold and the Romantics* (Copenhagen, 1958).

Shelley *Page 363*

This essay, a review of Edward Dowden's *Life of Percy Bysshe Shelley* (2 vols., 1886), was first published in *The Nineteenth Century* for January, 1888, then reprinted in *Essays in Criticism, Second Series.* Arnold's Notebook for 1888 shows that he intended to write a second essay on Shelley, perhaps on the poetry, but he never lived to complete it.

The lady whose Shelley story is told in the opening paragraph of the essay was Mrs. Fanny Kemble, the actress. (Marion Mainwaring, "Arnold on Shelley," *MLN,* LXVII, 1952, pp. 122–123) William A. Jamison, *Arnold and the Romantics* (Copenhagen, 1958).

Literature and Science *Page 381*

This essay is part of the century-long conflict between the advocates of a liberal education, especially through the instrumentality of the Greek and

Latin classics, and the advocates of a more practical or technical education, especially through the instrumentality of science. It was occasioned by an address, "Science and Culture," delivered by Thomas Henry Huxley, the naturalist, on the occasion of the opening of Sir Josiah Mason's Science College (later to become the University of Birmingham) on October 1, 1880. Mason had stipulated that his college was to make no provision for "mere literary instruction and education," and Huxley, supporting this view, quoted Arnold's essay on "The Function of Criticism at the Present Time" as asserting "that a criticism of life is the essence of culture" and "that literature contains the materials which suffice for the construction of such criticism." He himself believed, on the other hand, "that for the purpose of attaining real culture, an exclusively scientific education is at least as effectual as an exclusively literary education." Arnold's reply, "Literature and Science," was delivered as a Rede Lecture at Cambridge in 1882 and was published in *The Nineteenth Century* in August of that year. Fitted with a new introduction, it was then taken to America as one of the three discourses which Arnold delivered on his tour of 1883–84, and was reprinted in the volume *Discourses in America.* Along with Newman's *Idea of a University* it is one of the great defences of the humanistic tradition in education.

Friendship's Garland *Page 397*

Friendship's Garland, which reveals a side of Arnold's talent not apparent in any other of his works, belongs to the tradition of the literary hoax whereby a foreigner, visiting in England, comments upon its institutions to the dismay of a naive friend who attempts to explain their virtues. It owes something to Swift but more to Carlyle's *Sartor Resartus.* The visitor in this instance is a dogmatic young Prussian, Arminius, Baron von Thunder-ten-Tronckh, the history of whose family had been written by the famous Voltaire in *Candide.* He has come to England because he hopes to find the living descendant of Dr. Pangloss, the optimistic philosopher, among such Comtists and Liberals as Mr. Frederic Harrison and Mr. Robert Lowe. There he reluctantly suffers the adulation of a Grub Street hack named Matthew Arnold, who had previously made his acquaintance on the Continent and who now communicates his "Conversations, Letters and Opinions" to the public by the medium of letters to the *Pall Mall Gazette.* These letters, thirteen in all, were published at scattered intervals from 1866 to 1870 and were then collected into a book in 1871. Letters VI and VII, published on April 20 and 22, 1867, form a unit by themselves.

In the late '60's and early '70's Arnold's love of French culture had gradually given way to an admiration for Prussian efficiency, which is now embodied in the figure of Arminius. "I don't know," he writes in the fifth letter, "that I have ever described Arminius's personal appearance. He has the true square Teutonic head, a blond and disorderly mass of tow-like hair, a podgy and sanguine countenance, shaven cheeks, and a whity-brown moustache. He wears a rough pilot-coat, and generally smokes away with his hands in the pockets of it, and his light blue eyes fixed on his interlocutor's face."

Culture and Anarchy *Page 407*

The filiation of Arnold's thought is well seen in his transition from literary to social criticism. His literary criticism, the product of his ten years' appointment as Professor of Poetry at Oxford, culminated in *Essays in Criticism* (1865), the publication of which provoked an attack in the *Saturday Review* to which Arnold replied in an article, "My Countrymen," which was the germ of *Culture and Anarchy.* The opening section of *Culture and Anarchy* (now comprising the Introduction and "Sweetness and Light") was delivered as Arnold's concluding lecture as Professor of Poetry at Oxford.

The context in which Arnold wrote was that of the alarms and disturbances attendant upon the passage of the Second Reform Bill in 1867. The student would do well to read an account of this period in the histories by G. M. Trevelyan or E. L. Woodward, or in Dover Wilson's introduction to the Cambridge Press edition of *Culture and Anarchy.* Here the main events may be summarized briefly.

1866. March. Gladstone, in Earl Russell's Whig ministry, introduced a moderate franchise reform measure which, however, was opposed by a group within his own party led by Robert Lowe. The Whigs were defeated and Lord Derby, the Tory leader, formed a ministry with Disraeli as the chief figure.

July 23. Hyde Park riots. The Reform League, refused the use of the Park for a meeting, went on to Trafalgar Square, but the mob broke down the railings and milled about in disorder to the alarm of sober citizens. Spencer Walpole, the Home Secretary, showed himself unable to cope with the situation. John Bright, the Quaker radical, campaigned before mass meetings in the provinces.

1867. February. Parliament reconvened and Disraeli, seeing reform was inevitable, introduced a more radical measure than that sponsored by the Whigs the previous year.

Spring and Summer. Fenian and Trades Union disturbances, also riots in Wolverhampton and Birmingham caused by the anti-Catholic agitation of a Mr. Murphy.

June 10. Samuel Wilson, aged Colonel of the Royal London Militia, allowed a minor riot to proceed unchecked in the presence of his troops.

July. Chapter I of *Culture and Anarchy* published in the *Cornhill* (previously delivered as a lecture at Oxford in May).

August 15. Second Reform Bill passed, increasing the electorate from one-fifth to two-fifths of the adult male population.

1868. January–July. Last five chapters of *Culture and Anarchy* published in the *Cornhill.*

February. Disraeli succeeded Lord Derby as Prime Minister; defeated on Irish Church question (April).

November. General Election under the reformed franchise returned a liberal Parliament.

1869. January. *Culture and Anarchy* published in book form, with preface written in Christmas holidays.

February. The new Parliament convened.

As may be seen from the above chronology, Arnold's work is intimately involved with the events of the day and is, indeed, a kind of political pamphlet. But because it takes an enduring rather than a temporary view of the problem, it is also a political and educational classic. In this respect it may be contrasted with Carlyle's frenzied treatment of the crisis, in *Shooting Niagara, and After?* which proposes a quasi-military aristocracy; and it may also be compared with three classics, one of a remote time and two of the same age, which deal with the same problem in a similar way: Plato's *Republic,* Mill's *On Liberty,* and Newman's *Idea of a University.* By all three Arnold was influenced deeply.

Equality *Page 476*

This address, delivered at the Royal Institution of Great Britain, was published in the *Fortnightly Review* in March, 1878, and reprinted in *Mixed Essays* (1879). It provides a needed correction to *Culture and Anarchy,* in which Arnold was led, in his search for spiritual order, rather far toward the authoritarian conception of the state. In "Equality" he reaffirms his faith in the principles of the French Revolution and asserts that these principles cannot be realized on a spiritual level unless they are also embodied in the economic conditions of life. In particular he argues against unlimited freedom in the bequest of landed property. In the last chapter of *Culture and Anarchy* he had rather deprecated the importance of a Liberal nostrum, the Real Estate Intestacy Bill, which proposed that the land of a man who died intestate should be divided equally among his family instead of going exclusively to his eldest son. It is true that the basis on which he had done this was a distrust of the theory of "natural rights" and a view that the value of such measures depends on circumstances; and in "Equality" he continues this empirical approach. But his attitude toward the practical goal of social and economic democracy has changed. It is a part of a larger broadening and tempering of his views which occurred in the last decade of his life.

Preface to *Last Essays on Church and Religion* *Page 499*

Arnold's early religious position is difficult to ascertain, but it was probably undogmatic to the verge of agnosticism. Certainly when he began to write on the question, in 1863, he was already more concerned with preserving than destroying; that is, he assumed that a great deal of destruction had already taken place and that the mature ought to be beyond that point, building anew. This is the reason for his apparently perverse attitude towards the *cause célèbre* of Bishop Colenso in 1863. This South African ecclesiastic had belatedly discovered — what every Biblical scholar in Germany long had known — that not every statement in Genesis can be made to square with every other, and he inadvisedly published his findings in a work directed to the general reader, the *Critical Examination of the Pentateuch* (1862). Arnold, belonging to the "reverent" tradition of Biblical criticism, a tradition going back to Spinoza and including Coleridge, Strauss, Renan, and his own father, held that the important point was that, despite these factual errors, the spiritual truths of the Bible remained untouched. For Arnold the Bible was the literature of the Hebrew people. Its language was not the language of scientific statement but the language of poetry, "thrown out," as he says, to express imperfectly the sense of "an Eternal, not ourselves, which makes for righteousness." Unhappily, in the course of time this poetic language came to be taken literally, to be transformed from literature into dogma, and to give rise to a system of "*Aberglaube*," or extra-belief, not sanctioned by the original insight of the Hebrew people. It was the function of Jesus to renew and supplement this insight by his method of spiritual inwardness and his secret of self-renunciation and mildness, but once again in the hands of Paul and the later theologians the language which was originally intended to express imperfectly a subjective spiritual consciousness became hardened into a body of objective statements about history, cosmology, and metaphysics. In Arnold's day these statements could no longer be accepted, and the masses (so Arnold believed) were ready to reject the Bible altogether unless it could be presented to them for what it is — for literature, not dogma.

This was the message with which Arnold was principally concerned from 1869 to 1877 and which, in *Literature and Dogma,* he brought home to the largest circle of readers he ever enjoyed. *Literature and Dogma* is a long work and it cannot easily be excerpted, but fortunately, as Arnold was bidding farewell to the subject, he drew out its entire argument in one of the most simple and unmannered pieces he ever wrote, the Preface to *Last Essays on Church and Religion* (1877).

William Robbins, *The Ethical Idealism of Matthew Arnold* (Toronto, 1959); F. H. Bradley, *Ethical Studies* (1876); William Blackburn, "The Background of Arnold's *Literature and Dogma,*" *MP,* XLIII (1945), 130–39.

INDEX OF POETRY

Page numbers in italics refer to the Notes

INDEX OF CRITICISM

Page numbers in italics refer to the Notes

RIVERSIDE EDITIONS

Austen, Pride and Prejudice *ed.* Mark Schorer B1

Austen, Emma *ed.* Lionel Trilling B17

Brontë, C., Jane Eyre *ed.* Mark Schorer B35

Brontë, E., Wuthering Heights *ed.* V. S. Pritchett B2

Browning, Poems *ed.* Donald Smalley B3

*Butler, The Way of All Flesh *ed.* Daniel F. Howard B50

Byron, Don Juan *ed.* Leslie A. Marchand B40

*Chaucer, Selections from the Canterbury Tales and Other Writings *ed.* Robert A. Pratt B41

Conrad, Lord Jim *ed.* Morton Dauwen Zabel B23

Cooper, The Last of the Mohicans *ed.* William Charvat A29

Crane, The Red Badge of Courage and Other Writings *ed.* Richard Chase A46

Defoe, Moll Flanders *ed.* James Sutherland B31

Dickens, Bleak House *ed.* Morton Dauwen Zabel B4

Dickens, David Copperfield *ed.* George H. Ford B24

Dreiser, Sister Carrie *ed.* Claude Simpson A36

*Dryden, Selections *ed.* H. T. Swedenberg, Jr. B5

Eliot, Middlemarch *ed.* Gordon S. Haight B6

Emerson, Selections *ed.* Stephen E. Whicher A13

*Fielding, Tom Jones *ed.* James A. Work and Gerard E. Jensen B44

Franklin, Autobiography and Other Writings *ed.* Russel B. Nye A32

Hardy, Far from the Madding Crowd *ed.* Richard L. Purdy B18

Hardy, Tess of the d'Urbervilles *ed.* William E. Buckler B47

Hawthorne, The Scarlet Letter *ed.* Harry Levin A45

Howells, A Modern Instance *ed.* William M. Gibson A21

Howells, The Rise of Silas Lapham *ed.* Edwin H. Cady A28

James, The Ambassadors *ed.* Leon Edel A39

James, The Portrait of a Lady *ed.* Leon Edel A7

Keats, Selected Poems and Letters *ed.* Douglas Bush B42

Latin Poetry in Verse Translation *ed.* L. R. Lind C20

Malory, King Arthur and His Knights *ed.* Eugène Vinaver B8

Melville, Moby-Dick *ed.* Alfred Kazin A9

Meredith, The Egoist *ed.* Lionel Stevenson B27

*Mill, Autobiography *ed.* Lionel Trilling B22

Newman, Apologia pro Vita Sua *ed.* A. Dwight Culler B10

Norris, The Octopus *ed.* Kenneth S. Lynn A33

Poe, Selected Writings *ed.* Edward H. Davidson A11

Prose of the Victorian Period *ed.* William E. Buckler B30

Scott, Rob Roy *ed.* Edgar Johnson B12

*Shakespeare, Six Plays (Richard II, 1 Henry IV, As You Like It, Hamlet, King Lear, The Tempest) *ed.* S. F. Johnson B16

*Six Elizabethan Plays *ed.* Robert Cecil Bald B37

Six Restoration Plays *ed.* John H. Wilson B38

*Sterne, Tristram Shandy *ed.* Ian Watt B48

Swift, Gulliver's Travels *ed.* Louis A. Landa B49

Swift, Gulliver's Travels and Other Writings *ed.* Louis A. Landa B25

Ten Greek Plays in Contemporary Translations *ed.* L. R. Lind C19

Tennyson, Poems *ed.* Jerome H. Buckley B26

Thoreau, Walden *ed.* Sherman Paul A14

Trollope, Doctor Thorne *ed.* Elizabeth Bowen B43

Twain, Adventures of Huckleberry Finn *ed.* Henry Nash Smith A15

Whitman, Complete Poetry and Selected Prose *ed.* James E. Miller, Jr. A34

* In preparation